A History of
The Expansion of Christianity

Volume V
THE GREAT CENTURY
IN THE AMERICAS, AUSTRAL-
ASIA, AND AFRICA
A.D. 1800-A.D. 1914

A History of
THE EXPANSION OF CHRISTIANITY
(Volume V)

THE
GREAT CENTURY
IN THE AMERICAS, AUSTRAL-
ASIA, AND AFRICA
A.D. 1800-A.D. 1914

by

KENNETH SCOTT LATOURETTE

THE PATERNOSTER PRESS

ISBN: 0 85364 118 8

THE GREAT CENTURY

Copyright © 1943 by Harper and Row, Publishers
Published by special arrangement with Harper and Row, Publishers,
New York
Printed in the United States of America
This edition is distributed by The Paternoster Press
Paternoster House, 3 Mount Radford Crescent
Exeter, Devon, by arrangement with
The Zondervan Publishing House, Grand Rapids, Mich., U.S.A.

This Edition 1971

AUSTRALIA:
Emu Book Agencies Pty., Ltd., 511 Kent Street, Sydney, N.S.W.

SOUTH AFRICA:
Oxford University Press, P.O. Box 1141, Oxford House,
11, Buitencingle Street, Cape Town

In memory of

HARLAN PAGE BEACH

1854–1933

Contents

Chapter I

BY WAY OF INTRODUCTION.   I

Chapter II

BRITISH NORTH AMERICA. Roman Catholics; Protestants.   3

Chapter III

GREENLAND: THE DUTCH, DANISH, AND BRITISH WEST INDIES: BRITISH HON-   46
DURAS: BRITISH GUIANA: SURINAM.

Chapter IV

LATIN AMERICA. The crisis brought the Roman Catholic Church by political   68
revolution; the partial recovery; the coming of Eastern Christianity
through immigration; the entrance of Protestant Christianity through
missions to the Non-Christian Indians, commerce, immigration, and missions to Roman Catholics.

Chapter V

AUSTRALIA. Protestantism and Roman Catholicism among the whites and   130
the aborigines.

Chapter VI

NEW ZEALAND. Protestantism and Roman Catholicism among the Maoris   177
and the whites.

Chapter VII

THE ISLANDS OF THE PACIFIC. Protestant and Roman Catholic missions in   198
Tahiti and the Society Islands, the Cook or Hervey Islands, the Marquesas,
Pitcairn Island, the Tonga or Friendly Islands, the Samoan Islands, the

CONTENTS

Ellice Islands, the Fiji Islands, Rotuma, the New Hebrides, New Caledonia, the Loyalty Islands, the Solomon Islands, New Britain and the Bismarck Archipelago, New Guinea, Hawaii, Micronesia.

Chapter VIII

THE PHILIPPINE ISLANDS.   264

Chapter IX

THE EAST INDIES (the Dutch, Portuguese, and British Possessions).   275

Chapter X

MADAGASCAR AND SOME OF THE OTHER ISLANDS OFF THE SHORES OF AFRICA.   301

Chapter XI

AFRICA SOUTH OF THE SAHARA. The white churches in South Africa: mis-   319
sions to the non-whites in South Africa: German South-west Africa:
Bechuanaland: Rhodesia: Nyasaland: Angola: Portuguese East Africa:
German East Africa: British East Africa: Uganda: the Belgian Congo:
French Equatorial Africa: Rio Muni: Fernando Po: Cameroon: Nigeria:
Dahomy: Togo: the Gold Coast: the Ivory Coast: Liberia: Sierra Leone:
French Guinea: Portuguese Guinea: Gambia: Senegal: Upper Senegal:
Niger: Summary.

Chapter XII

BY WAY OF BRIEF SUMMARY AND ANTICIPATION.   465

BIBLIOGRAPHY.   471

INDEX.   507

MAPS (in rear of volume).

1. BRITISH NORTH AMERICA AND GREENLAND.

2. MEXICO, CENTRAL AMERICA, AND THE WEST INDIES.

3. SOUTH AMERICA.

4. AFRICA AND THE ADJACENT ISLANDS.

5. THE ISLANDS OF THE PACIFIC.

6. AUSTRALIA, NEW ZEALAND, THE EAST INDIES, AND THE PHILIPPINE ISLANDS.

In the current volume so wide and varied an area has been covered that the author has sought and received assistance from many individuals and institutions. It is a pleasure to record the debt, especially since as one does so the memory again becomes vivid of the generous help so ungrudgingly given. To mention by name all those who have been of service along the way would require a lengthy catalogue. Space must be taken, however, to acknowledge the obligation to Professor F. G. Harvey, who was indefatigable in gathering material on Australia and compiling it in usable form; to Chancellor Walter T. Brown, who out of his busy life took time to assemble from his colleagues a bibliography on Canada; to Dr. C. W. Keirstead, who graciously permitted quotations of data from an as yet unpublished study; to Professor B. K. Malinowski, who contributed from his vast stores of anthropological knowledge counsel on the sections having to do with primitive peoples; to Dr. Alfred Métraux, whose detailed familiarity through travel and reading with some sections of the interior of South America was the source of information which would otherwise have been missed; to the librarians of the Congregation for the Propagation of the Faith, the British Museum, New College, Edinburgh, and Yale University, whose unfailing efficiency and kindness made easily available the treasures of the collections over which they preside; to the Day Missions Library of the Yale University Divinity School and its long-suffering staff and especially to the late Professor Harlan P. Beach who did so much to assemble that amazing collection; and to Mrs. Charles T. Lincoln, who, sometimes in the face of ill-health, typed the manuscript from the author's difficult copy and made invaluable suggestions as to style. When these names are singled out, however, as they amply deserve to be, the author is also conscious of a much larger number—students, colleagues, acquaintances from many parts of the earth—who have aided with information and the stimulus of question and discussion. Whatever defects the volume may present would have been enormously greater had it not been for the help from these many friends.

A History of
The Expansion of Christianity

Volume V

THE GREAT CENTURY
IN THE AMERICAS, AUSTRAL-
ASIA, AND AFRICA
A.D. 1800-A.D. 1914

Chapter I

BY WAY OF INTRODUCTION

THIS volume is a continuation of the account of the expansion of Christianity in the nineteenth century which was begun in its predecessor. In the nineteenth century the spread of Christianity was so extensive, so many agencies, individuals, and movements had a part in it, and so many peoples and cultures were affected by it, that, even with rigid compression, the period cannot, as could each of the preceding three of our story, be confined to one volume. Three volumes are necessary if the history is to be told on a scale comparable with that employed for the earlier eras. This is in spite of the fact that the length of time is far the shortest of those thus far covered. In geographic extent, in movements issuing from it, and in its effect upon the race, in the nineteenth century Christianity had a far larger place in human history than at any previous time. It is, therefore, no obsession with recent events, no myopia born of interest in our own times, which has led to the dedication of as much space to the nineteenth century as to all the preceding eighteen. The apportionment is forced upon us by the rapid widening of the Christian stream and by the deepening influence upon the culture of mankind.

In the preceding volume, it will be recalled, we told of the forces which shaped what had long been the traditional home of Christianity, Europe, in this period and made their way from it to the rest of the world, we described the multiform ways in which, with unprecedented strength, the vitality inherent in Christianity expressed itself, we recounted the rise of the agencies through which Christianity expanded, we outlined the main characteristics of that expansion as contrasted with those of earlier eras, and we narrated the spread of Christianity in Europe and the United States of America with the attendant effects on the environment and by the environment.

In the present volume we are to move on to those portions of the Americas not included in the United States, to what, in the broadest use of that word, is termed Australasia, and to Africa south of the Sahara and its fringing islands. As can quickly be seen from the table of contents, we are to go first to Canada and Newfoundland, then to Greenland, to the British, Dutch, and Danish West Indies, and to British and Dutch Guiana, then to the huge area known best as Latin America, next to Australia, Tasmania, and New Zealand, then to the islands of the Pacific from New Caledonia and Norfolk Island in the South to Hawaii in the North, and from the Marquesas, Easter Island, and Pitcairn Island in the East to the Philippines and the East Indies in the West, to some of the islands adjacent to Africa, including especially Madagascar, and, finally, to Africa south of the Sahara.

At first glance it may seem that no logic or essential unity binds together these diverse areas and peoples and that the arrangement is purely an author's whim. On second thought it must be clear that among them all, in the nineteenth century, were common characteristics and that these lead us logically on to these lands from our chapters devoted to Europe and the United States. In these countries, as in the United States, European peoples, in the course of that expansion which was one of the outstanding world-wide phenomena of the nineteenth century, impinged upon peoples who for the most part were in primitive stages of culture. Except where they had already been touched by Christianity or, to a much less extent, by Islam, these primitive peoples were animists or near-animistic polytheists. Their cultures fairly quickly succumbed before that of the white man. Politically they rapidly became subject to the Westerner. In most of the areas in the temperate zones white settlers and their descendants soon constituted at least a substantial minority and usually a predominant majority of the population. The problems confronting Christianity were partly the winning of the non-European stocks, their protection against exploitation by the white man, and their successful and happy adjustment to the invading culture, and partly the continuation of the traditional allegiance of the immigrants to the faith and the moulding of the new nations which arose from white settlement. In grouping lands and peoples as we have done we are, therefore, moved by considerations other than the arbitrary convenience of the author.

The same questions concern us as through the preceding portions of our journey. What kinds of Christianity spread? Why did they spread? By what processes did they spread? Why was the spread more rapid in some places than in others? What effect did Christianity have upon its environment? What effects did the environment have upon Christianity?

In this volume, as in so much of our narrative, we are compelled to break new ground. No other comprehensive history exists of the planting and growth of Christianity in Canada, Australia, New Zealand, or South Africa. Nowhere else is there a balanced account embracing both Protestantism and Roman Catholicism in Latin America, the West Indies, the islands of the Pacific, Madagascar, or Africa south of the Sahara. Many detailed studies have been made of individual missions and denominations, but in attempting to give a well-rounded picture of the whole we are venturing the task of the pioneer.

Chapter II

BRITISH NORTH AMERICA. ROMAN CATHOLICS; PROTESTANTS

FOR those portions of North America which in the nineteenth century were part of the British Empire, the period opened, not with the even year of 1800, but with the years 1763 and 1783. By the peace of Paris, in 1763, as a result of the Seven Years' War France was excluded politically from North America except for two small islands off Newfoundland, St. Pierre and Miquelon. The process of elimination had been in progress for some time, various pieces of French territory having been progressively taken by the English during a series of wars lasting over two generations. For a brief time under Napoleon I, from 1800 to 1803, France reappeared as the possessor of Louisiana, but the famous sale of that vast region to the United States ended the short dream of renewed empire. In 1783, by the Treaty of Paris, Great Britain recognized the independence of the United States and thus formally admitted the loss of the most populous portion of her American possessions. The years 1763 and 1783, therefore, began a new period for British North America.

British North America, although deprived of what became the United States, was no inconsiderable area. Indeed, in 1914 in square miles it was slightly larger than the continental United States with Alaska. Since, however, so large a portion of it lay in the inhospitable North and so much of it was a mass of ancient rocks, its population was comparatively small, in 1914 slightly under eight millions.

The population was a mixture of various elements. The aborigines, the Indians and the Eskimos, remained, widely scattered. The French continued and, because of a high birth rate, multiplied rapidly. Some settlers moved in from south of the border, many of them those who, during the American Revolution, wished to remain under the British flag. Large numbers came from across the Atlantic, at first chiefly from the British Isles and later from the Continent of Europe. A few entered from the Far East.

Only gradually did the area approach political unity, and then did not fully attain it. In 1840 Upper and Lower Canada, the later provinces of Ontario and

Quebec, were brought together, and in 1849 self government in internal affairs was recognized by Great Britain. In 1867 this union was enlarged into a federal state by the inclusion of Nova Scotia and New Brunswick. In 1869 terms were made with the Hudson Bay Company to incorporate its huge possession, Rupert's Land, and in 1871 British Columbia was added. Prince Edward Island joined in 1873. Newfoundland chose to remain aloof. From Newfoundland the Labrador coast was administered. Here, then, was a huge nation, but sparsely settled, with Newfoundland and the Labrador as a separate administrative unit. Both commonwealths remained part of the British Empire.

In many ways the spread of Christianity in British North America paralleled that in the United States. Both were played upon by many of the same forces. In both there was the problem of the advancing frontier. In both the flood of immigration from the Old World was a challenge. Both had the Indian. Both experienced great changes due to the machine and the accompanying urbanization.

Yet the course of Christianity in British North America presented important contrasts to that in the United States.

In the first place, chiefly because of the French heritage, Roman Catholics were relatively more prominent than in the United States and geographically and racially constituted more of a solid block than in the latter country. Thus, while in the United States in 1890 the Roman Catholic Church had 33.8 per cent. and, in 1916, 37.5 per cent. of the church membership of the land,[1] in about 1881 it had approximately 42.4 per cent.[2] and in 1911 not far from 41.1 per cent. of the total church constituency of Canada.[3] In Newfoundland, the proportion of Roman Catholics was eventually somewhat smaller, in 1901 about 34 per cent. of the total church constituency.[4] Of the Roman Catholics more than half were in what on the eve of the British conquest had been the centre of French strength, Quebec.[5] There they were maintained as a compact enclave under their clergy. In Quebec Protestants were never more than a very small minority. Quebec, therefore, constituted a large overwhelmingly Roman Catholic entity, one for which no exact equivalent existed in the United States. However, Roman Catholicism was represented in all the other provinces, partly by the French and partly by immigrant stocks of other nationalities.

In the second place, Christianity in British North America differed from

---

[1] Department of Commerce, Bureau of the Census, *Religious Bodies, 1916*, Part I, p. 31.
[2] *The Statistical Year-book of Canada for 1890*, p. 422.
[3] *The Canada Year-book 1912*, p. 34.
[4] *The Encyclopædia Britannica*, 11th ed., Vol. XIX, p. 480.
[5] *The Statistical Year-book of Canada for 1890*, p. 423.

that in the great republic to the south in that it seems to have had the nominal allegiance of a much larger proportion of the population. Thus in 1911 more than 95 per cent. of the population of Canada was rated as possessing a church connexion[6] and in Newfoundland in 1901 nearly 100 per cent.[7] as against about 43.5 per cent. in the United States for 1910.[8] This difference even extended to the Indians, for in the United States by 1914 considerably less than half of the Indians acknowledged a formal relationship with the Church,[9] whereas in Canada by the beginning of the twentieth century at least approximately three-fourths and possibly nine-tenths were professedly Christian.[10] However, the figures for the two countries were not exactly comparable. Those for the United States were based upon actual church membership, while those for Canada embraced "adherents," a term which was not confined to formal membership. Even with this difference it seems clear that the proportion of those in British America calling themselves Christian was considerably higher than in the United States.

A third contrast was the absence in British North America of the large Negro element which was so marked in the United States. Some Negroes there were, but not nearly so formidable a segment of the population as in the latter country. The obvious reason for this difference was the lack of development, for climatic reasons, of the plantation system which flourished in slavery days in the southern part of the United States.

A fourth difference was the predominance of British stock—English, Scotch, Irish, and Welsh—especially the first three, in the non-French sections of the population of British America. Immigrants came from the Continent of Europe, but proportionately not in such quantities as to the United States.[11] This made for the preponderance in the Protestant membership of the standard denominations of the British Isles. The Church of England was relatively more prominent than was the Protestant Episcopal Church in the United States. Presbyterians, largely of Scotch and Scotch-Irish ancestry, and Methodists were the other two large denominations. Baptists were numerous, but relatively not so

[6] *The Canada Year Book 1912,* p. 34.

[7] *The Encyclopædia Britannica,* 11th ed., Vol. XIX, p. 480.

[8] Herman C. Weber, *1933 Yearbook of the American Churches* (New York, Round Table Press, 1933, pp. 400), p. 299.

[9] Vol. IV, Chap. 8.

[10] *The Encyclopædia Britannica,* 11th ed., Vol. V, p. 149.

[11] In 1911, of the population of 7,206,643, from 25 to 30 per cent. were of English origin, 13.85 per cent. of Scotch origin, 14.58 per cent. of Irish origin, 28.5 per cent. of French origin, 5.46 per cent. of German origin, leaving only 12.35 per cent. of other, including Indian, origin.—*The Canada Year Book 1912,* p. 22. This was a very different racial picture from that of the United States. For instance, in the latter in 1900 about a quarter were of predominantly German blood and in 1910 about 10 per cent. were Negroes.

much so as in the United States. The Lutherans, of German and Scandinavian provenance, were only small minorities,[12] and such bodies as the Dutch Reformed and the German Reformed scarcely entered into the picture.

With the fourth was associated a fifth difference. The Christianity of British North America was not so varied or so nearly a cross section of Christianity the world around as was that of the United States. Most of the types of historic Christianity were represented, through immigration, in British North America, but the Eastern Churches and the Protestantism of the Continent of Europe were much smaller proportionately than in the United States and the strong French element overweighted the Roman Catholic Church.

A sixth contrast was the much less prominent position held by those denominations which arose on the extreme radical wing of the Protestant Reformation. This probably was in consequence of the fact that in the migration to Canada from Europe the search for sanctuary played no such part it did in the initiation of several of the Thirteen Colonies. Thus Congregationalists, strong in the United States because of their place in the creation of New England and the source of many religious and reform movements, were less than one half of one per cent. of the population of Canada in 1911,[13] whereas in the United States in 1916 they constituted about three-quarters of one per cent. of the population.[14] In the United States, moreover, they provided a much larger proportion of the leadership in letters, morals, education, social reform and religion than in Canada. Baptists, who in Canada in 1911 were 5.31 per cent. of the population,[15] in the United States in 1916 were about 7 per cent. of the population.[16] If the proportion to those having a church connexion were taken, the percentages for Canada of each of these two groups would be only slightly larger, while those for the United States would be more than doubled.

A seventh difference was the absence, in British North America, of such large new indigenous religious denominations as those natives of the United States, the Disciples of Christ, the Church of Jesus Christ of Latter Day Saints (Mormons), and Christian Science. To be sure, in Canada these groups were represented, but they were imported and nothing comparable to them in magnitude sprang from the soil.

An eighth way in which the expansion and development of Christianity in

[12] In Canada in 1911 Lutherans were about 3.19 per cent. of the population (*The Canada Year Book 1912*, p. 34), while in the United States in 1916, although only about 2.5 per cent. of the population, they were nearly 6 per cent. of the church membership (Department of Commerce, Bureau of the Census, *Religious Bodies, 1916*, Part I, p. 20).
[13] *The Canada Year Book 1912*, p. 34.
[14] Department of Commerce, Bureau of the Census, *Religious Bodies, 1916*, Part I, p. 20.
[15] *The Canada Year Book 1912*, p. 34.
[16] Department of Commerce, Bureau of the Census, *Religious Bodies, 1916*, Part I, p. 20.

British North America was dissimilar to the United States was in the history of the frontier. In both areas the westward-moving frontier was of major importance. In Canada, however, there was nothing to correspond to the Mississippi Valley. Between fertile Eastern Ontario and the plains of Manitoba stretched a vast area of ancient rocks, studded with lakes and intersected by streams, but most of it unfitted for cultivation. The wave of settlement did not jump this barrier to any large extent until the last quarter of the nineteenth century, or not far from the time that the frontier was beginning to disappear in the United States. By then the railway and the mechanization of agriculture had made for notable changes in frontier society. Towns were more frequent, communications more rapid, and individual farmsteads and families were not so isolated as in the United States in the early days of white settlements west of the Appalachians. The kind of society which gave rise to camp-meetings was almost non-existent. Moreover, except in Alaska the frontier in the United States lacked the sub-Arctic and Arctic regions which formed so large a part of the area of Canada and Labrador. Frontier conditions, to be sure, for a time prevailed in Ontario, Quebec, the Maritime Provinces, and Newfoundland, but even here white settlement, being somewhat later than in the United States, was in a more mechanized age. The pioneer stage more quickly passed and did not leave the same kind of imprint on Christianity as in the United States.

It was possibly as an outgrowth of the last two factors that a ninth contrast arose. The Protestant Christianity of British North America did not become the source of such explosive, highly emotional religious movements as did that of the United States. No Great Awakening, no series of frontier revivals, no Finney, no Moody, emerged in British North America. The camp-meetings and revivals of the United States had repercussions in Canada but did not originate there. There was even less of originality in new revival movements than in the British Isles. No John Wesley, no Booth with his Salvation Army sprang from the soil. The Protestant Christianity of British North America displayed marked vigour but it was more sober and conservative and had less of the spark of brilliant genius than that of the mother country or of the great republic to the south.

While, therefore, the course of Christianity in British North America had many resemblances to that in the United States and the Christianity of the two areas possessed much in common, identity was strikingly absent.

In our narrative we turn first of all to the expansion of Roman Catholic Christianity.

In an earlier volume we sketched the story of the introduction of Roman

Catholic Christianity to Canada by the French and its spread by colonization and by missions to the Indians. The white population had found its occupation largely in the fur trade and because of the nature of that industry was widely scattered and relatively sparse. The chief towns were Quebec and Montreal and the major centres of white settlement were in their vicinity. Missions to Indians were also over broad reaches of territory. What had seemed the most promising, that to the Hurons, had enjoyed only a short life before it was wiped out by the invasions of the Iroquois. Due largely to the character of the Indian population and the vicissitudes of war, the dauntless heroism of the French missionaries had resulted in no large bodies of converts. Yet by 1763 through settlement and missions to Indians Roman Catholic Christianity was sprinkled widely, even though thinly, over much of what later became the Dominion of Canada. At that date there were said to be about 70,000 Roman Catholics in the land.[17] Of these the overwhelming majority were French.

British rule brought changes to Roman Catholic Christianity but did not place serious restraints upon it. To be sure, the immediate aftermath of the conquest was disheartening. Financial subsidies from France, such as grants to train priests, build churches, and towards the support of the bishop, were discontinued.[18] Rather than serve under the British heretics, numbers of the clergy went to France.[19] The suppression of the Jesuits in French domains about the time of the English conquest and the dissolution of the Society by the Pope in 1773 further weakened the Roman Catholic forces. However, in spite of these adversities and although the British were overwhelmingly Protestant and in face of the fact that in Great Britain at that time they suffered from political disabilities and from strong popular prejudice, in Canada Roman Catholics had the advantage of some favouring conditions. They were allowed religious liberty and the penal laws existing against their fellow believers in England were not extended to them.[20] Religious liberty had been promised by the capitulation of Quebec in 1759, by that of Montreal in 1760, and by the Treaty of Paris of 1763. It had been confirmed by the Quebec Act of 1774 and by the Constitutional Act of 1791.[21] Moreover, the Quebec Act accorded to the Roman Catholic clergy the right to collect their accustomed dues.[22] This gave to the bishops and clergy a fairly large income.[23] The leniency was partly out of the self-

[17] Oliver, *The Winning of the Frontier*, p. 79.
[18] Bracq, *The Evolution of French Canada*, p. 47.
[19] Morice, *History of the Catholic Church in Western Canada*. Vol. I, p. 53
[20] Lindsey, *Rome in Canada*, p. 120.
[21] Oliver, *op. cit.*, p. 92.
[22] Oliver, *op. cit.*, pp. 84-88.
[23] Pascoe, *Two Hundred years of the S.P.G.*, p. 136.

interest of the new rulers, for in light of their troubles with the Thirteen Colonies to the south, the British wished not to antagonize their French subjects. In 1764 the privilege of jury service was extended to the French and two years later Roman Catholics were allowed to practise in all the courts of Canada.[24]

Since the Treaty of Paris did not apply to that island, in 1762 and after 1763 the British governors for a time attempted to suppress Roman Catholicism in Newfoundland. However, to prevent dissatisfaction during the war in which the Thirteen Colonies obtained their independence, toleration soon became the custom. In 1782 a governor in effect granted religious liberty and in 1784 this concession was made formal.[25]

For some years the British administration in Canada sought to exercise the kind of control over the Roman Catholic Church which under the preceding regime had been wielded by the representatives of the French Crown. In theory no ordination was to take place and no assignment to a parish to be made without the consent of the governor.[26] For a time the attempt was made to prevent any direct communication with Rome or any exercise of authority by the Pope.[27] Early, too, the religious communities of men were forbidden to receive new members.[28]

Gradually restrictions were removed. In the War of 1812 between Great Britain and the United States the Roman Catholic bishop, Plessis, was loyal to the British and the parish priests exerted themselves in raising militia. The British Government, therefore, relaxed its pressure on the church and granted Plessis an allowance of £1,000 a year as "Catholic Bishop of Quebec," its first official recognition of the title.[29] Moreover, in 1816 the bishop obtained the consent of the British Government for the creation of new dioceses, although on the express condition that they should be subordinate to Quebec and be classed as *in partibus infidelium*. Between 1820 and 1822 four bishops were,

---

[24] Oliver, *op. cit.*, p. 81.

[25] Howley, *Ecclesiastical History of Newfoundland*, pp. 177-180.

[26] Lindsey, *op. cit.*, p. 127.

[27] Oliver, *op. cit.*, pp. 82-84; H. A. Scott in Shortt and Doughty, *Canada and Its Provinces*, Vol. XI, pp. 12ff.

[28] Scott in Shortt and Doughty, *op. cit.*, Vol. XI, pp. 21ff.

[29] Lindsey, *op. cit.*, p. 141. On the bishops of Quebec see Henri Têtu, *Les Eveques de Québec* (Quebec, Narcisse—S. Hardy, 1889, pp. 692), *passim*. On the early part of the history of the Roman Catholic Church under British rule, from 1760 through 1789, see Auguste Gosselin, *L'Église du Canada après la Conquête* (Quebec, Imprimerie Laflamme, 2 vols., 1916, 1917). For a vigorously unfavourable picture of Roman Catholicism in Canada, emphasizing the ignorance, fanaticism, and superstition said to have been fostered by the church, see Paul Théodore-Vibert, *La Nouvelle France Catholique* (Paris, Librairie Schleicher Frères, 1908, pp. x, 496), *passim*.

accordingly, consecrated. Never thereafter did the British place any obstacles in the way of expanding the hierarchy.[30]

In Newfoundland an Irish Franciscan, James Louis O'Donel, arrived in 1784 as the first prefect apostolic of the island. In 1796 he was made bishop and vicar apostolic. He, too, was loyal to the British Government and at one time helped discourage an incipient mutiny among the troops in St. Johns.[31] At the time that he became bishop three-fourths of the 35,000 who comprised the population of the island are said to have been Roman Catholics.[32]

During the French Revolution the antipathy of both the church and the British to that movement aided the church. More than thirty of the *émigré* priests were granted British passports to Canada and strengthened their church in that land.[33]

The French Canadians had large families and, accordingly, the growth of Roman Catholicism by natural increase was rapid. They were said to total 2,400,000 in 1901, of whom approximately two-thirds were in Canada and one-third in the United States.[34] In 1911 the French in Canada numbered slightly over 2,000,000, or nearly three-tenths of the total population.[35]

To the French were added other Roman Catholic elements by immigration from the other side of the Atlantic. Some came from the Highlands of Scotland. Indeed, the first bishop of Upper Canada was of Scotch birth.[36] In 1911 slightly over 1,000,000, or about one-seventh of the total population of Canada, were of Irish origin.[37] Of these, a large proportion were presumably Roman Catholics. In 1911 in Canada those of German provenance, some of whom were of that faith, were nearly 400,000, those from the Austro-Hungarian Empire, the majority of them probably Roman Catholic, totalled 129,103, Italians, practically all Roman Catholics, were 45,411, Poles, probably almost universally Roman Catholic, were 33,365, and Belgians, also with at least a nominal connexion with that faith, 9,593.[38] Although the Roman Catholics of Canada were French by a large majority, a substantial minority were from other nationalities.

The French in the Province of Quebec and to a certain degree the French

---

[30] Oliver, *op. cit.*, p. 104.
[31] Howley, *op. cit.*, pp. 186-204.
[32] Howley, *op. cit.*, p. 208.
[33] Lindsey, *op. cit.*, p. 142.
[34] Commons, *Races and Immigrants in America*, p. 97.
[35] *The Canada Year Book 1912*, p. 23.
[36] Scott in Shortt and Doughty, *op. cit.*, Vol. XI, pp. 26, 27; Hugh Joseph Somers, *The Life and Times of the Hon. and Rt. Rev. Alexander Macdonell, D.D., First Bishop of Upper Canada 1762-1840* (Washington, Catholic University of America, 1931, pp. lx, 232), *passim*.
[37] *Ibid.*
[38] *Ibid.*

in Ontario presented no especially grave problem to the Roman Catholic Church. The British conquest and rule intensified rather than weakened their loyalty to the faith. Some passed over to Protestantism,[39] but they were in the small minority. The Roman Catholic Church was the one institution which remained theirs, and became both the symbol and the bond of their French heritage. The movement of a large part of the population away from the church which was one of the striking features of the religious history of France in the Revolution and during much of the nineteenth century aroused their abhorrence rather than their emulation. They became extremely conservative in their Roman Catholicism. In the days of French rule Canada had shared the Gallicanism which prevailed in the home land and would have resented any direct supervision and direction from Rome. British rule and what was deemed the apostasy in France combined to strengthen the tie with the Holy See. Gallicanism did not die without a struggle, but ultramontanism increased until it became extremely strong.[40] In few lands did the Roman Catholic Church have so firm a hold upon all phases of the life of the people as it did over the French Canadians, especially in the Province of Quebec. Thus a pastoral letter of 1875 forbade the faithful to have recourse to the civil tribunals when they believed themselves to have suffered injustice at the hands of a priest, but to refer the case to an ecclesiastical court.[41] In elections to civil offices the parish priests are said to have intervened and to have given their support to particular candidates. So active were the bishops in politics that Rome felt constrained to order them to abstain from such participation.[42]

In what eventually were termed the Maritime Provinces active and successful attempts were early put forth to hold to the faith the Roman Catholic population. Some of these Roman Catholics were French. Some were Irish. Some were immigrants from the Scottish Highlands where Roman Catholicism had persisted since pre-Reformation days. French, Irish, and Scotch clergy served the various nationalities and the church prospered.[43] Roman Catholics were eventually between a fourth and a half of the population.

In Newfoundland Irish gradually entered. In 1763 slightly more than one-third of the population were Roman Catholics.[44] By 1827 some of English and

<hr />

[39] For glimpses of a few of these, see *The Life of Rev. Amand Parent, the First French-Canadian Ordained by the Methodist Church* (Toronto, William Briggs, 1887, pp. 235), *passim*.

[40] Lindsey, *op. cit.*, pp. 4, 9.

[41] Lindsey, *op. cit.*, p. 294.

[42] Lindsey, *op. cit.*, p. 271; Bracq, *The Evolution of French Canada*, p. 266; *The Autobiography of a Western Methodist Missionary*, p. 63.

[43] Brasseur de Bourbourg, *Histoire du Canada de son Église et de ses Missions*, Vol. II, pp. 111, 136-146, 169-172; Scott in Shortt and Doughty, *op. cit.*, Vol. XI, pp. 27ff.

[44] Howley, *Ecclesiastical History of Newfoundland*, pp. 165-169.

Protestant descent had become converts.[45] Nuns came from Ireland to carry on schools.[46] In 1844 about seven-tenths of the inhabitants were said to be Roman Catholics.[47]

In the West, where, except in certain communities, Roman Catholics were in the minority,[48] the church faced much the same problem as confronted it in the United States. It had to exert itself to hold to their faith the immigrants who traditionally belonged to it. This was true of those whose parentage was Canadian as well as of those who were from Europe.

Under British rule the Roman Catholic Church was under the necessity of starting almost afresh in the West. The few missionaries of French days had been Jesuits and the Jesuits were now in eclipse. However, before the close of the eighteenth century French Canadians and half-breeds, the result of mixture of the French with the Indians and apparently all of them Roman Catholics, began to penetrate to the West, some of them independently and some of them as employees of the Hudson Bay Company and the North-west Fur Company.[49] To the Red River Settlement, near the later city of Winnipeg, founded in 1811 by the Earl of Selkirk, came a number of Roman Catholics of several nationalities.[50] In 1818, largely at the instance of Lord Selkirk, the Bishop of Quebec sent two French-Canadian priests to the area with the double assignment of caring for the Roman Catholic settlers and winning the Indians.[51] In 1820 one of these, Provencher, was appointed bishop.[52] By 1843 the Red River Settlement contained 5,143 inhabitants of whom 2,798 were Roman Catholics and 2,345 Protestants.[53] In that year the first nuns arrived, as teachers.[54] Great difficulty was experienced in obtaining priests, partly because few were willing to face the hardships of the frontier. However, in 1845 came the first contingent of an order, the Oblates of Mary Immaculate, who were to have a large place in spreading the Roman Catholic faith in the West. Of recent origin, having been founded in France early in the nineteenth century, they had al-

---

[45] Pascoe, *Two Hundred Years of the S.P.G.*, p. 94.

[46] Howley, *op. cit.*, pp. 275ff., 371.

[47] *Notizie Statistiche delle Missioni di Tutto il Mondo Dipendenti dalla S.C. de Propaganda Fide*, pp. 1013ff.

[48] The only provinces in Canada, aside from Quebec, where they numbered more than five-sixths of the population, in which Roman Catholics even approached fifty per cent. of the population were Prince Edward Island and New Brunswick. In Nova Scotia in 1911 they were between a quarter and one-third, and in other provinces approximately between a fourth and a sixth of the population.—*The Canada Year Book 1912*, pp. 32, 33.

[49] Morice, *History of the Catholic Church in Western Canada*, Vol. I, pp. 55ff.

[50] Morice, *op. cit.*, Vol. I, pp. 65ff.

[51] Morice, *op. cit.*, Vol. I, pp. 91ff.; Oliver, *The Winning of the West*, pp. 171-175.

[52] Morice, *op. cit.*, Vol. I, p. 114.

[53] Morice, *op. cit.*, Vol. I, p. 171.

[54] Morice, *op. cit.*, Vol. I, pp. 183-186.

ready entered Canada. Since their object was missions to the underprivileged, they were appealed to by the opportunity to minister to settlers in the new country and by the challenge of the Indians. One of the original group of two Oblates, Alexander Antonin Taché, gave evidence of such zeal and ability that, in spite of his extreme youth, in 1850 he was appointed bishop as coadjutor and successor of Provencher.[55] Left in charge of the vast diocese by the death of his senior in 1853, Taché became the great organizer of his church in the West. Before his death (1894) he had seen the diocese subdivided and he himself had been made archbishop. Roman Catholic immigrants assisted in the development of the country. Some of them were recruited from Eastern Canada and the United States by missionaries.[56] Others came from the Old World.[57] More priests were brought in to care for them. Thus Albert Lacombe, a French Canadian with a dash of Indian blood in his veins, laboured in the West, first as a secular, and later as an Oblate. Although devoting most of his energies to the Indians, at times he also ministered to the white settlers.[58]

To the West migrated Ruthenians, Roman Catholic Uniates of the Greek rite. They began to come in the last decade of the nineteenth century. Eventually they numbered about 300,000, most of them farmers in Manitoba, Saskatchewan, and Alberta. In the new environment some of them were lost to Protestantism and some to the Russian Orthodox and to an independent Græco-Russian church, the Seraphimites. However, French Canadian and Belgian Redemptorist priests began to give them spiritual care and were allowed, for that purpose, to adopt the Byzantine rite. By 1909 over sixty mission stations existed among them, and in 1913 a bishop was appointed for them.[59]

To the West came also Germans[60] and Poles. Roman Catholic newspapers were begun in their languages.[61] Attempts were made to keep the German Roman Catholics apart in separate colonies.[62]

When the diocese of Regina was created (1910) it counted as its Roman Catholic population 18,000 French, 15,000 Ruthenians, 6,500 Germans, 2,800 English and Irish, 2,300 Poles, and 4,000 of other nationalities.[63]

In this Roman Catholic population of British North America, notably among

[55] Morice, *op. cit.*, Vol. I, pp. 226, 227.
[56] Morice, *op. cit.*, Vol. II, pp. 121, 150, 151.
[57] Morice, *op. cit.*, Vol. II, p. 152.
[58] Hughes, *Father Lacombe, passim.*
[59] Attwater, *The Catholic Eastern Churches*, pp. 87, 88; *The Catholic Encyclopedia*, Vol. VI, p. 750.
[60] On German Catholics in the West see Dawson, *Group Settlement. Ethnic Communities in Western Canada*, pp. 275ff.
[61] *Fides News Service*, Feb. 16, 1935.
[62] Dawson, *op. cit.*, pp. 275ff.
[63] Keirstead, *The Church History of the Canadian North-west*, p. 118.

the French, so loyal to their faith, religious orders and congregations flourished. Many were introduced from Europe, especially from France. In time Canada produced more vocations for the priesthood than were needed in the country, so that the orders found it a fertile recruiting ground for their missions in other lands. By 1889 at least thirty-three congregations of sisters had appeared in Canada, partly of native and partly of foreign origin.[64] Between 1889 and 1931 approximately sixty-four new congregations of sisters either were introduced into Canada or were organized there.[65] Numbers of men's orders and teaching brotherhoods also entered.[66] In 1899 an apostolic delegation was instituted for Canada. In 1909 a plenary council for the Roman Catholic Church in Canada was held. At that time the Church had thirty-four archbishops, bishops, vicars apostolic, and prefects apostolic, eight ecclesiastical provinces, twenty-nine dioceses, three vicariates, and two prefectures apostolic.[67]

Roman Catholic missions to the Indians and the Eskimos were extensive and far flung. In 1848 the two chief tribes of Indians in Labrador were mostly Roman Catholic.[68] In Acadia the Micmacs had largely been won in the days of the French occupation and in spite of a lack of clerical care which was not remedied until late in the nineteenth century held to their faith.[69] In 1842 the Jesuits re-entered Canada and before many years were labouring among the Indians of what was eventually known as the Province of Ontario, where their society had had such notable missions under the French regime. Their missions were scattered along the northern shores of Lakes Huron and Superior.[70] In the West the Oblates of Mary Immaculate were the major agency for Roman Catholic efforts for the Indians.[71] They were active among a number of tribes over the vast range of territory from Manitoba to British Columbia and from the southern border to the frozen North. In at least one instance we hear of an Indian language being reduced to writing and special characters devised for it.[72] In contrast with the pre-nineteenth century Spanish missions in the Americas but like most of the missions to the Indians in the United

[64] Le Canada Ecclesiastique, 1932, pp. 141-175.

[65] Le Canada Ecclesiastique, 1932, pp. 712-756. See also Scott in Shortt and Doughty, Canada and Its Provinces, Vol. XI, p. 88.

[66] Le Canada Ecclesiastique, 1932, pp. 125-140, 610-615, 620.

[67] Scott in Shortt and Doughty, op. cit., Vol. XI, p. 111.

[68] Pascoe, Two Hundred Years of the S.P.G., p. 97.

[69] Capucins Missionaires. Missions Françaises, pp. 54-56.

[70] Brasseur de Bourbourg, op. cit., Vol. II, pp. 274ff.; R. P. Lecompte, Les Missions Modernes de la Compagnie de Jésus au Canada (1842-1924) (Montreal, Imprimerie du Messager, 1925, pp. 76), passim.

[71] On the Oblates see Morice, op. cit., passim; Hughes, Father Lacombe, passim; Morice, Fifty Years in Western Canada, passim.

[72] Morice, Fifty Years in Western Canada, pp. 88, 89.

States, little effort was made to uproot the Indian from his old economic and tribal social structure and to induce him to settle down about the mission station and there begin an entirely new way of life, social and moral. Instead, the missionaries went to the Indians, sought to win them where they were and to alter only such customs as seemed to them in contradiction to Christian standards. This often entailed extensive travel, frequently accompanied by much hardship and danger. Here and there, usually with aid from the government, schools were conducted. Eskimos as well as Indians were reached. The first baptisms of Eskimos seem to have been in 1860.[73] As time passed, the state set aside reserves for the Indians and sought to persuade them to engage in agriculture after the manner of the whites.[74] The numbers involved were not large. In 1901 Indians, including half-breeds, in the Dominion of Canada were said to total 127,941.[75] Eskimos were reported to add another 5,000.[76]

Not many came to British North America from the Eastern Orthodox churches. In 1911 about 43,000 in Canada were listed as of Russian origin,[77] but most of them were not Russian by race.[78] A considerable group were Doukhobors, a religious sect of dissenters from the Russian Orthodox Church. Persecuted in Russia, they sought refuge abroad. In 1899, aided by the English Friends, a contingent arrived in Western Canada. Others followed until between 8,000 and 8,500 came.[79] In 1911 somewhat less than 6,000 Bulgarians and Rumanians, most of them recent arrivals and presumably Eastern Orthodox, were in Canada.[80]

The Protestant forms of Christianity enjoyed an even more rapid and extensive growth in British North America than did Roman Catholicism. This was to be expected. In 1763, because of the French background of the European occupation, very few Protestants were to be found in the land. By reason of the rule of Great Britain, a predominantly Protestant power, the majority of the nineteenth century immigration was from England and Scotland and was

---

[73] Morice, *History of the Catholic Church in Western Canada*, Vol. I, p. 292.
[74] Rogers, *Canada's Greatest Need*, p. 122.
[75] *The Canada Year Book 1912*, p. 23.
[76] Rogers, *op. cit.*, p. 125.
[77] *The Canada Year Book 1912*, p. 23.
[78] Woodsworth, *Strangers Within Our Gates*, p. 114.
[79] Woodsworth, *op. cit.*, pp. 115ff.; Dawson, *Group Settlement. Ethnic Communities in Western Canada*, pp. 1-91.
[80] *The Canada Year Book 1912*, p. 23.

Protestant by background.[81] Other large Protestant contingents came from Germany and Scandinavia and from the United States. Moreover, this movement took place during an age marked by a rising tide of life within Protestantism, and especially within British and American Protestantism. These currents made themselves powerfully felt in British North America. They contributed greatly to holding to their inherited faith those of Protestant ancestry and helped to make the Canadian Protestant churches active not only in winning the frontier and in retaining the allegiance of the immigrants, but also in reaching the non-Christian elements of the population and in sharing prominently in the Protestant foreign missionary enterprise.

Indeed, Protestantism seems to have been rather more successful in holding its traditional constituency in British North America than in the United States. While in the latter the percentage having a formal connexion with the Protestant churches increased in the 1800's, at the outset of the century the vast majority were without such a tie and the churches never fully closed the gap. In Canada, however, the overwhelming majority seem from the very first to have thought of themselves as affiliated with one or another of the churches.

In the spread of Protestant Christianity in British North America, both among whites and Indians, far more active assistance came from Great Britain than to the United States either in the nineteenth century or in pre-independence days. In the nineteenth century British missionary societies were decidedly more numerous and aggressive than in the seventeenth and eighteenth centuries. Naturally they directed their efforts to the British Empire rather than to the United States, where, during much of the century, antagonism to the British still lingered. Moreover, missionaries to the new settlements in British North America came also from the United States.

Extensive aid was given by societies and individuals connected with the Church of England. The Society for the Propagation of the Gospel in Foreign Parts, already venerable in 1763, contributed generously in men and money. By the opening of the twentieth century it had employed 1,597 missionaries, British and colonial, had assisted 921 stations, and had spent £1,891,154. It had laboured among both whites and Indians.[82] The Society for Promoting Christian Knowledge, slightly older than its sister society, assisted in the erection of

---

[81] In 1911 2,820,030, or more than half of those of non-French blood, were of British and Scottish origin.—*The Canada Year Book 1912*, p. 23.

[82] Pascoe, *Two Hundred Years of the S.P.G.*, pp. 192, 193; Mountain, *A Memoir of George J. Mountain*, pp. 173, 221, 341, 347; Clarke, *Constitutional Church Government*, p. 206. For a biography of one of its missionaries in Nova Scotia see William S. Bartlet, *The Frontier Missionary: A Memoir of the Life of the Rev. Jacob Bailey* (Boston, Ide and Dutton, 1853, pp. xi, 365).

churches and in the establishment of colleges and universities.[83] One of the most notable of the British missionaries was Charles James Stewart (1775-1837). A younger son of the Earl of Galloway and a graduate of Oxford, he felt called to devote himself to missions. He had thought of India but, hearing of the need in Canada, he went to that country. There for a time he was a travelling missionary, founding new churches. In 1826 he became (Anglican) Bishop of Quebec. A man of simple sincerity, he lived in ascetic fashion and devoted both his own fortune and his stipend to the advancement of the Church of England in the pioneer land. He repeatedly visited Great Britain and there stimulated the formation of the Upper Canada Clergy Society (later merged with the Society for the Propagation of the Gospel in Foreign Parts) and the Stewart Mission Fund, both to assist in nourishing his church.[84] In 1820 the Church Missionary Society sent John West to the Red River colony. For an even hundred years it supported missionaries to Indians and white settlers, sending in all 172 missionaries and 48 women workers and giving £834,113. Then in 1920 it withdrew, transferring its enterprises to the missionary society of the Church of England in Canada.[85] The Colonial and Continental Church Society, earlier the Colonial Church and School Society, aided with missions to the whites from Newfoundland to the Far West.[86] The New England Company, which had been organized in the seventeenth century to assist missions to Indians in New England,[87] withdrew its support from the latter when the Thirteen Colonies broke away from the British Empire and transferred most of its efforts to the parts of North America which remained in British hands.[88] Through Samuel Codner, who had been in Newfoundland and had been touched by the Evangelical revival, in 1823 there was formed in London by leading Evangelicals the Society for Educating the Poor of Newfoundland, later termed the Newfoundland and British North America Society for Educating the Poor and eventually the Church of England Society for Newfound-

[83] Allen and McClure, *Two Hundred Years: The History of the Society for Promoting Christian Knowledge*, pp. 312-330, 368-372; Bompas, *Diocese of Mackenzie River*, pp. 30, 31.

[84] Langtry, *History of the Church in Eastern Canada and Newfoundland*, pp. 43-50; Vernon, *The Old Church in the New Dominion*, p. 87; W. J. D. Waddilove, *The Stewart Missions. A Series of Letters and Journals Calculated to Exhibit to British Christians the Spiritual Destitution of the Emigrants Settled in the Remote Parts of Upper Canada* (London, J. Hatchard & Son, 1838, pp. xvi, 252), *passim*.

[85] Vernon, *op. cit.*, pp. 123-125, 132.

[86] Tucker, *From Sea to Sea the Dominion*, p. 45.

[87] Vol. III, pp. 219, 221.

[88] *History of the New England Company* (London, Taylor and Co., 1871, pp. xv, 353), *passim; Report of the Proceedings of the New England Company . . . during the years 1871-1872* (London, Taylor and Co., 1874, pp. xix, 413), *passim*.

land and the Colonies.[89] In 1854, through Lord Shaftesbury and others, the Mission to the Free Coloured Population of Canada was organized in England to aid those escaping from slavery in the United States.[90]

The Presbyterians of the British Isles and of the United States assisted in the establishment of Presbyterian churches in British North America. In 1825 the Glasgow Colonial Society was organized "for promoting the Moral and religious interests of the Scottish Settlers of British North America" and during the fifteen years of its existence sent out missionaries.[91] In 1765 at the invitation of settlers the Associate Synod of the Secession Church appointed two missionaries to Nova Scotia. Only one of these seems to have reached his destination. Other clergymen followed.[92] Ministers of the Associate Synod also went to what eventually became Ontario.[93] Assistance to the Presbyterian cause came from south of the Great Lakes from similar groups in the Thirteen Colonies. James Lyon, sent in 1764 by the Presbytery of New Brunswick, New Jersey, to Nova Scotia, was said to be the first Presbyterian clergyman since the brief early Huguenot efforts to labour within the bounds of the later Dominion of Canada.[94] From the Associate or Secession Synod formed in Philadelphia in 1753 came missionaries.[95] At least two individual congregations were offshoots of the Presbyterianism of the United States.[96] The Dutch Reformed Church of the United States sent a number of missionaries to Upper Canada, the later Ontario, among them Robert McDowall, who did much for the settlers in pioneer days. These efforts ceased about 1818 when the Presbytery of the Canadas was organized.[97] The Free Church of Scotland assisted those congregations in Canada who were in sympathy with it by aiding colleges with teachers and funds and by money and personnel for missions in the West.[98] Large numbers of young men came from Great Britain to the Presbyterian ministry in Western Canada.[99] In 1861 the Irish Presbyterian Church

[89] Mullins, *Our Beginnings*, pp. 1-12.

[90] Mullins, *op. cit.*, p. 21.

[91] Balfour, *Presbyterianism in the Colonies*, pp. 17-19.

[92] Robertson, *History of the Mission of the Secession Church to Nova Scotia and Prince Edward Island*, p. 20; M'Kerrow, *History of the Foreign Missions of the Secession and United Presbyterian Church*, pp. 37ff.

[93] M'Kerrow, *op. cit.*, pp. 106ff. For a United Presbyterian minister in Ontario from Scotland who had formerly been a missionary in South Africa, see Cochrane, *Memoirs and Remains of the Reverend Walter Inglis*, pp. 94ff.

[94] McNeill, *The Presbyterian Church in Canada*, pp. 4, 5.

[95] McNeill, *op. cit.*, p. 5.

[96] McNeill, *op. cit.*, pp. 5, 6.

[97] Gregg, *History of the Presbyterian Church in the Dominion of Canada*, p. 168; McNeill, *op. cit.*, p. 4.

[98] Balfour, *Presbyterianism in the Colonies*, p. 42.

[99] Keirstead, *The Church History of the Canadian North-west*, p. 264.

sent a missionary to Victoria, on Vancouver Island, a year before the Canada Presbyterian Church appointed its first missionaries to British Columbia.[100] Through its missionaries the Church of Scotland had a leading part in laying the foundations of Presbyterianism in British Columbia.[101]

Methodism in British North America owed its inception and much of its early growth to missionaries from the United States and the British Isles. It is said that the first regular Methodist preacher in Upper Canada was from the New York Conference. Numbers of the early Methodist itinerants there were from south of the border and employed on the Canadian frontier the methods which were proving so successful among the new settlements of the United States.[102] It was they who in 1805 introduced the camp-meeting, that recent development in the West.[103] The War of 1812 aroused resentment in Canada and made difficult the work of the Methodist preachers from the United States.[104] Methodist missionaries came from Great Britain.[105] For many years, indeed, a large number of Methodists in Canada were formally connected with the British rather than with the Canada Conference.[106] The Primitive Methodists and the Methodist New Connexion also received aid from the corresponding bodies in Great Britain.[107]

Congregationalism in British North America was deeply indebted to active help from the United States and Great Britain. Settlers from New England brought Congregationalism with them and some New England ministers visited or travelled among them.[108] The London Missionary Society sent missionaries to Canada and assisted with money.[109] In 1836, to give support to clergy in Canada the Congregational Union in London appointed a committee which eventually became the Colonial Missionary Society.[110] Numbers of Congregational ministers migrated to Canada from Great Britain.[111] The American Missionary Association interested itself in the Negroes who took

[100] Gordon, *The Life of James Robertson*, p. 80.
[101] *Ibid.;* McNeill, *op. cit.,* p. 103.
[102] Sanderson, *The First Century of Methodism in Canada*, Vol. I, pp. 27-32, 36-38.
[103] Sanderson, *op. cit.,* Vol. I, p. 44. On the camp-meeting and the revival on the Ontario frontier see M. A. Garland, *Some Phases of Pioneer Religious Life in Upper Canada before 1850* in *Ontario Historical Society Papers and Records,* Vol. XXV (Toronto, 1929), pp. 231ff.
[104] Sanderson, *op. cit.,* Vol. I, p. 97.
[105] Sanderson, *op. cit.,* Vol. I, pp. 89, 174.
[106] Sanderson, *op. cit.,* Vol. II, pp. 57, 58, 96.
[107] Sanderson, *op. cit.,* Vol. I, pp. 447, 449.
[108] Wood, *Memoir of Henry Wilkes*, pp. 20-23.
[109] Fergusson, *Historic Chapters in Christian Education in America,* p. 19; Wood, *op. cit.,* pp. 17, 23.
[110] Wood, *op. cit.,* p. 84.
[111] Wood, *op. cit.,* p. 44.

refuge in Canada from slavery in the United States. For a time in the 1820's and 1830's the American Home Missionary Society supported Congregational and Presbyterian missionaries in Canada.[112]

To the Baptists came some assistance from Great Britain. Thus with the aid of funds from England a college for the training of clergymen was opened in Montreal in 1838 and persisted until 1849.[113] In 1837 the Baptist Canadian Missionary Society was organized in England to collect funds for the Baptist cause in Canada.[114]

To the Moravians, largely immigrants from Russia, subsidies and men were contributed by their brethren in the United States and, to a less extent, from across the Atlantic.[115]

We now turn to a brief account of the planting of Protestantism in some of its more prominent forms in the various sections of British North America.

First we must speak of what were once known as Lower and Upper Canada, later the Provinces of Quebec and Ontario. The pre-emption of Lower Canada by French Roman Catholics kept Protestantism from being more than a minority faith in that region, but strong footholds were obtained, chiefly in the cities. Upper Canada, at the outset of the period containing few French, became the chief centre of Anglo-Saxon settlement and, accordingly, of Protestantism.

It was to be expected that the Church of England would be early represented. About the time of the British conquest John Ogilvie, a missionary of the Society for the Propagation of the Gospel in Foreign Parts among the Mohawk Indians, became chaplain of a regiment in Quebec and in and around that city organized congregations and made some converts from the Roman Catholics. After he left, these beginnings dwindled. By 1781 the English-speaking population of Upper and Lower Canada was said to be 6,000 and to be without a clergyman of the Church of England.[116] After the outbreak of the Revolution in the Thirteen Colonies fairly large numbers of Loyalists, those faithful to the British Crown, migrated to Canada, chiefly to Upper Canada.[117] One of these, John Stuart, a native of Virginia and for a time a missionary among the Mohawks, as an agent of the Society for the Propagation of the Gospel in Foreign Parts became the "father of the church in Upper

[112] Silcox, *Church Union in Canada*, p. 42.
[113] Fitch, *The Baptists of Canada*, pp. 118-121.
[114] Fitch, *op. cit.*, p. 114.
[115] Stocker, *A Home Mission History of the Moravian Church in the United States and Canada*, pp. 232ff.
[116] Langtry, *History of the Church is Eastern Canada and Newfoundland*, p. 40.
[117] Vernon, *The Old Church in the New Dominion*, pp. 57-66.

Canada."[118] In 1793 the Anglican diocese of Quebec was created. In 1839 it was divided and Toronto was made the seat of a bishop.[119] By 1843 there were said to be 60 clergymen in the diocese of Quebec[120] and by 1842 102 clergymen in the diocese of Toronto.[121] By 1863 two other dioceses had been created in Ontario.[122] Support came from the government in the form of the clergy reserves, one-seventh of all the lands in Upper Canada and of all lands in Lower Canada which were not already occupied by the French population set aside for the support of a "Protestant clergy." These became a bone of contention among the various denominations, for non-Anglicans, especially the Presbyterians, claimed the right to share in them. However, considerable income was derived from them for the clergy of the Church of England and eventually a portion of those in Upper Canada were commuted for a permanent endowment.[123] Although substantial help came in this fashion and from Great Britain, the settlers early began to organize for the extension of their church. In 1842, for instance, in Upper Canada a Diocesan Church Society was formed which within four years was supporting from ten to twelve missionaries within its area.[124] Later, when, in 1873, the Bishopric of Toronto was divided and the northern portion was constituted a separate see, the new ecclesiastical division became to a large degree a mission field of the Canadian church.[125]

Presbyterianism was strong in Upper and Lower Canada. As the prevailing faith in Scotland and in one of its forms, the Church of Scotland, enjoying a privileged position in that country, it was fairly certain to be prominent in lands settled from Great Britain. Some Presbyterians entered from the United States in the years between the Revolutionary War and the War of 1812. The predominant elements were from Scotland and Ireland.[126] Various strains of Presbyterianism were represented. When in 1818 a presbytery was formed in

---

[118] *Ibid.;* Pascoe, *Two Hundred Years of the S.P.G.,* pp. 154, 155.

[119] *The Church in Canada, No. II. A Journal of Visitation to a Part of the Diocese of Quebec by the Lord Bishop of Montreal in the Spring of 1843* (London, Society for the Propagation of the Gospel in Foreign Parts, 1844, pp. iv, 80), p. iii.

[120] *Ibid.*

[121] *The Church in Canada. A Journal of Visitation to the Western Portion of His Diocese by the Lord Bishop of Toronto in the Autumn of 1842,* pp. iii, iv.

[122] Langtry, *op. cit.,* pp. 201, 218. For a list of the bishops with brief chronological summaries of their careers, see Owsley Robert Rowley, *The Anglican Episcopate of Canada and Newfoundland* (Milwaukee, Wis., Morehouse Publishing Co., 1928, pp. xix, 280), *passim.*

[123] Pascoe, *op. cit.,* pp. 161-163.

[124] Pascoe, *op. cit.,* p. 160.

[125] Tucker, *From Sea to Sea the Dominion,* pp. 93, 94.

[126] McNeill, *The Presbyterian Church in Canada,* p. 6; Silcox, *Church Union in Canada,* p. 15.

Upper Canada independent of any of the Scottish churches it was partly with the hope that it would thus be easier to unite all the Presbyterians in the province in one organization.[127] The fulfilment of that hope, however, was to be postponed. The Disruption in Scotland (1843) was followed by one in Canada (1844) on similar lines.[128] The United Presbyterians formed themselves into a synod (1834) in connexion with the parent church in the mother country.[129] It was not until 1875 that a union merged all the Presbyterian bodies in the Presbyterian Church in Canada and it was even later that a few unreconciled congregations entered the union.[130] By the end of the century, however, a strong nation-wide Presbyterian body had come into being.

It was not strange that Methodism became one of the three most numerous Protestant denominations in British North America. The period of the settlement by Anglo-Saxon stock coincided with the rapid growth of the Methodist movement in Great Britain and the United States. Moreover, as in the United States, Methodism was singularly fitted to the frontier by message and organization. Soon after the British conquest a local preacher in the army at Quebec held services among the immigrants.[131] Methodists came from the British Isles and the United States. The Anglicans found that Methodist itinerant preachers were providing a ministry more adapted to the outlook of the settlers than were the clergy of the Church of England and that they were winning those who were traditionally of that body.[132] For a time the Methodism of the United States had a larger direct share in nourishing the Methodism of Upper Canada than did that of Great Britain. Indeed, the majority of the Methodists of Upper Canada were long affiliated with those of the United States. Until the War of 1812 Methodism in both Upper and Lower Canada was organizationally connected with the Methodist Episcopal Church of the United States and a considerable proportion of its preachers were from the United States. The War of 1812 brought difficulties and British preachers established themselves in Lower Canada and in parts of Upper Canada. In 1820 Upper Canada was allotted to the American and Lower Canada to the British preachers. In 1824 the Methodists of Upper Canada were organized into an annual conference, but still as a part of the Methodist Episcopal Church.[133] In 1828 this

---

[127] Balfour, *Presbyterianism in the Colonies*, p. 20.

[128] Balfour, *op. cit.*, pp. 29-31.

[129] McNeill, *op. cit.*, p. 16.

[130] McNeill, *op. cit.*, p. 47.

[131] Sanderson, *The First Century of Methodism in Canada*, Vol. I, pp. 23-26.

[132] Langtry, *op. cit.*, p. 47.

[133] Sanderson, *op. cit.*, Vol. I, pp. 105-109. For the lives of some of the preachers from the United States as well as the early history of Methodism in Canada, see by a participant, John Carroll, *Case and His Contemporaries; or the Canadian Itinerants' Memorial; Constituting a Biographical History of Methodism in Canada from Its Introduction into*

conference effected a peaceable separation from its parent and organized itself as the Methodist Episcopal Church in Canada.[134] In 1833 a union of this body with the British Conference was brought about which involved a change of name for the Canadian church to Wesleyan Methodist, the dropping of the episcopate, and some other alterations in polity. Between 1840 and 1847 the British Conference withdrew from its co-operation with the Canada Conference, but in the latter year the union was restored. In 1874, with other Methodist bodies in the Dominion, the Methodists of Lower and Upper Canada joined in the Methodist Church of Canada.[135]

Congregationalism appeared fairly early in Upper and Lower Canada.[136] The outstanding leader in its promotion, however, Henry Wilkes, did not begin his ministry there until the 1830's. Henry Wilkes (1805-1886) was born in Birmingham, England, the son of a Congregational manufacturer. In his late boyhood he came with his family to the New World and in Canada helped as a layman in more than one church. Although successful in business, he left it, in his middle twenties, to study for the ministry. This he did in Great Britain. In 1832 he returned to Canada and made a long exploring tour under the Canada Education and Home Missionary Society which had been formed in 1827 to provide clergymen, whether Presbyterian, Congregational, or Baptist, for destitute places. From 1833 to 1836 he was a pastor in Scotland, but he could not forget the need of Canada and in 1836 returned to become pastor of a struggling church in Montreal. He persuaded ministers to come out from England, had a part in bringing into being the Colonial Missionary Society, from 1853 was secretary-treasurer of the Canada Congregational Missionary Society to which funds came from both Canada and Britain, and was also principal of the Congregational college. The Congregational Union of Upper Canada and a similar body for Lower Canada were formed in the 1830's.[137] While, as we have said, Congregationalism did not become so prominent in Canada as in the United States, in the provinces of Ontario and Quebec it developed fairly strong centres.

Few Baptists were among the refugees from the revolting Thirteen Colonies

---

the Province, till the Death of the Rev. William Case in 1855 (Toronto, Samuel Rose, 4 vols., 1867-1874), *passim.*

[134] Sanderson, *op. cit.,* Vol. I, pp. 141-146. In 1811 there were 2,550 Methodists in Upper Canada and 2,792 in Lower Canada.—Sanderson, *op. cit.,* Vol. I, p. 62.

[135] Cornish, *Cyclopædia of Methodism in Canada,* pp. 15-19. Much of the history of Methodism in Canada is to be found in accounts of one of its leading figures in the two middle quarters of the nineteenth century. Egerton Ryerson, *The Story of My Life* and Sissons, *Egerton Ryerson. His Life and Letters.*

[136] There was a Congregational church formed in the city of Quebec in 1801.—Wood, *Memoirs of Henry Wilkes,* p. 17.

[137] Wood, *op. cit., passim.*

who migrated to Canada, for, in general, Baptists favoured independence from Great Britain. However, by 1800 more than one Baptist church had been organized in Upper and Lower Canada. At the outset the Baptists in what was later the western part of Ontario were from the United States, and those in the eastern part were largely from Scotland and England.[138] In 1819 an association was formed. In 1833 members from three associations organized the Missionary Convention of Upper Canada. In 1836 this was succeeded by the Upper Canada Baptist Missionary Society. In that year in the eastern part of Canada the Canada Baptist Missionary Society was constituted. Both bodies appealed to the Baptists of Great Britain for aid, for both were primarily for the extension of the Baptist cause in Canada.[139] In 1851 Baptists in Upper and Lower Canada are said to have numbered between 7,000 and 10,000.[140] In 1871 the membership was about 16,600.[141] In the following decade over a hundred churches were organized.[142] In 1890 there were 388 churches and 33,000 members. Much of the growth had been brought about by home missionary organizations.[143]

To Canada, and especially to Upper Canada, came Quakers, chiefly after the American Revolution and in the main from the United States as part of the westward migration to inviting virgin lands.[144]

In what became the Maritime Provinces of the Dominion of Canada, Nova Scotia, New Brunswick, and Prince Edward Island, the ecclesiastical, like the political history, until past the middle of the nineteenth century, was largely although not entirely distinct from that of Upper and Lower Canada.

The region came into the possession of Great Britain slightly earlier than did Upper and Lower Canada. When it passed into British hands a number of settlers entered from New England.[145] They brought with them Congregationalism. Until the American Revolution this was much stronger than the Church of England.[146] Indeed, before 1776 the Congregationalists were dominant in Nova Scotia. They asked and received a guarantee of civil and religious liberty.[147] The Congregational churches were founded spontaneously by the settlers and received little help from the outside. They experienced difficulty

[138] Fitch, *The Baptists of Canada*, pp. 102-108.
[139] Fitch, *op. cit.*, pp. 111, 114.
[140] Fitch, *op. cit.*, p. 131.
[141] Fitch, *op. cit.*, p. 152.
[142] Fitch, *op. cit.*, p. 153.
[143] Fitch, *op. cit.*, p. 155.
[144] Dorland, *A History of the Society of Friends* (Quakers) *in Canada*, pp. 50ff.
[145] Mackinnon, *Settlements and Churches in Nova Scotia, 1749-1776*, pp. 17-23.
[146] Mackinnon, *op. cit.*, pp. 60, 61, 70-76.
[147] Wood, *Memoir of Henry Wilkes*, p. 7.

in obtaining satisfactory pastors.[148] The Great Awakening spread from New England to Nova Scotia. Its great leader was Henry Alline (1748-1784). He was born in Rhode Island and as a lad was taken by his parents to Nova Scotia. There he was deeply stirred by the revival, became an indefatigable preacher, and before his early death from over-work had been the means of the conversion of hundreds and had done much to alter the moral tone of the settlements.[149] Out of the revivals came, as in New England, some Baptist churches.[150]

To this flourishing Congregationalism the American Revolution brought disaster. Most of the Congregationalists and their clergy sympathized with the revolting colonies. Large numbers moved out of British territory into the United States. In 1809 only four Congregational churches are said to have survived in Nova Scotia.[151]

Presbyterianism also entered before the American Revolution. It was brought in by Scotch settlers who had come by way of New Hampshire and by Scotch Highlanders and Scotch-Irish directly from the other side of the Atlantic. Presbyterian clergymen came, the first to reside in the future Dominion of Canada. Most of these were sent by the Associate Synod and the General Associate Synod, organs of small dissenting groups in Scotland, better known as the Burghers and Anti-Burghers.[152]

Although weak numerically, the Church of England had the advantage of being established by law through one of the earliest acts of the legislature of Nova Scotia.[153] The Society for the Propagation of the Gospel in Foreign Parts supported missionaries.[154]

The American Revolution not only weakened Congregationalism in Nova Scotia. It also brought to the later Maritime Provinces numbers of "Empire Loyalists," those who were not in accord with the independence of the Thirteen Colonies. Among these were missionaries of the Society for the Propaga-

---

[148] Mackinnon, op. cit., pp. 70-76.

[149] Mackinnon, op. cit., p. 83.

[150] Bill, Fifty Years with the Baptist Ministers and Churches of the Maritime Provinces, pp. 15, 16.

[151] Mackinnon, op. cit., pp. 60, 61, 70-76, 92; H. W. Barker in Church History, Vol. VII, pp. 371-380. Yet in the nineteenth century Congregationalism partially recovered.— Wood, op. cit., pp. 6, 51.

[152] Mackinnon, op. cit., pp. 49-51, 77-81; Robertson, History of the Mission of the Secession Church to Nova Scotia and Prince Edward Island, pp. 6, 18-25, 89.

[153] Langtry, History of the Church of England in Eastern Canada and Newfoundland pp. 23, 24.

[154] Mackinnon, op cit., p. 63; Vernon, The Old Church in the New Dominion, p. 81; Pascoe, Two Hundred Years of the S.P.G., pp. 107ff., 124ff.; Langtry, op. cit., pp. 14-16; Hawkins, Historical Notices of the Missions of the Church of England in the North American Colonies Previous to the Independence of the United States, pp. 354ff.

tion of the Gospel in Foreign Parts.[155] From then on the Church of England increased in strength. Numbers of the refugees from New England joined the Church of England. In 1787, Charles Inglis, formerly missionary of the society in several points in the Thirteen Colonies and rector of Trinity Church in New York City, was consecrated bishop of Nova Scotia but with a diocese which at the outset embraced much of British North America and Bermuda.[156] Aided by a grant from Parliament, the Society for the Propagation of the Gospel in Foreign Parts assisted in the support of clergymen.[157] It also contributed to the erection of churches.[158] While for a time the region suffered from a dearth of clergy, eventually this deficiency was made good.[159]

Not the Anglicans but the Presbyterians became numerically the strongest of the Protestant denominations in the Maritime Provinces. At the close of the American Revolution ex-soldiers of the Highland regiments joined the Highlanders who were already there.[160] A few ministers came from the Associate Synod and the General Associate Synod.[161] From the latter arrived, in 1786, James MacGregor. For more than forty years he traversed the region, often in the face of great hardships, preaching in Gaelic and English, organizing congregations, and erecting churches.[162] A younger colleague was Thomas McCulloch. He took a leading part in promoting education and in training clergy.[163] In 1817 most of the varieties of Presbyterians united in the Synod of Nova Scotia.[164] Missionaries came from the Church of Scotland, numbers of them as agents of the Glasgow Colonial Society.[165] In Nova Scotia in the Disruption of 1843 the majority of the clergy took the side of the Free Church.

---

[155] Eaton, *The Church of England in Nova Scotia and the Tory Clergy of the Revolution*, pp. 150, 155-157; Vernon, *op. cit.*, pp. 45-56; Pascoe, *op. cit.*, pp. 124ff.

[156] John Wolfe Lydekker, *The Life and Letters of Charles Inglis. His Ministry in America and Consecration as First Colonial Bishop, from 1759 to 1787* (London, Society for Promoting Christian Knowledge, 1936, pp. xv, 272. Based upon manuscript sources), *passim;* Anderson, *The History of the Church of England in the Colonies and the Foreign Dependencies of the British Empire*, Vol. III, p. 463; Langtry, *op. cit.*, pp. 26ff.

[157] Eaton, *op. cit.*, p. 221.

[158] Pascoe, *op. cit.*, p. 123.

[159] *Church in the Colonies, No. 16. Notes on a Visitation Tour Through Parts of the Diocese of Fredericton, New Brunswick, in 1846* (London, Society for the Propagation of the Gospel in Foreign Parts, 1846, pp. 26), p. 23; *The Church in the Colonies, No. III, A Journal of Visitation in Nova Scotia, Cape Breton, and along the Eastern Shore of New Brunswick, by the Lord Bishop of Nova Scotia in the Summer and Autumn of 1843* (London, Society for the Propagation of the Gospel in Foreign Parts, 1844, pp. ix, 72), *passim.*

[160] McNeill, *The Presbyterian Church in Canada*, p. 8.

[161] Robertson, *op. cit.*, pp. 255-258.

[162] McNeill, *op. cit.*, pp. 8, 9.

[163] McNeill, *op. cit.*, pp. 9-11.

[164] Robertson, *op. cit.*, p. 54; Balfour, *Presbyterianism in the Colonies*, p. 15.

[165] McNeill, *op. cit.*, p. 12.

In New Brunswick, in contrast, most of the ministers remained in the Synod of New Brunswick in Connexion with the Church of Scotland (organized in 1833) and only three withdrew (1845) to form the Synod of the (Free) Presbyterian Church of New Brunswick.[166] Regardless of their ecclesiastical affiliations, most of the early Presbyterian clergy had scanty incomes and depended partly upon farming for their support.[167] As the population grew and wealth increased, the older churches were able to join in sending out home missionaries. In 1875 fifty-three of these were employed to take possession of unoccupied points in the Maritime Provinces.[168] Presbyterianism had become firmly rooted and was propagating itself.

While not so numerous as Presbyterians, Methodists were prominent in the Maritime Provinces. Methodists were among the early settlers from Yorkshire. In 1779 a revival broke out among them and one of the converts, William Black, became an itinerant preacher. Some help came from the United States. Black and two others were ordained at Philadelphia in 1789 by Bishops Coke and Asbury and Black was appointed superintendent. In 1791 the New York Conference assigned preachers to Nova Scotia and New Brunswick.[169] However, more assistance was given by the British Conference. By 1816 nineteen missionaries had been sent. In 1799 Black himself went to England to ask for recruits and the following year returned with a party of missionaries.[170] By 1804 all the preachers from the United States had been withdrawn. The region was divided into missionary districts connected with the British Conference. In 1855 these were organized into the Conference of Eastern British America which in turn was affiliated with the British Conference. This was the arrangement until 1874, when Methodism in the Maritime Provinces was merged into the Methodist Church of Canada.[171] Canadian Methodism had finally attained its majority.

Next to the Presbyterians, the Baptists were the largest denomination in the Maritime Provinces. Here, indeed, by 1911 they were more numerous than

[166] Balfour, *op. cit.*, pp. 29-31; McNeill, *op. cit.*, pp. 14, 16.

[167] Robertson, *op. cit.*, p. 47.

[168] McNeill, *op. cit.*, p. 96.

[169] Sanderson, *The First Century of Methodism in Canada*, Vol. I, pp. 16-21.

[170] Marsden, *The Narrative of a Mission to Nova Scotia, New Brunswick and the Somers Islands*, pp. 3, 252.

[171] Carroll, *Cyclopædia of Methodism in Canada*, p. 15. On the Bible Christians, a division of Methodism introduced from Great Britain and to which the Bible Christian Missionary Society sent an agent in 1831, see John Harris, *The Life of the Rev. Francis Metherall and the History of the Bible Christian Church in Prince Edward Island* (London, Bible Christian Book Room, 1883, pp. vi, 111). On a Wesleyan Methodist, formerly an Irish Roman Catholic, see *The Autobiography of a Wesleyan Methodist Missionary, passim*.

in any other section of the Dominion.[172] This was no sudden achievement. The preaching of Henry Alline contributed to their growth.[173] Numbers of Negroes settled in the Maritime Provinces and the overwhelming majority of these became Baptists.[174] One of the early preachers among them was David George, who had been born a slave in Virginia, had run away, was caught, and was then converted through another Negro. When, during the American Revolution, the British evacuated Charleston, he went to Nova Scotia, preached to Negroes, and organized a Baptist church.[175] Most of the Baptists were, however, white. Until 1800 only individual churches existed. Beginning with that year associations of churches were formed.[176] Free Baptists, with an Arminian theology, and Regular Baptists, Calvinistic by tradition, were long separate.[177] Not until 1905 was a comprehensive union effected in the United Baptist Convention of the Maritime Provinces.[178] Many years earlier various organizations for home missions had assisted in the establishment of Baptist churches in all three provinces.[179] The denomination was later in taking form in Prince Edward Island than in the other two. The first Baptist preacher, a native of Scotland, came in 1814. Others followed from Nova Scotia and New Brunswick.[180] In general, the Baptist growth in the Maritime Provinces was an indigenous development, arising spontaneously from the convictions of the Baptists already there and with little help from the outside.[181]

To the Maritime Provinces came Quakers, some of them before the American Revolution and a few as Loyalists. Eventually, however, these early groups either returned to the United States or were absorbed ecclesiastically into the dominant denominations.[182]

In Newfoundland the Church of England became the largest of the Protestant denominations, with Methodism a fairly close second, with a substantial number of adherents of the Salvation Army, more than in any of the provinces of the Dominion of Canada, and with relatively small contingents of Presbyterians and Congregationalists.

As early as 1697 a clergyman of the Church of England settled in New-

---

[172] *The Canada Year Book 1912*, pp. 28, 29.

[173] Bill, *Fifty Years with the Baptist Ministers and Churches of the Maritime Provinces*, pp. 14, 15.

[174] Fitch, *The Baptists of Canada*, p. 65.

[175] Bill, *op. cit.*, pp. 19ff.

[176] Fitch, *op. cit.*, p. 15; Bill, *op. cit.*, p. 36.

[177] Fitch, *op. cit.*, pp. 15, 68-71, 74-85, 90, 96.

[178] Fitch, *op. cit.*, p. 15.

[179] Fitch, *op. cit.*, pp. 27, 55, 56, 86-88.

[180] Fitch, *op. cit.*, pp. 66, 67.

[181] The (English) Baptist Missionary Society gave financial aid to Acadia College, for the training of leaders.—Bill, *op. cit.*, p. 122.

[182] Dorland, *A History of the Society of Friends (Quakers) in Canada*, pp. 30ff.

foundland.[183] Soon after its organization, and, with at least one interval, throughout the eighteenth[184] and nineteenth centuries, the Society for the Propagation of the Gospel in Foreign Parts subsidized missionaries to the island. Yet at the close of the eighteenth century there was much religious destitution and in the first quarter of the nineteenth century the Roman Catholics were winning converts from among the nominal adherents to the Church of England. Until 1821, when a commissary was appointed, no provision had been made for episcopal supervision. In 1826 the island was added to Bishop Inglis's huge see. In 1839 a separate bishopric was created for Newfoundland and Bermuda.[185] In 1844 there came to Newfoundland as bishop a remarkable man, Edward Feild, who for the ensuing thirty-two years was the outstanding figure in the island. He lived in severely simple style, travelled extensively throughout his rough diocese, insisted that daily prayer be said in each of the churches, required every congregation to give to the central church fund, and was emphatic that the fisher folk who belonged to the church should contribute a tithe of their catch. He drew clergy from England by telling of the hardships they would have to face.[186] He improved, too, the theological seminary for the training of clergy which he inherited from his predecessor.[187]

In 1765 one of Wesley's preachers came to Newfoundland and while at Wesley's advice he became a missionary of the Society for the Propagation of the Gospel in Foreign Parts, he continued a Methodist in spirit. When, in 1773, wearied by opposition, he returned home, his work was continued by lay preachers. In 1774 and 1775 Methodist groups were formed. In 1785, at their request, Wesley sent them a missionary. From these beginnings Methodism grew, appealing as it did to the humble folk who were so large a proportion of the population.[188]

Congregationalism was begun in 1775 by John Jones, a soldier, who, having resigned from the army, returned in 1779 as pastor of the church in St. John's and continued there until his death, in 1800.[189]

[183] Langtry, *History of the Church in Eastern Canada and Newfoundland*, pp. 73ff.

[184] Hawkins, *Historical Notices of the Missions of the Church of England in the North American Colonies, Previous to the Independence of the United States*, pp. 346-353.

[185] Pascoe, *Two Hundred Years of the S.P.G.*, pp. 88-102. On one of the missionaries of this pioneer period, see [Edward Wix] *Six Months of a Newfoundland Missionary's Journal, from February to August, 1835* (London, 2d ed., 1836, pp. xi, 228).

[186] For one of these clergymen see R. H. Jelf, *Life of Joseph James Curling, Soldier and Priest* (Oxford, Fox, Jones & Co., 1910, pp. 64), *passim*.

[187] Wynne, *The Church in Greater Britain*, p. 67; Langtry, *op. cit.*, pp. 87ff.

[188] Sanderson, *The First Century of Methodism in Canada*, Vol. I, pp. 13ff.; Sutherland, *The Methodist Church and Missions*, pp. 68-84; James Lumsden, *The Skipper Parson on the Bays and Barrens of Newfoundland* (New York, Eaton and Mains, 1905, pp. 212), *passim*.

[189] Wood, *Memoir of Henry Wilkes*, pp. 2-5.

Politically part of Newfoundland was Labrador. Here on the rough coast, made harsh by its rocks and its long winters, fishermen established precarious settlements. At least in the first half of the nineteenth century, most of them were of English descent and were nominally members of the Church of England. Yet until 1848 they were given no clerical attention. The missions of the Moravians were to the Eskimos. Some of the fishermen married Eskimo women and their children tended to grow up without religious instruction. In 1848 Bishop Feild of Newfoundland visited the coast. Feild saw to it that missionaries were found for the area and that a church ship was assigned to it. He himself made repeated trips there, baptizing, confirming, and solemnizing marriages.[190] Methodist missionaries also came.[191]

The most famous mission to the Labrador fishermen was much later, and was by a physician, Wilfred Grenfell. While a medical student in London, Grenfell came in touch with Moody and two of the Moody converts, J. E. and C. T. Studd. As a result, he began devoting time to the underprivileged boys of the city. He next spent several years on the mission ships among the fishermen of the North Sea. In 1891 he heard of the need of the fishermen of Labrador and the north shores of Newfoundland and in 1892 made his first trip to the region. Then began a most remarkable mission which in time attracted wide and favourable attention. Athletic, practical, completely unselfish, and with unusual charm in his frank, direct approach to men, Grenfell sought, and with marked success, to improve the lot of the inhabitants of the bleak coast. His hospital ships and eventually small hospitals on shore cared for their illnesses. He started co-operative stores to buy and sell at fair prices. He fought liquor dealers. He initiated fox farms, a saw mill, and orphanages. He sent scores of boys to the United States for an education. He organized kindergartens, schools, and recreation. He enlisted the support of many in the United States and Great Britain, both financially and in giving periods of personal

---

[190] *Church in the Colonies, No. 19. A Visit to Labrador in the Autumn of MDCCCXLVIII by the Lord Bishop of Newfoundland* (London, Society for the Propagation of the Gospel in Foreign Parts, 1848, pp. 32), *passim; Church in the Colonies, No. 25. Newfoundland. Journal of a Voyage of Visitation in the "Hawk" Church Ship, on the Coast of Labrador and Round the Whole Island of Newfoundland in the Year 1849* (London, Society for the Propagation of the Gospel in Foreign Parts, 1850, pp. vi, 140), *passim; Church in the Colonies, No. 26. The Labrador Mission Letters of the Rev. H. P. Disney and the Rev. A. Gifford* (London, Society for Promoting Christian Knowledge, 1851, pp. 20), *passim.*

[191] For a personal narrative of one of these see Arminius Young, *A Methodist Missionary in Labrador* (Toronto, S. and A. Young, 1916, pp. 180), *passim.* For a popular account of another see Selby Jefferson, *Adventure for Christ in Labrador* (London, The Epworth Press, 1933, pp. 170), *passim.* For a summary account see Arminius Young, *One Hundred Years of Mission Work in the Wilds of Labrador* (London, Arthur H. Stockwell, no date, pp. 98), *passim.*

service. His enterprise outgrew the resources of its original sponsor, the Royal National Mission to Deep Sea Fishermen, and in 1912 the International Grenfell Association was incorporated. It drew its support from various local affiliated organizations in the United States and the British Isles.[192] His was one of the most notable efforts in the annals of mankind to transform wholesomely the life of a widely scattered and hard-pressed community.

In the great West from Lake Superior towards the setting sun extensive settlement did not take place until the last quarter of the nineteenth century. The mines, forests, and fisheries of British Columbia then proved a lure to many and the fertile prairies which stretched eastward from the Rocky Mountains began to be taken up by farmers, partly from the older sections of British North America, partly from the British Isles and the Continent of Europe, and partly from the United States. Down into the twentieth century the westward movement continued. Indeed, some of the most striking developments on the frontier were after 1900.

What had become the standard Protestant denominations of Canada felt a responsibility for the new regions and undertook extensive missions among them. Much of the growth of the churches was by spontaneous effort of the settlers themselves. Aid in clergy and funds came from the older portions of British possessions and from Great Britain. By 1914, so well had the situation been met, almost as large a percentage of the population confessed to a church connexion as in the older provinces. The proportion who did not do so was somewhat higher, but in no case, except in the sparsely settled North-west Territories, was it as much as two out of a hundred and even there it was less than one in ten.[193] As in the eastern portions of the Dominion, Christianity retained the formal allegiance of the overwhelming majority.

In British Columbia, Yukon, and the North-west Territories the Church of England was numerically the largest of the Protestant bodies. In the other provinces of the West the Presbyterians led. In all of the western provinces except Alberta, Saskatchewan, the North-west Territories, and Yukon the Methodists were third, in the first three of these political divisions they were

---

[192] A large amount of printed material exists on Grenfell's work. See especially Wilfred Grenfell, *Forty Years for Labrador* (Boston, Houghton Mifflin Co., 1932, pp. 372); Wilfred Grenfell, *A Labrador Doctor. The Autobiography of Wilfred Thomason Grenfell* (Boston, Houghton Mifflin Co., 1919, pp. 441); Norman Duncan, *Dr. Grenfell's Parish* (New York, Fleming H. Revell, 1905, pp. 155); *Work and Play in the Grenfell Mission. Extracts from the Letters and Journal of Hugh Payne Greeley and Floretta Elmore Greeley* (New York, Fleming H. Revell Co., 1920, pp. 192); Wilfred T. Grenfell, *Down North on the Labrador* (London, James Nisbet & Co., no date, pp. 229); Wilfred T. Grenfell, *Down to the Sea. Yarns from Labrador* (New York, Fleming H. Revell Co., 1910, pp. 226).

[193] *The Canada Year Book 1912*, pp. 28, 29.

second, and in Yukon fourth.[194] The Baptists were relatively not so prominent as in the Maritime Provinces, Congregationalism was very scantily represented, and the Lutherans loomed larger than in the East. With these exceptions the Protestantism of the West displayed much the same complexion as in the remainder of the Dominion.

The remarkable growth of the Church of England was due in large measure to personnel and funds from the British Isles. In 1820 the Hudson Bay Company sent out a chaplain. Beginning with 1850 the Society for the Propagation of the Gospel in Foreign Parts gave continuing assistance in men and money. By 1895 fourteen parishes had become self-supporting, but fifty-five missions to the settlers were still being subsidized.[195] The second Bishop of Rupert's Land (as much of the vast West was once known) was Robert Machray. He was consecrated in 1865 and died in 1904. In the former year Rupert's Land was served by eighteen clergy. In the latter year the area contained nine episcopal sees and about two hundred clergy. In this striking growth Machray was the moving spirit. He organized parishes, encouraged self-support, formed a synod made up of lay and clerical members, promoted schools, and established a college in which half of the active clergy in 1904 were graduates. Unselfish, moved by a high sense of duty, indomitable, hard-working, and hating cant, Machray was outstanding in the community and placed his stamp upon his church in that vast area.[196] In British Columbia the newly founded diocese was generously endowed by Miss Burdett-Counts.[197] Even into the twentieth century numerous reinforcements in the form of catechists, deacons, and priests and large subsidies from British societies came from the mother country.[198]

The Highlanders, Presbyterians, in the Red River Settlement, were long without clerical care by ministers of their own communion. However, in 1851 the pastor of a Toronto church induced one of his students, John Black, to go to them. There Black laboured for years and became the Nestor of a considerable presbytery. Intense of conviction and a powerful preacher, he inspired

[194] *Ibid.*

[195] Pascoe, *Two Hundred Years of the S.P.G.*, pp. 177-181; Rogers, *Canada's Greatest Need*, pp. 251ff.

[196] Robert Machray, *Life of Robert Machray, D.D., LL.D., D.C.L., Archbishop of Rupert's Land, Primate of All Canada, etc.* (London, Macmillan & Co., 1909, pp. xix, 468), *passim.*

[197] Wynne, *The Church in Greater Britain*, p. 52.

[198] H. H. Montgomery, *The Church on the Prairie* (London, Society for the Propagation of the Gospel in Foreign Parts, 5th ed., 1913, pp. 141), *passim*, especially pp. 18-27; J. Burgon Bickersteth, *The Land of Open Doors. Being Letters from Western Canada* (London, Wells Gardner, Darton & Co., 1914, pp. xxiv, 265); Pascoe, *Two Hundred Years of the S.P.G.*, pp. 181ff.

his parish to lay plans for wide missions of their church in the West. In his parish Manitoba College was founded, an institution in which many leaders of the church were educated.[199] The chief creator of Presbyterianism in the West was James Robertson (1839-1902). Born in Scotland, Robertson came with his family to Ontario in 1855. Part of his theological training he obtained in the United States. In 1873 he went west on an exploring expedition and the following year became pastor of Knox Church in Winnipeg. While there he helped to found Manitoba College. In 1881 he was appointed by the General Assembly as superintendent of missions for Manitoba and the North-west. Under his long and able leadership the Church Manse and Building Fund was organized. Through that and the Home Mission Committee of his church thousands of dollars were raised, hundreds of churches were erected, and scores of missionaries were subsidized. In all of this Robertson was the guiding and inspiring spirit, travelling, recruiting missionaries (largely Canadians), founding mission stations, and supervising the clergy.[200] Hs work was made possible by the loyal support of Presbyterians both in the older and the newer portions of the Dominion. In British Columbia the foundations of Presbyterianism were laid by clergymen from the British Isles. For a time, beginning in 1875, what was called the Presbytery of British Columbia, formed in that year, was in connexion with the Church of Scotland.[201]

In 1868 the Methodists of Canada appointed their first missionary, George Young, to the Red River Settlement.[202] Even earlier, in 1858, four missionaries had been sent to British Columbia.[203] The formation, in 1874, of the Methodist Church in Canada by the fusion of three bodies greatly furthered the prosecution of home missions.[204] The enterprise in the West was largely the work of Canadians from the older sections of the Dominion.[205]

Congregationalism entered the West about 1859, when through an agent of the Colonial Missionary Society a church was constituted in Victoria, British Columbia. This church, however, did not have a long life. In 1873 a representa-

---

[199] Balfour, *Presbyterianism in the Colonies,* p. 21; Oliver, *The Winning of the West,* pp. 189-191; MacBeth, *Our Task in Canada,* pp. 31, 32.

[200] Charles W. Gordon, *The Life of James Robertson* (Toronto, The Westminster Co., 1908, pp. 412), *passim;* Keirstead, *The Church History of the Canadian North-west,* pp. 215-220.

[201] McNeill, *The Presbyterian Church in Canada,* pp. 102, 103.

[202] George Young, *Manitoba Memories* (Toronto, William Briggs, 1897, pp. 364), pp. 26ff.

[203] Sanderson, *The First Century of Methodism in Canada,* Vol. II, pp. 134, 135.

[204] Sutherland, *The Methodist Church and Missions in Canada and Newfoundland,* p. 208.

[205] For examples see Wellington Bridgman, *Breaking Prairie Sod. The Story of a Pioneer Preacher in the Eighties* (Toronto, The Musson Book Company, 1920, pp. 265; autobiographical), *passim.*

tive was sent to Manitoba and in 1879 a church was gathered in Winnipeg.[206] The latter's first pastor, J. B. Silcox, became the outstanding leader of his denomination in that region. It was not until 1909 that the Congregational Church Extension Sociey of Western Canada was formed.[207] More loosely organized, Congregationalism was at a disadvantage when compared with the Anglicans, Presbyterians, and Methodists.

In 1869 the Baptists of Ontario sent a commission of two to explore the West. In 1873 the pioneer Baptist missionary, Alexander McDonald, arrived. A church was organized in Winnipeg in 1875, the first of the denomination in that part of the West. Others soon followed.[208] The first Baptist church in British Columbia came into being in Victoria in 1876, through one of that faith from Ontario.[209] In time associations were formed, then, in 1897, the Baptist Convention of British Columbia,[210] and in 1907 the Baptist Convention of Western Canada.[211]

Those of European blood but not of British birth or descent presented a challenge to the major Protestant denominations of British North America. Thus shortly before the American Revolution, in response to the British Government's offer of land to settlers, several hundred Protestants came to Nova Scotia from the Continent of Europe. Some of these were Lutheran and some Reformed. They turned to the Reformed and Lutherans of Pennsylvania for advice and clerical aid. Henry Melchior Muhlenberg, the leader of Pennsylvania Lutherans, is said to have advised them to adhere to the Church of England. This some of them did.[212] They were served by missionaries of the Society for the Propagation of the Gospel in Foreign Parts.[213] One of the Reformed settlers, a devout fisherman, was ordained by a presbytery temporarily constituted for that purpose by Presbyterian and Congregational ministers of the English-speaking colonials and served for many years.[214] Efforts were put forth by more than one denomination to win the Roman Catholic French. A few converts were made but they were an inconsiderable percentage of the French constituency.[215] About 1786 Mennonites began moving from Pennsyl-

[206] Silcox, *Church Union in Canada*, pp. 44, 45.

[207] Keirstead, *op. cit.*, p. 366.

[208] Fitch, *The Baptists of Canada*, pp. 232-235.

[209] Fitch, *op. cit.*, pp. 244-247.

[210] *Ibid.*

[211] Fitch, *op. cit.*, p. 254.

[212] Eaton, *The Church of England in Nova Scotia and the Tory Clergy of the Revolution*, pp. 69, 70, 74-76.

[213] Hawkins, *Historical Notices of the Missions of the Church of England in the North American Colonies Previous to the Independence of the United States*, pp. 358ff.

[214] McNeill, *The Presbyterian Church in Canada*, p. 3.

[215] Fitch, *op. cit.*, pp. 197-219; Balfour, *Presbyterianism in the Colonies*, p. 67; Wood, *Memoirs of Henry Wilkes*, p. 108; *The Autobiography of a Wesleyan Methodist Mis-*

vania to Upper Canada. More followed. A minister was ordained for them in 1801.[216] In the 1870's Mennonites from Russia settled in Manitoba on a reserve granted by the Canadian Government.[217] They tended to hold to their faith. In 1911 their chief centres were in Ontario, Manitoba, and Saskatchewan.[218] Mormons came from the United States to Ontario and the West.[219] Lutherans migrated from Germany, Scandinavia, and Iceland. Thousands of these settled in Ontario, but the great influx occurred late in the nineteenth and early in the twentieth century[220] while the Western provinces were being opened and it was here, especially in the prairie provinces, that the majority found homes.[221] The earliest ecclesiastical development among the Lutherans of the West seems to have been by those from Iceland. A synod of these was constituted in 1885.[222] Some of the bodies formed in the United States, such as the Augustana Synod, the Finnish Evangelical Church of America, the Norwegian Lutheran Church, the Danish Evangelical Lutheran Church, and the United Danish Evangelical Lutheran churches, extended their activities to their fellow nationals in Canada.[223] In 1861, as a result of efforts begun in 1850 by the Evangelical Lutheran Synod of Pittsburgh, the Evangelical Lutheran Synod of Canada was organized.[224]

Efforts were made by some of the predominantly Anglo-Saxon Protestant denominations to reach the Germans and Scandinavians. We hear of the American Unitarian Association establishing a mission among the Icelanders and winning several of their congregations.[225] The Presbyterians supported missionaries among the Galicians (mostly Roman Catholic Ruthenian Uniates), Hungarians, Doukhobors,[226] and Finns.[227] Baptists had missionaries among the Germans and Scandinavians.[228] Some Danes in New Brunswick became

sionary (formerly a Roman Catholic) (Montreal, E. Pickup, 1856, pp. 407), *passim;* Ninth Annual Report of the Foreign Evangelical Association, 1848, p. 24.

[216] Smith, *The Mennonites of America*, pp. 265-274.

[217] Smith, *op. cit.*, pp. 336-340; Keirstead, *The Church History of the Canadian Northwest*, pp. 493ff.

[218] *The Canada Year Book 1912*, p. 29; Dawson, *Group Settlement. Ethnic Communities in Western Canada*, pp. 95ff.

[219] Dawson, *op. cit.*, pp. 189ff.

[220] Keirstead, *op. cit.*, p. 12.

[221] *The Canada Year Book 1912*, p. 29.

[222] Keirstead, *op. cit.*, p. 447.

[223] Keirstead, *op. cit.*, pp. 461-477; *The Lutheran World Almanac . . . 1921*, pp. 125, 133, 135, 158, 159.

[224] Shortt and Doughty, *Canada and Its Provinces*, Vol. XI, p. 385.

[225] Keirstead, *op. cit.*, p. 45.

[226] Keirstead, *op. cit.*, p. 252.

[227] Arvi I. Heinonen, *Finnish Friends in Canada* (Toronto, Board of Home Missions of the United Church of Canada, 1930, pp. vii, 113), pp. 97ff.

[228] Fitch, *The Baptists of Canada*, pp. 176, 194, 269.

members of the Church of England.[229] The Greek Independent Church, drawn from former Ruthenian Roman Catholic Uniates, received aid from the Presbyterians. Several of its students for the priesthood were educated in (the Presbyterian) Manitoba College.[230] To care for the Negroes, slightly less than 17,000 in 1911,[231] various enterprises were initiated. The African Methodist Episcopal Church was introduced and by 1910 had about 3,000 members.[232] For the traditionally non-Christian immigrants something was done. The Methodists conducted missions for the Chinese and Japanese.[233] Some slight attempt was made to win the Jews,[234] but apparently even less in an organized fashion than in the United States. These instances are merely samples, chosen somewhat at random, of the endeavour of the larger Protestant denominations to cope with the newer immigration.

The Eskimos and Indians were the objects of extensive missions by the major Protestant denominations of British North America.

The Eskimos, in spite of their small number, perhaps 5,000, their primitive life, the inclemency of their northern habitat, and their necessarily thinly scattered and often impermanent dwellings, attracted much heroic devotion. In the eighteenth century the Moravians had opened a mission among them in Labrador. That enterprise continued. Several stations were established. Commerce was carried on and met much of the cost. By 1800 only 110 converts had been made, but in 1804 an awakening broke out which brought many into the Church and in 1904 all on the coast were said to be at least nominally Christian. Many were induced to settle down near the mission stations. Medical work was introduced, rather late, to be sure, to combat the native and imported diseases.[235] Missionaries of the Church of England also laboured among the Eskimos along the shores of Hudson Bay and near the mouths of the Mackenzie and Peel rivers.[236]

[229] Langtry, *History of the Church of England in Eastern Canada and Newfoundland*, pp. 164-166.

[230] Woodsworth, *Strangers Within Our Gates*, p. 138.

[231] *The Canada Year Book 1912*, p. 23.

[232] Woodsworth, *op. cit.*, p. 191.

[233] Woodsworth, *op. cit.*, pp. 186, 187, 296, 297; Sutherland, *The Methodist Church and Missions in Canada and Newfoundland*, p. 219.

[234] Woodsworth, *op. cit.*, p. 299.

[235] J. W. Davey, *The Fall of Torngak or The Moravian Mission on the Coast of Labrador* (London, S. W. Partridge & Co., 1905, pp. 288), *passim;* S. K. Hutton, *Among the Eskimos of Labrador. A Record of Five Years Close Intercourse with the Eskimo Tribes of Labrador* (London, Seeley, Service & Co., 1912, pp. xviii. 340), *passim;* A von Dewitz, *An der Küste Labradors. Oder: Innere Mission im Gebiet der Heidenmission* (Niesky, 1881, pp. 58; *passim*). *The Advance Guard. Two Hundred Years of Moravian Missions*, pp. 76ff.; Richter, *Die evangelische Mission in Fern- und Südost Asien, Australien, Amerika*, pp. 434-436; Grenfell, *Forty Years for Labrador*, p. 84.

[236] J. Lofthouse, *A Thousand Miles from a Post Office or, Twenty Years' Life and*

Missionaries of the Church of England were widely distributed among the Indians. Societies drawing their funds and much of their personnel from the British Isles had a major share in missions to the Indians. Although its objectives were primarily the white colonists, the Society for the Propagation of the Gospel in Foreign Parts did something for the Red Men. In the eighteenth century its agents laboured among the Indians of Nova Scotia and New Brunswick.[237] In Upper Canada, the later Ontario, in the eighteenth and nineteenth centuries, its missionaries served the Indians.[238] Beginning in 1820 with assistance to the chaplain of the Red River Settlement, the Church Missionary Society carried on extensive missions among several Indian tribes in the North and West.[239] Famous as a pioneer in an incredibly rough environment was John Horden (1828-1893), a missionary at the head of James Bay, who travelled prodigiously, erected churches, at least one with his own hands, and became the first Bishop of Moosonee, on the shores of Hudson Bay.[240] Fully as heroic was William Carpenter Bompas (1834-1906). Born and reared in London, successively the first bishop of three of the northern sees, he died, as he had lived, in harness.[241] In 1920, the larger part of the Indian population of the Canadian North-west having become at least professedly Christian, the Church Missionary Society withdrew.[242] The New England Company for a time after it discontinued its aid to the United States conducted missions among the Indians in New Brunswick, then, in 1822, transferred its efforts to the Mohawks and others of the Six Nations in Ontario, and later, as these took

Travel in the Hudson's Bay Regions (London, Society for Promoting Christian Knowledge, 1922, pp. vii, 184), *passim;* Arthur Lewis, *The Life and Work of the Rev. E. J. Peck among the Eskimos* (New York, A. C. Armstrong & Son, 1904, pp. xvi, 345), *passim.*

[237] Gould, *Inasmuch,* pp. 32-34.

[238] Gould, *op. cit.,* pp. 46-57; Pascoe, *Two Hundred Years of the S.P.G.,* pp. 165-175; Langtry, *History of the Church in Eastern Canada and Newfoundland,* p. 41; *The Church in Canada. A Journal of Visitation to the Western Portion of His Diocese by the Lord Bishop of Toronto in the Autumn of 1842,* pp. 7, 8, 46.

[239] Gould, *op. cit.,* pp. 83ff.; J. Hines, *The Red Indians of the Plains. Thirty Years' Missionary Experience in the Saskatchewa* (London, Society for Promoting Christian Knowledge, 1915, pp. 322; autobiographical), *passim;* Edward F. Wilson, *Missionary Work among the Ojebway Indians* (London, Society for Promoting Christian Knowledge, 1886, pp. 253; autobiographical), *passim; Snapshots from the North Pacific. Letters Written by Bishop Ridley, of Caledonia. Edited by Alice J. Janvrin* (London Church Missionary Society, 1903, pp. viii, 192), *passim; Metlahkatlah, Ten Years' Work among the Tsimsheean Indians* (London, Church Missionary Society, 1869, pp. 130), *passim.*

[240] Rogers, *Canada's Greatest Need,* pp. 172-179; Heeney, *Leaders of the Canadian Church,* pp. 137-170.

[241] H. A. Cody, *An Apostle of the North. Memoirs of the Right Reverend William Carpenter Bompas* (London, Seeley & Co., 1908, pp. 386), *passim.*

[242] Gould, *op. cit.,* pp. xi-xiii.

the Christian name, had an enterprise near Sault Ste. Marie and became active in British Columbia.[243]

The Presbyterians also had missions to the Indians. In 1866 James Nisbet was sent to the Crees of North Saskatchewan. Eventually a chain of stations was developed reaching from the Lake of the Woods to Vancouver Island.[244]

Methodists began to touch the Indians as early as 1823, in Ontario.[245] In time they had missions for them at centres stretching at intervals from Ontario to British Columbia.[246] One of the best remembered among their missionaries was James Evans (1801-1846). Born in England, as a young man he came to Canada and for a time was a teacher. Through a renewal of an earlier religious experience he devoted himself to the Indians, first in Ontario and later as superintendent of Methodist missions in the West. While in the West he reduced the Cree language to writing, devising for it a system of syllabic signs which were used to print literature in that tongue. It was unhampered by irregularities and was easily learned. A large proportion of the Crees eventually used it.[247] Other men and women laboured in various parts of the vast Dominion.[248]

Congregationalists[249] and Baptists[250] also had missions among the Indians, although much less extensive than those of the Church of England, the Presbyterians, and the Methodists.

In contrast with the United States, where increasingly the Federal Government assumed the burden of Indian schools in an education which was predominantly secular, in Canada the schools for the Indians were conducted by

[243] [Busk], *A Sketch of the Origin and Recent History of the New England Company*, pp. 17, 21, 30, 32.

[244] MacBeth, *Our Task in Canada*, pp. 64-66.

[245] George F. Playter, *The History of Methodism in Canada*, pp. 217, 218.

[246] Playter, *op. cit.*, pp. 227ff.; Sutherland, *The Methodist Church and Missions in Canada and Newfoundland*, pp. 237ff.

[247] John McLean, *James Evans, Inventor of the Syllabic System of the Cree Language* (Toronto, Methodist Mission Rooms, 1890, pp. 208), *passim*.

[248] For some of these missionaries see Thomas Crosby, *Up and Down the North Pacific Coast by Canoe and Mission Ship* (Toronto, The Missionary Society of the Methodist Episcopal Church, 1914, pp. xiv, 403), *passim;* James Woodsworth, *Thirty Years in the Canadian North-west* (Toronto, McClelland, Goodchild and Stewart, 1917, pp. xix, 259), pp. 14-97; Thomas Crosby, *Among the An-ko-me-nums or Flathead Tribes of Indians of the Pacific Coast* (Toronto, William Briggs, 1907, pp. 243), *passim;* John Semmens, *The Field and the Work: Sketches of Missionary Life in the Far North* (Toronto, Methodist Mission Rooms, 1884, pp. 199), *passim*. For an account of an Indian convert who was later a missionary to his own race, see *Life and Journals of Kah-ke-wa-quo-nā-by: (Rev. Peter Jones), Wesleyan Missionary* (Toronto, Anson Green, 1860, pp. xi, 424), *passim*.

[249] Wood, *Memoir of Henry Wilkes*, p. 154.

[250] Fitch, *The Baptists of Canada*, p. 271.

missionaries. The government made financial grants which often were sup-
plemented by the white churches.

As a result of Roman Catholic and Protestant missions, by 1914 a larger
proportion of the Indians of Canada were professedly Christian than of those
of the United States. In the Maritime Provinces and Quebec fully nine-tenths
of the Indians were Roman Catholics. In Ontario at least seven-eighths were
Christian, and of these about two-thirds were Protestants and a third Roman
Catholics. In the West in some areas practically all were Christian.[251] About
1914 baptized Protestant Indians numbered about 49,000.[252] Roman Catholics
were probably not far from the same total. This meant that at the end of the
period fully three-fourths and possibly more of the Indians of Canada bore the
Christian name.

Protestant Christianity made for profound changes in the life of the Indian.
The Protestant missionary fought the sale and use of alcoholic beverages. Like
his Roman Catholic brother, he sought to create a Christian family and he
conducted schools in which the Indian was aided in his adjustment to the white
man's ways. He promoted assimilation to the white man's culture. He worked
for improvement in physical cleanliness and he fought disease.[253]

When one attempts to appraise the effect of Christianity upon British North
America several facts stand out with great clarity.

It is obvious that in 1914 the vast majority of the whites, at least three-fourths
of the Indians, and some from among the small groups of Orientals thought
of themselves as Christians. In the course of the migration from the Old
World, very few had dropped their hereditary faith and some had had it
deepened.

Those of French blood were almost entirely Roman Catholic and were more
loyally so than were large numbers of the inhabitants of nineteenth-century
France. No such secularizing and anti-clerical movement developed in Canada
as in the mother country. In general, the non-French immigrants of Roman
Catholic background seem to have been held by the church. The secessions from
the Ruthenian Uniates affected only a minority.

Protestants constituted the large majority of the population. Extensive aid in
the gathering of Protestant churches had come from the British Isles and the
United States. So successful had been these efforts and so much vitality did the

---

[251] Warneck, *Geschichte der protestantischen Missionen*, pp. 234-237.
[252] Beach and St. John, *World Statistics of Christian Missions*, p. 59.
[253] For some of these results see *The Missionary Bulletin* (Toronto), Vol. XVI, No. 2,
passim.

developing Protestant denominations display that by 1914 the Canadians them-selves were bearing the chief brunt of caring for the new communities in the West and, a little later, of the missions to the Indians. They were also having an increasing share in the spread of their faith in other lands.[254] Indeed, even while missionaries were still coming to Canada from Great Britain, the Canadian churches were beginning to send missionaries to other countries.

No such spectacular and large-scale movements for the elimination of col-lective social practices repugnant to Christian ideals emerged in the nineteenth century from the Christianity of British North America as from the Protestant-ism of Great Britain and the United States. This was partly because of the absence of some of the evils which confronted the Christians of the mother country and of the great republic to the south. The few Negroes in the popula-tion did not create a major racial tension. Negro slavery, although for a time it existed, was never so serious as in the United States or the West Indies.[255] No such series of wars and of progressive forceful removals to new habitats punctuated the relations between whites and Indians as in the United States. No cruel exploitation of Indian labour marred the white man's advance as in the days of the establishment of the Spanish and Portuguese American empires. Not until nearly the close of the period did the rise of large cities and the de-velopment of industries begin to create the conditions with which Christians had been constrained to grapple in Western Europe and the United States. Moreover, by the time that much of the settlement of Canada was being ef-fected the battle had been partly won in the Occident against some of the earlier chronic ills and many attitudes and standards of Christian origin were accepted as a matter of course. Largely because of Christianity, prison reform, the hu-mane care of the insane, the blind, the deaf, and the dumb, and greater oppor-tunities for women were becoming general in the Western world. Between 1815 and 1914 war did not appear as an urgent major issue. The long frontier be-tween Canada and the United States was unfortified. The British navy guaran-teed security from attack by way of the ocean. The absence of much acute friction with the Indians was probably in part due to Christianity and to the benign treatment of the aboriginal races which that faith inspired. It has been suggested that, in contrast with the colonies out of which issued the United

---

[254] For a list of the Canadian Protestant societies which engaged in foreign missions at the close of the period see Beach and St. John, *op. cit.*, pp. 15, 16.

[255] On slavery in Upper Canada see W. R. Riddell, *An Official Record of Slavery in Upper Canada*, in *Ontario Historical Society, Papers and Records*, Vol. XXV. (Toronto, 1929), pp. 393-397. See also a more extended account, T. Watson Smith, *The Slave in Canada*, in *Collections of the Nova Scotia Historical Society*, Vol. X (Halifax, Nova Scotia Printing Co., 1899, pp. xi, 161), *passim.*

States, few settlements were made by radical Christian groups which came with the purpose of founding idealistic communities. The main motive of the British migration to Canada was economic and, accordingly, Canadian Protestantism was more conservative and less explosively idealistic than that of the United States.[256]

Yet Canadian Christianity and particularly Canadian Protestant Christianity espoused movements for reform. As a rule these came by contagion from the United States or Great Britain and were not indigenous. However, they found fertile ground and flourished. This was true of temperance organizations and prohibition sentiment. In 1898 desire for prohibition was said to be dominant in all the provinces except Roman Catholic Quebec.[257] The Young Men's and the Young Women's Christian Associations and the Young People's Societies of Christian Endeavour had an extensive growth.[258] The Salvation Army was prominent.[259] Early in the twentieth century organizations for social service and social welfare reflected the emphasis upon the "social gospel" in the United States.[260]

Especially notable was the influence of Christianity upon education. Fully as much as in the United States schools from primary to university grade owed their origin directly to the churches and much more than in the latter country remained under ecclesiastical auspices. Egerton Ryerson, an outstanding Methodist clergyman, was from 1844 to 1876 the superintendent of schools for Upper Canada. He insisted upon universal primary education supported by taxation, was the founder of the educational system of Ontario, and initiated Canada's system of teachers' training colleges.[261] As late as 1890 in most of the provinces of the Dominion the majority of the schools were under the control of the various denominations and had religious instruction as part of their curriculum. Even in Ontario, where the schools were undenominational, prayer and reading of the Bible were part of the daily procedure and the clergy were empowered to make arrangements for the teaching of religion.[262] In 1890 the structure of denominational schools was abolished in Manitoba, partly through Protestant opposition to the influence of the Roman Catholic clergy.[263] College after col-

---

[256] Silcox, *Church Union in Canada*, p. 16.

[257] Silcox, *op. cit.*, p. 80.

[258] Silcox, *op. cit.*, pp. 82-85.

[259] In 1911 it had 18,834 adherents in Canada, nearly two-thirds of them in urban and Protestant Ontario.—*The Canada Year Book 1912*, p. 29.

[260] Silcox, *op. cit.*, pp. 90-92.

[261] Ryerson, *The Story of My Life*, pp. 350, 351, 368-374.

[262] *The Statistical Year-book of Canada for 1890*, pp. 423, 424. See also Silcox, *op. cit.*, pp. 95, 96; Bracq, *The Evolution of French Canada*, p. 286.

[263] Oliver, *The Winning of the West*, p. 221.

lege was founded by the various denominations.[264] In the University of Toronto
a state institution became the nucleus of a federation in which the colleges of
several denominations joined without losing their identity,[265] thereby preserving a more pronounced sympathy with Christianity than was usual in state
universities in the United States. The University of Manitoba was a federation
of denominational colleges.[266] Education in Canada was largely the creation of
the churches and maintained a Christian emphasis.

The impress of the environment upon Christianity in British North America
was marked.

Obvious was the influence of the nations from which the population was
chiefly drawn—of pre-nineteenth century France upon the Roman Catholics,
and of Great Britain and the United States upon Protestantism. The effect of
the United States, because of the size and the proximity of that land, was larger
than its contribution to the population would have led one to expect. The
Christianity of Canada was chiefly that of France, the British Isles, and the
United States.

Because of its large French constituency and the tendency of the French
Canadians to keep apart, with their church as their distinctive institution, the
Roman Catholic Church in British North America was conservative. It was
less disposed to alter its methods than was the Roman Catholic Church
in the United States. This conservatism was as much the effect of the environment as was the malleability of the latter.

A development akin to that in Australia, New Zealand, and the United
States was the achievement of full equality of the various denominations before
the law. This took, in the main, the form of a successful struggle against the
privileged position of the Church of England. The contest centred around the
right of clergy other than those of the Church of England to officiate at marriages, the control of education, and the participation of other Protestant denominations in the "clergy reserves," which had been set aside in Upper and
Lower Canada by act of Parliament in 1791 for the support of the Protestant
ministry. Presbyterians were emphatic that, in view of the status of the Church

---

[264] Silcox, *op. cit.*, pp. 96, 97, 99; Langtry, *History of the Church in Eastern Canada,*
pp. 117-150, 162; Bill, *Fifty Years with the Baptist Ministers and Churches of the
Maritime Provinces*, pp. 66, 113, 122; Fitch, *The Baptists of Canada*, pp. 140-144; Wynne,
The Church in Greater Britain, p. 64; Robertson, *History of the Mission of the Secession
Church to Nova Scotia and Prince Edward Island*, pp. 220-236. On Roman Catholic colleges
see Bracq, *op. cit.*, pp. 300ff.
[265] Silcox, *op. cit.*, p. 97.
[266] Machray, *Life of Robert Machray*, p. 273.

of Scotland in Scotland, they must share with the Church of England in the rights accruing to the latter in colonies which were the common possession of Scotland and England. Methodists, with Egerton Ryerson as their chief spokesman, led in insisting that other denominations be admitted to an equal basis with these two. The advocates of equality won. In education the conflict was resolved partly by the setting up of separate denominational schools, especially colleges. The clergy reserves issue was settled first (1840) by granting the Church of Scotland establishment and providing for the sale of the lands and the division of the proceeds among the various denominations, and finally (1854) by secularizing the lands and assigning to public education the sums derived from them, but, in characteristic British fashion, safeguarding by pensions the vested rights of those individual clergymen who had previously drawn their support from the lands.[267] Except for the continuation in the Province of Quebec of the privileges enjoyed by the Roman Catholic Church before the British Conquest, eventually no exclusive state assistance was granted to any religious body.[268]

As in the United States, so in the Dominion of Canada, the churches tended to become ecclesiastically independent of those in the Old World and to develop national organizations as broad geographically as the political structure of the land. National unions of the same denominational families followed political union. The achievement of the federation of all Canada came in 1867. The first national ecclesiastical organizations followed. This was both an effect of the environment and an outgrowth of the inner vitality of Christianity.

Even the main details of these developments would prolong these pages unduly. The Church of England, whose bishops were long appointed by the Crown and received their consecration in England, and to which for many years clergy and funds came from the mother country, was somewhat slow to achieve self-government and a nation-wide structure. The secularization of the clergy reserves stimulated it to action. In 1853 the Synod of Toronto, the first of its kind in Canada, was held; in 1857 legal permission was obtained to constitute diocesan and provincial synods and to appoint a metropolitan; and in 1893 the first general synod convened, marking the full attainment of a national

---

[267] Oliver, *The Winning of the West*, pp. 142ff.; Clarke, *Constitutional Church Government*, pp. 207-209; Wynne, *The Church in Greater Britain*, p. 58; Sanderson, *The First Century of Methodism in Canada*, Vol. I, pp. 176-195; Langtry, *History of the Church in Eastern Canada*, p. 61; W. Stanford Reid, *The Church of Scotland in Lower Canada. Its Struggle for Establishment* (Toronto, Presbyterian Publications, 1936, pp. 192), *passim;* C. B. Sissons, *Egerton Ryerson. His Life and Letters*, Vol. I, pp. 23, 32, 34, 65, 66, 73-89, 129-131, 172, 184, 215, 253, 291, 368, 378, 402, 403, 442, 476, 481-489, 502, 503, 532, 533, 555, 556; Ryerson, *The Story of My Life*, pp. 213-249, 291-300, 378-382, 433-469.

[268] *The Statistical Year-book of Canada for 1890*, p. 421.

organization.[269] This did not include the diocese of Newfoundland. Among the Presbyterians various unions were effected which culminated, in 1875, in the formation of the Presbyterian Church in Canada.[270] By progressive steps the Methodists of Canada, once divided into several bodies largely representing imported differences, came together. The Methodist Church in Canada was organized in 1874 by a union of various bodies and in 1884 this in turn united with the other existing bodies to constitute the Methodist Church, Canada.[271] The Baptists did not coalesce into one national convention, but the three regional conventions in existence at the close of the period joined in the support of a common foreign mission society which was formed in 1911 by the fusion of the societies of the three conventions.[272] In 1906 the Congregational Union of Canada came into existence through the amalgamation of the Congregational Union of Ontario and Quebec and the Congregational Union of Nova Scotia and New Brunswick.[273] Through these nation-wide denominational organizations consolidation, especially in the Methodist, Presbyterian, and Baptist bodies, progressed further than in the United States.

A last and striking effect of the environment was the phenomenal progress made towards the union of different denominations into one body. This achievement was in large part a result of contact with the frontier. In the United States the frontier had bred impatience with denominational divisions inherited from older sections and Europe but the dissatisfaction had expressed itself in new denominations, notably the Disciples of Christ and the Christians, rather than in a merging of existing denominations. In Canada, in contrast, no fresh denominations of numerical consequence sprang up on the frontier and existing bodies tended to unite. The movement was strengthened by the Scottish dream, embodied more nearly successfully in the Church of Scotland than in England by the Church of England, of a single church embracing the entire nation. When the Presbyterian Church in Canada was formed (1875) its first moderator expressed the hope that all the Protestant churches of the Dominion would come together.[274] In 1889 the House of Bishops of the Provincial Synod of the Church of England in Canada appointed a committee to confer with representatives of other denominations on the possibility of church union, but

[269] Vernon, *The Old Church in the New Dominion*, pp. 3, 37, 171-174; Wynne, *op. cit.*, pp. 58, 60; Clarke, *op. cit.*, pp. 210-225, 237-239; Mountain, *A Memoir of George J. Mountain*, pp. 290-299.

[270] McNeill, *The Presbyterian Church in Canada*, pp. 16-32; Balfour, *Presbyterianism in the Colonies*, Vol. I, pp. 52-60.

[271] Sanderson, *The First Century of Methodism in Canada*, Vol. II, pp. 276-300, 403; Silcox, *Church Union in Canada*, pp. 50, 51.

[272] Silcox, *op. cit.*, p. 40.

[273] Silcox, *op. cit.*, p. 43.

[274] Silcox, *op. cit.*, p. 103.

nothing effective came of it. The need of co-operation in the West and the desirability of avoiding overlapping and duplication of efforts in new communities brought pressure towards unity. In 1902 at a meeting of the Methodist General Conference held, significantly, at Winnipeg, in the West, action was taken which led, after long negotiation, to the formation, in 1925, of the United Church of Canada by the Methodists, Congregationalists, and a majority of the Presbyterians.[275] Never before in the history of Protestantism had bodies of such different beliefs and polities come together on so large a scale.

In British North America Christianity enjoyed, in the nineteenth century, a phenomenal expansion. The Roman Catholic French multiplied through natural increase. To them were added other Roman Catholics by immigration. Protestantism had a particularly rapid growth. This was largely through immigration from the British Isles, but it was also by movements of population from the United States, and, in the latter part of the period, from the Continent of Europe. Protestantism was aided by extensive assistance in men and money from the United States, and especially from the British Isles. By the end of the nineteenth century, however, the Protestant churches of British North America were increasingly taking responsibility for the propagation of the faith in their own and other lands. The overwhelming majority of the white population had a more or less formal church connexion. Both Roman Catholics and Protestants engaged in efforts for the Indians and Eskimos which resulted in the conversion of most of these peoples. Christianity had marked effects in individual lives and on social customs and education. In Protestantism progress was registered towards a fusion of existing bodies into one national church. In British North America Christianity was vigorous and had become an integral and important part of the life of the new nation which was there emerging.

[275] Silcox, *op. cit.*, pp. 107-109. See also E. Lloyd Morrow, *Church Union in Canada. Its History, Motives, Doctrine and Government* (Toronto, Thomas Allen, 1923, pp. 450), *passim*.

Chapter III

GREENLAND: THE DUTCH, DANISH, AND BRITISH WEST INDIES: BRITISH HONDURAS: BRITISH GUIANA: SURINAM

IN ADDITION to the United States and British North America, in a few scattered sections in the New World, mostly islands, Protestant Christianity made extensive progress and usually became stronger numerically than Roman Catholic Christianity. These were territories over which flew the Dutch, Danish, or British flags, and so were under governments which were officially Protestant. They included Greenland, several islands in the West Indies, British Honduras, British Guiana, and Surinam (Dutch Guiana). In most of them the majority of the population were non-European by blood. Before the nineteenth century Christianity had begun to make headway among these groups, and between 1800 and 1914 it registered additional gains.

We turn first of all to the northernmost of the areas, Greenland. It will be recalled that Christianity was first introduced to Greenland by Scandinavian settlers near the close of the tenth century, that it persisted until at least the fifteenth century, but that it disappeared with the demise of the Scandinavian communities. It will also be remembered that it was reintroduced in the eighteenth century by Hans Egede and that two bodies, the Danish Lutheran state church and the Moravians, carried on missions among the Eskimos. The enterprises of both were continued throughout the nineteenth century.

The population among which the missionaries laboured was scattered along hundreds of miles of the bleak, narrow strip of indented coast between the sea and the ice sheet which covers the lofty interior. It was never large. In 1911 it was between 13,000 and 14,000, and this was about twice the size that it had been a century before.[1] All but a few hundred were under Danish administration. In 1911 less than 400 were Europeans. The remainder were Eskimos or a mixed stock emerging from the unions of Danes and Eskimos. Those with Danish blood were increasing. The pure-blooded Eskimos had suffered from adverse economic conditions and epidemics. In 1900 they were only

[1] *Greenland*, pp. 5, 6.

about half the total.[2] Almost all of the population was on the west coast. A very few were on the still more inhospitable east coast.

The missions of the state church were maintained by grants from the Danish government and by the Greenland Board of Trade through which the commerce of the island was conducted.[3] The missionaries were from Denmark. Natives of Greenland were trained to be schoolmasters and some of them became clergymen. As a rule, however, it was only those of mixed blood who were ordained. Pure-blooded Eskimos seem not to have had the stability of character or the mental qualities to fit them for so responsible a calling.[4]

The Moravians put forth their efforts exclusively for the pure-blooded Eskimos. They had central stations around which they sought to gather their charges, but also in time established out-stations.[5] The number under their supervision was the largest in 1854, 2,101. It then slowly declined and in 1899 was 1,623.[6]

As a result of the persistent efforts of the missionaries, by the close of the nineteenth century almost all of the Greenlanders were professing Christians.[7] Even those on the east coast were being reached.[8] Some of the latter had migrated to the southernmost of the Moravian stations and had there been instructed and baptized.[9] In the last decade of the nineteenth century the Danish authorities established a station of the state church at Angmagssalik, on the east coast.[10] Some of the Eskimos migrated from Angmagssalik to the west coast and there became Christians.[11] Only in the extreme north, on the west coast not far from Cape York, did a few pagans remain untouched by Christianity.[12]

Largely through the efforts of the missionaries and the teachers trained under them, most of the Greenlanders could read and write.[13] Literature in the Eskimo tongue was prepared, often at the cost of great labour. Thus Samuel Kleinschmidt (1814-1886), the son of a Moravian missionary, who

---

[2] Schulze, *200 Jähre Brüdermission*, Vol. II, pp. 5ff.

[3] *Greenland*, p. 13; Rink, *Danish Greenland. Its People and Its Products*, p. 283.

[4] Hutton, *A History of the Moravian Missions*, p. 243; Schulze, *op. cit.*, Vol. II, pp. 35, 36.

[5] Schulze, *op. cit.*, Vol. II, p. 7.

[6] Schulze, *op. cit.*, Vol. II, p. 12.

[7] Schulze, *op. cit.*, Vol. II, p. 15.

[8] I. Brodbeck, *Nach Osten. Untersuchungsfahrt nach der Ostküste Grönlands vom 2. bis 12. August 1881* (Niesky, Missions-Institut der Brüdergemeine, 1882, pp. 88), *passim*.

[9] Schulze, *op. cit.*, Vol. II, pp. 15, 16.

[10] F.C.P. Rüttel, *Ti Aar blandt Østgrønlands Hedninger* (Copenhagen, Gyldendalske Boghandel, 1917, pp. 253), *passim*.

[11] Rasmussen, *The People of the Polar North*, p. 285.

[12] Rasmussen, *op. cit.*, pp. 99ff.

[13] *Greenland*, p. 15.

served first under the Moravians and then under the Lutherans, devoted the major part of a celibate life to literary tasks and, later, to training Greenlanders. Among his achievements was the preparation of a grammar of the language and a new translation of the larger part of the Bible.[14] Hymnbooks were compiled, for the Moravians, in characteristic fashion, trained the Eskimos in singing and in instrumental music.[15]

The transition from paganism to Christianity brought some disruption in native society, partly because of the insistence of the missionaries on monogamy, partly through the discrediting of the leaders, the heads of the pre-Christian cult, and partly by prohibitions upon various native customs.[16] We hear of at least one ephemeral native religious movement, centring about a native "prophet" and embodying some ideas derived from Christianity.[17] Gradually the Greenlanders were brought into something approaching conformity to the requirements of the Church.

In 1900 the Moravians withdrew. This step was taken for several reasons, not the least of them being the realization that the population was now professedly Christian and that no confessed pagans remained in the areas in which the missions operated.[18] The Danish Lutheran state church was now left the sole ecclesiastical body in the island.

As we go southward we come next to the tropics and to a climate and populations markedly different from those of Greenland. Here, in the Dutch, Danish, and British West Indies, was a predominantly Negro population. Unlike the Negroes of the United States, it was not surrounded by a white majority. Whites were in the small minority. Assimilation to European culture was, therefore, slower and less complete than in the United States. However, the whites were the ruling class, and the Negroes, accordingly, tended to conform to their ways. At the dawn of the nineteenth century the white masters were nominally but not aggressively Christian. Christianity had barely begun to make headway among the Negroes. In the course of the nineteenth century great changes occurred. Thanks largely to the pressure of the Christian conscience on the home governments, the Negroes were emancipated. This action brought grave difficulties, among them the reluctance of the freedmen to work. The situation was aggravated by a prolonged economic depres-

[14] Schulze, *op. cit.,* Vol. II, pp. 22-26.
[15] Schulze, *op. cit.,* Vol. II, p. 24; Hutton, *op. cit.,* pp. 243, 245.
[16] Rink, *op. cit.,* pp. 140ff.; Rasmussen, *op. cit.,* pp. 289, 290.
[17] Rink, *op. cit.,* pp. 157, 158.
[18] Schulze, *op. cit.,* Vol. II, pp. 38-43; Hutton, *op. cit.,* pp. 242-245.

sion which was partly the result of liberation but chiefly because of the decline in the market price of the staple crop, sugar. Population increased, and the chronic poverty was aggravated. In spite of these adverse circumstances, Christianity made rapid headway. The Negro population became adherents of the faith. The churches and missions laboured valiantly to educate their constituencies. However, in some respects the masses remained distressingly far below Christian standards. The percentage of irregular unions and of illegitimate births was very high. Traces of African, pre-Christian cults persisted in the widely spread Voodoo and Obeah. Christianity made progress, but it did not solve some of the most serious of the problems which confronted it.

First we must mention the Dutch Islands in the West Indies. These comprised Curaçao, Oruba, and Bonaire, off the northern coast of Venezuela, and Eustatius, Saba, and part of St. Martin, east of the Virgin Islands. The largest, Curaçao, contained about 212 square miles. The total population early in the twentieth century was slightly less than 52,000. Only a small minority were Protestants. These were largely of the upper classes, of Dutch blood, and presumably were chiefly Protestant by heredity rather than through conversion. Among them were both Reformed and Lutherans.[19] The majority of the population were of Negro blood. These were predominantly Roman Catholic. Although in the seventeenth century the Dutch, under the stress of their bitter experience with the Spaniards, proscribed Roman Catholicism, that form of the faith already had a foothold. In the eighteenth and nineteenth centuries it made notable gains. Towards the close of the eighteenth century Dutch Franciscans arrived, but the paucity of priests of that order in Holland led to the abandonment by them of Curaçao. The greatest figure in the life of the Roman Catholic Church in the islands seems to have been M. J. Nieuwindt. He became prefect apostolic in 1824 and in 1842 was made the first vicar apostolic of the islands. In 1868, eight years after his death, the Dutch Dominicans were given the spiritual care of the Roman Catholics. A sisterhood had arrived under Nieuwindt. In 1900 four-fifths of the population were Roman Catholic.[20]

Somewhat different was the religious situation in the Danish West Indies, in the islands of St. Croix, St. Thomas, and St. John. As in the Dutch West Indies, the population was predominantly Negro. At the close of the nineteenth century it was slightly over 30,000. Of these, however, less than a fourth were Roman Catholics.[21] The majority were Protestants or had been to a greater or less extent under Protestant influence. The Moravian missions in-

[19] Amelunxen, De Geschiedenis van Curaçao, p. 178.

[20] The Catholic Encyclopedia, Vol. IV, pp. 569, 570; Missiones Catholicae . . . MDCCCXCII, pp. 485, 486; Amelunxen, op. cit., pp. 169-174.

[21] The Catholic Encyclopedia, Vol. XIII, p. 191.

augurated in the eighteenth century continued. On the eve of emancipation fully one-third of the entire population of St. Croix and St. Thomas were said to be members of the Church of England. In 1848 the Church of England in the two islands was placed under the Anglican Bishop of Antigua.[22]

A great change was effected by emancipation. This came by the act of government in 1848, more than a decade after it had been accomplished in the British West Indies. However, for some time the Danish administration had been convinced that the rising tide of anti-slavery sentiment would make the step inevitable. It had, accordingly, prepared for it by introducing schools for the slaves. These schools it entrusted to the Moravians. In them religious instruction was given, although the government insisted that this be non-sectarian. The Moravian missions, in large part supported by plantations the labour on which was by slaves, with consciences increasingly sensitive over the institution, a few years before the general emancipation obtained permission to manumit the Negroes owned by them. Freedom was followed by marked social changes. For a few years the churches under the Moravians prospered, but by the close of the nineteenth century, on one of the islands, St. Thomas, the economic and moral condition of the Negroes was reported to be deteriorating and the number having membership in the Moravian churches declined.[23]

Of the British West Indies the largest and most populous was Jamaica. At the close of the nineteenth century it had about 800,000 inhabitants. Of these the overwhelming majority were of Negro blood.

Here, as in most of the British West Indies, the abolition of slavery brought acute social and economic problems. Contrary to the desire of Buxton, who led in England the fight for emancipation and who wished the step to be taken gradually, the freeing of the Negroes was accelerated. The legislation was enacted in 1833 and was put into effect in 1834. Provision was made for forced labour under the guise of "apprenticeship" to continue until 1840, but this in turn was terminated in 1838.[24] The freedmen were either unwilling to work or demanded higher wages than plantation owners felt they could pay. Production on the plantations fell off sharply. This decline was accentuated by the withdrawal of the protective duties on sugar which had given the British West Indies an advantage in the market for that commodity in the British Isles.[25] To remedy the shortage of labour a few thousand coolies were imported

[22] Pascoe, *Two Hundred Years of the S.P.G.*, p. 213.

[23] Schulze, *200 Jähre Brüdermission*, pp. 134-142; Hutton, *History of the Moravian Missions*, pp. 230, 231; *Bericht von den Reisen und Verrichtungen der Brüder Breutel und Häuser auf den Dänisch-Westindischen Inseln vom December 1840 bis Mai 1841* (no place or date of publication, pp. 72), *passim*.

[24] Mathieson, *The Sugar Colonies and Governor Eyre, 1849-1866*, p. 1.

[25] Mathieson, *op. cit.*, pp. 4, 7.

on contract from India, but they never constituted a large element in the population.[26] Later, partly because of the development of a market for bananas, prosperity returned.

Roman Catholics were in the minority in Jamaica, but in the course of the nineteenth century their numbers increased and the provision for their spiritual care improved. For years after the English occupation (1655) the Roman Catholic form of the faith was forbidden. Of the belated beginnings made by Roman Catholics during the period of Spanish rule only slight traces were left. The Indians had died out in Spanish days and the subsequent Negro population was sparse when the English took possession. Not until 1792 was the Roman Catholic Church revived in the island. Some Roman Catholics, most of them French and Spanish, came from others of the West Indies. Irish Franciscans were sent and a few other priests entered. In 1837 three vicariates apostolic were created for the British West Indies and one of these included Jamaica. In that year Jesuits were sent and in 1852 the care of the Roman Catholics of the island was entrusted formally to that order. In 1894 this charge was transferred from the English province of the Society to the Maryland-New York province and priests came, accordingly, from the United States. Sisters of more than one congregation entered. Schools and churches were erected.[27] By immigration, births, and conversion the number of Roman Catholics rose in the nineteenth century from about 5,000 to about 13,000.[28]

The Church of England was said to have the largest communion roll in Jamaica of any religious body.[29] At the beginning of the nineteenth century the morale of that church was low. The white population was profligate and neglected religious observances and the clergy were reported to be more interested in making money than in the cure of souls.[30] Improvement came. In 1797 the colonial Assembly endeavoured to make better financial provision for church buildings and the clergy and directed that the latter give a portion of each Sunday to the religious instruction of slaves.[31] In 1815, partly to counteract the growing influence of the Wesleyans and to assist in propagating the faith among the slaves, the Assembly took steps towards an increase in the number of clergy.[32] In 1820 there was formed in England, to administer a fund

---

[26] Mathieson, op. cit., p. 135.

[27] Francis X. Delany, A History of the Catholic Church in Jamaica (New York, Jesuit Mission Press, 1930, pp. xi, 292), passim.

[28] Descamps, Histoire Générale Comparée des Missions, p. 580. In 1892 the total was 12,500.—Missiones Catholicae . . . MDCCCXCII, p. 489.

[29] Price, Banana Land, p. 12.

[30] Ellis, The Diocese of Jamaica, pp. 53-55.

[31] Ellis, op. cit., p. 46.

[32] Ellis, op. cit., pp. 56, 57.

arising from a seventeenth-century bequest of Robert Boyle, the Incorporated Society for the Conversion and Religious Instruction and Education of the Negro Slaves in the British West Indies.[33] In 1824 a bishopric bearing the name of Jamaica was created which included that island in its jurisdiction.[34] The financial support of the episcopate was derived from the British Government. Much of the income of the clergy was from grants voted by the Assembly.[35] In the tense feelings aroused over the agitation for emancipation and particularly because of a Negro insurrection in 1831, some of the white colonists, bitterly opposed to freedom for the slaves and regarding the Nonconformist missionaries as among its chief protagonists and as stirring up discontent among the blacks, formed the Colonial Church Union for the purpose of silencing these representatives of other denominations.[36] In the first flush of emancipation and before the moral and economic sag which eventually followed, the freedmen showed a marked hunger for education. The Church of England strove to meet the need. Even before emancipation the Church Missionary Society had begun to send out teachers and catechists for the Negroes.[37] It now reinforced its efforts, but in 1848 withdrew.[38] The Society for the Propagation of the Gospel in Foreign Parts also made grants for the education of the freedmen, but in 1865, with the exhaustion of the special fund from which it had financed them, discontinued its aid.[39] The Society for Promoting Christian Knowledge made appropriations for churches and schools extending over many years.[40] At the beginning of the year 1870, following a widespread trend in the British Empire, the Church of England was disestablished in Jamaica and thenceforward depended financially chiefly upon voluntary contributions.[41] The adjustment to the new status was painful. Once it was made, the church progressed. In 1861 the Jamaica Home and Foreign Missionary Society was organized. Through it scores of mission stations were opened in the island and a share was had in a mission in West Africa.[42] Something was done for the labourers from India and for the Chinese. Hospitality was offered to Syrians, members of one of the Eastern churches.[43] A theo-

[33] Ellis, op. cit., p. 58.
[34] Ellis, op. cit., pp. 47, 49.
[35] Ellis, op. cit., p. 62.
[36] Ellis, op. cit., p. 68.
[37] Ellis, op. cit., p. 66.
[38] Stock, History of the Church Missionary Society, Vol. I, pp. 346, 347.
[39] Classified Digest of the Records of the Society for the Propagation of the Gospel in Foreign Parts, pp. 229-232.
[40] Allen and McClure, Two Hundred Years: The History of the Society for Promoting Christian Knowledge, pp. 373, 445, 521.
[41] Ellis, op. cit., pp. 103-109.
[42] Ellis, op. cit., pp. 139-144, 147, 148.
[43] Ellis, op. cit., pp. 143-147.

logical college was maintained for the training of clergy. Through the Brotherhood of St. Andrew, introduced about 1896, laymen were enlisted and trained in the service of the Church.[44] By 1914 the Church of England was an increasingly vigorous factor in the life of the island.

Baptists were very numerous in Jamaica, more so than any other one denomination if all the various kinds of Baptists were included.[45] In 1783 a Negro from the United States, George Liele, or Lisle, began preaching. In the course of the next few years he and those stirred directly or indirectly by him gathered a number of Baptist congregations from among the blacks. Liele and several others of these preachers, notably Moses Baker, were of excellent character, but were superstitious and illiterate.[46] For a time in the fore part of the nineteenth century the Assembly attempted to prevent religious work by Nonconformists among those of Negro blood, thus embarrassing these preachers.[47] In 1814, in response to appeals from Liele and Baker, representatives of the Baptist Missionary Society began arriving from England.[48] These laboured primarily among the Negroes and were ardent advocates of emancipation. They were, accordingly, not popular with the rank and file of plantation owners. The latter laid at their doors the responsibility for the slave insurrection which broke out in December, 1831. Several of the missionaries were arrested and men professing attachment to the Colonial Church Union destroyed a number of Baptist chapels.[49] In view of the proximity of Haiti with its vivid examples, still fresh, of massacres of the whites, the venom against idealists who might upset the established order was understandable. When emancipation arrived, Baptist missionaries fought the apprenticeship system which followed it, declaring that it was little better than slavery.[50] When that in turn came to an end, they strove for higher wages for the blacks.[51] One of the Baptist missionaries, William Knibb, to make provision for the freedmen, bought landed estates to sell them in small parcels to the Negroes and thus to establish self-supporting communities.[52] Emancipation was followed by a rapid growth in the membership

[44] Ellis, *op. cit.*, pp. 155-159.

[45] Price, *Banana Land*, p. 12.

[46] Mathieson, *The Sugar Colonies and Governor Eyre, 1849-1866*, pp. 139, 140; Payne, *Freedom in Jamaica*, pp. 17, 18; Clarke, *Memorials of Baptist Missionaries in Jamaica*, pp. 9ff.

[47] Clarke, *op. cit.*, p. 30; Payne, *op. cit.*, pp. 18, 19.

[48] Payne, *op. cit.*, p. 19. For biographies of missionaries see Clarke, *op. cit., passim*; Clark, *The Voice of Jubilee*, pp. 137-253; Tucker, *Glorious Liberty*, p. 11.

[49] Payne, *op. cit.*, pp. 27-31; Phillippo, *Jamaica: Its Past and Present State*, pp. 164ff.; Hinton, *Memoir of William Knibb*, pp. 111ff.; Tucker, *op. cit.*, pp. 21ff.

[50] Payne, *op. cit.*, p. 49; Tucker, *op. cit.*, pp. 36ff.

[51] Hinton, *op. cit.*, pp. 286ff.

[52] Hinton, *op. cit.*, pp. 301ff.; Payne, *op. cit.*, p. 59.

of Baptist churches. The total rose from 10,838 in 1831 to 24,777 in 1839.[53] In 1860 and 1861 a revival broke out, with striking emotional features, which within a year brought 4,422 additions.[54] The awakening contributed to the appearance of itinerant preachers, some of them of unsavoury character, who sought to spread and perpetuate it.[55] A revolt which arose among the Negroes in 1865 was ascribed by some officials to the Baptists and severe treatment followed. However, the home government declared the most notable of the executions unwarranted.[56] In 1842 the Jamaica Baptist Association determined on self-support for the island, thus to relieve the Baptist Missionary Society of its responsibilities.[57] In that year, too, the Jamaica Baptist Missionary Society was formed with the West Indies as its contemplated sphere of activity.[58] There were dreams, moreover, of Christian Negroes going from Jamaica as missionaries to the Negroes of Africa. Beginning in 1843, over a span of years and at no little cost of life and health, quite a number went to Africa in connexion with the (English) Baptist Missionary Society.[59] Also commencing in the 1840's, with the aid of the Baptist Missionary Society a school was conducted for the purpose of training Jamaicans for the ministry.[60] After these brave attempts at financial independence and propagating the faith outside the island, the decades of economic depression which overtook Jamaica brought poverty to many of the clergy and churches. As prosperity returned the churches showed improvement.[61]

Jamaica was one of the islands visited by the much-travelled Thomas Coke in his energetic promotion of the incipient Methodism of the West Indies. He was first in the island in 1789. He soon sent from England a resident missionary.[62] Other missionaries followed. Efforts were directed especially to the Negroes, both slave and free. Chronic opposition developed from those who believed that the Methodists were preaching the equality of all men and were undermining the slavery on which the economic structure of the island was built. As in the case of the Baptists, violence was resorted to and various at-

[53] Hinton, *op. cit.*, p. 358.
[54] Henderson, *Goodness and Mercy*, p. 103; Edward Bean Underhill, *Life of James Mursell Phillippo, Missionary in Jamaica* (London, Yates & Alexander, 1881, pp. viii, 437), pp. 304-314.
[55] Henderson, *op. cit.*, p. 104.
[56] Tucker, *op. cit.*, pp. 76ff.
[57] Payne, *op. cit.*, pp. 68, 69; Tucker, *op. cit.*, pp. 57ff.
[58] Payne, *op. cit.*, p. 70.
[59] Payne, *op. cit.*, pp. 72ff.; Clark, *The Voice of Jubilee*, pp. 130ff.
[60] Payne, *op. cit.*, pp. 105ff.
[61] Price, *Banana Land*, pp. 62ff.
[62] Duncan, *A Narrative of the Wesleyan Mission to Jamaica*, pp. 8-10.

tempts, usually disallowed by the home government, were made by the local authorities to prevent Methodist activities for the blacks and mulattoes.[63] Yet the membership of the Methodist societies grew. In 1832 it was 12,835.[64] More and more Methodism was confined to those of Negro blood. The whites gravitated from it to the Church of England.[65] From the 1840's for about twenty years membership declined without a corresponding increase in quality.[66] This was in spite of a large influx from the revival of 1860. Out of the latter came antinomianism.[67] The discouragements of these decades were due in part to the economic difficulties under which the island laboured and in part to divisions in the mother church in Great Britain with a consequent retrenchment and a reduction of the missionary staff.[68] As these hindrances were left behind, conditions in Methodism improved. The gains were not due entirely or even primarily to economic factors. They were to be attributed in large part to the leadership of George Sargeant. Under him, in 1875, high schools and a theological college were opened to train native leaders.[69] In the 1880's Methodism in the West Indies became independent of that in Great Britain. A General Conference was formed, with Sargeant as its first president, and two Annual Conferences. Some of the clergy, however, were still recruited from the British Isles. Ecclesiastical independence did not prove an unqualified boon. Financially the load was too heavy, and in 1904, at the request of the two Annual Conferences, the Wesleyan Methodist Missionary Society resumed charge, reluctantly, of the West Indian Districts, including Jamaica. Reinforcements from Great Britain to the clergy were renewed.[70]

Although the Church of England, the Baptists, and the Methodists were the largest bodies represented in Jamaica, they were by no means the only ones. The Moravians ante-dated both Baptists and Methodists. They continued. After emancipation, in spite of poverty and of the fact that the membership was drawn from among the very poorest of those of Negro blood, progress was made towards self-support, the proportion of indigenous clergy to missionaries increased, and (in 1895) a society was formed to carry the Christian

---

[63] Duncan, op. cit., passim; Findlay and Holdsworth, The History of the Wesleyan Methodist Missionary Society, Vol. II, pp. 63-132.

[64] Duncan, op. cit., p. 267.

[65] Findlay and Holdsworth, op. cit., Vol. II, p. 358.

[66] Findlay and Holdsworth, op. cit., Vol. II, p. 365. On Methodism before 1850, with a description of its various stations and centres, see Peter Samuel, The Wesleyan-Methodist Missions in Jamaica and Honduras Delineated (London, 1850, pp. ix, 320); passim.

[67] Findlay and Holdsworth, op. cit., Vol. II, p. 374.

[68] Walker, The Call of the West Indies, pp. 96ff.

[69] Findlay and Holdsworth, op. cit., Vol. II, pp. 394-398.

[70] Findlay and Holdsworth, op. cit., Vol. II, pp. 444-473.

message to Africa. In 1912 the membership was 14,105.[71] The Presbyterians of Scotland despatched missionaries to the Negroes. The first arrived in 1800, the agent of the Scottish Missionary Society. In the course of the next three decades a few other appointees of that society came.[72] Beginning in 1834, the Synod of the United Secession Church sent missionaries.[73] The missionaries of the Scottish Missionary Society co-operated with those of the United Secession Church and in 1847 all were placed under the jurisdiction of the newly formed United Presbyterian Church. In 1849 the Presbyterians had about 4,000 communicants.[74] Later a theological college for training clergy was inaugurated.[75] A mission for the Indian labourers was begun.[76] When, in 1900, the Free Church of Scotland and the United Presbyterian Church coalesced to form the United Free Church of Scotland, the supervision of the Jamaica mission was transferred to the Foreign Mission Committee of the new body.[77] In 1843 the Established Church of Scotland had at least two congregations, primarily for the white colonists.[78] In 1837 Congregationalists of the United States began a mission which later was entrusted to the American Missionary Association. This body continued the enterprise until 1873, when it turned over its schools to the government and transferred its churches to the Baptists.[79] In 1834, moved by the need to follow up emancipation, the London Missionary Society sent its first representatives to Jamaica. In 1860 the churches connected with it had 1,691 members and its day schools 1,346 pupils. In 1867 the society decided that the Congregational churches established by its missionaries in the West Indies should prepare to stand on their own feet and assume the responsibility for the further spread of the faith in that area. It thereupon began a gradual reduction of its assistance. By 1885 the churches were technically independent, but from time to time the society continued to come to their relief with grants of personnel and money.[80] The Disciples of Christ sent a missionary in 1858.

[71] Schulze, *200 Jähre Brüdermission*, Vol. II, pp. 161-178; J. H. Buchner, *The Moravians in Jamaica. History of the Mission of the United Brethren's Church to the Negroes in the Island of Jamaica, from the year 1754 to 1854* (London, Longman, Brown & Co., 1854, pp. 175), *passim*.

[72] McNeill, *The Story of Our Missions. The West Indies*, pp. 21-23.

[73] McNeill, *op. cit.*, p. 23.

[74] McNeill, *op. cit.*, pp. 32-37. Also on this mission see Robson, *The Story of Our Jamaica Mission*, pp. 25-103.

[75] McNeill, *op. cit.*, p. 40.

[76] McNeill, *op. cit.*, pp. 54ff.

[77] McNeill, *op. cit.*, p. 58.

[78] Phillippo, *Jamaica. Its Past and Present State*, p. 285.

[79] Beard, *A Crusade of Brotherhood*, pp. 30, 53, 55.

[80] Lovett, *The History of the London Missionary Society, 1798-1895*, Vol. II, pp. 376-396.

Ten years later they discontinued the enterprise, but in 1876 resumed it.[81] In 1921 their churches had a membership of 2,457.[82] The British and Foreign Bible Society had auxiliaries on the island.[83] In the course of time still other denominations entered or sprang up—among them Seven Keys, Millennial Dawn, Pentecostal Holiness, Baptist Reformed Catholic Apostolic Church, and the Reformed Church of God.[84] The Seventh Day Adventists organized a conference in 1903.[85] The Church of God had several congregations.[86] The African Methodist Episcopal Church had an enterprise which flourished and then declined.[87] Jamaican Protestantism was variegated.

As a result of the extensive efforts of the several Christian bodies, something of Christianity penetrated to practically all of the Negroes of Jamaica. By the early part of the twentieth century nearly every home had some kind of connexion with a church or Sunday School.[88] However, a great deal of this was tenuous, and the majority failed to show much conformity to Christian standards. A very large proportion of the children were born out of wedlock.[89] In Myalism and Obeah paganism and witchcraft persisted, handed down in distorted form from the African heritage.[90] In some instances movements arose in which the non-Christian past was mixed with elements derived from Christianity.[91] Yet many examples were recorded of conformity to Christian standards, sometimes at no little cost.[92] Missionaries and churches were of major assistance in facilitating the adjustment of the former slaves to their new status of freedmen. Christian schools did much to raise the level of education and provide leadership. Even though financial self-support and complete independence of foreign leadership were not achieved, progress was made towards them. Negro missionaries were provided for Africa. The Negro churches leaned more on white aid than did those of the United States, but they gave evidence of a vigorous faith.

[81] *Survey of Service . . . Disciples of Christ*, pp. 477ff.
[82] *First Annual Report of the United Christian Missionary Society, Oct. 1, 1920-June 20, 1921*, p. 34.
[83] *The Hundred and Tenth Report of the British and Foreign Bible Society* (1914), p. 420.
[84] Price, *Banana Land*, pp. 27, 28.
[85] *1914 Year Book of the Seventh Day Adventist Denomination*, p. 149.
[86] *Year Book of the Church of God 1918*, pp. 196-198.
[87] *The Twenty-Fifth Quadrennial Report of the Parent Home and Foreign Missionary Department of the African Methodist Episcopal Church*, pp. 26-28.
[88] Price, *op. cit.*, p. 25.
[89] Price, *op. cit.*, p. 12; O'Rorke, *Our Opportunity in the West Indies*, p. 54.
[90] Price, *op. cit.*, pp. 154-166; Williams, *Voodoos and Obeahs*, pp. 142-208, 215, 216.
[91] Williams, *op. cit.*, pp. 149, 157, 172; Phillippo, *op. cit.*, pp. 270-274.
[92] For some of these see Price, *op. cit.*, pp. 134-138.

Trinidad, the second largest island of the British West Indies, was taken by the British from the Spaniards near the close of the eighteenth century. In 1914 its population was not far from a third of a million. The majority of its inhabitants were of Negro blood, but about a third were East Indians, brought in as labourers.

As was to be expected, the Spanish missionary enterprise had planted Christianity on Trinidad. When the island passed into the hands of the British, under the terms of capitulation the status of the Roman Catholic Church underwent no change. The new regime contributed to the support of the clergy. In 1820 Port of Spain, the capital of the island, was made the seat of a bishop. Later the see was raised to an archiepiscopate. The majority of the clergy were not of the local stock but were from England, Ireland, and France. The Dominicans, the Congregation of the Holy Ghost, the Order of Mary Immaculate, and the Augustinians were represented. There were some seculars.[93] The first of the Dominicans arrived in 1864. The Province of France, then that of Lyons, and eventually that of Ireland, supplied the members of the Order of Preachers.[94] The Sisters of St. Dominic and the Sisters of St. Joseph had charge of appropriate enterprises.

The Church of England made rapid strides on Trinidad. In 1836 it had only one clergyman besides the garrison chaplain. In that year aid began to come from the Society for the Propagation of the Gospel in Foreign Parts. In 1845 the colonial government divided the island into seventeen parishes and made provision for the clergy. As coolies were imported from India efforts were made to reach them through schools. In 1891 about a hundred of these Indians were being baptized each year.[95] After the emancipation of the Negroes the Church Missionary Society sent missionaries and school-teachers.[96] When the Church of England was disestablished in the West Indies, Trinidad became a separate diocese. Its first bishop, Richard Rawle, arrived in 1872, and through humble, devoted labour and extensive use of his private income did much to extend the church.[97]

The Methodists placed their first missionary on Trinidad in 1809, but opposition from the colonial authorities developed, stimulated in part by the ill will

[93] *The Catholic Encyclopedia*, Vol. XII, p. 291.

[94] Marie-Joseph Guillet, *Les Dominicains Français a l'Ile de la Trinidad (1864-1895)* (Tours, Marcel Cattier, 1926, pp. vi, 458), *passim*.

[95] *Classified Digest of the Records of the Society for the Propagation of the Gospel in Foreign Parts 1701-1892*, pp. 208, 209.

[96] Stock, *History of the Church Missionary Society*, Vol. I, p. 346.

[97] George Mather and Charles John Blagg, *Bishop Rawle. A Memoir* (London, Kegan Paul, Trench, Trübner & Co., 1890, pp. xii, 421), pp. 226ff.

of the Roman Catholics, and only a few converts were made. Many of such adherents as the Methodists had were immigrants from other islands.[98]

The London Missionary Society put a missionary in Port of Spain as early as 1809, but the antagonism of the local authorities to Nonconformists led in 1825 to the discontinuance of the enterprise.[99]

In 1867, through the initiative of J. Morton, the Canadian Presbyterians began efforts for the Indian immigrants on Trinidad. Literature in the appropriate languages was obtained from India. Schools were opened and were supported at first by subsidies from the proprietors of the estates and later by government grants. Preaching stations were instituted, churches were organized, and clergy and catechists were trained. In 1911 the mission counted 1,253 communicants, had about 11,000 pupils in primary schools, and maintained a secondary school, a college, and a home for girls. The liquor traffic was being fought.[100]

The Presbyterians of Scotland had in Trinidad a succession of missionaries, beginning in 1836, but the membership which they gathered seems never to have reached 1,000.[101]

Limitations of space forbid even a summary description of the others of the British West Indies island by island. Only generalizations can be made and a few of the developments chronicled.

Roman Catholics were numerous on some of the islands. In Dominica they constituted about three-fourths of the population (which, as was usual in the British West Indies, was overwhelmingly Negro).[102] In St. Kitts they were about a fifth of the population. In Grenada they were numerically in the ascendant.[103] Yet in Grenada Obeah was very prevalent among the nominal Christians.[104]

The Church of England was spread widely over the British West Indies. Just before and immediately after emancipation special assistance was given by the Society for the Propagation of the Gospel in Foreign Parts, the Society for Promoting Christian Knowledge, and the Church Missionary Society to

[98] Findlay and Holdsworth, *The History of the Methodist Missionary Society*, Vol. II, pp. 211-220, 408, 409, 452.

[99] Lovett, *The History of the London Missionary Society*, Vol. II, pp. 317, 318.

[100] *The Canadian Presbyterian Mission to East Indians. Trinidad, B.W.I. 1911* (Trinidad, Canadian Mission Council, 1911, pp. 60), *passim*.

[101] McNeill, *The Story of Our Missions. The West Indies*, pp. 85-88; Robson, *The Story of Our Jamaica Mission*, pp. 107-117.

[102] *The Catholic Encyclopedia*, Vol. XIII, p. 191.

[103] Findlay and Holdsworth, *op. cit.*, Vol. II, p. 41c.

[104] Hesketh J. Bell, *Obeah. Witchcraft in the West Indies* (London, Sampson Low, Marston & Co., 1893, pp. viii, 200), *passim*.

enable the church to care for the freedmen. The disestablishment which came to it in the second half of the nineteenth century in all of the islands except Barbados stimulated the Church of England to greater exertions. The hardship which followed called forth fresh support from private sources and from Anglican missionary agencies in Great Britain. In 1883 a comprehensive organization for the area was constituted through an association of the existing dioceses in an ecclesiastical province with an archbishop.[105] In Barbados the Church of England was especially strong.[106] In the dense population, chiefly Negro, about 200,000 in 1913, the church was well organized and salaries for the clergy continued to be paid from the colonial treasury. Here, on the endowment provided by the eighteenth-century bequest of Christopher Codrington, a college was established for training a clergy for the West Indies. The first head was the saintly Richard Rawle, later the first Bishop of Trinidad. Rawle also led in the organization of the West Indian African Mission, which laboured in what became French Guinea.[107] At almost the other extreme from Barbados were the thinly settled and many-islanded Bahamas. Here beginnings were made before the nineteenth century. Near the close of the eighteenth century Loyalists seeking refuge from the now independent Thirteen Colonies brought a marked accession of strength. Yet, at the beginning of the nineteenth century, the Church of England was weak. Only gradually was it built up. The successive bishops found the Bahamas poverty-stricken and difficult to traverse. One of them was drowned while on his episcopal journeys.[108] In Bermuda, with the aid of the Society for the Propagation of the Gospel in Foreign Parts, the Church of England did much for the education of the population and the proportion increased of couples whose marriage had been regularized.[109]

As might have been expected from its missionary character and the early leadership of Coke, Methodism was widely represented in the British West Indies. In its early stages in the islands, in the closing years of the eighteenth century and the opening decades of the nineteenth century, it frequently met with opposition, attempts at legal prohibition (eventually overruled by the home government), and even violence. However, its agents persevered and

---

[105] Pascoe, *Two Hundred Years of the S.P.G.*, pp. 194-197.

[106] In the 1820's Methodists who tried to effect a foothold were subjected to violence.— Shrewsbury, *Memorials of the Rev. William J. Shrewsbury*, pp. 129-204.

[107] O'Rorke, *Our Opportunity in the West Indies*, pp. 89ff.; Pascoe, *op. cit.*, pp. 196-206.

[108] O'Rorke, *op. cit.*, pp. 65ff.; Roscow Shedden, *Ups and Downs in a West India Diocese* (London, A. R. Mowbray & Co., 1927, pp. viii, 188), *passim;* Pascoe, *op. cit.*, pp. 223-227b.

[109] Pascoe, *op. cit.*, pp. 102ff.

won adherents from among both whites and Negroes.[110] At the time of emancipation there were said to be in all the West Indies 70 Methodist missionaries and 32,000 adult members, of whom 23,000 were ex-slaves. After emancipation additional missionaries were sent. By 1841, seven years after emancipation, the membership had about doubled.[111] The unsuccessful experiment with ecclesiastical independence in the latter part of the nineteenth century, chronicled a few paragraphs above, did not prove a severe check. Help came from Great Britain to wipe out the debts contracted under the West Indian conferences and the flow of clergy from the mother church was renewed.[112]

The Church of God won some adherents on Barbados and in Trinidad.[113] The British and Foreign Bible Society had auxiliaries.[114] The Seventh-Day Adventists, in the twentieth century so aggressive in their world-wide efforts, sent missionaries.[115] The African Methodist Episcopal Church reported enterprises on Trinidad and Barbados.[116]

On the mainland of Central and South America the possessions in the hands of predominantly Protestant powers were British Honduras, British Guiana, and Dutch Guiana.

British Honduras, or Belize as it was once called, need not long detain us. Its population was a mixture of Negroes, of Spaniards, of those of British blood, and of Indians of more than one tribe, some of them Caribs from the West Indies. Although English adventurers began arriving in the seventeenth century, it was not until late in the eighteenth century that their rights were formally recognized by Spain, and it was not until the nineteenth century that the British title emerged uncontested. A close connexion with Jamaica was long maintained. It was only in 1884 that the colony was formally separated from the administration of that island.

It was to be expected that, flanked by lands where Spanish culture prevailed and long claimed by Spain, British Honduras would have a large proportion of Roman Catholics. The region was so much on the fringe of Western civilization that Christianity of any kind was slow in gaining much of a foothold.

[110] Findlay and Holdsworth, *The History of the Wesleyan Methodist Missionary Society*, Vol. II, pp. 133ff.

[111] Walker, *The Call of the West Indies*, pp. 89-92.

[112] Findlay and Holdsworth, *op. cit.*, Vol. II, pp. 444ff.

[113] *Year Book of the Churches of God*, 1918, pp. 195, 198.

[114] *The Hundred and Tenth Report of the British and Foreign Bible Society*, pp. 421, 422.

[115] *1914 Year Book of the Seventh Day Adventist Denomination*, pp. 150-152.

[116] *The Twenty-fifth Quadrennial Report of the Parent Home and Foreign Missionary Department of the African Methodist Episcopal Church, 1912-1916*, p. 29.

In 1836 the area was placed ecclesiastically under the new Vicariate Apostolic of Jamaica. The Roman Catholic element was reinforced by refugees from an outbreak in Yucatán in 1848. In 1888 British Honduras was made a separate prefecture apostolic. By the close of the century the Jesuits were in charge. Roman Catholics then constituted about two-thirds of the population and, while still backward, subject to Obeah and to irregularity in their marital relations, were improving in education and in conformity to the requirements of their faith.[117]

Protestants were also present in British Honduras, but as minorities. Anglicans were represented chiefly by Negro labourers from Jamaica. On the eve of 1914 they were cared for by about fifteen clergy assisted by a few lay readers and catechists and supervised by a bishop. Improvement in morals was noted as a result of the missionaries' activities.[118] Methodists found their field among the Negroes and Caribs from the West Indies and among those of English descent. Their first missionary arrived in 1825. Progress was irregular and from time to time was interrupted by the ill-health or death of missionaries and by the neglect of the society in Great Britain. By 1913 about 2,000 members had been gathered and 9 clergy were employed.[119] The Baptists also inaugurated enterprises, partly in the native tongues.[120]

The Guianas, British and Dutch, adjoining each other on what once was the Spanish Main, were characterized by a low-lying alluvial plain from eighteen to fifty miles in width along the coast, and high lands, drained by rivers, in the interior. Most of the inhabitants were on the coastal plain.

At the dawn of the twentieth century the population of British Guiana (Demerara) was about 300,000. Of this about two-fifths were Negroes, another two-fifths were from India and Ceylon, chiefly Tamils, less than 10,000 were aborigines, about 12,000 were Portuguese, a few thousand were Chinese, and about 4,300 were Europeans other than Portuguese.[121] British Guiana was taken by Great Britain from Holland during the Napoleonic Wars and did not come permanently under the Union Jack until the close of that series of struggles. The Negroes were largely descendants of slaves, freed at the time of emancipation in the British Empire. The Portuguese, from Madeira, the

[117] *The Catholic Encyclopedia,* Vol. VII, pp. 449, 450; *Missiones Catholicae . . . MDCCCXCII,* p. 490.

[118] O'Rorke, *Our Opportunity in the West Indies,* pp. 84, 85. See also a narrative by a bishop of British Honduras, Herbert Bury, *A Bishop amongst Bananas* (London, Wells Gardner, Darton & Co., 1911, pp. xvi. 236), *passim.*

[119] Findlay and Holdsworth, *op. cit.,* Vol. II, pp. 290-297, 430-443, 482-488.

[120] Crowe, *The Gospel in Central America,* pp. 319ff.

[121] *The Encyclopædia Britannica,* eleventh edition, Vol. XII, p. 676. See somewhat different figures in *British Guiana,* p. 6. See also Rodway, *Guiana: British, Dutch, and French, passim.*

large element from India, and the Chinese portions of the population were in British Guiana because of efforts to supply the deficiency of cheap labour brought about by the freeing of the Negroes.[122]

Roman Catholics were not prominent in the population of British Guiana. At the close of the nineteenth and opening years of the twentieth century they numbered between 20,000 and 22,000. A large proportion of them were Portuguese, immigrants from Madeira. A vicariate apostolic was created in 1837. Jesuits and Ursulines gave leadership and instruction.[123]

The first Protestant effort for non-Christians in what later became British Guiana was made while that area was still under the Dutch, in the eighteenth century, by the Moravians. This was among the Indians in the vicinity of the Berbice River. The year 1738 was the date of beginning. For a time the enterprise seemed to flourish. Then a series of misfortunes overtook it, among them a Negro revolt in 1763 which wiped out some of the centres. In 1816 it was finally abandoned.[124]

The Church of England displayed a striking growth. At the beginning of the nineteenth century the region is said to have had only two clergymen, one of the Church of England, and one of the Dutch Reformed Church. Churches were erected, but as late as 1824 there were only three clergymen in the colony.[125] In 1826 British Guiana, previously under the Bishop of London, was placed under the jurisdiction of the Bishop of Barbados and the Leeward Islands. Aid began coming from the British societies. The Society for the Propagation of the Gospel in Foreign Parts undertook enterprises for the Negroes and the Indians. As in the West Indies, the need and opportunity brought by emancipation led to a large increase in the efforts of that society.[126] From 1827 through 1858 the Church Missionary Society conducted a mission for the Indians.[127] In 1842 a separate diocese was erected for British Guiana. Its first bishop was William Pierce Austin. Of large stature and endowed with great energy and endurance, he served for half a century and became the first Primate of the West Indies.[128] Both the Church of England and the Church

[122] Rodway, op. cit., pp. 123-128, 191-194; British Guiana, pp. 47-50.
[123] Missiones Catholicae . . . MDCCCXCII, pp. 486, 487; The Catholic Encyclopedia, Vol. VII, p. 62.
[124] Müller, 200 Jähre Brüdermission, Vol. I, pp. 93-105.
[125] Pascoe, Two Hundred Years of the S.P.G., p. 242.
[126] Pascoe, op. cit., pp. 242ff.
[127] Proceedings of the Church Missionary Society, 1827-1828, pp. 34, 130; 1857-1858, pp. 196, 197. See also J. H. Bernau, Missionary Labours in British Guiana (London, John Farquhar Shaw, 1847, pp. xi, 242), passim; W. T. Veness, Ten Years of Mission Life in British Guiana; Being the Memoir of the Rev. Thomas Youd (London, Society for Promoting Christian Knowledge, no date, pp. 136), passim.
[128] O'Rorke, Our Opportunity in the West Indies, pp. 119, 120; Farrar, Notes on the History of the Church in Guiana, pp. 16ff.

of Scotland (Presbyterian) received official recognition. In 1825 part of the colony was divided into parishes on the principle of assigning alternate ones to each of the two churches. However, the Church of England was by far the more active of the two. The establishment was continued until 1899.[129] Other denominations eventually shared in state aid. Not until after 1914 was this commuted through a proportionate distribution of interest-bearing government bonds among the various bodies.[130] Attempts were made to reach the several elements in the population. The Negroes were cared for. Much attention was paid to the aborigines.[131] Famous among the missionaries to them was William Henry Brett, who helped inaugurate (1840) the enterprise of the Society for the Propagation of the Gospel in Foreign Parts for the Indians and gave forty years of service.[132] Relatively few of the immigrants from India and Ceylon were won. In contrast with India, the majority of the converts were Brahmins.[133] About nine-tenths of the Chinese became Christians.[134] In 1892 the Church of England had 18,500 communicants, between three and four times the number of fifty years before.[135] Proportionately it had increased more rapidly than the population.

Methodism was introduced to Demerara (a section of the later British Guiana) by two freed Negroes who had been converted on Nevis, one of the West Indies. After an interruption in 1814 a continuing Methodist movement was inaugurated by a missionary. Vigorous and at times violent opposition developed from the local government and some of the whites on the ground that the Methodists would stir the Negroes to revolt. In spite of fluctuations the membership grew. Some converts were made from the Hindus. Internal dissensions and financial irregularities of one of the mission's chairmen proved a handicap. Yet Methodism continued.[136]

In 1807 the London Missionary Society inaugurated a mission in Demerara. It ministered chiefly to the Negroes, and in its early years, accordingly, the

[129] British Guiana, p. 33.

[130] White, Six Years in Hammock Land, p. 41.

[131] O'Rorke, op. cit., pp. 120-125.

[132] W. H. Brett, Mission Work among the Indian Tribes in the Forests of Guiana (London, Society for Promoting Christian Knowledge, no date, pp. xii, 260), passim; W. H. Brett, The Indian Tribes of Guiana: Their Condition and Habits (London, Bell and Daldy, 1868, pp. xiii, 500), passim; F. P. L. Josa, "The Apostle of the Indians of Guiana." A Memoir of the Life and Labours of the Rev. W. H. Brett, B.D. (London, Wells, Gardner, Darton & Co., 1888, pp. viii, 156), passim. Also on Indian missions see Farrar, op. cit., pp. 23-71.

[133] O'Rorke, op. cit., p. 126; Farrar, op. cit., pp. 67-70.

[134] O'Rorke, op. cit., pp. 126, 127.

[135] Farrar, op. cit., p. 208.

[136] Findlay and Holdsworth, The History of the Wesleyan Methodist Missionary Society, Vol. II, pp. 274-288, 377-384, 410-416; Bickford, An Autobiography, pp. 82, 83.

colonial authorities placed obstacles in its way in the fear that it would lead to a Negro rebellion. When, in 1823, some of the blacks revolted, one of the missionaries, John Smith, was accused of having incited them, was arrested and condemned, and died in prison (1824). Mission stations were also established in Berbice, another portion of what became British Guiana. After emancipation planters and the government took a more favourable attitude and subsidized education or actually encouraged religious instruction. In 1867 the London Missionary Society believed that the churches in British Guiana, now with 3,200 members, largely Negroes, had reached the point where they could begin to dispense with financial aid from Great Britain. No new missionaries were sent and grants were gradually reduced. In 1885 the churches became independent. Yet annual subsidies continued to be given and from time to time special assistance in personnel and funds was still sent.[137]

Numerically minor missions in British Guiana were by the Canadian Presbyterians, begun in 1896, for the East Indians;[138] the Seventh Day Adventists, organized in 1906;[139] the African Methodist Episcopal Zion Church;[140] and Lutherans (General Synod) from the United States. The last named gave fellowship and support to a congregation whose beginnings dated back to 1743.[141] The British and Foreign Bible Society had auxiliaries.[142]

By the close of the century the overwhelming majority of the Negroes, the Chinese, and, of course, of those of European descent were ostensibly Christian.[143]

Dutch Guiana (Surinam), the portion left to the Netherlands after the British conquest, was smaller than British Guiana. At the beginning of the twentieth century its population, too, was less than a third of that of its

---

[137] David Chamberlain, *Smith of Demerara* (London, Simpkin, Marshall, Hamilton, Kent & Co., 1923, pp. 110), *passim; The London Missionary Society's Report of the Proceedings against the Late Rev. J. Smith* (London, F. Westley, 1824, pp. vii, 204), *passim;* E. A. Wallbridge, *Memoirs of the Rev. John Smith, Missionary to Demerara* (London, Charles Gilpin, 1848, pp. xxvi, 274), *passim;* Lovett, *The History of the London Missionary Society, 1795-1895,* Vol. II, pp. 318-375, 389-396; L. Crookall, *British Guiana or Work and Wanderings among the Creoles and Coolies, the Africans and Indians of the Wild Country* (London, T. Fisher Unwin, 1898, pp. xii, 247), *passim;* Thomas Rain, *The Life and Labours of John Wray, Pioneer Missionary in British Guiana. Compiled chiefly from His Own Mss. and Diaries* (London, John Snow & Co., 182, pp. 376), *passim.*

[138] Beach and St. John, *World Statistics of Christian Missions,* p. 86.

[139] *1914 Year Book of the Seventh-day Adventist Denomination,* p. 151.

[140] *Quadrennial Report Board of Foreign Missions of the African Methodist Zion Church (1920-1924),* p. 19.

[141] White, *Six Years in Hammock Land,* pp. 42ff.

[142] *The Hundred & Tenth Annual Report of the British and Foreign Bible Society,* p. 422.

[143] Pascoe, *Two Hundred Years of the S.P.G.,* p. 251c.

western neighbour. This population, like that on the west, was mixed. Indians numbered about 2,000. Bush Negroes, or Marrons, the descendants of runaway slaves, living on the edges of the cultivated coastal plain, totalled about 10,000.[144] There were other Negroes, descendants of the freed slaves. Importation of Negroes stopped early in the nineteenth century with the abolition of the slave trade. Emancipation came in 1863. As in British Guiana, many of the freedmen proved unwilling to work on the plantations for wages which the employers felt able to pay. In efforts to meet the shortage of labour, Chinese, Javanese, and coolies from India were brought in. This added extensive non-Christian elements, early in the twentieth century amounting to about 6,000 Moslems and about 12,000 Hindus.[145]

Rome created a vicariate apostolic for Dutch Guiana in 1842. Near the beginning of the twentieth century Roman Catholics numbered not far from 14,000 and were served by Redemptorists, largely from Holland, and by one of the sisterhoods.[146]

The only Protestant bodies in Dutch Guiana with considerable followings were the Dutch Reformed, the Lutherans, and the Moravians. In 1908 the first had about 6,500 adherents, the second about 3,000, and the third, by far the largest in the colony, about 27,000.[147] There is room to say only a word concerning any of these, and that must be of the remarkable Moravian mission. This was begun in 1735. It had its first major development among the Indians. Before the end of the eighteenth century it had been extended to the Bush Negroes and to the slaves on the plantations.[148] In the nineteenth and twentieth centuries the Moravians laboured for Negroes, Bush Negroes, Indians, Javanese, Chinese, and the coolies from British India. Their chief numerical success was among those of Negro blood in the towns and on the cultivated coastal plain. For decades the mission was maintained through a profitable local business in which the missionaries found a livelihood. In the twentieth century steps were taken to divorce the business enterprise from the churches

---

[144] On the Bush Negroes, in the twentieth century still largely pagan, see Melville J. Herskovits and Frances S. Herskovits, *Rebel Destiny. Among the Bush Negroes of Dutch Guiana* (New York, McGraw-Hill Book Co., 1934, pp. xv, 366), *passim*; Morton C. Kahn, *Djuka. The Bush Negroes of Dutch Guiana* (New York, The Viking Press, 1931, pp. xxiv, 233), *passim*.

[145] *The Encyclopædia Britannica*, 11th ed., Vol. XII, pp. 680, 681; *Dutch Guiana*, pp. 5, 6.

[146] *The Catholic Encyclopedia*, Vol. VII, p. 63; *Missiones Catholicae . . . MDCCCXCII*, pp. 488, 489.

[147] Schulze, *200 Jähre Brüdermission*, Vol. II, p. 266. See a slightly different set of figures in *Dutch Guiana*, p. 16.

[148] See an extended account of these eighteenth-century missions in F. Staehelin, *Die Mission der Brüdergemeine in Suriname und Berbice im achtzehnten Jahrhundert* (Herrnhut, Verein für Brüdergeschichte, and Paramaribo, C. Kersten & Co., 3 vols. in 6 parts, no date), *passim*.

and towards making the latter self-supporting and self-governing. Schools were conducted and social clubs of various kinds organized.[149]

In the widely scattered islands and areas surveyed in this chapter the spread of Christianity from 1815 to 1914 had many common features. In all the faith made remarkable progress in winning adherents. Most of these were among the Negroes. Improvement in allegiance to the Church and in approximating to Christian ethical standards took place among the ruling white minority. The small Chinese enclaves proved responsive. Indians were reached with more difficulty, partly because they were few in number and were chiefly on the fringes of the white man's settlements in British Honduras and the Guianas and were more difficult of access. The immigrants in Trinidad, Jamaica, and the Guianas from India, Ceylon, and Java were resistant to Christianity. Relatively few converts were made among them. Except in a very few islands Protestants were more numerous than Roman Catholics. Protestants had many more missions and missionaries than did Roman Catholics. Marked advance was registered by Protestants in developing ecclesiastical organizations, in self-support, and towards an indigenous clergy. In no major denomination, however, was permanent full independence achieved from assistance in money and personnel from the parent bodies.

To Christianity must be chiefly ascribed the emancipation of the Negroes. Indirectly, therefore, Christianity was partly responsible for the economic and social revolutions which followed emancipation, and for the importation of labourers from China, India, Ceylon, and Java to fill the gaps on the plantations made by the unwillingness of the freedmen to work. It was through missionaries and the churches, usually with financial aid from the government, that most of the schools were founded and maintained and that progress was registered in literacy. Efforts, by no means lacking in success, were put forth towards regularity and permanence in marriage among the former slaves and their descendants. Yet, even with the amazing achievements of the period, much of ignorance remained, irregularity in sex relations persisted, a large percentage of the children were born out of wedlock, and survivals and developments from pagan religious beliefs and practices were marked, even among many of the professing Christians. Christianity was having progressively profound effects, but had not become fully self-sustaining.

[149] Schulze, *op. cit.*, Vol. II, pp. 257-361; H. Weiss, *"Ons Suriname"* (The Hague, Boekhandel van den Zendings-Studie-Raad, no date, pp. 186), *passim;* Hutton, *A History of the Moravian Missions*, pp. 250-265; Siegfr. Beck, *Die wirtschaftlich-soziale Arbeit der Missionsgeschäfte der Brüdergemeine in Suriname* (Herrnhut, Verlag der Missionsbuchhandlung, 1914, p. 31), *passim;* Gottfried U. Freitag, *Johannes King, der Buschland-Prophet* (Herrnhut, Verlag der Missionsbuchhandlung, 1927, pp. 88), *passim.*

Chapter IV

LATIN AMERICA. THE CRISIS BROUGHT THE ROMAN CATH-
OLIC CHURCH BY POLITICAL REVOLUTION; THE PARTIAL
RECOVERY; THE COMING OF EASTERN CHRISTIANITY
THROUGH IMMIGRATION; THE ENTRANCE OF PROTES-
TANT CHRISTIANITY THROUGH MISSIONS TO THE NON-
CHRISTIAN INDIANS, COMMERCE, IMMIGRATION, AND MIS-
SIONS TO ROMAN CATHOLICS

TO LATIN AMERICA the nineteenth century brought revolutionary
changes. On the mainland all the once vast possessions of Spain and
Portugal passed out of the hands of these nations. Some of the former Spanish
territories were acquired by the United States. More of them set up governments for themselves. Brazil became independent. Before the end of the century Spain lost what remained to her in the West Indies—Puerto Rico to the
United States and Cuba through independence assisted by the United States.
The Spanish section of the island of Haiti had earlier broken away to form the
Dominican Republic. Of the Latin countries of Europe, only France retained
territorial footholds in the New World. These were not extensive. On the
mainland was French Guiana. In the West Indies were a few French islands.
During the stormy opening years of the nineteenth century the wealthiest of
her West Indian holdings, on the island of Haiti, had been torn from France
by a Negro revolt. Of the French empire in North America only two small
fragments remained, the island groups of St. Pierre and Miquelon, off the
coast of Newfoundland.

In Latin America political revolution was followed by social revolution. In
the former Spanish domains the *creoles*, or American-born whites, took the
control from the European-born whites. In Mexico there were attempts to win
for the Indians, the mass of the population, better economic and social conditions. The former Spanish domains, once knit with the mother country into
a closed economic system, became open to the trade of the world. Immigration
from Europe poured into the east coast of the southern part of South America.
Foreign mercantile communities, at first especially of the British, arose in the

chief ports. Marked increases in population occurred, notably in the southern sections of South America.

Yet the changes could easily be exaggerated. The stratification of society remained much as it had been in colonial days. At the top were those of pure white blood, in several of the new nations a small minority. In some sections, especially in the South Temperate Zone, those of European blood constituted a majority. Between the pure whites and the darker races were the mixed bloods. At the bottom of the social ladder were the Indians and the Negroes. As in colonial days, Latin America still lived largely by the "extractive industries"— agriculture, stock-raising, and mining. Manufactures remained backward. It was as a source of food-stuffs, minerals, and various raw materials that Latin America was important in world economy.

What would be the fate of Christianity under these altered conditions? We have recounted[1] how in colonial days Latin America had been the scene of an extensive Roman Catholic missionary enterprise. Other forms of Christianity had not been permitted to enter. Those of European stock had been held to their traditional faith. Millions of the Indians had been won to Roman Catholic Christianity. Indeed, it was Latin America which had displayed the major expansion of Christianity in the sixteenth, seventeenth, and eighteenth centuries. Missions had been the characteristic instrument for pushing forward the frontier and assimilating it to Spanish authority and culture. Beginnings had been made towards the conversion of the Negroes who had been imported as slaves from Africa. Yet for the most part the Roman Catholic Christianity of Latin America had been passive. It had been directed by the state and its missions had been largely dependent upon the Crown for financial support. Its leadership was mainly from abroad. Right up to the eve of independence, most of its bishops were European-born. Those who manned its missions were chiefly from Europe. From it issued no important new movements: presumably it did not have enough vitality to give rise to them. The masses of its adherents among the aborigines were grossly ignorant. Most of its secular clergy were of poor quality. Like the civil government, the Church was kept rigidly in a colonial status. Now that independence had been achieved politically, could the Church make the adjustment and become an integral and growing force in the new age? Or would it be on the defensive, inextricably allied to the dwindling remnants of an order that was passing, the bulwark of a beleaguered and doomed minority who strove to conserve as long as possible the social and economic privileges which they had enjoyed under the old regime?

[1] Vols. III, Chaps. 3 and 4.

The immediate effect of the revolutions with which the nineteenth century was inaugurated seemed disastrous. In its internal life the Roman Catholic Church in Latin America suffered severely. The frontier missions to the Indians lapsed or, when continued, were enfeebled. In the very region in which Christianity had had its most triumphant advances in the three centuries which followed A. D. 1500, the existence of the faith appeared threatened.

Roman Catholic Christianity lived on. It recovered in part from the blows dealt by revolution and the establishment of governments independent of Europe. Here and there it made gains. These, however, were due almost entirely to reinforcements from Europe. Of itself Latin American Roman Catholicism put forth almost no fresh shoots. In this it was in striking contrast to the Christianity of the United States and Canada. Possible reasons for the difference are to be found in the fact that it had so long been paternalistically governed from Spain and Portugal and in the parallel fact that its membership was so largely made up of Indians and Negroes, who formed the majority of the population and who, although legally free, were in reality subject peoples. Among the large elements in these races in the United States and Canada who became Christians, whether Protestant or Roman Catholic, there was an almost equal lack of new movements. Since here, as in Latin America, Negroes and Indians were usually socially and economically subordinate to the whites, the imitativeness and lack of creativeness of the Christianity may have been due in part to this disadvantageous status. Then, too, a large proportion of the ruling white elements, from which leadership might otherwise have come, deemed the Church reactionary and obscurantist, and preserved only a formal connexion with it.[2] The Church in Spain, with which some contacts were maintained, itself suffered from attacks by anti-clericals, and its religious orders, which normally would have been the chief sources of personnel, were especially the objects of enmity.[3] Moreover, Spanish Christianity, like Spain itself, was decrepit. From it came in the nineteenth century no major new order and no great theology.

As the nineteenth century wore on, fresh forces threatened the disintegration of the inherited Christianity. New currents of thought, some of them anti-Christian and still more of them contrary to Roman Catholic Christianity, poured into a land once hermetically sealed. They especially affected the intelligentsia among the dominant classes. Positivism, the system of August Comte, entered and gained a small but influential following, particularly in

[2] Every, *South American Memories of Thirty Years*, pp. 5-10.
[3] Peers, *Spain. The Church and the Order*, pp. 61-91.

Brazil.[4] Renan had admirers.[5] Spiritualism became popular among the masses[6] and Theosophy among the educated.[7] Freemasonry, in Latin lands a rallying centre of anti-Christian and particularly of anti-Roman Catholic and anti-clerical elements, won footholds.[8]

In the revolutions which ushered in the independence of the Latin-American republics, religious discontent was at most a very minor factor. Here and there criticisms were directed against the wealth of the Church and against the Inquisition. The great "Liberator," Simon Bolivar, wished the separation of Church and state. In the struggle for independence the clergy were divided. As a rule the lower, native-born clergy favoured independence. In Mexico two of the earliest revolutionary leaders, Hidalgo and Morelos, were priests, and more than 100 priests and about 50 members of religious orders were in the armies which fought for independence. A leader in the revolt in Argentina was a Dominican, Ignacio Grela. In Brazil priests were early active for independence. In general the higher clergy, being Spanish-born, were opposed to independence. The division reflected the nature of the effort to throw off the Spanish yoke, the desire of the *creoles*, or American-born whites, to be freed from the domination of the *gachupines*, or Spanish-born whites. The Inquisition was also against the revolution. In general the leaders of the revolution, either from prudence or from religious conviction, observed respect for the Church's privileges.[9]

Independence and the creation of the new governments brought the Church problems and conflicts. The King of Spain wished to preserve his customary right of patronage and to appoint to the bishoprics of Spanish America. This might well prove a means towards reasserting his political authority. The new states refused to recognize this prerogative. They sought, moreover, to succeed to the powers over the Church which the king had formerly held. The clergy of Spain believed themselves to have presumptive priority to ecclesiastical positions in the former Spanish colonies. This the new governments, controlled as they were by *creoles*, would not admit. The opposing ambitions placed the Papacy in a most embarrassing position. If it granted the royal claims to patronage the Vatican would run afoul of the new regimes. If it declined to recognize

[4] Mackay, *The Other Spanish Christ*, pp. 167-170; Braga and Grubb, *The Republic of Brazil*, p. 44.

[5] Mackay, *op. cit.*, p. 172.

[6] Braga and Grubb, *op. cit.*, p. 43.

[7] Mackay, *op. cit.*, pp. 177-188; Braga and Grubb, *op. cit.*, p. 44.

[8] Nolte, *Missions-Annalen*, pp. 167ff.

[9] Mecham, *Church and State in Latin America*, pp. 45-73; Watters, *A History of the Church in Venezuela, 1810-1930*, pp. 53-70; Ryan, *The Church in the South American Republics*, p. 43; Mackay, *The Other Spanish Christ*, pp. 59-61; Silva Cotapos, *Historia Eclesiástica de Chile*, p. 202.

them, it would make more hazardous an already difficult ecclesiastical situation in Spain. Rome, dominated, not unwillingly, by an ultramontanism which sought to extinguish the power of the civil authorities over appointments to ecclesiastical posts and to extend the authority of the See of Peter, refused, so far as it dared, to grant to the successor governments the *patronato de Indias* once held by the Crown.[10] Moreover, hundreds of the Spanish-born clergy left America for the mother country and the crippled Church was badly under-staffed. Death added to the toll. In 1826 only 10 of the 38 bishoprics in Spanish America were occupied and soon only 5 of these were being actively admin-istered.[11] In 1847 Venezuela, which suffered especially heavily, had 200 less priests than at the end of the colonial period.[12]

These perplexing problems were not quickly solved. Friction was prolonged. The Papacy was slow to recognize the new governments and for some years seemed bent on assisting to restore the power of the Spanish Crown. In 1816 a Papal encyclical urged the bishops and archbishops to win their flocks to obedience to the King of Spain.[13] In 1817 the Papal Cardinal Secretary of State declared that he would receive no communication from the new governments.[14] In 1820 military successes of the revolutionists demonstrated the impossibility of re-establishing the Spanish rule and in that same year a revolt in Spain an-tagonized the Pope by setting up an anti-clerical government. The Papacy therefore became less unfriendly to the new order in the Americas.[15] In 1824, after King Ferdinand VII had had his full powers restored to him in Spain, the Pope issued an encyclical to the bishops and archbishops in America urging them to support the royal cause.[16] Confronted with the necessity of caring for Roman Catholics in Spanish America, for a time the Papacy endeavoured to meet the situation by appointing vicars apostolic. Although having episcopal powers and so being able to give leadership under Papal direction, they would presumably not be so direct an affront to the royal *patronato* as would the recognition (or, to use a more accurate word, preconization) of proprietary bishops selected in America without the approval of the King. This device proved unsatisfactory to both the monarch and the new governments.[17] In-deed, in 1830 the Mexican government declared that it would not receive vicars

[10] Mecham, *op. cit.,* pp. 2, 75; Watters, *op. cit.,* p. 89; Ryan, *op. cit.,* pp. 48ff.
[11] Watters, *op. cit.,* p. 89.
[12] Watters, *op. cit.,* p. 90.
[13] Ayarragaray, *La Iglesia en América y la Dominación Española,* pp. 183, 184; Mecham, *op. cit.,* p. 77.
[14] Mecham, *op. cit.,* p. 78.
[15] Mecham, *op. cit.,* p. 78, 79.
[16] Ayarragaray, *op. cit.,* p. 184; Mecham, *op. cit.,* p. 78; Mackay, *op. cit.,* p. 69.
[17] Ayarragaray, *op. cit.,* pp. 235ff.; Mecham, *op. cit.,* pp. 88-92, 102.

apostolic.[18] Deprived of episcopal leadership, for most of the sees were now vacant, the church in Latin America was rapidly becoming disorganized. Protestantism was entering. There was a threat of national churches with bishops appointed without reference to Rome. In spite of the opposition of Ferdinand VII, in 1827 the Pope confirmed candidates for the episcopate presented by the government of Colombia.[19] In 1831, 1834, and 1836 various sees in Mexico were filled without consulting the King.[20] In 1835, after the death of the intransigent Ferdinand VII (1833), Pope Gregory XVI formally recognized the independence of New Granada.[21] This paved the way for Papal recognition of other governments. Rome would not, however, immediately yield to the desire of the new republics to succeed to the *real patronato* and so to control the church in their domains.

Slowly partial recovery was made from the shock of revolution. The Roman Catholic Church regained some of its former strength and put itself in better condition to meet the unfriendly forces of the new day. Gradually Rome made better provision for the training of priests and the supervision of Latin-American affairs. In 1858 there was opened in Rome the *Collegio Pio-Latino-Americano Pontificio* for the education of students from Latin America. It had the endorsement and aid of Pope Pius IX, who had been Apostolic Delegate in Chile.[22] In 1899 there was held, in this college, a plenary council of Latin-American clergy.[23]

Reinforcements to the clerical ranks in Latin America came from various countries in Europe. To catalogue all of these would require more space than we can properly assign to them, for they were numerous. We can mention only a few. To Brazil came Portuguese Lazarists, Capuchins from the Tyrol and Italy, Jesuits from Austria, Germany, and Portugal, Mercedarians, Franciscans from Italy, Germany, and Holland, French Dominicans, Pallotines, Salesians of Don Bosco, Barnabites, Redemptorists from Austria and Holland, the Society of the Divine Word, Benedictines, Missionaries of the Holy Ghost, and German Missionaries of the Holy Family.[24] The Jesuits, the expulsion of whose society from the Spanish, Portuguese, and French domains had so seriously crippled the eighteenth-century Church, re-entered several of the new

---

[18] Ayarragaray, *op. cit.*, p. 290; Mecham, *op. cit.*, p. 103.

[19] Mecham, *op. cit.*, p. 100.

[20] Mecham, *op. cit.*, p. 104.

[21] Mecham, *op. cit.*, p. 105.

[22] *The Catholic Encyclopedia*, Vol. I, pp. 425, 426.

[23] *The Catholic Encyclopedia*, Vol. I, p. 426.

[24] Nolte, *Missions-Annalen*, pp. 55-58; Espey, *Festschrift zum Silberjubiläum der Wiedererrichtung der Provinz von der Unbefleckten Empfängnis im Süden Brasiliens 1901-1926, passim.*

states. There their career was by no means unchequered. They were expelled from more than one country but in some contrived to gain re-admission.[25] Franciscans, chiefly from Spain, had had a large part in pre-nineteenth century missions. Since the Franciscan colleges in Spanish colonial America from which the order had obtained much of its staff, drew their student bodies from Spain, the revolutions in the New World, so largely directed against the Spanish-born, deprived them of much of their personnel. In the nineteenth century Brothers Minor came from Italy to carry on the tradition. Late in the nineteenth and early in the twentieth century hundreds were added from Germany.[26] In 1844 Spanish Lazarists arrived in Mexico and before long were publishing a periodical and were in charge of two seminaries. In spite of the civil strife in the country and the distrust of political liberals, in 1868 they had six houses.[27] In 1899 a priest, Gerard Villota, founded at Burgos, Spain, St. Francis Xavier's College, known locally as the *Colegio de Ultramar*, for the training of clergy for Spanish speaking America. In 1920 Rome raised it to a Pontifical Seminary for Foreign Missions and then assigned it a field in Colombia.[28] Sisters of several congregations came, some from Europe, some from Canada, and some from the United States.[29] When, a few pages below, we summarize the nineteenth-century missions to the Indians, we shall see the large share which aid from Europe had in renewing the efforts to push forward the frontiers of Christianity.

The condition and status of the Roman Catholic Church differed from country to country and from administration to administration. Much more than in the colonial era when subordination to the home governments made for uniformity, there was diversity. In some areas the Church suffered more from political revolutions than in others. The sudden shifts in administration, many of them characterized by violence, which punctuated the nineteenth-century history of most of the Latin-American lands were often accompanied by an about face in official attitudes towards ecclesiastical affairs. A set of men closely allied with the Church would be ousted by anti-clericals. The anti-clericals, in turn, would be displaced by those who found part of their strength in the support of the Church. The anti-clericals usually were led by those who were affected by

[25] Mecham, *op. cit.*, pp. 148, 152, 168, 182, 183, 228, 235, 256, 285, 324, 334, 374, 375, 386, 387, 390, 420, 425; Crétineau-Joly, *Histoire de la Compagnie de Jésus*, Vol. VI, p. 316; Perez, *Compañia de Jesus en Colombia y Centro-América despues de su Restauracion*, pp. vii, 24ff., 79, 351.
[26] Lemmens, *Geschichte der Franziskanermissionen*, pp. 334, 342.
[27] Paradela, *Resumen Histórico de la Congregación de la Mission en España, desde 1704 a 1868*, p. 435.
[28] *Fides News Service*, Dec. 30, 1939.
[29] Silva Cotapos, *Historia Eclesiástica de Chile*, pp. 290, 291.

nineteenth-century intellectual, social, and political liberalism and generally but not always were inclined to be sceptical religiously. The clericals were alarmed by the disorders produced by the innovations and regarded the Church as a safeguard of civilized society. Most of the old aristocracy and the landed governing families supported the Church as a conservative institution, a bulwark of their position. Ecclesiastical leaders, to protect the position of the Church, entered into the political arena.

Relations with Rome were almost as varied. Characteristic was the struggle between the insistence of each state upon its right, as a successor to the old regime, to ecclesiastical patronage and to the choice of bishops once enjoyed by the Crown, and, frequently, the denial by the Papacy of that claim. In each case a *modus vivendi* was eventually reached, but that was different in the several states and was altered from time to time. Usually the right of patronage was ultimately conceded by the Papacy, either tacitly or formally.

This is not the place for the history of the relations of Church and state. We can make room only for a brief and incomplete outline. From it, however, some slight indication may be gathered of the shifting and often unfavourable conditions under which the Roman Catholic Church was constrained to carry on its ministry to the professedly Christian portions of the population and to extend its activities to the non-Christian Indians and Negroes and to the newer immigration. From the sketch, together with additional information interspersed in it, we shall gain some insight into the course of Roman Catholic Christianity in nineteenth-century Latin America. In general, while difficult and painful, by 1914 the adjustment had been accomplished. Losses suffered in the earlier stages of independence had been partly recouped. In some areas fresh gains had been made.

When the new nations began their independent careers, all for a time continued to recognize Roman Catholic Christianity as the state religion. However, beginning with the 1820's, in several countries violent anti-clerical opposition developed. This was aroused not so much by religious dissent or scepticism as by the power of the clergy in politics. As in colonial days the clergy had been in a fairly chronic state of feud with the civil officials, each side being jealous of its prerogatives and endeavouring to check the other, so now ecclesiastics often sought to control the government in what they believed to be the interests of the Church. The opponents of the clergy strove to achieve the abolition of tithes, the confiscation of church property, and the suppression of the religious orders. In the second half of the century the trend towards religious liberty and the separation of Church and state then so marked in the Occidental world made itself strongly felt. In several of the Latin-American nations the Church was disestablished. In some the change was accompanied by violence. From time to time restrictive legislation was passed.[30]

In Mexico the struggle between the Roman Catholic Church and the state was complicated by the condition of the masses, predominantly Indian and generally poverty-stricken and down-trodden, and by efforts at betterment, usually opposed by the higher ecclesiastical officials but at the outset with priests among the leaders. The pendulum swung repeatedly between support of the privileged position of the Roman Catholic Church and restrictions upon it. Down to the early 1830's the Church had, on the whole, gained in wealth and power. To be sure, between 1821 and 1830, largely because of the lack of bishops to effect ordinations, the number of clergy had declined by about a third. In 1821 the country contained only five bishops and it is said that in 1830 not a bishop remained. However, in the political disorder which marked the years immediately before and after independence, the Church was the most stable inclusive institution in the country and its wealth increased. In the 1830's there were attempts to curb the Church. For instance, the California missions were secularized and their property nationalized. A reaction followed which restored to the Church some of its power. Late in the 1850's a liberal government with Juárez as its chief figure placed greater restrictions on the Church than that institution had yet known in Mexico. Ecclesiastical holdings, except church buildings and other property directly used by the clergy, were confiscated, freedom of education was declared, government support was withdrawn from the vows which were at the foundation of the religious orders, religious toleration was proclaimed, marriage was made a civil contract, cemeteries were secularized, nunneries were partially suppressed, separation of Church and state was decreed, and the Mexican legation to the Vatican was withdrawn.[31] From this drastic trend a contrary movement set in. It aided in the establishment of the abortive empire of Maximilian. Maximilian himself, while punctilious in his observance of religious duties, was too liberal for the ecclesiastical authorities and lost their support. The liberal rebellion which eliminated him brought a confirmation of the separation of Church and state, civil marriage, the illegality of religious vows, and prohibition to religious institutions to acquire real estate or income from land. Díaz, the controlling power in Mexico from 1876 to 1910, at the outset was professedly a liberal. Yet under him, without a formal annulment of restrictions, the Roman Catholic Church gained in power. Its property increased, its schools more than doubled, new convents were founded, religious orders were restored, the numbers of

[30] Mecham, *Church and State in Latin America*, pp. 502-508.

[31] Wilfrid Hardy Callcott, *Church and State in Mexico 1822-1857* (Duke University Press, 1926, pp. 357), *passim;* Mecham, *op. cit.*, pp. 395-444.

priests more than trebled, the moral quality of the clergy improved, new churches were erected and old ones repaired, and eight new bishoprics and five new archbishoprics were founded. Catholic congresses convened.[32] However, in some places the Church was not able completely to regain the lost ground. In 1906 it was declared that in places in Yucatán no religious services had been held and that in sections of Lower California no mass had been celebrated for forty years.[33] When, in 1911, Diáz was swept into exile by the rising discontent, the revolution was directed in part against the Church.[34] After 1914 the anti-clerical tide was greatly intensified.

In Central America, as in Mexico, high ecclesiastical officials at first supported the independence movement as a means of being freed from the liberal anticlerical government then in power in Spain. They were speedily disillusioned, for from 1829 to 1839 the federation which controlled the region was in the hands of liberals who expelled the Archbishop, the Franciscans, the Dominicans, and the Recollets, decreed religious toleration, instituted civil marriage, and declared that the appointment to ecclesiastical dignities belonged to the nation. In 1839 a revolt brought the pro-clericals into power and dissolved the federation.[35] From 1839 to his death in 1865 Carrera, an ardent Roman Catholic, was dominant in Guatemala and was the most powerful individual in Central America. He restored its privileges to the Church, allowed the friars to return, and in 1852 had a concordat with Rome signed by Guatemala, the first with any American country, in which, in return for concessions, the president was promised the patronage to ecclesiastical appointments. After 1871 the liberals were again in the saddle in Guatemala, the Jesuits were expelled, religious orders were forbidden, all ecclesiastical property was nationalized, and civil marriage was inaugurated. In 1884, Rome, making the best of a bad situation, signed a new concordat.[36] In the smaller adjoining El Salvador developments closely paralleled those in Guatemala. In 1871 came the change from pro-clerical to anti-clerical policies. Church and state were separated and religious liberty was written into the constitution. Although the acquisition of property for endowment for religious purposes was forbidden, church property was not nationalized.[37] In Honduras ecclesiastical policies closely followed those of Guatemala.

[32] Callcott, *Liberalism in Mexico 1857-1929*, pp. 1-195; Mecham, *op. cit.*, pp. 445-460; David H. Strother (United States Consul-General in Mexico City), *Church and State in Mexico* (in Miscellaneous Documents of the House of Representatives, 2d session, 47th Congress, 1882-'83, Vol. XI, No. 39, pp. 87-91), p. 89.

[33] Callcott, *op. cit.*, p. 183.

[34] Mecham, *op. cit.*, pp. 460ff.; Callcott, *op. cit.*, pp. 196ff.

[35] Mecham, *op. cit.*, pp. 360-373.

[36] Mecham, *op. cit.*, pp. 373-379.

[37] Mecham, *op. cit.*, pp. 379-383.

After a generation of pro-clerical administrations, in 1880 the concordat with Rome was revoked, the separation of Church and state was effected, and in the course of the years various restrictions were placed on the Church. The era before 1914 closed with the Roman Catholic Church in Honduras poverty-stricken and suffering from a dearth of priests.[38] In Nicaragua the Roman Catholic Church enjoyed a more favourable position than in its three sister republics on the west. The anti-clerical reaction did not come in marked degree until 1894 and then did not go to such extremes as in the others. In 1909 the conservatives were once more in office and were sympathetic with the Church.[39] In Costa Rica relationships between Church and state were, on the whole, more harmonious than in any other Central American country. Although religious liberty was written into the constitution in 1871, the Roman Catholic Church was established by law and was subsidized by the government. In 1850 a separate bishopric was created for the country and in 1878 a seminary was founded to train priests. From 1833 to 1886 serious friction existed and for a time diplomatic relations with the Vatican were broken off. The chief executive of the republic enjoyed some of the ecclesiastical prerogatives once held by the King of Spain, for he possessed the right of patronage and no Papal documents could be published without his consent.[40] When, in 1903, Panama became an independent republic, Church and state were separated. Religious liberty was guaranteed, but religious instruction by Roman Catholics was allowed in the public schools and subventions were given to the schools of the Roman Catholic Church.[41]

Simon Bolivar, the Liberator, for about a decade succeeded in bringing the newly independent regions of Northern South America under one government, Great Colombia. This embraced the later Venezuela, Colombia, and Ecuador. Bolivar, although affected by the sceptical currents abroad in the Europe of his day and far from being a convinced Roman Catholic, respected the Church as a means of social control. Indeed, in his later years, appalled by the disorders which had followed freedom, he turned more and more to the Roman Catholic Church as a stabilizing institution and sought to facilitate an increase in the number of its clergy.[42] Before his death (December 27, 1830), Great Colombia had begun to break apart. In their ecclesiastical histories its successors differed from one another.

In Venezuela the hold of the Church was early weakened. The Church was

---

[38] Mecham, *op. cit.*, pp. 383-386.
[39] Mecham, *op. cit.*, pp. 386-388.
[40] Mecham, *op. cit.*, pp. 388-391.
[41] Mecham, *op. cit.*, pp. 391, 392.
[42] Mecham, *op. cit.*, pp. 107-121.

not disestablished. For more than three decades those in power were in general moderate conservatives. The tie between Church and state was continued. Yet the state usually insisted upon the right of patronage. Some curbs were placed on the Church and efforts were made to keep out foreign clergy. Strongly pro-clerical elements were seldom in control. Gúzman Blanco, who was master of the country from 1870 to 1889, took measures which weakened the Church. Religious foundations, parish schools, and even theological seminaries were ordered abolished. The training of priests was to be by the theological faculty of the state university. Indeed, except in a few centres, the Roman Catholic Church both lost its intellectual influence with the upper classes and became an object of contempt among the masses. After the end of the rule of Gúzman Blanco, the Church made some progress. Indeed, just before his overthrow, Sisters of Charity were introduced from France. Shortly afterwards Spanish Capuchins were brought in to aid in civilizing the Indians, a return to the frontier policy of the colonial regime. In 1894 Salesians were summoned to help with the schools. The Augustinians and the Dominicans returned. In 1900 provision was made for the establishment of theological seminaries. Yet in 1914 the Church was still weak.[43]

In the adjoining Colombia violent fluctuations occurred in the relations of Church and state and the ecclesiastical issue was again and again injected into politics. Until 1849, as in Venezuela, moderate conservatives were in control who adopted some liberal measures with restrictions on the Church. This was in spite of the fact that New Granada, as the country was then called, was the first Spanish American land to be recognized by the Holy See as independent (1835). Following recognition by the Pope, the hierarchy in New Granada was fully restored through Papal recognition and a Papal internuncio extraordinary was sent. However, the government of New Granada insisted upon its claim of patronage. From 1849 to 1880 the liberals were in the ascendant and the Church suffered severely. In 1850 the Jesuits were expelled. Measures repugnant to the Church were enacted, among them the annulment of tithes, of the right of asylum in churches, and of ecclesiastical courts. The seminary of the archdiocese was incorporated with the national college of San Bartolomé, thus withdrawing from the Church the education of its clergy. In 1853 Church and state were separated by constitutional enactment. When they protested, the archbishop and three of the bishops were exiled. For a brief period after 1855 the pressure on the Church was lightened and the Jesuits were permitted to return. However, from 1861 to 1867, under Tomás Mosquera, who was then

[43] Watters, *A History of the Church in Venezuela, 1810-1930, passim;* Mecham, *op. cit.,* pp. 121-140.

in power in the state, steps more drastic than any before them were taken. No clergyman was allowed to officiate without the authorization of the civil authorities, the Jesuits were again excluded, all church property except that used directly for religious purposes was confiscated, all religious houses were ordered suppressed, and several prelates were imprisoned or exiled. After Mosquera was banished (1867), the restrictions on the Church were somewhat relaxed, but until 1880 liberal anti-clericals were in control of the government. Conservatives then regained power and in general their policies prevailed until after 1914. In 1887 and 1888 a concordat with the Holy See was completed which accorded large privileges to the Church. Nomination to bishoprics and archbishoprics was conceded to the Pope, but with the counsel of the state. Although the Church remained independent of the state, the latter granted to the former financial subventions, marriages were regularized in a manner satisfactory to the Church, schools were to be in conformity with Roman Catholic morals and dogmas, and in them the Roman Catholic faith was to be taught and its religious exercises observed. Religious liberty was recognized, but the sentiment of the land was strongly Roman Catholic. During the remainder of the period before 1914 the Roman Catholic Church enjoyed a favoured position and registered substantial growth.[44]

For the first three decades after it separated from Great Colombia, or from 1830 to 1860, Ecuador had a chequered history, but in general Roman Catholic Christianity was recognized as the religion of the state and a vigorous popular religious conservatism curbed the entrance of Protestantism and the appearance of dissent. From 1860 to 1875, except for a four year interval, the land was dominated by García Moreno, the outstanding man in the history of the country and one of the greatest figures of Latin America. Moreno was a highly educated aristocrat who was convinced by what he saw in Europe of the disorders produced by liberalism that the only alternative to anarchy was the Roman Catholic faith and that the Church was needed to give moral discipline to the populace and unity to the nation. In 1862 he concluded with Rome a concordat which accorded more power to the Church and the Holy See than they had possessed under the Spanish regime. The civil authorities retained only a much reduced power of patronage, dissenting cults were forbidden, education was made to conform to the Roman Catholic faith, the hierarchy were given the right to prohibit books which seemed to them contrary to religion and good customs, ecclesiastical courts were maintained, and the government promised to aid in the conversion of the non-Christians in the land. Moreno brought

<hr/>

[44] Mecham, *op. cit.*, pp. 141-170. On the Jesuits during the early part of the period, see José Joaquin Borda, *Historia de la Compañia de Jesus en la Nueva Granada* (Piossy, S. Lejay et Cie. 2 vols., 1872), Vol. II, pp. 171-277.

in members of teaching orders, especially from France. He re-introduced the Jesuits to aid in higher education. He encouraged Rome to undertake the reform of the clergy. New bishoprics were created. He dedicated Ecuador to the Sacred Heart of Jesus. Shortly after his assassination (1875) an anti-clerical reaction occurred, but about 1881 the pendulum swung once more in favour of the Church. From about 1897 to 1914 and beyond, with one brief interruption, the anti-clericals were in power and placed restrictions upon the Church. A partial separation of Church and state was effected, efforts were made to secularize education, and religious liberty was enacted. However, the land remained predominantly Roman Catholic and religious toleration was not easily enforced.[45]

In Peru from the very dawn of independence Church and state preserved intimate and friendly relations. Most of the civil administrations were cordial to the Church and anti-clericalism never gained much headway. To be sure, at the outset most of the bishops were partisans of the old regime and were compelled to leave their sees. Many of the lower clergy were liberal and for a time encouraged the distribution of Bibles and the educational work of a Scottish Baptist minister, James Thomson, who was asked to undertake the organization of the country's educational system. Moreover, some of the monasteries were suppressed and the number of religious holidays was reduced. However, Roman Catholic Christianity was constitutionally recognized as the religion of the land and not until 1839 did the law allow even the private observance of any other cult. In 1874 the Pope conceded to the President of Peru such right of patronage as had been enjoyed by the Kings of Spain. Financial support was accorded the Church by the state. In the public schools, instruction in religion was given by the Church. Marriage, except for non-Roman Catholics and for them only beginning with 1897, was to be exclusively through the Church. Although in practice previously granted, it was only in 1915 that full religious liberty was finally legally conceded to Protestants. However, difficulty was increasingly encountered in obtaining recruits for the clergy and the deficiency was supplied in part by the importation of priests, largely from Spain. Many of these, unfortunately, viewed their posts as an opportunity to amass wealth.[46] Some French nuns came to conduct schools.[47]

In Bolivia Roman Catholic Christianity was recognized as the religion of

[45] Mecham, *Church and State in Latin America*, pp. 171-192 (the text of the concordat of 1862, translated, is on pp. 176-181) ; Ryan, *The Church in the South American Republics*, pp. 63-68; Kanters, *Le T. R. P. León Dehon*, p. 44.

[46] Mecham, *op. cit.*, pp. 193-219; Ryan, *op. cit.*, p. 72; Mackay, *The Other Spanish Christ*, p. 62.

[47] Lesourd, *L'Année Missionaire, 1931*, p. 246.

the country and legal permission for the public exercise of other forms of the faith was delayed until 1905. Yet the government insisted upon its right to ecclesiastical patronage, and the Pope, perforce, tolerated it, although he did not grant it formal recognition through a concordat. The state made financial contributions towards the support of the Church. On the other hand, by the year 1914 the Church had no authority over the public schools and could not give religious instruction in them during school hours. In spite of occasional efforts by the state to remedy the situation, in moral and intellectual quality and in training the majority of the parish clergy were very inferior. As the nineteenth century wore on they seem to have deteriorated rather than improved. The Christianity of the masses was debased and superficial.[48]

In Chile, from the early, somewhat turbulent years of independence, the Roman Catholic Church emerged comparatively unscathed. In the stormy period of revolution the diocesan seminaries were lost and the religious orders despoiled. Yet the national constitution which was adopted in 1833 and which remained the basic governmental document of the land until after 1914 recognized Roman Catholic Christianity as the religion of the republic and forbade the public exercise of any other cult. It also accorded to the President, as the head of the state, the power to name the higher ecclesiastical officials and to grant or refuse admission to Papal bulls, briefs, rescripts, or decrees of councils. The Papacy had no choice but to acquiesce. In 1840 Chile was given an archbishop. Two new dioceses were soon created and a faculty of theology was included in the reconstituted national university. In 1850 a society of labourers and artisans was formed under ecclesiastical auspices. The Archbishop undertook the reform of the religious orders. Sisterhoods were founded or introduced from abroad. The restriction of religious liberty was not rigidly enforced, and in 1865, in spite of the constitution, toleration was written into the laws. Tithes were abolished, but the state gave financial support to the Church. In the last quarter of the nineteenth century a determined assault was made by the liberals upon some of the privileges of the Church. Cemeteries were removed from the control of the Church, civil marriage was made compulsory, and civil registry of births, marriages, and deaths was instituted. However, the efforts to separate Church and state failed. Late in the nineteenth and early in the twentieth century the Roman Catholic Church, under able leadership, made striking advances. Schools, colleges, and a university were founded under Church direction. Associations for workmen were initiated under the supervision of priests. Although among the masses religious tolerance born partly

[48] Mecham, *op. cit.*, pp. 220-235.

of indifference increased, the Roman Catholic Church strengthened its organization.[49]

In colonial days the area which later became known as Argentina was largely a sparsely settled frontier country. It had not been so well covered by missions to the Indians as had some other regions. Christianity, represented by the Roman Catholic Church, had been much weaker than in such centres of Spanish power as Mexico and Peru. The first constitution of the Argentine Republic, then (1819) known as the United Provinces of La Plata, provided for the union of Church and state and for the control by the latter of presentation to the higher ecclesiastical posts. For a number of years the Church in Argentina, while orthodox in doctrine, was independent of the Papacy. For some years, too, in a time of near-anarchy, the hierarchy became extinct and the clergy fell into evil ways. In the 1820's while in control of the government, the remarkably able Bernadino Rivadavia set about the reform of the Church. He retained its independence of Rome but improved its organization and sought to reform the regulars. In 1831 a vicar apostolic appointed by the Pope on nomination by the government was able to take possession of the see of Buenos Aires. In 1834, but only after much controversy growing out of the national claim to the right of patronage, a Bishop of Buenos Aires was recognized by the state. Under the dictatorship of Juan Manuel de Rosas (1835-1852) the Church was completely subjected to the autocrat. The constitution of 1853, adopted after the overthrow of Rosas, continued the government's control of patronage and right to intervene in ecclesiastical matters and insured the financial support of the Church by the state. Within a few years working connexions were re-established with Rome. For a time relations with the Vatican remained uneasy and there was even an open break. In 1892 the breach was healed. Neither then nor later was a concordat concluded. The state retained its nomination to the episcopate, but friction quieted down. Yet the number of clergy remained inadequate to the population, civil marriage was in force, and the public schools, in which were enrolled the overwhelming proportion of the children receiving an education, did not allow religious instruction in school hours. In view of the religious history of Argentina, it is not surprising that in spite of reinforcements to the clergy from Spain and Italy the Roman Catholic Church was weaker than in some others of the Latin-American republics.[50]

[49] Mecham, *op. cit.*, pp. 246-268; Silva Cotapos, *Historia Eclesiástica de Chile*, pp. 186ff.; Francisco S. Belmar, *A Su Eminencia Reverendisima el Señor Cardenal Secretario de Estado de Su Santidad. Carta Demonstrativa del Patronato Canonico de la Republica de Chile* (Santiago, J. Nuñez, 1883, pp. 180), *passim*.

[50] Mecham, *op. cit.*, pp. 275-304; Ryan, *The Church in the South American Republics*, pp. 50-52.

No other South American land had so unhappy a history as Paraguay and in none other was the Roman Catholic Church so long or so abjectly subservient to the civil authority. The halcyon days of the great Jesuit mission in the seventeenth and eighteenth centuries had not disciplined the Indians in self reliance. The enterprise had been paternalistic in the extreme. The expulsion of the Jesuits had been followed by slave-raiders and by a decline in the morale of the Christian communities which the Franciscans and seculars, who succeeded to the missions, were powerless to arrest. The wars which accompanied independence brought decline.[51] After independence from Spain the land was dominated by dictators, first Francia, then Carlos Antonio López, and finally the latter's eldest son, Francisco Solano López. Although having a doctorate of theology and apparently desiring, in his able but capricious and often cruel way, the welfare of the Indian masses, Francia was scornful of religion, dominated the Church without reference to the Pope, held the clergy, ignorant and corrupt, completely under his thumb, and compelled them to act as his spies by telling him what they learned in the confessional. The elder López, although renewing relations with the Pope, kept the clergy in as servile a state as had his predecessor and required them to report to him the secrets of the confessional. The younger López also insisted on being master of the Church. His mad military ambitions brought upon Paraguay the armies of its neighbours and are said to have reduced the population by four-fifths. When, in 1870, he committed suicide, the new constitution made Roman Catholic Christianity the religion of the republic, but insisted that the head of the hierarchy be a Paraguayan. Relations were maintained with Rome, but the government chose the bishop. The number of clergy was pitifully inadequate. From 1881 to 1911 only sixty were graduated from the sole theological seminary in the country. Even in the twentieth century only about a third of the population were on the parish registers. Two-thirds, therefore, were without a formal church connexion.[52]

The Roman Catholic Church in Uruguay was crippled at the outset by weak-

[51] On the status of these Christian communities in the nineteenth century (largely in Eastern Boliva) see the following accounts by travellers:—Edward D. Mathews, *Up the Amazon and Madeira Rivers, through Boliva and Peru* (London, Sampson Low, Marston, Searle & Rivington, 1879, pp. xv, 402), *passim;* Franz Keller-Leuzinger, *The Amazon and Madeira Rivers. Sketches and Descriptions from the Note-book of an Explorer* (London, Chapman and Hall, 1874, pp. xvi, 177), pp. 142-169; Alcide d'Orbigny, *Fragment d'un Voyage au Centre de l'Amerique Méridionale* (Paris, P. Bertrand, 1845, pp. 584), *passim.* Yet these communities preserved their faith. The travellers speak of the Indian choirs at mass which kept up the music taught them by the Jesuits. Yet population had declined, economic conditions had deteriorated, and some of the seculars were of inferior character.

[52] Mecham, *op. cit.,* pp. 235-245; Elliott, *Paraguay,* pp. 65ff.

ness during the colonial period. To an unfavourable beginning was added after independence the handicap of prolonged civil disorder. In spite of the fact that its population were overwhelmingly of European stock, until past the middle of the nineteenth century Uruguay had a stormy career and rapidly changing governments subject to foreign interference. Only in the later years before 1914 did it make substantial progress. The constitution of 1830 remained the legal basis of the republic until after 1914. It named the Roman Catholic faith as the religion of the state but permitted religious toleration. It also gave the President the right of patronage. It was 1878 before the country obtained a bishopric of its own. Party struggles between the *Blancos*, conservatives and supporters of the Church, and the *Colorados*, liberals and anti-clericals, punctuated the decades and gradually led to restrictions upon the prerogatives of the Church. In 1918 the Church was disestablished. In 1914 only about a fourth of the population were communicants. The ecclesiastical organization was not extensive and the number of clergy was insufficient.[53] In view of the difficulties under which the Church laboured, this failure to gain a stronger hold on the people was not surprising.

No other Latin-American country had so broad an area or so large a population as Brazil. At the outset of the nineteenth century, Christianity, represented by the Roman Catholic Church, was not so strong as in some of the Spanish American lands. There had been missions to the Indians, several of them heroic and effective, but the Portuguese regime had never given such energetic support to missions to the aborigines as had the Spanish government. Huge areas in the vast interior remained completely untouched by Christianity and others, also large, were but superficially reached. Even among the white colonists the Church seems not to have been as vigorous as in the chief American centres of Spanish power. The course of independent Brazil was free from many sharp struggles between Church and state. From the severing of the ties with Portugal, in 1822, until 1889 the land was under Emperors of the Portuguese ruling house. This made for an easy transition for the Church. It was not difficult for Rome to acquiesce in the perpetuation by these monarchs of the same control over the Church as had been exercised by the Kings of Portugal, namely, that of patronage and of determining whether documents issuing from Rome should be allowed publication. In accord with the Portuguese tradition, especially of the eighteenth century, the Brazilian Church had pronounced Gallican tendencies, that is, it favoured a certain amount of freedom from the Vatican. The clergy were supported out of the public treasury. By the constitution of 1824 a modified religious liberty was granted. Yet

[53] Mecham, *op. cit.*, pp. 331-337; Ryan, *op. cit.*, pp. 73-75, 100.

the Church was not in a healthy condition. The clergy were corrupt, were infected with an easy-going liberalism, usually lived in concubinage, and were generally impecunious. The regulars were better off financially but were not numerous. The liberal and able Emperor Pedro II (reigned 1840-1888) sought the reform of the Church and especially of the religious orders. He asserted his right to name to all benefices without the advice of prelates. Foreign regulars and orders controlled from outside Brazil were excluded. The sharpest conflict between Church and state arose in the 1870's over the anti-Masonic campaign of ultramontane bishops. Freemasonry had become very strong. Many of the clergy and still more of the members of lay confraternities were affiliated with it. In spite of its antipathy to freemasonry, the Vatican deemed it the part of wisdom to wink at the situation. But two of the bishops were not so tolerant. They took action against freemasonry, and, for their pains, were ordered imprisoned. When, in 1889, Pedro II was deposed and exiled and a republic was inaugurated, through strong Positivist influence Church and state were completely separated (1890), state patronage was abolished, governmental subsidies were discontinued, and civil marriage was made compulsory and public instruction secular. Under the new conditions the Roman Catholic Church flourished.[54] Religious orders were revived and strengthened by the coming of foreign clergy. Orders heretofore unrepresented were introduced by missionaries from Europe.[55] Seminaries for the training of clergy were improved.[56] Yet the problems confronting the Church were vast. Several millions of freed Negroes, the last of the slaves having been emancipated in 1888, were to be reached. An immigration from Europe, largely Roman Catholic, had to be held to the faith. Thousands of Indians were still untouched. In the absence of resident priests, most of the rural communities were served religiously by relatively untrained lay leaders who presided at the public prayers and conducted funerals. Some of these laymen started ill-judged fanatical religious movements.[57]

French Guiana (Cayenne) need not long detain us. The population was small, about 50,000 in 1911. It was partly Negro and partly white and contained as well remnants of Indians. The emancipation of the slaves wrought a shortage

[54] Mecham, *Church and State in Latin America*, pp. 305-330; Ryan, *The Church in the South American Republics*, pp. 89ff.; F. Badaro, *L'Église au Brésil pendant l'Empire et pendant la République* (Rome Stabilimento Boutempelli, 1895, pp. xiii, 138), *passim*.
[55] Lemmens, *Geschichte der Franziskanermissionen*, pp. 274-276; Espey, *Festschrift zum Silberjubiläum der Wiedererrichtung der Provinz von der unbefleckten Empfängnis im Süden Brasiliens, 1901-1926, passim*. See a list of these orders with their dates of revival or introduction in Nolte, *Missions-Annalen der Missionare von der Hl. Familie*, pp. 55-58.
[56] Ryan, *op. cit.*, p. 93.
[57] Braga and Grubb, *The Republic of Brazil*, pp. 37, 38.

of labour which was partly met by further importations of Africans. The use of the possession by the French as a penal colony brought in undesirable white elements.[58] The majority of the population were nominally Roman Catholic. The earlier Jesuit missionaries were followed by the Holy Ghost Fathers and they in turn by their successors, the Congregation of the Holy Ghost and the Immaculate Heart of Mary, all Europeans. Brothers of Christian Instruction and Sisters of St. Joseph and of St. Paul of Chartres also aided the Church.[59] Some converts were made among the bush Negroes.[60]

The Island of Hispaniola (also known as Haiti), famous as the first strong centre of Spanish power in the New World, experienced difficult times in the nineteenth and twentieth centuries. During the period of the French Revolution and the Napoleonic Wars, French rule, which had prevailed in the western part of the island since 1697, was overthrown by revolts of the Negro majority. The white planter population was either killed or expelled. The Spaniards, who in 1795 were deprived by the French of the eastern part of the island, for a brief time (1809-1821) restored their flag over that section, only to have it again torn down. From 1822 to 1844 the eastern end was ruled from the western end. In the latter year the eastern portion became independent, as the Dominican Republic. From 1861 to 1865, Spanish rule was once more revived, only to be followed by a renewal of the republic. The state in the western end of the island was known as Haiti. The Spanish language prevailed in the Dominican Republic and French in Haiti. In the latter Negroes and mulattoes were dominant. In the former, although pure Negroes and mulattoes were in the overwhelming majority, there was a larger admixture of white blood.

Christianity in Hispaniola began the nineteenth century under adverse conditions. After the first flush of prosperity when, in the fore part of the sixteenth century, the island had been the centre of Spanish rule in the New World, a serious and prolonged decline set in. The Church shared in the decay. The prosperity which came in the eighteenth century with the French occupation of the western part of the island, was only in part reflected in the Church.[61] The Roman Catholic form of the faith was the nominal religion of the whites, but these constituted a small minority of the population. The Negroes, who were in the majority, had partly conformed to the culture of their masters and most of them had acquired a nominal Christianity. This, however,

[58] James Rodway, *Guiana: British, Dutch and French* (London, T. Fisher Unwin, 1912, pp. 318), pp. 139-152; *The Encyclopædia Britannica*, 11th ed., Vol. XII, pp. 682, 683.
[59] Schmidlin-Braun, *Catholic Mission History*, pp. 512, 513; *Missiones Catholicae . . . MDCCCXCII*, pp. 487, 488.
[60] Kahn, *Djuka*, p. 106.
[61] Schoenrich, *Santo Domingo*, pp. 185, 186.

was superficial in the extreme. Most of the priests were there primarily for the whites. They seem, moreover, to have been of inferior quality and to have been notorious for their greed.[62]

In the disorders in the first part of the nineteenth century the Church suffered severely. In Haiti long delay was experienced in reaching an agreement with Rome. In the interim, irregularity of episcopal administration proved a handicap. After several abortive attempts, in 1860 a concordat was entered into with Rome and thenceforward very little friction developed between Church and state. The right of the government to nominate the bishops and to approve of the appointment of parish clergy was recognized and some government financial support was promised. In 1861, accordingly, a hierarchy consisting of an archdiocese and four dioceses was established. Clergy came from France, and French brothers and sisters conducted schools and various charitable institutions.[63] Although some provision was made for training Haitians for the priesthood, the clergy remained predominantly French.[64] The church property was owned by the government. Religious toleration prevailed, but the vast majority of the population was nominally Roman Catholic.[65] Much of that faith, however, was a thin veneer. African cults survived in Voodooism and Obeah.[66]

In the Dominican Republic, the government regarded the property of the Roman Catholic Church as its own.[67] In contrast with Haiti, most of the clergy were native-born.[68] In 1884 an agreement with the Holy See was entered into whereby the latter appointed to the Archbishopric from nominees of the state and the state promised to pay the salary of the Archbishop and a few other ecclesiastical officials.[69] Some of the clergy were very lax morally, but others seem to have been of high character.[70] Through the efforts of one of them, Bellini, an insane asylum, an orphan asylum, and a college were founded.[71] A priest, Merino, was for a time President and gave the republic

[62] Mecham, op. cit., pp. 340, 341.

[63] Mecham, op. cit., pp. 342-346; J. N. Léger, Haiti, Her History and Her Detractors (New York, The Neale Publishing Co., 1907, pp. 372), pp. 186, 187; Schwager, Die katholische Heidenmission der Gegenwart, p. 45.

[64] Mecham, op. cit., pp. 345, 348; Huonder, Der einheimische Klerus in den Heidenländern, p. 248.

[65] Mecham, op. cit., pp. 346, 348.

[66] Mecham, op. cit., pp. 348, 349; Williams, Voodoos and Obeahs, pp. 95-97; Herskovits, Life in a Haitian Valley, pp. 139-248, 267-291.

[67] Welles, Naboth's Vineyard. The Dominican Republic 1844-1924, Vol. I, pp. 52, 53.

[68] Schoenrich, op. cit., p. 188.

[69] Schoenrich, op. cit., p. 186.

[70] Schoenrich, op. cit., p. 188.

[71] Schoenrich, op. cit., p. 189.

vigorous rule. He later became Archbishop.[72] While it was predominantly Roman Catholic, the Dominican Republic allowed religious liberty and freemasonry flourished.[73]

In Cuba under the Spanish regime all the bishops and most of the priests were appointed from Spain. In 1837-1841 much of the property belonging to the religious orders was secularized. After independence, partly because of its close Spanish connexions and its association with the old order, the Roman Catholic Church was attacked and Church and state were separated. Thanks largely to Leonard Wood, the Military Governor-General, an amicable adjustment was reached on some of the thorny issues. Both civil and ecclesiastical marriage were recognized. No religious instruction was allowed in the public schools, but religious bodies were permitted to establish schools of their own.[74]

In the French West Indies the population was said to be almost entirely Roman Catholic and was served by priests and nuns chiefly from France. Bishoprics were created in 1850 for Guadaloupe and Martinique,[75] succeeding prefectures apostolic.[76]

Throughout the Latin-American mainland the revolutions which ushered in political independence dealt serious blows to Roman Catholic enterprises for the Indians. As we have seen earlier,[77] the mission was the characteristic frontier institution of the Spanish colonial system. After the first wave of military conquest, it was through the mission that Spanish rule and Spanish culture advanced into new areas. Missions were found on the edges of the Spanish territories from California to Chile. To a somewhat less extent, missions performed a similar function in Brazil. Independence wrought havoc. For a generation or more Christianity not only ceased to advance among the Indians on the borders of Latin America. In many places it also actually lost ground.

A number of factors militated against the missions to the Indians. To a large degree the staffs had been made up of regulars from Europe. The independence movement was in part a revolt of American-born whites, the *creoles*, against the rule of European-born whites. Obviously the foreign-born clergy in the missions would be viewed with suspicion. Many of them would be compelled to leave the country. Latin American Christianity had always been too passive to supply many men for the missions. With the difficulties which overtook it as a result of independence and with its decline in morale, in the

[72] Welles, *op. cit.*, Vol. I, pp. 439-443.
[73] Schoenrich, *op. cit.*, pp. 195, 196.
[74] Mecham, *op. cit.*, pp. 354-359.
[75] *The Catholic Encyclopedia*, Vol. VII, p. 44; Vol. IX, p. 731.
[76] *Notizie Statistiche delle Missioni di Tutto il Mondo Dipendenti dalla S. C. de Propaganda Fide* (1844), pp. 626ff.
[77] Vol. III, Chap. 3.

nineteenth century it was even less capable of furnishing men to replace the foreign-born. In most of the new states the liberal or radical elements who led in the revolt against the old regime sought to curb the power of the Church. Generally one of their objects of attack was the religious orders. Since the missions were staffed by regulars rather than seculars, they were forced to bear much of the brunt of the animosity. For a time the new governments were probably unable, even had they been willing, to accord the same degree of financial support to the missions as had been given by the Crown. The internal disorder attendant upon the transition from the old to the new regime proved uncongenial to the missions, for the latter were essentially peaceful and seldom had more than a minimum of armed force as a defence.

The movement towards the passing of the missions was not new. The principle had long been recognized that the task of the missionary was temporary, that after the Indians around any centre had been converted and trained in Christian living the regulars should move on, presumably to begin their enterprise anew among a fresh group of non-Christians, and that their former wards should be incorporated into normal parish life administered by seculars. The frontier stage would then have ended and the Indians, now Christians and assimilated to European culture, would take their place in the colonial communities. In essence this was what was meant by "secularization." In practice the transition was usually long delayed.[78] In 1749 the Spanish Crown, moved by a growing coolness towards missions and religious orders, decreed the transfer of all parishes and missions in the Americas from the regulars to the seculars.[79] The command could not be immediately carried out, for many practical difficulties supervened.[80] However, the expulsion of Jesuits from the Spanish domains (1767) was followed by the transfer to the seculars of some of their former fields. Moreover, before the end of the eighteenth century some of the Franciscan missions were secularized.[81] In 1813 the Córtes of Spain ordered all missions in the New World which had been in existence more than ten years to be turned over to seculars and the regulars to found new missions.[82]

It was more than secularization which was wrought by independence, although at times that term was made a cloak for the change. With the outbreak of civil disturbances in Mexico towards the close of the first decade of the

[78] Geary, *The Secularization of the California Missions,* pp. 16-25.

[79] Geary, *op. cit.,* p. 25.

[80] Geary, *op. cit.,* pp. 32, 33.

[81] Geary, *op. cit.,* pp. 33ff.

[82] Geary, *op. cit.,* p. 31; Engelhardt, *The Missions and Missionaries of California,* Vol. I, p. 660.

nineteenth century, a repercussion of the Napoleonic occupation of Spain and the precursor of independence, supplies to the California missions were cut off, together with the annual allowances.[83] When (1827) in the progress of the movement for independence all of Spanish birth were expelled from Mexico, three Franciscan colleges which had been preparing men for the missions and whose student bodies were made up of Spaniards were closed. Two colleges, the one of Zacatecas and the one of Zapopan (founded in 1816), whose students were American-born, were allowed to continue. In 1859 these two institutions were suspended, with grave results for the missions.[84] In 1841 there were only six priests for all Lower California, four Dominicans and two Mercedarians.[85] In the meanwhile disease, notably epidemics of smallpox, had been wasting the scanty Indian population.[86] In 1833 the Mexican Government ordered the secularization of all the missions in Upper and Lower California and the division of the lands into individual holdings. Only gradually was the decree carried out. However, eventually secularization was largely accomplished. The Indians, at best never very enterprising or vigorous, unable to adjust themselves to the new, unfamiliar order, deteriorated.[87] The expulsion of the regulars from some of the states in Central America, especially after 1871, left thousands of Indians without clerical care.[88] In Venezuela the missions generally collapsed. For instance, in 1816 Capuchins from Catalonia had about 29 centres with about 21,000 Indians. In the following year they were arrested because they were Spaniards and had sided with the mother country. Only a minority escaped. The majority either died of exposure or hunger or were shot. Many of the Indians fled to avoid military service and those who had been under the supervision of the missions reverted to a wild condition.[89]

[83] Geary, *op. cit.*, p. 57; Engelhardt, *op. cit.*, Vol. I, p. 633.

[84] Lemmens, *Geschichte der Franziskanermissionen*, pp. 254-257. On the seminary of Zapopan see Luis de Nuestra Señora del Refugio de Palacio y Basave, *Historia Breve y Compendiosa del Colegio Apostolico de Propaganda Fide de N. Sra. de Zapopan* (Guadalajara, C. M. Zainz, 1925, pp. 112, 131, 22, vii), pp. 1-50.

[85] Engelhardt, *op cit.*, Vol. I, p. 683.

[86] Meigs, *The Dominican Mission Frontier of Lower California*, p. 155.

[87] Geary, *op. cit.*, pp. 144ff.; Meigs, *op. cit.*, p. 155; Engelhardt, *op. cit.*, Vol. I, pp. 678, 681, 682. For the continuation of some of the Franciscan efforts in California under the rule of the United States, see Charles Francis Saunders and J. Smeaton Chase, *The California Padres and Their Missions* (Boston, Houghton Mifflin Co., 1915, pp. xi, 418), p. 164.

[88] Schmidlin-Braun, *Catholic Mission History*, p. 684.

[89] *Informe sobre el Estado Actual de los Distritos de Reduccion de Indijenas Alto Orinoco, Central y Bajo Orinoco, y Medidas que Reclaman, Presentado a su Excelencia el Poder Ejecutivo por el Visitador Nombrado al Efecto* (Carácas, Diego Campbell, 1850, pp. 98), *passim*, especially the first chart in the appendix; *Capucins Missionaires. Missions Françaises*, p. 75; Rippy and Nelson, *Crusaders of the Jungle*, pp. 165, 166; Watters, *A History of the Church in Venezuela, 1810-1930*, p. 65.

In 1824 a government decree closed the Franciscan college in Ocapa, Peru, from which many priests had been supplied to a large number of missions in South America. One of the Franciscans remained by his Indians on a tributary of the Marañón, the Ucayali, and held them to the Christian faith.[90] The revolution in Bolivia destroyed all but one of the flourishing Franciscan missions among the Chiriguanos, on the north-western edge of the Gran Chaco. In 1814 some of the centres were plundered. Numbers of missionaries were imprisoned. Two died. Those who escaped found refuge in the college at Tarija. It was a quarter of a century before efforts for the non-Christian Indians could be resumed.[91] In 1817, when the independence of Chile seemed assured, all the Franciscans attached to the college at Chillán were Spaniards and all except one fled, taking refuge in Peru.[92] The years when independence was being secured brought distress to the missions as to the Church as a whole in Spanish America.

Before the middle of the nineteenth century recovery had begun. This was chiefly through reinforcements from Europe. The Latin American Church had too little vitality and was too frequently disturbed by its struggles with the state to provide many missionaries to the Indians. To be sure, in several instances missions were supported by the state and some natives of South America joined their staffs. However, there was little private giving. Only one missionary society seems to have come into being—in 1898 in Peru. South American Roman Catholics contributed only a pittance to the Society for the Propagation of the Faith.[93] It was from Europe that most of the men and the funds came for the nineteenth and twentieth century Roman Catholic enterprises among the Indians. As in colonial days, so after political independence, the Roman Catholic Church in Latin America was too passive and had too little initiative to concern itself much with even the non-Christians on its very borders. In several areas the lost ground was never fully regained. In others fresh advances were made. As the century wore on, thanks chiefly to the aid from Europe, progress was increasingly recorded. It continued to 1914 and beyond. Yet it is estimated that at the close of the nineteenth century there were in South America alone about two and two-thirds millions of pagan Indians.[94]

For the gains as for the earlier losses lack of space forbids a complete account. Only a few examples can be given. From them, however, may be gleaned

[90] Lemmens, *Franziskanermissionen*, pp. 303, 304.
[91] Lemmens, *op. cit.*, pp. 320, 321.
[92] Lemmens, *op. cit.*, p. 314.
[93] Schwager, *Die katholische Heidenmission der Gegenwart*, p. 71.
[94] Descamps, *Histoire Générale Comparée des Missions*, p. 583. Estimates greatly vary. Another, if British and Dutch Guiana be excepted, gives 1,322,000.—*The Catholic Encyclopedia*, Vol. XIV, p. 281.

something of an impression of the rather remarkable growth of these decades. The missions did not achieve the importance that had been theirs in the colonial period. With occasional exceptions, no longer did the state utilize them to push forward the frontier. Most of them were in remote districts among scanty populations which were not much in the public eye. Yet they were there and were not without effect.

In Mexico missions were renewed in 1872 by the Josephites among the Tarahumara,[95] the largest tribe of Indians north of Mexico City.[96] In 1900 the Jesuits took charge of the enterprise,[97] thus resuming a field which had been theirs in the seventeenth century.[98] Most of the Tarahumara became professedly Christian, but it was said that their knowledge of the faith was very superficial. Living in their remote mountain fastnesses, they maintained their life much as it had been before the coming of the Spaniards.[99] In 1895 priests from the Seminary of Saints Peter and Paul, in Rome, took over the bleak vicariate apostolic of Lower California among the unpromising and scanty Indian population.[100]

The Government of Venezuela fairly early made attempts to restore the missions which had been so badly disrupted in the struggle for independence. Presumably this was not as much from a religious motive as for the purpose of bringing order and civilization, an effort to revive the frontier policy of the Spanish colonial regime. In 1832 the Secretary of the Interior called attention to the decay of the missions and the need of active measures to renew them. Lack of funds and of priests proved a handicap.[101] In the 1840's fresh efforts were made. In 1841 a law was passed empowering the President to establish a system for the care of the Indians and to bring in priests from Europe. In the course of the decade several scores of priests entered, but the missions did not flourish. Some of the clergy died and many of the others seemed to prefer the cities to the rough and isolated life of a frontier missionary.[102] In 1882 further legislation was enacted on behalf of the Indians. In 1890 authority was given to bring in fifty Spanish regulars. In 1894 a plan for missions was outlined to be executed by Spanish Capuchins. Progress in giving effect to the programme appears to have been slow.[103] The Venezuelan missions did not

---

[95] Schmidlin-Braun, *Catholic Mission History*, p. 685.

[96] Bennett and Zingg, *The Tarahumara*, p. vii.

[97] *Revista de la Exposición Misional Española*, July, 1929, pp. 448-452.

[98] Bennett and Zingg, *op. cit.*, p. 355.

[99] Bennett and Zingg, *op. cit.*, pp. 296, 319, 320.

[100] Schmidlin-Braun, *op. cit.*, p. 685.

[101] Watters, *A History of the Church in Venezuela, 1810-1930*, p. 157.

[102] Watters, *op. cit.*, pp. 157-160.

[103] Watters, *op. cit.*, pp. 215-217; Freitag in *Zeitschrift für Missionswissenschaft*, Vol. XI, p. 174.

fully come back to the prosperity which they had enjoyed under the colonial regime.

In 1902 a convention was signed between Colombia and the Holy See whereby the administrative organization of missions and the delimitation of fields of activity were arranged and the government undertook to make grants of land and to give annual subsidies for the support of the enterprise.[104] Augustinians and Spanish Capuchins had been at work since the preceding decade, but now the efforts of these two bodies were strengthened, and other orders, including the Jesuits, entered the field.[105]

In its mountain fastnesses and valleys Ecuador contained many non-Christian Indians. In the turbulent initial decades of independence the missions which in colonial days had been conducted among them largely lapsed. Under the friendly regime of García Moreno some were renewed. In spite of the fact that during much of the time after Moreno's assassination (1875) the anticlericals were in power, as the years passed additional missions were established. Among those orders which either renewed or inaugurated enterprises between 1860 and 1914 were the Franciscans, with a missionary college in Quito and a vicariate apostolic;[106] the spiritual sons of John Bosco, the Salesians, who had a field among the difficult primitive Jivaros in a vast territory in Eastern Ecuador;[107] the Jesuits; and the Dominicans.[108]

In colonial days the valleys of the streams which drained the eastern slopes of the Peruvian Andes had been the scene of heroic missions of Jesuits and Franciscans. The expulsion of the Jesuits in the latter half of the eighteenth century had left (after a brief disappointing experiment with seculars) the Brothers Minor alone in the inhospitable region. The blow given the Franciscans in 1824 by the forced discontinuation of the college at Ocapa was not of long duration. In 1836 a presidential decree permitted the reopening of the college and the recruiting of new missionaries from Europe. Andreas Herrero, who during the vicissitudes of the revolutionary period had remained by his flock, was sent to the Old World for reinforcements. From his second trip to Europe, in 1836, he brought back ninety-three men, of whom nineteen were assigned to Peru and the remainder distributed over Chile and Bolivia. In the course of the nineteenth century new missions were opened and diction-

[104] Mecham, *Church and State in Latin America*, p. 164.

[105] Schmidlin-Braun, *op. cit.*, p. 681; Freitag in *Zeitschrift für Missionswissenschaft*, Vol. XI, pp. 170ff.; *Revista de la Exposición Misional Española*, Feb., 1929, pp. 214-221, March, 1929, pp. 273-279.

[106] Lemmens, *op. cit.*, p. 288.

[107] *Revista de la Exposición Misional Española*, Nov., 1928, pp. 75-78; Berg., *Die katholische Heidenmission als Kulturträger*, Vol. I, p. 224.

[108] Freitag in *Zeitschrift für Missionswissenschaft*, Vol. XI, pp. 175, 176.

aries and grammars were compiled for various tongues.[109] Augustinians and Spanish Dominicans also entered. In 1900, with the consent of the state, Rome created three prefectures apostolic for the uncivilized frontier and distributed them among the three orders.[110]

Herrero was also the pioneer in reviving the extensive Franciscan missions in Bolivia. Most of the staff which came to the New World as a result of his two trips to Europe were placed in Bolivia. The majority of these were Italians. To the older mission colleges of Tarija and Tarata he added new ones at La Paz and Sucre. Still later another was organized at Potosi. Some of the missions were of the type which prevailed in colonial days, in which the priests had the supervision of the entire life of the Christians, economic and civil as well as religious. In 1905, however, the civil administration was taken over by the state. To Italian Franciscans were added Brothers Minor from Germany and Austria. In accordance with the time-honoured tradition of missionaries among primitive folk, schools were conducted, dictionaries and grammars were prepared for several languages, and the beginnings of a Christian literature in the vernacular were made. Famous was Nicholas Armentia, of the College of La Paz, who in addition to compiling dictionaries and grammars for several tongues made valuable studies of the flora and fauna of the region and of the customs of the Indians. From time to time new centres were opened. Thousands of converts were gathered.[111]

The interruption brought to missions in Chile by the departure of the Spanish Franciscans (c. 1817) was not long continued. In 1837 Italian Brothers Minor came and were distributed to various areas. That same year the government founded in Castro a college for missionaries like the older one in Chillán.[112] In 1848 Italian Capuchins entered to take over part of the territory. These were succeeded (1889) by Spanish Capuchins.[113] They in turn were replaced by Bavarian Capuchins, the first of whom arrived in 1896. By 1927 less than 4,000 non-Christian Indians remained in their district, but in spite of marked progress in caring for the vast assignment, the missionaries were confessedly too few to give adequate spiritual oversight to their charges.[114]

---

[109] Lemmens, *op. cit.*, pp. 303-306; Bernardino Izaquirre, *Historia de las Misiones Franciscanas y Narracion de los Progresos de la Geografia en el Oriente del Peru* (Lima, Talleres Tipográficos de la Penitenciaría, Vols. X, XI, XII, 1925, 1926), *passim*.

[110] Schmidlin-Braun, *op. cit.*, p. 679.

[111] Lemmens, *op. cit.*, pp. 320-325; Freitag in *Zeitschrift für Missionswissenschaft*, Vol. XI, pp. 178-180; Berg, *Die katholische Heidenmission als Kulturträger*, Vol. II, pp. 301, 302; Schmidlin-Braun, *op. cit.*, p. 680.

[112] Silva Cotapos, *Historia Eclesiástica de Chile*, pp. 234, 235.

[113] Schmidlin-Braun, *op. cit.*, pp. 678, 679; Lemmens, *op. cit.*, pp. 314-316.

[114] Guido Beck von Ramberg, *Die Mission der bayerischen Kapuziner unter den Indianern in Chile* (Altötting, 1929, pp. 62), *passim*.

Into Paraguay, not yet fully recovered from the devastating experiences of the later part of the eighteenth and of the nineteenth century, came, in 1910, missionaries of the Society of the Divine Word. The Guarani language had changed since the days of the Jesuit missions. The older literature was, therefore, outmoded. A new literature had to be produced.[115]

Argentina embraced a huge area extending from the tropics on the North to the bleak, semi-arid regions in the South. Here were many tribes of aborigines, from the torrid Gran Chaco to Patagonia and Tierra del Fuego with their cooler climate. Over much of the area the aboriginal population was either non-existent or not numerous. It was found chiefly in the North and even there was sparse. In Patagonia its power was broken by wars in the last quarter of the nineteenth century and it tended to die out. In its place came white settlers—cattle raisers, sheep herders, and miners.

In Argentina Roman Catholic missions were widely extended. Until about the middle of the nineteenth century the missions dating from colonial days were badly disturbed by the disorder which attended the revolution and the early days of independence. In 1853 a Franciscan was given permission by the governor of one of the provinces to go to Europe for reinforcements. He returned with nineteen new recruits from Italy. In that decade three new Franciscan colleges were begun. By the end of the nineteenth century some of the missions had become thriving villages, with entirely Christian populations, but not far from 50,000 Indians were said still to be non-Christian.[116] These Franciscan enterprises were in the North. In the South, on the Patagonian plateau, the Salesians of Don Bosco had missions. The invitation came in 1872 from the Archbishop of Buenos Aires. Bosco himself accepted for them. The first band arrived in 1875.[117] A pioneer was Giovanni Cagliero who explored much of the region, later became bishop in it, and eventually was made a cardinal.[118] Within a few years most of the scanty aboriginal population in their territories, its earlier community life partly broken by wars with the whites, had become professedly Christian.[119]

Brazil contained more Indians than did any other of the South American countries. The vast Amazon Valley and the other extensive reaches of the largest of the Latin-American states held many thousands of aborigines. It is said, indeed, that in spite of the large increase of the population of Brazil by

[115] Berg, op. cit., Vol. II, p. 39.

[116] Lemmens, op. cit., pp. 332-334; Freitag in Zeitschrift für Missionswissenschaft, Vol. XI, p. 182.

[117] Ghéon, The Secret of Saint John Bosco, p. 177.

[118] Berg, op. cit., Vol. II, p. 302.

[119] Freitag in Zeitschrift für Missionswissenschaft, Vol. XI, pp. 181, 182.

immigration from Europe, from 1872 to 1912 the proportion of Indians to the whole rose from seven per cent. to thirteen per cent.[120] The Brazilian Indians varied greatly in the degree to which they adapted themselves to the white man's culture. Before 1914 many had been partly assimilated to it. Others remained comparatively untouched.[121] In the vast area of Matto Grosso in the closing years of the nineteenth and the opening years of the twentieth century Rondon carried on an extensive attempt, apart from Christian missions, to bring the Indians to adjust themselves to white civilization.[122] In the latter part of the nineteenth century and in the twentieth century Roman Catholic missionaries of a number of different orders undertook enterprises for the Indians. These were widely scattered. They ranged from the state of Rio Grande do Sul, in the extreme South, to the state of Pará in the North, and from the coast territories into Matto Grosso in the Centre, to the upper part of the Amazon Valley in the West, and to territory between Venezuela and British Guiana in the North-west. Missionaries from Europe bore the brunt of the labour for the non-Christians. Some orders served Roman Catholic colonists or native Brazilians of their faith as well as the pagan Indians. The Pallottini, the Society of the Divine Word, Italian Capuchins of more than one province, Jesuits, French Dominicans, Belgian Benedictines, the Holy Ghost Fathers, Italian Salesians, and Dutch Franciscans were among those who strove to reach the Indians.[123] Italian and German Franciscans were active.[124] Leadership for the Roman Catholic community was beginning to emerge from among the aborigines. We read of a bishop of Indian stock with a majority of full-blooded Indians among his clergy.[125]

The large Negro population of Brazil seems to have become Roman Catholic through the contagion of the prevailing faith about them rather than through much consciously planned missionary effort on their behalf. In Bahia the churches were said to have their chief support from those of Negro blood.[126]

[120] Cooper, *The Brazilians and Their Country*, p. 334.
[121] Cooper, *op. cit.*, pp. 332, 333.
[122] Cooper, *op. cit.*, p. 332; Freitag in *Zeitschrift für Missionswissenschaft*, Vol. XI, p. 184.
[123] Freitag in *Zeitschrift für Missionswissenschaft*, Vol. XI, pp. 183-186. For one of the Capuchins, see Adelheim Jann, *Candidus Sierro aus dem Kapuzinerorden Indianer-Missionär Ein Beitrag zur brasilianischen Missionsgeschichte* (Stans, Hans von Matt & Cie, 1915, pp. 214).
[124] Freitag in *Zeitschrift für Missionswissenschaft*, Vol. XI, pp. 183-186; J. C. Strömer, *Von Bahia zum Amazonenstrom. Das Arbeitsfeld der deutschen Franziskaner in Nordbrasilien* (Berlin, Buchverlag Germania, 1931, pp. 133), *passim;* Elsner, *Die deutschen Franziskaner in Brasilien*, pp. 81-87; Lemmens, *op. cit.*, pp. 275, 276.
[125] Huonder, *Der einheimische Klerus in den Heidenländern*, p. 38.
[126] Elliott, *Brazil*, p. 91.

To South America, mainly to Argentina and Brazil, but also to a less extent to Chile and Uruguay, came immigrants, mostly from Europe. The large majority of them were Italians, Spaniards, and Portuguese. They were, therefore, at least nominally Roman Catholics. Hundreds of thousands were Germans, and of these the majority were of that faith. This immigration constituted a challenge to the Roman Catholic Church. Could it be held to its Old World religious allegiance? Could it, in addition, be a fresh source of life from which would come a reinvigoration of the existing listless Roman Catholicism of the region? There were as well in Brazil thousands of Japanese, predominantly non-Christian. They, too, were an opportunity.

The figures of the immigration are impressive. Significant, too, were the sources of the new population. From 1857 to 1908 the arrivals in Argentina are said to have totalled 3,178,456. Of these 1,799,423 were Italians, 795,243 Spaniards, 188,316 French, 42,765 English, 59,800 Austro-Hungarians, 40,655 Germans, 28,344 Swiss, and 20,668 Belgians. Not all of these became permanent residents. A substantial proportion returned to Europe. Yet the majority threw in their lot with the country.[127] The influx was especially marked in the 1880's and after 1900. As early as 1895 approximately one-fourth of the population were foreign-born who had arrived after the age of eighteen. Most of those who came were agricultural and day labourers.[128] In Brazil early in the nineteenth century the state began to foster immigration. For at least a time the newly arrived were encouraged to group themselves by nationalities and to preserve their own languages and customs.[129] In the first half of the century many Germans came. From 1820 to 1915, 122,830 are said to have reached the country, and by about the latter year those of German blood in Brazil were said to total approximately 250,000.[130] With the dwindling of the flow of Germans not far from the middle of the nineteenth century, the coffee-growers of the state of São Paulo turned to Italy for labourers. Between 1820 and the end of 1915, 1,361,266 Italians are reported to have entered Brazil. By the latter year they and their descendants numbered over 2,000,000, the largest of the immigrant national bodies.[131] Most of the Italians were from the North of Italy.[132] From 1820 to the end of 1915 official records declared that there

[127] Albert B. Martinez and Maurice Lewandowski, *The Argentine in the Twentieth Century*. Translated by Bernard Miall from the French (New York, Charles Scribner's Sons, no date, pp. 376), p. 120.

[128] W. A. Hirst, *Argentina* (New York, Charles Scribner's Sons, 1910, pp. xxviii, 308), pp. 134-138.

[129] Elliott, *Brazil Today and Tomorrow*, p. 56.

[130] Elliott, *op. cit.*, pp. 57-60.

[131] Elliott, *op. cit.*, p. 60.

[132] Commons, *Races and Immigrants in America*, p. 78.

had come to Brazil, in addition to the Germans and Italians, 976,386 Portuguese, 468,583 Spaniards, 103,683 Russians, 78,545 Austrians, 52,434 Turk-Arabs, 28,072 French, 22,005 English, 15,608 Japanese, 10,713 Swiss, 5,435 Swedes, and 4,727 Belgians.[133] Of those listed as Russians, some were Poles, subjects of the Tsar.[134] Others of those from Russia were German by blood.[135] Immigration to Chile began shortly before the middle of the nineteenth century. It dwindled for a few years. Between 1881 and 1900, it revived. From 1900 to its virtual cessation in 1914 with the outbreak of the War of 1914-1918 it was closely regulated by law and on the average less than 2,000 a year entered. Of this immigration about three-fourths were Spaniards, but there were sprinklings of Germans, Swiss-French, and Canary Islanders.[136] In 1891, of the population of Uruguay about 70 per cent. were native and about 30 per cent. were foreign-born. Between 1884 and 1891 the net immigration, namely, the excess of entries over departures, was about 50,000. In the immigration Italians predominated with Spaniards next in numerical strength.[137] Large though this immigration was, it did not approach the size of the movement of population from Europe to the United States during the corresponding period. Moreover, although there were shifts of population to previously undeveloped regions and the opening of new areas played a large part in national history, notably in Brazil and Argentina, the expansion on the frontier did not assume such gigantic proportions as in the United States or even in Canada.

It seems probable that the Roman Catholic Church was neither so energetic nor so successful in holding the immigrants to their inherited faith as it was in the United States and Canada. The passive and crippled Roman Catholic Christianity of the older stock appears to have been no more aggressive in making provision for the immigrant than it was in trying to reach the non-Christian Indians. A much larger proportion of the immigrants than in the United States and Canada were Roman Catholic by heredity. Many of those in Spanish America were Spaniards and in Brazil were Portuguese. Presumably, therefore, they would be easily assimilated into the existing ecclesiastical structure. There is little evidence that much special effort was made to reach them. As a rule they were left religiously to themselves.[138] Most of such active attempts as were put forth to meet the problem of the immigrant appear to

[133] Elliott, *op. cit.*, p. 72.
[134] Denis, *Brazil*, pp. 275, 276.
[135] Denis, *op. cit.*, p. 277.
[136] L. E. Elliott, *Chile. Today and Tomorrow* (New York, the Macmillan Co., 1922, pp. x, 337), pp. 291-295.
[137] Bureau of American Republics, *Uruguay* (Washington, Bureau of American Republics, 1892, pp. vi, 347), pp. 53, 56.
[138] Braga and Grubb, *The Republic of Brazil*, p. 111.

have been by clergy from Europe. Of these clergy the majority were neither Spanish nor Portuguese.

A few concrete examples may serve to give an indication of what a complete study would present of the care of immigrant clergy for the immigrants. For years the Italians who were entering Rio Grande do Sul, the southernmost state of Brazil, were without clerical ministrations. Many of them gathered for such community prayers as could be led by laymen. In 1896, through the initiative of a local bishop, the Capuchins of Savoy commenced to come. They not only cared for their fellow Italians but also for the native Brazilians. In 1899 Sisters of St. Joseph began arriving to help with schools.[139] In 1835 Vincent Mary Pallotti founded in Italy the Pious Society of Missions, usually known as the Pallottines, primarily to serve the immigrants in America. Not far from 1914 it had established itself at a number of centres in South America and had fourteen missions in Brazil.[140] It is said that as late as 1924, in Rio Grande do Sul, of the 157,000 Germans who were nominally Roman Catholic, 30,000 had not affiliated themselves with their church.[141] We hear of one area in Brazil where German Franciscans served Italian immigrants.[142] In 1904 there were in Argentina a number of Spanish and Italian priests.[143] The Society of the Divine Word served some of the colonists.[144]

From Japan the Roman Catholics eventually sent a Jesuit to work among the Japanese in Brazil. Since the Japanese emigration societies sought to further the assimilation of their countrymen to Brazilian life, many of the Japanese, assuming that Roman Catholic Christianity was the religion of the land, adopted that faith.[145]

By 1935 some Uniates had migrated to South America. About 52,000 Ruthenians, Uniates, settled in Brazil and there were ministered to by 13 priests.[146] In Uruguay there were about 16,000 Maronites, presided over by a monk in Montevideo.[147] Syrian Jacobite Uniates were served by two priests in Argentina and one priest in Chile.[148]

In contrast with the United States, where the Roman Catholic Church owed its phenomenal growth in clergy and in physical plant largely to the immi-

[139] *Capucins Missionaires. Missions Françaises*, pp. 36-42.
[140] *The Catholic Encyclopedia*, Vol. XII, p. 107; Freitag in *Zeitschrift für Missionswissenschaft*, Vol. XI, p. 186.
[141] Braga and Grubb, *op. cit.*, p. 52.
[142] Espey, *Festschrift zum Silberjubiläum im Süden Brasiliens*, pp. 46, 115.
[143] Huonder, *Der einheimische Klerus in den Heidenländern*, p. 38.
[144] Freitag in *Zeitschrift für Missionswissenschaft*, Vol. XI, p. 184.
[145] Braga and Grubb, *op. cit.*, p. 111.
[146] Attwater, *The Catholic Eastern Churches*, p. 88.
[147] Attwater, *op. cit.*, p. 188.
[148] Attwater, *op. cit.*, p. 168.

grants, in Latin America the newcomers seem to have done little to care for themselves religiously. The initiative was mainly from Europe. This may have been due in part to the fact that in Latin America the immigration was chiefly from Southern Europe and that the Irish elements so prominent in the United States and from which so much of the leadership of the church in that country was derived was almost entirely absent. It was notorious that in the United States the Southern Europeans, while retaining a connexion with the church, were less enthusiastically Roman Catholic than were the Germans and the Irish. Possibly, too, the absence of such vigorous competition from Protestants as existed in the United States was a factor.

In the nineteenth century the Eastern churches were for the first time represented in Latin America. In the last decades of the century many Syrians, Arabic-speaking members of the Eastern Orthodox Church, went to South America, especially to Argentina. It is said that in 1887 there were 6,850 in Argentina and that in 1887-1915 136,449 Syrians came to Argentina and established schools, clubs, and churches for themselves. The majority adhered to the Orthodox Patriarch of Antioch and obtained clergy through him. Since in Syria many had attended Russian schools, the Holy Synod of Russia felt an interest in them and sent priests. For a time Russian influence grew. In 1905 some Syrians obtained clergy from the Orthodox Bishop of Ladik (Laodicea).[149] By 1917 there were in São Paulo Russian settlers with churches of the Russian type.[150] Syrian Orthodox also went to Brazil.[151] By 1932 Russian churches existed in Argentina, Brazil, Paraguay, and Uruguay and were under a superintendent.[152]

Protestant Christianity became much more extensive in Latin America than did the Eastern churches. Under the Spanish and Portuguese colonial regimes it had been rigidly excluded, but as the Latin-American countries achieved their independence these restrictions were relaxed and it became possible for Protestantism to gain admission. It was to be expected that Protestants would avail themselves of the weakening of the barriers against their form of the faith. In this great period of the spread of Protestantism, when the agents of

[149] Lübeck, *Die russischen Missionen,* pp. 57-59.
[150] Elliott, *Brazil,* p. 68.
[151] Braga and Grubb, *The Republic of Brazil,* p. 43.
[152] *Ibid.*

that wing of Christianity were penetrating to almost every portion of the globe, so large an area as Latin America would not be overlooked. Protestant Christianity entered in three ways—as missions to non-Christian Indians, through Protestant merchants, sailors, and immigrants, and by Protestant missions among Roman Catholics.

As early as 1833-1834 an effort was made by the American Board of Commissioners for Foreign Missions to explore the possibilities for missions to the Indians of Patagonia. Sea captains of the then widespread shipping of the United States brought news of the possible accessibility of these aborigines. Two men were sent to investigate, but after hearing their report the Board decided not to pursue the project.[153]

The most extensive of the efforts of Protestants to reach the non-Christian Indians of Latin America had their rise in Allen Francis Gardiner and were carried on through the Patagonian Missionary Society, later the South American Missionary Society. Gardiner was born in 1794, of a good English family. From boyhood he was in the royal navy and in 1826 he attained the rank of commander. As a young man he had a profound religious experience and for a time thought of becoming a clergyman. He did not do so, but about the age of forty he left the active service of the navy, and, after the death of his first wife, he decided to become a pioneer missionary. He went first to the Negroes of Natal. Then, after a few years, partly because he felt that area to be cared for by existing missionary societies, he explored (1838-1839) the possibilities of missions among the non-Christian Indians of Argentina and Chile.[154] For a time he turned his attention to New Guinea, but swung back to South America. After having sought in vain to induce the Church Missionary Society to enter that field, with a few friends he organized (1844) the Patagonian Missionary Society. A fruitless attempt to found a mission in Patagonia followed (1845). A journey to Bolivia (1847) seemed to give hope of a mission in that land. That also proved abortive. Gardiner again essayed the South American adventure, this time off Tierra del Fuego (1848). Once more he seemed to fail. Nor did he succeed in persuading the Moravians or the Presbyterian churches of Scotland to undertake the enterprise. In 1850 Gardiner and a group of six other men left for the inhospitable Tierra del Fuego, there

---

[153] Titus Coan, *Adventures in Patagonia. A Missionary's Exploring Trip.* With an introduction by Henry M. Field (New York, Dodd, Mead & Co., 1880, pp. xiv, 319), *passim; Report of the American Board of Commissioners for Foreign Missions, 1834,* pp. 99-102; *The Missionary Herald,* Vol. XXIX, p. 459, Vol. XXX, pp. 376-381, 397-402, 429-432, Vol. XXXI, pp. 20, 21, 37-41.

[154] Allen F. Gardiner, *A Visit to the Indians on the Frontiers of Chili* (London, R. B. Seeley and W. Burnside, 1841, pp. 194), *passim.*

to renew the endeavour. Within a few months the entire party died of exposure and starvation (1851).[155]

These unpropitious beginnings with their culminating disaster, far from terminating the mission, nerved its friends to greater efforts. Reinforcements were sent. The programme was adopted of establishing headquarters on one of the Falklands to which neophytes could be brought for training. Yet misfortune continued to dog the steps of the pioneers. In 1859, on an island off Tierra del Fuego a party of eight were killed by those to whom they had come to minister.[156] However, undeterred, the society persevered. It became the chief voluntary agency through which members of the Church of England endeavoured to reach South America. Its representatives laboured not only for non-Christian aborigines, but also for British merchants, sailors, and settlers, and for Roman Catholics. Waite Hockin Stirling (1829-1923), grandson of a baronet and nephew of an admiral, who in 1857 became secretary of the society and in 1862 the superintendent of its missions, in 1869 was consecrated Bishop of the Falklands with jurisdiction for the Church of England throughout South America except British Guiana. For decades he served his huge diocese, travelling almost incessantly.[157]

The original purpose of Gardiner, missions among non-Christian Indians, was cherished. For longer or shorter periods centres were maintained on islands off the south coast of Tierra del Fuego to give effect to the vision which had brought Gardiner to his death.[158] For a number of decades efforts, both intermittent and persistent, were made to win the aborigines of Patagonia.[159] In the vast, inland, only partially explored Chaco with its sparse and primitive aboriginal population stations were initiated with W. Barbrooke Grubb as

[155] John W. Marsh and Waite H. Stirling, *The Story of Commander Allen Gardiner, R.N., with Sketches of Missionary Work in South America* (London, James Nisbet & Co., 2d ed., 1868, pp. x, 176), *passim;* James Hamilton, *A Memoir of Richard Williams, Surgeon: Catechist to the Patagonian Missionary Society in Tierra del Fuego* (London, James Nisbet & Co., 1854, pp. viii, 255), *passim;* Sarah A. Myers, *Self-Sacrifice; or, The Pioneers of Fuegia* (Philadelphia, Presbyterian Board of Publication, 1861, pp. 300), *passim;* George Pakenham Despard, editor, *Hope Deferred, Not Lost; a Narrative of Missionary Effort in South America, in Connexion with the Patagonian Missionary Society* (London, James Nisbet & Co., 1854, pp. viii, 462), made up largely of journals and other original documents, *passim.*

[156] Young, *From Cape Horn to Panama*, pp. 31-42; G. W. Phillips, *The Missionary Martyr of Tierra del Fuego; Being the Memoir of Mr. J. Garland Phillips, Late Catechist of the Patagonian, or South American Missionary Society* (London, Wertheim, Macintosh, and Hunt, 1861, pp. xii, 255), *passim.*

[157] MacDonald, *Bishop Stirling of the Falklands, passim.*

[158] Young, *op. cit.,* pp. 48ff.

[159] Young, *op. cit.,* pp. 83ff.; *Life and Missionary Travels of the Rev. J. Furniss Ogle, M.A., from His Letters, Selected by His Sister, and edited by Rev. A. J. Wylie, LL.D.* (London, Longmans, Green and Co., 1873, pp. viii, 414), pp. 88-180.

their outstanding leader. These were first in the Paraguayan Chaco (beginning in 1888 through Adolpho Henricksen, who died in about a year as a result of hardships) and later (commencing in 1910-1911) in the Argentinian Chaco. Here the effort was made not only to win the Indians to the Christian faith, but also to raise the level of social, intellectual, economic, and physical living of the entire population, both Christian and non-Christian. Collective life and customs were modified and to some degree revolutionized. Grammars and dictionaries were compiled. Translations were made from the Old and New Testaments and the Prayer Book.[160] A mission was also conducted for the Araucanian Indians of Southern Chile, with churches, a hospital, and schools, including an industrial and agricultural institution.[161] Both the son and grandson of Captain Gardiner were active in the enterprise. Charles Darwin was so impressed with the achievements registered among peoples whom he had regarded as hopelessly degraded that he became a regular contributor to the funds of the society.[162]

For the Indians of the Chaco the San Pedro Mission to the Indians was organized in 1903 and carried on activities in Argentina and Bolivia.[163] The Bolivian Indian Mission, begun in 1907, obtained support from Great Britain and New Zealand.[164]

Protestant missions among the Indians and the mixed population, Indian, Negro, and white, of the Mosquito or Meskito Coast in Central America came about through the British connexion. For about two hundred years, from the middle of the seventeenth to the middle of the nineteenth century, the English claimed suzerainty in the region. Buccaneers and fugitive Negro slaves mingled their blood with that of the Indians. Yet some pure-blooded Indians persisted. In the second half of the nineteenth century the area passed by stages into the possession of Nicaragua. In 1849, after an exploratory expedition in 1847 by missionaries from Jamaica, the Moravians inaugurated a mission on the coast. Eventually the Moravians expanded to a number of centres, both among the mixed stock and the pure-blooded Indians. Especially after an awakening in

[160] W. Barbrooke Grubb, *A Church in the Wilds* (New York, E. P. Dutton and Co., 1914, pp. xv, 287), *passim;* Young, *op. cit.*, pp. 137ff.; *South American Missionary Society, Annual Report, 1910-1911*, pp. x, xi; Every, *The Anglican Church in South America*, pp. 40, 41, 53-58; Pride and Cowell, *South America*, pp. 31-38; R. J. Hunt, *The Livingstone of South America. The Life and Adventures of W. Barbrooke Grubb among the Wild Tribes of the Gran Chaco in Paraguay, Bolivia, Argentina, the Falkland Islands and Tierra del Fuego* (Philadelphia, J. B. Lippincott Co., 1933, pp. 347), *passim.*

[161] Young, *op. cit.*, pp. 165ff.; *South American Missionary Society, Annual Report, 1910-1911*, p. xii; Pride and Cowell, *op. cit.*, pp. 43-45.

[162] Young, *op. cit.*, p. 61; MacDonald, *op. cit.*, pp. 68-70.

[163] Beach and St. John, *World Statistics of Christian Missions*, p. 32.

[164] Beach and St. John, *op. cit.*, p. 46.

1881 which had some of the aspects of a mass movement, several stations were opened.[165] The Church of England, through the Society for the Propagation of the Gospel in Foreign Parts, was also represented, although not so extensively as the Moravians.[166] From 1830 to 1833 the Wesleyans had a mission, but without winning a reliable convert from among the Indians.[167]

Late in 1909 an independent missionary, Anna Coope, English-born but from the United States, went to Panama. She effected an entrance among the San Blas Indians and made some converts.[168]

The Protestantism which entered Latin America by immigration was decidedly varied. British merchants and sailors early became prominent in the main ports. As the dominant commercial people of the nineteenth century, the British took advantage of the disintegration which political independence brought to the restrictions on trade that had marked the Spanish and Portuguese colonial regimes. To give spiritual care to these British communities, consular chaplaincies were instituted in several of the ports. These were subsidized by the British Government. For years they were technically under the Bishop of London and, perforce, were without adequate episcopal supervision.[169] What seems to have been the first Protestant church building in nineteenth century Latin America was the Anglican chapel erected in Rio de Janeiro in 1819.[170] As time passed, British governmental grants were withdrawn and the chaplains were maintained chiefly by the voluntary subscriptions of the local residents.[171] In 1905, for instance, Buenos Aires, the largest city of the continent, contained seven congregations of the Church of England, each with its own clergy and self-supporting.[172] In addition to its efforts for the non-Christian Indians, the South American Missionary Society appointed and aided chaplains for British seamen and residents in several of the ports.[173] In 1869, as we have seen, an Anglican Bishop of the Falklands was consecrated with jurisdiction over his communion in all of South America except British Guiana.

[165] H. G. Schneider, *Moskito. Zur Erinnerung an die Feier des fünfzigjährigen Bestehens der Mission der Brüdergemeine in Mittel-Amerika* (Herrnhut, Missionsbuchhandlung, 1899, pp. viii, 230), *passim;* Schulze, *200 Jahre Brüdermission*, Vol. II, pp. 192-207.

[166] Pascoe, *Two Hundred Years of the S.P.G.*, pp. 236, 237.

[167] Findlay and Holdsworth, *The History of the Wesleyan Methodist Missionary Society*, Vol. II, pp. 296, 297.

[168] *Anna Coope, Sky Pilot of the San Blas Indians. An Autobiography* (New York, American Tract Society, 1917, pp. viii, 180), pp. 79ff.

[169] Every, *Twenty-Five Years in South America*, p. 81; Clarke, *Constitutional Church Government*, pp. 316, 317.

[170] Braga and Grubb, *The Republic of Brazil*, p. 50.

[171] Every, *op. cit.*, p. 88.

[172] Young, *From Cape Horn to Panama*, p. 114.

[173] Young, *op. cit.*, pp. 92ff.; Marsh, *Narrative of the Origin and Progress of the South American Mission*, pp. 17ff.

In 1900, after nearly a generation of travel, Bishop Stirling retired. In 1910 the diocese was divided, but each of the new sees was still huge.[174]

British settlers of other religious affiliations than the Church of England also came to Latin America. In 1825 Scotch colonists migrated in a group to a spot not far from Buenos Aires and in 1826, at their request, a Presbyterian minister was ordained and sent out to them. He remained in charge of their church and school until 1850.[175] At least two other Presbyterian places of worship were opened for Scotch settlers in the valley of the River Plate, one of them with the aid of the Colonial Committee.[176] In 1865 a Welsh Colony was founded at Chubut in Patagonia. Some of its members belonged to the Church of England. Some were Independents and had their own clergyman.[177]

In Callao, Peru, in the second quarter of the nineteenth century the American Seamen's Friend Society had a chaplain.[178]

Beginning in the 1850's Waldensees came from Italy to Uruguay. Eventually some found homes in Argentina. Most of them were farmers and kept their Italian dialect. They remained true to their Protestant faith. With the aid of funds from Italy a minister was sent them. Their outstanding clergyman, Armand Ugón, lived to a great age and was a leader in the community. Additional clergy were trained either in a Protestant theological seminary in Buenos Aires or in Italy. The Waldensees not only held to their faith but also had missions for Roman Catholics.[179]

After the Civil War in the United States numbers of Southerners, unhappy over the outcome of that struggle, migrated to Brazil, there to make a fresh start. Among them were Baptists, Methodists, and Presbyterians. The Southern branches of these denominations saw in them both a need and an opportunity and they became the nuclei for missions of these bodies.[180]

Of the extensive German immigration to Brazil a large proportion were Protestant by heredity. Partly through assistance from the Brazilian Govern-

[174] Every, op. cit., pp. 103, 105-109. For the narrative of one of the bishops, see E. F. Every, South American Memories of Thirty Years (London, Society for Promoting Christian Knowledge, 1933, pp. 210), passim. The best comprehensive description of the churches for English residents is in Every, The Anglican Church in South America, passim.

[175] Dodds, Records of the Scottish Settlers in the River Plate and Their Churches, pp. 6, 7, 136, 176, 185-204.

[176] Dodds, op. cit., pp. 235, 277.

[177] Hirst, Argentina, pp. 136, 161; Young, op. cit., pp. 123-125.

[178] Taylor, Our South American Cousins, p. 96.

[179] Ernesto Tron, Historia de la Iglesia de Colonia Valdense desde la Fundacion de la Colonia del Rosario Oriental hasta el Dia de Hoy (Montevideo, Imprenta "El Siglo Ilustrado," 1928, pp. 52), pp. 7-10, 23, 24, 26, 30, 43; Mackay, The Other Spanish Christ, p. 234.

[180] Braga and Grubb, op. cit., pp. 59-61.

ment, partly through their own efforts, and partly by aid from abroad, in time these formed strong churches. The Brazilian Government early gave stipends to the Protestant pastors who cared for the larger communities.[181] The smaller groups were not provided for in this fashion. As a result, many Protestant parents had their children baptized by Roman Catholic priests.[182] Some communities chose lay preachers, several of whom proved unworthy or incompetent.[183] Beginning in the 1860's, however, organizations in Germany commenced to take an active interest. In 1861 the Basel Mission began sending men. In 1867 these organized a synod. In 1881 ten Basel brothers were at work in Brazil.[184] Men also came from the Barmen seminary.[185] A *Deutscher Verein für Pastoration in Brazilien* was formed.[186] In the 1870's financial subsidies began coming for German Protestant churches in Brazil, Argentina, and Chile from the Evangelical Church of Prussia.[187] By the year 1914 assistance was derived from several bodies in Germany.[188] In time the strongest of the German Protestant churches in Brazil was the *Deutsche Evangelische Gemeinde*, in which both Lutheran and Reformed joined.[189] In 1900 the Missouri Synod, a strong, aggressive Lutheran body in the United States, inaugurated an enterprise in Brazil which ultimately brought several thousands into its fellowship.[190] Numbers of independent Protestant congregations were formed among the Germans in Brazil. There were also German Baptists and Seventh Day Adventists.[191]

German Protestants in Argentina, Uruguay, and Chile were gathered into churches. To assist in this process help came from Germany. A little was contributed from the United States.[192]

In 1908 a missionary from the United States assembled in Buenos Aires a congregation of Swedish Lutherans.[193]

---

[181] Schlatter, *Geschichte der Basler Mission 1815-1915,* Vol. I, p. 89; Mecham, *Church and State in Latin America,* p. 315.

[182] Schlatter, *op. cit.,* Vol. I, p. 89.

[183] Braga and Grubb, *op. cit.,* p. 50.

[184] Schlatter, *op. cit.,* Vol. I, p. 90.

[185] Braga and Grubb, *op. cit.,* p. 51.

[186] Schlatter, *op. cit.,* Vol. I, p. 90.

[187] Philip Schaff and S. I. Prine, editors, *History, Essays, Orations, and Other Documents of the Sixth General Conference of the Evangelical Alliance . . . 1873* (New York, Harper & Brothers, 1874, pp. iv, 773), pp. 650ff.

[188] *The Lutheran World Almanac, 1921,* p. 201.

[189] Braga and Grubb, *op. cit.,* p. 51. See also Tucker, *The Bible in Brazil,* p. 284.

[190] Braga and Grubb, *op. cit.,* pp. 51, 52.

[191] Braga and Grubb, *op. cit.,* p. 52.

[192] Schlatter, *op. cit.,* Vol. I, p. 90; O. von Barchwitz-Krauser, *Six Years with William Taylor in South America* (Boston, McDonald & Gill, 1885, pp. 332), *passim;* Arms, *History of the William Taylor Self-Supporting Missions in South America,* p. 83.

[193] Drach, *Our Church Abroad,* p. 96.

On Corn Island, off the coast of Nicaragua, the entire population of slightly less than 1,000, English-speaking, presumably largely of Negro blood and stemming from the British West Indies, were said to be Baptists.[194]

From Russia in 1877 came German-speaking Stundists.[195]

After the defeat of the Dutch republics of South Africa by the British, early in the twentieth century, some of the Boers, Reformed by faith, sought escape from the hated British rule by migration to South America.[196]

French-speaking Swiss Baptists came to Argentina and called a pastor from the mother country.[197]

In Argentina there were Dutch of the Reformed faith.[198]

Protestants, chiefly Anglicans, put forth efforts to reach the considerable Japanese immigration to Brazil.[199]

The Protestant Episcopal Church undertook to care, so far as possible, for the growing migration from the United States into Mexico, especially Northern Mexico.[200]

To the Canal Zone in Panama, especially during the building of the Canal in the early years of the twentieth century, came many Protestants as engineers and labourers, some from the United States and some·from the West Indies. For these not a little provision was made, notably by the Protestant Episcopal Church,[201] the Methodist Episcopal Church,[202] and the English Wesleyans.[203] Indeed, as early as the 1880's the Methodist synod of Jamaica sent representatives to care for its members who had gone to Panama to work on the Lesseps canal.[204]

Protestants were not content to restrict their efforts to non-Christian aborigines and to immigrants of their branch of the faith. They also endeavoured to reach the Roman Catholics of Latin America. In accordance with our purpose to centre our attention upon the spread of Christianity and to pass hurriedly

[194] Price, *Banana Land,* pp. 86-91.

[195] Browning, *The River Plate Republics,* p. 62

[196] Richter, *Die evangelische Mission in Fern- und Südost Asien, Australien, Amerika,* pp. 347, 348; Browning, *op. cit.,* p. 53.

[197] Browning, *op. cit.,* p. 54.

[198] *Eighty-Second Annual Report of the Missionary Society of the Methodist Episcopal Church, 1900,* p. 301; Beets, *Toiling and Trusting,* pp. 313-316.

[199] Braga and Grubb, *op. cit.,* pp. 81, 111.

[200] *Handbooks on the Missions of the Episcopal Church, No. vii, Mexico,* pp. 29ff.

[201] *Annual Report of the Board of Missions . . . September, 1, 1913 to September 1, 1914,* pp. 91, 92.

[202] *Annual Report of the Board of Foreign Missions of the Methodist Episcopal Church for the Year 1914,* pp. 260, 261.

[203] *The Ninety-Ninth Annual Report of the Wesleyan Methodist Missionary Society (1913),* pp. 185, 186.

[204] Findlay and Holdsworth, *The History of the Wesleyan Methodist Missionary Society,* Vol. II, p. 402.

over the enterprises for the winning of adherents of one communion by another, we must content ourselves with the barest of summaries, very incomplete, of this phase of the history of Christianity in Latin America. Moreover, in 1914, measured by numerical results, the effect of these Protestant missions to Roman Catholics was not particularly impressive. By that year the total communicant strength of the churches which had issued from them was somewhat less than 120,000. This total was considerably smaller than that of those Protestant bodies which by that date had arisen in the British West Indies and the Guianas from the previously non-Christian Negro population.[205] However, we must pay some attention to these Protestant efforts for Roman Catholics, for they were carried on by several hundred missionaries and eventually worked significant alterations in the religious picture in Latin America. In the quarter century after 1914 the churches arising from them more than quadrupled in size[206] and, moving towards independence of foreign assistance, became increasingly an integral part of the life of the region.

It is not surprising that Protestants felt impelled to carry their form of the faith to Latin America. The type of Roman Catholicism which they saw there seemed to them little if any better than paganism. They were scandalized by the lax morals of many of the clergy and by the ignorance and superstition of a large proportion of the masses. The sag in morale in the Roman Catholic Church which, as we have seen in the earlier sections of this chapter, was one of the consequences of the passing of the colonial regime, made the need for another type of Christianity appear even more imperative.

It was to be expected that some of the earliest Protestant enterprises for Roman Catholics would be by the British. The prominence of the British in nineteenth-century Protestant missions combined with the importance of British merchants and capital in the nineteenth-century economy of Latin America made such activity almost inevitable.

The British and Foreign Bible Society was early in the field. Between 1821 and 1824 several thousand Bibles and New Testaments in Spanish and Portuguese were distributed.[207] James Thomson, a Scot, an agent of the British and Foreign Bible Society and of the Lancastrian Educational Society, had for a brief time amazing success. He came to South America when the first flush of revolution was on the land, when the higher clergy, Spanish-born and in general opposed to independence, were discredited, and when many of the laity and the lower clergy, native-born, were inclined to be liberal and open to new

[205] Beach and St. John, *World Statistics of Christian Missions*, p. 59.
[206] Parker, *Interpretative Statistical Survey of the World Mission of the Christian Church*, p. 19.
[207] Canton, *A History of the British and Foreign Bible Society*, Vol. II, p. 83.

ideas. In Argentina he was made an honorary citizen and in Buenos Aires soon had about a hundred Lancastrian schools in operation with the Bible as a text-book. In Chile he was also made an honorary citizen. In Bogotá in a meeting held in a Dominican monastery he organized a Bible Society and enjoyed the friendship and assistance of some of the clergy.[208] He went on to Mexico (1827-1830, and again in 1842-1843) and there also at the outset was aided by several of the priests.[209] After the initial auspicious opening, in several areas a reaction seemed to undo most of what had been accomplished. The higher clergy, asserting themselves, forbade the faithful the possession of the Bibles thus distributed. The Bible Society at Bogotá disappeared.[210] Yet eventually the ground lost was more than regained. In the years 1856-1860 an agent of the British and Foreign Bible Society sold thousands of copies of the Bible in Colombia.[211] In the 1830's the Society is said to have succeeded in introducing copies of the Scriptures into Guatemala and Honduras.[212] In the 1840's an Englishman, Crowe, circulated Bibles and Protestant tracts and opened a Protestant school in Guatemala, but Roman Catholic opposition brought the enterprise to an early end.[213] In Brazil, Argentina, and Chile in the second half of the nineteenth century representatives of the Society were particularly active. By 1889 the Bible was being distributed in Brazil from forty-one sub-depots.[214] From 1863 to 1878 agents of the Society were again in Mexico and withdrew only because that country seemed a more natural field, for obvious geographical reasons, for the sister organization, the American Bible Society.[215]

What is said to have been the first Protestant sermon in Spanish in Argentina was preached in 1867 by John Francis Thomson. He was so polemical and anti-Roman Catholic that the attention he at first attracted among leading citizens was followed by a sharp revulsion.[216]

The South American Missionary Society extended its activities to Spanish-speaking Roman Catholics. Notably at Rosario and the adjacent Alberdi, in Argentina, and in Brazil, representatives of that organization laboured among Roman Catholics.[217]

---

[208] Mackay, *The Other Spanish Christ*, pp. 234-237; Canton, *op. cit.*, Vol. II, p. 84.
[209] Canton, *op. cit.*, Vol. II, pp. 86, 92-96, 347-350.
[210] Canton, *op. cit.*, Vol. II, pp. 92-96, 347-350.
[211] Canton, *op. cit.*, Vol. III, pp. 123-125.
[212] Grubb, *Religion in Central America*, p. 39.
[213] Crowe, *The Gospel in Central America*, pp. 528ff.
[214] Canton, *op. cit.*, Vol. III, pp. 125-142, Vol. IV, pp. 322-328.
[215] Canton, *op. cit.*, Vol. III, pp. 142-147.
[216] Mackay, *op. cit.*, p. 240.
[217] Young, *From Cape Horn to Panama*, pp. 102-113, 192, 193.

A unique and astonishing enterprise arose in Buenos Aires from the devotion of an Englishman, William Case Morris. Left motherless himself when little more than an infant, Morris conceived an especial interest in children, and particularly motherless children. While a clerk in Buenos Aires towards the latter part of the nineteenth century he began a school for children, primarily for the underprivileged. Eventually he was ordained in the Church of England and gave his entire time to his chosen work. Funds came from citizens of the city. In the course of the years tens of thousands of boys and girls passed through his schools. He sought to reach adults with the Christian message. He translated into Spanish a number of Protestant religious books. He lived on well past 1914, greatly beloved.[218]

In Paraguay a physician laboured among the nominally Roman Catholic Indian population in association with the South American Missionary Society.[219]

From an amalgamation of three societies, the South American Evangelical Mission, founded in 1897, the Help for Brazil Mission, begun in 1892, and the South American section of the Regions Beyond Missionary Union, there was inaugurated, in 1911, with headquarters in London, the Evangelical Union of South America.[220] This had missions in Brazil, Argentina, and Peru.[221]

The Help for Brazil Mission had been organized by Robert Reid Kalley, a Scotch physician, to assist Congregational churches which had arisen in Brazil, partly from his efforts. The first of these churches was organized in 1858. A convention of the Congregational churches was formed in 1913. Through them, in 1908, a Congregational Church was instituted in Lisbon, Portugal. It must be said that these churches, although called Congregational, declined to baptize infants and hence were nearly akin to the Baptists.[222]

In the 1890's two men from the East London Mission Institute, under the Missions Beyond Missionary Union, went to Cuzco, Peru. In spite of local opposition which led to temporary withdrawals, the enterprise persisted.[223]

The Christian Missions in Many Lands, as the overseas efforts of the

[218] Every, *South American Memories of Thirty Years*, pp. 21-33; Mackay, *op. cit.*, pp. 244, 245; *The South American Missionary Society Annual Report 1910-1911*, p. 5.
[219] J. W. Lindsay, *The Life of a Non-Professional Missionary* (London, World Dominion Press, no date, pp. 21), *passim*.
[220] Strong and Warnshuis, *Directory of Foreign Missions*, p. 29.
[221] *South America* (London, The organ of the Evangelical Union of South America, 1912-1915), Vol. IV, pp. 3ff. On the work of the Evangelical Union of South America in Brazil, see Frederick C. Glass, *With the Bible in Brazil* (London, Morgan & Scott, 1914, pp. 164), *passim*, and Fred. C. Glass, *Through the Heart of Brazil* (Liverpool, The South American Evangelical Mission, no date, pp. iv, 135), *passim*.
[222] Braga and Grubb, *The Republic of Brazil*, pp. 54-57.
[223] Wood in *Protestant Missions in South America*, pp. 152, 153.

Plymouth Brethren were generally known, were active in several Latin American countries.[224]

In 1898 the Canadian Baptists began the first continuing Protestant mission in Bolivia.[225]

The enterprises of the Protestants of the United States among the Roman Catholics of Latin America were far more prominent than were those of the Protestants of the British Isles.

At first thought this was to be anticipated. The United States and Latin America were in the same hemisphere. Although in practice wide divergencies appeared, on paper the framework of the governments of Latin America owed an obvious debt to the pattern given by the slightly older republic of the North. Through its Monroe Doctrine the United States exercised a benevolent although not always welcome semi-protectorate over Latin America. Beginning in 1889-1890 conferences of the American republics met from time to time at the instance of the United States. The Government of the United States was particularly active in the affairs of Mexico, Central America, and the Caribbean. Not far from the end of the period it built the Panama Canal.

Yet on second thought it was not so clear that the Protestants of the United States would or could interest themselves in religious conditions in Latin America, or at least in Latin America south of Central America and the Caribbean. Culturally Latin America and the United States were separated by a vast gulf. The one looked to Latin Europe, chiefly to France, Portugal, and Spain, for intellectual and spiritual fellowship. The other looked to Northern Europe, chiefly to Great Britain. The United States was suspect in Latin America as a potential aggressor, especially after its territorial gains at the expense of Mexico and its policies in Central America and the Caribbean. Among the vocal intellectuals it was often disliked and despised. In most of South America during this period the commerce and investments of the United States were much less than those of Great Britain. That, under these circumstances, the Protestant churches of the United States inaugurated extensive enterprises among the Roman Catholics of Latin America, including those of South America, was not to be automatically predicted. It was not due to either political or commercial imperialism. It came about partly through the missionary purpose of those churches which regarded the entire human race as their field and partly through a somewhat unrealistic idealism which exaggerated the community of interest brought by common republican institutions and cohabitation of the same hemisphere.

[224] Beach and St. John, *World Statistics of Christian Missions*, pp. 72-74.
[225] Browning, Ritchie and Grubb, *The West Coast Republics of South America*, p. 126.

In the first flush of peace which followed the end of the Napoleonic Wars and with the news of the independence movements in Latin America, the nascent foreign missionary interest of the churches of the United States was in part directed towards Latin America. Samuel J. Mills was intensely interested in Latin America and sought to induce the newly formed American Bible Society to extend its activities to the region.[226] In 1819 the American Bible Society sent 500 New Testaments to Buenos Aires for use in the public schools.[227] In the 1820's it helped in a number of ways in the preparation and distribution of the Scriptures in South America.[228] The United Foreign Missionary Society, organized in 1817 by the Presbyterians, the Dutch Reformed, and the Associate Reformed Church, had as one of its objectives Mexico and South America.[229] About 1820 the influential biographer of Mills was calling attention to what he believed to be the opportunity in Latin America.[230] In that same decade clergymen from the United States were residing in Buenos Aires and in 1827 a Sunday school there had a class for Spanish children.[231] In the 1830's and 1840's the Methodist Episcopal Church possessed agents in South America. In the 1840's they were at Rio de Janeiro and Buenos Aires.[232] Before 1850 the American Seamen's Friend Society had a chaplain at Valparaiso. The Foreign Evangelical Association shared in his support.[233]

It was not until the second half of the nineteenth century that Protestant missions from the United States assumed significant dimensions in Latin America. That they then became important was due to a variety of factors—chiefly the increase in religious liberty and political stability in Latin America, and the growing share of the churches of the United States in the entire Protestant foreign missionary enterprise. Up to 1914 the Latin-American missions from the United States enjoyed a rapid growth. As we are to see in the final volume, the War of 1914-1918 did not bring about any diminution in them. After 1914, indeed, they continued to increase. We can more conveniently survey the story if we summarize it country by country.

Being so near to the United States, with so long a joint boundary, Mexico was profoundly affected by the larger country. In the second half of the nineteenth century, Protestant missions from the United States began to flourish.

[226] Spring, *Memoirs of the Rev. Samuel J. Mills*, p. 116.
[227] Dwight, *The Centennial History of the American Bible Society*, Vol. I, pp. 56, 57.
[228] Dwight, *op. cit.*, Vol. I, pp. 75-82.
[229] Brown, *One Hundred Years*, p. 16.
[230] Spring, *op. cit.*, pp. 105-107.
[231] *Thirty-Second Annual Report of the Missionary Society of the Methodist Episcopal Church, 1851*, pp. 120, 121
[232] *Twenty-First Annual Report of the Missionary Society of the Methodist Episcopal Church, 1840*, p. 15; Tucker in *Protestant Missions in South America*, p. 77.
[233] *Twentieth Annual Report of the American Seamen's Friend Society, 1848*, p. 7.

In 1859 a Mexican celebrated what is said to have been the first Protestant communion in Mexico.[234] Miss Melinda Rankin, on her own initiative, but eventually aided by the American and Foreign Christian Union, an undenominational Protestant organization whose chief purpose was the spread of Protestant Christianity among Roman Catholics, in 1852 went to Brownsville, on the Texas side of the Rio Grande, to be as near to Mexico as possible. There she began a school, chiefly for Mexicans, until such time as their country should be open for Protestant efforts.[235] In 1865 she went to Monterey, seeking to make that the headquarters for Protestantism in Mexico. There before many years she purchased property for her enterprise and commenced the subsidizing of Mexican converts as missionaries among their own people.[236] In 1860 the American Bible Society sent an agent into Mexico. The following year two Mexicans joined a Protestant church in Brownsville.[237] Not far from that time a representative of the American Tract Society in Texas, James Hickey, an Irish convert from Roman Catholicism, because of his Union sympathies in the Civil War in the United States was forced to flee to Mexico. He went to Monterey, became an agent of the American Bible Society, and collected a congregation of converts.[238] In the 1860's Protestantism gained admission to Zacatecas, and in 1872, since the American and Foreign Christian Union could not do so, the Northern Presbyterians placed a missionary there.[239] In 1870 the Northern Baptists entered Monterey.[240] In 1873, because of lack of funds, the American and Foreign Christian Union turned over Miss Rankin's mission to the American Board of Commissioners for Foreign Missions.[241] Between 1870 and 1880 there had also entered Mexico the Northern Methodists (1873),[242] the Southern Presbyterians (1874),[243] the Southern Methodists, the Society of

[234] Camargo and Grubb, *Religion in the Republic of Mexico*, pp. 87, 88.

[235] Rankin, *Twenty Years among the Mexicans*, pp. 36ff.

[236] Rankin, *op. cit.*, pp. 120ff.

[237] Rankin, *op. cit.*, p. 88.

[238] Rankin, *op. cit.*, pp. 88, 89; Stewart, *Later Baptist Missionaries and Pioneers*, Vol. II, pp. 39-61.

[239] Rankin, *op. cit.*, pp. 141, 142.

[240] Rankin, *op. cit.*, p. 165.

[241] Rankin, *op. cit.*, p. 142. On some phases of the later development of that enterprise, see James Demarest Eaton, *Life under Two Flags* (New York, A. S. Barnes and Co., 1922, pp. viii, 297), pp. 74ff.

[242] On the Northern Methodists see *1873-1923. Souvenir Book of the Golden Anniversary or Jubilee of the Methodist Episcopal Church in Mexico* (Mexico, Casa Unida de Publicaciones, 1924, pp. 106), *passim; Thirteen Years in Mexico* (from *Letters of Charles W. Drees*), edited by *Ada M. C. Drees* (New York, The Abingdon Press, 1915, pp. 276), *passim;* John Wesley Butler, *History of the Methodist Episcopal Church in Mexico. Personal Reminiscences, Present Conditions and Future Outlook* (New York, The Methodist Book Concern, 1918, pp. 156), *passim.*

[243] On the Southern Presbyterians see Wm. A. Ross, *Sunrise in Aztec Land. Being an account of the Mission Work that has been carried on in Mexico since 1874 by the Pres-

Friends, and the Associate Reformed Presbyterian Church.[244] Through co-operating with a movement arising in the 1850's, partly from an indigenous secession from the Roman Catholic Church and partly through a clergyman from the United States, the Protestant Episcopal Church won a foothold in Mexico. Provision was later made by the Protestant Episcopal Church for the religious care of those from the United States who lived in Mexico, and in 1906 the Mexican movement and the one for the settlers coalesced.[245] Later a number of other societies commenced operations in the country, among them the Disciples of Christ.[246] In 1902 the International Committee of the Young Men's Christian Associations added its strength.[247]

This Protestant enterprise did not have an unobstructed course. The Roman Catholic clergy offered vigorous opposition and legal restrictions were long in being removed.[248] Most of the converts were from the lowly, for the country largely lacked a middle class and the upper classes generally held Protestantism in disdain.[249] Relatively few came from the pure-blooded Indian majority.[250]

Not far from 1915 there were about 22,000 Protestant communicants in Mexico.[251] Protestantism was weakest in the West. It was strongest in the North, where influences from the United States were potent, around Mexico City, and in Chiapas in the South.[252] It operated chiefly through evangelism and the gathering and strengthening of schools.[253] In many places its schools were pioneers of rural education.[254] In spite of the fact that it had been active for only slightly more than half a century, by 1914 Protestant Christianity, planted chiefly from the United States, was beginning to have some effect in Mexico.

In 1856 D. H. Wheeler was appointed by the American Bible Society as agent for Central America and was killed in an effort to circulate the Scriptures in that area.[255] The first continuing Protestant effort from the United States for the nominally Roman Catholic population of Central America was by the

byterian Church in the United States (Richmond, Presbyterian Committee of Publication, 1922, pp. 244), *passim.*

[244] Camargo and Grubb, *op. cit.,* p. 89.

[245] *Handbooks on the Missions of the Episcopal Church: No. VII. Mexico, passim.*

[246] *Survey of Service. Disciples of Christ,* pp. 441-456. For the other missions see Winton, *Mexico To-day,* table opposite p. 219.

[247] Winton, *op. cit.,* table opposite p. 219.

[248] Callcott, *Liberalism in Mexico, 1857-1929,* p. 109.

[249] Winton, *op. cit.,* p. 183.

[250] Camargo and Grubb, *op. cit.,* p. 99.

[251] Beach and St. John, *World Statistics of Christian Missions,* p. 74.

[252] Camargo and Grubb, *op. cit.,* p. 98.

[253] Winton, *op. cit.,* p. 187.

[254] Camargo and Grubb, *op. cit.,* p. 44.

[255] *Seventy-Second Annual Report of the American Bible Society . . . 1888,* p. 95.

Northern Presbyterians, and was not begun until 1882. John C. Hill and his wife then arrived, their travelling expenses met by the President of Guatemala. For a number of years Guatemala City was the only centre. Not until 1898 was another station opened.[256] More extensive was the Central American Mission. This was organized in 1890 through the initiative of C. I. Scofield. It was one of the undenominational enterprises, of which the China Inland Mission was the largest representative, which sought primarily to broadcast the Christian message, which did not directly solicit either missionaries or funds, and which paid no fixed salaries. Its first missionaries were appointed in 1891 and by 1902 it had thirty-three missionaries working in all five of the then existing republics of Central America.[257] In 1911 the American Baptist Home Mission Society gained a foothold in El Salvador.[258] Quakers of the California Yearly Meeting entered Guatemala early in the twentieth century and extended their operations to Honduras.[259] Through various agencies parts or all of the Bible were translated into several of the Indian tongues of the area.[260] In 1891 the Seventh Day Adventists made their way to the region.[261] The enterprises inaugurated by some of the other denominations among the Protestants in the Canal Zone later spread to the Spanish-speaking population. In 1862 the American and Foreign Christian Union had a missionary at Panama.[262] Central America was being penetrated by Protestantism.

In the Spanish-speaking North and West coasts of South America, with the exception of Chile, Protestantism, whether from the United States or elsewhere, did not win a very large following. This is said to have been because the culture inherited from colonial days persisted less altered than in the South and South-east.[263]

In Venezuela, what seems to have been the first resident Protestant missionary was an agent of the American Bible Society, who arrived in 1887 or 1888.[264] A former Capuchin held Bible classes in his house. For a time a church was assembled under the Southern Methodist Board.[265] In 1897 Theodore S. Pond

[256] Brown, *One Hundred Years*, pp. 825, 826.
[257] *The Central American Bulletin*, Vol. VIII, No. 4, Oct., 1902, pp. 4, 7; Grubb, *Religion in Central America*, pp. 33-36.
[258] White, *A Century of Faith*, pp. 201-207.
[259] Beach and St. John, *op. cit.*, p. 74.
[260] Grubb, *op. cit.*, pp. 41, 42.
[261] Beach and St. John, *op. cit.*, p. 74.
[262] *The Christian World*, Vol. XIII, p. 315.
[263] Baker, *Christian Missions and a New World Culture*, pp. 208-210.
[264] *Seventy-Second Annual Report of the American Bible Society . . . 1888*, p. 94; *Seventy-Third Annual Report of the American Bible Society . . . 1889*, p. 107.
[265] Brown, *op. cit.*, pp. 829, 830.

and his wife, representing the Northern Presbyterians, went to Caracas and there began a continuing mission of their denomination.[266] The Scandinavian Alliance Mission of North America followed in 1906 and the Seventh Day Adventists in 1911.[267]

From 1853 to 1869 the American and Foreign Christian Union had a man in Colombia.[268] Presbyterian missionaries from the United States entered Colombia in 1856. From that beginning, a substantial enterprise was gradually developed in Bogotá. Not many converts were made, but schools were opened, and eventually missionaries were placed at other centres.[269]

Loyally Roman Catholic Ecuador was very late in being penetrated by Protestant missionaries. In 1897, about the time that an anti-clerical government began to effect a modicum of religious toleration, W. E. Reed, at first connected with the Gospel Union of Kansas City, entered the country. In spite of bitter opposition he succeeded in remaining. Eventually he became associated with the Christian and Missionary Alliance and was the superintendent of its work in that republic.[270] The Seventh Day Adventists came in 1906.[271]

In Peru, the sojourn of James Thomson, of the British and Foreign Bible Society, in 1822-1824, was followed, about 1834, by a two months' visit in Lima by I. W. Wheelwright, agent of the American Bible Society for the west coast of South America.[272] From 1860 to 1864 the American and Foreign Christian Union had missionaries in Peru.[273] In 1888 Francisco G. Penzotti, representing the American Bible Society and sent from the Methodist mission in Argentina, took up his residence in Callao. He built up a large congregation, but he was imprisoned for his religious activities, and it was only after a sensational trial, finally before the supreme court, and through the pressure of public opinion in the United States that he was released (1891). The outcome of the case meant that the legal battle for the toleration of Protestantism was practically won.[274] In 1903 came the Holiness Church of California,[275] in 1906 the

---

[266] Brown, *op. cit.,* pp. 829-831.

[267] *Seventh-day Adventist Conferences, Missions and Institutions. Fifty-first Annual Statistical Report . . . 1913.*

[268] *The Christian World,* Vol. XXIV, p. 77.

[269] Brown, *op. cit.,* pp. 792, 793.

[270] W. F. Jordan, *Ecuador. A Story of Mission Achievement* (New York, The Christian Alliance Publishing Co., 1926, pp. 130), *passim.*

[271] *Seventh-day Adventist Conferences, Missions and Institutions. Fifty-first Annual Statistical Report . . . 1913.*

[272] *Annual Reports of the American Bible Society,* Vol. I, p. 787, 788.

[273] *The Christian World,* Vol. XXIV, p. 77.

[274] Browning, Ritchie, and Grubb, *The West Coast Republics of South America,* pp. 79, 80.

[275] Browning, Ritchie, and Grubb, *op. cit.,* p. 83.

Seventh Day Adventists,[276] in 1910 the Salvation Army, and in 1914 the Church of the Nazarene.[277]

In 1877 William Taylor began a tour of South America from which was to spring an extensive enterprise of the Methodist Episcopal Church on the west coast. William Taylor was a Methodist who had already had notable experience as an evangelist in California during the Gold Rush, in Australia, South Africa, Canada, Great Britain, and India. Later, as bishop of his church, he was to win an important place in missions in Negro Africa.[278] It was his programme to establish self-supporting missions. This was to be done through schools, staffed by recruits from the United States and sustained primarily by fees and subscriptions from local residents, foreign and native. Most of the missionaries were placed in Peru, but for a time some were also in Bolivia, Central America, and Brazil.[279] When, in 1884, Taylor was elected bishop for Africa, the care of the Latin-American missions was entrusted to the Transit and Building Fund Society of Bishop Taylor's Self-supporting Missions, formed especially for that purpose.[280] After a transition stage which was somewhat chequered organizationally, in 1904 these missions were taken under the care of the Missionary Society of the Methodist Episcopal Church on the same basis as its other enterprises.[281]

The way having been partly opened by Taylor's initiative, in 1891 the Methodists appointed T. B. Wood, long connected with the mission in that country, as presiding elder for the district of Peru.[282] They took over Penzotti's congregation in Callao and later extended their efforts to other cities.[283]

In Bolivia, after a loss of territory which cut it off from the coastal towns in which Taylor had inaugurated missions, Protestantism from the United States was late in obtaining a continuous footing. In the 1880's, Milne, of the American Bible Society, made his way into the country. Not until 1901, however, was a permanent mission begun from the United States. That was by the Methodists, entering from the west coast.[284] The Canadian Baptists and the

[276] Seventh-day Adventist Conferences, Missions, and Institutions. Fifty-first Annual Statistical Report . . . 1913.

[277] Browning, Ritchie, and Grubb, op. cit., p. 83.

[278] Taylor, Story of My Life, passim.

[279] Taylor, op. cit., p. 680; Taylor, Our South American Cousins, passim.

[280] Arms, History of the Williams Taylor Self-supporting Missions in South America, pp. 93-96.

[281] Arms, op. cit., pp. 188-208.

[282] Seventy-third Annual Report of the Missionary Society of the Methodist Episcopal Church . . . 1891, p. 56.

[283] Browning, Ritchie, and Grubb, op. cit., p. 82.

[284] Browning, Ritchie, and Grubb, op. cit., p. 126.

Plymouth Brethren had preceded them (in the 1890's).[285] After them came the Peniel Missionary Society (1906) and the Seventh Day Adventists (1907).[286]

In 1914 Chile had more Protestants than all the other republics of the west coast of South America combined. This may have been because the old order was not so strong there as in sections in which the colonial regime had been centred. Presumably, too, the temperate climate and the presence of fairly large groups of Protestant merchants and immigrants had a favouring influence. In 1845, in conjunction with the American Seamen's Friend Society, the Foreign Evangelical Society, later merged in the American and Foreign Christian Union, sent David Trumbull to Valparaiso as chaplain for British and American residents and seamen. In 1855 the congregation which he had gathered built the first Protestant church structure in the country.[287] A man of great charm and force of character, Trumbull made a strong impression on the Chileans. From time to time the American and Foreign Christian Union sent out additional missionaries. In 1873, at the request of the society and its missionaries because of shortage of its funds the Northern Presbyterians took over its interests.[288] The Northern Methodists continued and enlarged what had been begun by Taylor. Before the end of the nineteenth century the Seventh Day Adventists and the Christian and Missionary Alliance entered Chile. Not many years before 1914 came the Young Men's Christian Association.[289] In 1910 a Pentecostal movement began through the preaching of a former member of the Methodist mission. It was marked by emotional extravagances but by high moral demands and at first had its chief hold among the lower social and economic strata. It eventually assumed fairly large numerical dimensions.[290]

By 1914 Argentina contained slightly more Protestants who had been won from Roman Catholicism by missionaries from the United States than did Chile. Moreover, more organizations were represented.[291] Much of this activity was in and around Buenos Aires, and that centre had a much larger population than any city on the west coast. In the 1820's and again in the 1850's the Presbyterians made brief attempts at missions.[292] In 1858 the American Bible

[285] Beach and St. John, *World Statistics of Christian Missions,* p. 73.
[286] *Ibid.*
[287] Browning, Ritchie, and Grubb, *op. cit.,* pp. 27-29.
[288] *The Thirty-Seventh Annual Report of the Board of Foreign Missions of the Presbyterian Church in the United States of America, 1874,* p. 23; *The Christian World,* Vol. XXIV, p. 168.
[289] Beach and St. John, *op. cit.,* p. 72.
[290] Mackay, *The Other Spanish Christ,* pp. 247, 248.
[291] Beach and St. John, *op. cit.,* p. 72.
[292] Browning, *The River Plate Republics,* pp. 52, 53.

Society appointed an agent for the republics of the Plate area.[293] In 1836 the Methodists sent a man to Buenos Aires, but regular efforts to reach the Spanish-speaking population were not put forth until the 1860's.[294] By the end of the century Methodist activities were carried on at a number of points and included schools and a theological seminary.[295] The Christian Woman's Board of Missions (of the Disciples of Christ) entered Buenos Aires in 1906.[296] The Young Women's Christian Association came to Buenos Aires in 1890 and the Young Men's Christian Association in 1901.[297] The Christian and Missionary Alliance and the Seventh Day Adventists both entered in the 1890's. The first missionary of the Southern Baptists arrived in 1903.[298] The Methodists had by far the largest following.

In Uruguay by 1914, of the organizations from the United States, the Methodists, the Young Men's Christian Association, the Southern Baptists, the American Bible Society, and the Seventh Day Adventists were represented, with the Methodists leading in numbers.[299]

By 1914 the Methodists, the American Bible Society, and the Seventh Day Adventists had also established themselves in Paraguay.[300]

Of all the Latin-American countries, it was in Brazil that by 1914 Protestant missions from the United States achieved the most striking successes. Indeed, Protestantism as a whole was stronger in that land than in any other in Latin America. The reasons for this prosperity are not entirely clear. They are probably to be found partly in the fact that Brazil had a larger population and area than any other Latin-American state, partly in the early grant (even though incomplete) of religious liberty and the usually tolerant attitude of the government, partly in the substantial enclaves of Protestant emigrants, more considerable than in any other South American state (although by no means all of these groups were active in seeking to win their Roman Catholic neighbours to their form of the faith), partly in a certain receptiveness of Brazilians to new ideas from abroad, and partly in the weakening of the old patterns of life in the striking development in wealth and population which occurred in the South, the region (except in and around Pernambuco, where it was also

[293] *Seventy-second Annual Report of the American Bible Society . . . 1888*, p. 95.
[294] *Eightieth Annual Report of the Missionary Society of the Methodist Episcopal Church . . . 1898*, p. 271.
[295] *Eighty-third Annual Report of the Missionary Society of the Methodist Episcopal Church . . . 1901*, pp. 266ff.
[296] *Survey of Service, Disciples of Christ*, pp. 457ff.
[297] *International Survey of the Young Men's and Young Women's Christian Associations*, pp. 322ff.
[298] Beach and St. John, *op. cit.*, p. 72.
[299] *Ibid.*
[300] *Ibid.*

strong) in which Protestantism had its most marked growth.[301] Yet it must be said that in Argentina, especially around Buenos Aires, where many of these same factors were present, proportionately the growth of Protestantism at the expense of Roman Catholicism was much less striking. The causes for the difference are uncertain. Not even the existence of a much larger missionary body in Brazil is sufficient to account for it—at least as against Argentina. In Mexico, in which by 1914 the body of Protestants gathered from Roman Catholics by missionaries from the United States was less than half of that in Brazil, the missionary force coming from the United States was only a fourth smaller. It must also be said that in proportion to the population the number of Protestants in Brazil arising from missions from the United States was somewhat larger than in Mexico.[302]

It was not until the second half of the nineteenth century that Protestants from the United States planted a continuing missionary staff in Brazil. To be sure, in the second decade of the century the American Bible Society had begun to send the Scriptures to that country.[303] In the second half of the century the activities of the American Bible Society increased. Numbers of colporteurs travelled through the land, distributing the Bible.[304] In 1857 R. Nesbit lost his life on the upper reaches of the Amazon in an attempt to circulate the Scriptures.[305] In 1835 the Methodist Episcopal Church sent a representative to South America who preached in Rio de Janeiro for a few months. He was followed by another in 1836 who laboured chiefly among foreigners but gathered a Sunday school in which were a few Brazilians. Further Methodist missionaries arrived in 1838. In 1842 this Methodist effort was suspended.[306] From the comprehensive plans of William Taylor a few missions manned by Northern Methodists were begun in Brazil. These also were eventually discontinued.[307] Reaching north from Uruguay, for several years the Northern Methodists

[301] Mackay, *The Other Spanish Christ,* pp. 239, 240, suggests some of these reasons.
[302] About the year 1914 the Protestant churches founded in Brazil by missions from the United States had approximately 47,080 communicants as against 22,403 communicants in the Protestant churches in Mexico arising from missionaries from the United States and 4,911 in Argentina. Missionaries in Brazil from the United States numbered 282, as against 113 in Argentina and 219 in Mexico.—Beach and St. John, *op. cit.,* pp. 73, 74. In 1900 the population of Brazil was 17,318,556.—*Encyclopædia Britannica,* 14th ed., Vol. IV, p. 51. In 1900 that of Mexico was 13,607,219.—*Encyclopædia Britannica,* 14th ed., XV, p. 381.
[303] Braga and Grubb, *The Republic of Brazil,* pp. 48, 73.
[304] Hugh C. Tucker, *The Bible in Brazil. Colporter Experiences* (New York, Fleming H. Revell Co., 1902, pp. 293), *passim.*
[305] *Seventy-second Annual Report of the American Bible Society . . . 1888,* p. 95.
[306] Braga and Grubb, *op. cit.,* pp. 53, 54; G. E. Strobridge, *Biography of the Rev. Daniel Parish Kidder, D.D., LL.D.* (New York, Hunt & Eaton, 1894, pp. 357), pp. 87-135.
[307] Braga and Grubb, *op. cit.,* p. 62; Taylor, *Our South American Cousins,* pp. 347ff.

laboured in the southernmost section of Brazil, Rio Grande do Sul.[308] The spiritual sons of John Wesley were chiefly represented by the Methodist Episcopal Church, South. This was because of the immigration from the Southern states after the Civil War in the northern republic. In 1867 J. E. Newman arrived and became pastor of a church organized among these settlers. J. J. Ransom, who reached Brazil early in 1876, began preaching in Portuguese about two years later. Reinforcements came and numerous congregations arose.[309] For approximately a decade, 1851-1861, the American and Foreign Christian Union maintained missionaries in Brazil.[310] A missionary of the Presbyterians arrived in 1859. In 1862 what was said to be the first Presbyterian Church in the country was organized, and a presbytery in 1865.[311] Like the Southern Methodists, the Southern Presbyterians became interested in Brazil through the emigration from their section of the United States. In 1869 their first missionaries landed and others followed.[312] In 1888 the churches formed by the Northern and Southern Presbyterians came together in an autonomous Synod of Brazil.[313] This continued to be aided by missionaries from both the mother churches. Provision was early made for the training of an indigenous ministry and, partly through this leadership, Presbyterianism displayed a vigorous growth. In 1903, by a division, the Independent Presbyterian Church was formed, self-supporting from the very start.[314] It was also through the migration from the Southern states that the Southern Baptist Convention became sufficiently concerned about Brazil to appoint missionaries. On petition from the settlers, in 1879 a clergyman was sent. Soon two American churches were organized. Missionaries to the Brazilians sailed in 1881. The following year the first Brazilian Baptist church was organized. In 1894 the six existing Baptist churches associated themselves in a union. A national convention was formed in 1907. Membership rapidly increased.[315] In 1853 and again from

[308] Braga and Grubb, *op. cit.*, p. 62.

[309] Braga and Grubb, *op. cit.*, pp. 61, 62; *Annual Report of the Board of Missions of the Methodist Episcopal Church, South, June 1, 1876*, pp. 94-98.

[310] *The Christian World*, Vol. XXIV, p. 77.

[311] Brown, *One Hundred Years*, p. 795; Smith, *An Open Door in Brazil*, pp. 109, 110; Gammon, *The Evangelical Invasion of Brazil*, pp. 111, 112; George Hood, *Historical Sketch of the Missions in South America under the Care of the Board of Foreign Missions of the Presbyterian Church* (Philadelphia, Woman's Foreign Missionary Society of the Presbyterian Church, 1891, pp. 31), pp. 9ff.

[312] Smith, *op. cit.*, p. 127.

[313] Brown, *op. cit.*, p. 796; Gammon, *op. cit.*, pp. 125-128.

[314] Braga and Grubb, *op. cit.*, p. 87.

[315] Braga and Grubb, *op. cit.*, pp. 63, 64; Leon M. Reno and Alice W. Reno, *Reminiscences: Twenty-five Years in Victoria, Brasil* (Richmond, Educational Department, Foreign Mission Board Southern Baptist Convention, 1930, pp. 170), *passim;* T. B. Ray, *Brazilian Sketches* (Louisville, Baptist World Publishing Co., 1912, pp. 134), *passim;*

1859 to 1864 what proved to be abortive attempts were made on behalf of the Protestant Episcopal Church to found a mission in Brazil. In 1889 a continuing enterprise of the Episcopalians was begun in Rio Grande do Sul by J. W. Morris and L. L. Kinsolving. In 1899 Kinsolving was consecrated the first bishop of the *Egreja Episcopal Brasileira,* an independent church assisted by the Episcopalians of the United States. A successful beginning was early made in the training of a Brazilian clergy.[316] In 1894 the Seventh Day Adventists entered Brazil and began a thriving mission.[317] The pioneer secretary of the Young Men's Christian Association arrived in Brazil in 1893. A Young Men's Christian Association, the oldest on the continent, was organized in 1896.[318] It will be noticed that some of the larger denominations early became ecclesiastically independent of foreign control. This tended to reduce their foreign character.[319]

In Brazil the Protestant missions and churches made much of education. Schools, colleges, and theological seminaries were founded. The most noted was Mackenzie College, in São Paulo.[320] In 1908 the Lavras Agricultural School was inaugurated. It made important contributions to the agricultural side of the nation's life.[321] These schools, especially those of the Presbyterians, were eventually recognized to have been the cradle of the system of education later established by the government.[322]

In 1887 Protestants in Rio de Janeiro organized to form a hospital, an institution which ultimately became one of the best in the country.[323]

Puerto Rico seems not to have been touched by Protestant missions from the United States until after its cession to that country by Spain in 1898. On January 1st, 1899, the Stars and Stripes were raised over the island. Protestant missionaries at once entered. To prevent overlapping, the major denominations represented—Baptists, Congregationalists, Disciples of Christ, Methodists, Presbyterians, and United Brethren—agreed upon a division of fields. Within a

L. M. Bratcher, *Francisco Fulgencio Soren* (Nashville, Broadman Press, 1938, pp. 224), *passim.*

[316] *Handbooks of the Missions of the Episcopal Church, No. VI. South America,* pp. 60ff.

[317] *Seventh-day Adventist Conferences, Missions, and Institutions. Fifty-first Annual Statistical Report . . . 1913.*

[318] *International Survey of the Young Men's and Young Women's Christian Associations,* p. 326; Braga and Grubb, *op. cit.,* p. 77.

[319] Braga and Grubb, *op. cit.,* pp. 84, 85.

[320] Braga and Grubb, *op. cit.,* pp. 76, 77.

[321] Hunnicutt and Reed, *The Story of Agricultural Missions,* pp. 148ff.; Mackay, *The Other Spanish Christ,* p. 242.

[322] Braga and Grubb, *op. cit.,* p. 61.

[323] Braga and Grubb, *op. cit.,* p. 79.

few years an interdenominational union theological school was opened. Several other communions and societies established themselves. By 1915 not far from 9,000 communicants had been gathered, with the Baptists, Presbyterians, and United Brethren leading.[324]

The end of the Spanish-American War and the coming of independence brought for Cuba an extensive development of Protestant missions from the United States. Even before 1898, efforts had been made to reach the Cubans. Not long after the Civil War the Southern Methodists had been making contact with some of those who were in Key West.[325] As early as 1884 Protestantism had penetrated Cuba itself through two Spanish pastors, and then through a leader of the insurgents who, forced to flee from the island, had been converted while in New York.[326] When, on January 1st, 1899, a constitution went into effect guaranteeing religious liberty, the opportunity attracted a number of societies. By 1915 nine denominations had entered the country, and, in addition, the American Bible Society and the Young Men's Christian Association.[327] As in Puerto Rico, several of the societies joined in a territorial division of spheres of labour which tended to prevent a duplication of effort.[328] By 1915 nearly 17,000 communicants had been gathered.[329]

Protestantism made headway on the island of Haiti (formerly Hispaniola). It first gained a foothold in the western end, in the Negro state, Haiti, which was set up after the expulsion of the French. About 1816, at the request of the President of the republic, Pétion, two Wesleyan missionaries were sent from Great Britain. They won some converts, but in 1818, after the death of their patron, persecution set in and they were compelled to withdraw. However, the Wesleyans were able to continue through a Haitian pastor. In the following decade, at the invitation of the government, Negro colonists came from the United States. Among these were Protestant Christians who maintained their church life. English Baptist missionaries arrived. In 1861 a colony of Negro Methodists from New Haven, Connecticut, landed with their pastor.[330]

[324] Grose, *Advance in the Antilles*, pp. 208ff.; Stowell, *Between the Americas*, pp. 51ff.; White, *A Century of Faith*, pp. 184ff.; *Survey of Service. Disciples of Christ*, pp. 467-476; G. A. Riggs, *Baptists in Puerto Rico. Brief Historical Notes of Forty Years of Baptist Work in Puerto Rico* (Rio Piedras, no date, pp. 44), *passim;* Beach and St. John, *World Statistics of Christian Missions*, p. 75.

[325] *Annual Report of the Board of Missions of the Methodist Episcopal Church, South, June 1, 1875*, p. 70.

[326] Warneck, *Geschichte der protestantischen Missionen*, p. 255.

[327] Grose, *op. cit.*, p. 104; Beach and St. John, *World Statistics of Christian Missions*, p. 76.

[328] Grose, *op. cit.*, p. 107.

[329] Beach and St. John, *op. cit.*, p. 76.

[330] John W. Herivel, *Hayti and the Gospel* (London, Elliot Stock, 1891, pp. viii, 55), pp. 40ff.

In 1823 and again in 1845 Baptist missionaries came from the United States.[331] In 1851-1861 the American and Foreign Christian Union had a mission in Haiti which established four self-supporting churches.[332] In 1850 the American Bible Society sent an agent.[333] Negro Baptists and Methodists from the United States, the Protestant Episcopal Church (at first through a Negro clergyman), the Christian and Missionary Alliance, and the Seventh Day Adventists were present before 1915.[334] Through a business man who came from the United States (1889) the Free Methodists actively entered the Dominican Republic,[335] but it was not until after 1914 that Protestantism was largely represented in that portion of the island.

The compressed narrative of the past few pages may seem to be a somewhat arid catalogue of names, dates, and facts. To any who may have had the patience to make their way through it, however, it must be apparent that Protestant missions to Roman Catholics in Latin America, notably those from the United States, enjoyed a phenomenal growth in the half century before 1914. It was a time when in much of the world Protestantism, and particularly the Protestantism issuing from the United States, was displaying a pronounced expansion. In Latin America the period was chiefly one of pioneering and laying foundations. After 1914 both efforts and fruits were to multiply. In 1914, the transition year between eras, as a kind of augury of greater activity of the Protestant forces of the United States, the Committee on Co-operation in Latin America was formed. This was interdenominational and for comprehensive planning. Its headquarters were in New York City, but it eventually embraced ten regional groups in Latin America. It paved the way for more nearly unified Protestant action.[336]

To assess the effect of Christianity upon Latin America in the nineteenth century is difficult. At first sight the influence of the faith appears to have waned. Certainly the Church was neither so prominent or powerful as in the heyday of the Spanish and Portuguese regimes. Missions to the non-Christian Indians, while revived in the latter part of the nineteenth century, were by no means so widespread as in the colonial period. Much of nineteenth century religious scepticism entered from Europe and permeated the upper classes.

[331] White, *A Century of Faith,* pp. 209ff.
[332] *The Christian World,* Vol. XXIV, p. 75.
[333] Dwight, *The Centennial History of the American Bible Society,* Vol. I, pp. 219ff.
[334] Beach and St. John, *op. cit.,* p. 75.
[335] Stowell, *Between the Americas,* pp. 128ff.
[336] Parker, *Directory of World Missions,* p. 67.

The Roman Catholic Church was widely adjudged to be a bulwark of special privilege and of the remnants of the old order. As such it was distrusted by the liberal elements. Since the liberals were, on the whole, gaining ground, the Roman Catholic Church, and with it Christianity, appeared to be dwindling. Among the masses the Church seemed often not to be a moral force. In some areas the majority of the priests were grasping and licentious.[337] In certain sections church festivals were made the occasion for prolonged drunkenness.[338] Much of what the high-minded among both Roman Catholics and Protestants would brand as superstition flourished in the name of Christianity.[339] In several places, notably in Haiti, pagan cults survived among the Negroes, either openly or under thin disguises.

Yet Christianity continued as part of the warp and woof of life. Here and there were intellectuals who, although perhaps preserving no connexion, or at best only a slight connexion with the Church, had their ideals profoundly shaped by Christianity.[340] In 1892, following the *Rerum novarum* of Leo XIII, the *Federation de Circulos Católicos de Obreros* was formed in Argentina to promote the material and spiritual welfare of labour.[341] On several occasions the representatives of Pius X were arbiters between South American states.[342] Some priests and nuns were a constructive force morally, educationally, and in economic life.[343] In these and other ways, the influence of Roman Catholic Christianity was beneficent. The famous Christ of the Andes was witness to a continuing presence which made for peace.

Moreover, Protestant Christianity was beginning to be felt. Its effects were seen in the moral and spiritual transformation of individuals, in what to Latin America were new types of education,[344] and in wholesome recreation and physical culture.[345]

As in other areas and ages, so in Latin America in the nineteenth century, Christianity was profoundly affected by its environment. That environment was compounded of a number of elements. In it was the heritage from the

[337] Gamio, *Mexican Immigration into the United States*, p. 111; Mackay, *The Other Spanish Christ*, p. 119.
[338] Every, *South American Memories*, p. 86.
[339] See, for instance, Mackay, *op. cit.*, pp. 110-115.
[340] Mackay, *op. cit.*, pp. 159ff.
[341] *Anuario Católico Argentino, 1933*, pp. 331-338.
[342] Eckhardt, *The Papacy and World Affairs*, p. 165.
[343] Gamio, *op. cit.*, p. 111; Mackay, *op. cit.*, p. 119.
[344] As an example, see Braga and Grubb, *The Republic of Brazil*, p. 61.
[345] Mackay, *op. cit.*, pp. 251, 252.

Spanish and Portuguese Christianity of colonial days. That Christianity had been planted by zealous members of religious orders. It had in part reproduced the Spanish and Portuguese Christianity of the day. It had been intolerant. It had been passive. It had been dominated and in part financed by the Crown, and it had been led by foreign clergy. With some exceptions, the parish clergy, seculars, recruited increasingly from American-born youth, were inferior in character to the regulars who constituted the missionary force on the frontier. Then came the disturbances which ushered in political independence. The immediate effect of these was to lower the quality of Latin-American Christianity. In Church as in state separation from the mother countries was directed in part against officials of European birth. It therefore deprived the Church of many of its bishops. Conflicts between Rome and the new governments over the control of the Church punctuated much of the nineteenth century and further weakened the traditional Christianity. Struggles between clericals and anti-clericals and the entrance of scepticism from Europe dealt additional blows to the hereditary faith. The inherited Christianity was modified by the influx of Roman Catholics from Europe. To it was added, through immigration, a little of Eastern Christianity. It was augmented by Protestantism, partly through immigration and partly through missions. The immigrant Protestantism was chiefly from Germany. German Protestantism remained largely aloof from the rest of the religious life of the region. It was a bulwark of German tradition and language and constituted a brake on the process of assimilation. The Protestantism planted by missions was mainly from the United States. It was almost entirely the Protestantism of the older stock of that land. Baptists, Methodists, Presbyterians, Episcopalians, Congregationalists, and Disciples of Christ were represented, mainly the first three. There were also some denominations whose origin was purely in the United States, sprung from the Christianity of the older stock—principally Seventh Day Adventists. The Protestantism of the nineteenth-century immigration to the United States had but a slight part.

This Christianity, whether Roman Catholic, Eastern, or Protestant, was still predominantly passive. To be sure, much of its leadership and the rank and file of its clergy were native-born. In Brazil independent Protestant churches had begun to emerge. Yet numbers of the clergy were from abroad. Latin-American Christianity gave birth to no major new movements. It had but little active share in the propagation of the faith in other portions of the earth. Here it was in striking contrast with the Protestant and Roman Catholic Christianity of the United States and Canada. Yet in this it was akin to other phases of Latin-American culture. Latin America made no outstanding contribution to any phase of nineteenth-century culture. As under the Spanish and Portuguese colonial regimes it had been a recipient, so, in spite of political independence, it was still content to absorb ideas and institutions which came to it from without, modifying some of them, but originating nothing which was strikingly new.

Here and there were local modifications of Roman Catholic Christianity, movements usually within but sometimes outside the Church. Thus in Brazil the absence of resident priests in many communities and the conduct of the community prayers by local leaders brought much of the real religious life of the land under the immediate direction of laymen. Lay "saints" started fanatical movements. Usually they were Messiahs who professed to be heralds of a better age to which they would lead their followers.[346] Survivals of Indian or African paganism often mingled with Roman Catholic ceremonies.[347]

It may seem that we have allotted to Latin America a much smaller proportion of our space than the importance of the region warrants. If one were to take into account only geographic extent and the census, that criticism would be warranted. This work, however, is devoted to the history of the spread of Christianity. In proportion to the population the nineteenth century saw in Latin America less expansion of Christianity than in any other area of comparable size and population except possibly Europe (already overwhelmingly Christian in name) and parts of the interior of Asia. It may be, in fact, that if all the facts were known the record would be one of a net decline. Here was the region where in the preceding three centuries the major numerical spread of Christianity had occurred. Partly because of the methods employed in effecting that spread, in the fore part of the nineteenth century Christianity lost ground. In the latter part of the century recovery began. The revival, however, was because of reinforcements from Europe and the introduction of Protestantism from abroad rather than through life welling up from within the existing Latin-American church. After 1914 the tide of religious life continued to mount. Yet the impulse still came from without. The nineteenth century record of the Christianity planted in Latin America in the sixteenth,

[346] Braga and Grubb, *The Republic of Brazil*, pp. 37, 38; A. Métraux, "Messiahs of South America," in *The Inter-American Quarterly*, Vol. III, No. 2, pp. 53-60. For one of these religious leaders and the movement which arose and died with him, see R. B. Cunninghame Graham, *A Brazilian Mystic. Being the Life and Miracles of Antonio Conselheiro* (New York, The Dial Press, 1925, pp. xii, 238), *passim*.

[347] Braga and Grubb, *op. cit.*, pp. 13, 38, 39; Williams, *Voodoos and Obeahs, passim;* Melville J. Herskovits, *Life in a Haitian Valley* (New York, Alfred A. Knopf, 1937, ⸱p. xvi, 350, xix), pp. 139-291.

seventeenth, and eighteenth centuries is among the most thought provoking in the history of the faith. Clearly the lack of inner strength was not due to the fact that the Christianity was Roman Catholicism. In Europe and. in the United States and Canada in the nineteenth century that branch of the Christian movement displayed great vigour. Nor was it the absence of the stimulus given by the presence of Protestantism. The pulsing life in the nineteenth-century French Roman Catholic Church can scarcely be traced to contact with the numerically weak French Calvinism. Presumably the cause is to be found chiefly in the fashion in which Christianity was introduced and sustained during the colonial regime. Whatever the reason, the first part of the nineteenth century was a sorrowful one for Latin-American Christianity. The recovery of the latter part of the period and the diversification which developed came from the rising tide in Roman Catholic and Protestant Christianity in Western Europe and the United States. It was not indigenous. Whether the life flowing in from without could stir Latin-American religion to something more than an anæmia which required continuing transfusions from the more virile faith of other regions was, in 1914, an unanswered question.

Chapter V

AUSTRALIA. PROTESTANTISM AND ROMAN CATHOLICISM AMONG THE WHITES AND THE ABORIGINES

THE voyages of James Cook first directed the attention of the British in striking fashion to the Pacific. They were the precursors of the rise of new nations of British stock in Australia and New Zealand and of the occupation by the British of many of the islands of the South Pacific. Made in 1768-1770, 1772-1775, and 1776-1779, they opened to the astonished and eager eyes of the British a vast area, and islands and lands hitherto only vaguely known to Europeans. They came at a most opportune time. British industry and commerce were expanding. The British were rapidly assuming the position which they held in the nineteenth century of leadership in the machine age in manufactures and in overseas trade, of naval predominance, and of empire-building. Had Cook never lived or sailed the seas, the expanding British would probably have occupied Australasia. Here was a great portion of the world, but imperfectly held by peoples who could not stand against the white man with his superior tools and weapons. With the improvement of transportation brought by the inventions of the nineteenth century, the British, dominant in the world's commerce, could scarcely have failed to penetrate this to them remote section of the earth's surface. As the event happened, it was the exploits of Cook, the greatest of British maritime explorers, which opened the vast region to European eyes and furnished his government with the beginnings of a title to what eventually became its vast possessions in that quadrant of the globe.

Of the lands whose shores Cook charted, by far the largest was Australia. Here was an island so huge as better to deserve the appellation of continent. Its scanty population was in the stone age, divided into many small tribes, leading a non-agricultural, food-gathering, hunting, and fishing existence, and incapable either of effectively occupying the land or of offering successful resistance to white settlement. Although Australia extended northward into the tropics, more than half of its surface was within the temperate zone, and in spite of arid reaches in its interior much of it was eminently suitable for white settlement.

In 1788 a British colony was established in New South Wales, which had been so named by Cook. In less than seventy-five years towns and cities had been started on several widely separated harbours, population had poured in, much of the interior had been explored, and five states had been established —New South Wales, Victoria, South Australia, Western Australia, and Queensland. Tasmania, separated from the southernmost section of Australia by a comparatively narrow strait, had been settled. In 1900 these five states, together with Tasmania, united to form a federal government as the Commonwealth of Australia.

Almost spontaneously a comparison arises with that other large self-governing commonwealth within the British Empire with which we have already dealt. Australia and the Dominion of Canada were not far from the same size. Canada's area was about 3,750,000 square miles as against the approximately 3,000,000 square miles of Australia and Tasmania. In populations there was a marked difference. In 1921 that of Canada was 7,206,643[1] and that of Australia 4,445,005.[2] In contrast with Canada, Australia entirely lacked the French enclave which constituted more than a fourth of the population of its North American colleague. Nor did Australia have so extensive an immigration from the continent of Europe as did Canada. Its white stock was overwhelmingly of British descent—English, Scotch, Irish, and Welsh. For geographic reasons, Australia was not so subject to the influence of the United States as was Canada. The aborigines of Australia were only about two-thirds as numerous as those of Canada, approximately 75,000, if half-bloods were included.[3] In Canada the population, for climatic and historical reasons, was chiefly along the southern borders and was concentrated largely in the provinces of Ontario and Quebec. In Australia, also in part for reasons of geography, climate, and history, it was mainly on the coastal regions and was predominantly in the South-east.[4] Both commonwealths were new countries and had about them the flavour of the frontier. Having been settled predominantly in the nineteenth century when the machine age was well into its stride, they both displayed a marked urban development. In Australia in 1933 about one-third of the entire population was in the two cities of Sydney and Melbourne.[5] Since in the nineteenth century religious toleration was increasingly the practice in the British Isles, none of the British migration to either Canada or Australia was for the purpose of escaping religious persecution. In contrast

[1] *The Encyclopædia Britannica*, 14th ed., Vol. IV, p. 694.
[2] Wilson, *Official Year Book of the Commonwealth of Australia, No. 32, 1939*, p. 349.
[3] *The Encyclopædia Britannica*, 14th ed., Vol. II, p. 734.
[4] Wilson, *op. cit.*, p. 369.
[5] Wilson, *op. cit.*, pp. 352, 358.

with the United States, where religious idealism had played a large part in some of the original settlements in the colonial days and even in some of the westward movement on the frontier in the nineteenth century, in neither Canada nor Australia was it the outstanding factor in the migration of any influential group.

Australia presented some conditions peculiar to it which constituted problems, and, indeed, handicaps, to the spread of Christianity. At the outset it was a penal colony. The first permanent settlement, on Port Jackson, at what soon came to be called Sydney, was for convicts. Tasmania was used as an auxiliary station for them. For fully half a century Australia was a dumping ground to which these undesirable elements of the British Isles were forcibly expelled.[6] To be sure, many of the offences punished by transportation would in the later more humane years of the nineteenth century have been regarded as venial. By no means were all the convicts hardened criminals. Many were simply underprivileged individuals or political agitators who had run afoul of the existing social order. Increasingly, too, the settlers were those who had come of their own volition. By 1914 only a minority of the population were descendants of convicts. Yet at the beginning of white settlement, when the foundations of the new commonwealth were being laid, the convict element was prominent and was far from favourable soil for Christianity. Much of it was from the moral dregs of British society.[7] The concentration of so great a proportion of the population in a few large cities was also an obstacle, for here, as in Europe and America, the Church found difficulty in adjusting itself to the new conditions presented by the urban areas which sprang up, mushroom-like, in the machine age. In Australia, moreover, organized labour became a controlling force to a much greater degree than in pre-1914 Canada or the United States, and the general tendency for organized labour throughout the nineteenth century world was to drift away from Christianity and the Church and to be suspicious or even openly antagonistic to them. Then, too, mining camps, never conducive to strong church life, were prominent for a time. Climate and the nature of the land surface made pastoral life, the rearing of sheep, cattle, and horses, a major feature of the commonwealth. This

---

[6] In 1840 or 1841 transportation of convicts to New South Wales ceased. In 1852 the last convicts were disembarked in Tasmania. Until 1867 or 1868 a few were sent intermittently to Western Australia. The total number of convicts, both men and women, transported to Australia is said to have been 137,161.—Giles, *The Constitutional History of the Australian Church*, pp. 24, 25. Another account says that 83,290 were sent to New South Wales, 67,655 to Tasmania, and 9,718 to Western Australia.—*The Australian Encyclopædia*, Vol. I, p. 297.

[7] On the mixed character of the convicts see *The Australian Encyclopædia*, Vol. II, p. 582.

resulted in extensive ranches and a thinly scattered population. Over vast reaches towns and villages were few and parish life difficult or impossible. Only gradually was the size of holdings reduced and even then in great areas the density of population was so low as to render organized church life a problem.

On the other hand, some conditions favoured the building of Christianity into the life of the new nation. The overwhelming majority of the settlers were from the British Isles. The decades in which they were coming to Australia were marked by overflowing vitality in the religious life of the mother country. It was to be expected that this would make itself felt. Many of the settlers, issuing as they did from this background, would of their own volition transplant the Christianity to which they had been committed. Assistance in clergy and in funds would be given from the churches of Great Britain. In spite of the obstacles peculiar to Australia those professing some kind of connexion with the Church were almost exactly the same proportion of the population as in Canada.[8]

Much more than the Christianity of Canada, the Christianity of Australia reproduced that of the British Isles. In the absence of the French enclave and of extensive immigration from the continent of Europe, the Roman Catholicism of Australia was predominantly Irish. Whereas in Canada, largely because of the French element, the Roman Catholics were about two-fifths of the population,[9] in Australia they were only one-fifth of the whole.[10] The United States had far less effect upon the Protestantism of Australia than it did upon that of Canada, and continental European Protestantism was less strongly represented. The leading Protestant bodies were those which were outstanding in Great Britain—the Church of England, in 1921 with 44 per cent., and the Methodists and Presbyterians, each with about 11.5 per cent. of the population.[11]

This distribution of Protestant communions was quite different from that of Canada. There in 1921 Anglicans were 16.02 per cent., Methodists 13.19 per cent., and Presbyterians 16.04 per cent. of the population.[12] Baptists constituted only about 2 per cent. of the population of Australia[13] as against 4.8 per cent.

[8] In Canada in 1921 it was 97.5 per cent.—*The Encyclopædia Britannica*, 14th ed., Vol. IV, p. 695. In Australia in 1921 it was 96.9 per cent.—Wilson, *op. cit.*, p. 381.
[9] *The Canada Year Book 1912*, p. 34.
[10] Wilson, *op. cit.*, p. 381.
[11] *Ibid.*
[12] *The Encyclopædia Britannica*, 14th ed., Vol. IV, p. 695.
[13] Wilson, *op. cit.*, p. 381.

in Canada.[14] Congregationalists were 1.4 per cent. of the population of Australia in 1921[15] in comparison with .5 per cent. in Canada in 1911.[16]

Why the Church of England was so much stronger numerically in Australia than in Canada and the Methodists, Presbyterians, and Baptists so much weaker is not entirely clear. It may have been due in part to the greater urbanization of Australia, for the Church of England in Canada was especially prominent in the cities. It may have been because of the much higher proportion of English compared with Scotch stock in Australia as against Canada. This, however, would not account for the difference in the proportion of Methodism. That may have arisen from the proximity of the United States to Canada and to the fact that so much of Canadian Methodism stemmed from south of the border. Baptists and Congregationalists did not do so well in reproducing themselves as did the Methodists. In England and Wales Congregationalists were more than half as numerous as Wesleyans, and Baptists were about half as numerous.[17] In Australia Methodists outnumbered Congregationalists about eight to one and Baptists nearly six to one. The difference may have arisen in part from the fact that for some years state financial aid was given in Australia to the Anglican, Presbyterian, and Methodist communions, but very little to Congregationalists or Baptists. It may also have been because of better organization by the Methodists than by the Baptists and Congregationalists for propagating their faith. Possibly, moreover, the difference is to be ascribed to the fact that in the nineteenth century Methodism was still a young movement which was having a large growth in the British Isles, while the Baptists and Congregationalists had had their youthful period of rapid growth in the seventeenth century.

Although Australian Protestantism was overwhelmingly British, Lutheranism was represented by small bodies of immigrants from the continent of Europe, and two denominations of American origin, the Disciples of Christ and the Seventh Day Adventists, were, while very small minorities, widely distributed. Even the Disciples of Christ, however, owed their Australian foundation as much to contacts with Great Britain as with the United States.

We turn first of all to the spread of Protestant Christianity in Australia. It was this wing of the faith which was first introduced in organized form. In

---

[14] *The Encyclopædia Britannica,* 14th ed., Vol. IV, p. 695.
[15] Wilson, *op. cit.,* p. 381.
[16] *The Encyclopædia Britannica,* 14th ed., Vol. IV, p. 695.
[17] *The Encyclopædia Britannica,* 14th ed., Vol. VIII, p. 466.

one or another of its divisions it became the religion, either nominal or actual, of nearly four-fifths of the population.

As in the case of Canada, much assistance in the planting of Protestant Christianity came from the British Isles. Some of it was through financial subsidies. More was in clerical leadership. Most of it was given in the initial stages of Australia's life. Eventually, as we are to see a few pages farther on, Australian Protestantism not only provided its own support and its own clergy, but it also undertook the task of reaching new areas within Australia itself and sent missionaries to various islands in the Pacific and even to Asia.

Extensive aid came from the mother country to the Church of England in Australia. Between 1793 and 1900 the Society for the Propagation of the Gospel in Foreign Parts gave £253,598. From 1820 to 1898 £86,440 was contributed by the Society for Promoting Christian Knowledge.[18] The latter society also sent books and tracts. Its appropriations of money were used in part for the erection of churches and for educational institutions.[19] Thus these two bodies were fulfilling, in an area undreamed of when they were inaugurated, the purpose of their founders to assist religiously the overseas "plantations" of the Empire. The Colonial and Continental Church Society also made grants. Indeed, that organization, which came into being in 1861, had its roots partly in the earlier Australian Church Missionary Society. This in turn had grown out of the Western Australia Missionary Society founded by Frederick Chidley Irwin, a former governor of Western Australia.[20] From the Colonial Bishoprics Fund came contributions to the endowment of new bishoprics.[21] Between 1847 and 1857 Miss (afterwards Baroness) Burdett-Coutts gave £50,000 towards the extension of the colonial episcopate in Australia and elsewhere.[22] In 1851 Bishop Perry of Victoria reported that of the £14,000 spent in the diocese, £10,000 was derived from societies and friends in England.[23] From time to time bishops from Australia recruited clergy from England.[24]

Large assistance was given by the Presbyterian churches of the British Isles to the planting of Presbyterianism in Australia. Between 1866 and 1899 about

---

[18] Giles, *The Constitutional History of the Australian Church*, pp. 144, 145.

[19] Allen and McClure, *Two Hundred Years. The History of the Society for Promoting Christian Knowledge, 1698-1898*, pp. 330-346.

[20] Mullins, *Our Beginnings, being a Short Sketch of the History of the Colonial and Continental Church Society*, pp. 13-18.

[21] Giles, *op. cit.*, pp. 144, 145.

[22] Giles, *op. cit.*, p. 54; Goodman, *The Church in Victoria during the Episcopate of the Right Reverend Charles Perry*, p. 32.

[23] Goodman, *op. cit.*, pp. 150-154.

[24] Giles, *op. cit.*, p. 49; Goodman, *op. cit.*, p. 352; Matthews, *A Parson in the Australian Bush*, pp. 32-36.

two-thirds of the income of the Home Mission and Church Extension Fund of Queensland was from the Church of Scotland, the Free Church of Scotland, the Presbyterian Church of Ireland, and the United Presbyterian Church of Scotland.[25] To Victoria came clergy sent by the Colonial Committee of the Church of Scotland,[26] the United Presbyterians, and the Free Church of Scotland.[27] On more than one occasion the funds to bring out and support clergy from the mother country were raised in Australia.[28]

The help from British to Australian Methodism seems to have been chiefly in the sending of clergy.[29] So, too, assistance to the Congregationalists from their fellows in the British Isles appears to have been predominantly in men. The Colonial Missionary Society (organized in 1836) with headquarters in London was an agency through which at least some of the Congregational clergy were sent.[30] From Basel came pastors for German colonists.[31] The British and Foreign Bible Society made extensive grants of copies of the Scriptures. Between 1834 and 1854 these totalled 24,141 volumes. It operated largely through local Bible societies which were organized as auxiliaries to the parent society in London.[32]

Reinforcement was given to Australian Christianity through the visits of outstanding leaders from Great Britain and the United States. For instance, in the 1860's William Taylor, whom we have already met in California and South America and whom we are to see in both Africa and India, spent two prolonged periods in Australia, in itinerant preaching and in helping to raise money for Methodist chapels and schools.[33] In 1896 John R. Mott, from the United States, organized student Christian groups in a number of colleges and universities.[34]

It was natural that Christianity should put down its first roots in Australia in the oldest colony, New South Wales. Here, too, arose the most populous state of the commonwealth and the largest city.

---

[25] Hay, *Jubilee Memorial of the Presbyterian Church of Queensland, 1849-1899*, p. 8.
[26] Stewart, *The Presbyterian Church of Victoria*, p. 7.
[27] Campbell, *Fifty Years of Presbyterianism in Victoria*, pp. 35, 43, 44.
[28] Hay, *op. cit.*, p. 88; Stewart, *op. cit.*, pp. 30, 82-86; Cameron, *Centenary History of the Presbyterian Church in New South Wales*, p. 42.
[29] Bickford, *An Autobiography, passim*.
[30] *Annual Reports of the Colonial Missionary Society* (London, 1837ff.), *passim; The Sixth Report of the Congregational Home Missionary Society for New South Wales, passim; The First Report of the Van Diemen's Land Home Missionary and Christian Instruction Society* (1837), *passim*.
[31] Schlatter, *Geschichte der Basler Mission*, Vol. I, p. 93.
[32] Canton, *History of the British and Foreign Bible Society*, Vol. II, pp. 407, 410, 413, 417, Vol. V, pp. 257ff.
[33] Taylor, *Story of My Life*, pp. 255-326.
[34] Mathews, *John R. Mott*, pp. 112-114.

It was also to be expected that the Church of England should be the initial form of Christianity. In 1787, with the first consignment of convicts, there was appointed a chaplain of that communion. This was Richard Johnson. He was an Evangelical and seems to have owed his post to the great Evangelical reformer, William Wilberforce. It was a little group of leading Evangelicals who, convinced of the need of clerical care for the new penal settlements, brought pressure on the government to create a chaplaincy. The government gave Johnson a salary, but no funds with which to erect a church. The first building, a temporary structure at Sydney, Johnson put up at his own expense (but he was eventually reimbursed by the government). He served until 1801 and then returned to England.[35]

In 1793 there was appointed, as an assistant to Johnson, Samuel Marsden. Marsden had a much longer career in Australia than Johnson and a more extensive share in the planting of the faith. He, too, was an Evangelical. With only one trip back to England, Marsden served in Australia until his death (May 12, 1838). Practical, energetic, with widely ranging vision, Marsden had an important part not only in inaugurating Christianity in Australia, but also in assisting in its spread to other portions of the South Seas. In New South Wales he shared in plans for the moral and social improvement of women, aborigines, and convicts. He conducted two schools for orphans and erected a number of other schools, partly at his own expense. He was one of the first to develop agriculture in New South Wales. He dreamed of the conversion of the peoples of New Zealand and of the Society Islands. He was an adviser of the London Missionary Society, then in the pioneer stages of its enterprises in the South Seas. As we are to see in the following chapter, he had an outstanding part in the inception of missions to the Maoris of New Zealand.[36]

In the royal instructions received in 1790, provision was made for the Church by allotting to it 400 acres in each township for the maintenance of a clergyman and a schoolmaster.[37] One of the early Governors, Macquarie, was vigorous in promoting the erection of church buildings. Chiefly as the result of his initiative, by 1821, the close of his administration, six such structures were in use.[38]

[35] James Bonwick, *Australia's First Preacher, the Rev. Richard Johnson. First Chaplain of New South Wales* (London, Sampson Low, Marston & Co., 1898, pp. vii, 264), *passim;* Burton, *The State of Religion and Education in New South Wales,* p. 1; Giles, *The Constitutional History of the Australian Church,* pp. 39, 55-57.

[36] Marsden, *Memoirs of the Life and Labours of the Rev. Samuel Marsden, passim;* Johnstone, *Samuel Marsden, passim;* Elder, *The Letters and Journals of Samuel Marsden 1765-1838, passim;* Burton, *op. cit.,* pp. 8ff.

[37] Burton, *op. cit.,* p. 2.

[38] Whitington, *William Grant Broughton,* p. 51.

In 1823 episcopal provision was made for Australia and Tasmania by placing them under the Bishopric of Calcutta.[39] For the direct administration of New South Wales an archdeacon was appointed, Thomas Hobbes Scott. He arrived in 1825.[40] The second archdeacon, William Grant Broughton, reached his post in 1829. In 1836 he was consecrated the first Bishop of Australia. Broughton proved an able leader. In contrast with the low church, Evangelical Marsden, with his broad sympathies with other communions, Broughton was in touch with the rising Tractarian or Oxford movement and endeavoured to emphasize and strengthen the Church of England. He recruited additional clergy from the mother country. He helped to inspire the project for a central institution in England for training clergy for the colonies which led to the foundation (1848) of St. Augustine's College in Canterbury on the grounds where had once stood the monastery inaugurated by that Augustine who over twelve centuries before had introduced the Roman Catholic hierarchy to England. He stressed schools under Anglican auspices. He extended his travels to Tasmania and New Zealand, believing them to be in his territory. He began training an Australian clergy. He advocated the creation of additional bishoprics to give adequate leadership to the Church of England as it sought to care for the rapidly growing population of Australia. In consequence, in 1847 bishops for Melbourne, Adelaide, and Newcastle were consecrated. Already, in 1842, as Broughton had earnestly recommended, a bishop had been consecrated for Tasmania. Broughton himself became Metropolitan of the ecclesiastical Province of Australasia. He died (1853) while in England attempting to gain greater freedom for the Church of England in Australia from state control and the development of ecclesiastical autonomy in a form of organization in which bishops, clergy, and laity would be represented.[41]

The exacting limitations of space permit mention of only a few others of those who shared in laying the foundations of the Church of England in New South Wales. The first Bishop of Newcastle was William Tyrrell. A high churchman, unmarried, charming, systematic, hard-working, for thirty-two years he gave himself with devotion to his diocese and partly from his own income accumulated an endowment for his office.[42] Under Frederic Barker,

[39] Giles, *The Constitutional History of the Australian Church,* p. 57.
[40] Whitington, *op. cit.,* pp. 15-17.
[41] Whitington, *op. cit., passim;* Giles, *op. cit.,* pp. 43, 63; William Grant Broughton, *Sermons on the Church of England; Its Constitution, Mission and Trials,* edited by Benjamin Harrison (London, Bell and Daldy, 1857, pp. xliv, 360), pp. ix-xliv; P. A. Micklem, *Australia's First Bishop. A Brief Memoir of William Grant Broughton* (Australia, Angus & Robertson, 1936, pp. 58), *passim.*
[42] R. G. Boodle, *The Life and Labours of the Right Reverend William Tyrrell, D.D., First Bishop of Newcastle, New South Wales* (London, Wells Gardner, Darton & Co., 1881, pp. xii, 323), *passim.*

Broughton's successor, the Church of England continued its growth.[43] Edward Synge, as chaplain to Barker, travelled widely in what later became the diocese of Goulburn, inducing the settlers to promise subscriptions for clergy and the erection of churches.[44] Chalmers, the second Bishop of Goulburn, was trained at St. Augustine's College, became a missionary in Borneo, then served rural parishes in Australia, and was bishop from 1892 to 1901.[45]

Scotch immigration made inevitable the appearance of Presbyterianism in New South Wales. The founder of Presbyterianism in that colony was one of the most striking figures in the Australia of his day, John Dunmore Lang. To be sure, in 1809 settlers had erected a Presbyterian church building, but no clergyman came to answer their request.[46] Born in Ayrshire and educated in the University of Glasgow, Lang had his attention directed to Australia by a brother who had preceded him to New South Wales and had written him of the religious needs of the traditionally Presbyterian portion of the population. In 1822 he was ordained with the express purpose of forming a church in Sydney in connexion with the Church of Scotland. The following year he arrived in Australia.[47] He came at his own expense.[48] In 1824 a Presbyterian church was organized in Sydney.[49] A man of great physical and mental vigour, Lang had an energetic career. He was a pioneer, with large dreams. He foresaw a great future for Australia. He believed that the colonies in the eastern part of the continent would form a federation, would soon become fully independent of Great Britain, and would spread far and wide in the southern and eastern world British institutions and Protestant Christianity.[50] Before the Disruption in Scotland he had come to believe that the Church should be independent of financial support by the state. This conviction was reinforced and implemented by what he saw of the voluntary principle while on a tour

---

[43] William M. Cowper, *Episcopate of the Right Reverend Frederic Barker, D.D., Bishop of Sydney and Metropolitan of Australia* (London, Hatchards, 1888, pp. xv, 428), *passim*.

[44] Wynne, *The Church in Greater Britain*, p. 81.

[45] W. Charles Pritchard, *A Memoir of Bishop Chalmers* (Melbourne, Melville & Mullen, 1904, pp. 160), *passim*. See for another pioneer J. W. Eisdell, *Back Country, or the Cheerful Adventures of a Bush Parson in the Eighties* (Oxford University Press, 1936, pp. 175), *passim*.

[46] Lang in Burton, *op. cit.*, p. 12; Cameron, *Centenary History of the Presbyterian Church in New South Wales*, p. 2.

[47] Cameron, *op. cit.*, pp. 4-6; Lang, *An Historical and Statistical Account of New South Wales*, Vol. II, p. iv; John Dunmore Lang, *A Sermon Preached on Sunday, June 15, 1823 . . . in Sydney . . .* (Sydney, Robert Howe, 1823, pp. 18), *passim*.

[48] Lang, *An Historical and Statistical Account of New South Wales*, Vol. II, p. 404.

[49] Lang in Burton, *op. cit.*, p. 12.

[50] John Dunmore Lang, *The Australian Emigrant's Manual* (London, Partridge and Oakey, 1852, pp. xvi, 93), *passim;* John Dunmore Lang, *Freedom and Independence for the Golden Lands of Australia, the Right of the Colonies and the Interest of Britain and of the World* (Sydney, F. Cunninghame, 2d ed., 1857, pp. xi, 400), *passim*.

of the United States.[51] Lang was a member of the first Legislative Council of the colony and later served other terms on it.[52] He made several trips to Great Britain. Through them he induced a number of additional clergy to go to Australia. He also strove to augment the emigration of Protestants to the new country to offset the state-aided influx of Irish Roman Catholics. In this he met with substantial success.[53] He fostered education and was largely responsible, partly through gifts of himself and his family, for the founding of a college.[54]

When his ire or his convictions were aroused Lang was outspoken in denouncing men and measures.[55] He was a major cause of more than one division in Australian Presbyterianism. In 1832 he with four others formed the first presbytery in the country.[56] Late in 1837, meeting difficulty in obtaining admission to the presbytery of the clergy whom he had recently brought with him on one of his trips to Scotland, he, with them, formed a separate body, the Synod of New South Wales. In 1840 the presbytery and the synod united to constitute the Synod of Australia, in connexion with the Established Church of Scotland.[57] In 1842 he broke with the Synod of Australia and was deposed by it from the ministry. The difference arose partly from a rebuke to him from the synod for prolonged absence from his parish (while on one of his overseas journeys), partly from his growing and emphatically asserted conviction that the Church should not receive financial aid from the state, and partly on the accusation of ecclesiastical and financial irregularities, and of slander, schism, and contumacy.[58] The presbytery in Scotland of which Lang was a member confirmed the deposition, but Lang brought legal action against

[51] John Dunmore Lang, *Three Lectures on the Impolicy and Injustice of Religious Establishments or the Granting of Money for the Support of Religion from the Public Treasury* (Sydney, Robert Barr, 1856, pp. 76. Lectures delivered in 1842), *passim;* Lang, *An Historical and Statistical Account of New South Wales,* Vol. II, pp. 437-447.

[52] Lang, *An Historical and Statistical Account of New South Wales,* Vol. II, pp. 437-447.

[53] Cameron, *op. cit.,* pp. 9, 20-24; Lang, *Historical Account of the Separation of Victoria from New South Wales,* pp. 27-29.

[54] Lang, *An Historical and Statistical Account of New South Wales,* Vol. II, pp. 450-456; Cameron, *op. cit.,* pp. 4-6.

[55] *Australia: or Facts and Features, Sketches and Incidents of Australia and Australian Life . . . by a Clergyman thirteen years resident in the interior of New South Wales* (London, Longmans, Green & Co., 1867, pp. xiii, 286), pp. 239, 240.

[56] Cameron, *op. cit.,* p. 7.

[57] Cameron, *op. cit.,* pp. 10-13; *Correspondence with the Colonial Office on the Part of the General Assembly's Colonial Committee and the Rev. Dr. Lang . . . Relative to the Divisions in the Presbyterian Church of New South Wales* (Edinburgh, 1839), *passim.*

[58] Lang, *An Historical and Statistical Account of New South Wales,* Vol. II, pp. 437-447; *An Authentic Statement of the Facts and Circumstances of the Deposition of Dr. John Dunmore Lang from the Christian Ministry by the Synod of Australia, in Connexion with the Church of Scotland, in the Year 1842* (Published by order of the Presbytery of Sydney, 1860, pp. 16), *passim;* Cameron, *op. cit.,* pp. 14-19.

the General Assembly of Scotland and the latter hastened to direct the presbytery to reinstate him. The Synod of Australia later rescinded its deposition.[59]

As may have been gathered from the preceding paragraph, Presbyterianism early shared with the Church of England financial support by the state. This was to be expected, since in Scotland it was the state church, as was the Church of England in England.[60]

The Disruption in Scotland, brought about over the question of the connexion of the Church with lay proprietors and the state, had been brewing in the months when the issue over Lang was acute. Feeling over the latter had been accentuated by Lang's positive stand against dependence of the Church upon the state. For a time the Synod of Australia tried to keep on friendly terms with both the Church of Scotland and the Free Church, but each of the home bodies insisted upon an unequivocal stand. This led (1846) to division in Australia and the formation of the Synod of Eastern Australia by those who sympathized with the Free Church position. The Synod of Eastern Australia forswore all aid from the state.[61] In 1864 a union was effected which embraced not only this body and the synod from which it had separated, but also the United Presbyterians.[62]

The union gave fresh impulse to efforts of the Presbyterian churches to extend their form of the faith in New South Wales. Growth had been slow in the days of division. One of the first acts of the General Assembly of the united church was to adopt a Home Missions and Church Extension Scheme. Through an agent in London clergy were obtained from the mother country. Provision was also made for training a native ministry.[63] Through John Miller Ross, who had developed a similar plan for the Presbyterian Church of England, a Sustentation Fund Scheme was inaugurated which endeavoured out of a central treasury to assure a minimum salary to each minister.[64]

Experiencing, as it was, a rapid growth in the British Isles in the nineteenth century and reaching out in missions to many different parts of the world, Methodism could not but spread to so important a British colony as New South Wales. Methodism entered Australia, in the spontaneous fashion to be expected of it, through immigrant laymen. In 1812 the first class meeting assembled in Sydney. Others soon followed.[65] Together they appealed to the

[59] Cameron, op. cit., pp. 28, 29.

[60] Hamilton, A Jubilee History of the Presbyterian Church of Victoria, p. 5; Cameron, op. cit., pp. 33ff.

[61] Cameron, op. cit., pp. 33-66.

[62] Cameron, op. cit., pp. 31, 32, 67-85.

[63] Cameron, op. cit., p. 172.

[64] Cameron, op. cit., pp. 88, 89, 92-96, 101, 102.

[65] Colwell, A Century in the Pacific, pp. 223-227.

Methodist Conference in Great Britain for aid. In response, Samuel Leigh was sent. Trained as a Congregationalist, Leigh had come to reject Calvinism and had joined the Wesleyans. He was first appointed a missionary to Canada, but unsettled conditions in that country led to the cancellation of his passage and, instead, he was transferred to Australia. Governmental permission was obtained for him to go as a schoolmaster. He reached Sydney in 1815. He travelled widely, preaching, organizing Sunday schools and Methodist classes. Samuel Marsden welcomed his coming. He won the confidence of the benevolently minded Governor Macquarie and was aided by him in the formation of a branch of the British and Foreign Bible Society. He organized an asylum for the poor and a tract society. At his request, Walter Lawry was sent to assist him and arrived in 1818. After a few crowded years Leigh's health failed. At Marsden's suggestion he then turned his attention to New Zealand and in 1820, after a nine months' visit to that region, went to England to prepare himself for the new venture. We are to meet him again in the next chapter as a missionary to the Maoris.[66]

From the British Conference came more missionaries to nourish the rising Australian Methodism. George Erskine, who had sailed with Thomas Coke to inaugurate the Wesleyan enterprise in Ceylon, had failed in health, was transferred to New South Wales, and arrived in 1822. He became the first General Superintendent of the mission.[67] By 1830, however, Methodism in New South Wales had reached a low ebb. Leigh and Erskine had worn themselves out and were infirm and spent. As second General Superintendent was appointed, in 1831, Joseph Orton, who had been a missionary in Jamaica. Under him Methodism enjoyed a marked revival and extension.[68]

In 1840 Methodism in New South Wales could count seven ministers and 308 members, in 1845 nine ministers and 1,391 members, and in 1850 fourteen ministers and 2,093 members.[69] With 1851 came the discovery of gold and a great influx of population. In the meantime Methodism had been introduced into other parts of Australia.

In the 1850's the British Conference felt that Australasian Methodism was approaching maturity and that the time had come for it to stand on its own

[66] Strachan, *The Life of the Rev. Samuel Leigh,* pp. 13-83; Keeling, *What He Did for Convicts and Cannibals. Some Account of the Life and Work of Rev. Samuel Leigh,* pp. 19-53; Bickford, *Christian Work in Australasia,* pp. 15-18; Colwell, *The Illustrated History of Methodism,* pp. 41ff.; Colwell, *A Century in the Pacific,* pp. 231, 235, 236; Findlay and Holdsworth, *The History of the Wesleyan Methodist Missionary Society,* Vol. III, pp. 13-36.
[67] Colwell, *A Century in the Pacific,* pp. 235-241.
[68] Findlay and Holdsworth, *op. cit.,* Vol. III, pp. 49ff.
[69] Bickford, *op. cit.,* pp. 38-41.

feet. With the encouragement of the British Conference, in 1855 the first Australasian Conference met in Sydney and adopted the plan submitted by the mother body as the basis for the Australasian Wesleyan Methodist Connexion, partly independent of the parent church.[70]

Thus embarked upon a more nearly autonomous career, Australian Methodism continued to grow. In 1878 in New South Wales it numbered 89 ministers and 5,283 members.[71] Revivals in England in the 1880's were reflected in Australia. Fresh efforts were made to meet the problems presented by the growing cities.[72] In 1883, for instance, William George Taylor, a native of Yorkshire and for a number of years a missionary in Australia, was appointed to a down town church in Sydney which had been left stranded by the movement of its membership to the suburbs and transformed it into the successful Central Methodist Mission.[73]

Because of the enterprise of the London Missionary Society begun in the South Seas in 1790's, English Congregationalists early had contact with Australia. Several of the original group who went to Tahiti later settled in New South Wales. In 1809 some of these attempted to form a Congregational church but were discouraged by Marsden, the senior chaplain of the colony, from carrying through their project. Even so liberal a Church of England clergyman as he objected to the proposed administration of the sacraments by a layman.[74] Partly through the efforts of former Tahitian missionaries, in 1829 a congregation was assembled in a private home. A chapel was built (completed, 1833) and the church in it was ministered to for several years by W. Jarrett. In 1840 Ross was sent out by the Colonial Missionary Society, which had been organized in London in 1836 to establish Congregationalism in the British possessions.[75] In 1864 Camden College was founded both as a boys' school and to train a ministry.[76]

Baptists traced the beginning of their denomination in New South Wales to John McKaeg, a Highland minister. He began preaching in Sydney in 1831. Early in 1834 he resigned from the little church which had been organized.[77] In 1834 John Saunders arrived, sent in response to a request to the

[70] Findlay and Holdsworth, op. cit., Vol. III, pp. 134-140.

[71] Bickford, op. cit., p. 51.

[72] W. G. Taylor in Colwell, A Century in the Pacific, p. 691.

[73] William George Taylor, The Life-Story of an Australian Evangelist with an Account of the Origin and Growth of the Sydney Central Methodist Mission (London, The Epworth Press, 1920, pp. 347), passim.

[74] Colwell, A Century in the Pacific, p. 226.

[75] Kiek, An Apostle in Australia, pp. 42-62; Harvey, Notes on Australian Church History (Ms.); The Third Annual Report of the Colonial Missionary Society, 1839, p. 24.

[76] Harvey, op cit.

[77] A. Crowther Smith in The Christian Century, Vol. XLVIII, p. 885.

Baptist Missionary Society.[78] In the course of the next thirty years several other Baptist churches were assembled.[79]

Quakers were not numerous. As early as 1834 a few in sympathy with them were found in Sydney.[80] In 1906 there were only 184 Quakers in New South Wales.[81]

The Churches of Christ entered New South Wales about 1851. Gradually congregations and Sunday Schools arose.[82]

The first Young Women's Christian Association in Australia was organized in Sydney in 1880.[83]

Two years later, in 1882, the Salvation Army entered Sydney.[84]

In 1895 the Seventh Day Adventists gained a foothold.[85]

To minister to the Germans who came in some numbers to New South Wales, pastors were sent from schools at Hermannsburg, Basel, and Neuendettelsau.[86] These, it will be noted, represented the Pietist tradition and gave that trend to the German Christianity of the area. The Missouri Synod of the United States extended its efforts to Australia.[87] Lang also had several missionaries ordained to labour among the Germans.[88]

In 1872 New South Wales contained, in addition to Anglicans, Presbyterians, and Wesleyan Methodists, the largest Protestant bodies, twenty-five Congregational chapels, twenty-four Baptist chapels, forty-two Primitive Methodist chapels, two German Lutheran, four Evangelical Lutheran, three Christian Israelite chapels, and one chapel each of Unitarians, United Methodists, and unconnected Independents.[89]

In the nineteenth century Victoria was the second colony in Australia in population. Melbourne, its metropolis, was, after Sydney, the largest city in Australasia. Although a few hundred former convicts were sent in under the technical name of "exiles," except for one abortive attempt which was thwarted by popular feeling in the colony Victoria never contained a penal establishment.[90] About a generation later in being settled than was the area about Syd-

[78] Harvey, *op. cit.*
[79] *Ibid.*
[80] Backhouse, *A Narrative of a Visit to the Australian Colonies,* p. 233.
[81] *The Society of Friends in Australasia . . . 1906, passim.*
[82] Maston, *Jubilee Pictorial History of Churches of Christ in Australasia,* p. 305.
[83] *Outline Sketch of the Young Women's Christian Associations in Australasia,* p. 7.
[84] Harvey, *op. cit.*
[85] *Statistical Report of Seventh-Day Adventist Conferences and Missions for . . . 1905,* p. 4.
[86] Theile, *One Hundred Years of the Lutheran Church in Queensland,* pp. 20, 21.
[87] Theile, *op. cit.,* p. 38.
[88] Cameron, *Centenary History of the Presbyterian Church in New South Wales,* p. 27.
[89] Lang, *An Historical and Statistical Account of New South Wales,* Vol. II, p. 449.
[90] *Victoria, The First Century,* pp. 155ff.

ney, in 1838 what was later Victoria had a population of less than 4,000. In 1851 it was given a separate government, distinct from that of New South Wales. That year it had 77,435 inhabitants. Then came the discovery of gold, and within a decade the population jumped to more than 500,000.[91] In 1921 Victoria contained approximately 1,500,000 persons.[92]

By statistics of 1876, the Church of England seems to have been outstripped in numerical strength in Victoria by both the Presbyterians and the Wesleyans.[93] However, the first public worship in the area of the later Victoria was conducted, in 1803, by an Anglican chaplain.[94] Services were held in Portland, beginning in 1834. About 1836, when Melbourne was laid out, a plot was reserved for the Church of England, a small wooden building was put up, and a congregation was served by laymen.[95] In 1838 William G. Broughton, as Bishop of Australia, visited Port Phillip, on which Melbourne was then arising, planned the erection of a church, and saw to the appointment of a resident chaplain.[96] Ten years later, in 1848, there arrived the first Bishop of Melbourne, Charles Perry. Perry had had a remarkable record as a student at Cambridge, as senior wrangler, first Smith's prizeman, and first classman in the classical tripos. Through personal experience he was a warm Evangelical, and it was on the recommendation of the Evangelical Henry Venn that he was appointed to the episcopate.[97] Aid came from the Society for the Propagation of the Gospel in Foreign Parts.[98] Sympathetic assistance was also given by Charles Joseph LaTrobe, who had been trained for the Moravian ministry and who in the early years of Perry's episcopate was the administrative head of the colony.[99] Perry was indefatigable in travel and in labours for the Church and for education. In the first three and a half years of his tenure, the number of clergy increased from three to twenty-three.[100] Then came the gold rush and

---

[91] *The Encyclopædia Britannica*, 14th ed., Vol. XXIII, pp. 135, 136.
[92] Wilson, *Official Year Book of the Commonwealth of Australia, No. 32, 1939*, p. 349.
[93] Bickford, *Christian Work in Australasia*, p. 123.
[94] *Victoria, The First Century*, p. 429.
[95] Harvey, *Notes on Australian Church History*, (Ms.).
[96] Pascoe, *Two Hundred Years of the S.P.G.*, p. 404; Goodman, *The Church in Victoria during the Episcopate of the Right Reverend Charles Perry, First Bishop of Melbourne*, pp. 17-24.
[97] Goodman, *op. cit.*, pp. 33-58.
[98] Pascoe, *op. cit.*, p. 406.
[99] Goodman, *op. cit.*, p. 43.
[100] Goodman, *op. cit.*, pp. 60ff.; *Church in the Colonies. No. 33. Australia. Diocese of Melbourne. A Statement of the Progress, Condition, and Prospects of the Church, being the Substance of an Address Delivered by the Lord Bishop of Melbourne . . . 11th June, 1855* (London, Society for Promoting Christian Knowledge, 1855, pp. 63), *passim*. For an account by a clergyman who reached Melbourne in 1863, see Alex. Pyne, *Reminiscences of Colonial Life and Missionary Adventure in both Hemispheres* (London, Elliot Stock, 1875, pp. xii, 434), pp. 228ff.

brought fresh problems. In 1853, encouraged by increases in state funds due to the production of gold, the Legislative Council of the colony appropriated £30,000 a year and later £50,000 for the support of the various denominations. Of these sums about half went to the Church of England.[101] The grants were discontinued in 1875.[102] By 1881 local contributions had become so dependable that the Society for the Propagation of the Gospel in Foreign Parts withdrew its subsidies.[103] From time to time additional bishoprics were created in Victoria, and in 1905 Melbourne was made the seat of an archbishop.[104]

The first Presbyterian clergyman to reach Port Phillip was James Clow. He had been a chaplain of the East India Company in Bombay, India, and, after being forced home, on a pension, by impaired health, decided to come to Australasia. He reached Port Phillip late in 1837. There he gave leadership.[105] Early the following year another Presbyterian minister arrived, James Forbes, one of the clergy brought from Scotland by Lang and encouraged by that large-visioned pioneer to go to the new settlement at Melbourne.[106] Forbes appealed to the Colonial Committee of the Church of Scotland for reinforcements. In response, three were appointed.[107] Since no one was sent to respond to the plea for Gippsland, to the east of Melbourne, in 1851 a clergyman was despatched there from Sydney by Lang.[108] The first presbytery in the Port Phillip district was organized in 1842.[109] The Disruption in Scotland had its echoes in Victoria, but for several years division was avoided. Then, in 1847, for conscience's sake and at no small personal sacrifice, Forbes resigned from the Scots Church which he had built up, and with two other ministers and an elder organized the Free Presbyterian Synod of Australia Felix.[110] In 1847 came a clergyman of one of the bodies, the Relief Church, which in Scotland in that year were merging to form the United Presbyterian Church. It, too, stood for the support of the Church by voluntary offerings rather than by the state. Lang, agitating for similar principles, had prepared the minds of a number in Melbourne to welcome a minister of these convictions.[111] In the next five

---

[101] Goodman, *op. cit.*, pp. 159-177; Hamilton, *A Jubilee History of the Presbyterian Church of Victoria*, pp. 68, 80, 81.

[102] Pascoe, *op. cit.*, p. 408.

[103] Pascoe, *op. cit.*, p. 409.

[104] Harvey, *op. cit.*

[105] Macdonald, *One Hundred Years of Presbyterianism in Victoria*, pp. 13-17; Stewart, *The Presbyterian Church of Victoria 1859-1909*, pp. 1-6; Hamilton, *op. cit.*, p. 7.

[106] Hamilton, *op. cit.*, p. 9; Macdonald, *op. cit.*, pp. 17, 18.

[107] Hamilton, *op. cit.*, p. 13.

[108] Hamilton, *op. cit.*, p. 16.

[109] Hamilton, *op. cit.*, p. 17; Macdonald, *op. cit.*, p. 23.

[110] Macdonald, *op. cit.*, pp. 24-30; Stewart, *op. cit.*, pp. 26-28; Cameron, *op. cit.*, p. 40; Hamilton, *op. cit.*, p. 36; Campbell, *Fifty Years of Presbyterianism in Victoria*, p. 33.

[111] Macdonald, *op. cit.*, pp. 30, 31: Hamilton, *op. cit.*, p. 45.

years ten more United Presbyterian clergymen reached the colony, more than to the other two Presbyterian bodies.[112] In 1852, when it had surmounted some of the more pressing difficulties which attended the first few years of its existence, the Free Church of Scotland took up a collection which resulted in sending about twelve of its clergymen to Victoria.[113] In 1859, after long negotiations, a union was effected of most of the Presbyterians of Victoria. This was due chiefly to Irving Hetherington, who succeeded Forbes as pastor of the Scots Church. The first moderator of the united body was the first Presbyterian clergyman to make his home in Victoria, James Clow.[114] Union was followed by rapid growth. Provision was made for training a native ministry and deaconesses.[115] Between 1859 and 1904 the number of ordained ministers rose from 56 to 185.[116] An active organization for home missions and church extension carried Presbyterianism into new settlements and strove to meet the changes brought by shifts in population.

Among the settlers who came in 1832 to what later became Victoria were several Methodists. In 1836 James Orton, the General Superintendent who did so much to put Australian Methodism on its feet, visited the infant Melbourne and held what is said to have been the first public religious service in that city. Not long thereafter a Methodist Society was organized and in 1838 a chapel was built. Orton served the group in 1840 and in the following year a resident minister arrived.[117] In 1849 the Primitive Methodists sent John Ride to Melbourne and under him erected a building.[118] In 1851 came Joseph Townend of the Wesleyan Methodist Association, later the United Methodist Free Church.[119] The great influx of population brought by the discovery of gold (1851) stimulated the Methodists to give it spiritual care. In 1852 the Methodist Immigrants' Home was founded for the temporary housing of new arrivals. The goldfields were visited and services were held for the miners. Reinforcements were sent from Great Britain. By the year 1855 Victoria held twenty Methodist circuits with seventeen regular ministers assigned to them.[120]

[112] Hamilton, op. cit., p. 95.
[113] Macdonald, op. cit., pp. 32-35; Hamilton, op. cit., pp. 74, 75.
[114] Macdonald, op. cit., pp. 37-63; Stewart, op. cit., p. 36.
[115] Stewart, op. cit., pp. 46-51.
[116] Macdonald, op. cit., pp. 51, 67.
[117] Findlay and Holdsworth, The History of the Wesleyan Methodist Missionary Society, Vol. III, pp. 82-87; Colwell, A Century in the Pacific, pp. 279-282.
[118] E. H. Sugden in Colwell, op. cit., p. 283.
[119] Autobiography of the Reverend Joseph Townend with Reminiscences of his Missionary Labours in Australia (London, W. Reed, United Methodist Free Churches' Book-room, 1869, pp. iii, 252), pp. 84ff.
[120] Findlay and Holdsworth, op. cit., Vol. III, pp. 92-100; E. H. Sugden in Colwell, op. cit., pp. 283-287. For an account of one of the new clergyman who came, a native of Great Britain who for about fifteen years before being appointed to Victoria was a missionary in the West Indies, see Bickford, An Autobiography, passim.

In the 1860's a Church Building and Loan Fund was established and a college was founded for the training of an indigenous ministry.[121] When, in 1875, state aid to churches was discontinued and, near the same time, another fresh influx of population was brought by the opening of new land to settlement, the Methodists organized a home missionary society to meet the challenge.[122] In 1886, fifty years after James Orton had conducted the first public religious service, one-tenth of the population of approximately 1,000,000 were counted as Methodists, and the denomination possessed in Victoria 480 churches, 109 ministers, 33 home missionaries, 751 local preachers, 4,691 Sunday school teachers, and 40,459 Sunday school scholars.[123]

Congregationalism had its inception in the future Victoria when, in 1837, Port Phillip was visited by a layman, Henry Hopkins, from Tasmania, who asked the Colonial Missionary Society to send out a clergyman and contributed a sum towards the expense. In 1838 the clergyman, William Waterfield, arrived. A church was formed in 1839 and not long thereafter a building was erected on land given by the government. Additional clergymen came and at more places religious work was begun. The advent in 1854 of three able men sent by the Colonial Missionary Society gave a notable impetus to the denomination. In 1860 a continuing Congregational union was formed at Melbourne, an earlier effort, in 1852, having lapsed. In 1861 a college was opened for the training of clergy.[124]

Baptist laymen began in 1838 public services of their denomination in Melbourne. They met in a tent. In 1842 a clergyman arrived from England and in 1843 a church was organized. In the next few years other churches were formed in the colony, and in 1862 they constituted an association. With slight exceptions the Baptists declined to receive aid from the state and protested against it on principle. Both General and Particular Baptists had churches. In 1871 a home missionary society was organized, partly to train men for the ministry and partly to found new Baptist churches. For a number of years Baptists and Congregationalists co-operated in theological education. In 1889 Baptists inaugurated a theological college of their own. Churches multiplied, in both city and country.[125]

In 1882 the Salvation Army was introduced to Melbourne.[126] Before 1906

[121] E. H. Sugden in Colwell, op. cit., pp. 287, 288.
[122] Watsford, Glorious Gospel Triumphs as Seen in My Life and Work in Fiji and Australia, pp. 172-176.
[123] Watsford, op. cit., p. 258.
[124] Harvey, Notes on Australian Church History (Ms.); Victoria. The First Century, p. 431; Twenty-first Annual Report of the Colonial Missionary Society, 1857, pp. 23-28.
[125] F. J. Wilkin, Baptists in Victoria. Our First Century 1838-1938 (Melbourne, The Baptist Union of Victoria, 1939, pp. xvi, 211), passim.
[126] Harvey, op. cit.

the Friends had a monthly meeting.[127] In 1898 the first gathering of Christian Scientists in Melbourne was assembled.[128] In 1853 Disciples of Christ began to hold services. By 1862 about six Churches of Christ, as they were known, had come into being in Victoria, entirely by lay effort. Preachers came from England and evangelists from America. In 1882 the Disciples of Christ in Victoria numbered about 2,700 and in 1903 about 6,000.[129] In 1888 the Seventh Day Adventists entered Victoria and seventeen years later had 723 members.[130] As in New South Wales, so in Victoria, German immigrants were cared for spiritually by pastors from such missionary training centres in Germany as Basel, Hermannsburg, and Neuendettelsau.[131]

Tasmania, or Van Diemen's Land, as the white men first called it, is not far from the size of Scotland. Its initial influx of whites began more than thirty years before that of the adjacent Victoria and less than twenty years after that of New South Wales. As in the latter colony, much of the original white migration was an involuntary one, of convicts. Convicts long constituted a substantial proportion of the population. Not until 1853 did their importation cease. In that year Tasmania was granted representative institutions and three years later responsible government. In both population and area it was the smallest of the six states of the commonwealth. In 1921 it contained 213,780 persons. A somewhat larger proportion of its people were classified as rural than in any of the other five states.[132] Its chief city, Hobart, was the smallest of the leading cities of the commonwealth.

Organized Christianity entered Tasmania coincidently with the second British settlement, in 1804. The first one had been made the preceding year, on the estuary of the Derwent. The second one was also on the Derwent and was the beginning of Hobart.[133] The colony was composed chiefly of convicts. With it was a chaplain, a clergyman of the Church of England, Robert Knopwood.[134] Provision was also early made for the spiritual care of Launceston, the first permanent community on the northern part of the island, on the Tamar.[135] From 1835 to 1842 the Society for the Propagation of the Gospel in Foreign Parts aided in the construction on the island of sixteen churches and

---

[127] *The Society of Friends in Australasia . . . 1906, passim.*

[128] *Christian Science Journal, Vol. XXX,* p. 663.

[129] Maston, *Jubilee Pictorial History of Churches of Christ in Australasia,* pp. 149-155.

[130] *Statistical Report of Seventh-day Adventist Conferences and Missions for . . . 1905,* p. 4.

[131] Theile, *One Hundred Years of the Lutheran Church in Queensland,* pp. 20, 21.

[132] Wilson, *Official Year Book of the Commonwealth of Australia, No. 32—1909,* pp. 349, 356.

[133] Walker, *Early Tasmania,* pp. 1-102.

[134] Walker, *op. cit.,* p. 64; Bickford, *Christian Work in Australasia,* p. 242.

[135] Walker, *op. cit.,* pp. 103ff.; Harvey, *op. cit.*

eight parsonages.[136] While still archdeacon, Broughton visited Tasmania.[137] Soon after he was consecrated bishop, he appointed an archdeacon, William Hutchins, for the island.[138] On a visit in 1838, he noted an improvement in "the moral and religious condition of the inhabitants" since his previous one, five years before.[139] When, in 1842, a bishopric of the Church of England was created for the island, about 18,000 out of the 60,000 population were convicts.[140] Of the total population, approximately two-thirds were counted as connected with the Church of England and so were its responsibility.[141] The first incumbent of the new see was Francis Russell Nixon, an Oxford graduate who had already achieved distinction in the church in his native land.[142] His high church tendencies aroused opposition among his clergy,[143] particularly since he possessed strength of both intellect and will. He served his diocese loyally, and, when, after twenty-one years, he retired to England, it was with health shattered by the hardships of the post, especially by the difficulties of the necessary travel.[144] A later bishop, Henry Montgomery, who held the see from 1889 to 1901, travelled almost incessantly, going to the remote corners of the island, giving instruction and administering confirmation. He was active, too, in the Australian Board of Missions, visited Melanesia, and organized the diocese of Carpentaria, on the northern part of the continent.[145]

What is said to have been the first Presbyterian service held in Tasmania was on January 12th, 1823, by Archibald MacArthur, who had been sent from Scotland in response to a request from settlers in Hobart. His salary was paid by his parishioners and the government.[146] Other Presbyterian clergymen came.[147] In 1835 the first presbytery was organized, with Lang, who had so

[136] Pascoe, *Two Hundred Years of the S.P.G.*, p. 429.

[137] *Ibid.*

[138] Giles, *The Constitutional History of the Australian Church*, pp. 56, 69.

[139] Pascoe, *op. cit.*, p. 429.

[140] Pascoe, *op. cit.*, pp. 429, 430.

[141] Thomas Hay Forster, *Account of a Voyage in a Convict Ship: with Notes of the First Itinerating Missionary in Tasmania* (Westminster, The Society for the Propagation of the Gospel in Foreign Parts, 1850), p. 4.

[142] Giles, *op. cit.*, p. 51.

[143] Henry Phibbs Fry, *Answer to the Right Reverend F. R. Nixon, D.D., Lord Bishop of Tasmania; Being a Vindication of the Clergy Condemned for Asserting the Right of Private Judgment* (Hobart Town, J. Walch & Sons, 1853, pp. 211, xvi, 36), *passim*.

[144] Giles, *op. cit.*, p. 51. On one of his trips see Francis R. Nixon, *The Cruise of the Beacon: A Narrative of a Visit to the Islands of Bass's Straits* (London, Bell & Daldy, 1857, pp. 114), *passim*.

[145] M. M., *Bishop Montgomery. A Memoir* (Westminster, The Society for the Propagation of the Gospel in Foreign Parts, 1933, pp. xi, 109), pp. 28-39.

[146] Bickford, *Christian Work in Australasia*, p. 246; Harvey, *op. cit.*

[147] Harvey, *op. cit.*

large a share in founding Presbyterianism in Australia, as the first moderator.[148] There was division after the Disruption in Scotland, but in 1896 reunion was effected.[149]

In 1820 Benjamin Carvosso, who had been appointed by the Methodist Missionary Society, spent a few days at Hobart. A little later in the same year three Methodist soldiers started a class meeting.[150] In 1821, Leigh, as General Superintendent in the South Seas, stopping at Hobart, appointed to Tasmania one of the men whom he had brought with him from England.[151] During the 1840's and 1850's the churches attained self-support.[152] In 1854 Methodism counted in Tasmania twenty-three chapels, eleven other preaching-places, and eight ministers. In 1874 these had risen to ninety-seven chapels and other preaching-places, and fifteen ministers.[153]

Congregationalism in Tasmania owed its beginnings to a layman of Hobart, Henry Hopkins. He sent to England for an Independent minister. In response came Frederick Miller, who arrived in Hobart in 1830. In 1832 a church was organized. More clergymen came from the mother country.[154] In 1834, the Congregationalists, although still few in number, formed what was at first called the Van Diemen's Land Colonial Missionary and Christian Instruction Society. This brought out missionaries, partly with the aid of the Colonial Missionary Society, and in time supported several stations and aided weak churches.[155]

In 1834 a Baptist minister arrived in Tasmania. In 1835 Baptist churches were organized in Hobart and Launceston. The Baptists grew, in part through the extensive gifts of William Gibson and his family.[156]

In 1832, two Quakers, under an inner compulsion to go on "a religious mission" to the South Seas, landed at Hobart and began their ministry, working against the prevailing intemperance and seeking to inculcate better treatment of the dwindling aborigines. They visited other parts of the island, but it was

---

[148] John Dunmore Lang, *The True Glory of a Christian Church. A Sermon Preached at the Opening of St. Andrews, or the Scots Church, Hobart Town, Van Diemen's Land, on Sabbath, the 15th of November, 1835* (Sydney, Henry Bull, 1835, pp. xiii, 20), pp. v-ix.

[149] Harvey, *op. cit.*

[150] Findlay and Holdsworth, *The History of the Wesleyen Methodist Missionary Society,* Vol. III, pp. 66, 67.

[151] Findlay and Holdsworth, *op. cit.,* Vol. III, p. 68.

[152] Findlay and Holdsworth, *op. cit.,* Vol. III, p. 79.

[153] Colwell, *A Century in the Pacific,* pp. 269-277.

[154] Harvey, *Notes on Australian Church History* (Ms.).

[155] *The Twenty-Third Report of the Tasmanian Colonial Missionary and Christian Instruction Society in Connection with the Tasmanian· Congregational Union* (Hobart Town, Burnet, 1859), *passim.*

[156] Harvey, *op. cit.*

at Hobart that in about the year 1833 they opened what is said to have been the first Friends' meeting in the Southern Hemisphere. There, too, they organized a monthly meeting. The following year a yearly meeting convened.[157] The Society of Friends did not attain large dimensions. In 1906 it reported only 142 members in Tasmania.[158]

The Disciples of Christ were first represented in Tasmania in 1865, but aggressive effort did not begin until 1872. Then, as the result of a year's preaching by a visiting minister, a church was organized in Hobart. Other churches followed, but at the beginning of the twentieth century the total membership was only about 500.[159]

The Seventh Day Adventists entered in 1901 and within five years had a little over 200 members.[160]

Although the first permanent settlement in South Australia was not until the 1830's, about three decades after that in Tasmania, the population of the younger colony grew more rapidly and by 1914 made the state in that respect the third largest in Australia. The chief city, Adelaide, became the fourth in size in the commonwealth. The overwhelming majority of the people of South Australia, indeed, were in the relatively small south-eastern section, in and not far from Adelaide.[161]

In contrast with New South Wales and Tasmania, the original settlement in South Australia was not by convicts but by those who came out voluntarily. In the first contingent were members of the Church of England who formed among themselves a committee affiliated with the Society for the Propagation of the Gospel in Foreign Parts. With the aid of that society the material to build a church was purchased and sent out on one of the earliest vessels which sailed for the colony. A chaplain, C. B. Howard, was appointed, who with his own hands helped to erect the church.[162] By the time the first bishop was consecrated, in the year 1847, eleven years after the colony was founded, five clergymen of the Church of England were already at work. The first bishop

---

[157] James Backhouse and Charles Tylor, *The Life and Labours of George Washington Walker, of Hobart Town, Tasmania* (London, A. W. Bennett, 1862, pp. xii, 556, 12), pp. 12-288.

[158] *The Society of Friends in Australasia. List of Members Constituting the General Meeting for Australia . . . New Zealand*, 1906, *passim*.

[159] Maston, *Jubilee Pictorial History of Churches of Christ in Australasia*, pp. 133.

[160] *Statistical Report of Seventh-day Adventist Conferences and Missions for . . . 1905*, p. 4.

[161] For a description of South Australia in 1876 see William Harcus, *South Australia: Its History, Resources, and Productions* (London, Sampson Low, Marston, Searle, & Rivington, 1876, pp. xv, 430), *passim*.

[162] Pascoe, *Two Hundred Years of the S.P.G.*, pp. 115, 116. On the early days of the Church of England in South Australia see G. H. Jose, *The Church of England in South Australia, 1836-1856* (Adelaide, Church Office, 1937, pp. 70), *passim*.

was Augustus Short (1802-1883). A graduate of Oxford with first class classical honours, for a time tutor and lecturer at Christ Church, and later Bampton lecturer, he brought to his post unusual gifts of mind. Like so many of his generation of Oxonians, he had fallen under the spell of the Tractarian Movement. However, he was only a moderately high churchman. In 1851 state support of the church in the colony was discontinued and Short was compelled to raise funds. He also travelled extensively among the new and often widely scattered settlements and ranches of his huge diocese. While eager to have the Anglican Church in Australia hold true to its connexion with the Church of England, he wished for it liberty of action. He obtained for his diocese an organization of laity, clergy, and bishop, freed from the state. In 1882, now an old man and in failing health, he retired to England.[163]

Short's successor was George Wyndon Kennion. Under him a home mission society was founded, a mission steamer was equipped to minister to the settlers along the Murray, the chief river of Australia, and more than forty churches were added to the diocese.[164]

The first Presbyterian clergyman to reach South Australia arrived in 1837, from the United Secession Church. In 1839 a Presbyterian church was organized. As usual, various branches of Presbyterianism were represented, the United Presbyterian Church, the Church of Scotland, and, after the Disruption in the mother country, the Free Church. In 1865 the three were brought together in a union, the Presbyterian Church of South Australia.[165]

By 1876 the Methodists, if all their various branches be included, possessed in South Australia about five times as many churches as the Anglicans with more than three times the number of sittings. In churches in that year they outnumbered the Presbyterians nearly twenty to one and in sittings more than thirty to one.[166] Relatively the Methodists were more numerous in South Australia than in either New South Wales or Victoria. The captain of the vessel which brought the first contingent of settlers was a Methodist and Methodists were prominent in the early stages of the colony. Of their own initiative, the Methodist settlers early began forming themselves into classes. Indeed, a Methodist society seems to have been organized among the first colonists on their way out. Local preachers were soon appointed from among the members. Through a shipwreck, a minister joined the colony in 1838 and

[163] Whitington, *Augustus Short, First Bishop of Adelaide, passim;* Giles, *The Constitutional History of the Australian Church,* p. 5.
[164] Harvey, *Notes on Australian Church History* (Ms.).
[165] *Ibid.*
[166] Bickford, *Christian Work in Australasia,* p. 163.

organized the Methodists. Other ministers came, and Methodism experienced the rapid growth of which the statistics give evidence.[167]

Congregationalism was introduced into South Australia in 1837 by T. Q. Stow, sent by the Colonial Missionary Society.[168] In 1850 a Congregational Union was formed for the colony. In 1859 it had at least fifteen centres and seventeen ministers, and had begun a chapel building society and a fund to assist the disabled and aged among its clergy.[169]

About 1836 the first Baptist church in South Australia was organized in the cottage of a British Baptist who, having wished to be a missionary and having found all other doors closed, had gone on his own resources to the new colony.[170] In the course of time ministers came who had been trained by the famous London Baptist preacher, C. H. Spurgeon.[171] Incidentally, the prominence of preachers trained by Spurgeon brought a certain disadvantage to the Baptists. These preachers were accustomed to great "tabernacles." As population moved away from the centres of the cities, this method proved ill adapted to the new situation and by the time the Baptists awoke to the problem the suburban areas had been largely occupied by other denominations.

The Churches of Christ were introduced to South Australia in 1847 by a group from Scotland. Eventually additional churches arose and evangelists from Great Britain and the United States aided in the growth of the denomination.[172]

Lutheranism was represented in South Australia by immigrants from Germany. In one instance a pastor came with his flock from Silesia to the new country.[173]

It was in Adelaide in 1880 that a mission was begun using the methods of the Salvation Army. An appeal was made to London for assistance. In 1881, in response to it, officers reached Adelaide and formally established the Army, the first unit in Australia.[174]

---

[167] Findlay and Holdsworth, *The History of the Wesleyan Methodist Missionary Society,* Vol. III, pp. 101-120; Bickford, *op. cit.,* pp. 135-138; Colwell, *A Century in the Pacific,* pp. 301-310.

[168] Bickford, *op. cit.,* pp. 160, 161.

[169] *Report of the Proceedings of the Tenth Annual Meeting of the Congregational Union of South Australia, held April 19th, 20th and 21st, 1859* (Adelaide, J. T. Shawyer, 1859, pp. 8), *passim.*

[170] Mrs. W. H. Hinton, *Ethel Ambrose Pioneer Medical Missionary* (London, Marshall, Morgan & Scott, no date, pp. 255), pp. 15ff.

[171] Bickford, *op. cit.,* p. 162. For the story of the Baptists in South Australia see H. Estcourt Hughes, *Our First Hundred Years. The Baptist Church of South Australia* (Adelaide, S. A. Baptist Union, 1937, pp. 349), *passim.*

[172] Maston, *Jubilee Pictorial History of Churches of Christ in Australasia,* pp. 19ff.

[173] Bickford, *op. cit.,* p. 163.

[174] Harvey, *op. cit.*

Although the largest of the states in area, although permanent settlement in it began early, in the 1820's, and in spite of the fact that several thousand convicts were sent to it, Western Australia grew slowly. In 1890 it had a population of only 46,290, and in 1900, after a gold rush, still merely 179,708.[175] Its one large city, Perth, held about half of this meagre total. Down to 1914 its chief dependence was upon pastoral pursuits and mining.

For years the only clergyman in Western Australia was the chaplain at Perth, a priest of the Church of England. In 1836 the Western Australia Missionary Society, which had been organized in Great Britain to provide clergy for the colony, sent out its first missionary.[176] Others followed. Through the assistance of the Society for the Propagation of the Gospel in Foreign Parts in providing an endowment, in 1857 Western Australia was made a separate diocese.[177] As population grew and the Anglican Church expanded, Western Australia was created (1913) an ecclesiastical province, with three dioceses.[178] The Church of England had taken firm rootage.

Methodism reached Western Australia in 1830, with the arrival of a vessel which had been chartered by two Yorkshire Wesleyan families and which had a number of others of that denomination on board. Public services were begun through that familiar Methodist missionary instrument, the local preacher. In 1833 came another Methodist contingent. Until 1840 Methodism depended upon the lay leadership of local preachers. In that year a clergyman, formerly in Newfoundland, was sent as a missionary from Great Britain, but until 1852 he was without a colleague. It was not until 1900 that a separate Methodist conference was formed. Largely because of this slow development and the lack of aid from the outside, Methodism was weaker in Western Australia than in some others of the Australian states.[179]

Presbyterianism was even later than Methodism in developing in Western Australia. In 1878 there was only one Presbyterian church in the entire colony. The following year the colonial committees of the Church of Scotland and the Free Church joined in sending out a clergyman. In 1886 the Free Church of Scotland commissioned a clergyman to establish a church at Fremantle. In 1892, when the first presbytery was formed, it comprised only three congregations. By 1901 two other presbyteries had been organized, and in that year a

175 *The Encyclopædia Britannica*, 14th ed., Vol. XXIII, pp. 529, 532, 533.
176 Mullins, *Our Beginnings, being a Short Sketch of the History of the Colonial and Continental Church Society*, pp. 13ff.
177 Pascoe, *Two Hundred Years of the S.P.G.*, pp. 424-427.
178 Giles, *The Constitutional History of the Australian Church*, p. 131.
179 Findlay and Holdsworth, *The History of the Wesleyan Methodist Missionary Society*, Vol. III, pp. 120-126; Brian Wibberley in Colwell, *A Century in the Pacific*, pp. 336-358.

general assembly was constituted. Help came from Scotland, and in the twentieth century a vigorous effort was made to reach out into the state through lay missionaries.[180]

By 1878 Congregationalists had three churches in Western Australia.[181] The Colonial Missionary Society gave assistance in funds and missionaries, but the beginnings were usually due to the initiative of laymen. Late in the nineteenth century active extension began, largely through the leading church in Perth, and the formation of more churches followed.[182]

Although there seem to have been a few Baptists in Western Australia as early as 1878,[183] apparently it was not until 1894 that the first Baptist services were held. These were in Perth, conducted by a layman. In the 1890's several churches sprang up, a Baptist Union of Western Australia was formed, and organized missionary effort was begun for some of the new settlements.[184]

The Churches of Christ came into being in Western Australia through a missionary from the South Australia Conference. He reached Perth in 1891 and a church was soon organized. Others followed, and a conference was convened in 1898.[185]

The Seventh Day Adventists did not make their way to Western Australia until 1902.[186]

Queensland, eventually third in population of the Australian states, was originally part of New South Wales. Settlement began around Moreton Bay, where the city of Brisbane, eventually the fourth in size of the Australian cities, was to arise. When, in 1859, Queensland was separated from New South Wales and made a distinct colony, it had a white population of about 20,000. Some of these were convicts or ex-convicts. In the next few years, partly because of the development of gold-mining, the population grew rapidly. Aside from the manufactures and commerce of Brisbane, Queensland eventually depended chiefly upon pastoral pursuits for its prosperity. The importation of labourers, "Kanakas," from the Pacific islands, for the sugar plantations, from 1862 to 1904, followed by its prohibition and the subsequent deportation

---

[180] Bickford, *Christian Work in Australia*, p. 186; Harvey, *Notes on Australian Church History* (Ms.).

[181] Bickford, *op. cit.*, p. 186.

[182] Harvey, *op. cit.*

[183] Bickford, *op. cit.*, p. 186.

[184] Leslie J. Gomm, *Blazing New Trails. The Story of the Life and Work of William Kennedy, Pathfinder, Preacher, and Pioneer* (Glebe, J. H. Packer, 1935, pp. 208), pp. 35-39, and *passim*.

[185] Maston, *Jubilee Pictorial History of Churches of Christ in Australasia*, pp. 81ff.

[186] *Statistical Report of Seventh-day Adventist Conferences and Missions for . . . 1905*, p. 4.

of most of the immigrants, brought to Queensland a racial problem and a challenge to Christianity.[187]

Beginning with 1840, the Society for the Propagation of the Gospel in Foreign Parts began sending missionaries to Moreton Bay. In 1859 the Moreton Bay district was made a separate diocese of the Church of England. Within three years the number of clergymen rose from three to sixteen. So rapid was the growth of the church in the Diocese of Brisbane in self-support, that in 1881 the society withdrew its aid. In 1892 a new see was created in the central part of the colony with Rockhampton as its seat. The sparsely settled northern portion of Queensland was more slowly cared for, but in 1878 a bishop was consecrated for it. Before leaving England for his new post he sent out twenty missionaries to his diocese.[188] In 1891 a mission was begun among the "Kanakas," and thousands were soon brought under instruction. Removed from their accustomed environment and placed under the direction of the whites, these labourers proved receptive to the Christian message.[189]

It was that pioneer of Australian Presbyterianism, Lang, who in 1845 held the first service of his denomination in what later became Queensland. With his vision of a great nation in Australia, he had induced some immigrants to come to the region. In 1849 a Presbyterian church was formed in Brisbane, and two years later a minister for it was obtained from the Free Church of Scotland.[190] In 1863, with the cordial approval of their church in New South Wales, the Presbyterians in the colony formed the Presbyterian Church of Queensland.[191] In 1876 an institution was opened for the training of clergy.[192] Presbyterianism was well planted.

It is not clear just when Methodism first appeared in the Moreton Bay district. In 1847 a class was established by a young man and his wife from the South who later became missionaries in the Fiji Islands. In 1863 Queensland was made a Methodist District, but until 1893 it was ecclesiastically attached to New South Wales. In that year it was given a distinct conference with two districts. Beginning in 1894 other Methodist bodies—the Primitive Methodists, some of the United Free Methodists, and the Bible Christians—joined with this Wesleyan Methodist body to form a union. In 1913 the united church

[187] The Encyclopædia Britannica, 14th ed., Vol. XVIII, pp. 845, 846; Bickford, op. cit., pp. 67, 68.
[188] Pascoe, Two Hundred Years of the S.P.G., pp. 410-414.
[189] Pascoe, op. cit., pp. 412, 414a.
[190] Hay, Jubilee Memorial of the Presbyterian Church of Queensland, 1849-1899, pp. 2, 5.
[191] Hay, op. cit., p. 1; Cameron, Centenary History of the Presbyterian Church in New South Wales, p. 46.
[192] Hay, op. cit., pp. 136ff.

had had 99 ministers, 48 home missionaries, 439 local preachers, and 10,000 members and probationers.[193]

To Queensland the Colonial Missionary Society sent personnel and money to stimulate the development of Congregationalism. In 1849 a group of Congregationalists began meeting in Ipswich. In 1853 they formed a fellowship which was served by an appointee of the Colonial Missionary Society and became the mother church of their denomination in Queensland. A Congregational Union was constituted in 1861.[194]

The Baptists in Queensland organized their own church in 1855, after having joined for six years with Presbyterians and Congregationalists in a United Evangelical Church.[195]

The Churches of Christ dated their inception in Queensland from meetings in a private home in 1871. Continuing Churches of Christ were not organized until 1882, when two evangelists arrived from other parts of Australia. Beginning with 1883, annual conferences were held.[196]

Lutheranism in Queensland traced its origin to Lang. Lang had at heart the welfare of the aborigines near Moreton Bay and prevailed upon Johannes E. Gossner of the Bethlehem Church in Berlin to send a party of missionaries to care for them. Gossner, it will be remembered,[197] had dreamed of self-supporting missionaries. The initial party gathered by Gossner was composed largely of artisans and clergymen and, coming in 1838, settled not far from Brisbane. A second missionary party arrived in 1844. Because of the disintegration of the aborigines under the pressure of the surrounding white population, the mission did not prosper. Some of the missionaries remained, took up farms, and became the nucleus of the Lutheranism of Queensland. By 1859 about 2,000 Germans had come to Queensland, and from 1862 to 1873 immigration added largely to them. Between 1870 and 1890 about 2,000 Scandinavians augmented the Lutheran constituency Clergy were obtained with difficulty. Some came from the Hermannsburg Mission, the Gossner Mission, and Basel. As in several other parts of Australia, divisions entered into the Lutheran body. These were due partly to national cleavages and partly to what were termed confessional differences. The strong Missouri Synod of the United States was

[193] H. Youngman in Colwell, *A Century in the Pacific*, pp. 363-373; Findlay and Holdsworth, *op. cit.*, Vol. III, pp. 143, 144.
[194] *Sixty-fourth Annual Report of the Colonial Missionary Society*, p. 26; Kiek, *An Apostle in Australia*, p. 64.
[195] Harvey, *Notes on Australian Church History* (Ms.).
[196] Maston, *Jubilee Pictorial History of Churches of Christ in Australasia*, pp. 103ff.
[197] Vol. IV, pp. 91, 267.

represented. One synod was connected with the state church of Prussia. Not until after 1914 was substantial progress towards union registered.[198]

Northern Australia combined a vast area with a sparse population. In 1921 it had less than 4,000 of white blood.[199] In addition there were aborigines, of whom we are to say more a few paragraphs below. Before 1911 Northern Australia was politically a part of South Australia. It was then handed over to the Commonwealth. Provision was made for it religiously through the initiative of the churches in the more thickly settled portions of Australia and by assistance from Great Britain. In 1873 Methodists held a meeting in Adelaide to establish a mission in the Northern Territory. To the money which they raised they asked the missionary society in Great Britain to add. A missionary was placed at the chief town.[200] In 1900, as a result of an earlier meeting of the bishops of Australia, a bishop was consecrated for a diocese of the Church of England for the Northern Territory and the portion of Queensland which bordered on the Gulf of Carpentaria.[201] The first incumbent was Gilbert White. He had already laboured as a clergyman in Queensland. As bishop he undertook long and arduous journeys in his difficult diocese and cared for both whites and aborigines.[202]

The Christianity of Australia was not, like so much of the Christianity of Latin America, passive. To be sure, as we have seen in the past few pages, in its early stages financial help was given it by the churches of the British Isles. For years, moreover, clergy continued to come from the mother country. For several decades the colonial governments contributed financial subsidies. However, very early the Protestants of Australia not only took much of the initiative in founding churches, but eventually they also bore the entire financial load, produced and trained most of their own leadership, both clerical and lay, and began to propagate their faith in other lands. As in Canada, so in Australia, before the last quarter of the nineteenth century the state had ceased to subsidize the churches. As was natural, the churches of Australia found their chief mission field among the aborigines of their own country and among the primitive peoples of the islands of the Pacific. However, they also had a few missions in Asia.

To detail the many enterprises through which the Protestants of Australia

[198] Theile, *One Hundred Years of the Lutheran Church in Queensland, passim.*

[199] Wilson, *Official Year Book of the Commonwealth of Australia, No. 32—1939,* p. 349.

[200] Colwell, *A Century in the Pacific,* p. 322; Bickford, *An Autobiography,* p. 276; Findlay and Holdsworth, *The History of the Wesleyan Methodist Missionary Society,* Vol. III, p. 101.

[201] Pascoe, *Two Hundred Years of the S.P.G.,* p. 424.

[202] An autobiography of the first bishop is Gilbert White, *Thirty Years in Tropical Australia* (London, Society for Promoting Christian Knowledge, 1918, pp. viii, 264).

undertook to strengthen Christianity in their own land and to extend it abroad would require a volume. Here we must content ourselves with picking out, almost at random, a few examples. In 1850 six Anglican bishops in Australia and New Zealand met and among other achievements established an Australasian Board of Missions to spread the Christian message among the non-Christians in the Western Pacific.[203] In 1825 an Auxiliary of the Church Missionary Society was organized in New South Wales.[204] From time to time in the later decades of the nineteenth century, a clergyman in Melbourne sent reinforcements to the India missions of the Church Missionary Society and by 1888 was raising for that purpose funds up to £2,000 a year.[205] A Victorian Church Missionary Society was founded in 1856.[206] In 1892, through the stimulus given by a deputation from Great Britain, in connexion with the Church Missionary Society, Church Missionary Associations were instituted in New South Wales and Victoria.[207] Similar associations in Tasmania, South Australia, and Western Australia united with the one in Victoria.[208] In New South Wales[209] and South Australia[210] funds were raised for the extension of the Church of England in these colonies. In 1845 the Presbyterian Church Society of Australia Felix was constituted to further "religious instruction and Divine worship in the district of Port Phillip."[211] In 1868 the Presbyterian Church of New South Wales assumed the support of a missionary to the New Hebrides.[212] The Women's Missionary Association of the Presbyterian Church of New South Wales was formed in 1891 and sent missionaries to India.[213] In 1892 a Presbyterian Women's Missionary Union was organized in Queensland.[214] As early as 1820 Leigh began among Australian Methodists an auxiliary of the missionary society of the mother country.[215] In the 1840's Australian Methodists inaugurated funds for home missions.[216] In 1855, when Methodism in

[203] Pascoe, *Two Hundred Years of the S.P.G.*, p. 398; Goodman, *The Church in Victoria during the Episcopate of the Right Reverend Charles Perry*, pp. 134ff.
[204] Stock, *History of the Church Missionary Society*, Vol. III, p. 674.
[205] Stock, *op. cit.*, Vol. III, p. 673.
[206] Johnstone, *A History of the Church Missionary Society in Australia and Tasmania*, p. 195.
[207] Johnstone, *op. cit.*, pp. 218ff.; Strong and Warnshuis, *Directory of Foreign Missions*, p. 1.
[208] Strong and Warnshuis, *op. cit.*, p. 1.
[209] Giles, *The Constitutional History of the Australian Church*, p. 45.
[210] Whitington, *Augustus Short, First Bishop of Adelaide*, p. 156.
[211] Ross, *Colonization and Church Work in Victoria*, p. 177.
[212] Cameron, *Centenary History of the Presbyterian Church in New South Wales*, pp. 105ff.
[213] Cameron, *op. cit.*, pp. 111ff.
[214] Hay, *Jubilee Memorial of the Presbyterian Church*, p. 194.
[215] Colwell, *The Illustrated History of Methodism*, p. 114.
[216] Colwell, *op. cit.*, pp. 429ff.

Australasia formed an autonomous organization with its own conference, a missionary society was constituted to which the mother church entrusted much of its responsibilities in the Pacific islands.[217] Australian Methodism also had home mission societies[218] and a Church Sustentation and Extension Society.[219] In 1851 the Congregationalists of New South Wales organized a home mission society. This was assisted by the Colonial Missionary Society of London, but by far the major part of its income was from contributions from Australia.[220] In Tasmania, beginning as far back as 1828, the Congregationalists had a missionary society associated with the London Missionary Society.[221] In 1837 they organized a Colonial Missionary and Christian Instruction Society.[222] By 1910 the Laymen's Missionary Movement had taken firm root in Australia.[223]

A few immigrants of non-European stock and from a non-Christian background entered Australia. That no more came was due to the restrictive policy adopted to ensure a "white Australia." To these pagans the Protestants of Australia gave attention. Efforts were made to reach the Chinese. Several of these were by the Anglicans and were attended with hundreds of baptisms.[224] The Presbyterian Church of New South Wales supported Chinese Christians to labour among their countrymen.[225] The Methodists had converts from among the Chinese.[226]

As we have seen a few paragraphs above, the Church of England reached numbers of the "Kanakas" of Queensland. Yet, after several years of successful effort for them, as late as 1897 no church was set aside for their use and in some instances members of white congregations objected to their presence at public worship.[227]

There were Anglican missions to Jewish and Syrian immigrants.[228]

The most numerous bodies of traditionally non-Christian peoples faced by

---

[217] Strong and Warnshuis, *op. cit.*, p. 3; Bickford, *An Autobiography*, p. 132; Carruthers, *Lights in the Southern Sky*, pp. 31-33.

[218] Colwell, *A Century in the Pacific*, pp. 249ff., 256; Carruthers, *Memories of an Australian Ministry*, p. 180.

[219] Colwell, *A Century in the Pacific*, p. 247.

[220] *The Fourth Annual Report of the Congregational Home Missionary Society for New South Wales, 1854, passim.*

[221] *Thirty-third Report of the Tasmanian Missionary Society, 1859, passim.*

[222] *The Twenty-third Annual Report of the Tasmanian Colonial Missionary and Christian Instruction Society in Connection with the Tasmanian Congregational Union, 1859, passim.*

[223] Carruthers, *Memories of an Australian Ministry*, p. 181.

[224] Johnstone, *A History of the Church Missionary Society in Australia and Tasmania*, pp. 284-299.

[225] Cameron, *op. cit.*, p. 107.

[226] Johnstone, *op. cit.*, pp. 284-299.

[227] Pascoe, *Two Hundred Years of the S.P.G.*, p. 414a.

[228] Johnstone, *op. cit.*, p. 299.

the churches of Australia within their own borders were the aborigines. Both to the state and to the Church the aborigines constituted an unusually difficult problem. In race and culture they were very different from the white settlers who flooded into the country. Food gatherers rather than agriculturalists, they required a great deal of land and could not easily be fitted into the agricultural and urban civilization introduced from Europe. Their tribal organization and their customs were poles apart from the political and social structure of the whites.[229] At the very outset of the contacts between the two races clashes occurred. Some of the whites treated the blacks with incredible cruelty and sought to rid the land of them as though they were vermin.[230] Often the aborigines were demoralized by the white man's vices. In the unequal contest the aborigines rapidly declined in numbers. Those who had inhabited Tasmania entirely died out, and that in spite of efforts by the government to afford them protection and to give them Christian instruction.[231] In Australia proper they dwindled from about 250,000 or 300,000 in 1788, divided into probably about 500 tribes,[232] to about 50,000 pure bloods and about 25,000 of mixed blood in 1938.[233] The decline was most marked in the states with the largest white population, New South Wales, Victoria, and South Australia. The survivors were the most numerous in Queensland, Western Australia, and the Northern Territory.

So strong were the disintegrating forces that both state and Church fought a rearguard action. They could slow down but could not prevent the decay of the native race. Through their efforts, however, and especially those of the missionaries, hundreds of the aborigines were helped to make a wholesome adjustment to the new day so rudely thrust upon them and even to enter upon a richer life than their fathers had known. We can give the space only to some of the efforts in their behalf.

The government made various attempts to protect the aborigines and to facilitate their adaptation to the white man's world. Sometimes this was by setting aside special areas for them. Sometimes it was by schools. In all the government settlements religious work was undertaken.[234]

Of the various Christian bodies, the Church of England engaged in the

---

[229] See a brief description by Elkin in Needham, *White and Black in Australia*, pp. 13-37, with a select bibliography. A semi-popular account is N. W. Thomas, *Natives of Australia* (London, Archibald Constable and Co., 1906, pp. xii, 256).

[230] Pascoe, *op. cit.*, p. 418.

[231] James Bonwick, *The Lost Tasmanian Race* (London, Sampson Low, Marston, Searle, and Rivington, 1884, pp. 214), *passim*, especially pp. 172-175.

[232] Elkin in Needham, *op. cit.*, p. 22.

[233] Wilson, *Official Year Book of the Commonwealth of Australia, No. 32—1939*, p. 408.

[234] Bleakley in Needham, *op. cit.*, pp. 38-62.

most extensive of the enterprises for the aborigines. Samuel Marsden, famous as a pioneer clergyman of the Church of England, was interested.[235] The primary motive which led, in 1825, to the formation of the Auxiliary of the Church Missionary Society in New South Wales was the aborigines. From 1823 to 1825 a clergyman, an appointee of the Church Missionary Society, was in charge of a government institution for aborigines in New South Wales. From 1826 this society did something for them.[236] From 1831 to 1842 the Church Missionary Society was engaged in an undertaking in close connexion with the government.[237] In 1848 Bishop Short, of Adelaide, advocated educating the aborigines in the same schools with the whites, but he also wished government reserves and industrial training.[238] Two years later, Archdeacon Hale of that diocese opened a training institution for young aborigines and by 1872 from this beginning a Christian village had arisen. Since, however, the whites desired the rich lands occupied by the natives, the blacks were removed to a government settlement.[239] The diocesan board of missions which was organized in Melbourne in 1851 had the aborigines among its objectives, and in 1862 a lay missionary for them was appointed.[240] The Church Missionary Society of Victoria maintained several missions among the aborigines. In at least two of these, at Lake Condah and Lake Tyers, orderly Christian communities arose. In spite of these efforts the blacks declined in numbers.[241] In Western Australia the Anglicans had missions.[242] Famous in the annals of efforts of the Church of England for the natives were two clergymen, John Brown Gribble and E. R. Gribble, father and son. In 1880 the elder Gribble began a mission in New South Wales. Later he headed a new mission in Western Australia. In 1892 he inaugurated an enterprise at Yarrabah, in the northern part of Queensland, which became the most successful of the Anglican missions to the aborigines. There, where the natives were rotting with disease, drink, and opium, a settlement was founded with school, church, and fields in which the blacks were taught to lead a settled, industrious existence. Remarkable changes for good were wrought in many individuals. The younger generation proved sound and the birth rate began to increase. E. R. Gribble, who

---

[235] Johnstone, op. cit., pp. 164-182.

[236] Pitts, The Australian Aboriginal and the Christian Church, p. 98; Johnstone, op. cit., pp. 163, 164, 184.

[237] Stock, The History of the Church Missionary Society, Vol. I, pp. 360, 361.

[238] Whitington, Augustus Short, First Bishop of Adelaide, p. 92.

[239] Pascoe, op. cit., pp. 419, 420; Needham, op. cit., p. 84; Whitington, op. cit., p. 97.

[240] Goodman, The Church in Victoria under the Episcopate of the Right Reverend Charles Perry, pp. 381-408.

[241] Johnstone, A History of the Church Missionary Society in Australia and Tasmania, pp. 271-274.

[242] Pascoe, op. cit., pp. 426, 427a.

grew up on the frontier, tor a time after his father's death was in charge of Yarrabah and later was Protector of the Aborigines successively in Queensland and Western Australia.[243] Aided by Christians from Yarrabah, in 1908 the Church Missionary Association of Victoria opened a station on the Roper River, in Northern Australia.[244] In 1905 the Anglicans founded a station on Mitchell River,[245] on the eastern side of the Gulf of Carpentaria, and in 1913 on Forrest River, not far from Cambridge Gulf, in the northern part of Western Australia.[246]

In the 1850's W. Ridley, a Presbyterian, for two or three years had a mission among the aborigines in New South Wales.[247] In 1891 the Presbyterians inaugurated a mission on the Batavia River on the Cape York Peninsula in Queensland.[248] Eventually they had three stations in Queensland.[249]

In South Australia in the 1850's the Aborigines' Friends' Association was organized. It sought to protect the blacks and opened some missions for them.[250]

For a few years in the 1820's the Methodists had a school at Parramatta in New South Wales under William Walker.[251] In the following two decades the Methodists conducted an heroic but unsuccessful mission in Victoria. In the 1850's another fleeting effort was made in Western Australia.[252] In 1915 still another attempt was made in North Australia.[253]

With their characteristic zeal to carry the Christian message to primitive and backward peoples, the Moravians were early active among the Australian aborigines. In 1850 two Moravians landed at Melbourne. In the following two decades a station at Lake Boga in Victoria was tried but was disrupted by the gold rush, and one at Lake Koperamana in South Australia proved too difficult. Two continuing stations were begun in Victoria, with August Hagenauer as their outstanding figure. Presbyterians assisted with funds. In the first

[243] White, *Round About the Torres Straits*, pp. 10-20; Pascoe, *op. cit.*, p. 414d; E. R. Gribble, *Forty Years with the Aborigines* (Sydney, Angus and Robertson, 1930, pp. 235), *passim*.

[244] Johnstone, *op. cit.*, pp. 274-278; White, *op. cit.*, pp. 30-40.

[245] White, *op. cit.*, pp. 21-29.

[246] Pitts, *op. cit.*, pp. 113-119.

[247] Cameron, *Centenary History of the Presbyterian Church in New South Wales*, pp. 25, 109, 110.

[248] Hay, *Jubilee Memorial of the Presbyterian Church of Queensland*, pp. 110-122.

[249] Frank H. L. Paton, *Glimpses of Mapoon. The Story of a Visit to the North Queensland Mission Stations of the Presbyterian Church* (Melbourne, Arbuckle, Waddell & Fawckner, 1911, pp. 59), *passim*.

[250] Needham, *White and Black in Australia*, pp. 46, 50, 57, 92.

[251] Needham, *op. cit.*, pp. 68, 69; Findlay and Holdsworth, *The History of the Wesleyan Methodist Missionary Society*, Vol. III, pp. 34, 35, 43, 46, 47, 149, 150.

[252] Findlay and Holdsworth, *op. cit.*, Vol. III, pp. 151ff.

[253] Needham, *op. cit.*, p. 115.

decade of the twentieth century, since their constituencies were dying out, both stations were discontinued. At the outset the Presbyterian missions in Queensland were manned by Moravians.[254]

German Lutherans maintained missions for the aborigines of Queensland, South Australia, and Central Australia.[255]

Two undenominational societies, the United Aborigines' Mission and the Aborigines' Inland Mission had enterprises.[256]

These various undertakings, although bringing transformation of life to numerous individuals and for many making the coming of the white man a blessing rather than a curse, seemed unable long to stem the tide which was drowning the doomed race. Only in remote areas in the tropics where the white man did not yet care to settle were the unfortunate blacks able to survive in any large numbers. Here missions and government strove, with partial success, to halt the destruction.

In Australia the record of the relation of the aborigines to the white man and his culture and of the attempts of Christians to deal with the problem was different from that in Canada. In Australia less attention seems to have been devoted to the issue. Such as was given to it appears to have been further from success. At the outset of the nineteenth century Australia probably had about twice as many aborigines as Canada. By 1914 it probably had only two-thirds as many. In neither dominion did the aborigines make a thoroughly satisfactory accommodation to the white man's world. In both suffering and frustration were all too prevalent. Yet in Australia there seems to have been more cruelty and ruthless extermination than in Canada. The contrast may have been due in part to racial and cultural differences between the aborigines of Australia and those of Canada which made the adjustment somewhat less painful for the latter. It may also have been due in part to the fact that in Australia there were fewer missions for the natives, whether by Protestant or by Roman Catholic.

In proportion to those having a church connexion, Roman Catholic Christianity was not so prominent in Australia as in the United States or Canada. In 1921 21.8 per cent. of those in Australia with a church affiliation were

---

[254] H. G. Schneider, *Missionsarbeit der Brüdergemeine in Australien* (Gradau, Verlag der Unitäts-Buchhandlung, 1882, pp. viii, 207), *passim;* Schulze, *200 Jahre Brüdermission,* Vol. III, pp. 563-614.

[255] Needham, *op. cit.,* pp. 75, 103, 104, 115, 116.

[256] Needham, *op. cit.,* pp. 101, 102.

Roman Catholics.[257] This was in contrast with 37.5 per cent. of the church membership of the United States in 1916[258] and with 41.1 per cent. of the total church constituency of Canada in 1911.[259] The figures for Australia given above are from the census taken by the government. The statistics compiled by the Roman Catholic Church are smaller. They indicate that in 1921 17 per cent. of the population belonged to that body.[260] If these latter figures are correct, numerically Roman Catholic Christianity was relatively a declining force in Australian life, for ten years before, in 1911, the statistics gathered by that church showed 19.4 per cent. of the population as being of that faith.[261] Another set of figures declares that about 1872 the Roman Catholic percentage of the population was not far from 25.[262] In contrast, in the United States the proportionate strength of the Roman Catholic Church was increasing between 1890 and 1916 and in Canada between 1881 and 1911 was about stationary.

Australian Roman Catholicism was predominantly Irish both in the origin of its membership and in its clergy.[263] This was partly because of the fact that in the first decades of white settlement numbers of the convicts sent to the colony were from Ireland. Many Irish came because of the famines in their native island in the second quarter of the nineteenth century.[264] Even after the importation of convicts ceased, the Irish continued to arrive. As late as the first decade of the twentieth century, of those leaving Ireland 1.4 per cent. had Australia as their destination.[265] To the Irish were added some Italian and German Roman Catholics, but these were in the minority.[266]

The Irish Roman Catholic convict settlers were compelled to wait for many years for regular clerical care by priests of their own church. Feeling in Great Britain against Roman Catholicism was strong and until 1829 legal disabilities

[257] Wilson, *Official Year Book of the Commonwealth of Australia, No. 32—1939*, p. 381. This gives the total number of Roman Catholics in 1921 as 1,134,002.

[258] Department of Commerce, Bureau of the Census, *Religious Bodies. 1916*, Part I, p. 31.

[259] *The Canada Year Book 1912*, p. 34.

[260] *The Australasian Catholic Directory for 1921*, table after p. 250, gives as a total 925,108 Roman Catholics.

[261] *The Australasian Catholic Directory for 1910*, table after p. 193, gives as a total 852,202 Roman Catholics.

[262] Balangero, *Australia e Ceylan*, p. 127. About 1838 one of the Roman Catholics estimates his co-religionists as one-third of the population of New South Wales—Ullathorne, *The Catholic Mission in Australasia*, p. 7.

[263] Balangero, *op. cit.*, p. 129.

[264] *Ibid.*

[265] *The Australasian Catholic Directory for 1929*, p. 337.

[266] *The Australasian Catholic Directory for 1929*, p. 335. For the life of a Jesuit who laboured among the Germans see Johann Nep. Faigl, P. *Johann Nep. Hinteröcker, Priester der Gesellschaft Jesu und apost. Missionar in Australien* (Linz, F. J. Ebenhöch-schen Buchhandlung, 1875, p. 239).

were not appreciably lightened. In the early days of the colony Roman Catholic prisoners were required to attend the services conducted by the Anglican chaplains.[267] On the charge of being implicated in the abortive rebellion of 1798 in Ireland, two priests were sent to Australia (1800 and 1801) as convicts. Of these one was pardoned and recalled in 1802. The other was placed on Norfolk Island and officiated there for a time, but he, too, later was allowed to return to Ireland.[268] In 1803 Dixon, another priest involved in the affair of 1798 and who had been deported in 1800, having shown "exemplary conduct" was granted conditional emancipation and permitted to perform his clerical functions, but the following year, since the meetings of Roman Catholics were alleged to be centres for the formation of political conspiracies, Dixon was deprived of his rations and allowances as a chaplain. In 1808 he left the country.[269] The Irish bishops seemed indifferent to the fate of their Australian co-religionists.[270] In 1817 an Irish priest, Jeremiah Francis O'Flynn, reached Australia, under appointment by Rome as Prefect Apostolic for New South Wales. However, the Vicar Apostolic of London, who claimed jurisdiction, felt aggrieved at the assignment, O'Flynn came to Australia in face of the refusal of permission from the appropriate British secretary of state, and, after a few months of religious work, he was arrested and sent to England.[271] In 1819, Slater, the recently consecrated Vicar Apostolic of the Cape of Good Hope, had his jurisdiction extended to Australia and busied himself in seeking priests for that part of his diocese.[272] In 1819 he obtained two priests from Ireland, and these were appointed by the government as chaplains to the Roman Catholic prisoners. They arrived in 1820. One of them remained in New South Wales and the other went to Tasmania.[273] These began a succession of priests.[274] After a brief time Mauritius was also placed under Slater. It was as vicar general of Slater's successor that Ullathorne came to Australia (1833).[275] In 1834 John Bede Polding, a Benedictine, was consecrated Vicar Apostolic for Australia.[276]

---

[267] Ullathorne, *A Reply to Judge Burton, passim.*

[268] O'Brien, *The Dawn of Catholicism in Australia,* Vol. I, p. 115.

[269] *Ibid.;* Burton, *The State of Religion and Education in New South Wales,* pp. 13-15; Ullathorne, *op. cit.,* pp. 7, 8.

[270] O'Brien, *op. cit.,* Vol. I, pp. 139, 140.

[271] O'Brien, *op. cit., passim;* Ullathorne, *The Catholic Mission in Australasia,* p. 8; Ullathorne, *A Reply to Judge Burton,* p. 10.

[272] O'Brien, *op. cit.,* Vol. II, p. 180; Birt, *Benedictine Pioneers in Australia,* Vol. I, pp. 9ff.

[273] O'Brien, *op. cit.,* Vol. II, pp. 206, 207; Ullathorne, *The Catholic Mission in Australasia,* pp. 10, 11.

[274] Ullathorne, *op. cit.,* pp. 10, 11; Ullathorne, *A Reply to Judge Burton,* p. 25.

[275] Birt, *op. cit.,* Vol. I, pp. 127, 158ff.

[276] Birt, *op. cit.,* Vol. I, pp. 226ff.

At the insistence of Ullathorne and Polding, who believed that Australia could best be reached by a comprehensive hierarchy, in 1842 Polding was created archbishop, and a bishop, Robert William Willson, was consecrated for Hobart.[277] Ullathorne was selected for bishop for Adelaide, but declined, and Francis Murphy was appointed.[278] By 1869 the hierarchy had increased to an archbishop and seven bishops.[279] In 1888 Tasmania was created a separate province, with Hobart as the seat of the archbishop.[280] Late in the nineteenth century Patrick Francis Moran, Archbishop of Sydney, was a cardinal.[281]

In the later decades in which financial assistance was given the churches by the government, the Roman Catholics were accorded a share. For instance, when in 1855 the legislature of Victoria appropriated £50,000 for religious purposes, the sum allocated to the Roman Catholics was second only to that allotted the Church of England.[282] In the 1830's in New South Wales stipends were paid to several Roman Catholic chaplains and subsidies to Roman Catholic schools.[283] In 1836 in New South Wales the chief denominations were placed on a basis of full equality before the state and government subsidies were set aside for the salaries of priests and the building of churches.[284]

In Australia the Roman Catholic Church developed its usual features of organization and life and was propagated and strengthened by means already familiar to us in our earlier accounts of the United States and Canada. Members of religious orders entered, both regular clergy and lay brothers. Sisterhoods appeared. Seminaries were begun for the training of a native clergy. In 1910 the Roman Catholic Church counted in Australia 1,443 churches, 738 secular and 230 regular clergy, 466 brothers, 5,081 sisters, 3 seminaries, and 85 charitable institutions.[285] This was a striking growth from the unpromising beginnings made scarcely a century before. Parochial schools and higher schools were stressed, as a means of nurturing children and young people in the Christian faith. In 1910 these institutions had an enrolment of 112,315.[286] In

[277] Birt, op. cit., Vol. II, pp. 1ff. Incidentally, Broughton, the Anglican bishop, resented what he deemed an encroachment on his see by the appointment by Rome of an "Archbishop of Sydney" and protested publicly against it.—Broughton, Sermons on the Church of England, pp. xxiv-xxxi.

[278] Birt, op. cit., Vol. II, p. 98.

[279] The Proceedings of the Second Provincial Council of Australia, held in Melbourne April 1869 . . . (Melbourne, S. V. Winter, pp. 24), passim.

[280] Harvey, Notes on Australian Church History (Ms.).

[281] Ibid.

[282] Hamilton, A Jubilee History of the Presbyterian Church of Victoria, pp. 80, 81.

[283] Burton, op. cit., pp. 106-110; Ullathorne, A Reply to Judge Burton, pp. 13-17, 62.

[284] Ullathorne, op. cit., pp. 41-44.

[285] Australasian Catholic Directory for 1910, after p. 193.

[286] Ibid.

1914 an Apostolic Delegation was created for Australia, to facilitate relations with Rome.[287]

The Roman Catholic Church in Australia, so far as the white population was concerned, was confined chiefly to those who by heredity were attached to it. A few converts were made from Protestantism. Thus in the 1840's two of the clergy of the Church of England, under the impulse of the Oxford Movement, paralleled what some of their brethren in England were then doing, and went over to the Roman Catholics.[288] This, however, was exceptional.

Roman Catholics were not content to restrict their attention to the whites. They also sought to win the aborigines. Much less prominent in Australia than the Protestants, their missions to the blacks were not so numerous as were those of the latter. Moreover, most of these were manned, not by those of Australian but of European birth. Never were their enterprises for the Australian aborigines nearly so extensive as were those of the Roman Catholics of Canada for the Indians and Eskimos. This was probably in part because the Roman Catholics were not relatively so strong in Australia as in Canada. As we saw a few paragraphs above, the contrast was one which was shared with Protestants. The reason for it is by no means clear. Even as late as the 1830's, the Roman Catholics had been too engrossed in establishing themselves among the whites to do more than baptize a few of the children of the aborigines who were in danger of death and include some of the youths in their schools.[289] In 1843 a short-lived mission was inaugurated by Passionists from Italy on land near Brisbane granted by the government.[290] In 1846 Spanish Benedictines began a mission in Western Australia. This had Salvado as its chief figure. With its centre at New Norcia, it became the most successful of all the Roman Catholic enterprises for Australian aborigines.[291] In 1906 the Benedictines opened another mission on the Drysdale River, in the extreme north of Western Australia.[292] In 1877 a priest, D. McNabb, obtained from the government a grant of land in Queensland for a reservation for the blacks, but the opposition of white neighbours compelled its cancellation (1885).[293] In 1882 a group of Jesuits began a mission near Port Darwin, in North Aus-

[287] *Australasian Catholic Directory for 1921*, p. 11.

[288] *The Autobiography and Reminiscences of William Macquarie Cowper, Dean of Sydney*, p. 49.

[289] Ullathorne, *The Catholic Mission in Australasia*, p. 47.

[290] Walter, *Australien*, pp. 129, 130.

[291] Walter, *op. cit.*, pp. 130ff.; *Australasian Catholic Directory for 1907*, p. 102; Needham, *White and Black in Australia*, pp. 78-80.

[292] Walter, *op. cit.*, pp. 134, 135.

[293] Needham, *op. cit.*, p. 96; Walter, *op. cit.*, p. 135.

tralia, but after ten years felt constrained to retire.[294] In the 1890's Trappists from France inaugurated a mission at Beagle Bay, in the northern part of Western Australia. Handicapped by lack of funds, they gave up the undertaking and returned home. The Pallotini Fathers replaced them (1901), led by George Walter, who had been a missionary in the Cameroons.[295] The Roman Catholics found that it was practically hopeless to induce adult aborigines, with their roving habits, to submit themselves to the discipline of the mission and its settled life. They emphasized, therefore, the training of the children. If they could have them from a tender age, they found less difficulty in inculcating an orderly life with agricultural and industrial crafts.[296] As in the earlier frontier missions in Latin America, the Roman Catholics endeavoured to build around the mission station a community of Christians, removed so far as possible from contamination by non-missionary whites and under the close supervision of the white clergy.

The Eastern Churches were but scantily represented in Australia, for very few immigrants came from Eastern Europe and Western Asia. The census of 1921 showed only 5,372 professing allegiance to the Greek Orthodox faith.[297]

What effect did Christianity have upon Australia, this land where a young nation was arising so rapidly from immigration and where a new civilization was bringing disruption to a bewildered, angry, scattered population of primitives?

In the new nation of European blood which was established some results were fairly obvious. The overwhelming majority of the population, in 1921 96.9 per cent.,[298] professed to have some connexion with one or another of the Christian churches. After aid from abroad in their early stages, these churches became self-supporting financially and in time produced practically all their clergy. Not content with meeting the needs of their own country, several of these churches were propagating their faith among the islands of the Pacific and, to a lesser degree, in Asia. The churches undertook responsibility for much of the education of Australia. This was partly to meet the need for

[294] Needham, op. cit., p. 97.
[295] Walter, op. cit., pp. 140ff.; Daisy Bates, The Passing of the Aborigines (London, John Murray, 1938, pp. xviii, 258), pp. 9-21.
[296] Walter, op. cit., pp. 136-139.
[297] Wilson, Official Year Book of the Commonwealth of Australia, No. 32—1939, p. 381.
[298] Ibid.

schools and partly to ensure religious rearing for their youth. By the establishment, in 1825, through royal charter, of the Church and School Corporation, all of the education of New South Wales was entrusted to the clergy of the Church of England.[299] Even when, in 1844, the decision was made in New South Wales to adopt a national system of education, schools of the various denominations, both Protestant and Roman Catholic, were still subsidized from state funds.[300] The New South Wales Public School League for making Primary Education National, Secular, Compulsory, and Free, formed in 1874, had in its inception a Baptist clergyman as its leading spirit.[301] In Victoria in 1851 some schools were maintained by the several churches with government grants, others were under the British and Foreign Society, attended only by Protestants and managed like denominational schools, and still others were state institutions, but admitting clergymen of all denominations to give religious instruction to their children. Only in the 1870's did Victoria adopt a system of free, secular, compulsory state education.[302] Down to 1914 secondary education was left almost entirely to ecclesiastical and private initiative.[303] Many colleges were founded and maintained by the churches.[304] In accordance with time-honoured Christian tradition, organizations connected with the churches gave medical care to the poor and aid to underprivileged women and children.[305] Clergy on the frontier took it upon themselves to protect women left alone with the children while the men were away at work for weeks at a time.[306] In Australia, as in Great Britain, the United States, and Canada, Christians organized to fight intemperance, gambling, prostitution, immoral literature, and "Sabbath desecration." They had a large part in obtaining woman's suffrage and in prison reform.[307]

Less tangible and more difficult to measure with accuracy were some other

[299] Lang, *An Historical and Statistical Account of New South Wales*, Vol. II, p. 408; Cameron, *Centenary History of the Presbyterian Church in New South Wales*, p. 5.

[300] C. J. Prescott in Colwell, *A Century in the Pacific*, pp. 611-613.

[301] Kiek, *An Apostle in Australia*, p. 108.

[302] J. Alex. Allan, *The Old Model School. Its History and Romance, 1852-1904* (Melbourne University Press, 1934, pp. xxiii, 225), pp. 1-3; E. H. Sugden in Colwell, *op. cit.*, pp. 288, 289.

[303] C. J. Prescott in Colwell, *op. cit.*, pp. 618-620.

[304] Cameron, *op. cit.*, pp. 150ff.; E. H. Sugden in Colwell, *op. cit.*, p. 292; Bickford, *An Autobiography*, p. 275; Whitington, *Augustus Short, First Bishop of Adelaide*, p. 169. For the history of one of these see Watson A. Steel in collaboration with Charles W. Sloman, *The History of All Saints College, Bathurst 1873-1934. Compiled from Available Records and Personal Reminiscences* (Australia, Angus & Robertson, 1936, pp. 217).

[305] Burton, *The State of Religion and Education in New South Wales*, p. 251; Stewart, *The Presbyterian Church of Victoria*, p. 86.

[306] Bickford, *op. cit.*, p. 140.

[307] Cameron, *op. cit.*, pp. 115, 116; Hay, *Jubilee Memorial of the Presbyterian Church of Queensland*, p. 182; Kiek, *op. cit.*, pp. 193ff.

results. The transformation of individual lives through the ministrations of the churches and the inward compulsion of the faith could seldom be appraised with accuracy, but here, as elsewhere, was one of the potent results of Christianity. The training given by Methodism to its local preachers in public speech and in social and moral idealism nurtured some of the outstanding leaders for the initial stages of the labour movement. Cardinal Moran, speaking for his church, gave backing to organized labour.[308] The Australian-wide organization of the Church of England ante-dated political union and by its example contributed to the formation of the Commonwealth of Australia. As in Canada and the United States, the prevailing Protestantism reinforced political democracy.

Christianity and the churches could not entirely save the aborigines from cruel and callous treatment by the whites. Nor could they fully ensure to the blacks a successful transition to the world of the dominant white man. They did much, however, to arouse the public conscience and to obtain protective governmental action. By their missions they aided hundreds to achieve a happy adjustment to the new order.

Environment placed its mark upon the Christianity of Australia. To be sure, this Christianity was to a very large degree that of the British Isles of the nineteenth century. In the religious as in the other sides of its life, Australia gave evidence of its colonial status. Yet in its Christianity as in its other phases the transplanted culture underwent changes.

One inter-related group of features which arose out of the environment was the early demotion of the Church of England from its position as the only ecclesiastical fellowship supported by the state, the eventual withdrawal of all state aid to the churches, and the complete dependence of the latter upon voluntary contributions. This was partly because the Church of England had to face the presence of a Presbyterianism which in Scotland was the established church and because other denominations insisted upon equal access to a public purse which was dependent upon general taxation. It was partly due to the increasing disfavour with which the nineteenth century Occident viewed the union of Church and state. State support of public worship ceased in South Australia in 1851,[309] in 1862 in New South Wales (except that it was to be continued through the lifetime of the individual clergymen who then benefited

[308] Matthews, *A Parson in the Australian Bush*, pp. 306, 307.
[309] Whitington, *op. cit.*, p. 80.

by it),[310] in Tasmania in 1868,[311] in Victoria by an act of 1871, and in Western Australia in 1895 by the grant of lump sums to the Church of England and to the Roman Catholic, the Presbyterian, and the Wesleyan communions.[312]

Another feature was increased self-government by the Church of England as against the Erastianism in the mother country, with an important share given to the laity in the councils of the church. Diocesan synods were developed in which the bishop, clergy, and laity participated.[313] Since his salary was derived from voluntary subscriptions, the parishioners exercised a greater control over their pastor than was true in the Church of England in the home land. Lay representation was more common in the conferences of Australian than of British Methodism.[314]

As in Canada, the atmosphere of a new country bred impatience with ecclesiastical differences inherited from Great Britain and furthered church union. This first became apparent in the coming together of the various branches of the same denominational families. As we have seen, the several divisions of Presbyterianism tended to be erased,[315] and the diverse bodies of Methodism to coalesce.[316] In the twentieth century the movement went further. In the first decade of that century negotiations looking towards union began between the Presbyterians, the Methodists, and the Congregationalists.[317]

Some of the denominational families developed Australian-wide ecclesiastical structures. The Church of England early took steps in this direction. The Australian bishops met in 1850 and again in 1868. Out of the latter gathering issued, in 1872, a General Synod.[318] Yet strong centralization did not come. The isolation through which in each colony the Church of England had developed as a distinct unity was not fully surmounted. The bond of union was more the inheritance of a common tradition than visible outward organization.[319] The Anglican churches in Australia did not become fully autonomous

[310] Bickford, *Christian Work in Australasia*, pp. 51-53.

[311] Giles, *The Constitutional History of the Australian Church*, pp. 135-143.

[312] Giles, *op. cit.*, p. 144.

[313] Giles, *op. cit.*, pp. 75-92, 97-102; Goodman, *The Church in Victoria during the Episcopate of the Right Reverend Charles Perry*, pp. 4, 221-251.

[314] H. T. Burgess in Colwell, *A Century in the Pacific*, p. 322.

[315] Stewart, *The Presbyterian Church of Victoria*, p. 44; *An Apology for Presbyterian Union in Australia, and a Plea for Non-Intervention on the Part of the Scottish Churches. Addressed to the Members of the ensuing General Assembly of the Free Church of Scotland* (Glasgow, James R. Macnair, 1861, pp. 15), *passim*.

[316] Colwell, *The Illustrated History of Methodism*, pp. 609ff.; E. H. Sugden in Colwell, *A Century in the Pacific*, pp. 293-295; H. T. Burgess in Colwell, *A Century in the Pacific*, pp. 327-333.

[317] Carruthers, *Memories of an Australian Ministry*, pp. 242-248.

[318] Giles, *The Constitutional History of the Australian Church*, pp. 146-157; *The Autobiography and Reminiscences of William M. Cowper, Dean of Sydney*, p. 171.

[319] Giles, *op. cit.*, p. 9.

but legally remained parts of the Church of England of the mother country.[320] The Presbyterians achieved a federal union which preserved much of the autonomy of the church of each state. The first Federal Assembly met in 1888. At the last meeting of that body, in 1901, a new union was adopted and an Assembly of the Presbyterian Church of Australia was formed.[321] As far back as 1855 a conference convened of Congregational ministers and delegates from the several Australian colonies.[322] At irregular intervals other gatherings assembled. The Congregational Union of Australia and New Zealand was constituted in 1888 and was revived in 1903.[323] In 1855, largely from the initiative of the mother church, a comprehensive Australasian Wesleyan Methodist Connexion came into being.[324]

Several features affecting more than one denomination seem to have arisen from the Australian environment. As was to be expected in a new country, a free and easy style of preaching, in contrast to the dignified, reserved type prevailing in Great Britain, was popular. There was little leisure for mature scholarship. No new major denominations emerged, but, true to its colonial status, Australia conserved the ones inherited from the mother country. The churches were strongest in the rural sections. In the great cities, so characteristic of the land, church attendance was relatively small. In Sydney and Brisbane, possibly because of a climate which encouraged outdoor life and sports through much of the year, and possibly because of a tradition inherited from the days when convicts were a prominent element of the population, the churches did not seem to have so strong a hold as in the South.

Individual denominations developed peculiarities which partly distinguished them from the parent bodies in Europe. Presbyterianism and Methodism were mixtures of the various British types—English, Scotch, Scotch-Irish, and Welsh. Although the Church of England was accused of clinging too closely to the British forms of organization, to a framework of officialdom unadapted to the new country, and to the parish system for parishes which were too large,[325] it developed at least one method which was peculiarly fitted to the thinly scattered population of the pastoral *hinterland*. Partly at the suggestion of Bishop Westcott of Durham, in the mother country, not far from the close of the nineteenth century, what were known as Bush Brotherhoods were formed. By 1908 four of these had come into being. They provided a kind of community

[320] Giles, *op. cit.*, p. 166.
[321] Cameron, *Centenary History of the Church in New South Wales*, pp. 191-195.
[322] *Report of the Van Diemen's Land Congregational Union, Dec. 1855, passim.*
[323] Harvey, *Notes on Australian Church History* (Ms.).
[324] Findlay and Holdsworth, *The History of the Wesleyan Methodist Missionary Society*, Vol. III, pp. 140ff.
[325] Matthews, *A Parson in the Australian Bush*, p. 7.

life for the unmarried clergy who, perforce, spent much of their time in solitary travel over their vast districts. Four or five times a year the members would gather at the centre for fellowship.[326] One observer from the continent of Europe noted in the Roman Catholic churches a certain severity and simplicity in architecture and in services,[327] but that was probably an inheritance from Great Britain rather than due to Australia.

In sharing in the creation of the new nation in Australia Christianity displayed pronounced vitality. Although the motive of white settlement was overwhelmingly the desire for greater economic and social opportunity, and although at the outset convicts constituted a large element of the population, Christianity succeeded in making itself an integral part of the life of the rising commonwealth. The Christianity was predominantly that of the British Isles of the nineteenth century. Numerically its largest element was Anglican, with the various trends of nineteenth-century English Anglicanism represented. Presbyterianism was brought by immigrants from Scotland, Ireland, and England. Methodism was prominent, as was natural from the increasing place which it won for itself in the British Isles of the nineteenth century. Baptists, Congregationalists, and Quakers formed a part of Australian Christianity, but not so large as of the Christianity of the mother country. Their failure to achieve greater prominence may have been because their type of organization did not so readily lend itself to propagation in the new land. It may also have been because they were products of sixteenth- and seventeenth-century movements in British Christianity rather than of those of the eighteenth and nineteenth centuries. The latter more largely flowed into and through Methodism. Yet the prominence won by the Baptists in the United States in the nineteenth century suggests that these are insufficient answers to the question. Roman Catholic Christianity owed its strength chiefly to the Irish immigration. Lutheranism was dependent upon relatively small contingents from the continent of Europe.

This Christianity was planted partly with assistance from the churches of the British Isles and to a much less extent from Europe and the United States, but owed its growth chiefly and increasingly to the conviction and initiative of the Australians themselves. It displayed marked inner vitality.

[326] Matthews, *op. cit.*, pp. 32-36. For the life of a clergyman on the frontier before the foundation of these brotherhoods, see John Davies Mereweather, *Diary of a Working Clergyman in Australia and Tasmania . . . 1850-1853* (London, Hatchard & Co., 1859, pp. viii, 369), *passim*.

[327] Balangero, *Australia e Ceylan*, pp. 156-165.

Whether Christianity somewhat relaxed its grip in the process of being transplanted is not clear. The overwhelming majority of Australians professed to be Christians, but there were some indications that their avowed faith was losing its hold. The presence of rapidly growing cities, a problem which here as elsewhere plagued the church of the nineteenth and twentieth centuries, was not completely met. The outdoor life and the emphasis on sports detracted from attention to organized religion. The virile labour movement, while at the outset with strong Christian elements in its leadership, drifted towards secularism. Yet this Australian Christianity continued to be vigorous. It sought to protect and win the aborigines. It helped to shape the life of the country, notably in ideals, morals, and education. It undertook the spread of its faith to the islands of the Pacific and here and there in Asia.

Chapter VI

NEW ZEALAND. PROTESTANTISM AND ROMAN CATHOLICISM AMONG THE MAORIS AND THE WHITES

NEW ZEALAND displayed a number of resemblances to Australia. Like the latter, before the coming of the white man it was inhabited by a dusky people of "backward" culture. Also like the latter, in the seventeenth century it was discovered but not occupied by the Dutch. James Cook was the first European to map its shores with any degree of fulness, as he had been for the shores of Australia. The white settlers in both Australia and New Zealand were chiefly from the British Isles and the majority of them arrived in the nineteenth century. In both lands dominions arose which while eventually self-governing remained within the British Empire. In both the white population tended to cluster in cities.

The contrasts between Australia and New Zealand were, however, marked. New Zealand was wholly within the temperate zone and possessed an equable climate favourable to white settlement. Australia was chiefly tropical and subtropical and much of its expanse was forbidding to Europeans. Yet New Zealand was so much smaller than Australia that, while having on the average more people to the square mile, by 1914 it could boast only a little over a fourth as large a population. In 1916 this was slightly above 1,000,000.

Markedly different, too, was the fate of the aborigines of the two lands. At the advent of the Europeans, the populations were probably not far from the same size. In both the coming of the white man was followed by rapid decline. Yet the aborigines of New Zealand dwindled for partially different reasons than did those of Australia. In New Zealand it was the intensification of intertribal wars by the introduction of iron and of fire-arms which wrought the most spectacular damage. This was not true in Australia. The aborigines of New Zealand offered more vigorous resistance to the white man than did those of Australia. The former eventually achieved a more successful adjustment to the culture of the whites than did the latter. Indeed, by 1914 they had become an integral, self-respecting part of the life of the new nation. They had once more begun to increase in numbers and their blood and that of the whites were mingling in a fashion which gave promise of the ultimate fusion of the two.

The diversity between the courses of the aborigines arose in part from contrasts in race and in culture. In New Zealand the aborigines were Maoris, Polynesians. The first ancestors of the Maoris seem not to have come to New Zealand until the tenth century or afterwards and the greatest influx was not until the fourteenth century. In Australia the blacks were of darker and smaller stock who probably had been much longer in the land. A hard but not impossible struggle for existence appears to have been at least in part responsible for a certain sturdiness of physique and character in the Maoris. In contradistinction from the Australian blacks, who had not passed beyond the food-gathering stages, the Maoris engaged in agriculture as well as in hunting and fishing. Their cannibalism was presumably not a religious act but for the purpose of increasing their supply of meat. In their art and some of their crafts they were much ahead of the Australian natives. In Australia the aborigines were widely scattered. In New Zealand they were largely concentrated on the North Island. The South Island had relatively few.[1]

In contrast with Canada, where the first efforts to win the Indians to the Christian faith were approximately concurrent with the initial white settlements, and with Australia, where resolute organized enterprises in behalf of the aborigines lagged about a generation behind the first colonization by the British, in New Zealand missionary activity among the Maoris antedated by about a quarter of a century the first extensive permanent immigration from the British Isles. In New Zealand the missionary effort for the aborigines was more extensive and more successful than was that in Australia. In both it was predominantly Protestant and chiefly by representatives of the Church of England.

It was Samuel Marsden who inaugurated the first Christian mission to the Maoris. For many years after his arrival in 1794 a leading figure in the religious life of New South Wales, with the breadth of interest and the practical initiative which characterized him, Marsden expanded his activity to New Zealand. Across the years Marsden gave hospitality to several Maoris who in one way or another had come to New South Wales.[2] These contacts begot in him a high respect for the native capacities of that people, kindled his imagina-

---

[1] On the Maoris see Elsdon Best, *The Maori* (Wellington, Harry H. Tombs, 2 Vols., 1924), *passim*.

[2] For accounts of contacts with white men by which Maoris left New Zealand, see Robert McNab, *From Tasman to Marsden. A History of Northern New Zealand from 1642 to 1818* (Dunedin, J. Wilkie & Co., 1914, pp. xiv, 236), pp. 86ff.

tion, and led him to wish to begin a mission among them. While on leave in Great Britain, in 1807 and 1808, Marsden persuaded the then youthful Church Missionary Society to appoint two mechanics to introduce useful arts among them. His belief, shared by the London Missionary Society in its earlier venture in the South Seas, was that the teaching of crafts and orderly labour to primitive peoples was a necessary preparation to making converts from among them. The first recruits reached Australia in 1810. Discouraging delays, due in part to the fear of sea captains for the ferocity of the Maoris and to deeds of violence by both whites and Maoris, prevented for more than four years the inauguration of the mission. Eventually, late in 1814, Marsden, then fifty years of age, himself headed a party, now grown to several missionary families and five Maori chiefs, which went to New Zealand. They landed at the Bay of Islands, near the northern tip of the North Island. There, on Christmas Day, 1814, Marsden conducted what seems to have been the first Christian service in New Zealand.

Marsden kept in close touch with the enterprise. He made seven other trips to New Zealand. His last was in 1837, when he was in his seventy-third year. He himself conducted a school for Maoris in Parramatta, in New South Wales. There were grievous disappointments. A few of the missionaries succumbed either to drink or to sexual irregularities. Some engaged in trade to the detriment of their calling. One of the Maori chiefs who seemed to be the most promising in his interest in the Christian message used contacts made through the mission to obtain fire-arms to gain the advantage in his wars with his enemies. Yet some of the missionaries proved worthy. Notable among these were two brothers, William Williams and Henry Williams. They arrived in the 1820's and each was to give about half a century to the Maoris. Several of the later generations of the Williams family served the Maoris as clergymen. Converts gradually began to come. The first baptism was that of a chief, in 1825. In 1838, the year after Marsden's last visit, the Church Missionary Society had in New Zealand a staff of 35 missionaries and 51 schools. Communicants numbered 178 and 2,176 persons were counted as attending public worship. In the 1830's new stations were opened, some of them well within the main part of the North Island. Cattle, sheep, horses, and new plants and seeds were introduced. The missionaries did much to reduce in frequency the wars which the coming of fire-arms had made so deadly. The language was given written form. Hymns, catechisms, the liturgy, and portions of the Bible were translated into it. By 1841 in some of the tribes the old religious practices were passing. Slavery was also going. Cannibalism, infanticide, and suicide were dying out. Polygamy was becoming less common. Marsden, however, was not to live to see the full fruition of his dreams.[3]

Marsden was also largely responsible for the inauguration of a Wesleyan mission to the Maoris. It was at his suggestion that Samuel Leigh, a pioneer Methodist clergyman in Australia, visited New Zealand (1819). In England on health leave in 1820, Leigh induced his missionary society to authorize the expansion of their work to New Zealand and by touring the country raised the means for the support of the new undertaking. In 1822 he arrived at the Bay of Islands. A station was opened at Whangaroa Bay, north of the Bay of Islands. Within a few months Leigh was forced by ill health to return to Australia, but colleagues carried on the enterprise. In 1826 the entire band of missionaries was forced by the violence of the Maoris to seek refuge in Sydney. However, undaunted, the following year the mission was renewed at Hokianga, also near the northern tip of the North Island. In 1830 the first convert was baptized. Others followed.[4]

To the Anglicans and Methodists were added, late in the 1830's, the Roman Catholics. In the 1830's Bishop Polding of Sydney baptized two children of Maori chiefs who had been sent to Australia by an Irish sailor.[5] The pioneers in New Zealand were French priests of the recently founded Marists, the Society of Mary of Lyons and Belley. The French, in the early flush of the

---

[3] John Rawson Elder, editor, *The Letters and Journals of Samuel Marsden, 1765-1838* (Dunedin, Coulls Somerville Wilkie, 1932, pp. 580), *passim;* H. C. Fancourt, *The Advance of the Missionaries. Being the Expansion of the C.M.S. Mission South of the Bay of Islands, 1833-1840* (Wellington, 1939, pp. xix, 129), *passim;* Ramsden, *Marsden and the Missions, passim;* John Liddiard Nicholas, *Narrative of a Voyage to New Zealand, Performed in the Years 1814 and 1815, in Company with the Rev. Samuel Marsden* (London, James Black and Son, 2 vols., 1817), *passim;* Johnstone, *Samuel Marsden,* pp. 128ff.; Stock, *The History of the Church Missionary Society,* Vol. I, pp. 204-215; John Rawson Elder, editor, *Marsden's Lieutenants* (Dunedin, Coulls Somerville Wilkie, 1934, pp. 280), *passim;* William Yate, *An Account of New Zealand and of the Formation and Progress of the Church Missionary Society's Mission in the Northern Island* (London, Seeley and Burnside, 1835, p. 310), pp. 165ff.; J. B. Marsden, editor, *Memories of the Life and Labours of the Rev. Samuel Marsden* (London, The Religious Tract Society, [1880], pp. viii, 326), pp. 47ff.; Williams, *Christianity among the New Zealanders, passim;* Phyllis L. Garlick, *Peacemaker of the Tribes. Henry Williams of New Zealand* (London, The Highway Press, 1939, pp. vi, 76), *passim.*

[4] Findlay and Holdsworth, *The History of the Wesleyan Methodist Missionary Society,* Vol. III, pp. 165-222; Alexander Strachan, *The Life of the Rev. Samuel Leigh* (London, The Wesleyan Mission House, 1870, pp. vi, 418), pp. 82-216, 303-377; Keeling, *What He did for Convicts and Cannibals . . . Rev. Samuel Leigh,* pp. 66ff.; Ramsden, *Marsden and the Missions,* pp. 91ff., 175ff.; J. G. Turner, *The Pioneer Missionary. Life of the Rev. Nathaniel Turner, Missionary to New Zealand, Tonga, and Australia* (London, The Wesleyan Conference Office, 1872, pp. viii, 335), *passim;* Alfred Barrett, *The Life of the Rev. John Hewgill Bumby, with a Brief History of the Commencement and Progress of the Wesleyan Mission in New Zealand* (London, John Mason, 1853, pp. vi, 254), *passim.*

[5] Ullathorne, *The Catholic Mission of Australasia,* pp. 48, 49.

renewal of their missionary enthusiasm which followed 1815, were inaugurat-. ing missions in the Pacific. In 1836 Jean Baptiste François Pompallier was named the first Vicar Apostolic of Western Oceania. In 1838 he landed in New Zealand and celebrated in the home of an Irish settler the first mass said on that island group. In 1842 New Zealand was created a separate vicariate apostolic. Pompallier was continued as its head. He and his colleagues rapidly extended their labours among the Maoris in the North Island. Translations were made of prayers and the creed.[6] Friction arose between Roman Catholics and Protestants. Wesleyans and the representatives of the Church Missionary Society, since both were of the Evangelical strain in British Protestantism, had preserved amicable relations, but the coming of the Roman Catholics brought tension.[7]

To the disturbances created by the arrival of Roman Catholic missionaries were added the much graver conflicts and the disintegrating influences which accompanied the rapid growth of white immigration. These were to continue until the 1870's.

The most powerful of the missionary organizations represented in New Zealand, the Church Missionary Society, fought vigorously in England the leading project for colonizing the islands. It pled the disruption which this would bring to the noteworthy progress which had been achieved by the mission among the Maoris.[8] The Aborigines' Protection Society gave warning of the damage to the Maoris which could be anticipated from white coloniza-tion.[9] However, both societies were defeated. In 1840 British sovereignty was extended to New Zealand. The missionaries strove to have this step taken in such fashion as would safeguard the interests of the Maoris. Already they had co-operated with James Busby who in 1833 had been sent as British Resident to the Bay of Islands and had endeavoured to help him to exercise some re-straint over the frequently lawless European population.[10] Now, in 1840, they gave assistance to William Hobson, the first British Governor of New Zealand, when he negotiated with Maori chiefs the Treaty of Waitangi. By this agree-ment the Maoris acknowledged the sovereignty of Queen Victoria and in return were given the rights of British subjects and were guaranteed the full, ex-

---

[6] *Fishers of Men* (Author, place of publication, publisher, and date not given, pp. 131. Under ecclesiastical imprimatur, 1938, composed largely of translations of documents), *passim; The Catholic Encyclopedia*, Vol. XI, p. 41; Pompallier, *Early History of the Catholic Church in Oceania*, pp. 34ff.

[7] Taylor, *The Past and Present of New Zealand*, pp. 56-59; Findlay and Holdsworth, *op. cit.*, Vol. III, pp. 223, 234; Williams, *op. cit.*, pp. 335ff.

[8] Stock, *op. cit.*, Vol. I, pp. 427, 428; Harrop, *England and New Zealand*, p. xvi.

[9] *Fifteenth Annual Report of the Aborigines' Protection Society*, p. 4.

[10] Scholefield, *Captain William Hobson, First Governor of New Zealand*, p. 61.

clusive, and undisturbed possession of their lands. Both Hobson and the missionaries thus sought to protect the Maoris against exploitation by the whites.[11] Although some of the Maoris accused the missionaries of despoiling them of their lands,[12] the Treaty of Waitangi became the basis of the later incorporation of the race into the structure of the new commonwealth on something approaching a basis of equality.[13]

Land hungry white settlers were ill content with an arrangement which kept them from access to some of the best soil of New Zealand. Encroachments on the Maoris' territories followed. Missionaries and their supporters in Great Britain protested, and sometimes to good effect.[14] Missionaries also strove to persuade the Maoris not to resist by force of arms and probably did much to prevent a general anti-white rising.[15]

In spite of the efforts of missionaries and of white officials, wars broke out between Maoris and whites, first in the 1840's and then, more extensively, in 1860. By the close of the year 1865 the main force of Maori opposition had been broken, but not until 1871 were the last of the scattered Maori forces subdued.[16]

Unrest and war did not entirely stop the spread of Christianity among the Maoris.[17] In 1854, just after his first governorship of New Zealand, Sir George Grey reported that all but about 1 per cent. of the Maoris had made a profession of Christianity.[18] This did not mean that they had been accepted as full members of the Church. Indeed, only a small percentage were communicants.[19] Yet they called themselves Christian and had been somewhat affected by the faith.

The progress of the Church of England, which had the largest following of any of the Christian bodies among the Maoris, was facilitated by the arrival, in 1842, of the first Anglican Bishop of New Zealand, George Augustus Selwyn.[20] At times Selwyn brought controversy.[21] His high churchmanship

[11] Pinfold, *Fifty Years in Maoriland*, p. 99; Scholefield, *op. cit.*, pp. 9, 10; Jacobs, *New Zealand*, p. 85.

[12] Scholefield, *op. cit.*, p. 91.

[13] Scholefield, *op. cit.*, pp. 9, 10.

[14] Harrop, *England and New Zealand*, p. 203.

[15] Pascoe, *Two Hundred Years of the S.P.G.*, p. 437.

[16] Condliffe, *A Short History of New Zealand*, pp. 97ff.; Shrimpton and Mulgan, *Maori & Pakeha*, pp. 127ff., 199ff.; Lady Martin, *Our Maoris*, pp. 45-52, 144ff.

[17] For pictures of an Anglican mission station in 1859, see J. W. and E. Stack, *Further Maoriland Adventures*, edited by A. H. Reed (Dunedin, A. H. and A. W. Reed, 1938), pp. xv, 255), pp. 190ff.

[18] Stock, *The History of the Church Missionary Society*, Vol. I, pp. 446, 447.

[19] Williams, *Christianity among the New Zealanders*, p. 345, gives the number of communicants, presumably only of the Church of England, as 2,893 in 1849, a total which had about trebled in the preceding five years.

[20] On Selwyn see H. W. Tucker, *Memoir of the Life and Episcopate of George Augustus Selwyn, D.D.* (London, William Wells Gardner, 2 vols., 1879), G. H. Curteis, *Bishop*

was in contrast with the traditions of the staff of the Church Missionary Society. He was possessed, too, of marked energy and positive convictions which did not easily yield to opposition. However, he was a man of single-hearted devotion, of high integrity, of outstanding intellectual gifts, of iron physique, and of unflinching courage. He ministered to both whites and Maoris, travelling through his pioneer diocese in the face of great physical hardships. He was one of the most distinguished figures in the colony, gave remarkable leadership to his church among both races, and, as we are to see in the next chapter, extended his mission beyond New Zealand into other islands of the South Pacific.

The disturbances of these decades brought grave developments in the collective life and the incipient Christianity of the Maoris. The demoralization attendant upon contact with the whites was accentuated. Drunkenness increased.[22] The decline in population continued. New cults developed which were a compound of Christianity, Maori ideas, and the individual characteristics of their leaders. The "King Movement" of the 1850's and the 1860's, while more political than religious, embodied suggestions from the Bible. An attempt in the face of the encroachments by the whites and of enervating inter-tribal wars to unite the Maoris under a king, it led to disastrous warfare with the whites.[23] More nearly a distinct religion was the movement usually denominated by the name Hau Hau, but also known as Pai Marire. Arising out of the sense of injustice bred by the advance of the whites, it was in part an anti-foreign reaction. On at least one occasion it became violently anti-missionary.[24] It was a compound of various elements—indigenous, Protestant, Roman Catholic, and from the Old Testament. It was inaugurated by a prophet who claimed to have revelations from the Angel Gabriel. The magic associated with it was believed to render its votaries invulnerable to the white man's bullets. It persisted after the suppression of the wars which it had helped to

Selwyn of New Zealand and of Lichfield (London, Kegan Paul, Trench & Co., 1889, pp. xiv, 498); Louise Creighton, *G. A. Selwyn, D.D., Bishop of New Zealand and Lichfield* (London, Longmans, Green and Co., 1923, pp. xi, 180); C.J.S. and L.F.S., *Annals of the Diocese of New Zealand* (London, Society for Promoting Christian Knowledge, 1847, pp. x, 247).

[21] Findlay and Holdsworth, *op. cit.*, Vol. III, p. 224; Stock, *op. cit.*, Vol. I, pp. 432-434.

[22] John Noble Coleman, *A Memoir of the Rev. Richard Davis, for Thirty-Nine Years a Missionary in New Zealand* (London, James Nisbet and Co., 1865, pp. xii, 457), pp. 376, 378.

[23] Taylor, *The Past and Present of New Zealand*, pp. 120ff.; Stock, *op. cit.*, Vol. II, pp. 627, 628; Condliffe, *op. cit.*, pp. 101ff.

[24] See a first hand account in Grace, *A Pioneer Missionary among the Maoris*, pp. 134ff.

inspire.[25] Late in the 1870's another Maori prophet, Te Whiti, arose, who preached not war but peace and, when the white authorities feared in him a new revolt and sent troops against him, he had the women and children march to welcome them with song and dance.[26]

Although many of the Maoris fought the whites and were caught up in these native religious movements, the majority remained peaceful[27] and were affiliated with one or another of the denominations introduced from abroad. Of these bodies, the Church of England continued to attract the largest following. Clergy were ordained from among the Maoris, twenty-three by the close of 1872,[28] and thirty-six from 1873 to 1895 inclusive.[29] The Church Missionary Society gradually withdrew, entrusting its responsibilities to the Church of England in New Zealand which had arisen through white settlement. In 1883 the administration of the mission was transferred to a local Maori Mission Board under the bishops, and with a diminishing subsidy from the parent society. In 1903 the subsidy was discontinued.[30] Eventually each diocese took the responsibility for the Maoris within its own borders.[31] Of the churches of foreign origin represented among the Maoris, the Roman Catholics ranked next to the Church of England in numerical strength, the Methodists third, and the Mormons fourth.[32] There were a few Presbyterians[33] and Seventh Day Adventists.[34] German missionaries, of the North German Missionary Society, entered in the 1840's.[35] Some settled on the Chatham Islands, east of New Zealand, where Maori teachers, Anglican and Methodist, had already introduced Christianity.[36] From 1876 to 1900 the Her-

[25] Pinfold, Fifty Years in Maoriland, pp. 102, 103; Buller, Forty Years in New Zealand, pp. 343ff.; Tucker, Memoir of the Life and Episcopate of George Augustus Selwyn, Vol. II, pp. 197, 208; Taylor, op. cit., pp. 147ff.; Grace, op. cit., pp. 256, 257.

[26] Condliffe, op. cit., pp. 113, 114; Shrimpton and Mulgan, op. cit., pp. 311-313; MacDougall, The Conversion of the Maoris, pp. 109, 110.

[27] On some of these see Grace, op. cit., pp. 96, 108, 109.

[28] Stock, The History of the Church Missionary Society, Vol. II, p. 640. On one of these clergymen see Lady Martin, Our Maoris, pp. 175ff.

[29] Stock, op. cit., Vol. III, p. 553.

[30] Stock, op. cit., Vol. IV, pp. 389, 390.

[31] Strong and Warnshuis, Directory of Foreign Missions, p. 7.

[32] Keesing, The Changing Maori, p. 142.

[33] MacDougall, op. cit., pp. 124, 125; Elder, The History of the Presbyterian Church in New Zealand 1840-1940, pp. 244-250, 337. About the year 1844 James Duncan, a Presbyterian missionary, began work among the Maoris.—Dickson, History of the Presbyterian Church of New Zealand, pp. 31-38.

[34] Keesing, op. cit., p. 142.

[35] Richter, Die evangelische Mission in Fern- und Südost-Asien, Australien, Amerika, p. 232. A biography of one of these missionaries, also containing mention of others of the mission, is L. Tiesmeyer, Eine deutsche Missionsarbeit auf Neu-Seeland. Lebensgeschichte des Missionars I. Fr. Riemenschneider (Bremen, W. Valett & Co., 1875, pp. vi, 142).

[36] Buller, op. cit., pp. 321, 322.

mannsburg Mission, which came at the suggestion of German colonists, had a small enterprise.[37] Schools were conducted by the various missions and a Christian literature was developed in the Maori tongue.[38]

Gradually, thanks in no small degree to Christianity, the tide which seemed to be sweeping the Maoris into the limbo of extinct races turned. In the 1890's the Maoris, after a prolonged discouraging decline in numbers, began to increase.[39] Progress was made against the gross intemperance which for years had wrought demoralization.[40] Missionaries first by their teachings and then the white government by its police measures brought to an end the internecine wars which fire-arms had so greatly intensified.[41] The Maoris were making their adjustment to the white man's world.

The rapid and extensive settlement of New Zealand by white colonists from the British Isles which entailed such grave problems to the Maoris began in 1840. Long before that year whites had been coming to New Zealand. It was only then, however, that systematic occupation began. It was to that year that the Commonwealth of New Zealand really traced its foundation.

The planned colonization of New Zealand arose from the project of Edward Gibbon Wakefield. A man of outstanding ability, Wakefield early cast a cloud over his career by an unfortunate matrimonial adventure which in his young manhood cost him a term in Newgate Prison. Back of him was Quaker blood, with kinship to so notable a social reformer as Elizabeth Fry. Possibly it was this strain which led him to frame his ambitious plan for colonization. Through him came much of the earliest settlement of South Australia. More extensive was his contribution to New Zealand.[42]

Into all the phases of Wakefield's programme we must not take time to go. Of its essence was the attempt to induce men and women of excellent character to become colonists, in contrast with the convicts who constituted a large proportion of the earliest migration to Australia. Wakefield was impressed with the fashion in which the religious purpose of some of the earliest settlements in the Thirteen Colonies had helped to shape the United States and viewed with favour the founding of similar groups, each of which should

[37] Richter, op. cit., p. 233.
[38] Pinfold, op. cit., pp. 104-107.
[39] Keesing, The Changing Maori, pp. 83-87.
[40] Stock, op. cit., Vol. III, p. 556.
[41] Donne, The Maori Past and Present (London, Seeley Service & Co., 1927, pp. 287), p. 208; Elder, The Letters and Journals of Samuel Marsden, p. 46.
[42] A. J. Harrop, The Amazing Career of Edward Gibbon Wakefield, passim.

centre about a particular denomination.[43] He was not interested in their religious views except as they brought colonists of a high type.[44]

Wakefield's dream was not entirely realized. New Zealand was settled around several centres which for a time remained somewhat distinct. Two of these, as we shall see in a moment, at the outset bore the stamp of particular communions. This, however, was not true of all. In Auckland, on the northern part of North Island, and near the strongholds of the early missionary enterprise, the Church was more prominent than in the towns to the South, on or near Cook Strait, Wellington, Nelson, and New Plymouth, which arose out of the enterprise of Wakefield's organization, the New Zealand Company.[45] To Wakefield's disgust, Selwyn made his headquarters at Auckland and supported the missionaries.[46] These latter Wakefield heartily disliked.

From the beginning, the Church of England was active among the settlers who came under the New Zealand Company. A chaplain sent by the Society for the Propagation of the Gospel in Foreign Parts accompanied some of the earliest immigrants and arrived in 1840.[47] In 1838 Bishop Broughton of Australia visited New Zealand and exercised some direction over its religious life.[48] To promote the growth of the Church of England in the new colony, the New Zealand Church Society was formed.[49] It was partly at its instance that in 1841 Selwyn was appointed Bishop of New Zealand.[50] The New Zealand Company gave generous grants of money for the use of the Church of England in Wellington, New Plymouth, and Nelson.[51]

It was largely on the initiative of Wakefield that there arose, in the South Island, a settlement built around the Church of England. The leading spirit was John Robert Godley, a graduate of Christ Church, Oxford. Wakefield, however, continued to push the project and to devote to it thought and energy. The original plan contemplated a colony composed entirely of communicants of the Church of England, with a bishop, clergy, churches, schools, and a

---

[43] Edward Gibbon Wakefield, *A View of the Art of Colonization, with Present Reference to the British Empire* (London, John W. Parker, 1849, pp. xxiv, 513), pp. 155-165.

[44] Harrop, *England and New Zealand*, p. 247.

[45] Condliffe, *A Short History of New Zealand*, pp. 84, 85; Purchas, *A History of the English Church in New Zealand*, p. 128. In 1842, out of Auckland's population of 1,900, 1,100 were considered to belong to the Church of England.—*New Zealand Part I. Letters from the Bishop to the Society for the Propagation of the Gospel together with extracts from his Visitation Journal, from July, 1842, to January, 1843* (London, The Society for the Propagation of the Gospel, 1844, pp. ix, 111), *passim*.

[46] Purchas, *op. cit.*, pp. 128, 147.

[47] Pascoe, *Two Hundred Years of the S.P.G.*, p. 434.

[48] Giles, *The Constitutional History of the Australian Church*, p. 66.

[49] Jacobs, *New Zealand*, p. 85.

[50] Pascoe, *op. cit.*, p. 435; Jacobs, *op. cit.*, p. 101.

[51] Jacobs, *op. cit.*, p. 102.

college. To bring this about the Canterbury Association was formed and the promise of one block of a million acres with the exclusive privilege of naming until 1858 those who should be allowed to purchase land in the settlement was obtained from the New Zealand Company. The initial large body of colonists, 1,512 in number, sailed on eight ships from September, 1850, to January, 1851. As the centre of the colony the city of Christchurch was founded. Disappointments marked the early days of the enterprise. The funds for the maintenance of the clergy were insufficient and some of the latter, if they did not have private means, became all but destitute. Difficulties were encountered in selling land. Yet when in December, 1856, the first bishop of the new see of Christchurch, Henry John Chitly Harper, arrived, procured in England by Selwyn, he found five churches, nine clergymen, and a population of about 5,000, of whom 70 per cent. were members of the Church of England.[52] Christchurch came to have the outward appearance and the atmosphere of an English cathedral and university town. It centred around its cathedral and college, a bit of the old world set down in the antipodes.[53]

Under the energetic leadership of Selwyn and through a fairly large colonization from the British Isles, the Church of England enjoyed a rapid growth. Soon after his arrival, Selwyn began St. John's College for the training of clergy, catechists, and school-teachers. Within a few years eight of its students had been admitted to deacon's orders.[54] In 1858 Selwyn became Metropolitan of New Zealand, and the bishoprics of Wellington, Waiapu, and Nelson were created and made subject to him. The Diocese of Christchurch was at first a suffragan of Sydney, but in 1858 it also was put under Selwyn.[55] In 1844 Selwyn held a synod, said to have been the first of its kind in the Church of England since the silencing of Convocation in England in 1717.[56] A second one convened in 1847.[57] Finding his precedent in part in the Catholic Church of the early Christian centuries and in part in the Protestant Episcopal Church of the United States, in 1850 Selwyn suggested a plan of church government resem-

[52] Pascoe, *op. cit.*, pp. 439, 440; Purchas, *op. cit.*, pp. 147-153; Harrop, *op. cit.*, p. 248; Jacobs, *op. cit.*, pp. 178, 181-185; Samuel Butler, *A First Year in Canterbury Settlement* (London, Longmans, Green, Longmans, Roberts & Quen, 1863, pp. x, 162), *passim;* Harrop, *The Amazing Career of Edward Gibbon Wakefield*, pp. 150-167.

[53] For a description of Christchurch in the 1880's see G. E. Mason, *Round the Round World on a Church Mission* (London, Society for Promoting Christian Knowledge, 1892, pp. x, 379), pp. 261ff.

[54] *Church in the Colonies, No. 7. New Zealand, Part II. Journal of the Bishop's Visitation Tour from August to December, 1843* (London, The Society for the Propagation of the Gospel, 3d ed. 1847, pp. 64), p. 61.

[55] Clarke, *Constitutional Church Government*, pp. 168ff.

[56] Giles, *The Constitutional History of the Australian Church*, p. 76.

[57] Jacobs, *New Zealand*, pp. 165-167.

bling that of the latter.[58] In 1857 a conference of bishops, clergy, and laity met to frame a constitution for the church.[59] In 1859 the first general synod assembled, made up of these same three elements.[60] The Church of England in New Zealand was coming of age and was displaying a vigorous life which enabled it to grow and to adapt itself to its new environment. It was rapidly increasing the number of its communicants and of its clergy.[61] In the 1920's Anglicans were almost the same proportion of the population of New Zealand as of Australia—43.66 per cent. in New Zealand in 1925[62] and 44 per cent. in Australia in 1921.[63]

Presbyterianism was proportionately more than twice as strong in New Zealand as in Australia. In the former in 1925 it constituted 25.42 per cent.[64] and in the latter in 1921 only about 11.5 per cent. of the population.[65] Relatively, too, it was more prominent than in Canada, even if only the Protestant elements of both commonwealths are taken into consideration. The reason for this greater strength is not clear. It may have been in part because the first extensive settlements of New Zealand were made on or shortly before the Disruption in Scotland and became a natural outlet for the new burst of energy released by the birth of the Free Church. Certainly the Presbyterian clergy of New Zealand were largely from the Free Church.

The first Presbyterian minister in New Zealand, John Macfarlane, sailed from Glasgow in 1839 with a shipload of immigrants under the New Zealand Company. He and the group soon settled in Wellington.[66] In 1842 preliminary steps were taken towards organizing a Presbyterian church in Auckland.[67] In 1843 a minister of the Church of Scotland arrived and began services.[68] Not until 1849 was the first building finished. Early in that same year there came a minister sent by the Free Church of Scotland in response to the request of a local group. A new church building was opened in 1850.[69]

In 1849 there was begun, on South Island (sometimes called Middle Island),

[58] Jacobs, *op. cit.*, pp. 186, 187.

[59] Jacobs, *op. cit.*, p. 224.

[60] Jacobs, *op. cit.*, p. 243.

[61] See figures in Jacobs, *op. cit.*, pp. 423-427, 438, 451, 457. For a picture of the life of the Church of England in New Zealand in the 1880's see William Garden Cowie, Bishop of Auckland, *Our Last Year in New Zealand, 1887* (London, Kegan Paul, Trench & Co., 1888, pp. 403), *passim.*

[62] *The Encyclopædia Britannica*, 14th ed., Vol. XVI, p. 395.

[63] Wilson, *Official Year Book of the Commonwealth of Australia, No. 32—1939*, p. 381.

[64] *The Encyclopædia Britannica*, 14th ed., Vol. XVI, p. 395.

[65] Wilson, *op. cit.*, p. 381.

[66] Dickson, *History of the Presbyterian Church of New Zealand*, pp. 18-30; Elder, *The History of the Presbyterian Church of New Zealand 1840-1940*, pp. 25-32.

[67] Comrie, *The Presbytery of Auckland*, p. 17.

[68] Dickson, *op. cit.*, p. 59.

[69] *Ibid.;* Comrie, *op. cit.*, pp. 23ff.

at Otago, a settlement of Presbyterians which was the counterpart of that of the Anglicans at Christchurch. On the eve of the Disruption in Scotland George Rennie, a Scotchman interested in reform, together with William Carghill, had dreamed of a Scotch Presbyterian settlement in New Zealand.[70] In 1843, not long after the Disruption, a company was formed "for the purpose of promoting the emigration of persons belonging to the Free Kirk."[71] In 1844 an exploring party fixed on Otago. The name of the settlement was to be New Edinburgh, but was altered to Dunedin, an old Celtic designation of Edinburgh.[72] The organization which until 1852 carried through the project was called the Association of Lay Members of the Free Church of Scotland, but usually and more briefly the Otago Association. It entered into an agreement with the New Zealand Company for the purchase of land and its resale to colonists.[73] Of the sums paid for the land a proportion was to be set aside for an endowment for education and the Church.[74] In 1845 the project received the blessing of the General Assembly of the Free Church of Scotland.[75] The members of the Otago Association were mainly communicants of the Free Church of excellent social standing who were moved by philanthropic purposes.[76] The original settlers were for the most part idealists who dreamed of founding a model Christian state.[77] The initial shiploads arrived in March and April, 1848.[78] The first minister of the colony was Thomas Burns, a nephew of the poet, Robert Burns. Thomas Burns had been active in recruiting the early contingents.[79] In 1854 the Presbytery of the Church of Otago was constituted with Thomas Burns as senior moderator.[80] On the model of a Free Church institution suggested by Chalmers, a Sustentation Fund was inaugurated towards the equalization of the salaries of ministers.[81] In 1861, only a few years after the founding of Dunedin, gold was discovered in the vicinity and a mining population flocked in, largely from elements quite out of sympathy with the purposes of the colony, and partly disrupted the life of the

[70] Harrop, *The Amazing Story of Edward Gibbon Wakefield*, p. 150; Hocken, *Contributions to the Early History of New Zealand* [*Settlement of Otago*], pp. 7ff.; Elder, *op. cit.*, pp. 37, 38.

[71] Stead, *The Story of Social Christianity*, Vol. II, p. 238.

[72] Gillies, *The Presbyterian Church Trust*, pp. 5-7, 16.

[73] Gillies, *op. cit.*, pp. 30-38.

[74] Gillies, *op. cit.*, pp. 3, 4, 10.

[75] Gillies, *op. cit.*, p. 7.

[76] Ross, *The Story of the Otago Church and Settlement*, p. 16.

[77] Ross, *op. cit.*, pp. 22-25.

[78] Hislop, *History of the Knox Church, Dunedin*, pp. 1-12.

[79] Ross, *op. cit.*, pp. 16, 52-54; Hocken, *op. cit.*, pp. 17-26; Elder, *op. cit.*, pp. 42-44.

[80] Gillies, *op. cit.*, p. 18; Elder, *op. cit.*, p. 50.

[81] Ross, *op. cit.*, p. 240.

community. Ministers were appointed to visit the gold fields in rotation and an appeal was sent to Scotland for more clergy.[82] In 1864 the crest of the flood passed and an ebb set it, but the population of Otago Province did not again fall much below 55,000.[83] So large had the colony grown that in 1864 the Otago Presbytery was divided into three and in 1866 a synod met.[84] Between 1866 and 1881 about thirty clergymen came from the British Isles.[85] In the 1870's a theological college was opened for the training of clergy in New Zealand and steps were taken by the synod to aid young men preparing for the ministry.[86]

Elsewhere in New Zealand Presbyterianism also displayed a rapid increase. In 1848 there landed at Nelson a minister sent by the Colonial Committee of the Free Church in response to a request from a local group.[87] In 1850 W. Kirton of the Church of Scotland arrived at Wellington and served there for thirteen years.[88] In 1857 three ministers from the Free Church and two elders formed the Wellington Presbytery. The congregation connected with the Church of Scotland remained aloof until 1874.[89] About the year 1853 Norman McLeod of the Highlands of Scotland, after serving Gaelic-speaking communities on Cape Breton, when threescore years and ten led a company of his parishioners to Australia (1851) and then (1854) to New Zealand. There, reinforced by others from Nova Scotia, a Highland colony arose ruled by McLeod in patriarchal fashion.[90] In 1859 a clergyman, P. Barclay, sent by the Colonial Committee, took charge of the Presbyterians in Napier.[91] In 1856 a Free Church minister, C. Fraser, arrived at Lyttelton, in the Canterbury district, and did much to extend Presbyterianism in that region.[92] In the years 1871 and 1872 seventeen Presbyterian ministers, most of them of the Free Church, came to New Zealand.[93]

Eventually there arose two Presbyterian churches in New Zealand, one embracing North Island and the northern provinces of the South Island, and the other Otago and the southern part of South Island. An attempt at union in 1861 failed, partly because the Otago body held more tenaciously than did

[82] Ross, *op. cit.*, p. 113.
[83] Ross, *op. cit.*, p. 181.
[84] Ross, *op. cit.*, p. 201.
[85] Ross, *op. cit.*, pp. 210-212.
[86] Ross, *op. cit.*, p. 201.
[87] Dickson, *History of the Presbyterian Church of New Zealand*, p. 109.
[88] Dickson, *op. cit.*, p. 48; Elder, *op. cit.*, p. 34.
[89] Dickson, *op. cit.*, p. 56.
[90] Dickson, *op. cit.*, p. 78; Shrimpton and Mulgan, *Maori & Pakeha*, p. 282; Elder, *op. cit.*, pp. 62, 63.
[91] Dickson, *op. cit.*, p. 130; Elder, *op. cit.*, pp. 63, 64.
[92] Dickson, *op. cit.*, pp. 151, 165.
[93] Dickson, *op. cit.*, p. 97.

the northern church to the forms inherited from Scotland. In 1901, after protracted preliminary stages, the union was accomplished.[94]

The northern church, in 1878 recognized by the state as "the Presbyterian Church of New Zealand,"[95] early took active steps for church extension in its part of the islands.[96] Until past the close of the nineteenth century, the majority of its clergy continued to come from the British Isles. Of its ninety ministers in 1899, forty-three were from the Free Church of Scotland, eleven from the Irish Presbyterian Church, eight from the Church of Scotland, four from the English Presbyterian Church, and five from the Congregational fellowship. Only the minority were trained in New Zealand.[97] Moreover, in 1899 it was reported that six counties north of Auckland with a population of 14,000 were without a minister.[98]

The New Zealand Presbyterians began to propagate their faith in other lands. In 1867-1869 the Otago church commenced giving assistance to missions in the New Hebrides.[99] Late in the 1860's the northern church began its mission in the same island group.[100] The Otago synod also carried on a mission among the Chinese who were attracted to the gold fields in the vicinity.[101] In the first decade of the twentieth century New Zealand Presbyterianism inaugurated missions in South China near Canton, and in the Punjab, in India.[102]

Methodism was the third largest of the Protestant denominations in New Zealand, but relatively it was not so prominent as in Australia and Canada. The presence of Methodist missionaries to the Maoris in advance of extensive white colonization ensured early care for the latter when it began. A Methodist missionary visited Auckland within its first year, formed a class, and appointed a local preacher to conduct services.[103] Auckland, indeed, became in time a Methodist stronghold. In 1874, in the province of Auckland, Methodism had 27 churches with 573 members and 5,351 adherents. In 1912 it had 95 churches, 4,134 members, and 19,580 adherents.[104] It was a Methodist missionary to the Maoris who preached, in 1840, on the first immigrant ship to reach Port Nicholson, the harbour on which Wellington arose. Methodist churches were

[94] Ross, op. cit., p. 387; Dickson, op. cit., p. 277; Elder, op. cit., pp. 158-178.
[95] Dickson, op. cit., p. 283.
[96] Dickson, op. cit., pp. 301-305. On the spread in the Presbytery of Auckland, see Comrie, The Presbytery of Auckland, passim.
[97] Dickson, op. cit., p. 379.
[98] Dickson, op. cit., p. 307.
[99] Ross, op. cit., pp. 265-270; Elder, op. cit., p. 274.
[100] Strong and Warnshuis, Directory of Foreign Missions, p. 8; Elder, op. cit., pp. 272, 273.
[101] Ross, op. cit., p. 260.
[102] Elder, op. cit., pp. 280-308.
[103] Morley in Colwell, A Century in the Pacific, pp. 578, 579.
[104] Morley in Colwell, op. cit., pp. 381, 382.

built. The Primitive Methodists entered in 1847.[105] Methodism was represented in New Plymouth from the very beginning, for some of the original settlers were from Devon and Cornwall, where they had been connected with that branch of the faith.[106] Methodism was also prompt in gaining a foothold in the Anglican Christchurch and the Presbyterian Dunedin. In the former there were Methodists among the initial arrivals and in the first year of the colony a local preacher delivered the first Methodist sermon. In 1854 a church building, then the largest structure in the city, was erected.[107] In Port Chalmers, on which Dunedin was to rise, a Methodist missionary to the Maoris was on hand to welcome the original contingent of white colonists and preached to them. Not until 1857, however, did a class meeting come into being in Dunedin.[108] In 1872 New Zealand Methodists had 3 districts, 29 circuits, 119 churches, 45 ministers, 181 local preachers, and 2,658 members.[109] In 1874 the first New Zealand Methodist Conference was held, in Christchurch.[110] In 1913, after a series of efforts which began at least as early as 1881, a union of the various Methodist bodies in New Zealand was consummated. Methodists then had 199 ministers, 453 churches, 27,781 members, and 92,636 adherents.[111]

The first Baptist church in New Zealand was organized at Nelson in 1851 through a clergyman, Decimus Dolamore, who, on landing, found a group who were about to send to England for a minister. Other churches followed in various parts of the islands. In 1882 the Baptist Union of New Zealand was formed. It undertook both home and foreign missions. In 1882 Baptists numbered 2,023 and in 1912 5,494.[112]

Independents (Congregationalists) had a church and a minister in Wellington as early as the 1840's.[113]

Quakers were but scantily represented. In 1906 only 285 were recorded in all New Zealand.[114]

Seventh Day Adventists dated their entrance into New Zealand from 1889, but grew slowly. In 1905 they had only 415 members.[115]

Roman Catholics not only conducted a successful mission among the Maoris.

[105] Morley in Colwell, *op. cit.,* pp. 382, 383.
[106] Morley in Colwell, *op. cit.,* p. 387.
[107] Morley in Colwell, *op. cit.,* pp. 391, 392.
[108] Morley in Colwell, *op. cit.,* p. 399.
[109] Turner, *The Pioneer Missionary,* pp. 224, 225.
[110] Bickford, *Christian Work in Australasia,* p. 288.
[111] Morley in Colwell, *op. cit.,* pp. 406, 407.
[112] John Laird in *The Chronicle,* Vol. I, pp. 115-121, 124.
[113] Dickson, *History of the Presbyterian Church of New Zealand,* p. 43.
[114] *The Society of Friends in Australasia . . . 1st December, 1906,* pp. 58-73.
[115] *Statistical Report of Seventh-Day Adventist Conferences and Missions for the year ending Dec. 31, 1905,* p. 4.

They also became numerous among the white population. As in Australia, they were predominantly Irish. Orders and congregations of priests, lay brothers, and sisters entered to serve them and to hold them to the faith. Prominent were the priests of the Society of Mary, the Mill Hill fathers, the Redemptorists, the Marist Brothers, the Sisters of Our Lady of Mercy, the Sisters of Our Lady of the Mission, Sisters of St. Joseph of Nazareth, and Sisters of St. Joseph of the Sacred Heart (of Australian origin).[116] In the 1840's Pompallier, the first Vicar Apostolic in New Zealand, broke with the Superior-General of his own order, the Marists, on the issue of the power of the bishop over his clergy. This led Pompallier to separate himself from the Society of Mary. The latter withdrew its priests in the diocese of Wellington. Pompallier remained in charge of Auckland.[117] Franciscans came (1860) at Pompallier's invitation to fill the gap left by the Marists, but various difficulties, including conflicts with Pompallier and his successor, led to their withdrawal (1872).[118] Rome provided for additional episcopal supervision of New Zealand. In 1848 Wellington was made the seat of a bishop and in 1887 was raised to a metropolitanate. In 1848 Auckland was also made the seat of a bishop with Pompallier as the first incumbent. In 1869 Dunedin and in 1887 Christchurch were given that status.[119] In 1892 New Zealand was said to have about 90,000 Roman Catholics, of whom more than 5,000 were Maoris.[120] By 1910 the number was reported to have increased to 130,376.[121]

As in Australia, the outstanding denominational groups of the British Isles held the lead in New Zealand—the Anglicans, the Presbyterians, and the Roman Catholics. They were not grouped regionally as in the mother country, but they were forced to live together. In general, however, they corresponded to the racial divisions of the colonists. The Church of England was strongest among the English, the Presbyterians among the Scotch, and the Roman Catholics among the Irish. To these were added the Methodists. As in Australia, Congregationalists and Baptists were relatively not so prominent as in Great Britain.

Some of the effects of Christianity upon New Zealand were fairly obvious. In 1914 the overwhelming majority of the population were at least nominally Christian.

[116] *Missiones Catholicae, 1927*, pp. 374, 375.
[117] Pompallier, *Early History of the Catholic Church in Oceania*, p. 6.
[118] Lemmens, *Geschichte der Fraziskanermissionen*, pp. 337, 338.
[119] *Missiones Catholicae . . . MDCCCXCII*, pp. 530-534.
[120] *Ibid.*
[121] *Australasian Catholic Directory for 1910*, after p. 193.

This included most of the Maoris. The missionaries gave written form to the language of the Maoris and prepared a literature in it, including translations of the Bible and of various other Christian books. Schools for the Maoris were instituted. Seeds and domestic animals were introduced. Much was done to prevent the wars among the Maoris which had been intensified by the introduction of fire-arms. Cannibalism disappeared. The missionaries sought to safeguard the Maoris from exploitation by the whites and to lessen the demoralization brought by the less desirable elements of European culture. They were by no means entirely successful. Neither did they completely fail. They and Maori Christian leaders accomplished much in keeping the peace between the whites and a large proportion of the Maoris. That the latter had begun to make their adjustment to the white man's world and by the end of the nineteenth century to increase once more in numbers was due in no small degree to Christianity.

Among the whites Christianity produced its characteristic fruits. There were active efforts against the sale and use of intoxicants.[122] Orphanages were founded by both Protestants[123] and Roman Catholics.[124] Some educational institutions were maintained, including Roman Catholic parochial schools.[125] To give them economic opportunity the Salvation Army brought out to New Zealand young men to labour on the farms. In various ports the churches, the Salvation Army, and the Young Men's Christian Association made provision for meeting the steamers to welcome immigrants and to assist them to their destinations.[126]

Although at the outset the clerical leadership of the churches was entirely from abroad, from the beginning the laity assumed most of the support of the clergy and often took the initiative in organizing churches and in sending for clergy. New Zealand Christianity, too, had sufficient vitality to undertake foreign missions. These were chiefly in the islands of the Pacific, but several were in Asia.[127]

Some results were more difficult to appraise. The effects upon individual lives were not easily dissociated from the effects of other forces. In the Canterbury and Otago communities Christianity was patently a cause of the initial settlements and helped to mould the local life. It is not clear, however, whether

[122] Ross, *The Story of the Otago Church and Settlement*, pp. 236-239.
[123] Pinfold, *Fifty Years in Maoriland*, pp. 149, 150; Elder, *The History of the Presbyterian Church in New Zealand 1840-1940*, pp. 339-342.
[124] *Missiones Catholicae, MDCCCXCII*, pp. 530-534.
[125] *Ibid.*; Jacobs, *New Zealand*, p. 411; Elder, *op. cit.*, pp. 358ff.
[126] Pinfold, *op. cit.*, pp. 135, 136.
[127] Pinfold, *op. cit.*, p. 171; Strong and Warnshuis, *Directory of Foreign Missions*, pp. 6, 7.

Christianity was a major factor in shaping the ideals of the commonwealth as a whole. In so far as Christianity was a contributory factor to nineteenth-century Anglo-Saxon democracy and humanitarianism (and in the preceding volume it became clear that it was), it was potent in the life of New Zealand, for New Zealand was strongly democratic. Beyond its part in creating an atmosphere in which such projects flourished, it is not certain that Christianity was responsible for the specific measures of the advanced social legislation which characterized New Zealand.[128] Nor can it be determined just how far the Christian faith, undoubtedly vital in many of the population, contributed to the courage with which New Zealanders met the prolonged economic depression of the 1880's.

The environment helped to give to New Zealand Christianity its distinctive features. The fact that the immigration was overwhelmingly from the British Isles was responsible for the British character of the Christianity. Since the immigration began then, the British Christianity which was introduced was that of the nineteenth century. This may seem to be so obvious as to be a banality. Yet it helps to account for differences between the Protestantism of New Zealand and that of the United States. The former lacked features which came to the latter through the part which groups fleeing from seventeenth-century religious persecution had in the original settlements. For instance, with some exceptions the former did not give rise to so many novel religious movements as did the latter. The exceptions were among the Maoris, where oppression by the whites, with a certain rough parallel to the seventeenth-century persecutions in Europe, helped to give rise to distinctive and somewhat bizarre sects. It must also be noted that here and there pre-Christian beliefs of the Maoris filtered into the nominally Christian white society and were adopted by some of the colonists.[129] In contrast with Canada and Australia, where for a time the state accorded financial support to the Church, in New Zealand no church was ever established by law.[130] This may have been because extensive settlement by the whites began so late in the nineteenth century that, since establishment was being challenged in the older British colonies, it could not easily be adopted. In New Zealand, as in Australia and

[128] For a description of this legislation see Hugh H. Lusk, *Social Welfare in New Zealand* (New York, Sturgis & Walton, 1913, pp. 287), *passim*. George Grey, Governor and later Premier, who was a potent advocate of democratic liberalism in New Zealand, in part owed his idealism and especially his courage and constancy to a warm Christian faith—Henderson, *Sir George Grey*, pp. 2-4, 19, 20, 242ff., 275-278.

[129] Donne, *The Maori, Past and Present*, p. 211.

[130] Harper, *Letters from New Zealand*, p. 321.

Canada, it was the opposition of rival groups to special privileges for the Church of England which militated against establishment. To be sure, two-thirds of Selwyn's salary once came from the imperial government and when that grant was withdrawn the proposal was made (1844) that the colonial government assume it. In spite of the fact that a bill had already passed to create "an ecclesiastical establishment," the Presbyterians and Roman Catholics were able to defeat the suggestion.[131] Grants, too, came to the churches from the New Zealand Company and the Canterbury Association, but these were partly in the form of endowments[132] and were not large enough to nullify the principle of voluntary support by the laity. Church attendance seems to have been better in New Zealand than in Australia.[133] This may have arisen from the absence of the convict element in the original population. It may also have been in part from a climate which did not so clamantly encourage sports and outdoor life. As in the United States, Canada, and Australia, denominational organizations were gradually formed on a national scale and corresponded with political and geographic patterns. As in these other three lands, too, the latter part of the period witnessed movements, congenial to a new country with its trend away from tradition, to soften the ecclesiastical divisions inherited from the mother country.

New Zealand was another of the nations which arose in the nineteenth century through European colonization in a land which previously had been but sparsely peopled by a non-European race of primitive culture. Since in that century the leading empire-builders and colonizers were the British, New Zealand arose from migration from the British Isles. Because Great Britain was predominantly Protestant and because the nineteenth century was marked by pronounced vitality in Protestantism, and especially in Anglo-Saxon Protestantism, New Zealand became predominantly Protestant, with vigorous churches which not only held the allegiance of the majority but also reached out to spread their faith to other lands, particularly among the island peoples of the South Pacific. Except for inconsiderable numbers of Jews and Orientals, the minority outside the fold of the Protestant spheres of influence were in the Roman Catholic Church. Since in New Zealand the Roman Catholic constituency was prevailingly Irish, that branch of the faith was espoused with the ardent loyalty created by the long years when it had been the symbol and

---

[131] Dickson, *History of the Presbyterian Church in New Zealand*, p. 39.

[132] Dickson, *op. cit.*, pp. 122, 123; Jacobs, *New Zealand*, p. 432; Harper, *op. cit.*, pp. 323-326.

[133] Harper, *op. cit.*, p. 333.

channel of Celtic Irish nationalism against the English overlords. Both Protestants and Roman Catholics reached the Maoris in advance of the flood of white colonization. Between them they won the majority of that people to the Christian faith and gave striking assistance in effecting accommodation to the white man's world. New Zealand was professedly Christian and bore deeply in its life the imprint of that faith. As in the United States, Canada, and Australia, and in contrast with Latin America, the Christianity introduced from Europe was not passive, but active.

Chapter VII

THE ISLANDS OF THE PACIFIC. PROTESTANT AND ROMAN CATHOLIC MISSIONS IN TAHITI AND THE SOCIETY ISLANDS, THE COOK OR HERVEY ISLANDS, THE MARQUESAS, PITCAIRN ISLAND, THE TONGA OR FRIENDLY ISLANDS, THE SAMOAN ISLANDS, THE ELLICE ISLANDS, THE FIJI ISLANDS, ROTUMA, THE NEW HEBRIDES, NEW CALEDONIA, THE LOYALTY ISLANDS, THE SOLOMON ISLANDS, NEW BRITAIN AND THE BISMARCK ARCHIPELAGO, NEW GUINEA, HAWAII, MICRONESIA

FROM Latin America, Australia, and New Zealand we turn naturally to the islands of the Pacific, lying between and adjacent to these other lands. They were like them in being the home of primitive peoples among whom the impinging cultures of the Occident brought revolutionary changes. Moreover, Christianity was introduced to several of these islands from the United States, Australia, and New Zealand.

Before the latter part of the eighteenth century some of the islands of the Pacific had been touched by white men. In the sixteenth century the Spaniards disclosed several of them to European eyes. In the seventeenth and eighteenth centuries many of them had been seen by the Dutch. It was Cook's voyages in the second half of the eighteenth century which were chiefly responsible for revealing them to the English-speaking world. Coming, as they did, on the eve of the nineteenth century and the great expansion of the British Empire, Cook's expeditions were most timely and directed the attention of merchant adventurers and missionaries to this hitherto unrecognized region. In the course of the nineteenth century the cultures of most of the smaller islands were transformed by the coming of the white man. The old largely disappeared. On some of the larger islands, however, only the coastal fringes were altered.

The white man's invasion took a number of forms. Often its initial impact was comprised of beach-combers, the flotsam and jetsam of the white man's commerce, men of depraved morals who contaminated and degraded native life. Much of it had commerce as its vehicle. Traders, whalers, and sealers came to the islands. More often than not they sought only gain, and with callous disregard of the welfare of the aborigines. As in New Zealand, they sold fire-arms which intensified the tribal wars. They misused women. They carried off men and women to work on plantations in an indentured labour which frequently differed little from slavery. Seeing them break the time-honoured taboos with impunity, the natives did likewise and the old forms of social control were weakened or vanished.

The missionaries, the chief subject of this chapter, constituted another phase of the white man's influx. In contrast with the other, they had as their primary aim the welfare of the islanders. Some of them were bungling and did unnecessary damage to those whom they had come to help. Some were shocked by the costume, or lack of costume, of the natives and sought to induce them to wear the white man's clothes. Unwashed and unadapted to the local conditions, the clothing often bred disease. Customs were uprooted which seemed to the missionary unchristian, but which in some instances were either morally neutral or could not be destroyed without working more immediate harm than good. Occasionally a missionary succumbed to temptations accentuated by the alien environment and brought opprobrium upon his profession. More frequently he became a prisoner to the routine of his task. Yet many lived nobly and intelligently and were an inestimable boon to those to whom they devoted their lives. Sometimes the missionary preceded the trader. Sometimes he followed him. Between the two was usually marked antipathy. The missionary fought the demoralization which the trader brought and the latter was resentful and often actively hostile.

Eventually the officials of white governments were added to the beachcombers, the traders, and the missionaries. During the early part of the nineteenth century the British Government only reluctantly acquired fresh territories in the Pacific. The expense and the trouble involved were held to be but poorly compensated by the returns. The French, the other major nineteenth-century builders of an overseas empire, were even more slow to assume responsibilities in that area. However, as the century wore on, a race for colonial possessions set in. By 1914 all of the Pacific had been parcelled out. The British had the lion's share. The French were next. The Germans somewhat tardily appeared and picked up groups which no one else had taken. The United States annexed Hawaii and acquired part of Samoa and stepping stones to the Philippines and the Far East. The Dutch moved eastward from their old footholds in the Indies. The officials of the white governments increasingly regimented the natives and brought them more and more into conformity with the white man's laws and customs.

To governments was added immigration. In no group of islands did the white man constitute a majority. In some groups, however, the white man's need for labour for his plantations brought an influx from Asia, America, and Europe. This was especially marked in Fiji and Hawaii. In the former the immigration was from India. In the latter it was more varied. In Hawaii the original Polynesian population became a minority. Chinese constituted elements in several other island groups. To some of the French islands Indo-Chinese labourers were imported.

It was, then, a varied impact through which the white man's culture worked the disintegration of the aboriginal cultures and supplanted them. The missionary, as the main agent for the entrance of Christianity, was only one of several instruments of the revolution.

The peoples of the Pacific to whom this white civilization came were not of one race or one culture. The Pacific was often regarded as being divided into Polynesia, Melanesia, and Micronesia. These compartments corresponded roughly to the facts. They represented both racial and cultural differences. However, racial composition varied from island group to island group. Languages were even more numerous. While the cultures were what are usually termed primitive, they were not all of one level or of the same pattern.

For many of the island peoples the impact of the white man meant a shrinking population. In some instances the decline may have begun before the advent of the whites. Certainly chronic warfare, infanticide,[1] and small families seem to have been common. Where decrease was in progress, the white man accentuated it. The coming of the white man worked adversely in a number of respects. The introduction of fire-arms with the consequent intensification of inter-tribal wars, the sale of liquor, the recruiting of labour for white plantations in other islands, the passing of the old culture, a loss of interest in life due to the disappearance of traditional incentives and to despair, and new diseases (such as colds, influenza, dysentery, measles, smallpox, and venereal disorders) to which the natives had not built up the partial resistance which the whites, long accustomed to them, had developed—all these contributed to the destruction, although in just what proportion it is difficult to say. Probably disease was the most nearly universal factor. In some islands, most tragically in the Marquesas, almost complete depopulation ensued. In several recovery eventually began.[2]

It was in the midst of this setting that Christianity was introduced and

[1] Ellis, *Polynesian Researches*, Vol. I, pp. 248-294.

[2] Stephen H. Roberts, *Population Problems of the Pacific*, pp. 58-128. Diseases introduced by the white man seem to have been a most important cause of depopulation. For a few examples see Williams, *A Narrative of Missionary Enterprises in the South Seas*, pp. 264-267; Delmas, *Essai d'Histoire de la Mission des Iles Marquèses*, p. 160.

grew. In some of the groups and islands the pre-Christian cults disappeared and the entire population became at least nominally Christian. In others, mostly the larger islands, by 1914 the adoption of Christianity had only begun but was continuing.

The forms of Christianity which were propagated were predominantly Protestant. This was to be expected. The chief commercial and colonizing power, Great Britain, was overwhelmingly Protestant. Near by were Australia and New Zealand, where an active Protestant Christianity was arising. Hawaii passed into the control of the United States, also largely Protestant. Some Protestant missionaries were from France and Germany. Roman Catholic missions at the outset were French, the result of French leadership in nine-teenth-century Roman Catholic missions and of French imperialism in the Pacific. Later, with the emergence of Germany as a colonial power, came German Roman Catholic missions.

Christian missionaries reduced languages to writing, translated the Bible into them, and began the preparation of other literature. They introduced schools. In some islands they directed the creation of a new culture after the destruction of the old. Here and there, before the coming of control by the white man's governments, they were advisers to the native rulers.

In numbers of the islands adherence to Christianity was wrought by mass movements. An initial period of resistance to the faith but marked by the conversion of a few individuals was followed by the rapid breakdown of the non-Christian cults and the adoption of the new faith by practically the entire population. In other islands, usually the larger ones, Christianity made its way among only a portion of the people.

The Christianity thus planted had sufficient vigour to impel those who professed it to support their own churches and often to go as missionaries to other islands. Indeed, scores of native Christians went as missionaries to distant islands and quite alien peoples, many at the cost of their lives.

The totals entailed were not large when compared with some other sections of the world. In 1914 the population of all the islands with which this chapter is to deal was not much over 2,000,000. Because it was scattered over many islands and archipelagos we must devote to it a somewhat larger proportion of our space than would be justified by an allotment based upon a strictly per-centage basis. Even then we shall be compelled to omit a few of the smaller enterprises and to pass over others with only brief mention.

We shall pursue our narrative group by group and occasionally island by island. We shall speak of both Protestant and Roman Catholic enterprises.

The story will seem somewhat disjointed, for it is impossible to arrange it in any strictly logical order either by geography or by chronology.

It seems fitting to begin with Tahiti (Otaheite in some of the earlier orthography), and the Society Islands, as Cook had christened them. It was here that Cook (although he was not the first European to discover the islands) observed the transit of Venus (1769), the initial occasion which brought him to the Pacific.[3] It was to Tahiti that there came the earliest of the groups of Protestant missionaries who sought to win the Pacific islanders to their faith. This was from the newly organized London Missionary Society. William Carey had been enthralled by the published narratives of Cook's voyages and had dreamed of going to Tahiti and disproving Cook's prophecy that the island would never become the scene of a Christian mission.[4] However, he was diverted to India by the enthusiastic John Thomas.[5] The honour of actually initiating the enterprise belongs, more than to any one else, to T. Haweis, a clergyman of the Church of England and chaplain to Lady Huntingdon, the famous patroness of Wesley and Whitefield and foundress of Lady Huntingdon's Connexion. As early as 1788 or 1789 Haweis, thrilled by the accounts of the recent voyages to the South Seas, had attempted, in vain, to send missionaries there. As one of the first Board of Directors of the London Missionary Society he pled for a mission to that region. He argued, not without reason, that China and Japan were practically sealed against Christianity, that in India and in Moslem lands the prevailing faiths were comparatively impervious to Christian preaching, and that the religions of the South Seas would prove less resistant.[6] For the enterprise there was enlisted James Wilson, who in his late youth, after a life of adventure, had retired from the sea and had entered upon a profound religious experience.[7] A ship, the *Duff*, was purchased and equipped. It sailed in August, 1796, commanded by Wilson, with a contingent of thirty missionaries, six wives, and three children. Of these only four were ordained. The rest of the men were artisans. It was believed that the natives must be "civilized" before they could understand and appreciate the Christian message. It was expected that the missionaries could support themselves in the salubrious and fertile islands. The *Duff* landed most of its party on Tahiti, but it also took some to Tongatabu in the Tonga or what Cook had called the Friendly Islands, and left one on the Marquesas.[8]

---

[3] Carrington, *Life of Captain Cook*, pp. 8off.
[4] S. Pearce Carey, *William Carey*, pp. 39, 53.
[5] Carey, *op. cit.*, pp. 96, 97.
[6] Lovett, *The History of the London Missionary Society*, Vol. I, pp. 117-122.
[7] Lovett, *op. cit.*, Vol. I, pp. 122ff.
[8] *A Missionary Voyage to the Southern Pacific Ocean, Performed in the Years 1796, 1797, 1798, in the Ship Duff, Commanded by Captain James Wilson, Compiled from the*

The enterprise proved much more difficult than had been anticipated. In 1798 eleven out of the eighteen on Tahiti, discouraged, took the opportunity given by a passing ship and went to New South Wales. The acquisition of the language was far from easy. Two of those who remained took non-Christian Tahitian wives and were cut off by the mission.[9] In 1798 three of the men left on Tongatabu were massacred. All but one of the others, disheartened, left the island for Australia. The exception had "gone native."[10] By 1799 the man who had been left on the Marquesas returned to England.[11]

The island of Tahiti and the smaller adjacent island of Eimeo had been brought under the rule of one of the native chiefs, Pomare, with the aid of fire-arms and some Europeans. Although remaining firmly loyal to his old cult, Pomare befriended the missionaries.[12] When, in 1803, Pomare died, he was succeeded by a son, who likewise took the name of Pomare, and was also favorably disposed towards the missionaries.[13] Yet many of the islanders held the missionaries responsible for the increase in deaths from the imported diseases.[14] In 1808 civil war drove Pomare II from Tahiti to Eimeo. The missionaries felt constrained by the disorders also to go to that island.[15]

The flight to Eimeo proved the turning point. While on that island, in close company with the missionaries, Pomare II, perhaps in part because of loss of faith in the religion which had failed to save him from his fate, professed Christianity and asked for baptism.[16] While that was not at once given him, he henceforth sided with Christianity. When in 1815 Pomare II succeeded in restoring his authority over Tahiti, his victory meant the triumph of the new faith. He led in espousing it and toured the island urging his subjects to accept it. The old gods and their cults were overthrown and Tahiti and Eimeo became nominally Christian. Church buildings were erected and the Sabbath was kept.[17] In 1819 Pomare II was publicly baptized.[18] By 1825 most of the

---

Journals of the Officers and the Missionaries . . . by a Committee Appointed for that Purpose by the Directors of the Missionary Society (London, T. Chapman, 1799, pp. c. 420), *passim.*

[9] Lovett, *op. cit.,* Vol. I, pp. 146ff.

[10] Lovett, *op. cit.,* Vol. I, pp. 169ff.

[11] Lovett, *op. cit.,* Vol. I, pp. 174, 175.

[12] Lovett, *op. cit.,* Vol. I, pp. 181, 182; Ellis, *Polynesian Researches,* Vol. II, pp. 51-67.

[13] Lovett, *op. cit.,* Vol. I, p. 183.

[14] Ellis, *op. cit.,* Vol. II, p. 65.

[15] Ellis, *op. cit.,* Vol. II, p. 79; Lovett, *op. cit.,* Vol. I, p. 192.

[16] Ellis, *op. cit.,* Vol. II, pp. 87ff.; Lovett, *op. cit.,* Vol. I, pp. 194-197.

[17] Lovett, *op. cit.,* Vol. I, pp. 208-215.

[18] Lovett, *op. cit.,* Vol. I, p. 209. For a picture of the situation between 1817 and 1822 see letters in William Ellis, *Memoir of Mrs. Mercy Ellis, Wife of Rev. William Ellis* (Boston, Crocker & Brewster, 1836, pp. 286), pp. 72-124.

population of Eimeo had been given that rite.[19] In many respects Pomare II proved a disappointment to the missionaries. He drank to excess and in matters of sex did not conform to Christian standards.[20] Yet, like that of many of the monarchs of Northern Europe when the conversion of that region was under way, his advocacy was decisive.

To the deepening of the incipient Christianity the missionaries set themselves with devotion. In the language, already reduced to writing, a literature was inaugurated. A printing press and a printer were sent out and in 1817 began the issuance of books.[21] Schools were organized. The entire Bible was translated and, printed in Great Britain, in 1840 was introduced in its new dress.[22] With the advice of the missionaries, but apparently at the instance of the natives, a code of laws was framed embodying the new ideals, and in 1819 was promulgated by Pomare II.[23]

The results of these laws were not altogether happy. Some wondered whether the stern penalties placed on adultery were not contributory to the professional prostitution which arose.[24]

Reinforcements came from Great Britain.[25] The most notable among them was John Williams, who became one of the outstanding missionaries in the South Seas. Born in 1796, the year that the *Duff* sailed, as a lad of eighteen, while an apprentice, he was converted in a Dissenting chapel and two years later was appointed by the London Missionary Society to the South Seas. In 1817 he and his bride reached Tahiti.[26] We are to meet him again, a daring and resourceful pioneer.

Assisted by these additions to its ranks, the mission carried its message to others of the Society group. Even before the missionaries established a residence on them, several of the islands quickly followed the example of Tahiti. Led, as on Tahiti, by their chiefs, they destroyed their idols and became nominally Christian.[27] In 1820 several, the island of Raiatea foremost among them, adopted the substance of the laws which had been enacted on Tahiti the previous year.[28]

[19] Lovett, *op. cit.*, Vol. I, p. 224.
[20] Lovett, *op. cit.*, Vol. I, pp. 227, 228.
[21] Ellis, *Life of William Ellis*, pp. 46-48.
[22] Murray, *The Bible in the Pacific*, pp. 3, 4.
[23] Ellis, *Polynesian Researches*, Vol. III, pp. 134ff.
[24] Lovett, *op. cit.*, Vol. I, p. 328.
[25] Lovett, *op. cit.*, Vol. I, p. 238. See an account of a visit by a Quaker in the 1830's which was extended to several others of the islands of the Pacific and gives vivid pictures of the missions of that day, but which seems not to have issued in organized results, in *Memoirs of the Life and Gospel Labours of Daniel Wheeler* (London, Harvey and Darton, 1842, pp. xxviii, 793), pp. 311ff.
[26] Northcott, *John Williams Sails On*, pp. 13-29.
[27] Ellis, *Polynesian Researches*, Vol. II, pp. 167ff.
[28] Ellis, *op. cit.*, Vol. III, p. 143.

The missionaries endeavoured to instruct the neophytes in the faith thus adopted *en masse*. Schools were introduced. In contravention of the native attitude which wished to assign to the chiefs the leading place in the Church which they had enjoyed in the old cults, the missionaries attempted to reproduce the kind of organization which they had known in the democratically governed Independent churches in Great Britain.[29] As a by-product of the change to the new faith, the natives began to don costumes of European style. Although sometimes encouraged by the missionaries, this seems to have been done more from the desire to imitate their teachers and the visiting traders with their supposedly superior civilization than from any sense of moral or religious duty.[30]

It is not strange that out of Christianity, so recently and in many instances so superficially adopted, new movements should spring up which departed from the teaching of the missionaries. In 1828 a cult, the Mamaia, arose. Its leader proclaimed himself to be Jesus Christ and promised his followers a sensuous paradise.[31]

More serious complications followed the advent, in 1834, of French Roman Catholic missionaries. In 1834 priests of the Congregation of Picpus established themselves on the Gambier Islands, south-east of the Society Islands, and within four years the entire population is said to have embraced Christianity.[32] From the Gambier Islands, in 1836, two of the Picpus Fathers came to Tahiti. The native authorities compelled them to leave. A second attempt, in 1837, met with a similar fate. Complaint was made to the French Government, and in 1838 a French man-of-war constrained the Queen, Pomare IV, to grant the same privileges to Roman Catholic as to Protestant missionaries.[33] This was followed by an extension of French authority over Tahiti, at first, in 1842, in the form of a protectorate, and eventually, through various stages, by formal annexation as a French colony (1880).[34] Increasing restrictions were placed on the English missionaries and in 1886 the London Missionary Society formally withdrew.[35] In the meantime, in 1863, at the request of the islanders, who did not wish to become Roman Catholics, missionaries of the Société des Missions Évangéliques arrived. The French Protestants thus fell heir to the responsibil-

[29] Ellis, *op. cit.*, Vol. III, pp. 56-58.
[30] Ellis, *op. cit.*, Vol. II, pp. 388ff.
[31] *The Encyclopædia Britannica*, 14th ed., Vol. XXI, p. 755.
[32] Louvet, *Les Missions Catholiques au XIXme Siècle*, p. 514.
[33] Louvet, *The History of the London Missionary Society*, Vol. I, pp. 306-311; Wilks, *Tahiti*, pp. 14ff.
[34] Louvet, *op. cit.*, pp. 517, 518; Wilks, *op. cit.*, pp. 8off.
[35] Lovett, *op. cit.*, Vol. I, pp. 326-339; On a missionary of the London Missionary Society who was unintentionally shot, in 1844, during hostilities between the French and the Tahitians, see Joseph A. Millar, *Memoir of the Rev. Thomas S. McKean, M.A.* (London, John Snow, 1847, pp. xxiv, 208), *passim*.

ities of their British brethren. About three-fifths of the population were affiliated with them.[36] Under the French protection the Picpus Fathers re-entered. In 1848 the islands were made a separate vicariate apostolic. The Picpus Fathers and sisters and lay brothers eventually won about a fourth of the population.[37] The Mormons and the Seventh Day Adventists gathered a few adherents.[38] The Society Islands remained professedly Christian, but of a somewhat different ecclesiastical complexion than in the first half of the nineteenth century.

Christianity was introduced into the Paumotu or Low Archipelago, between the Gambier and the Society Islands, in 1817 by natives who adopted it while in Tahiti and carried it back with them.[39] The group had later been entered by Mormon missionaries when, in 1849, the Picpus Fathers made their first efforts to win it. Not until 1874 did this order begin a continuing enterprise. By 1888 between four-fifths and nine-tenths of the population had become Roman Catholics.[40]

The Picpus Fathers were also the instruments for introducing Roman Catholic Christianity to Easter Island, that strange, isolated point of land, with its mysterious monolithic statues, on the eastern outskirts of the Pacific. Between 1864 and 1868 the entire population, Polynesian with some Melanesian admixture, was won. Exploitation by white adventurers brought disturbances. A distressing decline in population, due partly to disease, continued. The missionaries left (1871), taking with them to the Gambier Islands about 300 of their adherents. Later the Archbishop of Santiago de Chile was given jurisdiction. By 1914 there was no resident priest and the few remaining natives carried on a form of worship based on what the French missionaries had taught them.[41]

Because of its connexion with Tahiti, the strange story of Pitcairn Island

---

[36] Pannier et Mondain, *l'Expansion Française Outre-Mer et les Protestants Français*, pp. 107, 108; Richter, *Die evangelische Mission in Fern- und Südest-Asien, Australien, Amerika*, pp. 193, 194. See also Th. Arbousset, *Tahiti et les Îles Adjacentes. Voyages et Séjour dans ces Îles, de 1862 à 1865* (Paris, Grassart, 1867, pp. vii, 368), pp. 182ff., where a first hand account is given, with documents, of the entrance of the French Protestants; Ed. Ahne, *Dans les Îles du Pacifique* (Paris, Société des Missions Évangéliques, 1931, pp. 57), pp. 33ff.

[37] Pannier et Mondain, *op. cit.*, p. 113; *Missiones Catholicae . . . MDCCCXCII*, p. 544; Louvet, *op. cit.*, pp. 518, 519.

[38] Pannier et Mondain, *op. cit.*, p. 113. On the Seventh Day Adventists see Gates, *In Coral Isles*, pp. 61ff.

[39] Ellis, *Polynesian Researches*, Vol. III, pp. 304-308.

[40] Louvet, *op. cit.*, pp. 519, 520.

[41] Louvet, *op. cit.*, pp. 520, 521; *Malpelo, Cocos, and Eastern Islands. Handbooks Prepared under the Historical Section of the Foreign Office.—Nos. 141 and 142* (London, H. M. Stationery Office, 1921, pp. 62), pp. 35ff.; Mouly, *Île de Pâques. Île de Mystère* (Bruges, Librairie de l'Oeuvre St. Charles, 1935, pp. 168), *passim*.

must be noted here. In 1787 the *Bounty* was sent to Tahiti to bring samples of the bread-fruit tree to the West Indies. While in the South Seas, some of the crew, driven to desperation by the severity of the captain, William Bligh, mutinied (April, 1789), and put him and the loyal part of the crew adrift in the ship's launch. Nine of the crew of the *Bounty*, together with twelve women and six men of the Pacific Islanders, largely from Tahiti, made their way on that craft to the uninhabited Pitcairn Island. There they established their residence, cut off from the outside world and from possible punishment by the British authorities. Then followed a sad tale of violence and death, until only two of the mutineers were left, with the women and the children which had come of the unions. The two survivors (before long reduced by death to one), sobered by the tragedies through which they had passed, took it upon themselves to teach the Christian faith to this company. For this they used the Bible and the Prayer Book. As a result, when the island was eventually rediscovered by passing ships, an orderly community was found, regular in its religious observances, devout, and seemingly a model of the Christian virtues.[42] Late in 1890 the island was visited by the mission ship which the Seventh Day Adventists had that year equipped for the Pacific and all the inhabitants were said to have been won to that form of the faith.[43]

On the Marquesas Islands, inhabited by Polynesians, efforts to establish a mission were made by the London Missionary Society in 1797, in 1821, in 1825, in 1828, in 1829, and in 1834. In several of these, Christians from the Society Islands were utilized.[44] Some Marquesans, too, were in Protestant mission schools in the Society Islands and Hawaii.[45] In 1833 a mission to the Marquesas was undertaken from Hawaii, where for several years the American Board of Commissioners for Foreign Missions had had a prosperous enterprise.[46] In 1853 more persistent efforts were undertaken by Hawaiian Christians from the churches founded by the American Board. By 1870 these had established four churches in the Marquesas.[47] After 1862 reinforcements from

[42] A fairly large literature has accumulated about Pitcairn Island. An early account, embodying a number of documents, is Thos. Boyles Murray, *Pitcairn: The Island, the People, and the Pastor* (London, Society for Promoting Christian Knowledge, 1860, pp. 414). A more popular account is W. Y. Fullerton, *The Romance of Pitcairn Island* (London, The Carey Press, no date, pp. 112). A more recent study, carefully done, and based upon manuscripts, published records, and a personal sojourn on the island, is Harry L. Shapiro, *The Heritage of the Bounty. The Story of Pitcairn through Six Generations* (New York, Simon and Schuster, 1936, pp. xv, 329).

[43] Gates, *In Coral Isles*, pp. 37-59.

[44] Ellis, *op. cit.*, Vol. III, pp. 319, 320; Murray, *Forty Years' Mission Work in Polynesia and New Guinea*, pp. 1-11.

[45] Ellis, *op. cit.*, Vol. III, p. 316.

[46] Strong, *The Story of the American Board*, p. 68.

[47] Strong, *op. cit.*, pp. 230, 231.

Hawaii ceased, but until early in the twentieth century some of the staff remained.[48] Since in the course of the nineteenth century the Marquesas had passed under French rule, the Hawaiian Evangelical Association, through whom the mission had long been conducted, transferred its responsibilities to the French Protestants. The latter maintained only a small staff.[49]

In 1839 the first Roman Catholic missionaries arrived, Picpus Fathers, with a French expedition which occupied the islands. The initial baptism was that of a young chief, in 1839. In 1843 the French Government limited the number of priests on the Marquesas to eight, each of these to be accompanied by a lay brother, but it agreed to give financial support to this staff. In 1847 Sisters of St. Joseph of Cluny arrived. In 1848 the Marquesas were created a vicariate apostolic. About the year 1849, a native chief and chieftainess were exiled by the French to Tahiti and later were returned to the Marquesas. They thereupon sought religious instruction and (1853) were baptized with numbers of their families. Soon afterwards several other chiefs were baptized. Then followed (until 1860) the happiest period of the mission. However, in the 1860's anti-clerical officials were in power, in 1861 the state subvention was discontinued, and in 1864 an epidemic of smallpox carried off hundreds of the population. In 1870 there was talk of abandoning the mission, but the Pope opposed so drastic a step.[50] In 1892, out of an estimated population of 5,000, about 2,800 were counted as Roman Catholics.[51]

To the south and east of Tahiti lay the Austral or Tubuai Islands, inhabited by Polynesians. About the year 1820 Christianity entered through contact with the island of Raiatea, recently won to the faith through the London Missionary Society. Some of the people of Rurutu, one of the Austral group, driven by contrary winds, came to Raiatea, were greatly impressed by what they saw, and took missionaries back with them. The missionaries were natives from Raiatea and met with immediate success.[52]

It was also from the Society Islands that Christianity first came to the Hervey or Cook Islands. The peoples of both groups were Polynesians and nearly enough related linguistically to be able to communicate without interpreters. Here the pioneer was John Williams. John Williams was one of those adventurous spirits who can never be content in conventional channels but who are always pressing on to new frontiers. In him the urge which makes some men explorers and empire-builders was transmuted by his religious faith into a

[48] *Fortieth Annual Report of the Hawaiian Evangelical Association, July, 1903,* p. 47.
[49] *Societé des Missions Évangéliques . . . May, 1902,* p. 85.
[50] Delmas, *Essai d'Histoire de la Mission des Îles Marquises, passim.*
[51] *Missiones Catholicae . . . MDCCCXCII,* p. 536.
[52] Williams, *A Narrative of Missionary Enterprises in the South Seas,* pp. 57-67.

passion for spreading Christianity among islands where it had never before been preached. In 1821, while on a trip to New South Wales on health leave, he touched at one of the Cook group, Aitutaki, told a chief of the overthrow of idolatry in the Society Islands, and received an invitation to send teachers. As a result, when in 1822 Williams returned, the population already called themselves Christians.[53] Williams spent a considerable period of time on the chief island, Rarotonga. Here, and on the other islands of the group, with the aid of native missionaries from the Society Islands and of reinforcements from Great Britain, Christianity speedily displaced the older cults.[54] Useful crafts were introduced.[55] In the 1830's a complete translation of the New Testament into Rarotongan was printed in England by the British and Foreign Bible Society. This was followed, 1847-1851, by the entire Bible.[56] On Rarotonga a college was built for the training of native missionaries.[57] From it teachers went out to the New Hebrides, Samoa, the Loyalty Islands, and New Guinea. They had a remarkable part in spreading Christianity in the Pacific.[58] Yet in 1879 a visitor reported that on at least one of the islands, while the population was professedly Christian, the native chiefs were continually interfering in Church affairs and that the native pastors were too lax in Church government.[59]

In 1894 Roman Catholicism was brought to the Cook group by the Picpus Fathers.[60]

In spite of the fact that the Cook Islanders became professedly Christian, depopulation continued until near the close of the nineteenth century and was then not entirely arrested. The islanders were, moreover, seriously deficient not only in physical but also in moral stamina.[61]

From the Cook Islands Christianity in its Protestant form spread to the Penrhyn Islands, about 600 miles north. It was carried to them chiefly by some

[53] Williams, *op. cit.*, pp. 67-79.

[54] Williams, *op. cit.*, pp. 95ff. For one of the missionaries see *Selections from the Auto-biography of the Rev. William Gill* (London, Yates and Alexander, 1880, pp. iv, 316), *passim*, and William Wyatt Gill, *Life in the Southern Isles; or Scenes and Incidents in the South Pacific and New Guinea* (London, The Religious Tract Society, 1876, pp. viii, 360), *passim*. See also Gill, *Gems from the Coral Islands*, Vol. I, pp. 20ff.

[55] Williams, *op. cit.*, pp. 167, 168.

[56] Murray, *The Bible in the Pacific*, pp. 27-30.

[57] J. P. Sunderland and A. Buzacott, *Mission Life in the Islands of the Pacific, Being a Narrative of the Life and Labours of the Rev. A. Buzacott* (London, John Snow and Co., 1866, pp. xxii, 282), pp. 131ff.

[58] Lovett, *The History of the London Missionary Society*, Vol. I, p. 353.

[59] Gill, *Jottings from the Pacific*, pp. 39-44.

[60] Schwager, *Die katholische Heidenmission der Gegenwart*, p. 42.

[61] Burton, *The Call of the Pacific*, pp. 33-35, citing the report of the New Zealand Resident-Commissioner of the Cook Islands for 1908.

of their inhabitants who had been driven to the Hervey Islands by a storm, had there come in contact with the faith, and had brought it back with them. Within a year of the return of these wanderers, most of the images of the old cult were destroyed, chapels built, and schools begun.[62]

The island of Niue, also known by the forbidding name Savage, while nearer to the Tonga Islands than to the Hervey group, eventually shared with the latter a political connexion with New Zealand. With the Hervey group, in 1901 it came under the administration of New Zealand. To its inhabitants, predominantly of Polynesian stock, Christianity arrived, as it did at the outset to the Society and the Hervey Islands, through the London Missionary Society. John Williams made an unsuccessful attempt to introduce the faith.[63] In 1840 another effort also failed. In 1846 a native of Niue who had become a Christian in Samoa was placed on the island as a teacher. In 1849 a Samoan and his wife were landed as teachers.[64] Several hundred converts had been made, and, indeed, all but a minority of the population were professedly Christian,[65] when, in 1861, W. G. Lawes, one of the ablest of the missionaries to the Pacific Islands, was assigned to Niue. He found that Christianity had already worked a remarkable change in the lives of the population. Under him and his brother the faith continued to make progress.[66] In time not only was practically the entire population professedly Christian, but also most of the children were in school.[67] Yet by 1914 morality was reported to be deteriorating, partly through the influence of natives who had been abroad and had acquired the vices of the white man.[68]

Not far to the west of Niue are the Tonga, or Friendly Islands.[69] Numbering several score and for the most part low-lying, they had, at the dawn of the nineteenth century, a population with Polynesian elements, possibly Malay-Polynesian, which, in the third quarter of that century, totalled about 50,000.[70] The two chief islands were Tongatabu and Vavau. Haabai, a group of smaller islands, lay between these two.

[62] Lovett, *op. cit.*, Vol. I, pp. 370, 371; Gill, *Gems from the Coral Islands*, Vol. II, pp. 265ff.

[63] Williams, *op. cit.*, pp. 275ff.

[64] Lovett, *op. cit.*, Vol. I, pp. 418, 419.

[65] Murray, *Missions in Western Polynesia*, pp. 356-390.

[66] King, *W. G. Lawes*, pp. 22-46.

[67] Lovett, *op. cit.*, Vol. I, p. 420.

[68] Cousins, *Isles Afar Off*, p. 79.

[69] For an account of missions in the Friendly Islands written for children, but containing much useful information, see Sarah S. Farmer, *Tonga and the Friendly Islands with a Sketch of their Mission History for Young People* (London, Hamilton, Adams & Co., 1855, pp. vi, 427).

[70] Burton, *op. cit.*, p. 39.

The initial effort to introduce Christianity was by missionaries deposited on Tongatabu by the *Duff*, in 1797. However, this attempt proved abortive. Three of the group were killed (1798) in the course of a civil war in which they declined to participate, one took a native wife and abandoned his faith, and in 1801 the others seized the opportunity offered by a passing ship and went to New South Wales.[71] Native Christians from others of the South Sea Islands were later sent by the London Missionary Society, but when, in 1830, John Williams visited Tongatabu, he found the Wesleyans so successful that he readily agreed to leave the field to them.[72]

It was through one of the New South Wales refugees from the London Missionary Society's first mission that a Wesleyan, Walter Lawry, became interested in the Tonga Islands. He and that other pioneer of Methodism in Australia, Samuel Leigh, urged on British Methodists the opportunities in Tonga and New Zealand, and the two enterprises were authorized simultaneously (1820). In 1822 Lawry, his family and several companions, artisans, landed on Tongatabu. They were welcomed by a chief, but after fourteen months Lawry was compelled by his wife's health to withdraw and without his leadership the mission languished.[73] In 1826 it was renewed by John Thomas and a companion. Thomas was the real founder of the Wesleyan mission in the Tonga group. A blacksmith from Worcestershire, with slight formal education and with uncertain health, he was to spend more than a quarter of a century in the Tonga Islands and was to see the large majority of the population become professedly Christian.[74] The first few months were discouraging, but reinforcements arrived, among them Nathaniel Turner, who already had had missionary experience in New Zealand.[75] The first efforts were on Tongatabu, but the chiefs of some of the other islands asked for missionaries. In 1830 one of these chiefs, Taufaahau of Haabai, was baptized, taking the name of George. Converts were also made on Vavau. In 1834 a mass movement occurred, beginning on Vavau and rapidly extending to other islands, including Haabai. It was marked by weeping, the public confession of sins, and the joy of conversion. On Haabai Taufaahau became a class leader and in 1835 freed

---

[71] Lovett, *op. cit.*, Vol. I, pp. 169-173. The one who had "gone native" eventually returned to England and resumed his Christian faith. See his story in *An Authentic Narrative of Four Years' Residence at Tongataboo* (London, Longman, Hurst, Rees, and Orme, 1810, pp. 234).

[72] Williams, *op. cit.*, pp. 280-284.

[73] Findlay and Holdsworth, *The History of the Wesleyan Methodist Missionary Society*, Vol. III, pp. 267-276.

[74] G. Stringer Rowe, *A Pioneer. A Memoir of the Rev. John Thomas, Missionary to the Friendly Islands* (London, T. Woolmer, 1885, pp. 136), *passim;* Findlay and Holdsworth, *op. cit.*, Vol. III, pp. 277-284.

[75] Turner, *The Pioneer Missionary . . . Nathaniel Turner*, pp. 91ff.

his slaves. The movement spread to Tongatabu, but less widely, and still encountered resistance from the adherents to the old cults. In the various islands thousands became church members.[76] In Tongatabu the anti-Christian party resorted to war (1837 and 1840). Eventually Taufaahau became king in Tongatabu as well as on Haabai and Vavau, although for a time he had to face armed resistance.[77] In 1839 he proclaimed a code of laws embodying Christian principles.[78]

In 1854 Methodism in the Tonga Islands passed out of the control of the mother society in Great Britain and became a charge of the newly constituted Australasian Conference.[79] It was the Methodism of Australia and New Zealand which now became responsible for assisting the nascent Christianity. In 1862 Taufaahau, or King George as he was often called, granted a constitution to his kingdom.[80] J. E. Moulton, a missionary recently from England by way of Australia, became the head of Tobou College, on Tongatabu, which was opened in 1866 for the education of young chiefs for posts in the government. A curriculum combining European learning with manual training was developed and the institution won for itself a prominent place in the life of the islands.[81]

In the 1880's what was known as the Free Church arose. Shirley Baker, the chairman of the Tonga district of the Wesleyan church, became prime minister of the kingdom. King George apparently became convinced, presumably at least in part under the influence of Baker, that annexation by Great Britain was impending and that a church with British connexions, as was the Methodist body in the islands, was at once a compromise and a threat to independence. Whatever the motive, the Free Church was so called because, while remaining Methodist in polity, it was independent of the former tie with the church in New South Wales. It became the state church and into it flocked the majority of the Christians. Only a minority remained true to the foreign affiliation. When, in 1890, Baker was forcibly deported by the British authorities, the Free Church continued. In spite of its nationalist character it long had as its president a foreign clergyman, J. B. Watkins. Moulton became the chairman

---

[76] Moulton in Colwell, *A Century in the Pacific,* pp. 420-422; Findlay and Holdsworth, *op. cit.,* Vol. II, pp. 287-309.

[77] Moulton in Colwell, *op. cit.,* pp. 424, 425.

[78] Findlay and Holdsworth, *op. cit.,* Vol. III, pp. 326, 327.

[79] Findlay and Holdsworth, *op. cit.,* Vol. III, p. 337. For glimpses of Methodism in the Tonga group on the eve of separation from the parent society, see Lawry, *Friendly and Feejee Islands,* pp. 13-76; Lawry, *A Second Missionary Visit to the Friendly and Feejee Islands in the Year MDCCCL,* pp. 1-116; West, *Ten Years in South-Central Polynesia,* pp. 1-404.

[80] Moulton in Colwell, *op. cit.,* p. 426.

[81] Moulton in Colwell, *op. cit.,* pp. 426ff.; Moulton, *Moulton of Tonga,* pp. 44-88.

of the organization which embraced the minority who retained fellowship with Australian Methodism. Gradually friendly relations between the two Protestant churches were re-established. The extension of a British protectorate over the islands in 1900 did not essentially alter the ecclesiastical situation. In 1902 Moulton completed a revision of the translation of the Bible. In earlier translations it had been available for many years.[82] Whether through the Free Church or the Methodist Church, Protestant Christianity was becoming better equipped and more deeply rooted.

Early in the twentieth century, the Church of England entered Tonga in the person of Bishop Willis, who had withdrawn from Hawaii when the Anglican enterprise in that area was made over to the Protestant Episcopal Church of the United States. He built a church and opened up various places of worship, but his following was small.[83]

Although Protestantism, either in its Free Church or in its Methodist form, became the faith of the large majority of the population of the Tonga group, Roman Catholicism also gained entrance and won adherents. The Roman Catholics were late in arriving. When they came they found Protestantism already strongly entrenched. The leading chiefs, favourable to that form of the faith, at first resisted the introduction of a rival variety. In 1837 Pompallier, whom we met in the preceding chapter as the first Vicar Apostolic of Western Oceania, was refused permission to place priests on the islands. Late in 1841 and early in 1842 Pompallier returned and, supported by a French warship, was able to establish a footing.[84] One of the Marists then brought in, Chevron, spent many years in the islands and came to be called the Apostle of Tonga. Taufaahau (King George) offered opposition. Converts were slow in coming. In 1855 the commander of a French gunboat obtained from Taufaahau the promise of toleration for Roman Catholicism and in the next few years recurring visits of French men-of-war made for freedom for Roman Catholic activities. Yet the Roman Catholic community grew but slowly. The controversy over the Free Church which disrupted the Methodist body led to the further increase of Roman Catholics. By the beginning of the twentieth century, they numbered about 3,000. They were under the care of eleven Marist and three native priests and were also served by Sisters of the Third Order Regular of Mary.[85]

[82] Moulton in Colwell, *op. cit.*, pp. 430-437; Moulton, *Moulton of Tonga*, pp. 95ff.; Murray, *The Bible in the Pacific*, pp. 70-75; Martin, *Missionaries and Annexation in the Pacific*, pp. 95, 96.
[83] Hands, *Polynesia*, pp. 30, 31.
[84] Pompallier, *Early History of the Catholic Church in Oceania*, p. 78.
[85] Piolet, *Les Missions Catholiques Françaises au XIXe Siècle*, Vol. IV pp. 135-148; Blanc, *L'Heritage d'un Évêque d'Océanie*, pp. 172ff.

Wallis or Uvea Island, north of Tonga and west of Samoa, seems to have owed its introduction to Christianity to converts from Niuatobatabu, an island south of Samoa, whose population had become Christian in the 1830's through zealous products of the great mass movement of 1834 on Vavau. The initial attempt was by a party led by the chief of Niuatobatabu and was terminated by the massacre of the entire party. Other Christian missionaries, natives of the Tonga group, arrived later with a letter of commendation from King George. They gathered a few converts, but met with such stubborn opposition from the Roman Catholics that they eventually withdrew.[86] In 1837, only a short time after the fatal ending of the first Protestant attempt, Bataillon, a Marist priest, introduced by the Vicar Apostolic, Pompallier, and accompanied by a lay brother, began the Roman Catholic mission. In spite of initial persecution, within a few years a mass movement occurred. In 1842 Bataillon reported that Pompallier, during a four months' stay, had baptized and confirmed the entire population, more than 2,000 in number.[87] In 1842 Bataillon became the first Vicar Apostolic of Central Oceania.[88] A seminary was begun and in 1886 four native priests were ordained.[89] In 1886, largely in consequence of the labours of the missionaries, Wallis Island was made a French protectorate.[90]

Fotuna, slightly to the west and south of Wallis Island and, like it, peopled by Polynesians, appears to have made its first acquaintance with Christianity through the Marists. In 1837 a Marist priest, Pierre Louis Marie Chanel, and a lay coadjutor were placed on the island. Chanel had gathered a few catechumens when, in 1841, he was killed by some of the islanders. At Pompallier's request, and to the great alarm of the populace, a French gunboat was sent. In 1842 new missionaries were landed on the island and hundreds were soon baptized. Before long the island was professedly Christian. As on Wallis Island, the population eventually began to increase.[91]

The Samoan or Navigators Islands contained one of the largest bodies of Polynesians. In 1839 the population was estimated to be 56,600. In 1930 the pure native stock numbered only slightly less than 50,000.[92] Christianity was first propagated in Samoa by those who had been won in the Tonga Islands.

[86] Findlay and Holdsworth, *The History of the Wesleyan Methodist Missionary Society*, Vol. III, pp. 321-325.
[87] Bataillon in *Annales de la Propagation de la Foi*, Vol. XIII, pp. 5-34, 338ff., Vol. XV, pp. 399, 400; Pompallier, *Early History of the Catholic Church in Oceania*, pp. 18-32.
[88] Louvet, *Les Missions Catholiques au XIXe Siècle*, pp. 524, 525.
[89] Huonder, *Der einheimische Klerus in den Heidenländern*, pp. 251-258.
[90] Piolet, *op. cit.*, Vol. IV, p. 106.
[91] Piolet, *op. cit.*, Vol. IV, pp. 114-123; Blanc, *L'Heritage d'un Évêque d'Océanie*, pp. 228ff.
[92] Keesing, *Modern Samoa*, pp. 15-32.

Some of these were Tongans and some were Samoans who had been in Tonga.[93] In 1830 John Williams visited the islands and placed there a Samoan chief who had become a Christian while in Tonga.[94] With the chief were sent Christian Tahitians as missionaries. In 1832 Williams was back and discovered that the population of Manua, the easternmost of the Samoan group, called themselves Christians and were asking for missionaries. He learned, too, that Christianity had made marked progress on the two largest islands, Savaii and Upolu.[95] Conversion tended to be by groups and tribes. The Samoans built chapels, and white men who had drifted into the islands, some of unworthy character, administered baptism and the communion.[96] The London Missionary Society took advantage of the remarkable opportunity. In 1835 missionaries arrived from the Society Islands and in 1836, largely at the instance of Williams, reinforcements, the first permanently resident British missionaries of the London Missionary Society in the islands, came from England.[97] Williams dreamed of extending Christianity to every island of importance between Samoa and New Guinea.[98] Of the band of missionaries which he brought to the South Seas in 1838, three settled on Samoa.[99] By 1840 the main islands, Savaii, Upolu, and Tutuila, were covered with a network of mission stations, with a missionary at the chief point in each. Progress was most rapid on Tutuila, less distracted by wars and contacts with non-missionary foreigners. The missionaries endeavoured, sometimes with success, to compose the wars. Converts multiplied. Occasionally marked religious movements occurred which the missionaries denominated revivals. The Bible was translated. A printing press was brought in. Schools were begun. On Upolu, Malua Institution was started for the training of a native ministry.[100] The organization of the church tended to conform to the old social structure, with its clans and chiefs, rather than to supplant it.[101]

[93] Findlay and Holdsworth, *op. cit.*, Vol. III, pp. 339, 340.

[94] Williams, *A Narrative of Missionary Enterprises in the South Seas*, pp. 303ff.

[95] Williams, *op. cit.*, pp. 375ff.

[96] Lovett, *The History of the London Missionary Society*, Vol. I, p. 374.

[97] Lovett, *op. cit.*, Vol. I, p. 375.

[98] Williams in *The Missionary's Farewell; Valedictory Services of the Rev. John Williams, Previous to His Departure for the South Seas* (New York, D. Appleton & Co., 1938, pp. 141), p. 88.

[99] Lovett, *op. cit.*, Vol. I, p. 375.

[100] Lovett, *op. cit.*, Vol. I, pp. 379-403; Murray, *Forty Years' Mission Work in Polynesia and New Guinea*, pp. 17ff.; Murray, *The Bible in the Pacific*, pp. 39-47; Turner, *Nineteen Years in Polynesia*, pp. 95ff.; *Missionary Life in Samoa, as Exhibited in the Journals of the Late George Archibald Lundie during the Revival in Tutuila in 1840-41* (Edinburgh, William Oliphant and Sons, 1846, pp. v, 294), *passim*; Charles Phillips, *Samoa, Past and Present: A Narrative of Missionary Work in the South Seas* (London, John Snow and Co., no date, pp. 96), *passim*.

[101] Lovett, *op. cit.*, Vol. I, p. 396; Keesing, *op. cit.*, pp. 399, 400.

Instead of reproducing the congregational polity familiar to them in Great Britain, the missionaries developed a type of Presbyterianism. They retained the direction, however, holding positions akin to those of bishops.[102] In the course of time practically all the Samoans regarded themselves as Christians. Of these the large majority were affiliated with the churches founded under the auspices of the London Missionary Society.

Efforts were also made to reach the Chinese coolies on the plantations. Some of the Samoan Christians supported a Chinese who engaged in that labour.[103]

Substantial minorities of the Samoans attached themselves to other forms of Christianity. Of these the largest groups were the Methodists and the Roman Catholics.[104] Much smaller followings were attracted by the Mormons and the Seventh Day Adventists.

The Christianity which was first introduced to Samoa was from Tonga and was therefore Methodism. The Tahitian missionaries brought by John Williams were forbidden by the chief in whose domains they laboured to accept the urgent invitations which came from other tribes. The Tongan Methodism continued to spread, and the denominational alignment conformed to divisions between tribes. The news of the prosperity of the faith reached Tonga. Before long a Samoan chief asked for a British missionary. The Tonga Synod therefore sent Peter Turner, in 1835. A mass movement to Christianity followed Turner's arrival. In twenty months the Methodist converts rose from 2,000 to 13,000. However, at the London headquarters the London Missionary Society and the Wesleyan Methodist Missionary Society had agreed on a division of their fields in the Pacific Islands, and Samoa had been allotted to the former. When, in 1836, its first resident representatives of the London Missionary Society arrived, they told Turner of the arrangement. Turner and the Tonga Synod protested to their society, but in vain. His London superiors ordered Turner out of Samoa. In 1839 he yielded and went. Turner's converts were unwilling to allow a foreign agency thus summarily to decide their religious affiliations. Many held to their Methodism. They appealed to King George of Tonga. King George responded by a personal visit to Samoa and by sending

---

[102] Lovett, op. cit., Vol. I, p. 401.

[103] Cousins, Isles Afar Off, p. 67.

[104] Murray, Forty Years' Mission Work in Polynesia and New Guinea, p. 444, says that c. 1875 out of a total native population of 34,265, 26,493 were affiliated with the London Missionary Society, 4,794 with the Wesleyan Methodists, 2,852 with the Roman Catholics, and 126 with the Mormons. By 1926 the numbers were 30,459 affiliated with the London Missionary Society, 6,742 with the Wesleyan Methodists, 6,889 with the Roman Catholics, 1,251 with the Mormons, and 27 with the Seventh Day Adventists.— Keesing, op. cit., p. 398.

Tongan Methodists to assist their Samoan fellows. However, deprived of European leadership, Samoan Methodism became involved in tribal intrigues, lost followers to the London Mission and to the Roman Catholics, and began to incorporate non-Christian practices.[105] In 1857 the recently formed Australian Methodist Missionary Society, stirred by reports of the sad condition of the Samoan Methodists and not feeling itself bound by the self-denying abstention of the British mother society, sent a missionary to mend the situation. Others followed and were aided by Tongan teachers. Friendly relations were established with the London Missionary Society's representatives. Yet many difficulties were encountered, including the intertribal wars which racked the islands in the last four decades of the nineteenth century and which ended only with the establishment of foreign rule through division between the United States and Germany. Methodism never regained the position which it had held in the 1830's.[106]

It was in 1845 that Roman Catholic Christianity first entered Samoa. In that year a missionary party arrived from Wallis Island, sent by Bataillon, the Vicar Apostolic of Central Oceania. Some Samoans who had accepted the faith on that island came with it. The group had as its nucleus three French Marists (two priests and a lay coadjutor) and two catechists, natives of Wallis.[107] The outstanding Marist missionary, Louis Elroy, later Vicar Apostolic of Central Oceania and the Navigators Islands, arrived in 1856.[108] Protestant Christianity had already spread so widely that the Roman Catholics had difficulty in making headway. Moreover, the inter-tribal wars proved an obstacle. However, the divisions among the Protestants, especially the weakness in the Methodist forces after the withdrawal of Peter Turner, created a favourable opportunity. Some Methodists became Roman Catholics.[109] The number of priests, catechists, churches, and Christians rose fairly steadily, and more than doubled in the forty years between 1866 and 1906.[110] Roman Catholicism became especially strong among the increasing mixed-blood portion of the population. Eventually it had about four times as many adherents among them as did any other denomination. This seems to have been the fruitage of the schools conducted for children of mixed parentage.[111]

[105] Findlay and Holdsworth, *The History of the Wesleyan Methodist Missionary Society*, Vol. III, pp. 338-357.

[106] Findlay and Holdsworth, *op. cit.*, Vol. III, pp. 357-362; Danks in Colwell, *A Century in the Pacific*, pp. 490-505; *George Brown . . . An Autobiography*, pp. 29-65.

[107] A. Monfat, *Les Premiers Missionaires de Samoa* (Lyon, Librarie Catholique Emmanuel Vitte, 1923, pp. viii, 335), pp. 177ff.

[108] Piolet, *Les Missions Catholiques Françaises au XIXe Siècle*, Vol. IV, pp. 172, 173.

[109] Findlay and Holdsworth, *op. cit.*, Vol. III, p. 356.

[110] Schmidlin, *Die katholischen Missionen in den deutschen Schutzgebieten*, p. 194.

[111] Keesing, *Modern Samoa*, p. 399.

By the close of the nineteenth century the Samoans had become a Christian people. The annexation of the islands by Germany and the United States did not bring any essential change in their religious life. The German and American governments might be restive under a situation in which British and French missionaries possessed such marked influence, but they made no very vigorous attempt to change it.[112] The Samoans were loyal to their churches and at times were so zealous in erecting church buildings that the American colonial authorities sought to curb projects which resulted in large debts.[113] Many beliefs of pre-Christian days persisted and mingled with the imported faith,[114] but this was not unlike the condition which had prevailed in Western and Southern Europe in the first generations after its formal conversion.

The Tokelau group, comprising several scores of coral islets, lies about 350 miles north-west of Samoa. In 1921 its population was not far from 1,000.[115] In the 1850's and 1860's Roman Catholic Christianity reached it from Wallis Island and later from Samoa.[116] Protestant Christianity, represented by the London Missionary Society, came in the 1860's from Samoa.[117] Before the end of the century the population, Polynesian, seems all to have become Christian.

The Ellice Islands, coral atolls with a Polynesian population of Samoan antecedents, west and slightly north of the Tokelau Islands, adopted Protestant Christianity in the 1860's and 1870's. They seem to have heard of it first from the captain of a passing trading vessel. Then it came to them from shipwrecked Christians from the Penrhyn Islands. From time to time missionaries of the London Missionary Society and of the American Board of Commissioners for Foreign Missions visited them. Teachers from Samoa were introduced by the former society. The population were so eager to learn of the new faith that slavers seeking labourers for Peru were able to lure many of them away with the promise to teach them the desired religion.[118]

The volcanic island of Rotuma, about half way between the Ellice and the Fiji Islands, had a population of between 2,000 and 3,000. The population seemed to have affinities with the Polynesians but its language was related more nearly to that of Fiji. In 1839, while on the voyage which ended in his martyrdom, John Williams put two native teachers on the island.[119] It was, how-

---

[112] Keesing, op. cit., pp. 403, 404.
[113] Keesing, op. cit., p. 403.
[114] Keesing, op. cit., pp. 408-410.
[115] *The Encyclopædia Britannica*, 14th ed., Vol. XVII, p. 13.
[116] Piolet, op. cit., Vol. IV, pp. 176-182.
[117] Lovett, *The History of the London Missionary Society*, Vol. I, pp. 420-422.
[118] Murray, *Forty Years' Mission Work in Polynesia and New Guinea*, pp. 375-423. See a brief account by a visitor in 1872, in Gill, *Jottings from the Pacific*, pp. 11-27. Gill reported the process of conversion not yet completed.
[119] Lovett, op. cit., Vol. I, p. 376.

ever, the Wesleyans rather than the London Missionary Society who were the chief means of the introduction of Christianity. Native Methodist teachers entered from both Tonga and Fiji. By 1864, in spite of persecution, and with only an occasional visit by a white missionary, about 1,200 were professedly Christian, and there were 22 local preachers and 230 persons meeting in class. In 1864 William Fletcher was appointed to the island as a resident missionary. During his eleven years there he translated the New Testament into the vernacular. Other Methodist missionaries followed him.[120]

The first Roman Catholic missionary to put foot on Rotuma was the pioneer, Pompallier. He touched there in 1837 on his way to New Zealand but did not begin a mission. In 1846 Bataillon, the initial Vicar Apostolic of Central Oceania, sent two missionaries. These found Methodists from Tonga already at work. Partly because of opposition from the Methodists, few converts were made. In 1853, discouraged, the two priests went to Fotuna, accompanied by several of the neophytes. However, in 1859 a Rotumian catechist and in 1861 two Fotunian catechists were placed on the island. They laboured to such good effect that the number of Roman Catholics grew. In 1868 two French missionaries were sent to Rotuma. In spite of the effort of a French naval officer to obtain toleration for the Roman Catholics, the chiefs who had adhered to Methodism sought by war to oppose the spread of the rival form of the faith. In the 1880's the intervention of the British Government brought enforced toleration. In 1887 Rome detached Rotuma from the Vicariate Apostolic of Central Oceania and put it under the newly founded Vicariate Apostolic of Fiji. This action, with the early advent of new missionaries, brought renewed life to the Roman Catholic minority.[121]

The Fiji Islands have a larger land area than any of the groups thus far covered in this chapter. In contrast with these latter, moreover, with their predominantly Polynesian populations, Fiji was peopled primarily by Melanesians. The Polynesian strains in the islands were in the minority.[122] How numerous the population was when intimate contacts with the white man began is not certain. Estimates varied from 70,000 to 300,000.[123] Decline in population began early[124] and was a marked feature of the nineteenth century. From a total of 104,625 in 1892 the Fijians dwindled to 87,096 in 1911.[125]

---

[120] Bennett in Colwell, *A Century in the Pacific*, pp. 466, 467; Findlay and Holdsworth, *The History of the Wesleyan Methodist Missionary Society*, Vol. III, pp. 467, 468.
[121] Blanc, *Histoire Religieuse de l'Archipel Fidjien*, Vol. II, pp. 253-288.
[122] Thomson, *The Fijians*, pp. 10ff.
[123] Roberts, *Population Problems in the Pacific*, p. 89; Williams and Calvert, *Fiji and the Fijians*, Vol. I, p. 102.
[124] Williams and Calvert, *op. cit.*, Vol. I, p. 103.
[125] Roberts, *op. cit.*, p. 90.

Physically they were well built. They possessed a culture of their own, were excellent in agriculture, and are said to have constructed better houses and more seaworthy boats than any others of the Pacific Islanders.[126] War between the tribes and between village and village was common.[127] Life was cheap. Widows were strangled on the death of their husbands. Some of the old and infirm were killed or were allowed to die of starvation. Cannibalism had developed, although its origin is unknown and the extent to which it was practised has been a subject of disagreement.[128] Religion included ancestor worship and gods who spoke through a priesthood, usually hereditary and with marked influence.

Tasman in the seventeenth century and Cook in the eighteenth century sighted the Fijis but did not land. In the last decade of the eighteenth century and in the first decade of the nineteenth century white men began to arrive. Vessels in search of sandal wood stripped the islands of that commodity. Whalers and purchasers of *bêche-de-mer*, the sea-slug prized by Chinese gourmands, followed them. Fire-arms were introduced. They made inter-tribal wars much more deadly. Chiefs who possessed them became powerful and gathered about them confederacies of weaker tribes.[129] Before the appearance of the missionaries, contacts with the white man were beginning a cultural revolution.

It was not until 1874 that Great Britain formally annexed the islands. In the meantime there was native government. The most powerful of the chiefs, Thakombau, had gradually, by war and diplomacy, made himself the master of the larger part of the islands. In 1871 he had been declared sovereign of all Fiji, but he had not conquered the interior, his government was deeply in debt, the resident Europeans were dissatisfied, and the chiefs were persuaded to cede the country to Great Britain.[130]

In the latter part of the nineteenth century a further complication arose through the presence of coolies from abroad. The plantations developed by the white man required labour. The Fijians provided an inadequate supply. New Hebrideans and Solomon Islanders were brought in but proved unsatisfactory. Thousands were introduced from India under contract. In 1907 indentured adults numbered 11,689.[131] After their terms were over, many Indians remained in the islands. In 1911 the total Indian population of Fiji was 40,286,

---

[126] Burton, *The Fiji of To-day*, p. 53; Burton, *The Call of the Pacific*, p. 81.
[127] Thomson, *op. cit.*, pp. 85 ff.
[128] Thomson, *op. cit.*, pp. 102ff.; Henderson, *Fiji and the Fijians*, pp. 50-100.
[129] Thomson, *op. cit.*, pp. 85, 86, 100.
[130] Thomson, *op. cit.*, pp. 21-55.
[131] Burton, *The Fiji of To-day*, p. 270.

an increase of 23,181 in ten years.[132] Since the overwhelming majority were non-Christian, they constituted a problem and a challenge to the Church.

Christianity effectively entered Fiji from the Tonga Islands and under Methodist auspices. To be sure, in 1830 John Williams had landed two Tahitian teachers on the islands, but their influence was slight.[133] Moreover, he had agreed to leave Fiji to the Wesleyans.[134] That was logical, because Tongans had long been going to the Fijis and it was natural that Methodism, having become strong in Tonga, should take advantage of the traditional connexion between the two groups. Under the enthusiasm of the great mass movement of 1834 in which Christianity made such notable strides in Tonga, and in view of reinforcements about to arrive from England, it was decided that at last the time was ripe to extend the Methodist mission to Fiji. In 1835 two British missionaries went to Lakemba, one of the Fiji group near Tonga, where a number of Tongan Christians were already residing.[135] Since the chiefs on Lakemba would not accept Christianity against the wish of their superiors on the larger islands, one of the missionaries soon moved to Viti Levu, the outstanding one of the group. Reinforcements came from England, bringing with them a printing press. By 1840 beginnings had been made in the translation and printing of the New Testament and in conducting schools. Conversions were slow, partly because the chiefs were fearful of the effects of the new faith upon the old social and political structure.[136] By 1841, however, Christianity had triumphed on the small islands of Ono-i-lau. There the population had had their faith shaken in the old gods when, in 1835, the customary offerings had failed to stem a disastrous epidemic. They had heard rumours of Jehovah and decided to turn to him. The missionaries sent them a convert as a teacher. War between Christians and non-Christians followed, but the former prevailed.[137]

The early missionaries to the Fijis included some able men—among them John Hunt, who from a farm labourer had become a Methodist minister,[138] David Cargill, who was adept in languages, Richard Burdsall Lyth, a surgeon

[132] Brummitt, A Winter Holiday in Fiji, p. 135.

[133] Findlay and Holdsworth, The History of the Wesleyan Methodist Missionary Society, Vol. III, p. 370; Burton and Deane, A Hundred Years in Fiji, p. 22.

[134] Williams, A Narrative of Missionary Enterprises in the South Seas, p. 284.

[135] Findlay and Holdsworth, op. cit., Vol. III, pp. 371, 372; Williams and Calvert, Fiji and the Fijians, Vol. II, pp. 4ff.

[136] Henderson, op. cit., pp. 101-118; Murray, The Bible in the Pacific, p. 84.

[137] Henderson, op. cit., pp. 168ff.; Williams and Calvert, op. cit., Vol. II, pp. 52ff.

[138] George Stringer Rowe, A Missionary Among Cannibals; or, the Life of John Hunt (New York, Phillips & Hunt, no date, pp. 286. Made up largely of extracts from Hunt's journals and letters), passim.

who was the founder of modern medical practice in Fiji,[139] James Calvert, a skilled printer as well as clergyman,[140] and Thomas Williams, whose keen observations of native life became a treasure house of information for the old culture.[141]

The frequent wars retarded the spread of Christianity. The missionaries urged the Christians not to fight and this increased the enmity of the leading non-Christian chief, Thakombau, who felt his forces weakened by the unwillingness of his Christian subjects to take up arms.[142]

In spite of wars and opposition, Christianity continued to gain. From time to time movements broke out marked by deep emotion and contrition for sin and accompanied by conversions.[143]

The progress of the new faith was accelerated by the conversion of Thakombau. In 1854 he openly espoused Christianity. In 1857 he was publicly married to the one esteemed his chief wife, dismissed his other wives, and was baptized. He seems to have been moved to this step by illness and reverses in war, which had come to him in spite of his loyalty to the old religion. A letter from King George of Tonga urging him to become a Christian may also have had some effect.[144] Fully as important as the conversion of Thakombau was the victory in battle in 1855 of the Christian forces, headed by Thakombau and aided by King George, against the non-Christians. The old gods were discredited.[145] By 1856 there were 4,000 church members and 30,000 attendants at worship.[146] Before many years open paganism had largely retreated to the hills. To be sure, as late as 1867 Thomas Baker was killed, the only missionary martyr in the islands, but two of the murderers were later baptized and the son of one of the slayers became a local preacher.[147] The

---

[139] Henderson, op. cit., pp. 127ff.

[140] G. Stringer Rowe, James Calvert of Fiji (London, Charles H. Kelly, 1893, pp. xi, 304) ; R. Vernon, James Calvert, or, From Dark to Dawn in Fiji (New York, Fleming H. Revell, no date, p. 160).

[141] G. C. Henderson, The Journal of Thomas Williams, Missionary in Fiji, 1840-1853 (Sydney, Angus & Robertson, 2 vols., 1931) ; Williams and Calvert, Fiji and the Fijians, Vol. I, passim.

[142] Williams and Calvert, op. cit., Vol. II, pp. 309, 310.

[143] Williams and Calvert, op. cit., Vol. II, pp. 269, 270; Joseph Waterhouse, Vah-ta-ah, the Feejeean Princess (London, Hamilton, Adams, and Co., 1857, pp. 64), passim. On the state of Christianity in 1847 see Lawry, Friendly and Feejee Islands, pp. 175ff., and in 1850 see Lawry, A Second Missionary Visit to the Friendly and Feejee Islands in the year MDCCCL, pp. 117ff.

[144] Williams and Calvert, op. cit., Vol. II, pp. 333ff.; Joseph Waterhouse, The King and People of Fiji (London, Wesleyan Conference Office, 1866, pp. xii, 435), pp. 251ff.

[145] Henderson, Fiji and the Fijians, pp. 264-270.

[146] Henderson, op. cit., p. 261.

[147] Bennett in Colwell, A Century in the Pacific, p. 468.

annexation of the islands by Great Britain (1874) prepared the way for the final blows to the non-Christian faiths.[148]

Various motives seem to have shared in moving the Fijians to accept Christianity. Of some we cannot be entirely sure. Perhaps the Fijians themselves were not always certain of them. The victory of Christians in warfare furthered the change of faith, for by the test of combat the Christian God had been proved more powerful than the old deities.[149] Indeed, on at least one occasion victorious Christians gave the vanquished pagans the choice of death or conversion.[150] One chief embraced Christianity because in a time of drought the prayers of non-Christian priests failed to bring relief but rain fell copiously during the Christian service on Sunday.[151] The cures of disease wrought by missionaries and Christian teachers won some.[152] A priest of the old cult ascribed his conversion to a dream in which his pagan god bowed to the earth before the Christian God.[153] Some of the Fijians seem to have been sincerely convinced that their past lives had been evil and that they had need of repentance and salvation.[154]

Of basic importance in the achievement of the conversion of the Fijians were the missionaries. Their preaching, their training of teachers, their translation and printing of the Bible, their creation of a system of elementary schools, their systematic preparation of inquirers for church membership, and their own devotion had marked results.[155]

The effects of Christianity upon the Fijians were striking. Largely because of Christianity, cannibalism came to an end and, after an initial intensification of warfare by the interjection of the new faith as a further cause of contention, inter-tribal warfare diminished. Indeed, for a time missionaries strictly forbade Christians to engage in war and later only reluctantly modified their pacifism to permit Christians to defend themselves.[156] When they resorted to war, the Christians were sometimes more magnanimous to the defeated foe than earlier custom would have enjoined.[157] Monogamous marriage was insisted upon. The strangling of widows came to an end. Christian missionaries counteracted the

---

[148] Burton and Deane, *A Hundred Years in Fiji*, p. 56.
[149] Henderson, *op. cit.*, pp. 268-270.
[150] Henderson, *The Journal of Thomas Williams*, pp. 34, 52.
[151] Henderson, *The Journal of Thomas Williams*, pp. 60-65.
[152] Henderson, *The Journal of Thomas Williams*, p. 415.
[153] Henderson, *The Journal of Thomas Williams*, p. 389.
[154] Lawry, *A Second Missionary Visit to the Friendly and Feejee Islands in the Year MDCCCL*, p. 158.
[155] Henderson, *Fiji and the Fijians*, pp. 142-167, 230.
[156] Henderson, *Fiji and the Fijians*, pp. 242-260.
[157] Watsford, *Glorious Gospel Triumphs as Seen in My Life and Work in Fiji and Australasia*, p. 71.

demoralizing influences of many of the whites who settled in the islands and who were not restrained by any considerations of Christian morality. They reduced the language to writing, and, in addition to the translation of the Bible,[158] began the preparation of a literature. For seventy years they bore the main burden of education. In each village a school was established to teach reading, writing, arithmetic, and religion. A Central Training Institution was developed.[159] Eventually (1908) a theological institution was established and an excellent native ministry was brought into being.[160] The status of women was altered.[161] As in so many others of the Christian communities in the South Seas, Christianity stimulated the natives to go as missionaries to other peoples. Several scores of Fijian Christians went to New Guinea, New Britain, the Solomon Islands, and North Australia to propagate their faith.[162]

The decision, in 1874, to extend British sovereignty over the Fijis was favoured by the Wesleyan missionaries. The immediate impulse to consummate it seems to have been due in part to the humanitarian desire, stirred by Presbyterian missionaries in the New Hebrides, to stop the horrors of the kidnapping of labourers from the New Hebrides and the Solomon Islands for Fijian plantations.[163]

The Methodists were not content with reaching the Fijians. They also sought to win to their faith the labourers from India. Several years after the first of the coolies arrived in the islands the Methodists obtained an Indian Christian to begin the efforts for them.[164] Missionaries of white blood joined in the enterprise. The task was not easy. In contrast with the Fijians, whose primitive culture and faith gave way fairly quickly to that of the European, the Indians were adherents of either Hinduism or Islam, religions which have never yielded readily to Christianity.[165] By 1910 four clergymen, four women, and six or eight Indians were engaged in this phase of the mission. There were day schools, Sunday schools, and an orphanage. Yet only 72 church members had been gathered and only 1,000 could be said to be attendants at public worship.[166]

British settlers entered Fiji. Since the majority of these were professedly

---

[158] Murray, The Bible in the Pacific, p. 84.
[159] Burton and Deane, A Hundred Years in Fiji, p. 87.
[160] Mann, Education in Fiji, pp. 23, 24; Burton and Deane, op. cit., pp. 72ff.
[161] Burton and Deane, op. cit., pp. 94ff.
[162] Burton and Deane, op. cit., p. 116.
[163] Martin, Missionaries and Annexation in the Pacific, p. 77.
[164] Ross, Churches and Church Workers in Fiji, p. 30.
[165] Burton, The Fiji of To-day, pp. 322ff.
[166] Burton, The Call of the Pacific, p. 110; Brummitt. A Winter Holiday in Fiji, pp. 142ff.

members of the Church of England, in 1870 a clergyman of that communion came to care for them. In the course of the next forty years a few others followed. Early in the 1880's the Anglican enterprise was extended to the Melanesians who had been brought into the islands as labourers and for whom the Church of England was conducting missions in their native islands. Eventually a missionary of the Church of England was sent to the Indians. In 1908 Suva, in the Fijis, became the seat of the Diocese of Polynesia of the Church of England which had been created in that year.[167]

In 1876, through the initiative of the Presbyterian Church of New Zealand, a Presbyterian church was organized in Fiji for the white settlers of that denomination. Long gaps, however, existed between the pastorates of resident ministers.[168]

In the 1890's the Seventh Day Adventists came and in 1914 had ten churches and 136 members.[169]

Roman Catholic Christianity also entered the Fijis. Here, as in so many others of the islands of the Pacific, the missionaries were Marists. In 1842 Pompallier, as Vicar Apostolic of Western Oceania, placed a native catechist on Lakemba, the island of the Fiji group near to Tonga, where the Wesleyans had established a foothold a few years before. In 1844 Bataillon, as Vicar Apostolic of Central Oceania, put some European missionaries on Lakemba. Difficulties with the Wesleyans were encountered. In 1851, when the mission seemed about to perish, Bataillon brought reinforcements. Additional stations were opened. Yet difficulties continued. The inter-tribal wars of the period brought embarrassment. The Wesleyans made much more rapid headway than the Roman Catholics and opposed the latter. They had been earlier in the field and had the advantage of the powerful backing of King George of Tonga. There was Roman Catholic opposition to the annexation of Fiji by Great Britain. However, the Roman Catholic mission made progress, even though slowly. In 1861, following the intervention of a French corvette in behalf of some converts, several villages embraced the faith. In 1863 Fiji was separated from the Vicariate Apostolic of Central Oceania and was created a Prefecture Apostolic. As late as 1870, no native chief was a Roman Catholic. Most of the chiefs, indeed, were hostile. For years, in spite of the arrival, in 1882, of the vanguard of the Third Order Regular of Mary, sisters to aid the men who had heretofore carried the entire burden, the missionary personnel

[167] Hands, *Polynesia*, pp. 25-32; Pascoe, *Two Hundred Years of the S.P.G.*, pp. 456-459b; Ross, *op. cit.*, pp. 37-47; C. W. Whonsbon Aston, *Levuka Days of a Parson in Polynesia* (London, Society for Promoting Christian Knowledge, 1936, pp. 95), *passim*.

[168] Ross, *op. cit.*, pp. 49-76.

[169] Watson, *Cannibals and Head-Hunters in the South Seas*, pp. 64-73; *Seventh-day Adventist Conferences and Missions of . . . 1914*; Gates, *The Coral Isles*, pp. 137ff.

was not numerous. Even with the inauguration of some new centres, in 1887 the number of Roman Catholics showed an actual loss of more than half in the preceding quarter of a century. The total on the rolls was only about 6,000 as compared with about 13,000 in 1863. The decline was ascribed in part to the paucity of missionaries. The Roman Catholic cause also suffered from its supposed identification with France in contrast with the Wesleyans, who could assert that they were British and of the same faith as the ruling power. In 1887 the Fijis were raised to a Vicariate Apostolic and were combined ecclesiastically with Rotuma. For Vicar Apostolic an experienced Marist missionary, Julien Vidal of Samoa, was chosen. Under him reinforcements came and new stations were opened.[170] Schools were maintained by Marist Brothers, Marist Sisters, and Sisters of St. Joseph of Cluny. Differing from the extensive education to the many by the Wesleyans, the Roman Catholic schools gave a more intensive and possibly a more efficient education to the few.[171] Efforts were made to improve the women in physical cleanliness.[172] In spite of the devotion of the missionaries, Roman Catholics remained a minority. Not long before 1914 the government census counted 7,148 Roman Catholics as against 78,542 Methodists.[173]

The New Hebrides are a group of islands, largely rugged and of volcanic origin, to the east of the Fijis. With them are usually associated the smaller Banks and Torres Islands which lie slightly to the north of the main group. The New Hebrides, in turn, fall into the northern group, which includes the largest islands, and the southern, with Erromanga, Tanna, and Aneityum as the larger ones. At the outset of the nineteenth century the population was predominantly Melanesian, but in many islands had traces of Polynesian blood. The people were said to be of lower grade than those of many others of the Pacific Islands. Tribal warfare, cannibalism, and the killing of widows were prevalent. In 1910 the total population was reported to be between 60,000 and 65,000.[174] This was very much less than at the advent of the white man. The decrease was due to a variety of factors, among them diseases which came with the white man, the introduction of fire-arms with the resultant intensification of tribal wars, and emigration to plantations in Queensland and other sections in the South Seas.[175] The first Europeans to see the New Hebrides

[170] Blanc, *Histoire Religieuse de l'Archipel Fijien, passim.*
[171] Mann, *Education in Fiji,* pp. 26, 27.
[172] Ross, *Churches and Church Workers in Fiji,* p. 34.
[173] Brummitt, *A Winter Holiday in Fiji,* p. 157.
[174] *New Hebrides. Handbooks Prepared Under the Direction of the Historical Section of the Foreign Office* (London, H. M. Stationery Office, 1920, pp. 31), *passim.* For a description of much of the old structure of society see Rivers, *The History of Melanesian Society,* Vol. I, pp. 189ff.
[175] Speiser in Rivers, *Essays on the Depopulation of Melanesia,* pp. 25ff.

were the Spaniards, in 1606. In 1773 Cook explored their coasts, giving them the name which they later bore. In the first half of the nineteenth century came white sailors and traders, some of whom divested the islands of their sandal-wood. The recruiting of labour for Queensland, Fiji, and New Caledonia commenced in the second half of the nineteenth century. Both France and Great Britain became interested in the new islands and in the 1880's began to extend their control over them. In 1906 a condominium was established by the two countries, an administration whose weaknesses were the occasion for severe criticism.

Christianity first arrived in the New Hebrides through that intrepid pioneer of the London Missionary Society, John Williams. In November, 1839, Williams came, expecting to introduce Samoans as missionaries. Apparently he looked upon the New Hebrides as the key to the islands in the South-west Pacific. He put three Samoans on Tanna, but, on November 20th, he was killed on Erromanga.[176] His murder may have been in retaliation for cruel treatment received from some white men who a short time before had been there in search of sandal-wood.[177]

The news of the tragedy stimulated the London Missionary Society to fulfil Williams's dream. In 1840 a missionary party was sent from England. When, in 1842, after a delay in Samoa, it reached Tanna, it found the Samoan teachers safe. For a time the missionaries lived on Tanna, but after a few months were forced out, presumably because the inhabitants held them responsible for an epidemic of dysentery.[178] In 1841 Samoan Christians were placed on the island of Futuna, for its language was akin to that of Samoa.[179] Before many months they were killed. They were accused of having caused an epidemic which was sweeping the island.[180] In 1841 Samoan missionaries had also been landed on Aneityum.[181] In 1845 these were found to be making some progress and additional Samoans were sent to aid them.[182] By 1845 Samoan teachers had renewed Christian efforts on Tanna.[183] Yet in 1846 two of them were killed on the charge of causing disease and in 1848 Rarotongans were commissioned to the island to strengthen what was left of the Christian community.[184]

In 1848 white missionaries, John Geddie and his wife, and one other, were

[176] Ebenezer Prout, *Memoirs of the Life of the Rev. John Williams, Missionary to Polynesia* (London, John Snow, 1843, pp. viii, 618), pp. 565ff.

[177] Turner, *Nineteen Years in Polynesia*, pp. 2, 3.

[178] Turner, *op. cit.*, pp. 4ff.

[179] Gunn, *The Gospel in Futuna*, p. 6.

[180] Turner, *op. cit.*, pp. 363-365.

[181] Lovett, *The History of the London Missionary Society*, Vol. I, p. 406.

[182] Turner, *op. cit.*, pp. 365-372.

[183] Turner, *op. cit.*, pp. 373-381.

[184] Turner, *op. cit.*, p. 438.

stationed on Aneityum.[185] Geddie had been reared in Nova Scotia, in a family which was interested in missions in the South Seas, and had been a pastor. The moving spirit in the formation of a missionary society among the Presbyterians of Nova Scotia, he was sent to the Pacific as the first appointee of that organization. After a period in Samoa, he was conveyed to Aneityum by the ship which served the various stations of the London Missionary Society. Then followed discouraging years of slow beginnings. Yet reinforcements came in the persons of John Inglis and his wife from the Reformed Presbyterian Church of Scotland.[186] By 1854 more than one-half of the population had become Christians. By 1860 the New Testament had been translated and about half the population had been taught to read. Further personnel arrived from Nova Scotia and Scotland. Some of these were placed on other islands. In spite of the murder of two of them,[187] on Erromanga in 1861 because of an epidemic of measles which was bringing many deaths, Christianity continued to spread in the southern islands through the Presbyterian missions. When Geddie died, in 1872, all the population of Aneityum were said to be Christians.[188]

In the propagation of Christianity in the southern portions of the New Hebrides, as we have already suggested, Christians from the Pacific had a large share. Samoans and Rarotongans were important in the first stages of the introduction of the faith. Later, Christians from Aneityum were prominent as pioneers in various islands. To be sure, the native missionaries were under the direction of the white missionary and often were given stipends by him, but frequently they were for months and even years without the personal supervision of the whites and more than one of them paid for their devotion with their lives.[189]

Erromanga proved peculiarly difficult. It was not only the scene of the murder (1839) of John Williams and James Harris. It also had as martyrs (1861) George Nichol Gordon and his wife from Nova Scotia, and, a few years later (1872) James Douglas Gordon, a younger brother of George Nichol Gordon. However, other missionaries came, and by the close of the century it was called a Christian island.[190]

[185] Patterson, *Missionary Life Among the Cannibals: Being the Life of the Rev. John Geddie, passim;* James W. Falconer, *John Geddie* (Toronto, Board of Foreign Missions, Presbyterian Church in Canada, 1915, pp. 118), *passim; Letters of Charlotte Geddie and Charlotte Geddie Harrington* (no place, publisher, or date, pp. 79), *passim.*
[186] Inglis, *In the New Hebrides, passim;* Inglis, *Bible Illustrations from the New Hebrides, passim.*
[187] Murray, *The Martyrs of Polynesia,* pp. 94ff.
[188] Patterson, *op. cit.,* p. 508.
[189] Inglis, *Bible Illustrations from the New Hebrides,* pp. 219-253.
[190] H. A. Robertson, *Erromanga, the Martyr Islc,* edited by John Fraser (London, Hodder and Stoughton, 1902, pp. xx, 467), *passim.*

Tanna also was a hard field, but here, too, by the close of the nineteenth·
century Christianity was making notable gains.[191]

Famous as a missionary in the New Hebrides was John G. Paton. In 1858,
after having served in the Glasgow City Mission, he went out under the
Reformed Presbyterian Church of Scotland. He first resided on Tanna, but
after four years was driven off by natives who hated Christianity as the supposed cause of their diseases and as destructive of their old customs. He then
went as an appointee of the Presbyterian Church of Victoria to the neighbouring and smaller island of Aniwa and had the pleasure of seeing its population
become professedly Christian. In his later years he raised money in Great
Britain and Australia for the mission, especially for a boat, the *Dayspring*, to
ply among the islands.[192]

Presbyterians of Canada, Scotland, Australia, and New Zealand eventually
joined in supporting the mission in the New Hebrides. By 1914 seven Presbyterian bodies and the John G. Paton Mission Fund shared in the enterprise.[193]
Part of the expense was met by trade in which the missionaries engaged.

By 1914, in addition to Aneityum, Erromanga, and Aniwa, five other islands,
Futuna, Efate, Nguna, Tongoa, Epi, and Paama, were said to be Christian.[194]
In Futuna it was recorded that the third generation of Christians were a
marked advance on the first and second generations, that Christianity reduced
quarrelling, and was accompanied by literacy, honesty, greater diligence, and
chastity.[195] In Nguna the missionary whose residence bridged the transition
from paganism to Christianity was Peter Milne (1834-1924). Born and reared
in Scotland, he went to the New Hebrides from the Presbyterian Church of
New Zealand, in 1870 was assigned to Nguna, by 1896 had seen that island
become Christian, and by the following year had witnessed the same change
on six other adjacent islands. This meant that the villages, led by their chiefs,
had renounced their non-Christian cults and that the majority of the people

[191] *Agnes C. P. Watt. Twenty-five Years' Mission Life on Tanna, New Hebrides. Biographical Sketch and Introduction by T. Watt Leggatt* (Paisley, J. and R. Parlane, 1896,
pp. 385), *passim;* Langridge, *The Conquest of Cannibal Tanna, passim;* Murray, *Missions
in Western Polynesia*, pp. 133-170; Frank H. L. Paton, *Lomai of Lenakel. A Hero of the
New Hebrides* (London, Hodder and Stoughton, 1903, pp. xii, 315), *passim.*
[192] *John G. Paton, Missionary to the New Hebrides. An Autobiography. Edited by His
Brother* (New York, Fleming H. Revell Co., 3 Parts, 1889-1898), *passim;* Maggie Whitecross Paton, *Letters and Sketches from the New Hebrides. Edited by Her Brother-in-law,
James Paton* (New York, A. C. Armstrong and Son, 1895, pp. xi, 382), *passim;* Langridge and Paton, *John G. Paton. Later Years and Farewell, passim.*
[193] Frank H. L. Paton, *Glimpses of the New Hebrides* (Melbourne, Foreign Missions
Committee, Presbyterian Church of Victoria, no date, pp. 94), p. 6.
[194] *Ibid.*
[195] Gunn, *The Gospel in Futuna, passim,* especially pp. 160-164.

were attending school and church.[196] The conversion of Tongoa took place under the ministry of Oscar Michelsen, a native of Norway and an immigrant to New Zealand, who went to the New Hebrides in 1878 from the Otago Presbyterian Church to help Milne and soon took over the task on Tongoa.[197] On Epi and Paama the work of conversion (by missionaries from New Zealand) was not completed until after 1900.[198]

As New Zealand, through its Presbyterian churches, had a large part in winning the southern islands of the New Hebrides to the Christian faith, so also it was from New Zealand that the Church of England reached out to the northern islands of that group. Through a clerical error in the letters patent which described his diocese, George Augustus Selwyn, the first Anglican Bishop of New Zealand, was given jurisdiction over a vast area in the Pacific.[199] He therefore became Bishop of New Zealand and Melanesia. With his customary courage and initiative, he took this large responsibility seriously. His duties in New Zealand engrossed his attention for the first years of his episcopate, but in 1848 he made a tour through a number of the island groups of the Pacific, and, among other places, touched at Aneityum.[200] In the following year he was again at Aneityum.[201] He was the moving spirit in forming (1850) the Australasian Board of Missions in which the Anglicans of Australia and New Zealand joined in undertaking the Melanesian Mission.[202] His plan was to gather boys from the islands, take them to New Zealand for training, and return them to their homes as missionaries.[203] Between 1848 and 1852 he visited more than fifty islands in the Pacific.[204]

To assist him in the Melanesian enterprise Selwyn brought to the Pacific,

[196] Alexander Don, *Peter Milne (1834-1924)*, *Missionary to Nguna, New Hebrides, 1870-1924, from the Presbyterian Church of New Zealand* (Dunedin, Foreign Missions Committee, P.C.N.Z., 1927, pp. 296), *passim*, especially p. 267.

[197] Oscar Michelsen, *Cannibals Won for Christ: a Story of Missionary Perils and Triumphs in Tongoa, New Hebrides* (London, Morgan and Scott, no date, p. 188), *passim*; G. Kurze, *Wie die Kannibalen von Tongoa Christen wurden* (Leipzig, Verlag der Akademischen Buchhandlung, 1894, pp. viii, 110), *passim;* Michelsen, Misi, *passim*.

[198] Maurice Frater, *Midst Volcanic Fires. An Account of Missionary Tours Among the Volcanic Islands of the New Hebrides* (London, James Clarke & Co., no date, pp. 228), pp. 167 ff.; Alexander Don, compiler, *Light in Dark Isles. A Jubilee Record and Study of the New Hebrides Mission of the Presbyterian Church of New Zealand* (Dunedin, Foreign Missions Committee, P.C.N.Z., 1918, pp. 195, v), pp. 28-37.

[199] Tucker, *Memoir of the Life and Episcopate of George Augustus Selwyn*, Vol. I, pp. 72, 73.

[200] Tucker, *op. cit.*, Vol. I, pp. 253ff.

[201] Tucker, *op. cit.*, Vol. I, p. 291.

[202] Armstrong, *The History of the Melanesian Mission*, p. 14; Creighton, *G. A. Selwyn*, pp. 73, 74.

[203] Creighton, *op. cit.*, p. 72.

[204] Creighton, *op. cit.*, p. 83.

in 1855, John Coleridge Patteson. Patteson was the son of a distinguished judge and had for mother a niece of the poet Samuel Taylor Coleridge. Patteson was athletic and daring, a man of great charm and of rare devotion and beauty of spirit.[205] Under Selwyn's tutelage and with his companionship Patteson served his apprenticeship in the many islands of his huge field. Selwyn made his last voyage through the islands in 1859.[206] In 1861 Patteson was consecrated the first Anglican Bishop of Melanesia.[207] He proved an intrepid pioneer and an extraordinarily able linguist. Following the methods of Selwyn, he gathered boys for training, first in a centre in New Zealand and then, because it was nearer and its climate was more suitable, in Norfolk Island.[208] Through the islands of his great diocese he sailed until, 1871, he met his death at the hands of natives on Nukapu of the Santa Cruz group, apparently in revenge for some of the islanders who had been carried off by other white men as labourers for Fiji.[209]

Among the groups which Patteson visited were the New Hebrides. From them he brought boys to be educated and returned.[210] In 1877 a son of George Augustus Selwyn, John Selwyn, was consecrated Bishop of Melanesia.[211] Both the Bishops Selwyn were eager not to compete with the Presbyterian missions. Since these were in the southern islands of the New Hebrides, they did not attempt to establish the Anglican communion there, but confined themselves to the northern islands, partly in the Banks group. By 1895 the Melanesian Mission counted on three islands 1,050 baptized and 1,550 under instruction, out of a population of 13,000.[212] The white members of the Melanesian Mission were said to make a careful study of native customs and to seek to have Christianity bring as little dislocation as possible in native life.[213] Yet the Melanesian Mission was also declared to be slow in introducing an industrial education which was adapted to conditions in the islands.[214]

The Torres Islands, north of the Banks Islands, small, deficient in water, with a fierce population numbering less than 2,000 in 1895, were a field of the

---

[205] Yonge, *Life of John Coleridge Patteson,* Vol. I, pp. 1-106; Paton, *Patteson of Melanesia,* pp. 9-36.

[206] Tucker, *op. cit.,* Vol. II, p. 79.

[207] Yonge, *op. cit.,* Vol. I, pp. 316-319.

[208] Paton, *op. cit.,* pp. 123ff.

[209] Yonge, *op. cit.,* Vol. II, pp. 378-384.

[210] Yonge, *op. cit.,* Vol. II, pp. 172, 249.

[211] How, *Bishop John Selwyn,* p. 112.

[212] Montgomery, *The Light of Melanesia,* pp. 234-247. On one of these islands, Raga or Pentecost, see an account by a missionary to it, Etta Mason, *On Our Island* (London, Society for Promoting Christian Knowledge, 1926, pp. 96), *passim.* See also *The Isles That Wait* by a Lady Member of the Melanesian Mission, pp. 16ff.

[213] Jacomb, *The Future of the Kanaka,* pp. 150, 151.

[214] Jacomb, *op. cit.,* p. 148.

Melanesian Mission. Bishop John Selwyn visited them in 1880 and by the end of the century several score of their inhabitants had been baptized.[215]

Roman Catholic missionaries also came to the New Hebrides. The first arrived in 1848, refugees from New Caledonia. They did not remain long. Until 1900 the New Hebrides were attached to the Vicariate Apostolic of New Caledonia, and that island absorbed the energies of such Marists as could be spared for the vicariate. An attempt in 1875 to educate New Hebridean children in New Caledonia failed because of the difficulty of acclimatization. In 1887, at the request of French officials who wished to use them to offset the British influence of Protestant missionaries, Marists were sent to the New Hebrides. Reinforcements followed. The chief efforts were on Mallicollo, Ambrym, and Espiritu Santo, where Protestantism had not made much headway. Yet missionaries of each of the two branches of Christianity were jealous of the other and the acrimony was heightened by the Anglo-French rivalry for the control of the islands. About 1900 the New Hebrides were created a prefecture apostolic and were said to have about 1,000 Roman Catholic Christians and about 3,000 catechumens.[216]

By 1914, as a result of Protestant and Roman Catholic missions, Christianity had been firmly planted in the New Hebrides. Protestantism was under British and Roman Catholicism under French leadership. The former was much stronger numerically than the latter. It was said that the natives distrusted the French more than the English and, therefore, were not inclined to heed the Roman Catholic as much as they did the Protestant missionaries.[217] Protestants especially had reduced languages to writing, had developed schools, and had made the beginnings of a printed literature. Protestant missionaries fought, in time with no little success, the sale of alcoholic drinks, so demoralizing to the islanders.[218] They also vigorously opposed the decoying of the young men from the islands to the plantations of Queensland, Fiji, and New Caledonia and eventually had the traffic put under the ban.[219] On at least one island the custom of having marriages arranged by the parents or by the chiefs was fought—whether wisely or not we need not attempt to decide.[220] Modern medical care was introduced. Cannibalism and inter-tribal wars were either

[215] Montgomery, *op cit.*, pp. 103ff., 247.
[216] Piolet, *Les Missions Catholiques Françaises au XIXe Siècle*, Vol. IV, pp. 333-342.
[217] Jacomb, *op. cit.*, p. 177.
[218] Rivers, *Essays on the Depopulation of Melanesia*, p. 47; Langridge, *The Conquest of Cannibal Tanna*, p. 173.
[219] Rivers, *op. cit.*, p. 47; Langridge and Paton, *John G. Paton. Later Years and Farewell*, p. 16; Inglis, *In the New Hebrides*, pp. 198ff.; Michelsen, *Misi*, p. 97.
[220] Michelsen, *op. cit.*, p. 181.

brought to an end or were greatly reduced in frequency. A new culture, in which Christianity was an important factor, was being produced.

Partly because of their geographical propinquity and partly because shortly after the middle of the nineteenth century they passed under French rule, New Caledonia and the adjacent Isle of Pines and Loyalty Islands may be considered together. To their native population, a mixture of Melanesian and Polynesian elements, were added, chiefly in the second half of the nineteenth century, labourers from others of the Pacific Islands and from Annam and Java, European convicts, and free white settlers. The climate was not so hot and was more favourable to European settlers than was that of the New Hebrides. The size, the possibility of developing plantations, and the rich mineral deposits of New Caledonia accounted for the rather larger white settlement and a greater demand for foreign labour than we have had occasion to note on most of the islands with which this chapter has thus far dealt.

Christianity seems to have been introduced to the Loyalty Islands before it came to New Caledonia. It appears to have come first to Maré about 1834 in the person of a native of Tonga. In 1841 an agent of the London Missionary Society put two Samoan Christian teachers on Maré. In that same decade a Rarotongan missionary planted Christianity on the largest of the Loyalty archipelago, Lifu. In 1856 Christians from Maré brought their faith to another of the group, Uvea. Beginning with the 1850's the London Missionary Society introduced white representatives. The coming of Roman Catholic missionaries soon backed by French political power brought complications. With the establishment of French authority, attempts were made to expel the missionaries of the London Missionary Society, chiefly because, being British, they were supposedly inimical to French power. By the close of the year 1887 the Loyalty Islands were left, for a time, without a British missionary.[221] Yet Protestant Christianity persisted. In the 1890's there were said to be about 8,000 Protestants and about 3,000 Roman Catholics.[222] Not until 1921 did the London Missionary Society finally withdraw.[223] From the Loyalty Islands, indeed, through migration, Protestant Christianity penetrated to New Caledonia.[224] French Protestants came to the rescue. In 1883 the French Government placed a French Protestant pastor on Maré. In 1897 the Société des Missions Évangéliques of Paris sent a representative. In the twentieth century its mis-

[221] Lovett, *The History of the London Missionary Society*, Vol. I, pp. 410-417; S. M'Farlane, *The Story of the Lifu Mission* (London, James Nisbet & Co., 1873, pp. viii, 392), *passim;* Murray, *Missions in Western Polynesia*, pp. 266-356.

[222] Leenhardt, *La Grande Terre*, p. 34.

[223] *The Hundred and Twenty-Seventh Report of the London Missionary Society*, p. 95.

[224] Leenhardt, *op. cit.*, pp. 35ff.

sionaries were of assistance both in the Loyalty Islands and in New Cale-donia.[225]

Although Protestants were in the majority in the Loyalty Islands, in New Caledonia itself and on the Isle of Pines Roman Catholics had the ascendancy. In 1843 a French corvette brought to New Caledonia Douarre, the first Vicar Apostolic of the island, and four Marists.[226] Inter-tribal wars made the first years of the mission precarious. In 1847, aroused by disease and famine which they attributed to the missionaries, the natives killed a lay brother, Blaise Marmoiton.[227] A French ship rescued the surviving missionaries and took them and their converts off the island.[228] Refuge was found on Fotuna, now Christian.[229] When the enterprise was revived, the missionaries first established footholds on Aneityum, in the New Hebrides, and, especially, on the Isle of Pines. There was thought of abandoning New Caledonia completely, but fear of occupation by the British and the Church of England contributed to a decision to continue. In 1851 the Roman Catholic mission was renewed.[230] In 1853 France annexed New Caledonia and under its protection the future of the mission was assured. Occasional revolts by some of the chiefs were sup-pressed. The missionary staff was reinforced. In 1855 Sisters of the Third Order of Mary arrived, followed, in 1860, by Sisters of St. Joseph of Cluny, for schools and for hospitals. Later came Little Sisters of Mary and Little Sisters of the Poor. The state gave support to the Church. From 1863 to 1870 an energetic governor of anti-clerical tendencies brought embarrassment to the missionaries, but his successor was more friendly. Provision was made for hospital and clerical care for the convicts. At first the missionaries opposed colonization by free whites or any attempt to deprive the natives of their lands. Eventually they had no choice but to acquiesce in the presence of white settlers. They provided schools for both whites and blacks. By the beginning of the twentieth century Roman Catholics among the aborigines numbered about 11,000.[231]

[225] Ph. Delord, *Mon Voyage d'Enquête en Nouvelle-Calédonie Août-Septembre, 1899* (Paris, Maison des Missions Évangéliques, 1901, pp. 241), *passim;* Leenhardt, *op. cit., passim;* Maurice Leenhardt, *Le Cathécumène Canaque* (Paris, Société des Missions Évangéliques, 1922, pp. 40), *passim;* Rey Lescure, *Un Brick une Piroque. Coup d'œil sur la Missione de Nouvelle-Calédonie* (Paris, Société des Missions Évangéliques, 1929, pp. 91), *passim.*

[226] Salinis, *Marins et Missionnaires. Conquête de la Nouvelle-Calédonie 1843-1853,* pp. 1-14.

[227] V. Courant, *La Martyr de la Nouvelle-Calédonie, Blaise Marmoiton, Frère Coad-juteur de la Société de Marie (1812-1847)* (Lyon, Librarie Catholique Emmanuel Vitte, 1931, pp. 256), *passim;* Verguet, *Histoire de la Première Mission Catholique au Vicariat de Mélanésie,* pp. 237ff.

[228] Salinis, *op. cit.,* p. 64.

[229] Dubois, *Les Missions Maristes d'Océanie,* p. 22.

[230] Salinis, *op. cit.,* pp. 65ff.

[231] Piolet, *Les Missions Catholiques Françaises au XIXe Siècle,* Vol. IV, pp. 276-332.

The Santa Cruz Islands, made memorable by the tragic death of Bishop Patteson, became, quite naturally, a field of the Melanesian Mission. In 1878, through friendships arising from his return of shipwrecked natives of the islands the year before, Bishop John Selwyn succeeded in obtaining a foothold for his mission. In 1880 he gained entrance to.the largest of the group, Santa Cruz.[232] Eventually native teachers and then white missionaries were placed on the islands, schools were opened, and some converts were won.[233]

The Solomon Islands lie north and west of the Santa Cruz group. They are much larger than the latter, rugged and with a high rainfall and considerable areas of fertile soil. In the nineteenth century the population was predominantly Melanesian, but displayed variety and had a number of reciprocally unintelligible languages. The Solomon Islanders showed marked skill in the shaping of weapons and in building canoes and houses. They were enthusiastic headhunters. The islands were first seen by white men in the sixteenth century when Spaniards from Peru visited them and gave some of them the names which they still bear. White men then lost sight of them and did not again visit them until the latter part of the eighteenth century. In the first half of the nineteenth century traders were frequent. In the second half of the century came "blackbirding ships," in search of labourers for Queensland and Fiji. They were often guilty of cruelties which were painfully reminiscent of the slave trade at its worst and left behind them bitterness. It was 1903 before "blackbirding" finally ceased. The British declared a protectorate over some of the islands in 1893 and over others in 1899 and 1900. In 1899 the British and German Governments delimited their spheres of influence, the north-western-most going to the Germans and the others, the bulk of the group, to the British. The European governments endeavoured to enforce their conceptions of order, but did not adequately penetrate some of the remoter interior portions of the islands.

Roman Catholicism was the first form of Christianity to essay entrance to the Solomons. Franciscans were with the Spanish expedition of the sixteenth century, but established no foothold.[234] The next attempt was in 1845 by Marists led by Épalle, the first Vicar Apostolic of Micronesia and Melanesia. In endeavouring to effect a landing on the island of Ysabel Épalle was mortally wounded.[235] This blow did not immediately end the mission. For several

[232] How, *Bishop John Selwyn*, pp. 177-187.
[233] Armstrong, *The History of the Melanesian Mission*, pp. 190, 245, 269, 275, 331, 351, 361; Montgomery, *The Light of Melanesia*, pp. 123ff.
[234] Vol. III, p. 310.
[235] Verguet, *Histoire de la Première Mission Catholique au Vicariat de Mélanésie*, pp. 87ff.

years the Marists struggled on, but without much success.[236] In 1852 the Propaganda allowed the Marists to withdraw and to concentrate their energies on other parts of the vast field in the Pacific. The responsibility for the Solomon Islands was transferred to the recently founded Foreign Missionary Society of Milan.[237] In spite of the martyrdom of one of its missionaries, this society in turn failed to establish a continuing enterprise and withdrew.[238] In 1897 Rome returned the islands to the care of the Marists. It divided the group into two prefectures apostolic, placing the southern one under the Vicar Apostolic of Fiji and the northern under the Vicar Apostolic of Samoa.[239] Both vicars apostolic moved promptly to begin to fill their assignments.[240] In the southern prefecture the initial contingent arrived in 1898, comprised of the vicar apostolic, three priests, and a number of Fijian catechists.[241] Headquarters were set up on Sura, an uninhabited island, and, accordingly, removed from the violence which had made difficult the earlier attempts. Here a school was begun and from here trips were made to other islands and pupils obtained. Before many years a catechism, prayers, and hymns had been put into the language. In 1910 a school for catechists was founded on Sura. In 1912 the Southern Solomons were made a vicariate apostolic.[242] In 1904 Sisters of the Third Order Regular of Mary arrived and opened the first school for girls.[243] Advance, however, was slow.[244] Again and again a station had to be left vacant because of the illness of the missionaries.[245] Not until 1910 did rapid gains begin to be made.[246] In the Northern Solomons the Marists concentrated their attention on the children, bringing them into a head station away from their pagan parents, drawing from them their catechists, and through them founding substations with schools in a radius of about two hours' travel from the central one. This permitted adequate supervision.[247] In 1912 in the northern vicariate apostolic there were twelve priests, four lay brothers, eleven sisters, four catechists, twelve schools with 443 pupils, 480 baptized Christians, and 649 catechumens.[248]

---

[236] Verguet, op. cit., pp. 106-200.

[237] Piolet, op. cit., Vol IV, p. 365.

[238] Piolet, op. cit., Vol. IV, pp. 365, 366; Blanc, Histoire Religieuse de l'Archipel Fidjien, Vol. II, pp. 153, 154.

[239] Piolet, op. cit., Vol. IV, p. 366; Blanc, op. cit., Vol. II, p. 154.

[240] Piolet, op. cit., Vol. IV, pp. 367, 368; Blanc, op. cit., Vol. II, pp. 154ff.

[241] Dubois, Les Missions Maristes d'Océanie, p. 27.

[242] Raucaz, In the Savage South Solomons, pp. 84-101.

[243] Raucaz, op. cit., p. 70.

[244] Raucaz, op. cit., p. 174.

[245] Raucaz, op. cit., p. 115.

[246] Raucaz, op. cit., p. 118.

[247] Berg, Die katholische Heidenmission als Kulturträger, Vol. I, p. 345.

[248] Schmidlin, Die katholischen Missionen in den deutschen Schutzgebieten, p. 189.

In 1851 and again in 1852 Bishop G. A. Selwyn, with his boundless energy and widely ranging vision, visited the Solomon Islands.[249] Patteson repeatedly toured their shores. He brought boys from them to be trained in the school which was eventually placed on Norfolk Island. He took them back to serve as teachers. He was grieved when one of these lapsed into his pre-Christian faith. He was pained by the havoc which the "blackbirders" were working.[250] Bishop John Selwyn also cruised among the Solomons.[251] By the beginning of the twentieth century there were Christians along the south-eastern fringes of Ysabel, on the Floridas, a group of islands south of Ysabel, on the larger island of Guadalcanar, on the island the other side of the Floridas, Mala, on the smaller island of Ulawa, south of Mala, and on San Cristoval or Bauro, the southernmost of the large islands of the Solomons. Chapels had been built and schools organized. Most of the resident work had been accomplished by natives who as boys had been educated on Norfolk Island, but supervision was given by the successive bishops in their long itineraries on the mission craft.[252] There were, too, a few resident missionaries.[253] The progress of Christianity was especially marked on the Floridas, partly because they were smaller islands which could be penetrated more easily than the larger ones. Here as early as 1888 a gathering of the chiefs was held under Christian auspices by which laws were passed in partial conformity with Christian ideals.[254]

Another non-Roman Catholic mission in the Solomon Islands, not so large as that of the Anglicans, was the South Sea Evangelical Mission.[255] Its founder was Florence S. H. Young. Miss Young came from an English family which had provided Baring Brothers with a partner and the navy with two admirals. Her father was a loyal member of the Plymouth Brethren. Reared in New Zealand and Australia, while a young woman living on a plantation in Queensland Miss Young began religious work among the labourers from the New Hebrides and the Solomon Islands. In 1886 she inaugurated, with the encouragement of George Müller,[256] the Queensland Kanaka Mission. Then

[249] Tucker, *Memoir of the Life and Episcopate of George Augustus Selwyn*, Vol. II, p. 7.
[250] Paton, *Patteson of Melanesia*, pp. 59, 102, 120, 122, 175, 177, 178; Armstrong, *The History of the Melanesian Mission*, pp. 63, 68, 85.
[251] How, *Bishop John Selwyn*, pp. 188-192; Armstrong, *op. cit.*, pp. 227, 233., 267ff.
[252] Frances Awdry, *In the Isles of the Sea: the Story of Fifty Years in Melanesia* (London, Bemros & Sons, 1902, pp. xiv, 147), pp. 50-110; *The Isles that Wait*. By a Lady Member of the Melanesian Mission, pp. 72ff.; Montgomery, *The Light of Melanesia*, pp. 160ff.
[253] See the biography of one of these in Ellen Wilson, *Dr. Welchman of Bugotu* (London, Society for Promoting Christian Knowledge, 1935, pp. 117), *passim*.
[254] Armstrong, *op. cit.*, p. 268. See also Montgomery, *op. cit.*, pp. 203ff., 247.
[255] Florence S. H. Young, *Pearls from the Pacific* (London, Marshall Brothers, [1925], pp. 256), *passim*.
[256] Vol. IV, p. 154.

she responded to the appeal of Hudson Taylor and for several years was with the China Inland Mission. In 1902 she returned to Australia and resumed her labours with the Queensland Kanaka Mission. That enterprise had prospered in her absence. Converts began returning to the Solomon Islands and on the northern end of the island of Mala (or Malaita) propagated their faith. In 1900 and 1902 unattached white missionaries went to the Solomons, but at least two of them soon died. In 1904 the Solomon Island branch of the Queensland Kanaka Mission was formed with a supporting council from Sydney and Melbourne. In general principles it resembled the China Inland Mission, for it was undenominational and issued no direct appeals for funds. The first party of missionaries, with Miss Young among them, arrived in the Solomon Islands that same year and made their headquarters on Mala with the Christian community gathered by the repatriated labourers. When, in 1906, the Kanaka labourers were deported from Queensland in the effort to preserve Australia for the whites, the Queensland Kanaka Mission saw its erstwhile field melting away and was transformed into the South Sea Evangelical Mission. A mission ship was built, a medical missionary was appointed to accompany it, and visits were paid to numbers of places in the islands. Some of the Queensland converts were found to have succumbed to the pressure of their non-Christian surroundings and to have apostatized, but others had become earnest missionaries. Schools were established. The number of Christians grew.[257]

Early in the twentieth century the Methodists of Australia began a mission to the Solomon Islands. In 1879 and again in 1899, George Brown, one of the great leaders of Australian Methodist missions, passed through them. Some of the Solomon Islanders who as labourers in Fiji had become Christians through contact with the Methodists asked that a mission be started on their native shores. In 1901 the Australian Methodists decided to heed their request. They endeavoured to enter islands and areas unoccupied by other Protestant organizations. In 1902 the first contingent of missionaries arrived, made up of whites and of South Sea Islanders from Fiji and Samoa. The initial station was placed on New Georgia. Eventually centres were opened on several other islands, converts were won, and schools were opened.[258]

By 1914 the Seventh Day Adventists had made a small beginning which was to be the prelude to a larger growth.[259]

[257] See a description by a disinterested anthropologist of the work of the Melanesian (Anglican) Mission and the South Sea Evangelical Mission in H. Ian Hogbin, *Experiments in Civilization. The Effects of European Culture on a Native Community of the Solomon Islands* (London, George Routledge & Sons, 1939, xvii, 268), pp. 173ff.

[258] *George Brown . . . An Autobiography*, pp. 515ff.; J. F. Goldie in Colwell, *A Century in the Pacific*, pp. 561-585.

[259] Watson, *Cannibals and Head-Hunters in the South Seas*, pp. 211ff.

North and west of the Solomons are islands which for a time were known collectively as the Bismarck Archipelago. The chief ones are New Britain (also once called New Pomerania), New Ireland (also once denominated New Mecklenburg), New Hanover, and the Admiralty Islands (or Manus). The population was Melanesian with a strong admixture of Papuans. Early in the twentieth century it numbered not far from 150,000. For many decades the islands were counted a British possession, but in 1884 became a German protectorate.[260]

The introduction of Christianity to the Bismarck Archipelago was by the Australian Methodists. In 1874, at the suggestion of George Brown, who had had fourteen years in Samoa, the decision was made to begin a mission there. This was the first mission initiated by the Australian Methodist Church. The following year, Brown himself went to the islands, accompanied by several Fijian and Samoan volunteers. Footholds were gained. Reinforcements came. Death, sometimes by disease, sometimes by violence from those whom the missionaries had come to serve, made heavy inroads on the staff, both of the Fijians and Samoans and of the whites. The news that their fellows had been killed and eaten only stimulated more Fijians to apply for the hazardous enterprise.[261] When, in 1881, Brown retired from residence in the islands, Benjamin Danks continued in charge.[262] By 1912 the Methodist mission could report 189 churches, over 200 catechists and teachers, 3,600 native church members, 6,000 children in school, and 21,000 adherents.[263] Translations of the New Testament were made in at least two dialects and other literature was prepared. Industrial education was developed.[264] After the islands were brought under German rule, German Methodist missionaries came to reinforce the staff.[265]

Roman Catholic Christianity began to be represented in the Bismarck Archipelago in 1882, when a few French priests accompanied an ill-starred venture at white settlement. They did not undertake direct missions for the aborigines, but the episode directed the attention of Rome to the islands and the Propaganda sent out priests of the Congregation of the Holy Heart of Jesus of Issoudun. In 1890 New Pomerania was made a vicariate apostolic, and Couppé, a Frenchman of great energy and organizing ability, was placed

[260] Burton, *The Call of the Pacific*, pp. 190ff.
[261] *George Brown . . . Autobiography*, pp. 69ff.
[262] *In New Britain. The Story of Benjamin Danks, Pioneer Missionary, from His Diary*, edited by Wallace Deane (Australia, Angus & Robertson, 1933, pp. x, 293), *passim*.
[263] Burton, *op. cit.*, p. 203.
[264] Danks in Colwell, *A Century in the Pacific*, pp. 522-525.
[265] Danks in Colwell, *op. cit.*, p. 527.

at its head. The colonial regime insisted upon keeping the Roman Catholic and the Methodist mission in different spheres, to avoid competition. Reinforcements came chiefly from Germany, from Hiltrup, where there was a mission house of the Holy Heart of Jesus. Much emphasis was placed upon schools and orphanages. Late in the 1890's a mass movement occurred and in the three years 1894-1897 over 3,000 were baptized. By 1912 there were under Bishop Couppé 31 head-stations, 102 sub-stations, 37 priests, 43 lay brothers, 34 sisters, 83 catechists, 49 women catechists, and 20,417 Roman Catholics.[266]

By far the largest of the islands which we must consider in this chapter is New Guinea or Papua. Its backbone is a tangled range of mountains whose highest peaks, although only a short distance south of the equator, reach well above the timber line into the region of glaciers and perpetual snow. On the northern coast is a somewhat lower mountain chain. Dense forests cover much of the land. There are huge cultivable plains. Numerous rivers, some of them of large size, drain the interior. In the nineteenth century the population was a mixture of Negritos, Papuans, and Melanesians, with the Papuans in the majority. Early in the twentieth century it was in excess of half a million. By 1914 several hundred whites were living on the island, most of them, naturally, along the coast. By the close of the nineteenth century the island had been parcelled out among the Netherlands, Great Britain, and Germany. Approximately the western half fell to the Netherlands and will be mentioned when, two chapters below, we speak of the Netherlands East Indies. The British began developing interests and making claims to territories on the south coast, and in the division, the south-eastern section of the island fell to them. The north-eastern portion passed into the control of Germany and came to be denominated Kaiser Wilhelm's Land. In 1905 the British portion was transferred to the Commonwealth of Australia.[267]

In the eastern half of New Guinea the first organized efforts to introduce Christianity seem to have been by the London Missionary Society, in 1871. The directors of that society had long contemplated a mission to New Guinea, and in 1870, when Roman Catholics were placing obstacles in the way of their enterprise in the Loyalty group, they decided that the time was opportune to assign Samuel McFarlane of the island of Lifu to this new field.[268] When McFarlane laid the project before the Christians of Lifu and asked for volunteers, every native pastor and every student in the seminary offered for the

---

[266] Schmidlin, *Die katholischen Missionen in den deutschen Schutzgebieten*, pp. 168-182; Leo Brenninkmeyer, *15 Jahre beim Bergvolke der Baininger* (Hiltrup, Herz-Jesu-Missionshaus, 1928, pp. 96), *passim*.

[267] *British New Guinea (Papua)* (London, H. M. Stationery Office, 1920, pp. 69), pp. 1-21.

[268] Lovett, *The History of the London Missionary Society*, Vol. I, p. 431.

dangerous undertaking. McFarlane was joined by A. W. Murray, of the Samoan mission.[269] Some of the Lifu teachers were placed on an island in the Torres Straits, between Australia and New Guinea. Others were put on New Guinea itself. In 1872 Christians from the Hervey Islands were brought. for the south-east coast, where a lighter-skinned people seemed akin to these Polynesians.[270] In 1874 W. G. Lawes, who had served his missionary apprenticeship on Niue or Savage Island, was transferred to New Guinea. McFarlane made his headquarters on Murray Island, near the mouth of one of the largest streams of New Guinea, the Fly River. Here he established a training school from which he hoped that the graduates would go, as from a kind of Iona, to be missionaries on the mainland.[271] Lawes held that the best results could be obtained by living with the people at a fixed centre on or near the mainland and by placing teachers wherever possible and paying them frequent visits.[272] Both McFarlane and Lawes were to have many years in the New Guinea field. Lawes fixed his residence at Port Moresby, an important *entrepôt* on the south-east coast, and from there made his itineraries.[273] During his service of about three decades the enterprise of his society in New Guinea made substantial progress.

In 1877 there came to New Guinea under the London Missionary Society one of the great pioneer missionaries of the South Seas, James Chalmers, also known by his South Sea name, Tamate. Born in 1841, in Scotland, the son of a stonemason, he was reared in simple circumstances which helped to develop in him a strong physique, dauntless courage, abounding energy, and a passionate love for the sea. In 1867 he arrived in Rarotonga, and there spent ten years among a population already professedly Christian. On New Guinea, Chalmers travelled extensively, both along the coast and in the interior, seeking locations for teachers from the Pacific Islands, and making peace between warring tribes. While in general he and Lawes favoured the annexation of the south-eastern part of New Guinea as a lesser evil than possession by some other European power, they both endeavoured to safeguard the natives from forced labour and from the loss of their lands. In 1901 Chalmers was killed by the natives on an island east of the delta of the Fly River.[274]

---

[269] McFarlane, *Among the Cannibals of New Guinea*, pp. 12, 13.

[270] McFarlane, *op. cit.*, pp. 25ff.; Murray, *Forty Years of Mission Work in Polynesia and New Guinea*, pp. 445ff.

[271] McFarlane, *op. cit.*, pp. 81ff.

[272] Lovett, *op. cit.*, Vol. I, p. 448.

[273] King, *W. G. Lawes*, pp. 62ff.

[274] Richard Lovett, *James Chalmers: His Autobiography and Letters* (New York, Fleming H. Revell Co., no date, pp. 511), *passim*; James Chalmers and W. Wyatt Gill, *Work and Adventure in New Guinea, 1877-1885* (London, The Religious Tract Society,

By the close of the nineteenth century much, although not all, of the pioneer work of the London Missionary Society in New Guinea had been accomplished. Numbers of centres had been opened along most of the south coast of the British portion of the island and some converts had been made.[275] In 1907 there were 15 English missionaries, 139 ordained missionaries, 15 native preachers, 2,646 church members, 105 schools, and 3,370 scholars.[276] Through one of the white missionaries, Charles W. Abel, who eventually raised funds for his work independently of the society, an important mission was developed on and near the island of Kwato, not far from the extreme south-easterly tip of New Guinea. Here natives were trained in crafts, industries, and sports to provide them with wholesome substitutes for the inter-tribal wars which had given zest to life in their pre-Christian days.[277] The London Missionary Society had begun the most extensive enterprise of any of the British missionary agencies.[278]

Not so large as the territory covered by the London Missionary Society was that delimited as the field of the Australasian Board of Missions (Methodist). In 1890 the General Conference of the Methodist Church of Australia decided to accept the invitation of the Governor of New Guinea to begin a new mission on that island. That same year the London Missionary Society, the Methodists, and the Anglicans agreed to a division of territory which assigned the south-east coast to the first, the islands off much of the north-east coast to the second, and (all these within the British portion of New Guinea) most of the north-east coast to the third.[279] That doughty Methodist pioneer, George Brown, set out to survey the region allotted to his denomination. This wise preliminary having been accomplished, in 1891 Brown conducted a large party

---

1885, pp. 342), *passim;* James Chalmers, *Pioneering in New Guinea* (London, The Religious Tract Society, 1887, pp. x, 343), *passim;* James Chalmers, *Pioneering in New Guinea, 1877-1894* (New York, Fleming H. Revell Co., no date, pp. xiv, 255), *passim;* William Robson, *James Chalmers* (New York, Fleming H. Revell Co., no date, pp. 160), *passim.*

[275] Lovett, *op. cit.,* Vol. I, p. 466.

[276] G. Currie Martin, *The New Guinea Mission* (London, London Missionary Society, 1908, pp. x, 99), p. 81.

[277] Russell W. Abel, *Charles W. Abel of Kwato* (New York, Fleming H. Revell Co., 1934, pp. 255), *passim;* Charles W. Abel, *Savage Life in New Guinea* (London, London Missionary Society, no date, pp. 221), *passim;* Thompson, *My Trip in the "John Williams,"* pp. 14ff.

[278] For a brief account which combines history with a description of current conditions in the fourth decade of the twentieth century, see Cecil Northcott, *Guinea Gold. The London Missionary Society at Work in the Territory of Papua* (Westminster, The Livingstone Press, 1936, pp. 101), *passim.* For a description of a tour late in the nineteenth century, see Thompson, *op. cit.,* pp. 14-111.

[279] *George Brown . . . Autobiography,* pp. 465-468.

of white and Pacific Island missionaries to inaugurate the enterprise.[280] In 1924, after a third of a century, the Methodists counted 96 churches, 23 European and 22 Pacific Island missionaries, 67 Papuan teachers, 58 local preachers, 3,510 church members, and 6,314 day school scholars.[281]

The Church of England entered New Guinea not far from the time of the beginning of the Methodist enterprise and made itself responsible for a much larger territory than did the latter. In 1886 the General Synod of the Church of England in Australia declared that the recent annexation by Great Britain carried with it an obligation for the Church to make provision for the spiritual care of both settlers and natives.[282] The leader of the new undertaking was Albert Alexander Maclaren.[283] Although of Scotch descent and in his early childhood in the Scottish Kirk, Maclaren was reared in England and was confirmed and grew up in the Church of England. He was trained at St. Augustine's Missionary Training College in Canterbury. Denied by uncertain health the fulfilment of his dream of serving in Africa, in 1877 he went to Australia. When the appeal was made for men to inaugurate the new mission he responded. In 1890 he went to New Guinea on a preliminary visit. In 1891 the beginnings were made of a continuing mission, at Dogura, on the north-east coast, less than a hundred miles from the East Cape. Late in December of that year Maclaren died. In spite of this discouraging inception, the mission was reinforced. Both whites and South Sea Islanders were added to the staff. In 1896 the first baptisms were administered. Early in 1898 a bishop was consecrated for what had been created a diocese.[284] Additional centres were opened and increasingly converts were gathered.[285] In 1914 the mission had a staff

---

[280] *George Brown . . . Autobiography*, pp. 473ff. For an autobiography of one of the group who put in many years in New Guinea, see William W. Bromilow, *Twenty Years among Primitive Papuans* (London, The Epworth Press, 1929, pp. 316), *passim*.

[281] John Wear Burton, *Our Task in Papua* (London, The Epworth Press, 1926, pp. 124), p. 91.

[282] White, *Round About the Torres Straits*, p. 59.

[283] Frances M. Synge, *Albert Maclaren. Pioneer Missionary in New Guinea. A Memoir* (Westminster, The Society for the Propagation of the Gospel in Foreign Parts, 1908, pp. xxi, 171), *passim;* Edgar Rogers, *A Pioneer of New Guinea. The Story of Albert Alexander Maclaren* (Westminster, The Society for the Propagation of the Gospel in Foreign Parts, 1920, pp. viii, 172), *passim*.

[284] White, *op. cit.*, pp. 67-70.

[285] Arthur Kent Chignell, *Twenty-one Years in Papua. A History of the English Church Mission in New Guinea (1891-1912)* (London, A. R. Mowbray & Co., 1913, pp. xv, 157), pp. 57ff.; Arthur Kent Chignell, *An Outpost in Papua* (London, Smith, Elder & Co., 1911, pp. xii, 375), *passim;* Gilbert White, *A Pioneer of Papua. Being the Life of the Rev. Copland King* (London, Society for Promoting Christian Knowledge, 1929, pp. 91), *passim;* [J. O. Feetham], *The Church in New Guinea. A Tour of the Island* (London, Office of the New Guinea Mission, 1918, pp. 32), *passim;* Gilbert White, *Francis de Sales Buchanan, Missionary to New Guinea* (London, Society for Promoting Christian Knowledge, 1923, pp. vii, 59), pp. 27ff.

composed of the bishop, 9 priests, 6 white laymen, 13 white ladies, 24 South Sea Islanders, 16 Papuans, and 8 pupil teachers, and counted 18 churches, 22 schools, 1,318 pupils, 2,345 baptized, and 1,354 communicants. It was making provision for the religious care of the whites in Port Moresby, the chief European settlement in the British part of New Guinea.[286]

On the eve of 1914 the Seventh Day Adventists entered New Guinea, and after that year had a growing enterprise.[287]

What in the 1880's became the German portion of New Guinea was not far from the size of Germany. As was to be expected, German Protestant missions saw in it a duty and an opportunity. In 1886 and 1887, not long after the German occupation, two societies began operations, the Neuendettelsau and the Rhenish.

The Neuendettelsau Mission had as its outstanding figure Johann Flierl. German born and trained, Flierl had previously spent seven years as a missionary among the aborigines of Central Australia. He arrived in 1886 and in spite of the unfriendly climate was to have a long life in the island.[288] Additional missionaries came. The society was handicapped by not possessing extensive missions elsewhere in the South Seas from which to draw Pacific Islanders to augment and aid their staff. However, by 1906 eight stations had been opened, and each of these had small but growing congregations. Improved types of agriculture were introduced. Schools were conducted for training native Christians to be missionaries among their own people. Congregations were encouraged to send out members, supported by themselves, to propagate the faith, but still under the supervision of the white missionary. Following the example of several of the older missions in the Pacific, a steamship was operated to facilitate communication between the various centres along the coast and in the islands and to open up new areas. Outposts were also early planted among the hill tribes. Numbers of tribes and several different language areas were reached.[289] By 1910, 13 mission stations had been established, about 2,000 had been baptized, about 500 pupils were in the schools,

[286] Report of the New Guinea Mission for the Year Ending 31st March, 1914 (Sydney, Central Depot, A.B.M. Office, pp. 44), passim.

[287] Watson, Cannibals and Head-Hunters in the South Seas, pp. 172ff.

[288] Johann Flierl, Dreissig Jahre Missionsarbeit in Wüsten und Wildnissen (Neuendettelsau, Verlag des Missionshauses, 1910, pp. 134), passim; John Flierl, Forty-Five Years in New Guinea, translated by M. Wiederaenders (Columbus, The Lutheran Book Concern, 2d ed., 1931, pp. 204), passim; Johann Flierl, Führungen Gottes. Ein Rückblick auf meinem Lebensgang und auf meine 20jahrige Thätigkeit in der Mission (Neuendettelsau, Verlag des Missionshauses, 1899, pp. 172), passim.

[289] Joh. Flierl, Christ in New Guinea (Tanunda, South Australia, Auricht's Printing Office, 1932, pp. 208), passim; Johann Flierl, Gottes Wort in den Urwäldern von Neuguinea (Neuendettelsau, Verlag des Missionshauses, 1929, pp. 171), passim; Richter, Die evangelische Mission in Fern- und Südost-Asien, Australien, Amerika, pp. 280-287.

and it was estimated that the mission's influence was being felt by approximately 10,000 natives.[290]

In 1887 the first missionaries of the Rhenish Mission in Barmen came to New Guinea. The following year they opened their initial station, on Astrolabe Bay. The Rhenish Mission used much the same methods as the Neuendettelsauers. However, it had fewer stations and a smaller body of converts.[291]

It was scarcely to be expected that Roman Catholic would be as prominent as Protestant missions in the British portion of New Guinea. Even though by the end of the nineteenth century the British Government accorded complete toleration to all branches of the Church and to missionaries of all nations, the fact that Protestants were preponderant in the British Isles favoured a similar Protestant predominance in the British colonies. Yet the Roman Catholics were represented in British New Guinea. In 1884 missionaries of the Holy Heart of Jesus of Issoudun opened a station on Thursday Island, in Torres Strait. There the presence of Roman Catholic Filipinos afforded an opening.[292] In 1885 a foothold was obtained nearer New Guinea proper, on Yule Island, just off the south coast about midway along the British section. From here exploratory journeys were made. Sisters of the Holy Heart of Issoudun arrived. In 1889 a vicariate apostolic was created for New Guinea and one of the pioneer priests, Verjus, was named the first bishop. By 1900 25 stations had been founded, served by 2 bishops, 20 priests, 14 lay brothers, and 78 sisters. About 3,000 converts were counted.[293]

In Kaiser Wilhelm's Land, the German section of New Guinea, Roman Catholicism was represented by the Society of the Divine Word. In 1895 the Propaganda requested the society to undertake the task. The following year the region was made a prefecture apostolic with Eberhard Limbrock as its first head. The difficulties were many. The untoward climate claimed a heavy toll of missionary life. The languages were numerous. Yet progress was made.[294] On Limbrock's initiative the mission developed plantations from which copra was sold to help defray its expenses. Somewhat more tardily, rice culture was introduced.[295] By the end of the year 1912 there were 25 priests, 24 lay brothers, and 37 sisters at work, 18 head stations had been opened, and

[290] Joh. Flierl, *Gedenkblatt der Neuendettelsauer Heidenmission in Queensland und Neu-Guinea* (Neuendettelsau, Verlag des Missionshauses, 1910, pp. 94), pp. 84-86.

[291] Richter, *op. cit.*, pp. 280-287; I. W. Thomas, *Von Nias nach Kaiser-Wilhelms-Land . . . ein Reisejahr* (Gütersloh, C. Bertelsmann, 1892, pp. 140), *passim*; G. Kunze, *Im Dienst des Kreuzes auf ungebahnten Pfaden* (Barmen, Verlag des Missionshauses, 4 parts, 1897), *passim*.

[292] Piolet, *Les Missions Catholiques Françaises au XIXe Siècle,* Vol. IV, p. 370.

[293] Piolet, *op. cit.,* Vol. IV, pp. 379-386.

[294] Schmidlin, *Die katholischen Missionen in den deutschen Schutzgebieten,* p. 160.

[295] Hagspiel, *Along the Mission Trail,* Vol. III, pp. 125-128, 132-136.

the number of Christians was 2,410. Schools had been begun and medical care undertaken.[296] By the time the World War of 1914-1918 changed the political ownership of the land, the Society of the Divine Word had gained so firm a footing that its enterprise continued and grew.

By 1914 the fringes of the British and German portions of New Guinea had been reached by Christianity. Both Protestantism and Roman Catholicism were represented. The coast and some of the islands along the coast had been sprinkled with stations. Here and there the hinterland had been penetrated. A few thousand converts had been made. Several communities had become professedly Christian. Some of the many languages had been reduced to writing, and a Christian literature had been produced. However, only a beginning had been made. The larger proportion of the population were as yet completely or relatively untouched.

From New Guinea we move north of the equator. Here, still in the tropics, we come to the Hawaiian Islands, volcanoes, living and dead, rising out of the ocean floor and one of them towering nearly 14,000 feet above sea level. Hawaii presented Christianity with the most complex racial problem which it faced in the Pacific Islands. When Europeans first arrived, it had a Polynesian population. To this were added by 1914 whites from the United States, English, Germans, Scandinavians, Chinese, Japanese, Koreans, Portuguese, Puerto Ricans, Spaniards. Filipinos, and some others. The native Hawaiian stock shared the usual fate of the Polynesians in their contacts with the white man and declined. From an estimated 400,000 (probably excessive) when Captain Cook visited the islands in the 1770's, it sank to about 142,000 in 1823, 130,313 in 1832, 44,088 in 1878, and 29,834 in 1900. The demand for labour for the sugar (and, later, pineapple) plantations brought in the larger proportion of the aliens. Beginning in the 1870's Portuguese entered from the Azores and Madeira. Spaniards, in smaller numbers, arrived from Malaga. Beginning about 1906 came Filipinos. A few Gilbert Islanders were introduced but proved unsatisfactory. Chinese, Japanese, and Koreans immigrated by the thousands. By 1900 they constituted more than half of the population, with the Japanese leading. In 1920, out of a population of 255,912, Japanese were 42.7 per cent., Chinese 9.2 per cent., pure Hawaiians 9.3 per cent., and 7 per cent. were of mixtures of Hawaiians with other stocks.[297] The majority of the population, then, was from non-Christian peoples. Of the elements which were from Christian peoples, much more than half were Roman Catholic. However, in

[296] Schmidlin, *op. cit.*, p. 163; Johannes Tauren, *Die Missionen in Neu-Guinea* (Post Kaldenkirchen, Missionsdruckerei Steyl, 1931, pp. 36), pp. 17-36.

[297] *The Encyclopædia Britannica*, 14th ed., Vol. XI, pp. 268, 269; Roberts, *Population Problems in the Pacific*, pp. 316ff.

1914 those traditionally Protestant were dominant in the political, social, and economic life of the islands.

The time gap between the establishment of white contacts with Hawaii and the first organized attempts to propagate Christianity was greater than in most of the island groups of the Pacific. The effective disclosure of Hawaii to the European world, as for so many others of the Pacific Islands, began with the visits of Captain Cook, in the 1770's. The great explorer was killed there, in 1779. Ships and sailors from the United States and Europe soon began to frequent the islands. A political development ensued which was akin to that which had followed the advent of the white man in Tahiti, Tonga, and Fiji. By utilizing the fire-arms which came from the whites, an extraordinarily able chief, Kamehameha I, consolidated all the islands but one under his rule and founded the Hawaiian kingdom.[298] By his death (1819) intercourse with the whites had begun to bring not only a decline in population but also the disintegration of the old culture and the accompanying religion. Shortly after Kamehameha's demise deliberate infraction of taboo and the abandonment of some of the old religious rites by influential leaders loosened the hold of the traditional cults.[299] It was to a people and a culture in a state of flux that the first Christian missionaries came.

An interesting contrast can be drawn between the introduction and progress of Christianity among the Polynesians of New Zealand, the Maoris, and among the Polynesians of Hawaii. In New Zealand intimate contact with missionaries and the rapid spread of Christianity preceded the full onslaught of non-missionary Europeans and their culture. In Hawaii the two phases of the impact of the whites came in the opposite chronological order. In New Zealand the occupation of the land by the white man gave rise to bitter wars and contributed to the rise of strange religious movements among the Maoris. In Hawaii the transition to white rule was made much later, was accomplished peacefully, and did not entail the emergence of new religious sects.

Before the arrival, in 1820, of the first band of Christian missionaries, a knowledge of Christianity had filtered into Hawaii. A few of the early white settlers held to the faith in which they had been nurtured and by example acquainted some Hawaiians with it.[300] George Vancouver, the British explorer, who visited the islands three times in the 1790's, is said to have given to the chiefs instruction in Christianity and to have promised to try to have mission-

---

[298] On the history and customs of Hawaii before the coming of the missionaries see Dibble, *History of the Sandwich Islands*, pp. 1-137; James Jackson Jarves, *History of the Hawaiian Islands*, pp. 9-106.

[299] Bingham, *A Residence of Twenty-One Years in the Sandwich Islands*, pp. 72-79.

[300] Restarick, *Hawaii, 1778-1920, from the Viewpoint of a Bishop*, pp. 18-25, 28-39.

aries sent from England.[301] In 1819 two chiefs were, at their own request, baptized by the Roman Catholic chaplain of a visiting French ship.[302]

It was missionaries, mostly from the Congregational churches of New England, sent by the American Board of Commissioners for Foreign Missions, who were to bring the majority of the Hawaiians in touch with the Christian faith and were to gather a large proportion of them into church membership.

This New England enterprise had its immediate origin in the presence of a number of Hawaiian youths in the United States and in the effort to train them to return as missionaries to their own people. For several years ships from the United States had been visiting the Hawaiian Islands as the "crossroads of the Pacific." On them some Hawaiians had found passage. The most memorable was Henry Obookiah (or Opukahaia), who, as we saw in the preceding volume,[303] found his way to New Haven, was taught by one of the tutors of Yale College, attracted the attention of Samuel J. Mills, of the group who inspired the formation of the American Board of Commissioners for Foreign Missions, was one of those for whom the school at Cornwall, Connecticut, was organized, but died (1818) before he could return to Hawaii.[304] In 1819, the year after Obookiah's death, and in part because of the impulse given by that sad event, a party of missionaries sailed from Boston. It consisted of two clergymen, a physician, two school masters, a printer, a farmer, seven wives, several children, and three Hawaiians from the Cornwall school. It reached Hawaii in 1820. To their awed and grateful surprise, the missionaries were greeted with the news that taboo had been abandoned, idols destroyed, and that those who had attempted to restore them had been defeated in war.[305]

From the successor of Kamehameha I the missionaries obtained a hesitant permission to land. They began to acquire the language. They addressed themselves to the chiefs and especially to members of the royal house. They were

---

[301] Restarick, *op. cit.*, pp. 25, 26.

[302] Yzendoorn, *History of the Catholic Mission in the Hawaiian Islands*, pp. 18, 20.

[303] Vol. IV, p. 84.

[304] [E. W. Dwight], *Memoirs of Henry Obookiah, a Native of Owhyhee and a Member of the Foreign Mission School, Who Died at Cornwall, Conn., Feb. 17, 1818, aged 26 years* (New Haven, 1818, pp. 109), *passim*.

[305] Bingham, *op. cit.*, pp. 57-70; Anderson, *The Hawaiian Islands*, pp. 45-49. On this first missionary party, its members, and their descendants, see Emily C. Hawley, *The Introduction of Christianity into the Hawaiian Islands* (Brattleboro, E. L. Hildreth & Co., 1922, pp. 84ff.). On one of the women of the first party, with vivid accounts of life in Hawaii, see *Life and Times of Mrs. Lucy G. Thurston, Wife of Rev. Asa Thurston, Pioneer Missionary to the Sandwich Islands, Gathered from Letters and Journals . . . Selected and Arranged by Herself* (Ann Arbor, S. C. Andrews, 1882, pp. x, 30), *passim*. On one of the Thurston children see *The Missionary's Daughter: A Memoir of Lucy Goodale Thurston, of the Sandwich Islands* (New York, American Tract Society, 1842, pp. 219), *passim*.

helped by Christian chiefs from Tahiti who, with a British missionary, called in Hawaii on their way to the Marquesas there to promote the faith. Being Polynesians and speaking a language akin to that of Hawaii, the Tahitians were able to allay many fears. In 1823 numbers of the chiefs professed to be Christians. Before her death, in 1823, the influential widow of Kamehameha I and mother of the reigning king was baptized.[306] About the year 1825 Kapiolani, a woman from a leading family, showed her loyalty to the new faith by descending into the crater of Kilauea, the great live volcano of the islands, and defying the goddess, Pele, who was supposed to preside there.[307]

By the end of its first decade the American mission had made remarkable progress. Reinforcements had been received. Part of the Bible had been translated and printed. Public Christian services were largely attended. Laws had been passed by the native government to restrain drunkenness, prostitution, and gambling and to secure the observance of Sunday, even though attempts at enforcement aroused the violent indignation of foreign residents and visiting sailors. Thousands were in schools and other thousands in what were known as moral and religious societies.[308]

By the close of 1837, however, about half the population were still unreached by the direct influence of the mission and the number of pupils in the schools was declining. At one time more than a third of the population were in school. Now only about a sixth were enrolled.[309] The missionary body numbered eighty-seven and there were seventeen churches.[310]

In 1836 there began a mass movement into the Church, similar to those which we have noticed on several of the island groups of the Pacific and not unlike those in other sections and periods of the spread of Christianity. The missionaries termed it the Great Awakening and used many of the methods with which they were familiar in the revivals in the United States. Since these, too, were mass movements, the adaptation to the Hawaiian situation was not so much a *tour de force* as might at first sight have been supposed. "Protracted meetings" were held. Huge crowds attended. Efforts were made through personal conferences to ensure the sincerity and the intelligent and informed action of all who sought admission to the Church. As a result of the Great

[306] Anderson, *History of the Sandwich Islands Mission*, pp. 19-43; Bingham, *op. cit.*, pp. 81-205.
[307] Bingham, *op. cit.*, pp. 254-256.
[308] Anderson, *op. cit.*, pp. 44-98; Bingham, *op. cit.*, pp. 206-364.
[309] Anderson, *op. cit.*, pp. 120, 121.
[310] Anderson, *op. cit.*, pp. 134, 135. For pictures of missionary life see Sereno Edwards Bishop. *Reminiscences of Old Hawaii* (Honolulu, Hawaiian Gazette Co., 1916, pp. 61), *passim*, and Mary Dillingham Frear, *Lowell and Abigail. A Realistic Idyll* (New Haven, Privately Printed, 1934, pp. xvi, 324), *passim*.

Awakening, in the three years 1839-1841 over 20,000 were received into church membership, or about a sixth of the population.[311] Opportunely for the instruction of the converts, the translation of the entire Bible was completed (1839).[312] As time passed the rate of accessions to the Church declined. After 1843, when 5,296 were admitted, the number in any one year never again reached 2,000.[313] Yet through these additions Hawaii was fast becoming professedly Christian.

Efforts were made by missionaries and native Christians to make effective the faith thus professed. In 1840, after careful discussion, a written constitution for the state was adopted which declared that no law should be enacted contrary to the Bible and that religious liberty should be observed. A code of laws was also framed which was a compound of old customs with the newly imported principles.[314] Substantial church buildings were erected, including a notable one in Honolulu undertaken at the instance of the king and the major chiefs.[315] In 1839 a school was begun for the young chiefs, with missionaries in charge. In it were educated three who later ruled as monarchs.[316] With the encouragement of the missionaries, provision was made for the division of part of the land in such fashion as to permit private ownership by individuals. It was hoped that by this means industry, the better cultivation of the soil, and thrift would be encouraged.[317] Whether the institution of ownership in severalty was wise may be open to debate,[318] but the missionaries believed that the immediate results were good. One missionary bought abandoned land in the hope of inducing the natives to stay on it and furthered the development of sugar plantations to give them work.[319] Missionaries entered the employment of the government, although usually first severing their official connexion with the mission. One became a judge; another, government printer.[320] Gerrit Parmele Judd, who came to Hawaii as a missionary physician, served in many capacities—as member of the treasury board, as recorder and translator, as min-

---

[311] Anderson, *op. cit.*, pp. 140-157; Bingham, *op. cit.*, pp. 498-530; Coan, *Life in Hawaii* pp. 42-60; Dibble, *History of the Sandwich Islands*, pp. 341ff.

[312] Anderson, *op. cit.*, p. 135; Bingham, *op. cit.*, p. 531.

[313] Anderson, *op. cit.*, pp. 166, 167.

[314] Bingham, *op. cit.*, pp. 561ff.

[315] Bingham, *op. cit.*, pp. 570ff.

[316] Bingham, *op. cit.*, pp. 162, 163; Gulick, *The Pilgrims of Hawaii*, pp. 180, 181.

[317] Anderson, *op. cit.*, p. 173; Gulick, *op. cit.*, p. 266; Oliver Pomeroy Emerson, *Pioneer Days in Hawaii* (Garden City, Doubleday, Doran & Co., 1928, pp. xiii, 257), pp. 140-143; Hobbs, *Hawaii*, pp. 37ff.

[318] See some of the changes and problems brought by the alteration in land tenure ir Hobbs, *op. cit.*, pp. 48ff.

[319] Ethel M. Damon, *Father Bond of Kohala* (Honolulu, The Friend, 1927, pp. ix, 284), pp. 178ff.

[320] Robertson in *The Centennial Book*, pp. 31ff.

ister of foreign affairs, as minister of the interior, as minister of finance, and in reality if not in name as premier.[321] William Richards, a clergyman, was what might be termed minister of education, although at the outset with the more modest designation "chaplain, teacher, and translator for the King," and was succeeded in that post by another clergyman, Richard Armstrong, father of Samuel C. Armstrong, who became famous as the creator of Hampton Institute in the United States.[322]

In 1863, forty-three years after the arrival of its first missionaries, the American Board of Commissioners for Foreign Missions, deeming the Hawaiian Christian community able to assume self-government, turned over its work to the Board of the Hawaiian Evangelical Association.[323] In preparation for this step the Hawaiian Evangelical Association, which had heretofore consisted of the missionaries of the American Board who were resident in the islands, together with other resident ministers of foreign birth in sympathy with them, was enlarged to include all native and foreign Congregational and Presbyterian clergymen in Hawaii, Micronesia, and the Marquesas, and lay delegates elected by the local ecclesiastical bodies. For a number of years other preparations had been made for ecclesiastical independence. A native ministry had been trained, and the larger churches of early days, with missionaries as pastors, had been divided into smaller ones with natives in charge.[324] It was reported that in spite of the continued decline of the population, there were 19,679 members in good standing, that the nation had been Christianized, the language reduced to writing, with books in it on science, literature, and religion, the Bible put in the mother tongue, the law of Christian marriage everywhere recognized, public worship attended as well as in the majority of Christian countries, Sunday better observed than in most parts of the world, and intemperance, except among foreigners, rarer than in any other portion of the earth's surface. Hawaiians trained in the schools of the mission occupied leading places in Church and state.[325] This estimate by the American Board of the success of its mission indicates as do few other brief statements its ideals

---

[321] *Dictionary of American Biography*, Vol. X, pp. 229, 230; Jarves, *History of the Hawaiian Islands*, pp. 174, 182, 190.

[322] Samuel Williston, *William Richards* (Cambridge, Mass., privately printed, 1938, pp. 91), pp. 48ff.; *Richard Armstrong* (Hampton, Normal School Press Print, 1887, pp. 120), *passim*.

[323] *Fifty-third Annual Report of the American Board of Commissioners for Foreign Missions, 1863*, pp. 23, 24; Anderson, *The Hawaiian Islands*, pp. 315ff.

[324] Anderson, *History of the Sandwich Islands Mission*, pp. 280ff.

[325] *Fifty-third Annual Report of the American Board of Commissioners for Foreign Missions, 1863*, pp. 132-135. On the mission press see Howard M. Ballou and George R. Carter, *The History of the Hawaiian Mission Press, with a Bibliography of the Earlier Publications*, in *Papers of the Hawaiian Historical Society, No. 14* (Honolulu, 1908, pp. 44), pp. 9-44.

and programme.[326] The American Board did not immediately withdraw all help. It continued the salaries of some of its former missionaries. Down through 1904 it made grants-in-aid to several enterprises.[327] It assisted the North Pacific Institute, which trained Hawaiians to be missionaries to the Gilbert Islands and pastors of Hawaiian churches. It subsidized the boarding school for boys at Hilo. It contributed towards missions to the Chinese and Japanese in the islands.[328] Yet, in general, the churches which had been founded in Hawaii were, from 1863 onwards, independent of control or financial support from the United States.

The Hawaiian Evangelical Association, the heir of the American Board, continued a vigorous life. It long maintained missions in the Marquesas and Micronesia. It nourished the life of the native Hawaiian churches. Significantly, however, most of its leadership was of white stock. The Hawaiians did not assume much initiative.[329] This was also true of the Woman's Board of Missions, organized in 1882, which paralleled with efforts by and for that sex some of the enterprises of the general society.[330]

The Hawaiians were a waning race. Before the first missionaries arrived, as we saw a moment ago, they had begun to decrease in numbers. Missionary efforts did not arrest the decline. The success of the missionaries in winning the native stock was followed by the influx of additional racial elements, largely non-Christian by tradition, which constituted a new challenge. The Hawaiian Evangelical Association, undiscouraged, engaged in efforts, some of them successful, to reach this immigration, especially the Chinese, the Japanese, and the Portuguese. Missionaries for them were maintained and churches and social centres were built.

In the 1880's something of an anti-Christian reaction occurred among the native Hawaiian stock, both among the common people and the rulers, with a revival of the old cults.[331] This, however, seems to have been only temporary.

---

[326] On adverse criticism of the mission by a British Consul-General, see Manley Hopkins, *Hawaii* (London, Longman, Green, Longman and Roberts, 1862, pp. xxiii, 423), pp. 376-393. On a reply to some criticisms of missionaries, see Walter F. Frear, *Anti-Missionary Criticism with Reference to Hawaii* (Honolulu, Advertiser Publishing Co., 1935, pp. 45), *passim*.

[327] *Ninety-fourth Annual Report of the American Board of Commissioners for Foreign Missions, 1904*, p. 152.

[328] Strong, *The Story of the American Board*, pp. 444, 445.

[329] *Annual Reports of the Hawaiian Evangelical Association*, 1823ff. On one of the Japanese pastors, a graduate of the Doshisha, see Takie Okumura, *Seventy Years of Divine Blessings* (no place or publisher, 1939, pp. ii, 191), *passim*.

[330] *Annual Reports of the Woman's Board of Foreign Missions* (Honolulu, 1883ff.).

[331] Blackman, *The Making of Hawaii*, pp. 88-91.

The descendants of the American Board missionaries were prominent in the later life of the islands. They were leaders in religious, business, and civic life. A son of a missionary, Sanford B. Dole, was outstanding in the movement which overthrew the monarchy and worked for annexation to the United States. He was the first president of the republic and the first Governor of the Territory of Hawaii after annexation.[332] The missionary families contributed to the dominant society in Hawaii a note of idealism which helped, among other things, towards a peaceful adjustment of the complex racial problems brought by immigration.

Although Congregationalism, introduced and nourished by the American Board of Commissioners for Foreign Missions, became the most influential element in the religious life of Hawaii, several other Christian communions entered.

The Anglicans were represented. Several families of that faith early settled in Honolulu. Beginning in 1840 regular services were held by a lay reader.[333] King Kamehameha IV while on a visit to Great Britain was greatly attracted by the Church of England and his Queen wrote Queen Victoria asking for a bishop for his realm.[334] Request was also made by the Hawaiian Government to the Protestant Episcopal Bishop of California for a clergyman. None could be sent.[335] In 1861 T. N. Staley was appointed and consecrated in England as Bishop of Honolulu. The following year he arrived in his diocese. One of his early acts was to baptize the Queen, Emma. Not long thereafter the King, the Queen, and several of the leading officers of state were confirmed.[336] Vigorous criticism was voiced by some of the representatives of the American Board and their friends on the ground that the islands were already being well cared for by the existing mission and that the Anglican mission was an intrusion. The fear was also expressed that a government tax might be imposed to support the new enterprise of what for a time was called the Reformed Catholic Church and that Bishop Staley might prove the precursor of annexation by Great Britain.[337] Differences in ecclesiastical polity also made for friction. In spite of opposition, the Anglican mission grew. Schools were opened. Reinforcements came from Great Britain and from the Protestant Episcopal

---

[332] *Dictionary of American Biography*, Vol. V, pp. 358, 359.
[333] Restarick, *Hawaii, 1778-1920, from the Viewpoint of a Bishop*, p. 55.
[334] Staley, *Five Years' Church Work in the Kingdom of Hawaii*, pp. 13ff.
[335] Restarick, *op. cit.*, pp. 59, 60.
[336] Restarick, *op. cit.*, pp. 63, 64; Staley, *op. cit.*, pp. 24-28.
[337] Staley, *op. cit.*, pp. 52, 53, 86, 89, 110-113; Anderson, *The Hawaiian Islands*, pp. 331ff.; W. Ellis, *The American Mission to the Sandwich Islands: a Vindication and an Appeal, in Relation to the Proceedings of the Reformed Catholic Mission at Honolulu* (Honolulu, H. M. Whitney, 1866, pp. 77), *passim*.

Church in the United States.[338] However, partly because of the dissatisfaction of some of his European flock over his high churchmanship, Bishop Staley found his course stormy, and in 1870 he resigned.[339] In 1872 he was followed as bishop by Alfred Willis, also from England.[340] While the Anglican Church did not have a large following, it continued to be patronized by royalty. The last two Hawaiian monarchs, King Kalakaua and Queen Lilioukalani, were confirmed by Willis.[341] Moreover, it was in a school conducted by Bishop Willis that a lad who later came to be known as Sun Yat-sen, the most influential Chinese of the second and third decades of the nineteenth century, received his first training in English and the impressions of Christianity which eventually led to his acceptance of that faith.[342] In consequence of the annexation by the United States, in 1901 Willis resigned and in 1902 the Protestant Episcopal Church assumed charge.[343] Henry Bond Restarick became bishop. Under him the Anglican communion enjoyed a healthy growth. It served both whites and Hawaiians and had missions and churches for Chinese, Japanese, and Koreans.[344] However, it remained a minority, although a prominent minority.[345]

The Mormons, or the Church of Jesus Christ of Latter Day Saints, sent their first missionaries in 1850. The Book of Mormon was translated (1855) and within a few years about 4,000 converts were claimed. Discouragements followed, and in 1858 the missionaries withdrew. In the 1860's a fresh start was made. The numbers of neophytes grew.[346] In 1896 about one-sixth of the Hawaiians who professed a religious connexion were said to be of that faith.[347] In 1910 the membership numbered 8,170, most of whom were Hawaiians, but some of whom were part Hawaiian, Orientals, and whites.[348]

In 1857 the American Methodists started a mission which lapsed in 1860. In 1886 a Methodist pastor from Japan began attempts to reach his fellow-countrymen. In 1890 a clergyman came from California to superintend Meth-

---

[338] Staley, op. cit., pp. 51ff.

[339] Restarick, op. cit., pp. 120, 121.

[340] Restarick, op. cit., pp. 136, 137.

[341] Restarick, op. cit., pp. 142, 177.

[342] Henry Bond Restarick, Sun Yat Sen (Yale University Press, 1931, pp. xvii, 167), pp. 11-19.

[343] Restarick, Hawaii, 1778-1920, from the Viewpoint of a Bishop, pp. 178ff.

[344] Restarick, op. cit., pp. 216ff.; Henry Bond Restarick, My Personal Recollections (Honolulu, Paradise of the Pacific Press, 1938, pp. 343), pp. 310ff.

[345] Handbooks of the Missions of the Episcopal Church, No. VIII. Hawaiian Islands (New York, The National Council of the Protestant Episcopal Church, 1927, pp. 95), pp. 33ff.; R. B. Anderson in The Centennial Book, 1820-1920, pp. 70, 71.

[346] Gulick, Mixing the Races in Hawaii, pp. 149, 150; Coan, Life in Hawaii, pp. 101-103.

[347] Blackman, The Making of Hawaii, p. 91.

[348] Gulick, op. cit., p. 150.

odist efforts and to be in charge of an Anglo-Saxon church in Honolulu.[349] By 1898 six Japanese preachers were at work on at least two islands.[350] In 1905 a new organization was set up for Methodist efforts and an arrangement was entered into with the Hawaiian Evangelical Association by which duplication of enterprises was prevented and a comprehensive plan for covering the islands was agreed upon. The Methodists were not to approach the Hawaiians nor the Congregationalists the Koreans.[351] In 1913 the Methodists reported missions among Filipinos, Japanese, and Koreans.[352]

In 1894 the Salvation Army entered Honolulu and in time spread to a number of other centres in the islands.[353]

The Seventh Day Adventists arrived in 1895[354] but by 1914 had made only a slight beginning.

We hear also of the Disciples of Christ and of the Lutherans.[355]

The large majority of the Protestant missions and missionaries in Hawaii, as the past few paragraphs reveal, were from the United States. This was because of geographic proximity and the extensive commercial American contacts with the islands.

Roman Catholic missions at the outset were not from the United States but from the Continent of Europe and were French-speaking. In 1824, four years after the baptism of the two Hawaiian chiefs by the chaplain of a visiting French ship, Jean Rives, who had gone to Europe with the royal party, sought in France Roman Catholic missionaries for Hawaii. He obtained them from the Picpus Fathers. In 1828 the first missionaries reached Hawaii. The survivor of the two chiefs was friendly. Moreover, before the arrival of the mission a group of foreigners and Hawaiians had been meeting in Honolulu for Roman Catholic prayers and a few of the Hawaiians had been baptized. Opposition arose from the Protestants, and in 1831 the King ordered the priests out of his realms. He professed not to wish idolatry, for so he regarded Roman Catholicism, to be reintroduced when his domains had been so recently rid of it in another form, or to see his land religiously divided. The command was carried out. Two lay brothers, however, remained. In 1833 Rome created the

---

[349] Gulick, *op. cit.*, p. 159.
[350] *Eightieth Annual Report of the Missionary Society of the Methodist Episcopal Church* (1898), pp. 336, 337.
[351] Gulick, *op. cit.*, p. 159.
[352] *The Annual Report for the Board of Home Missions and Church Extension of the Methodist Episcopal Church for . . . 1913*, p. 11.
[353] Gulick, *op. cit.*, pp. 161, 162.
[354] *Seventh-Day Adventist Conferences and Missions for . . . 1905.*
[355] *Eighty-third Annual Report of the Missionary Society of the Methodist Episcopal Church* (1901), pp. 360-363.

Vicariate Apostolic of Oriental Oceanica and included in it Hawaii. In 1839 the commander of a French frigate obtained by threat of force toleration for Roman Catholicism, the gift of a site for a church, and the release of those imprisoned for their faith. Following the permission thus wrested from the unwilling government, reinforcements arrived and a church was built. Schools were inaugurated. In the 1840's a separate vicariate apostolic was created for Hawaii. More recruits were obtained from abroad. The influx of Portuguese labourers brought additional burdens and opportunities, for the immigrants were Roman Catholics and required spiritual care. Still later, chiefly in the period after 1914, came Filipinos, also Roman Catholics and therefore a responsibility. Efforts, too, were made for the Japanese. Various charitable institutions were founded.[356] In 1896 Hawaii contained almost as many Roman Catholics as Protestants. That branch of the faith was especially strong among the Portuguese, but about a third of the Hawaiians and about two-fifths of the part-Hawaiians who claimed a church connexion were Roman Catholics.[357]

The most famous of the Roman Catholic missionaries was Joseph Damien de Veuster (1840-1889), better known as Father Damien and often called the apostle to the lepers.[358] A Fleming by birth and rearing, of sturdy farming stock, in his late teens he joined the Picpus Fathers, and in 1863 came to Hawaii under that order. In 1873 he volunteered for the leper colony at Molokai and there served devotedly until the dread disease silenced him. He brought about improved housing conditions, a more regular provision of supplies by the government, and better care for the children. Three years before his death there came to help him Joseph Dutton, a convert, an American, who was attracted by what he had heard of him and as a lay brother gave himself to the lepers, especially in institutions founded, as it chanced, by Protestants.[359]

West and south of Hawaii are clusters of islands scattered over hundreds of miles of ocean and known collectively as Micronesia. They are made up principally of four groups, the Mariana, the Caroline, the Marshall, and the Gilbert Islands. Most of them are low-lying, many of them atolls. The land

---

[356] Yzendoorn, *History of the Catholic Missions in the Hawaiian Missions, passim.*
[357] Blackman, *The Making of Hawaii*, p. 91.
[358] Irene Caudwell, *Damien of Molokai* (New York, The Macmillan Co., 1932, pp. xi, 203), *passim;* Vital Jourdan, *Le Père Damien de Veuster* (Paris, Maison-Mère, 1931, pp. xvi, 541, including many of Damien's letters), *passim;* John Farrow, *Damien the Leper* (New York, Sheed & Ward, 1937, pp. xx, 230), *passim;* Ewald Henseler, *Der Apostel von Molokai* (Kirnach-Villingen, Verlag der Schulbrüder, 1930, pp. iv, 127), *passim;* Robert Louis Stevenson, *Father Damien. An Open Letter to the Reverend Dr. Hyde of Honolulu* (New York, Charles Scribner's Sons, 1916, pp. 53), *passim.*
[359] Charles S. Dutton, *The Samaritans of Molokai. The Lives of Father Damien and Brother Dutton among the Lepers* (New York, Dodd, Mead and Co. 1932, pp. xiv, 286), pp. 124-278.

surface of all Micronesia totals only a little more than 1,000 square miles and its population at the dawn of the twentieth century was less than 100,000.

The first white men to see the Marianas were those of Magellan's famous expedition early in the sixteenth century. The Marianas were then inhabited by the Chamorros, an Indonesian people seemingly akin to the Polynesians. Late in the seventeenth century they were conquered by Spain and an infiltration of Filipino and Spanish blood followed. Held by Spain until late in the nineteenth century, when the largest of the group, the island of Guam, passed to the United States and the rest to Germany, they naturally early became a field of Spanish Roman Catholic missionary effort. Jesuits in the seventeenth century were followed by Augustinians in the eighteenth century and the population became professedly Christian. In 1907, after the German annexation, Rhenish-Westphalian Capuchins entered the German portions. In 1901 Spanish Capuchins came to Guam.[360]

In 1900 the American Board of Commissioners for Foreign Missions sent missionaries to Guam. Parts of the Bible were translated and a few converts were made, but in 1910 the missionaries were withdrawn. American Baptist missionaries arrived in 1911.[361]

The Caroline Islands stretched over a wide expanse and had a Micronesian population. In the eighteenth century they were the scene of Roman Catholic missionary effort. In the last quarter of the nineteenth century they became a Spanish possession, and were a field of the Spanish Capuchins. Since in 1899 they passed into the hands of Germany, in 1904 the Rhenish-Westphalian Capuchins came. In 1905 the Carolines were made a prefecture apostolic. By 1914 Roman Catholics were about 5 per cent. of the population. On some islands the proportion was much higher. On Ponape by 1911 it was two-thirds.[362]

Protestant missions to the Carolines were begun by the American Board of Commissioners for Foreign Missions. Its first party included several Hawaiian Christians and arrived in 1852. They found that on one island a white trader had already made some converts. Stations were founded on the islands of Ponape and Kusaie. A succession of ships, five of them with the name of

---

[360] Schmidlin, *Die katholischen Missionen in den deutschen Schutzgebieten*, pp. 204-206; Laura Thompson, *Guam and Its People. A Story of Culture Change and Colonial Education* (New York, American Council, Institute of Pacific Relations, 1941, pp. xii, 308), pp. 144-158.

[361] Strong, *The Story of the American Board*, p. 451; F. M. Price in D. L. Pierson, *The Pacific Islanders*, pp. 229-248.

[362] Schmidlin, *op. cit.*, pp. 199-203; Kilian Müller, *Ponape im Sonnenlicht der Oeffentlichkeit* (Cologne, J. P. Bachem, 1912, pp. 80), *passim*; Georg Fritz, *Ad majorem Dei gloriam. Die Vorgeschichte des Aufstandes von 1910/11 in Ponape* (Leipzig, Dieterich'sche Verlagsbuchhandlung, 1912, pp. 105), pp. 34ff.

Morning Star, were operated by the mission to connect the stations in this and other groups. Eventually the Hawaiian Evangelical Association joined with the American Board in the enterprise. Converts were made and some of these became missionaries to other islands.[363] The Spanish annexation was followed by misunderstandings with the new rulers and by persecution. For a time the missionaries withdrew.[364] The transfer to Germany was followed by the re-entrance of missionaries of the American Board. A hearty welcome was given them. However, after a few years it seemed best for them to remove from some of the islands in favour of Germans from the Jugendbund für Entschiedenes Christentum in connexion with the Liebenzell Mission.[365] In the meantime, in 1902 and 1903 a mass movement had made Kusaie outwardly Christian.[366] Since 1879 it had been the centre on which training schools for the Gilbert and Marshall Islands had been located.[367]

Christian missions in the Marshall Islands were begun in 1857, on Ebon. The first missionaries were welcomed by islanders who had become acquainted with one of them in Kusaie.[368] Eventually others of the islands were reached, including Nauru, rich in phosphate deposits and with foreign as well as native labourers.[369]

After the German occupation, Roman Catholic missionaries of that nationality came (1899) to the Marshall Islands from the Hiltrup house of the Holy Heart of Jesus. By 1911 they had opened eight stations and several schools and had counted 950 baptisms.[370]

In the Gilbert Islands the American Board began a mission in the same year that it inaugurated one in the Marshall Islands. Here Hawaiian Christians were very active. Here, too, laboured Hiram Bingham, son of one of the original contingent in Hawaii. He became famous for his translation of the Bible and the preparation of other literature in the native tongue.[371] In 1899 a missionary of the London Missionary Society from Samoa began an enterprise in the southern islands of the Gilbert group. By 1914, thanks in part to

[363] Strong, *op. cit.,* pp. 227-249; Bliss, *Micronesia,* pp. 7-106.

[364] Bliss, *op. cit.,* pp. 107ff.; Strong, *op. cit.,* pp. 445ff.

[365] Strong, *op. cit.,* p. 453; Richter, *Die evangelische Mission in Fern- und Südost-Asien, Australien, Amerika,* p. 248.

[366] Strong, *op. cit.,* p. 451.

[367] Fensham and Tuthill, *The Old and the New in Micronesia,* p. 49. For a description of the missions of the American Board on the Carolines early in the twentieth century, see T. C. Bliss in D. L. Pierson, *op. cit.,* pp. 207-225.

[368] Bliss, *op. cit.,* pp. 63, 64, 135-139; Fensham and Tuthill, *op. cit.,* pp. 70-74.

[369] *The One Hundred and Third Annual Report of the American Board of Commissioners for Foreign Missions,* 1913, pp. 187-189.

[370] Schmidlin, *op. cit.,* pp. 182-187.

[371] Strong, *op. cit.,* pp. 237, 241; *Dictionary of American Biography,* Vol. II, pp. 276, 277; Fensham and Tuthill, *op. cit.,* pp. 63-70.

the use of Samoan and Gilbertese teachers, there were 30 churches with 2,000 members, 7,500 attending public worship, and 3,000 children in schools.[372]

This chapter has of necessity been crowded with details and with accounts of many island groups and peoples. More than in most of its predecessors, therefore, some kind of summary is required. Again we can best approach it by way of our familiar categories.

The Christianity which was carried to the islands of the Pacific was both Roman Catholicism and Protestantism. The Roman Catholic missionaries were mostly French. They were not so prominent or so influential as were the Protestants. The Protestants were predominantly British and the majority were Congregationalists and Methodists. In the New Hebrides there were Presbyterians. There were some strong Anglican missions. In the French possessions were a few French Protestant missionaries. In the German territories were some Germans. In the northern islands Americans, especially American Congregationalists, were the most numerous.

It is interesting that the Christianity most strongly represented, Congregationalism and Methodism, and which had the largest numerical growth was that which in its origin had been made up of dissenting minorities and which had emphasized individual conversion. Although in the Pacific it continued to seek individual conversions and endeavoured to admit to church membership only those who could show evidence of that experience, it spread largely by mass movements. It is even more interesting that Congregationalism should have been so prominent. Relatively it loomed larger than in any other major non-Anglo-Saxon area except Turkey. Although in its motherlands it stressed the individual more than did most Protestant groups, in the Pacific it came in contact with peoples whose traditional pattern of life was tribal and collective. Probably the Congregational tradition of the local church as an entity and the record in Great Britain of the Cromwellian commonwealth and in the United States, and especially in New England, of seeking to mould the entire life of the community kept the contrast in the Pacific from being starkly anomalous and facilitated the reciprocal adaptation of the imported and the indigenous patterns.

The reasons for the spread of Christianity were many. Some of them are readily determined. Others are more difficult and some are probably impossible to discover. Obviously the power of the white man and his culture was a factor. The education which the missionary offered seemed to the native

[372] Cousins, *Isles Afar Off*, pp. 81-85.

to give him the tools which made the white man superior. So, too, the might of the white man, so much greater than that of the native, might be attributed to the white man's God. For some the character of the missionary had an appeal. Force was almost never employed to induce acceptance of Christianity, but occasionally the punishment meted out by a European ship of war for the harsh usage of missionaries wrought fear, prevented further violence, and rendered the islanders more amenable to what the foreigner brought. The rapid collapse of the native cultures under the impact of the white man's advance broke down the resistance of the indigenous institutions and religions and prepared the way for the acceptance of Christianity and of the social and moral ideals which its representatives sought to inculcate. Sometimes the missionary came early in the history of that impact and shared with the trader the rôle of a pioneer of the new order. Usually he was at least slightly behind the explorers and the first traders and occasionally, as in Hawaii, he did not arrive until the disintegration of the old culture was well under way. Whether early or late in reaching an island group, Christianity found its course facilitated by the progressive decrepitude of what it was seeking to supplant.

On a first rapid survey of the story, one is led to venture the generalization that something in the Polynesian race or culture favoured the adoption of Christianity. With occasional exceptions, the islands in which the Polynesian stock was predominant became professedly Christian earlier than did those in which Melanesian and Micronesian blood prevailed. Polynesian Christians, too, more generally became eager emissaries of the new faith to other islands and even to Melanesians and Micronesians than did the Christians of these latter two racial strains. On more careful investigation, however, one is led to inquire whether the difference is not chronological rather than racial. In general Christian missionaries reached the Polynesians in force before they did the islands inhabited by the Melanesians and Micronesians. When it came to the latter Christianity had much the same course as among the former. There were the same initial resistance, the same stage of individual conversions, the same subsequent mass movements into the Church, and something of the same readiness to carry the faith to other peoples.

Of obvious importance in the spread of Christianity was the zeal of the missionaries, whether white or native. It must also be clear that something in Christianity, no matter what its variety, and even though imperfectly understood and still more imperfectly applied, appealed to a hunger in the native heart and brought a response.

The processes by which Christianity spread in the various groups were largely of the one pattern. Usually white missionaries were first, although on more than one occasion Christians from other islands were the pioneers and, much more infrequently, a white trader was the initial teacher of the new faith. Generally a period of opposition followed, but occasionally the missionaries were eagerly welcomed. If there was opposition, converts at first came one by one in a thin stream. Sooner or later a mass movement brought a large proportion of the population into the Church. As a rule in this mass movement, the heads of the group, the chiefs, led the way. Very early the language was reduced to writing, portions of the Bible translated, and schools started. In several groups, after the mass conversion, the laws and the social structure were partly recast to bring them, so far as possible, into conformity with Christian patterns.

The effects of Christianity were many. If the entire group became Christian, the pre-Christian cults disappeared. The missionary fought drink and sexual irregularity and struggled to bring the family to Christian standards. In this he was by no means entirely successful. Even after a generation of nominal Christianity, drunkenness and adultery were all too common among church members.[373] Yet, when the difficulties are remembered, the advance was amazing. Moreover, the missionary strove to make peace[374] and to eliminate the inter-tribal warfare which had been intensified by the importation of fire-arms. Often he himself went about completely unarmed. Where Christianity prevailed, cannibalism and head-hunting disappeared. The missionary struggled to prevent the exploitation of the natives by white traders and by those who were recruiting labour for the white man's plantations. It was through the missionaries that the native languages were reduced to writing and the beginnings of a literature prepared. Most of such schools as existed in the Pacific Islands were inaugurated by the missionaries and the majority remained under the direction of the Church. Sometimes the missionary has been accused of accelerating, even though unintentionally, the decline in the population by inducing the natives to don European clothes. Drenched by tropical showers and too infrequently washed, the clothes are said to have increased disease.[375] If the missionary contributed to the decline, it was only to a minor degree. Often depopulation had begun before his advent. The epidemics which were a major factor in producing it usually came in quite independently of him. Indeed, he fought them. Nor was he the sole factor in the introduction of the white man's clothing. This would have come in without him through imitation of the dominant whites. Probably the missionary was sometimes un-

[373] Lovett, *James Chalmers*, pp. 82, 87; Hogbin, *Experiments in Civilization*, pp. 209ff.
[374] For some instances out of many, see Berg, *Die katholische Heidenmission als Kulturträger*, Vol. III, pp. 260ff.
[375] Rivers, *Essays on the Depopulation of Melanesia*, pp. 7ff.

wise in his guidance of the transition from the old culture to the new. That at best was a most difficult task and it would have been strange had he not been guilty of occasional blunders. What must be remembered, however, is the indubitable fact that the disintegration of the native cultures would have occurred had never a missionary come to the islands. Commerce and the extension of political control by the whites would have brought it about. That was unmistakably demonstrated in Hawaii before the arrival of the first missionaries. The missionary modified, generally for good, the impact of the white man and his culture. He strove to protect the native against some of the most demoralizing and degrading aspects of that impact. He took the lead in assisting the native to make positive adaptations by acquiring the learning requisite in the new day. He sought to advise him in reconstructing his social institutions. More important still, Christianity brought forth its characteristic fruits in transformed, noble lives. These may have been in the minority. For the majority, as in most lands, the accepted Christianity, while working important moral and spiritual changes, was fairly superficial. Among some, however, Christianity nourished a type of character for which there can be only admiration.

Many of the native Christians were impelled by their faith to become teachers of their own people or missionaries to other tribes and islands, often at great peril and even at the cost of life itself.[376] One must remember, moreover, what their Christianity did for the white missionaries. It sent them from their homes and sustained them in the face of severe trials. A very few of them succumbed to the fierce temptations about them and proved unworthy of their calling. Some sank into uninspired mediocrity. But many were centres of courage and unselfish living.

The effect of the environment on Christianity was neither so striking nor so obvious as was the effect of Christianity upon the environment. Outwardly the majority of the Christians conformed to the types of worship, organization, and creeds which had been brought them. Only rarely did indigenous movements develop which were at variance with what had been inculcated by the missionary. Undoubtedly pre-Christian attitudes persisted and in the minds of the converts the new was interpreted in terms of the old.[377] That is what almost always happens with the coming of a new religion to any milieu. Probably the outstanding effect of the environment was the degree to which the imported Christianity was dominated by the white man. Not only were the outward forms which had been introduced by the missionary preserved.

---

[376] See some of these in Paton, *The Kingdom in the Pacific*, pp. 73ff.
[377] Hogbin. *ob. cit.*, pp. 184ff.

The missionary also continued to direct the churches. Financial self-support made rapid progress. Clergy were trained. The young churches contributed both personnel and money to carry the faith to other islands. Yet the white man usually remained in control. This was to be expected. It was paralleled in the Christianity of the Indians of the Americas and to a less degree among the Negroes of the West Indies. It was but a counterpart of the situation in the political and economic phases of life. In these the islanders were largely brought into submission to the white man. They also copied his dress and his manners. It is not surprising that in their religion they continued to look to the white man for leadership.

It remained an unanswered question whether a religious life so dependent on the white man would survive if the latter were to withdraw. If it endured, presumably it would develop fresh forms. What these would be no one could foretell. Possibly the changes brought by the political developments after 1914 and especially after 1940 would shed light on the outcome. Whatever the future might hold, parallels would probably continue to be found among the other non-European peoples with whom this volume deals. All faced much the same conditions and displayed variations of the same patterns.

The nineteenth century record in the spread of Christianity among the Pacific Islanders is one of the most spectacular in the history of that or of any other faith. Within the course of a hundred years, often within a generation, Christianity displaced the native cults, eliminated some of the social practices most contradictory to its tenets, and contributed to the construction of new societies. In other areas greater numbers were affected. In none was a more extensive change wrought in so brief a span of time. In the impact of the white man's culture, so much of it grasping and sordid, the Christian missionaries, in spite of mistakes and weaknesses, introduced a constructive force which transformed for good many individuals, helped to offset the degrading elements in the white man's approach, and in more than one island assisted in making the new order a vast advance over the old.

Chapter VIII

THE PHILIPPINE ISLANDS

IN THE Philippine Islands the nineteenth century began late. There the Napoleonic Wars with their invasion of the mother country were followed by no such revolutionary consequences as in Spanish America. The Philippines were cut off by the changes in America from their traditional tie with Mexico, but they remained under Spanish rule. Only slowly did the forces at work in the nineteenth century Occident become potent. Even while the neighbouring Japan was being made over by its renewed contact with the West, the Philippines slumbered, living with relatively slight alterations the kind of life which had been introduced by the Spanish conquest in the sixteenth century. To be sure, now and again revolts broke out, but until the close of the century these were not of any basically different pattern from others which had punctuated the Spanish period. Manila and some other ports were opened to foreign commerce. Although with trade came ideas, these were slow in penetrating even a minority. Spain extended her rule here and there in the mountains and against the Moslem Moros in the South, to parts of the islands which had not heretofore acknowledged it, but this was only a continuation, now slowing down, of the conquest begun years before.

Yet the Philippines could not be hermetically sealed against the currents which were flowing so strongly in the rest of the world. In the third quarter of the century a governor representing the liberal ideas then in vogue in Spain wrought a few changes. The digging of the Suez Canal facilitated communication with the mother country. Masonry, of the Continental anti-clerical, politically liberal type, was introduced. More Spaniards came to the islands. A few Filipinos, profiting by the wealth which trade was bringing, sent their sons to Europe to complete their education. In the 1880's a handful of these intellectuals organized in Spain an association for Philippine reform. In the 1890's a society was secretly brought into being in the Philippines which sought the expulsion of the friars and the destruction of the Spanish regime. In 1896 open rebellion broke out. Rizal, a young physician trained in Europe and a liberal, was executed, a fate which later made him the national hero.

Then, in 1898, came the Spanish-American War followed by the transfer of the Philippines to the United States. Revolutionary changes ensued. The United States, while suppressing the armed opposition, entered upon a course which was avowedly designed to prepare the Filipinos for self-government. Secular public education was inaugurated by a corps of hundreds of American school-teachers, missionaries of the new order.[1] Representative government was introduced and developed. Railroads and highways were constructed, a programme of public health was framed, improvements were made in agriculture, changes were effected in the currency and in weights and measures, the knowledge and use of the English language were fostered, and a civil service system was planned. The islands throbbed with new life. The nineteenth century had at last entered in full force.[2]

In one basic respect the United States continued the policy of Spain. American, like Spanish rule, was paternalistic. While the new regime was designed to be a school in self-government, it was both pedagogue and guardian, guiding the development of its wards and giving protection from the rough and tumble world into which the islanders would be thrown when once the coveted independence was granted.

The religious development of the Philippines paralleled the other phases of the islands' history. Until the American occupation the Roman Catholic Church was the dominant force in the religious life. Thanks to the missionary efforts of the sixteenth, seventeenth, and eighteenth centuries,[3] the majority of the Filipinos were Roman Catholic Christians. Only in mountain fastnesses and in the southern islands, where Islam had gained entrance before the arrival of Christianity, were there many confessed non-Christians. The combination of nationalist revolt and annexation by the United States brought striking changes. These were three-fold: nationalist movements tore away large minorities from the Roman Catholic Church, Protestant Christianity was introduced, and in the endeavour to meet the new conditions alterations were made in the Roman Catholic leadership and programme.

This story we must now undertake in somewhat greater detail, but still, because of the limitations of space, only in summary. Since by the year 1800 the majority of the Filipinos were already Christians, since in the nineteenth century only relatively few converts were made from among the non-Christians, and since most of the developments were within the Christian community

[1] Vincent R. Catapang, *The Development and Present Status of Education in the Philippine Islands* (Boston, The Stratford Co., 1926, pp. xvii, 137), pp. 64ff.; Alzona, *A History of Education in the Philippines*, pp. 189ff.

[2] For a brief survey of this history see Barrows, *History of the Philippines*, pp. 205-355. On Rizal see Austin Craig, *Lineage, Life, and Labors of José Rizal, Philippine Patriot* (Manila, Philippine Education Company, 1913, pp. xv, 287), *passim*.

[3] Vol. III, chap. 12.

rather than by expansion, we cannot, under the avowed purpose of these volumes, give the proportion of our space to the Philippines which, if this were a general history of Christianity, the numerical strength and strategic importance of the islands would demand.

Through the efforts of the Spanish missionaries of the sixteenth, seventeenth, and eighteenth centuries, the Philippines had become the first predominantly Christian land in the Far East. This was a remarkable achievement. It was paralleled by the conversion not far from the same time of the populations of some of the smaller islands of the Netherlands East Indies and, as we have seen in the last chapter, by the acceptance of Christianity in the nineteenth century by the peoples of numbers of the other islands of the Pacific. In all of these instances Christianity and European civilization came hand in hand to folk of primitive or near-primitive culture and, as has often been the case where an advanced religion and culture have impinged upon primitive cults and civilizations, won a quick and relatively easy victory. Yet the Filipinos continued to be the largest body of non-European Christians in the Pacific.

In the nineteenth century Spanish civilization and Roman Catholic Christianity were still pushing forward their frontiers in the Philippines. To be sure, during the Napoleonic Wars few reinforcements could be sent to the distant islands.[4] In Mexico, moreover, the liberals confiscated in the 1830's the real estate and other property which belonged to the Philippine missions, thus reducing the latters' support.[5] For a time in the first half of the century, because of the conflict between Rome and the Government of Spain, some of the bishoprics were vacant.[6] However, in the nineteenth century advance went on. One estimate declares that in the course of the century the Christian population increased from 4,000,000 to 7,000,000, and that of the gain 2,000,000 were from natural increase and 1,000,000 by conversion.[7] Beginning about the year 1850 the Spanish authorities embarked upon a renewed effort to subjugate the non-Christian peoples of the islands.[8] Much of this was by military means. Some of it was also by missions. In 1859 the Jesuits, who had been expelled in the eighteenth century, returned to the islands. They resumed missions among the Moros and the government entrusted to them the pacification of

[4] Galarreta, *Vida del Martir Ilmo Jerónimo Hermosilla*, p. 57, says that from 1805 to 1825 the Dominican Province of the Holy Rosary, which covered the Philippines and some other parts of the Far East, obtained only twenty-seven new recruits.
[5] Mecham, *Church and State in Latin America*, p. 412.
[6] Schmidlin-Braun, *Catholic Mission History*, p. 634.
[7] *Ibid.*
[8] Keesing, *Taming Philippine Headhunters*, p. 26.

much of the southern region.[9] In the 1880's determined attempts were made by the Manila authorities to extend their authority over the mountain peoples of Northern Luzon. These were by the joint action of the army and the missionaries.[10] In 1862 the initial contingent of Spanish Lazarists arrived. The Archbishop of Manila placed them in charge of his seminary for the training of native clergy.[11] By 1899 they had graduated 323. At least two other seminaries in the islands were put in the hands of the Lazarists.[12] In Manila the Dominican institution, the University of Santo Tomás, trained hundreds in theology.[13] In the 1890's the Dominicans founded three colleges in various parts of the islands.[14] More missionaries came from Spain. The Franciscans recruited them from the lowliest ranks of society and educated them at the expense of pious foundations, for this was said to fit them to mix with the poor.[15] The Dominicans also prepared at least some of their men in special institutions in Spain.[16] As in the previous centuries, the Church was still largely in the hands of the religious orders. Their members were overwhelmingly Spaniards. The secular priests, who were in part Filipinos and mestizos, were said to be ignorant and immoral.[17] They had only a minority of the parishes, in 1870 181 out of 792.[18] The Church, like the state, was as heretofore under the tutelage of Spaniards. The fees charged by the friars and the ownership of land by the religious orders were chronic sources of unrest.[19]

As the nineteenth century progressed, the Filipino seculars began to be more and more restive under the domination of the Spanish regulars. One of the causes of the revolt of the 1890's was hatred of the friars. The outstanding leader of the rebellion, Aguinaldo, declared that regulars had usurped the just prerogatives of the Filipino seculars and had appropriated the land. He claimed for Filipino priests the right to become bishops.[20] In 1899 Aguinaldo appointed head of the Filipino church a Filipino priest, Gregorio Aglipay y Labayan. The appointment was approved by an ecclesiastical assembly convened by Aglipay. The purpose was not to seek independence of Rome but to obtain

---

[9] Alzona, op. cit., p. 165.
[10] Keesing, op. cit., p. 66.
[11] Paradela, Resumen Histórico de la Congregación de la Missión en España, 1704-1868, pp. 461-471.
[12] Alzona, op. cit., p. 150.
[13] Los Dominicos en el Extremo Oriente, p. 272.
[14] Los Dominicos en el Extremo Oriente, pp. 93ff.
[15] Feodor Jagor, in Blair and Robertson, The Philippine Islands, Vol. XXVIII, pp. 290ff.
[16] Los Dominicos en el Extremo Oriente, pp. 171ff.
[17] Manuel Bernaldez Pizarro, in Blair and Robertson, op. cit., Vol. LI, pp. 203ff.
[18] Alzona, op. cit., p. 152.
[19] Forbes, The Philippine Islands, Vol. II, pp. 53-56.
[20] Report of the Philippine Commission to the President (Washington, Government Printing Office, Vol. I, 1900, pp. vii, 264), Vol. I, p. 130.

the appointment of Filipino bishops.[21] Another leader, Don Isabelo de los Reyes y Florentino, was sent to Europe to seek Papal recognition. Rome failed to agree to the choice of Filipino bishops. On his return from Europe, the disappointed Reyes formed an organization which (1902) declared a schism from Rome and elected Aglipay as its head. At first Aglipay demurred, but, when the American regime declined to evict the friars from their lands, he accepted. He became the Archbishop of the Independent Catholic Church of the Philippines (also called the Iglesia Filipina Independiente, or the Filipino Independent Church) and several priests were elected bishops. The movement rapidly gained momentum and carried numbers of priests and hundreds of thousands of Filipinos along with it. Contact was had with the Protestants and much emphasis was placed upon putting the Bible into the hands of the laity.[22] Under the influence of Reyes, who had been in touch with radical thought in Europe, the new church took on a theologically liberal tinge and sought fellowship with the Unitarians. It experienced great difficulty in obtaining and training a competent body of clergy.[23] Moreover, by court action in 1906 it lost possession of the Roman Catholic church buildings which it had claimed.[24] In 1918, however, it had about a seventh of the church edifices of the country.[25]

Not nearly so numerous as the Aglipayan movement were the adherents of the Colorum sect. The Colorums arose about the middle of the nineteenth century. They had their origin in a religious brotherhood founded in 1841 by Filipino laymen. When a dispute broke out with the parish priest over the size of the fee for saying the masses which this fellowship had as part of its collective purpose, the priest ordered the society dissolved. It refused, became secret, and was partly dispersed by troops sent against it at the instigation of the clergy. It lived on under the name of Colorum. Colorum persisted as a secret religious organization whose members looked upon themselves as pilgrims to Jerusalem, expected the end of the world to come very soon, and professed to hold to the love of God and of their neighbours. As late as the 1920's the government took forcible action against it, but it managed to survive.[26]

[21] The Philippine Liberal, September, 1933, pp. 12-14.

[22] The Philippine Liberal, October, 1933, pp. 12, 13, 15; Stuntz, The Philippines and the Far East, pp. 488ff.

[23] Laubach, The People of the Philippines, pp. 137ff.; Osias and Lorenzana, Evangelical Christianity in the Philippines, p. 129.

[24] Richter, Die evangelische Mission in Fern- und Südost-Asien, Australien, Amerika, p. 172; Forbes, The Philippine Islands, Vol. II, p. 62.

[25] Census of the Philippine Islands, 1918, Vol. IV, Part I, pp. 38, 39.

[26] Robert G. Woods in Asia. Vol. XXXII, pp. 450-454, 459, 460.

In 1899 there sprang up in the northern part of the island of Luzon a cult calling itself the *Guardia de Honor*.[27] From the *Guardia de Honor* there issued a Filipino prophet who proclaimed, also in Northern Luzon, a faith called *Sapalada*, which declared that a native culture-hero would appear and relieve the mountaineers of their burdens.[28]

In the years 1908-1910 the Tungud movement swept across part of the island of Mindanao.[29]

The various indigenous movements were in part the effect of the environment upon the transmitted Roman Catholic Christianity, reactions against the paternalism of the Spanish-dominated Church. They found especial opportunity when the old order was weakened by the transition to the rule of the United States and were furthered by the rising tide of nationalism.

Protestantism entered almost immediately after the transfer of the Philippines to the United States and was propagated by missionaries from that country. This was to be expected. The period was one of rapidly mounting enthusiasm in the churches of the United States for foreign missions. The new regime brought the religious toleration which had not existed in Spanish days. The Philippines appealed to American idealism as both an opportunity and an obligation. Within a few years several of the Protestant denominations came to the islands. Indeed, except for the contribution of the British and Foreign Bible Society, Protestantism in the islands sprang entirely from missions from the United States. It enjoyed a rapid growth. This was partly because the old patterns of life had been weakened by the shift of political masters, partly because the connexion with the United States gave it prestige, partly because of dissatisfaction with the Roman Catholic Church and a religious hunger not met by that branch of the faith as it existed in the Philippines, and partly because of the zeal of the missionaries.[30] Whereas in 1898 Protestantism had not been permitted in the islands, in 1921 it had 486 houses of worship, or more than a sixth as many as the Roman Catholic Church,[31] and about the year 1914 it counted 204 missionaries and 46,444 communicants.[32]

As early as 1838 the British and Foreign Bible Society made grants for the distribution of the Bible in Manila.[33] In the 1880's portions of the New Testa-

[27] Keesing, *Taming Philippine Headhunters*, p. 81.

[28] Keesing, *op. cit.*, pp. 81, 232.

[29] Keesing, *op. cit.*, p. 233.

[30] Brown, *The New Era in the Philippines*, pp. 210ff.

[31] *Census of the Philippine Islands, 1918*, Vol. IV, Part I, pp. 38, 39.

[32] Beach and St. John, *World Statistics of Christian Missions*, p. 67. Also on the progress of Protestantism see Brown, *op. cit.*, pp. 196-209, and Charles W. Briggs, *The Progressing Philippines* (Philadelphia, The Griffith and Rowland Press, 1913, pp. 174), pp. 139ff.

[33] Canton, *A History of the British and Foreign Bible Society*, Vol. II, p. 404.

ment translated into one of the Filipino vernaculars by a former Dominican, Lallave, were introduced to the islands, but attempts of agents of the Society to establish a continuing residence failed.[34] In 1898, however, translations into two others of the vernaculars of portions of the New Testament made in Europe by Filipinos, one of them Reyes, and printed in Madrid, were ready. After the American occupation they were quickly brought in. Representatives of the British and Foreign Bible Society were soon travelling widely through the islands. In 1900 the British and Foreign Bible Society and the American Bible Society divided the territory between them.[35] Translations were made into still other vernaculars. In 1919 the British society withdrew and left the territory to the American society.[36]

In 1898, only shortly after Commodore Dewey had won his famous victory over the Spanish fleet at Manila and before the formal annexation of the islands by the United States, at the instance of the Presbyterians a conference of several of the Protestant mission boards was convened in New York City which laid down the principle that American societies should enter the Philippines and that the territory should be divided between them to prevent duplication of effort.[37] So nearly simultaneously that a pleasant dispute arose as to which had first arrived, the Northern Methodists and the Northern Presbyterians sent representatives to survey the situation. The latter had a temporary agent there in December, 1898. The former could point to Bishop Thoburn, who made an official visit to the islands in March, 1899.[38] Neither lost any time in taking advantage of the doors so unexpectedly opened. Both denominations built up large enterprises. Notable was Silliman Institute, a college, later a university, developed by the Presbyterians at Dumaguete, on the Island of Negros.[39]

Other American denominations quickly followed. In 1900 came the Northern Baptists, with Eric Lund, who had been in charge of their mission in Barcelona, as their pioneer. He was accompanied by a Filipino who, as a student of engineering, had been one of his converts in Spain.[40] In 1901 the United

---

[34] Canton, *op. cit.,* Vol. V, pp. 150, 151; H. W. Munger in *Missions,* Vol. XXIV, pp. 147-150; Stuntz, *op cit.,* pp. 395, 396.

[35] Canton, *op. cit.,* Vol. V, pp. 147-150, 154-158; Dwight, *Centennial History of the American Bible Society,* Vol. II, pp. 503-511; Stuntz, *op. cit.,* pp. 397ff.

[36] Ryan, *Religious Education in the Philippines,* p. 59.

[37] Brown, *One Hundred Years,* pp. 861-864.

[38] Rodgers, *Forty Years in the Philippines,* p. 2; Ryan, *Religious Education in the Philippines,* pp. 47-52; Osias and Lorenzana, *op. cit.,* p. 83; Stuntz, *op. cit.,* pp. 420ff.

[39] Rodgers, *op. cit.,* pp. 74ff.

[40] H. W. Munger in *The Chronicle,* Vol. I, p. 167; John Marvin Dean, *The Cross of Christ in Bolo-Land* (New York, Fleming H. Revell Co., 1902, pp. 233), pp. 112ff.

Brethren in Christ arrived. They organized their first church in 1904.[41] In 1901 came also the first missionaries of the Disciples of Christ.[42] The Protestant Episcopal Church early took steps to enter the Philippines. In 1899 its Brotherhood of St. Andrew sent some of its members to co-operate with the army chaplains in religious and social work among the American troops. In 1901 Charles H. Brent was elected bishop of the newly formed missionary district which embraced the islands. Brent proved to be a man of devotion, wide vision, and abounding energy. He felt that his church should not seek to win converts from among the Roman Catholic population, for this seemed to him to have an unsavoury smack of proselytism from a sister communion. However, in Manila he built an imposing cathedral, carried on religious activities for the American population, and inaugurated efforts for the Chinese and a hospital and orphanage. He also saw that missions were begun for the Moslem Moros and for the pagan Igorots.[43] In 1902 the American Board of Commissioners for Foreign Missions sent its first missionary to the Philippines. He established a centre at Davao, on the Island of Mindanao.[44] In 1902 the Christian and Missionary Alliance came. Its headquarters were in Zamboanga in Mindanao.[45] In the first decade of the twentieth century the Seventh Day Adventists included the Philippines in their widely flung fields.[46]

To these denominations were added other movements. That characteristic feature of nineteenth-century American Protestantism, the Sunday school, flourished. The first one was organized in 1900 and a Sunday School Union for the islands was formed in 1911.[47] The Young Men's Christian Association made its first contacts through the American army and navy. Later it developed units in Manila and in several smaller centres.[48]

From the very beginning, Protestants, confronted with a united Roman Catholic Church and entering almost simultaneously through several denominations, began machinery for co-operation. In 1900 the Ministerial Alliance

---

[41] Drury, *History of the Church of the United Brethren in Christ*, pp. 608-610; Laubach, *op. cit.*, p. 190.

[42] *Survey of Service . . . Disciples of Christ*, pp. 425ff.; Laubach, *op. cit.*, p. 191.

[43] *Handbooks on the Missions of the Episcopal Church. No. III. Philippine Islands* (New York, The National Council of the Protestant Episcopal Church, 1923, pp. 58), *passim;* Eleanor Slater, *Charles Henry Brent. Everybody's Bishop* (Milwaukee, Morehouse Publishing Co., 1932, pp. viii, 128), pp. 19-30.

[44] *The Ninety-third Annual Report of the American Board of Commissioners for Foreign Missions, 1903*, p. 132; *The Ninety-Fourth Annual Report of the American Board of Commissioners for Foreign Missions, 1904*, p. 131.

[45] Beach and St. John, *op. cit.*, p. 67; Laubach, *op. cit.*, p. 193.

[46] Gates, *In Coral Isles*, pp. 245ff.; Laubach, *op. cit.*, p. 194.

[47] Ryan, *op. cit.*, pp. 67, 68.

[48] *International Survey of the Young Men's and Young Women's Christian Associations*, p. 318.

was formed. In 1901 the Evangelical Union of the Philippine Islands was constituted by representatives of six organizations. It early suggested a division of territory among the member denominations.[49] It also furthered joint action in other undertakings. In 1907 the Union Theological Seminary was inaugurated in Manila by the Presbyterians and Methodists. Later at least three other denominations assisted it.[50]

Filipino nationalism, so marked in politics and in the Roman Catholic Church, affected Protestantism. Before 1914 several congregations hived off from the mother bodies· In 1909, for instance, Nicolas Zamora, the first Filipino ordained by the Protestants, led in the formation of the Methodist Evangelical Church of the Philippines.[51]

Threatened by nationalistic schisms, by the dissolution of the tie between Church and state, by the expulsion of some of the friars,[52] and by Protestantism, the Roman Catholic Church took vigorous steps to retain the hold which long endeavour had given it in the Philippines. Rome led the way and placed the islands under the supervision of a newly created Apostolic Delegation. A little later, in 1910, four new bishoprics were created.[53] The purchase by the civil government in 1903 of over 410,000 acres of the frairs' lands[54] provided the orders with large funds and diverted from them some of the antagonism which had been engendered by their landlordism. As a result of the visit to Rome in 1902 of William Howard Taft on behalf of the United States, the Vatican agreed to replace some of the Spanish bishops by Americans and not to send back to the Philippines friars who were obnoxious to their flocks. The number of friars in 1903 was only 246 as against more than 1,000 in 1898.[55] This gave opportunity for the Roman Catholic Church to introduce fresh blood into its clergy. American Archbishops of Manila were appointed. Several Filipino priests were raised to the episcopate, in part meeting the demands for a national clergy which had contributed to the schisms.[56] Some of the bishops in the United States made room for Filipinos in their diocesan seminaries, and thus in time returned to the islands native-born clergy who had become acquainted with English and with the American spirit.[57] Numbers of American priests came directly from the United States. Among these, however, were

[49] Laubach, op. cit., pp. 203, 204; Rodgers, op. cit., pp. 162ff.
[50] Osias and Lorenzana, op. cit., p. 154; Rodgers, op. cit., p. 166; Ryan, op. cit., p. 60.
[51] Rodgers, op. cit., p. 176.
[52] For some of the losses see Cartas Edificantes de los Misioneros de la Compañia de Jesús en Filipinas, 1898-1902, pp. 17ff., recounting Jesuit reverses in Mindanao.
[53] Schwager in Zeitschrift für Missionswissenschaft, Vol. IV, pp. 212, 213.
[54] Forbes, The Philippine Islands, Vol. II, pp. 57, 58.
[55] Forbes, op. cit., Vol. II, p. 60.
[56] Forbes, op. cit., Vol. II, p. 64.
[57] Schwager in Zeitschrift für Missionswissenschaft, Vol. IV, p. 216.

those who found the adjustments too difficult and went back home.[58] The Roman Catholic Church in the United States, its capacities strained by the task of caring for the mounting flood of immigration from Europe, had little energy to spare for this new American possession. Once order was restored by the new regime, numbers of Spanish regulars and lay brothers flocked to the islands, recruiting the diminished ranks of the old orders and making possible the reoccupation of some of the lost territory.[59] Several new, non-Spanish orders sent representatives from Europe. The Mill Hill Fathers, especially Dutch and Tyrolese, came in 1906 and performed a notable service in pushing forward the frontiers of Christianity among the Igorots.[60] Scheutvelders, members of the Congregation of the Immaculate Heart of Mary, mainly Dutch and Belgians, in 1907 began arriving in Northern Luzon and within a few years established a number of stations.[61] Dutch Missionaries of the Holy Heart of Jesus entered in 1908.[62] In 1909 came the Society of the Divine Word. In its field in Northern Luzon it not only cared for the Christians, but also carried on missions for the pagans.[63] Many of the Roman Catholic schools reorganized their courses of study and introduced the teaching of English.[64] The ancient University of Santo Tomás, maintained by the Dominicans, added courses in dentistry and civil engineering and a school of medicine.[65] Additional schools, well housed and equipped, were opened in Manila and the provinces.[66] Money was coming from the United States and Europe to assist the new enterprises.[67] The Roman Catholic Church was recovering from the blows dealt it during the transition to the new order and was here and there registering fresh gains. It had not suffered so severely as it had in Latin America in the upheavals that ushered in the nineteenth century.

The Spanish colonial period which had begun in the sixteenth century con-

---

[58] Schwager in *op. cit.*, Vol. IV, p. 214.

[59] *Ibid.; Cartas Edificantes de los Misioneros de la Compañia de Jesús en Filipinas, 1898-1902*, pp. 169ff.

[60] Schwager in *Zeitschrift für Missionswissenschaft*, Vol. IV, p. 215; Berg, *Die katholische Heidenmission als Kulturträger*, Vol. I, p. 225.

[61] Keesing, *Taming Philippine Headhunters*, p. 82; Schwager in *Zeitschrift für Missionswissenschaft*, Vol. IV, p. 225.

[62] Schwager in *op. cit.*, Vol. IV, p. 215.

[63] Joh. Tauren, *Die Missionen der Gesellschaft des Göttl. Wortes in den Heidenländern. Die Missionen auf den Philippinen* (Post Kaldenkirchen, Missionsdruckerei Steyl, 1931, pp. 29), pp. 12ff.; Hagspiel, *Along the Mission Trail*, Vol. I, pp. 120ff.

[64] Alzona, *A History of Education in the Philippines, 1565-1930*, p. 342.

[65] *Los Dominicos en el Extremo Oriente*, p. 66.

[66] Alzona, *op. cit.*, p. 342.

[67] Schwager in *Zeitschrift für Missionswissenschaft*, Vol. IV, pp. 219, 220.

tinued but little altered until 1898. The long, latterly somnolent rule of Spain in the Philippines was not without lasting results. Under the relatively mild and benevolent Spanish sway, Roman Catholic Christianity had become the faith of the large majority. This majority, although still divided in language, had begun to be welded into a nation with a cultural bond whose origin was European and Christian. It was upon the foundations laid by Spain and the Roman Catholic Church that the twentieth century structure of the Philippine Commonwealth was built. Without them the American achievements would have been impossible.

In the brief sixteen years between 1898 and 1914, the end of the period covered in this volume, revolutionary changes were wrought. The coming of the United States swept the Filipinos into mid-current in the stream of nineteenth-century life. Democratic ideals were inculcated and democratic institutions were set up. A state system of secular education was introduced. Religious toleration was instituted.

The religious life of the islands could not but be affected by the new day. The first result was the weakening of Roman Catholic Christianity by revolts against the Spanish friars and by the appearance of extensive nationalistic schisms and of Protestantism. By the year 1914, however, the position of Christianity in the islands was strengthened rather than weakened. The schismatic movements, enfeebled though they were by the lack of adequate leadership, helped to make Christianity a more conscious possession of the Filipinos and a more integral part of their new national life than would probably otherwise have been the case. A virile Protestantism introduced by the vigorous churches of the United States both added variety and enhanced the vitality of the Christianity of the islands. The Roman Catholic Church, aroused by these defections and this competition from a torpor which was compounded of a decadent Spanish Roman Catholicism and a tropical environment, began to show new life. Reinforcements from the more energetic churches of Belgium, Holland, Germany, and the United States brought fresh blood. New methods were adopted and progress was registered against old abuses. Both Protestants and Roman Catholics not only raised the level of the religious and moral life of the professedly Christian community, but also won fresh converts from the non-Christian minorities. In general the opening years of the twentieth century witnessed a striking advance in Filipino Christianity.

Chapter IX

THE EAST INDIES (THE DUTCH, PORTUGUESE, AND BRITISH POSSESSIONS)

FROM the Philippines it is but an easy step to the East Indies, or, as they are also known, the Malay Archipelago. Indeed, the two groups really belong together. Physically they are one in being the fringing islands of Southeastern Asia. Racially they have much in common. The distinction between them arises partly from the political division brought by European imperialism. The Philippines were a Spanish possession which passed into the hands of the United States. The East Indies became predominantly Dutch in ownership with a small remnant of the once extensive Portuguese dominion and with larger fragments acquired in the nineteenth century by the British and the Germans. Moreover, the East Indies have close connexions with the islands of the Pacific with which we dealt in the chapter before the last.

The East Indies cover a vast area and embrace a wide variety of peoples, languages, and cultures.[1] From east to west they stretch across more than 3,000 miles, or a distance not far from the width of the continent of North America. From north to south they extend over approximately 1,500 miles. They embrace the huge islands of New Guinea, Borneo, and Sumatra, islands of medium size such as Java and Celebes, and many smaller ones. In the period with which we here have to do, the population was predominantly Papuan and Malay, but these stocks were divided into many tribes and peoples. To them were added smaller contingents of Arabs, Indians, Chinese, and Europeans. In the course of the nineteenth century the population increased. By 1914 it was more than 40,000,000. About three-fourths of this was on Java and its smaller neighbour, Madura. The East Indies had received successive waves of culture from Asia and Europe and included peoples of advanced civilization and of primitive cultures. Religiously it was divided. Java was overwhelmingly Moslem, the result of contact with Arab Moslem traders before

[1] Excellent brief descriptive surveys are in a set of handbooks prepared under the direction of the Historical Section of the (British) Foreign Office and published in London by H. M. Stationery Office in 1920. These include the titles *Dutch Borneo, Dutch Timor and the Lesser Sunda Islands, Java and Madura, Dutch New Guinea and the Molucca Islands, Celebes, Sumatra,* and *Portuguese Timor.*

the Portuguese and Dutch eras. Islam was also strongly represented on other islands, notably in Sumatra, Borneo, and Celebes. In Java Islam overlaid earlier strata of animism, Hinduism, and Buddhism. Hinduism survived on the island of Bali, immediately to the east of Java, and among a small minority in Java. The hundreds of thousands of primitive folk were chiefly animists.

By the year 1914 the larger part of the East Indies had been brought under Dutch control. The Dutch had entered at the close of the sixteenth century. In the seventeenth century they greatly reduced but did not entirely eliminate the Portuguese holdings and made themselves dominant in the archipelago. In the latter part of the eighteenth century their power declined. In 1798 the East India Company, through which they had administered the islands, was abolished and a new form of supervision was devised. During the Napoleonic Wars the British took over the Dutch possessions. After the coming of peace the ownership was restored to the Netherlands. In the second half of the nineteenth century and the fore part of the twentieth century the Dutch greatly extended their rule. By 1914 they were masters of all but the eastern half of Timor, which was what remained of the once extensive Portuguese domains, the eastern part of New Guinea, which was divided between the British and the Germans, and portions of the northern sections of Borneo, which were parts of the British Empire.

Most of the gains achieved by Christianity in the East Indies were among primitive peoples of animistic faith. These folk were in the minority. From the Moslem majority and the diminished Hindu enclaves very few converts were made. In the animistic tribes there was a race between Islam and Christianity. Sometimes the advance of Islam was more rapid than was that of Christianity.

We turn first to the spread of Christianity in the Dutch East Indies. To this we must give the largest part of this chapter. We will then speak briefly of Portuguese Timor and finally of the British portions of Borneo. British and German New Guinea we covered in the chapter before last.

As we have seen in an earlier volume,[2] Christianity was introduced to the East Indies in the sixteenth century by the Spaniards and the Portuguese. This was in its Roman Catholic form. With the establishment of Dutch rule came the prevailing faith of the new masters, Calvinistic Protestantism. Ministers and their assistants were supported by the East India Company with the active interest of the churches of the Netherlands. As a result, a state church arose which by the year 1800 had a membership of between 65,000 and 200,000, chiefly in Amboina, Ceram, the Banda Islands, Timor, Talaud, Sangi, Roti, and Batavia.

[2] Vol. III, chap. 11.

In the nineteenth century, as was to be expected in colonies of a country which had achieved its independence under that banner, the form of Christianity propagated was chiefly Protestantism. Eventually Roman Catholic missionaries were permitted. The majority of the missionaries, both Protestant and Roman Catholic, were Dutch. It was upon this greatest of the Dutch colonial possessions that Dutch Christians concentrated most of their foreign missionary efforts. Yet there were in addition extensive German missions. There were also missions, although much less prominent, from Great Britain and the United States.

During much of the nineteenth century, especially in the first half, the attempts to spread Christianity encountered serious handicaps at the hands of the state. The colonial administration was bent upon making the East Indies financially profitable to the Dutch. A policy of exploitation of the natives was adopted. From the fear of arousing Moslem opposition and so of jeopardizing Dutch incomes, the East Indian Government was neutral religiously and at times almost hostile to Christianity.[3] It even impounded a Javanese translation of the New Testament to prevent its distribution.[4] In 1838 when a Javanese desired baptism, for five years the government opposed objections.[5]

However, the existing Christian communities persisted and beginnings were made of fresh enterprises. The colonial administration maintained the policy of its predecessor, the East India Company, and paid the salaries of the clergy. In other words, there continued to be a state church. Early in the nineteenth century King William I, in an attempt to strengthen Holland after the weaknesses brought by the Napoleonic Wars, sought to bring all of his Protestant subjects into one ecclesiastical body. In the mother country he did not succeed, but his wishes were carried out in the colonies. In 1820 a royal decree declared that all the Protestant churches in the East Indies should be merged. In that year a Commission for the Affairs of the Protestant Churches in the Netherlands East and West Indies was set up at the Hague of which the majority were clergy in active service. It had the power to examine and ordain missionaries and teachers of religion for the Indies. In Batavia there was a council of clergymen and officials who advised the Governor-General in ecclesiastical affairs. Not until 1854 was the actual union consummated in the East Indies. That year the Lutheran Church in Batavia united with the Reformed Church. Each Protestant in the East Indies was supposed to be a member of

---

[3] On the history of the government permits for missionaries in the first half of the nineteenth century and the changes which came later, see Franken-van Driel, *Regeering en Zending in Nederlandsch-Indië*, pp. 46ff.

[4] Vandenbosch, *The Dutch East Indies*, pp. 196, 232, 233.

[5] Vandenbosch in *The International Review of Missions*, Vol. XXIII, p. 210.

the united state church.[6] However, this Indian Church was not very aggressive in propagating its faith among non-Christians. The paternalistic support and direction by the East India Company, followed, in the nineteenth century, by a similar connexion with the colonial government, kept it from having much initiative of its own. In this it was not unlike the Roman Catholic churches which had arisen in Latin America under the patronage of the Spanish and Portuguese Crowns. It was mainly through representatives of missionary societies of the Occident that fresh conversions were made.

The chief channel of new religious life in the early years of the nineteenth century was the Netherlands Missionary Society. Formed in 1797 in part through impulses issuing from the London Missionary Society, it was, like its British prototype, meant to be representative of no one denomination. Most of its founders were clergymen of the Dutch Reformed Church. It maintained friendly relations with that body and found in it most of its constituency, but it remained independent.[7] The majority of its missionaries were Dutch, but a number were of German birth.[8] Some were trained in its own school in Holland, some were from Jänicke's school in Berlin, and still others from the famous missionary institution in Basel.[9] Many of its missionaries were appointed by the colonial government to positions in the state church. In connexion with these relationships, misunderstandings and friction with the government frequently arose, partly because much of the time the situation was not regularized by precise agreement between the state and the society.[10] In spite of these difficulties, the Netherlands Missionary Society helped to provide spiritual oversight for the Christian communities which had arisen in the pre-nineteenth century era. Its agents also pushed forward the frontiers of Christianity among non-Christian tribes. This they did especially in the Moluccas, Timor, and the South-west Islands. Famous among the missionaries of the first half of the nineteenth century was Joseph Carel Kam, who arrived in 1815 and laboured until his death in 1833. He was known as a man with a burning heart and as "the apostle to the Moluccas." He travelled widely, was a great organizer, and urged upon the society the sending of more missionaries.[11] He baptized scores of Moslems and pagans. Notable also was the progress

[6] Vandenbosch, *op. cit.*, p. 228; Richter, *Die evangelische Mission in Nederlandisch-Indien*, p. 19.

[7] Rauws *et alii*, *The Netherlands Indies*, pp. 45-49.

[8] See the list of missionaries of the first hundred years of the society in *Gedenkboek uitgegeven ter Gelegenheid van het Honderjarig Bestaan van het Nederlandsche Zendelinggenootschap* (Rotterdam, M. Wyt & Zonen, 1897, pp. 197, iii), pp. 37ff.

[9] Richter, *op. cit.*, p. 21.

[10] Rauws, *op. cit.*, pp. 51-53.

[11] Rauws, *op. cit.*, p. 51; Richter, *op. cit.*, p. 23; Dijkstra, *Het Evangelie in Onze Oost*, pp. 68-71; Kruijf, *Geschiedenis van het Nederlandsche Zendelinggenootschap*, pp. 104-106.

achieved among the pagan peoples in Minahassa, the north-eastern peninsula of the island of Celebes. The region became famous for its coffee and spices. Its native population was intelligent and lighter-hued than most of its neighbours. Here missionaries of the society entered in 1822 and found only a few hundred Christians. By 1870, or in slightly less than half a century, efforts had so far borne fruit that the region could be called a Christian country. Two missionaries whose terms of service spanned more than half of this period were Johann Friedrich Riedel and Johann Gottlieb Schwartz, both of them from Jänicke's school.[12] Many of the congregations which arose from the efforts of the missionaries in Amboina, Minahassa, and the South-west Islands were incorporated into the Indian Church.[13] The Netherlands Missionary Society was adding to the Christian nuclei created in the preceding period.[14]

The first half of the nineteenth century saw, in addition to the growing and fairly extensive enterprise of the Netherlands Missionary Society, a number of efforts, most of them fleeting, of British and American missionaries. During the British occupation, the English Baptists began missions in Amboina, manned by Jabez Carey, a son of William Carey, and in Java and Sumatra. The one on Amboina did not long continue, but those in Java and Sumatra persisted until the middle of the century.[15] In 1814 the London Missionary Society helped make possible the arrival in Java of Kam and two other agents of the Netherlands Missionary Society.[16] In the days before 1842 when China was still closed to the residence of all but a few of the Protestant missionaries, Medhurst, of the London Missionary Society, two representatives of the Protestant Episcopal Church, and a woman who was independent of any mission board came to Batavia and there for longer or shorter periods laboured among the Chinese who were to be found in that port.[17] In 1833 two representatives of the American Board of Commissioners for Foreign

[12] Richter, *op. cit.*, pp. 25-27; Kruijf, *op. cit.*, pp. 295ff.; N. Grundemann, *Johann Friedrich Riedel, ein Lebensbild aus der Minahassa auf Celebes* (Gütersloh, C. Bertelsmann, 1873, pp. 285), *passim*.

[13] Rauws, *op. cit.*, pp. 53, 54.

[14] For a survey of the Dutch East Indies at the middle of the nineteenth century, showing the status of Christianity and especially of the activities of the Netherlands Missionary Society, see L. J. van Rhijn, *Reis door den Indischen Archipel in het Belang der Evangelische Zending* (Rotterdam, M. Wijt & Zonen, 1851, pp. xx, 655, 28), *passim*.

[15] Pearce Carey, *William Carey* (New York, George H. Doran Co., 1923, pp. xvi, 428), pp. 299-306; *Periodical Accounts Relative to the Baptist Missionary Society*, Vol. V (1813), pp. 140, 384, Vol. VI, pp. 318, 319; *Annual Report of the Committee of the Baptist Missionary Society*, 1819, p. 23, 1822, pp. 17, 18, 1839, p. 23, 1840, p. 23. Mention of these missions last appears in the report for 1849.

[16] Lovett, *The History of the London Missionary Society*, Vol. I, p. 105.

[17] Kenneth Scott Latourette, *A History of Christian Missions in China* (New York, The Macmillan Co., 1929, pp. xii, 930), pp. 213, 220, 225, 252.

Missions, Samuel Munson and Henry Lyman, arrived in Batavia, the one to study Chinese and the other Malay. The following year, while seeking to penetrate the interior of Sumatra, they were killed and eaten by Bataks.[18] The tragedy was penitently remembered by the Bataks when in after years many of them became Christians.[19] Later attempts in that same decade by the American Board to found a mission in the East Indies did not have enduring success.[20]

The initial half of the nineteenth century also witnessed the beginnings of German missions. In 1835, through a suggestion which originated with Medhurst, the Rhenish Missionary Society sent several missionaries to Banjermasin, in the south-eastern part of Borneo. Efforts were made to win the Dayaks, but only a few converts had been made, and those chiefly among slaves who had lost their freedom through debt and had been bought by the missionaries and used as servants, when in 1859 an uprising cost the lives of several of the missionary staff.[21]

In the second half of the century and in the first decade and a half of the twentieth century a marked expansion occurred in missionary efforts. This paralleled the growth which characterized the history of Christianity in many other parts of the world.

Here, too, as in so much else of the contemporary world, augmented missionary activity went almost *pari passu* with an increase in the territory controlled by the overlords from the Occident and with a growing humanitarianism which insisted that the white man's rule must be for the benefit of the coloured races. By 1914 the Dutch had greatly enlarged the areas under their flag. Between 1848 and 1870 a rising tide of sentiment in Holland brought to an end the forced "culture system" by which the natives had been required to till the soil in a fashion which had resulted in ruthless exploitation for the benefit of the Netherlands. This reform was due to a variety of factors, not all of them religious or even moral. However, a leader in the fight for a lightening of the burdens of the East Indians was W. R. Baron van Hoevell, who had been a preacher in Batavia. Forced out of his post by his advocacy of reform, he returned home, obtained election to the States General, and from that vantage demanded that colonial policy should have as its cornerstone not profit

---

[18] Strong, *The Story of the American Board*, pp. 116-118; Wm. Thompson, *Memoirs of the Rev. Samuel Munson and the Rev. Henry Lyman, Late Missionaries to the Indian Archipelago, with a Journal of Their Exploring Tour* (New York, D. Appleton & Co., 1839, pp. 196), *passim; The Martyr of Sumatra: A Memoir of Henry Lyman* (New York, Robert Carter & Brothers, 1861, pp. 437), *passim.*

[19] Warneck, *50 Jahre Batakmission in Sumatra*, p. 17.

[20] Strong, *op. cit.*, p. 118.

[21] Bonn, *Ein Jahrhundert Rheinische Mission*, p. 43.

for the Dutch but the material and intellectual welfare of the Indies.[22] In the later decades of the nineteenth century Christian parties (both Protestant and Roman Catholic) grew in political power. In 1890 they gained control of the government and after a long fight obtained the subsidization of private schools, which included those maintained by missions.[23] In 1901 a coalition of these parties formed a ministry under Abraham Kuyper, a man of striking versatility and energy. They insisted upon what was known as the "ethical policy," that, as was said in the speech from the throne in 1901, "as a Christian power the Netherlands" was under obligation to better the position of native Christians, to support Christian missions, and to imbue the whole conduct of the colonial government with the consciousness that the Netherlands had a moral duty to the peoples of the archipelago. Under the impulse of this policy Dutch administration was extended over some of the native states where the regime was said to be bad, more tasks were undertaken for the benefit of the Indonesians, education was fostered, measures which had as their object the promotion of the economic welfare of islanders were inaugurated, steps were taken towards the development of democratic institutions, careful studies were made of the economic life of Java and Madura, and the expert knowledge of specialists was applied to the conservation of native life and customs and the assimilation of Western innovations in ways which would bring as little as possible of violent deracination.[24] As part of the change of policy in favour of Christian missions, in 1890 the provision which had hitherto prevailed that schools subsidized by the government could give no religious instruction was repealed. As a result mission schools multiplied.[25] Christians were trying, with some degree of success, to constrain the government to afford greater opportunity for missionaries and to apply to colonial administration the principles of their faith.

The movement was akin to the contemporary one in the British Empire which idealized the rule of non-Europeans by Europeans as "the white man's burden" and to the similar one in the United States which regarded the Philippines as a trust to be administered in behalf of the material and spiritual welfare of the Filipinos.

The increase in the influence of Christianity in Dutch colonial policy came in large part out of religious revivals in the Netherlands which began in the

---

[22] Vandenbosch, *The Dutch East Indies*, pp. 48-50.

[23] Vandenbosch, *op. cit.*, p. 196. On the history of government subsidies to mission schools, see Franken-van Driel, *Regeering en Zending in Nederlandsch-Indië*, pp. 3-38.

[24] Vandenbosch, *op. cit.*, pp. 52-54; Schrieke, *The Effect of Western Influence on Native Civilization in the Malay Archipelago*, pp. 44, 45.

[25] Vandenbosch, *op. cit.*, p. 235.

1830's. These had their rise among the lower classes but spread rapidly, acquired leaders of marked intellectual vigour, and in political life gave birth to parties representing the convictions which they proclaimed.[26] In their nature and effect they were counterparts of the awakenings which in Great Britain had brought about the abolition of slavery in the Empire and were contributing to a greater benevolence in British colonial policy and which in the United States were issuing in anti-slavery and other reform movements. Roman Catholics were also increasing in number in Holland and were forming a Catholic party which on occasion entered into coalition with the Protestant ones.

The revivals which augmented the impact of Christianity upon colonial administration also contributed to new missionary societies. The increase in religious conviction brought religious controversy. To many the Netherlands Missionary Society with its inclusive and tolerant attitude towards sectarian differences seemed over-lax. The rise of the middle class and its demands for a larger voice in church affairs contributed to divisions. Moreover, the currents of liberal thought then flowing in Protestantism were felt in Holland and helped to accentuate the differences between those affected by them and those touched by the revivals. Pietistic and revivalistic strains, while distrustful of the new liberalism, were in turn looked upon askance by many of the theologically conservative. The result was both an augmentation and a division of the missionary forces.[27] The Netherlands Missionary Society continued, but a number of other organizations appeared.

A brief summary of the new societies which arose out of the complex religious movements in Holland should help to make clear both the variety of channels through which Protestant Christianity penetrated to the East Indies and the vigour of the movements through which they came into being. In 1864 many of the orthodox, impatient and distressed over the refusal of the Netherlands Missionary Society to take a clear-cut stand in favour of their doctrinal position, withdrew from that body and associated themselves with other missionary organizations.[28] While many of the Mennonites co-operated with the Netherlands Missionary Society, others founded, in 1847, the Mennonite Missionary Union (*Doobsgezinde Zendingsvereeniging*). Part of the support of the new body was derived from Mennonites in Germany and the Ukraine. From Germany and the Ukraine came missionaries. Being farmers, when they reached Java they employed agriculture as an avenue for mission

[26] Vandenbosch in *The International Review of Missions*, Vol. XXIII, p. 211.

[27] Rauws *et alii*, *The Netherlands Indies*, pp. 56-58; Richter, *Die evangelische Mission in Niederländisch-Indien*, pp. 38, 39.

[28] Rauws, *op. cit.*, p. 58.

work.[29] In 1847 there was also formed, at Hemmen, the Association of Christian Workmen (*De Christen Werkman*). It had as its purpose the sending of laymen who would make their living in trade, the handicrafts, or industry, and by word and example would aid in the propagation of their faith. It obtained some recruits through Gossner, of Germany, whose missionary society had ideals not uncongenial to those of the Dutch group. By the year 1858 about fifty were sent to the Indies, but the movement dwindled. Numbers of those commissioned met an early death through the unfavourable climate.[30] Many of those dispatched by the Association of Christian Workmen became affiliated with the Society for Home and Foreign Missions (*Genootschap voor in-en uitwendige Zending*), which was organized in 1851 in Batavia and which displayed much zeal in distributing Christian literature and in training as clergymen, colporteurs, and evangelists those who had been born in the Indies.[31] One of those associated with the latter body was F. L. Anthing, who gathered a staff of natives for evangelistic efforts.[32] In 1850 a religious awakening broke out in Ermelo, in Holland, and its leader, H. W. Witteveen, founded an independent missionary society which sent several men to the East Indies. However, the Ermelo movement did not have a long organized existence and the missions which it established passed into the hands of other societies.[33] In the 1850's a congregation arose in Java in the country house of Mrs. Le Jolle, later Mrs. van Vollenhoven. Out of this came the Salatiga Mission in Central Java. A society to help support it was organized in Utrecht.[34] The Neukirchen Mission, founded in 1882, in the Rhineland in Germany, formed a connexion with the Salatiga enterprise, and in this was aided by Dutch friends through the Salatiga Committee.[35] In 1855 the Java Committee (*Het Java Comité*) was born out of a missionary address in Amsterdam on Java. Gradually it grew, sending out and supporting missionaries.[36] The Netherlands Missionary Union (*Nederlandsche Zendings-Vereeniging*) came into being in 1858 among some who felt the Netherlands Missionary Society was too inclusive and hence too lax. It excluded from membership all who did not believe in the divinity of Christ.

[29] Boissevain, *De Zending in Oost en West*, pp. 173ff.; Rauws, *op. cit.*, p. 61; Nederlandschen Studenten Zendings-Bond, *Hedendaagsche Zending in Onze Oost*, pp. 81ff.

[30] Rauws, *op. cit.*, pp. 61-63; Dijkstra, *Het Evangelie in Onze Oost*, Vol. I, p. 163; Richter, *op. cit.*, p. 45.

[31] Rauws, *op. cit.*, pp. 63, 64; Richter, *op. cit.*, p. 45.

[32] Richter, *op. cit.*, p. 45.

[33] Dijkstra, *op. cit.*, Vol. I, pp. 164, 165; Rauws, *op. cit.*, p. 64.

[34] Rauws, *op. cit.*, pp. 64, 65; Nederlandschen Studenten Zendings-Bond, *op. cit.*, pp. 95ff.; Kühnen in Boissevain, *op. cit.*, pp. 182ff.

[35] Rauws, *op. cit.*, p. 125.

[36] Rauws, *op. cit.*, p. 65; Nederlandschen Studenten Zendings-Bond, *op. cit.*, pp. 109ff.; Duijker in Boissevain, *op. cit.*, pp. 201ff.

At first distrusted for its democratic and non-ecclesiastical leanings and the association of its founder with the Plymouth Brethren, it soon affiliated itself with the Dutch Reformed Church and became an organ of the theologically conservative elements of that body. Until 1913 its only field of operation in the East Indies was in West Java.[37] In 1859 the Utrecht Missionary Union (*Utrechtsche Zendings-Vereeniging*) was organized, somewhat on the model of the Basel Mission, by laymen and clergymen who objected to the theological inclusiveness of the Netherlands Missionary Society on the one hand and to the non-ecclesiastical trends then seen in the Netherlands Missionary Union. In 1905 it united with the Netherlands Missionary Society in the training of its representatives. It operated in several islands of the East Indies.[38] In the year 1860 or 1861 the Dutch Reformed Missionary Union (*Nederlandsche Gereformeerde Zendingsvereeniging*) was constituted on the basis chiefly of the articles of the Dutch Reformed Church. Conservative theologically, it became connected with the Christian Reformed Church, which adhered to strict Calvinism.[39] In 1892 some of the members of the Christian Reformed Church withdrew and formed another body. In 1906 this organized a committee for foreign missions.[40] In 1887 there came into being the *Comité tot Voorziening in de Godsdienstige Behoeften van de Gevestigde Inlandsche Protestantsche Christengemeenten op de Sangi- en Talaud Eilanden*, or, to give it its abbreviated English name, the Sangi and Talaud Committee. Its purpose was to provide the government with personnel for the churches in the Sangi and Talaud Islands, just south of the Philippines. On it were represented the Netherlands Missionary Union and the Utrecht Missionary Union, and, later, the Netherlands Missionary Society.[41] This multiplicity of societies represented a complex and puzzling picture to those unfamiliar with the nineteenth-century religious history of Dutch Protestantism.

In addition to these bodies, others were brought into being for special purposes. The Netherlands Bible Society, organized in 1814, interested itself in the East Indies as well as in some other areas. It published translations of the Bible or parts of the Bible into the native languages and sent out specialists on language to make or revise them.[42] The *Centraal Comité Depok*, or Depok

[37] Rauws, *op. cit.*, p. 66; Dijkstra, *op. cit.*, Vol. I, pp. 165, 166; Nederlandschen Studenten Zendings-Bond, *op. cit.*, pp. 123ff.

[38] Rauws, *op. cit.*, p. 67; Dijkstra, *op. cit.*, Vol. I, pp. 166, 167; Nederlandschen Studenten Zendings-Bond, *op. cit.*, pp. 143ff.

[39] Rauws, *op. cit.*, p. 68; Dijkstra, *op. cit.*, Vol. I, pp. 167, 168, 170-172.

[40] Rauws, *op. cit.*, p. 70.

[41] Rauws, *op. cit.*, p. 69.

[42] Rauws, *op. cit.*, p. 73; Nederlandschen Studenten Zendings-Bond, *op. cit.*, pp. 221ff. See lists of the translations made by this and other agencies in Rauws, *op. cit.*, pp. 171-176.

Central Committee, had as an objective the establishment and maintenance of a seminary at Depok, near Batavia, opened in 1878, for the training of native evangelists. It also prepared teachers who could act as pastors.[43] In 1905 there was formed the Committee of Assistance for the Christian School for Daughters of the Javanese Nobility.[44] In 1881 an association arose for the support of a school for upper class girls of Minahassa.[45] In 1910 the Union for Christian Dutch Education for the Native Population in the Netherlands Indies (*Vereeniging voor Christelijk Hollandsch Onderwijs ten Behoeve van de Inlandsche Bevolking in Nederlandsch-Indië*) was inaugurated and assisted other societies in establishing schools-and obtaining teachers.[46] In the eighth decade of the nineteenth century Lutherans of Holland organized a society for home and foreign missions and a few years later began sending missionaries to the Batu Islands, off the west coast of Sumatra.[47] In 1884 an association was constituted to assist the Rhenish Missionary Society.[48]

The movement for co-operation which as the nineteenth century progressed became strong in Protestant circles had repercussions in Holland and the Netherlands Indies. In 1880 the first Netherlands Indies Mission Conference was held in the seminary at Depok and at a second conference, in 1881, the Netherlands Indies Missionary Alliance was called into existence.[49] In 1887 a General Mission Conference, for consultation between the societies, was convened in Holland and thereafter held annual meetings.[50] In 1906 what was known as the Missions Consulate was instituted in the Netherlands Indies, with the object of representing Protestant missions in that area in their relations with the state. In it joined nearly all the Protestant missionary bodies of the Indies.[51]

Numerous though the Dutch societies were, for the most part they sprang from the common background of Calvinism. Their differences arose in large degree from the varieties in the adherence to or departure from Calvinism in the Dutch churches. Most of the Protestantism propagated by the Dutch possessed striking family likenesses.

Although the majority of the Protestant organizations seeking to propagate Christianity in the Netherlands East Indies were Dutch, there were a few

[43] Rauws, *op. cit.*, p. 74.
[44] Parker, *Directory of World Missions*, p. 42.
[45] Parker, *op. cit.*, p. 45.
[46] *Ibid.*
[47] Parker, *op. cit.*, p. 44; Rauws, *op. cit.*, p. 69.
[48] Parker, *op. cit.*, p. 44.
[49] Rauws, *op. cit.*, p. 74.
[50] Rauws, *Overzicht van het Zendingswerk in Ned. Os-ten West-Indië*, p. 7.
[51] Baron van Boetzelaer van Dubbledam (the first missions consul), in *The International Review of Missions*, Vol. XXII, pp. 233ff.; Rauws, *op. cit.*, p. 9.

non-Dutch societies, some of them outstanding. The Rhenish Missionary Society continued and, as we shall see in a few moments, with phenomenal success. From the United States came the Methodist Episcopal Church. With the ambition to realize the dream of Wesley which made the world his parish, this his spiritual child was planting missions in many lands. As an expansion of its enterprise in India, in 1885 the Methodist Episcopal Church entered Singapore. From there it branched out into the Malay Peninsula and to the Philippines. It is not surprising that in the first decade of the twentieth century it placed representatives in Java and Sumatra.[52] Directed from its headquarters in London, in 1894 the Salvation Army made its debut in Java. It spread widely through the islands.[53] In 1899 came the ubiquitous Seventh Day Adventists, but it was not until 1906 that their first resident missionaries arrived.[54]

The activities of these various Protestant agencies were widespread. With devotion and courage, several missions addressed themselves to the Moslems who were in the overwhelming majority on the most populous of the islands, Java. Some missionaries were in Borneo, some in the Moluccas, some in Celebes, others in New Guinea, and still others in Sumatra and its adjacent islands. Numerically the most successful of the enterprises were among the animistic peoples.

The ecclesiastical body with the largest membership was the state church, the so-called Protestant Church in the Netherlands Indies.[55] It was the outgrowth of pre-nineteenth century efforts at conversion, of Dutch migration, and of nineteenth- and twentieth-century missions. In the reports of its numerical strength there was marked discrepancy. An account giving the totals in the year 1910 placed the native membership at 279,000.[56] One set of figures for about the year 1924 ascribed to it a baptized membership of 352,146.[57] A set of statistics for the year 1925 declared that European members, most of them Dutch, totalled 121,784 and that native-born members totalled 525,731.[58] Yet government figures for the year 1925 seem to say that the native members were 450,826,[59] and an account for 1930 placed the number of European mem-

[52] Nathalie Toms Means, *Malaysia Mosaic. A Story of Fifty Years of Methodism* (Singapore, The Methodist Book Room, 1935, pp. 145), pp. 15, 94, 117ff.; Elizabeth Harper Brooks, *Java and Its Challenge* (Pittsburgh, 1911, pp. 196, pp. 84ff.
[53] Rauws, *The Netherlands Indies*, pp. 128-130.
[54] Gates, *In Coral Isles*, pp. 225-243.
[55] See a geographic description in *Atlas der Protestantsche Kerk in Nederlandsch Oost-Indië* (Weltevreden, Java, Bestuur over de Protestantsche Kerken in Nederlandsch-Indië, 1925, pp. vi, 166), *passim*.
[56] Warneck, *Geschichte der protestantischen Missionen*, pp. 451, 453.
[57] Beach and Fahs, *World Missionary Atlas*, p. 101.
[58] Richter, *Die evangelische Mission in Niederlandisch-Indien*, p. 32.
[59] *Ibid*.

bers at about 100,000 and of native members at between 500,000 and 600,000.[60] Striking disagreement also existed over the number of communicants, for the first set of figures, 352,146, professed to include only those who fell in this category, and the second set declared that of the total of 647,515 Christians communicants were only 153,632. Slightly less than half of the non-European membership seems to have been in Minahassa, the fruits of the marked mass movement of the nineteenth century. Most of the others were in Celebes (aside from Minahassa), Amboina, Saparoea, Ceram, Ternate, Halmahera, Timor, and others of the Little Sunda Islands. A few thousand were in Sumatra. The majority of those in Java were Europeans or had come from other parts of the Netherlands Indies.[61] Many Eurasians, from the mixture of Dutch and native blood, were in the church. In Java, although that island was almost solidly Moslem, some converts had been gathered. The state church was, however, recruited chiefly from Europeans and former animists. It seemed to be largely passive, depending upon the government for its financial undergirding and upon Holland for its leadership. The lack of vitality was said to be due in part to the fact that so many members were officials, and hence transient, and in part to the large Eurasian contingent which looked to Europeans for leadership.[62] However, as we are to see in the seventh volume, after 1914 the state church gave indications of more vigorous life.

Next in numerical size to the state church were the bodies of Christians which arose out of the efforts of the Rhenish Missionary Society. These were mostly in Sumatra and its fringing islands and chiefly among the Bataks. The Bataks were a sturdy, active folk, related to the Malays, and living in the high interior of Sumatra where the altitude provided a less enervating environment than the lowlands. Away from the coast, they were relatively untouched by the Islam which had spread by the trade routes and as late as the middle of the nineteenth century, in spite of a beginning of penetration by Islam, they were still predominantly animists.[63] Before the year 1861 various efforts had been made to reach the Bataks, among them the one by Munson and Lyman which came to an early and tragic end. The Netherlands Bible Society sent Neubronner van der Tuuk to study the language and translate into it part of the Scriptures. So well did he do his work that his grammar, dictionary, and Biblical translations remained standard down into the twentieth century.[64] When, in 1859, Rhenish missionaries were driven out of Borneo by an uprising,

[60] Rauws, *Oversicht van het Zendingswerk in Ned. Oost- en West-Indië*, pp. 60-62.
[61] Richter, *op. cit.*, pp. 32, 33.
[62] Vandenbosch, *The Dutch East Indies*, p. 230.
[63] Richter, *op. cit.*, pp. 80-82.
[64] Richter, *op. cit.*, pp. 83, 84.

the news of this undertaking directed their attention to the Bataks. In 1861 the pioneers of the Rhenish Batak mission entered Sumatra. As was to be expected, the first years were ones of opposition and slow progress. Sometimes stations were burned. Islam offered competition. Not until 1890 did the government permit missionaries in all parts of the Batak territory. Eventually, however, the entire region was covered and more than a third of the Bataks became Christians. The fact that only one mission was in the area was of advantage. A comprehensive plan for reaching the Bataks was adopted with a programme and organization for touching the life of every church, school, Christian, and pupil. From the beginning, self-support was fostered in the churches. With the assistance of state subsidies, a system of schools was developed. The customary law of the Bataks, the *adat*, and the hereditary social structure were taken over where not obviously inconsistent with Christian principles. Thus the transition to Christianity was eased and brought about, so far as possible, in conformity with Batak traditions and with as little abrupt break with the past as was compatible with the ideals of the new religion. Bataks were trained to fill the posts of teacher-preacher, lay assistants or presbyters, and clergy. Christian colonies went out to other parts of Sumatra and became centres for the spread of the faith. Modern medicine was introduced. Over all the structure of the Batak Christian communities the missionaries exercised a paternalistic direction. In 1901 a missionary society was organized to carry the faith to Bataks who had migrated to the coastal cities of Java and Sumatra. At one time a native cult, Pormalim, arose which had the Ten Commandments and the Lord's Prayer, called Mary "God's wife," and through lustrations and a stupefying beverage sought to be sanctified. However, it did not long flourish. In many ways the picture resembled that in other animistic communities in the Pacific which had been won to the Christian faith.[65] By 1914 the churches

[65] Richter, *op. cit.*, pp. 84-99; Bonn, *Ein Jahrhundert Rheinische Mission*, pp. 51ff.; Spiecker, *Die Rheinische Mission auf Sumatra, Nias und den andern westlich von Sumatra gelegenen Inseln, passim;* Gottfried Simon, *Unter den Mohammedanern Sumatras* (Bethel bei Bielefeld, Anstalt Bethel, 1926, pp. 175), *passim;* Joh. Warneck, *Unsere batakschen Gehilfen, wie sie arbeiten und wie an ihnen gearbeitet wird* (Gütersloh, C. Bertelsmann, 1908, pp. 134), *passim;* J. Warneck, *Madju. Ein Gang durch die Batakmission* (Barmen, Missionshaus, 1928, pp. 61), *passim;* G. Warneck, *Nacht und Morgen auf Sumatra, oder Schilderungen und Erzählungen aus dem Heidenthum und der Mission unter den Battas* (Barmen, Missionshaus, 1872, pp. v, 150), *passim;* Joh. Warneck, *50 Jahre Batakmission in Sumatra* (Berlin, Martin Warneck, 2d ed., 1912, pp. 301), *passim;* H. Irle, *In Gottes Schule. Lebensbild einer Missionarin* (Barmen, Missionshaus, 2d ed., 1925, pp. 109), pp. 68ff.; J. Merle Davis, *The Batak Church* (Department of Social and Industrial Research of the International Missionary Council, 1938, pp. 32), *passim;* "God First," or *Hester Needham's Work in Sumatra. Her Letters and Diaries arranged by Mary Enfield* (London, The Religious Tract Society, 1899, pp. 320), *passim.* Materials from the Batak mission are included in Joh. Warneck, *The Living Christ and Dying*

connected with the Rhenish mission in Sumatra had a membership of 159,024, of whom 71,373, or nearly one-half, were communicants.[66] As among many other peoples of primitive culture, missionaries and the Church were the means of introducing the Bataks to an advanced civilization and of helping them to make a wholesome adjustment to the impact of the white man.

Notable among the Rhenish missionaries to the Bataks were Ludwig Ingwer Nommensen (1834-1918) and Johann Warneck. Born to poverty, from his boyhood Nommensen was inured to hardship and physical labour, admirable preparation for the pioneering which he was to do in Sumatra. He arrived in that island in 1862, the year after the inception of the mission. He became the mission's organizer and leader. A man of indomitable will, wise, far-seeing, a friend and a father to his people, he placed upon the nascent Christian community the stamp of his personality and his faith.[67] Johann Warneck, the son of the distinguished scholar in the field of missions, Gustav Warneck, came to Sumatra in 1892 and for a time was on the frontier. He returned to Germany in 1910, but in 1920 was back as head of the Batak enterprise.[68]

The island of Nias, off the west coast of Sumatra, also became the scene of a successful undertaking of the Rhenish society. In 1861, while waiting in one of the Sumatran ports for an opportunity to go inland, one of the refugees from the Borneo mission came in touch with some of the people of Nias who were there as labourers. In 1865 a residence was effected on Nias itself. For the first twenty-five years progress was slow, but the Bible was translated into the vernacular. Then the Dutch expanded their rule to include the entire island. With the extension of their authority Christianity also gained adherents.[69] In 1914 the Rhenish society counted 17,795 members on the island.[70] Eventually about half the population was Christian.[71] As among the Bataks, a church identified with the life of one people came into being, for the Christians were of one folk and were under one mission.

The Rhenish missionaries also undertook to reach other islands off the west coast of Sumatra, the Batu and Mentawei groups and Enggano.[72] Some of

Heathenism, translated from the third German edition (New York, Fleming H. Revell Co., no date, pp. 312), *passim.*

[66] *Jahresbericht der Rheinischen Missions-Gesellschaft . . . 1914,* p. 174.

[67] Joh. Warneck, *D. Ludwig I. Nommensen. Ein Lebensbild* (Barmen, Missionshaus, 3d ed., 1928, pp. 142), *passim;* Bonn, *op. cit.,* pp. 139-147; Schlunk, *Grosse Missionsführer der Kirchengeschichte,* pp. 139-151.

[68] Richter, *op. cit.,* pp. 94, 95.

[69] Richter, *op. cit.,* pp. 99-113; Bonn, *op. cit.,* pp. 69ff.; Spiecker, *op. cit.,* pp. 185ff.

[70] *Jahresbericht der Rheinischen Missions-Gesellschaft . . . 1914,* p. 174.

[71] Rauws *et alii, The Netherlands Indies,* p. 116.

[72] Richter, *op. cit.,* pp. 109-113; Spiecker, *op. cit.,* pp. 28-45; Bonn, *op. cit.,* pp. 75-79.

them continued at the original centre of their society in the Netherlands Indies, in the southern part of Borneo.[73]

The Sangi (Sangir) and Talaud (or Talaur) Islands were a region in which Protestant Christianity made striking progress. At the dawn of the nineteenth century the peoples there were predominantly animistic. Islam had gained a foothold and Christianity, propagated under the auspices of the East India Company, had several thousand nominal adherents. In the nineteenth and twentieth centuries missionaries of more than one society entered. The colonial government gave some financial assistance, but inadequate for the needs of the missionaries. Eventually more than two-thirds of the population bore the Christian name.[74]

To the island of Halmahera the Utrecht Missionary Union sent missionaries in 1866. Progress was slow, partly because of the presence of Islam. Plantations of coffee, cocoa, and cocoanut palms were set out, improvements were made in the cultivation of rice, and a few thousand Christians were gathered.[75]

The Dutch part of New Guinea saw its first resident Protestant missionaries in 1855, when, with the financial aid of the colonial government, the Society for Home and Foreign Missions sent two of the Gossner men to the region. A few years later came representatives of the Utrecht Missionary Union. Progress was slow. Not until 1875 did the Utrecht missionaries have their first baptisms. With the extension of Dutch rule in the fore part of the twentieth century, the native cultures began to disintegrate and Christianity made more rapid gains. By the year 1934 slightly more than one-fourth of the population were Christians.[76]

One of the most interesting enterprises was among the Toradjas, inland from Posso, in the central part of Celebes. The Toradjas were of more than one tribe and speech, animists, head-hunters, and short of stature. To them came, in the 1890's, A. C. Kruyt, of the Netherlands Missionary Society, from a missionary family which had served in Java, and N. Adriani, sent by the Netherlands Bible Society, from a family of scholars and with a careful academic preparation behind him. They were the first Europeans to live in that part of the country and preceded Dutch officials by more than a decade. For years their efforts appeared fruitless. They first travelled about the region, investigating it, and familiarizing themselves with the people, the language, and the customs. They told of their religion, but they had few converts. To a

[73] *Jahresbericht der Rheinischen Missions-Gesellschaft . . . 1914*, p. 171.
[74] Coolsma, *De Zendingseeuw voor Nederlandsch Oost-Indië*, pp. 633-673; Richter, *op. cit.*, pp. 125-127.
[75] Richter, *op. cit.*, 131, 132; Coolsma, *op. cit.*, pp. 730ff.
[76] Richter, *op. cit.*, pp. 136-138; Rauws, *op. cit.*, p. 116.

Toradja, becoming a Christian meant separation from his own community, not only the living but also the dead, for the ancestral cult was prominent. A few schools were opened, but they had little influence. Moreover, Kruyt and Adriani felt it better that the Toradjas should come to Christianity by their natural groups, led by their chiefs. In 1905 the Dutch Government, as part of its policy of expanding its rule, began bringing the Toradjas under its administration, built roads, commenced the collection of taxes, compelled the building of houses on the new roads, sought to extirpate head-hunting, and in other ways disrupted the old customs. The Toradjas, bewildered and discouraged by the passing of their hereditary culture and spiritually confused and uncertain, turned to the missionaries, for they knew that these white men were friendly and familiar with their ways. From all sides came requests for schools and teachers, not so much from the desire for learning as from the wish to escape from uncertainty, to be told how to avoid conflict with the new administration, and to have the children trained for the new order. The Toradjas listened to the missionaries, not with any hunger for the Christian message, but because they deemed Christianity part of that white man's civilization which the state was forcing on them. Appreciating the situation, the missionaries did not seek to take advantage of it to rush the Toradjas into the Church. Gradually, through hearing the missionaries, the Toradjas became familiar with Christian teachings. About 1909 they began coming by small groups, often led by their chiefs. A mass movement set in and before two decades had elapsed the majority had adopted the new faith. The missionaries strove to make as little break as possible with the pre-Christian culture. Important native festivals were continued, with such adaptations as would fit them to Christian ideals. Western culture, brought in by the Dutch colonial regime, had dissolved the animistic community into individuals. The Christian congregations were the new community. As among the Bataks and in Nias, Minahassa, and some other areas, the Church became an integral part of the people and its life.[77]

Although Java had about three-fourths of the population of the Netherlands East Indies, it contained only a small percentage of the native Christians of the archipelago. This was chiefly because the vast majority of its people were Moslems. Except through strong political and social pressure, Islam has never yielded many converts to Christianity.

Yet in Java in the course of the nineteenth and twentieth centuries converts

[77] A. C. Kruyt in Schrieke, *The Effect of Western Influence on Native Civilization in the Malay Archipelago*, pp. 3-9; Vanderbosch, *The Dutch East Indies*, p. 233; H. Kraemer and A. E. Adriani, *Dr. N. Adriani* (Amsterdam, H. J. Paris, 1930, pp. 213), *passim;* N. Adriani, *Verzamelde Geschriften* (Haarlem, De Erven F. Bohn, N.V., 3 vols., 1932), *passim;* Richter, *Die evangelische Mission in Niederländisch-Indien*, pp. 118-123.

from Islam to Protestant Christianity, although only a few thousands, were more numerous than those made in all the rest of the world during the period. This was partly because the island was under Dutch rule and partly because Islam sat more lightly on the Javanese, who in the course of their history had yielded allegiance to Hinduism and Buddhism before they had become followers of the Prophet, than upon some other Moslem peoples.

For many years the colonial administration was decidedly cool towards efforts to win the Javanese to Christianity, presumably because it feared that they would give rise to unrest among the Moslems and bring serious problems to the state. Missionaries often met with difficulty in obtaining permits to establish residence.[78] However, not far from the middle of the nineteenth century several lay Christians, feeling the effects of the religious revivals which were then stirring Holland, began on their own initiative to spread their faith. In Surabaia two Christian groups thus arose, one around a retired Dutch naval officer, Embde, and his Javanese wife, who sought to induce the converts to adopt Dutch ways, and the other around Coolen, a Eurasian, who wished the converts to remain Javanese so far as possible, told them the Bible story through the familiar puppet shadow plays, and utilized Javanese music. Out of the Embde-Coolen movements came Christian communities whose members eventually numbered about 19,000.[79] In the southern part of mid-Java lived Mrs. Philips, the wife of a government inspector of indigo plantations. In the third quarter of the nineteenth century she was active in propagating Christianity among the labourers on the plantations. She had three native helpers, of whom Sadrach became the best known. In ten years about 1,000 Javanese were baptized. Although he was in close touch with missionaries, Sadrach allowed his converts to keep some of their pre-Christian beliefs and practices. Eventually he had a following of between 6,000 and 7,000. For a time the *Gereformeerde Zendingsvereeniging* had close connexions with him, but a break occurred. The majority followed Sadrach.[80] A few pages above we noted the movement at Salatiga around Mrs. Le Jolle, later Mrs. van Vollenhoven. It was in association with this that the Salatiga Mission arose.

---

[78] For a picture of Christianity in Java about the middle of the century, see *Berichten omtrent de Evangelisatie van Java, medegedeeld door J. F. G. Brumund, Predikant te Soerabaja, uitgegeven door H. A. G. Brumund, Predikant te Amsterdam* (Amsterdam, Johs. van der Hey en Zoon, 1854, pp. xxxvi, 164). See also, for a slightly later time, P. Jansz, *Java's Zendingveld, beschouwd na de Beoordeeling door S. E. Harthoorn in zijn Werkje: De Evangelische Zending in Oost-Java* (Amsterdam, H. de Hoogh, 1865, pp. 204).

[79] Richter, *op. cit.*, pp. 41-43; S. E. Harthoorn, *De Evangelische Zending en Oost-Java. Eene Kritische Bijdrage* (Haarlem, A. C. Kruseman, 1863, pp. vii, 205), pp. 150-174.

[80] Richter, *op. cit.*, pp. 42, 43, 63-65; Coolsma, *De Zendingseeuw voor Nederlandsch Oost-Indië*, pp. 157, 158, 170-176, 196-198.

After Mrs. Le Jolle-van Vollenhoven returned to Holland, her enterprise was carried on by de Boer, a farmer's son from Ermelo. Following the device of his father-in-law, a Mennonite missionary, de Boer acquired land on which he formed colonies of Christians. The Neukirchen brothers came to assist him and later took over his work.[81] In West Java several societies laboured among the Moslem Sundanese and the large bodies of Chinese.[82] On the north coast of Central Java the Mennonites developed Christian communities through bringing the converts together in colonies.[83] Numerically the strongest of the Protestant efforts among the Javanese Moslems was that of the Netherlands Missionary Society. It was built on the beginnings made by Embde and Coolen and had as its great pioneer J. E. Jellesma, sometimes called the Apostle to the Javanese. Although he died in 1858 after only ten years in the country, within that brief decade he had gathered more than 2,000 Christians in several Christian villages. This method of creating Christian communities was followed by his successors. Land was reclaimed from the virgin forests and Christian settlements established on it. Two other great figures in this mission were the Kruyts, father and son. Educational and medical enterprises were developed. By 1894 the number of Christians was about 6,000, and in 1929 about 18,000.[84] To the eastern tip of Java immigrants came from the overcrowded eastern provinces. Among these were many from the island of Madura. Here, in 1879, arrived J. P. Esser, for the Java Committee. Here, too, came as settlers Christians who had been associated with the enterprises of the Netherlands Missionary Society. Because of this connexion the Java Committee collaborated with the older sister organization.[85] Through these various agencies strong churches were arising among the Javanese.[86]

In the Timor Archipelago the state church was very strong, and at one time and another the Netherlands Missionary Society had fairly extensive activities. On the island of Sumba or Soemba in the 1880's the Christian Reformed Church took over the missionary enterprise.[87]

[81] Richter, op. cit., pp. 43, 58-60; Coolsma, op. cit., pp. 189ff.

[82] Richter, op. cit., pp. 56, 57; S. Coolsma, Twaalf Voorlezingen over West-Java (Rotterdam, D. van Sijn & Zoon, 1879, pp. viii, 260), passim; B. Alkema, Kiekjes uit de Soendalanden (The Hague, Boekhandel van den Zendings-Studie Raad, 1911, pp. 173), passim.

[83] Richter, op. cit., pp. 61, 62.

[84] Richter, op. cit., pp. 70-74; Kruijf, Geschiedenis van het Nederlandsche Zendelinggenootschap, pp. 508ff.

[85] Richter, op. cit., pp. 74, 75; Nederlandschen Studenten Zendings-Bond, Hedendaagsche Zending in Onze Oost, pp. 116-118.

[86] For a description of missions in Java in the early and mid-1890's, see E. Nijland, Schetsen uit Insulinde, pp. 1-160; F. Lion Cachet, Een Jaar op Reis in Dienst der Zending (Amsterdam, J. A. Wormser, 1896, pp. viii, 879), passim.

[87] Nijland, op. cit., pp. 363ff.

Roman Catholic missions in the Dutch East Indies were to have a phenomenal growth after 1914, but they were late in making much headway. The promising beginnings of the sixteenth century under Portuguese rule were all but obliterated under the strongly Protestant Dutch East India Company. In the nineteenth century and until after 1914 Roman Catholic missions were much less numerous and prominent than were Protestant missions. In 1892 there was but one vicariate apostolic for all the islands, and it contained only 47 European missionaries, 27 churches, 7 chapels, and 54,490 Roman Catholics, and of the latter about 8,500 were soldiers.[88] By 1913 there were still only 82 priests, 39 lay brothers, and 46 sisters, ministering to 46,950 "coloured" and 35,336 European Roman Catholics.[89] This minority position and inconsiderable increase arose from the fact that Roman Catholicism was not strong in Holland and, as against Protestantism, was regarded with disfavour by Dutch colonial officials. Yet, beginning late in the eighteenth century, restrictions in Holland were gradually removed and Roman Catholics began to prosper in numbers and organization. It was the growth of Roman Catholicism in Holland which was chiefly responsible for the remarkable expansion in the Indies after 1914. To this story we are to revert in the seventh volume. Here we can only summarize the beginnings.

The renewal of active Roman Catholic effort in the Dutch possessions came in 1808. Holland was then under the rule of Louis Bonaparte, a Roman Catholic, and two priests of that faith were permitted to go to the East Indies to care for their co-religionists. Other priests followed and in 1842 a vicariate apostolic was created for the islands.[90] Under an agreement of 1847 between the Roman Catholic Church and the East Indian Government and through subsequent arrangements, the former body was accorded subsidies towards the support of its personnel and its public worship.[91] Yet the state attempted to keep Roman Catholic missionaries out of territories where Protestants were at work—as it also did Protestants from Roman Catholic areas.[92] It was only slowly, for instance, that clerical ministrations were permitted in the strongly Protestant Minahassa to those natives of that region who, converted to Roman Catholicism while serving as soldiers in Java, had returned home.[93] For a time in the 1830's representatives of the Société des Missions Étrangères of

[88] *Missiones Catholicae . . . MDCCCXCII*, pp. 244-246.

[89] Schwager in *Zeitschrift für Missionswissenschaft*, Vol. III, p. 315.

[90] Schwager in *Zeitschrift für Missionswissenschaft*, Vol. III, p. 310; *Missiones Catholicae . . . MDCCCXCII*, p. 244; Van der Velden, *De Roomsch-Katholieke Missie in Nederlandsch Oost-Indië, 1808-1908*, pp. 13-101.

[91] Vandenbosch, *The Dutch East Indies*, p. 229.

[92] *Capucins Missionaires. Missions Françaises*, p. 80.

[93] Schwager in *Zeitschrift für Missionswissenschaft*, Vol. III, p. 311.

Paris essayed to establish themselves in Nias and Sumatra, but the unfriendliness of the government to non-Dutch missions discouraged them.[94]

The coming of the Society of Jesus, in 1859, brought new vigour to the Roman Catholic cause. About half of the Jesuits gave themselves to the Europeans and about half to the natives.[95]

In the course of time other orders followed. In 1903 the Dutch Holy Heart of Jesus missionaries were entrusted with the Moluccas and with the Kei Islands, off Dutch New Guinea. In 1905 Dutch Capuchins were assigned to a prefecture apostolic in Sumatra.[96] In 1913 the Society of the Divine Word was given the care of the Little Sunda Islands (with the exception of Flores), to which the Jesuits had ministered since 1864. In 1914 Flores was added to the field of the Society of the Divine Word.[97] Brothers of St. Aloysius (Oudenbosch), Ursulines, Franciscan Sisters, Sisters of Our Lady of Mercy, and Sisters of the Society of Jesus, Mary, and Joseph also came.[98] Roman Catholics of several orders and congregations were sharing in the spread of their form of the faith in this vast Dutch empire.

During the fore part of the nineteenth century, Portugal retained several of the Little Sunda Islands which had been hers since the sixteenth and seventeenth centuries. Here were Roman Catholic Christians descended from converts made in the days of Portuguese vigour. In the early years of the nineteenth century they were sadly neglected. In 1859 the Netherlands bought a clear title to some of the islands. Portugal, however, retained possession of the eastern part of Timor. Ecclesiastically Portuguese Timor was under the Bishop of Macao. About the year 1913 it was served by Portuguese Jesuits, seculars, and some sisters, but the republican government in Portugal expelled the Jesuits and the sisters.[99] In spite of the long continued Roman Catholic efforts, the majority of the population remained non-Christian.[100]

In 1914 the north coast of Borneo, with its hinterland, was under British control. British Borneo was composed politically of Sarawak, an independent

[94] *Ibid.*
[95] Schwager in *Zeitschrift für Missionswissenschaft*, Vol. III, p. 314.
[96] *Ibid.;* Fijen and Hamelijnck, *Missie-Schetsen uit Tropisch Nederland*, pp. 59ff., 126ff.
[97] Hagspiel, *Along the Mission Trail*, Vol. II, pp. 74ff.; Joh. Thauren, *Die Mission in Hollandisch-Indien. Das Apostolische Vikariat der Kleinen Sundainseln* (Post Kaldenkirchen, Missionsdruckerei Steyl, 1931, pp. 64), pp. 26ff.; Fijen and Hamelijnck, *op. cit.*, pp. 111ff.
[98] Van der Velden, *op. cit.*, pp. 305ff.
[99] Schwager in *Zeitschrift für Missionswissenschaft*, Vol. III, pp. 328, 329; Schmidlin, Braun, *Catholic Mission History*, p. 643.
[100] *Portuguese Timor* (London, H. M. Stationery Office, 1920, pp. 26), p. 10.

state under British protection and ruled by the Brooke family, founded by a remarkable adventurer, James Brooke; of the small island of Labuan, administered from the Straits Settlements; of Brunei, a sultanate, its past glory much decayed, now a British protectorate, and of British North Borneo, governed by the British North Borneo Company. The area was well watered and rugged and was the home of many different tribes. Chinese settlers were numerous. Through their East India Company the British had long been interested in the region, but the active, continuing extension of their control dated from the 1840's. It was then that James Brooke became Rajah of Sarawak,[101] that the British suppressed piracy off Brunei, and that Labuan was ceded to Great Britain. The British North Borneo Company was chartered in 1881.[102] It was, in other words, in that latter two-thirds of the nineteenth century, so marked by the building of colonial empires by European peoples, that the British obtained these footholds in the East Indies.

Christian missions accompanied British rule and took advantage of its protection. Islam had already entered the country and had gained adherents, but as a rule it sat rather lightly on its professed constituencies. The religion of the vast majority was animism or animism with a thin veneer of Islam.[103] There were many headhunters.

It was through James Brooke that Christianity was introduced. Brooke desired the welfare of his subjects. He had suppressed piracy and he wished to give the land the benefit of the faith of his mother country.[104] Funds were collected in England and in 1847 Francis Thomas McDougall was appointed as the first missionary to the region. McDougall proved peculiarly fitted for the pioneer post. He came from stock which had served in the navy and army. He was trained as a surgeon and had then graduated from Oxford where he was a notable oarsman and where, caught up in the religious awakening then stirring that university, he formed the purpose of taking holy orders. He and a colleague arrived in Kuching, the chief city of Sarawak, in 1848. McDougall began both medical and educational work. The schools proved a fruitful means of rearing a Christian community. Progress was made among the Chinese. In 1855 McDougall was consecrated bishop. In 1868, because of failing health, he resigned and took a vicarage in England.[105] So well had he laid the founda-

---

[101] Baring-Gould and Bampfylde, *A History of Sarawak under its Two White Rajahs, 1839-1908*, pp. 61ff.

[102] Rutter, *British North Borneo*, pp. 115ff.

[103] Gomes, *Seventeen Years Among the Sea Dyaks of Borneo*, pp. 194ff.; Baring-Gould and Bampfylde, *op. cit.*, pp. 443-446; Rutter, *op. cit.*, pp. 290ff.

[104] Baring-Gould and Bampfylde, *op. cit.*, p. 446; Currey, *Borneo*, p. 57.

[105] Charles John Bunyon, *Memoirs of Francis Thomas McDougall, D.C.L., F.R.C.S.,*

tions that the church continued to expand. Under his successors the language
of the Sea Dayaks was reduced to writing, and the mission was extended to
North Borneo. In North Borneo the Europeans on the rubber estates, in
Labuan, and in the towns were also to be cared for. By 1914 Christianity had
been planted in a number of centres, schools established, medical care given,
and the beginnings of a native clergy, Chinese, had been made.[106] Before
1914 nothing was done in Brunei.[107]

Methodism entered Sarawak in 1901 in the persons of a Chinese colony. The
Rajah Charles Brooke wished to bring to his domains Chinese Christian
farmers who by their example would demonstrate to his Dayak subjects the
possibilities of making a living through agriculture. In response there arrived
from Fukien Province Chinese who had become Christians through the
American Methodist mission. While in Hongkong, on their way to Borneo,
Bishop F. W. Warne, of the Methodist Episcopal Church, who was passing
through the port, heard of them, went with them on the remainder of their
journey, and helped to introduce them to their new home. To care for them
and aid them in their difficult adjustment an American from the Methodist
force in Malaya was appointed to them. After a short term he was succeeded,
in 1903, by a younger man, James M. Hoover. Hoover reached Borneo in
1903 and, with an occasional furlough, served until his death in 1935. His was
a remarkable achievement. He brought courage to the disheartened colonists,
organized schools, and introduced electric lights, power machinery for the
hulling of rice, and better methods of transportation. He left behind him a
strong and prosperous Christian community.[108]

Roman Catholic Christianity was also represented. In the seventeenth century a mission had been founded at Brunei, but this lapsed. In the 1850's a
Spaniard, Quarteron or Cuarteron, a sea captain, believing that he was about
to perish in a shipwreck, vowed that if spared he would become a missionary.
In 1855 he came to Brunei as prefect apostolic, assisted by Italian priests. The
death toll was heavy. Quarteron remained until 1879, but his enterprise disintegrated and he left.[109] In 1881 arrived the Mill Hill Fathers, a society with

Sometime Bishop of Labuan and Sarawak and of Harriette His Wife. By Her Brother
(London, Longmans, Green and Co., 1889, pp. 368), *passim;* Green, *Borneo*, pp. 103-117.
    [106] Gomes, *op. cit.*, pp. 105-119, 240-251; Green, *op. cit.*, pp. 123ff.
    [107] Currey, *op. cit.*, pp. 64-71; Ruth Henrich, *No Richer Harvest. The Story of the
Church in Borneo* (London, Society for Promoting Christian Knowledge, 1934, pp. 72),
pp. 40ff.; Green, *op. cit.*, pp. 117-122.
    [108] Frank T. Cartwright, *Tuan Hoover of Borneo* (Cincinnati, The Abingdon Press,
1938, pp. 186), *passim.*
    [109] Baring-Gould and Bampfylde, *op. cit.*, pp. 448, 449; Schmidlin-Braun, *Catholic
Mission History*, p. 642; Descamps, *Histoire Générale Comparée des Missions*, p. 555.

English headquarters, although with many Dutch in its personnel. Their centre was at Kuching, but their sphere embraced the British zone of influence. They laboured among the Chinese and inland among the indigenous tribes. In one of their mountain stations they established an agricultural colony. They had schools. In 1913 they counted 14 head stations, 11 sub-stations, 16 schools, and about 3,000 Christians.[110]

The kind of Christianity which came to the East Indies was to a large degree determined by the political complexion of the colonial regimes. In the largest portion, that controlled by the Dutch, it was predominantly Protestant and from Holland, chiefly from the Dutch Reformed churches. There were strong missions from Germany. Some Protestant missions, very much in the minority, were from the British Isles and the United States. After lapsing with the Dutch conquest (except in the greatly shrunken remnants of the Portuguese possessions), Roman Catholic missions, aided by the growing tolerance in Holland in the nineteenth century, were renewed shortly after 1800. However, they were much more restricted territorially than were Protestant missions and even in 1914 had only a small fraction of the Christians of the islands. In the diminished enclave, centring in Timor, which remained to Portugal, it was Portuguese Roman Catholicism which was propagated. In the British territories on the northern shores of Borneo, the Church of England and the Roman Catholic Mill Hillers, also with English headquarters, were in the majority, with a smaller but vigorous American Methodist mission completing the picture.

As in the other islands of the Pacific basin, the reasons for the spread of Christianity were to be found in part in the vigorous colonial and commercial expansion of European peoples, especially in the latter part of the pre-1914 century, and in part in the rising tide of vitality of the churches of Western Europe and the United States. They were also to be discovered in the collapse of native cultures, especially those of the primitive peoples, under the impact of the white man. As these cultures and their attendant religions disintegrated, the resistance to Christianity weakened. Christianity came with the prestige of the seemingly all-powerful European. The various factors combined to produce a phenomenal growth in the Christian communities after the middle of the nineteenth century.

[110] Schwager in *Zeitschrift für Missionswissenschaft*, Vol. III, pp. 326-328; E.v.R.W., *Felix Westerwoudt, Missioner in Borneo*, translated from the Dutch by T. W. Lefeber (Maryknoll, Catholic Foreign Mission Society of America, 1924, pp. xi, 115), *passim*.

Christianity spread largely through the representatives of missionary societies in the Occident supported by the contributions of many individuals. However, the Dutch colonial government subsidized much of the missionary effort, and although the rank and file of its membership was passive and as yet did little to propagate its faith, a state church, dating from pre-nineteenth century days, was very prominent. The overwhelming proportion of the accessions to Christianity was from the animists and not from the Moslems who constituted the majority of the population, yet more thousands were won from the latter than in all the rest of the world by Protestants and Roman Catholics in the nineteenth century. Conversion was largely by groups, notably in Celebes, in the Sangi and Talaud Islands, among the Bataks, and in the island of Nias.

The effects of Christianity were many.[111] Several languages were reduced to writing and the beginnings of a literature were made. The Bible was translated in whole or in part into a large number of tongues.[112] In areas of large Christian populations the percentage of literacy was much higher than in those in which the proportion of Christians was small.[113] Particularly was education brought to women. The status of women was profoundly altered.[114] Modern medical care was furthered. Here and there new crops and improved methods of agriculture were introduced. Changes in morals followed the acceptance of the Christian faith. As always, Christianity worked a religious revolution among its adherents. To peoples bewildered by the coming of Western culture, the Christian faith made for poise, courage, and hope. Head-hunting was discouraged. Such practices as trial by ordeal of those accused of being sorcerers, witches, and were-wolves were fought. More of individualism appeared. The idea of progress found entrance.[115] In some of these latter innovations it is hard to disentangle the results of the colonial administration from those of missions. It must be remembered, however, that the growing humanitarianism of the colonial government which marked the latter half of the nineteenth century, with its sense of responsibility and trusteeship for the welfare of the native races, arose in some degree from the religious awakenings which in Holland found political expression in avowedly Christian parties. Christianity was bringing new life, righting age-long ills, curbing the selfish exploitation of one race by another, and seeking to enrich the lives of individuals and groups.

As elsewhere, the environment was having its effect upon the imported

[111] See H. Th. Fischer, *Zending en Volksleven in Nederlands-Indië* (Zwolle, 1932, pp. 205), pp. 43ff.
[112] Kilgour in Rauws *et alii, The Netherlands Indies*, pp. 171-176.
[113] Rauws, *op. cit.,* p. 142.
[114] Vandenbosch, *The Dutch East Indies*, p. 197.
[115] Schrieke, *The Effect of Western Influence on Native Civilizations in the Malay Archipelago*, pp. 237-247.

faith. Here and there, as among the Bataks, Christianity was becoming the tribal religion. Where this was the case, in the ecclesiastical structure many features of the pre-Christian social organization persisted. Sometimes these were consciously perpetuated by the missionary. Pre-Christian festivals were often carried over, modified in such fashion as to make them consistent with Christian ideals. Here and there pre-Christian practices which were declared by the more inflexible to be superstitious were permitted Christians. As yet the Christianity, whether Protestant or Roman Catholic, in the state church or under the missionary societies, was largely passive and was directed by the white clergy. As in the political and the economic realms, so in the Church, the colonial status persisted. The Indonesians were the wards of the white man. There were stirrings of independence. As yet, however, these were comparatively unimportant. Rather fewer indigenous cults, syncretistic combinations of Christian and pre-Christian beliefs, appeared than in some other lands where primitive peoples had been won to the faith. These were to multiply after 1914. Not until after 1914, moreover, did the Christians take much initiative in propagating their faith among other tribes or seek to manage their own churches. Yet Christianity was taking root. The subsequent period was to demonstrate that it was no exotic, but was becoming an integral part of the life of the archipelago.

Chapter X

MADAGASCAR AND SOME OF THE OTHER ISLANDS OFF THE SHORES OF AFRICA

MADAGASCAR constitutes a convenient and logical transition from the Islands of the Pacific and the East Indies to Africa. Although it is near to Africa, separated from that continent merely by the Mozambique Channel, at its narrowest point only about 250 miles wide, its population is akin in language and race to the Malays, Polynesians, and Melanesians. Infiltrations of African blood are to be found, but as a rule only as minority strains. Traces of Arab and Indian stocks are due to early commercial contacts with these peoples.

In size, Madagascar is one of the largest islands in the world. Its length, from north to south, is about 900 miles, and its width averages about 250 miles. In area, of the islands of the earth only Greenland, New Guinea, and Borneo exceed it. It is more than twice the size of Great Britain or the Main Island of Japan.

In physical structure, Madagascar has coastal plains, broad in the West, narrower in the East, rising abruptly to an elevated inner plateau. None of its mountains exceeds 10,000 feet in height.

The larger part of the island lies within the tropics, and the climate is largely determined by this fact.

The population, denominated collectively the Malagasy, is divided into a number of tribes. These differ in racial stock and in culture. In general one language has prevailed, although with several dialects. Some cultural practices, moreover, have been common to all tribes, but with variations. For so large an island, the population was and is comparatively sparse. Early in the twentieth century it was said to be about 2,750,000.[1] Whether, as had so many other peoples, it had declined with the coming of the white man, we do not know. One estimate made in the first half of the nineteenth century placed the total at about 4,450,000 and declared that evidence existed that this was smaller than it had once been.[2]

[1] *The Encyclopædia Britannica*, 11th ed., Vol. XVII, p. 274.
[2] Ellis, *History of Madagascar*, Vol. I, p. 114.

Of the tribes, the Hòva acquired political supremacy in the course of the nineteenth century and succeeded in bringing most of the island under their sway. Their home was in Imèrina, an elevated portion of the central plateau, from 4,000 to 6,000 feet above sea-level. They were akin to the Malays, were of lighter complexion than the other tribes, energetic, quick in intelligence, and keen traders.[3] They had their capital at Antanànarìvo, on a long rocky ridge in Imèrina.

In culture the Malagasy were by no means as backward as were many of their kinsfolk in the Pacific Islands at the dawn of the nineteenth century. They possessed arts and crafts which apparently they had brought with them when they settled on Madagascar. Contacts with the Arabs and possibly with the Indians had presumably added to their cultural heritage. They were removed from the primitive stage and yet could not be called highly civilized.

In religion the Malagasy were largely animists, with traces of a rudimentary polytheism. They had neither temples, images, priestly class, nor regular times of worship.[4] Presumably, then, this religion would, like others of its kind, yield more readily to Christianity than would an advanced system.

In the sixteenth and seventeenth centuries efforts were made by Roman Catholic missionaries to introduce Christianity to Madagascar, but without enduring success.[5] In the eighteenth century the island suffered from European pirates and slave-hunters. There were several attempts by the French to found colonies, but with the outbreak of the French Revolution attention was deflected and they came to naught.[6]

Christianity was reintroduced early in the nineteenth century, under circumstances which for several years greatly furthered its spread. Some time before 1800 Imèrina was united politically under a line to Hòva chiefs. In the first decade of the nineteenth century there came to the throne Radàma I. This prince proved able and ambitious. He used the slave trade to provide himself with European arms and through these extended his rule. In other words, he was doing what native chiefs in several of the groups of Pacific Islands were accomplishing in the first half of the nineteenth century, employing the newly introduced weapons of the white man to reduce other tribes to his sway and build up a kingdom. During the Napoleonic Wars the British seized from the French the island of Mauritius and, while not completely eliminating these

[3] Sibree, *The Madagascar Mission,* pp. 10, 14.

[4] Sibree, *op. cit.,* pp. 18, 19; Henry Rusillon, *Un Culte Dynastique avec Evocation des Morts chez les Sakalaves de Madagascar le "Tromba"* (Paris, Librairie Alphonse Picard et Fils, 1912, pp. 194), *passim.*

[5] Vol. III, pp. 244, 245.

[6] Ellis, *op. cit.,* Vol. II, pp. 34-92.

hereditary enemies from that section of the ocean, succeeded them in their influence in Madagascar. In 1817 the British Governor Farquhar, of Mauritius, entered into a treaty with Radàma I by which the latter agreed to end the slave trade in his domains in return for an annual payment of money, arms, and other equipment.[7] Radàma was eager to introduce European crafts and education. At this juncture there came, in 1818, representatives of the London Missionary Society.

Since 1796, or almost from the time of its formation, the London Missionary Society had been contemplating inaugurating an enterprise in Madagascar. Governor Farquhar encouraged them in this plan.[8] Two missionary families were sent, but death took a heavy toll and soon only David Jones was left, and he had lost his wife and child. In 1820 Jones succeeded in reaching Antanànarìvo in the train of the British agent who was renewing the treaty with Radàma. Radàma seems to have had little interest in Christianity as such, but he saw in Jones a means of obtaining the teachers of European culture which he wished and through him wrote to the directors of the London Missionary Society asking for missionaries on the condition that they would also send skilful artisans to make his "people workmen as well as good Christians."[9] He also dispatched ten Malagasy boys to England there to be educated by the society at the expense of the government.[10] Jones opened a school in Antanànarìvo which had as its first pupils youths of princely blood and soon the king erected a building for it. Reinforcements arrived from Great Britain, some of them the artisans who had been requested. Before many years preaching in Malagasy was begun, and portions of the Bible were translated and printed, together with a catechism and a hymn book. Not all of the artisans were an asset and those of the Malagasy boys who returned after their period of training in England did not prove of help. Moreover, Radàma moved too rapidly for many of his people and the conservatives lamented the passing of the old ways. Baptisms were few. Yet through the schools a knowledge of Christianity was rapidly spreading.[11]

Radàma I died in 1828 and was succeeded by one of his wives, Rànavàlona. Rànavàlona owed her throne to officials who opposed the innovations and

[7] Ellis, op. cit., Vol. II, pp. 93-195.
[8] Ellis, op. cit., Vol. II, pp. 202-205.
[9] Lovett, The History of the London Missionary Society, Vol. I, pp. 675, 676.
[10] Lovett, op. cit., Vol. I, p. 676.
[11] Hayes, David Jones, pp. 24-85; Lovett, op. cit., Vol. I, pp. 674-684; Ellis, op. cit., Vol. II, pp. 205-411; Keturah Jeffreys, The Widowed Missionary's Journal; Containing some Account of Madagascar and also, a Narrative of the Missionary Career of the Rev. J. Jeffreys; who died . . . July 4, 1825 (Southampton, 1837, pp. x, 216), passim.

were ardently loyal to the old cults. Eventually vigorous attempts were made to stamp out the new faith.

For the first few years of Rànavàlona's reign the restrictions on the propagation of Christianity tightened, but not sufficiently to prevent active efforts by the missionaries or the acceptance of the faith by some of the Malagasy. After a brief period the missionaries were permitted to continue their schools. Two churches were formed of the Malagasy converts. Crowds came to the public services and prayer meetings were spontaneously held in private homes. The translation of the Bible was pushed to completion. In 1830 the entire New Testament was printed. In 1836 the full Bible was finished and the first copies came off the press. The work of the artisan missionaries in training Malagasy in useful crafts and in making soap from native materials gained favour with the Queen. Yet Rànavàlona early broke off relations with Great Britain, and, after progressive steps against the acceptance of the faith by the Malagasy, in 1835, alarmed by the increase in the popularity of Christianity, she forbade her subjects participating in any but the hereditary religious customs of the country. In 1836 the missionaries were ordered off the island. Most of them found refuge in Mauritius.[12]

From 1836 until the death of Rànavàlona I, in 1861, was a period of persecution. Violence was by spasms and was not equally acute throughout the quarter of a century. The number of Christians actually put to death was not large. We hear of a martyrdom of a young woman in 1837, of the spearing of nine Christians in 1840, of the spearing of others and of deaths by the poison ordeal in 1842, and of the execution of eighteen in 1849 near the royal palace, fourteen of them by casting them over a cliff and the other four by burning. In 1857 twenty-one were stoned to death and others were hurled over cliffs or killed by the poison ordeal. Thousands of others were fined, flogged, deprived of their official rank, or sold into slavery. Many fled to Mauritius.[13]

In spite of the persecution, Christianity survived and continued to spread. This was in part because the anti-Christian measures were not persistently enforced. It was in part from the devotion of the Malagasy Christians. They continued to meet in secret, to cherish the Bible and other Christian books, transcribing them by hand when printed copies ran short. Often they bore torture without flinching and without vindictiveness. Moreover, the London Missionary Society sent a representative, William Ellis, who had served his

[12] Hayes, *op. cit.*, pp. 85ff.; Ellis, *The Martyr Church,* pp. 59-113; Sibree, *The Madagascar Mission,* pp. 27-36.
[13] Ellis, *The Martyr Church,* pp. 114-197, 269; Sibree, *op. cit.,* pp. 37, 38; J. J. Freeman and D. Jones, *A Narrative of the Persecution of the Christians in Madagascar* (London, John Snow, 1840, pp. viii, 297), *passim.*

missionary apprenticeship in Tahiti. Three times Ellis landed on Madagascar and at the third attempt he was allowed to come to the capital and had a friendly audience with the Queen. He was able to give encouragement to Christians and reported that their ranks were growing.[14]

It was during the reign of Rànavàlona I, so adverse to Christianity, that Roman Catholicism was reintroduced to Madagascar. This was the work of a French secular, Henri de Solages (1786-1832), the son of a marquis. Since his seminary days in St. Sulpice Solages had wished to become a missionary. He especially fixed his eyes on the Pacific, where he hoped to compensate to the church the losses suffered in Europe. In 1829 he was appointed Prefect Apostolic of the Isle of Bourbon or Réunion, a French possession near Madagascar. He wished, from this vantage point, to see missions undertaken in the Pacific and on Madagascar. He himself went to Madagascar, hoping to obtain freedom for Roman Catholic schools, but died on the way to Antanànarìvo.[15] He was followed by Dalmond, who acquired footholds on the French island of Sainte Marie off the east coast and on the island of Nossi Bé off the north-west coast. Dalmond became Prefect Apostolic of the French Comoro Islands (between Madagascar and Africa) and Madagascar. In response to his appeal, French Jesuits came. Although three of the Jesuits obtained temporary entrance to Antanànarìvo in the wake of a French merchant, they did not succeed in remaining. Various attempts to gain admission elsewhere failed. The Jesuits had to content themselves with posts on Sainte Marie, Nossi Bé, and the Comoros.[16]

The death of Rànavàlona I inaugurated a new day of prosperity for Christianity. Under her successors tolerance and then active favour were shown to the faith. Her son, who followed her on the throne as Radàma II, was not a Christian, but he was friendly to the missionaries, attended Christian instruction, and bore patiently and even penitently the reproaches of one of them for his chronic drunkenness.[17] Upon hearing the news of the death of Rànavàlona I, William Ellis set out for Madagascar, soon reached Antanànarìvo, was cordially received by the King, and aided the Christians in taking advantage of the new situation. Reinforcements soon arrived from Great Britain and

---

[14] Ellis, *op. cit.*, pp. 174-227, 268; William Ellis, *Three Visits to Madagascar during the years 1853-1854-1856* (London, John Murray, 1859, pp. xvii, 476), *passim;* Ellis, *Life of William Ellis*, pp. 213ff.

[15] Georges Goyau, *Les Grandes Desseins Missionnaires d'Henri de Solages (1786-1832)* (Paris, Librairie Plon, 1933, pp. vii, 295), *passim.*

[16] Schwager, *Die katholische Heidenmission der Gegenwart*, pp. 153, 154; La Vaissière, *Histoire de Madagascar*, Vol. I, pp. 33ff.

[17] Ellis, *The Martyr Church of Madagascar*, pp. 258-260.

generous grants of funds were made by the London Missionary Society for the erection of memorial churches to the martyrs.[18]

In 1863 Radàma II was put to death in a palace revolution. For him was substituted a wife and cousin who took the name of Ràsohèrina. Although Ràsohèrina did not become a Christian, during her reign the faith continued to spread.[19] On her demise, in 1868, she was succeeded by a cousin whose reign name was Rànavàlona II.

At the coronation of the new Queen none of the symbols of the native cult was allowed and within a few months Rànavàlona II and her husband, the Prime Minister, were baptized. Not long thereafter a church was organized in the palace. In September, 1869, the charms and "idols" in Imèrina were gathered and burned. The Hòva had broken with their old religion. Much the same movement was occurring among another tribe, the Bètsilèo.[20] As in so many other countries and islands, including numbers of the groups of the Pacific, a mass movement to Christianity was under way, led by the monarch.

The news of the revived opportunity for the spread of Christianity, coming after the persecutions and martyrdoms, stimulated the strengthening of the staffs of organizations already at work and the inauguration of enterprises by other societies. During the five years from 1869 to 1873 inclusive the London Missionary Society sent twenty-one missionaries to Madagascar, nearly trebling its representation,[21] and in the latter year it dispatched a deputation of two to visit the island and give counsel to the London board of directors.[22] Under Radàma II and Ràsohèrina the Jesuits and the Sisters of St. Joseph obtained a footing at Antanànarìvo. Ràsohèrina sent her adopted children to a Roman Catholic school. In 1866 Brothers of Christian Schools reached the capital.[23] A treaty with France, in 1868, guaranteed to the French freedom to practise their religion.[24] Only three-fifths as many Jesuits arrived in the decade beginning with 1869 as in the preceding ten years,[25] but this may have been in part because of the distress in France brought by the Franco-Prussian War and

[18] Ellis, *The Martyr Church of Madagascar*, pp. 238-307; Ellis, *Madagascar Revisited*, pp. 1-301.

[19] Ellis, *Madagascar Revisited*, pp. 302ff.

[20] Ellis, *The Martyr Church of Madagascar*, pp. 373ff.; Sibree, *The Madagascar Mission*, p. 45; James Sibree, *Madagascar and Its People. Notes of a Four Years' Residence* (London, The Religious Tract Society, 1870, pp. 576), pp. 471ff.

[21] Lovett, *The History of the London Missionary Society*, Vol. I, p. 737; Sibree, *The Madagascar Mission*, p. 47.

[22] Joseph Mullens, *Twelve Months in Madagascar* (London, James Nisbet & Co., 1875, pp. xiii, 334), *passim*.

[23] Schwager, *Die katholische Heidenmission der Gegenwart*, p. 155; La Vaissière, *Histoire de Madagascar*, Vol. I, pp. 345ff.

[24] La Vaissière, *op. cit.*, Vol. II, p. 10.

[25] La Vaissière, *op. cit.*, Vol. II, pp. 479, 480.

the transition from the Second Empire to the Third Republic.[26] In spite of handicaps, of the favoured position accorded Protestantism by the state, and the complaint that Roman Catholic children were being compelled to attend Protestant schools, in 1882 the Roman Catholic missions counted 44 priests, 22 lay brothers, 20 sisters, 20,000 children in schools, and 80,000 baptized and catechumens. They had spread to more than one section and tribe.[27] Partly at the instance of William Ellis, the Friends Foreign Mission Association entered Madagascar. Its first representatives arrived in 1867. They and the other Quakers who followed them worked in close and friendly co-operation with the London Missionary Society.[28] In 1862 the Anglican Bishop Ryan of Mauritius visited Antanànarìvo.[29] With the hearty approval of representatives of the London Missionary Society, the Church Missionary Society sent two men who reached the island in 1864.[30] In the same year two representatives of the Society for the Propagation of the Gospel in Foreign Parts arrived.[31] The societies of the Church of England directed most of their attention to other tribes than the Hòva.[32] The latter, when Christian, were predominantly Congregationalists, thought of that form of Christianity as the Queen's, and sometimes rebaptized the Anglican converts out of supposed loyalty to Hòva rule.[33] About 1870, with the growth of the Anglican missions, the suggestion began to be made that a bishop be appointed for Madagascar. To this objection was made in England, largely in Nonconformist circles and, for a time, by the London Missionary Society. When, in 1874, a bishop was sent out, it was by the Society for the Propagation of the Gospel in Foreign Parts and consecrated not through the Church of England, but through the Scottish Episcopal Church. The Church Missionary Society thereupon withdrew.[34] The bishop

---

[26] La Vaissière, op. cit., Vol. II, pp. 86ff.

[27] Schwager, op. cit., p. 155. On the spread among one of the tribes, see [Dubois], La Mission de Madagascar Bètsilèo, pp. 12-14. See also Mission Catholique des RR.PP. Jesuites à Madagascar (Antanànarìvo, Imprimerie de la Mission Catholique, 1888, pp. 49), passim.

[28] [William Johnson], Review of the Work of the Friends' Foreign Mission Association from 1867-1800 (Antanànarìvo, The Friends' Foreign Mission Association, 1880, pp. viii, 103), pp. 21ff.

[29] The Gospel in Madagascar: a Brief Account of the English Mission in that Island. Second edition, with a Preface and an Additional Chapter by the Lord Bishop of Mauritius (London, Seeley, Jackson, and Halliday, 1863, pp. 264), pp. 223ff.

[30] Stock, The History of the Church Missionary Society, Vol. II, pp. 473, 474.

[31] Pascoe, Two Hundred Years of the S.P.G., p. 375.

[32] For work among a branch of the Sakalava tribe see George Herbert Smith, Among the Menabe; or, Thirteen Months on the West Coast of Madagascar (London, Society for Promoting Christian Knowledge, 1896, pp. viii, 112).

[33] Stock, op. cit., Vol. II, p. 477.

[34] Stock, op. cit., Vol. II, pp. 478-480; Pascoe, op. cit., pp. 377, 378; McMahon, Christian Missions in Madagascar, pp. 40, 41.

took up his residence at Antanànarìvo, and eventually a cathedral was erected there for him.[35] In Norway, among the friends of missions, the news of the persecutions had aroused deep concern. The end of the persecutions brought rejoicing and in 1866 two representatives of the Norwegian Missionary Society reached the island.[36] This society, it will be recalled,[37] had arisen in part out of the revival in Norway of which Hans Nilson Hauge was the leading spirit. The Norwegians laboured in friendly co-operation with the London Missionary Society. Although they had a centre in Antanànarìvo, they found an important field to the south of Imèrina, among the Bètsilèo. They later extended their efforts still farther among two other tribes, the Sakalava, who occupied a large area on the west coast,[38] and the Bara, south of the Bètsilèo,[39] and to the south-east coast.[40] Some Norwegian Lutherans from the United States entered the service of the Norwegian Missionary Society. Funds, too, had come to that society from America. In 1892, only two years after its formation, the United Norwegian Lutheran Church, an American body, arranged with the Norwegian Missionary Society to assume responsibility for the southern part of Madagascar.[41] In 1894 what later came to be called the Lutheran Free Church, an offshoot from the United Norwegian Lutheran Church and also American, took over the western half of the field of the parent body.[42] By 1895, then, Christianity was being propagated in Madagascar by the London Missionary Society, the Jesuits aided by the Brothers of Christian Schools and the Sisters of St. Joseph, the Society for the Propagation of the Gospel in Foreign Parts, English Quakers, and Norwegian Lutherans from both Norway and the United States.

The third of a century from the death of Rànavàlona I, in 1861, to the French occupation, in 1895, saw the fairly continuous growth of Christianity. As the pioneer of Christianity in the nineteenth century and enjoying, as it did, a favoured position with the ruling Hòva power, the London Missionary Society was the chief channel for the spread of Christianity. In 1870 there were

[35] Webster, Madagascar, p. 37.
[36] Burgess, Zanahary in South Madagascar, p. 123; Johnson, Det förste Hundredaar av Madagaskars Kirkehistorie, pp. 105ff.
[37] Vol. IV, p. 92.
[38] Burgess, op. cit., p. 127; Røstvig, Sakalaverne og deres Land, pp. 83ff.; Birkeli, Fra tamarindernes land, pp. 107ff.
[39] Burgess, op. cit., p. 128.
[40] Horne, Til Seier gjennem Nederlag. Missionen paa Sydostkysten af Madagascar, pp. 29ff.; A. Walen, Madagaskars Sydostkyst (Stavanger, Det Norske Missionsselskab, 1887, pp. 114), passim.
[41] Burgess, op. cit., pp. 137-151; Drach, Our Church Abroad, pp. 113-120; Andrew Burgess, Ra-ha-la-hi-ko. My Brother in Madagascar (Minneapolis, Augsburg Publishing House, 1938, pp. 224), p. 27.
[42] Burgess, Zanahary in South Madagascar, p. 154.

said to be associated with it more than 260 churches, with over 20,000 members and over 130,000 adherents. By 1880 this number had grown to 1,024 churches, 68,227 members, and 225,460 adherents. In 1890 there were reported to be 1,223 churches, 59,615 members, and 248,108 adherents. The smaller number of members in 1890 as against 1880 is said to have been more than offset by an improvement in moral quality and in intelligent faith.[43] In 1868 the Madagascar Congregational Union, known as the Six-Monthly Meeting because it gathered twice a year, came into being. This became the apex of a modified Presbyterian system of ecclesiastical organization with something of an admixture of episcopacy. In 1873 the Six-Monthly Meeting undertook to carry the Christian faith to parts of the island as yet untouched and thus took on missionary functions.[44] In 1869 a theological college was opened in Antanànarìvo for the training of pastors and of assistants to the missionaries.[45] Great emphasis was placed upon schools. Nearly every congregation had one of them meeting in the church building. A normal school for the training of teachers was early begun.[46] Dispensaries were opened, Malagasy were given training in medicine and surgery, and books were prepared to be a medium for European medical knowledge.[47] In 1889 the revision of the translation of the Bible was completed.[48] Sunday schools and Societies of Christian Endeavour were introduced and fostered.[49] Although the London Missionary Society had its centre among the Hòva and on Imèrina, it carried the faith to some other provinces and tribes.[50] Here was a vigorous and growing Christian community, still largely under foreign direction, but with a rising native leadership and increasing native support, adapting its inherited Congregational organization to meet local conditions, and a means not only of nourishing its members in the Christian faith and of winning others, but also of introducing some phases of European culture.[51]

[43] Lovett, *The History of the London Missionary Society,* Vol. I, pp. 744-747.
[44] Sibree, *Fifty Years in Madagascar,* pp. 163-170.
[45] Sibree, *op. cit.,* pp. 105ff.
[46] Sibree, *The Madagascar Mission,* p. 54.
[47] Sibree, *The Madagascar Mission,* p. 61; W. Burns Thomson, *Reminiscences of Medical Missionary Work* (London, Hodder and Stoughton, 1895, pp. xv, 248), pp. 156-170.
[48] Sibree, *The Madagascar Mission,* p. 63.
[49] Sibree, *op. cit.,* pp. 67, 68.
[50] Lovett, *op. cit.,* Vol. I, pp. 756ff.
[51] On this period see material in the following biographies of missionaries of the London Missionary Society: Edward and Emrys Rowlands, *Thomas Rowlands of Madagascar* (London, The Livingstone Press, no date, pp. 122); C. F. A. Moss, *A Pioneer in Madagascar, John Pearse of the L.M.S.* (London, Headley Brothers, 1913, pp. xv, 261); Thomas T. Matthews, *Notes of Nine Years' Mission Work in the Province of Vonizongo, North West, Madagascar* (London, Hodder and Stoughton, 1881, pp. vi, 164); T. T. Matthews, *Thirty Years in Madagascar* (London, The Religious Tract Society, 1904, pp. 384); J. A. Houlder, *Among the Malagasy. An Unconventional Record of Missionary*

To this rapid expansion of Christianity French imperialism brought important changes. The French had long cherished an ambition to control the island. As in so many other parts of the nineteenth-century world, the British and the French clashed. Here as elsewhere Britain was associated with Protestantism and France with Roman Catholicism. Until the 1880's, British influence was usually the stronger. From 1883 to 1885 the French waged a desultory war on Madagascar and the treaty which brought peace stipulated that the foreign relations of Madagascar should be directed by France. In 1890, Great Britain, in return for concessions in Zanzibar, agreed to the French protectorate. In 1894 demands were presented which were designed to make France supreme. They were refused and in 1895 French troops took possession of Antanànarìvo. The following year the Queen was constrained to resign and was exiled and Madagascar was declared a French colony.[52] A new period in the history of the island had opened.

The changes wrought in the missionary and ecclesiastical situation by the establishment of French rule were two-fold. In the first place, the coming of the French brought embarrassment to Protestant missions and reinforced Roman Catholic Christianity. In the second place, anti-clericalism on the part of the French colonial authorities disturbed the programmes of both Protestants and Roman Catholics.

The transformation of Madagascar inevitably altered the relative strength of the various types of Christianity represented. The time was one of friction between the French and the British over their rival territorial ambitions in Africa. In 1898 the Fashoda incident brought the two nations to the brink of war. While the tension was eased by a Franco-British agreement of 1899 and by the progressive bettering of relations having as a mile post the formation of the *Entente Cordiale* between the two powers in 1904, British missions found it impossible to hold the leading place which had been theirs when the country was independent and when British commerce and diplomacy were potent. In 1895 and 1896 a rebellion broke out which was directed against the French

---

Experience (London, James Clarke & Co., 1912, pp. xiii, 320). Two biographies of Friends' missionaries which in part or in whole fall in these years are P. Doncaster, editor, *Faithful unto Death. A Story of the Missionary Life in Madagascar of William and Lucy S. Johnson* (London, Headley Brothers, 1896, pp. xxi, 277); A. J. and G. Crosfield, *A Man in Shining Armour. The Story of the Life of William Wilson* (London, Headley Brothers, no date, pp. 278).

[52] All of the biographies in the preceding note devote part of their space to the coming of French rule. British accounts of the war of the 1880's are S. Pasfield Oliver, *The True Story of the French Dispute in Madagascar* (London, T. Fisher Unwin, 1885, pp. viii, 279), and George A. Shaw, *Madagascar and France* (London, The Religious Tract Society, 1885, pp. 320).

and also against Christianity. It was anti-foreign, an attempt to oust or destroy all phases of the cultural and political influences which had culminated in the French conquest. In places it was also directed against the Hòva, to take advantage of the embarrassment of that people by the French attack to rise against their rule. Church after church was burned and some deaths of Christians were recorded.[53] The French Resident-General who was appointed late in 1896 at first had the conviction that the London Missionary Society was inimical to the French and must be curbed. The new administration ordered the teaching of French in the extensive mission schools, a requirement which brought difficulties.[54] The Roman Catholics are said to have declared that to be Protestant was to be English and that to be Catholic was to be French.[55] To strengthen the Protestant cause the Société des Missions Évangéliques de Paris sent representatives. A pioneer deputation arrived in 1896. Soon missionaries began to come. The London Missionary Society turned over to them nearly 500 of its congregations and a number of its schools. By 1908 the French Protestants had more missionaries than any one British society. They worked in close amity with the London Missionary Society and the English Friends.[56] Missionaries of the Society for the Propagation of the Gospel in Foreign Parts continued. The Anglican form of the faith spread spontaneously, at first entirely apart from foreigners, in the North.[57] The Norwegian Missionary Society did not suffer from the same suspicions as did the British organizations. Its foreign staff, already, in 1898, more numerous than that of any British body, remained the largest of any of the Protestant groups.[58] The Roman Catholics greatly augmented their forces, partly by the entrance of additional orders

[53] Sibree, *The Madagascar Mission*, pp. 77, 78; McMahon, *Christian Missions in Madagascar*, p. 114; Webster, *Madagascar*, pp. 44, 45.

[54] Sibree, *op. cit.*, pp. 79, 80.

[55] Mondain, *Un Siècle de Mission Protestante à Madagascar*, p. 311.

[56] Mondain, *op. cit.*, pp. 312ff.; Paul Barnaud, *Mon Voyage à Madagascar* (Paris, Société des Missions Évangéliques, 1921, pp. 383), *passim;* G. S. Chapus and G. Mondain, *L'Action Protestante à Madagascar* (Antanànarivo, Imprimerie L.M.S., no date, pp. 63), pp. 35ff.; A. Boegner and Paul Germond, *Rapport sur la Délégation à Madagascar . . . (Juillet 1898—Février 1899)* (Paris, Maison des Missions Évangéliques, 1899, pp. 277), *passim;* H. Rusillon, *Un Petit Continent, Madagascar* (Paris, Société des Missions Évangéliques, 1933, pp. viii, 414), pp. 343ff.; Jane Pannier, *Jean Bianquis* (Paris, Société Évangéliques, no date, pp. 230), pp. 87-100.

[57] G. L. King, *A Self-made Bishop. The Story of John Tsizehena, "Bishop of the North, D.D."* (Westminster, The Society for the Propagation of the Gospel in Foreign Parts, 1933, pp. x, 58), *passim.*

[58] Griffith, *Madagascar*, pp. 78, 79. On the Norwegian missions under French rule, see Johnson, *Det förste Hundredaar av Madagaskars Kirkenhistorie*, pp. 128ff.; H. Hansen, *Beitrag zur Geschichte der Insel Madagaskar besonders im letzten Jahrzehnt. Auf Grund norwegischer Quellen* (Gütersloh, C. Bertelsmann, 1899, pp. viii, 437), pp. 192ff.

and societies. The Jesuit province of Lyons, which had been in charge of the island, called to its aid the Jesuits of Champagne.[59] In 1896 the Lazarists took over the southern part of the island, and in 1898 the Holy Ghost Fathers were given charge of a portion of the North.[60] A nineteenth-century community of French origin, the Missionaries of La Salette, also entered.[61] In 1905 the ecclesiastical map differed substantially from that of 1895.

In 1905, about the time of the separation of Church and state in France, a new Governor-General, representative of the anti-clericalism which had brought about that event, was appointed to Madagascar. Through him measures were taken which curbed the churches and the missions and encouraged the old native cults. As in France, the church buildings were made the property of the state. Restrictions were placed on erecting new buildings and on preaching to non-Christians. The holding of schools in church buildings was forbidden. Since most of the Christian village schools were conducted in the churches and chapels, this ruling was a severe blow. Only those teachers were allowed to continue who held a French certificate and who knew the French language. Christian Endeavour Societies, the Six-Monthly Meeting of the churches, and the Young Men's Christian Association were proscribed, presumably because they were suspected as possible nurseries of Malagasy nationalism.[62] The attempt was being made to consolidate French rule and to reduce the power of the Church.

These various actions by the government retarded but did not permanently check the growth of Christianity. The estimated Protestant church-membership rose from 41,134 in 1898 to 66,264 in 1908 and to 74,817 in 1918. The estimated number of adherents to Protestantism was 86,416 in 1898, 218,188 in 1908, and 449,126 in 1918.[63] Roman Catholics were said to total approximately 170,000 in 1905[64] and approximately 210,000 in about the year 1911.[65] It is difficult to determine statistically which was stronger, Protestantism or Roman Catholicism, for the figures of the two wings of the Christian movement were not

[59] [Dubois], *La Mission de Madagascar Bètsilèo, passim; Léon Derville, Madagascar-Bètsilèo. Ils ne sont que Quarante. Les Jesuits chez les Bètsilèos* (Paris, Dillon et Cie, 1930, pp. 126), pp. 11, 12.
[60] Schwager, *Die katholische Heidenmission der Gegenwart*, p. 156.
[61] Schmidlin-Braun, *Catholic Mission History*, p. 660.
[62] Richter, *Geschichte der evangelischen Mission in Afrika*, pp. 659-662; Sibree, *Fifty Years in Madagascar*, pp. 288-298; Webster, *Madagascar*, p. 52.
[63] Griffith, *Madagascar*, pp. 78, 79. On a Quaker missionary of the period, see *For He Loveth Our Nation. A Record of the Life and Work of William Edward Gregory. By His Wife* (London, Allenson & Co., no date, pp. vii, 248), *passim*.
[64] Schwager, *Die katholische Heidenmission der Gegenwart*, pp. 157, 158.
[65] Streit, *Atlas Hierarchicus*, p. 102.

comparable. It is clear, however, that both increased in the fore part of the twentieth century.

May we summarize this already too condensed account of one of the most remarkable stories in the entire course of the expansion of Christianity?

The kind of Christianity which spread in Madagascar was British, Norwegian, and French Protestantism, with the English Congregationalists leading the way, and French Roman Catholicism.

The reason for the spread was to be found at first in a combination of burning missionary zeal, British commercial ambition, and the desire of the Malagasy, and especially the Hòva, the leading tribe, for Western culture. At the outset, as in so many lands, encouragement was given by the prince. Persecution followed but was not severe enough to prevent the continuing expansion of the faith. The movement towards Christianity was eventually vastly accelerated by the favour and then the conversion of the head of the state. Annexation by France modified the spread and gave opportunity and incentive for French Protestantism and Roman Catholicism. The fact that it made headway at the outset and chiefly among the Hòva and that the Hòva were first the political leaders, and then, after the French conquest had deprived them of that position, the most active traders of the island, greatly promoted the spread of Christianity.[66]

The effect of Christianity upon its environment was seen in part in the winning of the allegiance of a growing number of the Malagasy and the emergence of strong churches which were progressively more self-supporting and self-propagating. Among the other results were the end of the slave trade, brought about largely by the pressure of Christianity on the British conscience, the initiation of Western types of education, the preaching of human worth and the equality of men, the dignifying of human labour, the elevation of the status of women, the substitution of monogamy for polygamy and polyandry, the overthrow of the witch-doctor and fetishism, better housing, the fight for temperance, the introduction of Sunday, and the translation and circulation of the Bible.[67] We hear, too, of training in industries and agriculture, and of the introduction of new kinds of trees and the promotion of forestry.[68]

The effects of the environment were various. To the trend towards cooperation among Protestants which was so marked a feature of the twentieth

[66] A. M. Chirgwin, *Wayfaring for Christ* (London, Edinburgh House Press, 1932, pp. 160), pp. 18-20.
[67] Rusillon in *The International Review of Missions*, Vol. XXIII, pp. 530-538.
[68] Berg, *Die katholische Heidenmission als Kulturträger*, Vol. I, p. 302.

century throughout the world must be attributed a gathering in London of representatives of the various societies at work in Madagascar, the sending of a joint delegation to the island in 1913, the holding of an inter-mission conference in that year, and an agreement upon a delimitation of territory among the seven Protestant bodies in such fashion as to prevent overlapping and to ensure the bringing to the entire island of the Christian message as interpreted by Protestants.[69] The organization of the churches planted by the London Missionary Society displayed an adaptation of the English congregational model to the Malagasy setting. In the course of a religious awakening which swept across some of the provinces in 1904 we hear of visions, faith-healing, and the exorcism of evil spirits which seem to owe much to the inherited background.[70] Local indigenous sects also arose, but as minorities.[71] In spite of the presence of many Malagasy preachers and much zeal of native Christians in spreading the faith, the white missionaries were still in control. Here as among most of the non-European peoples penetrated by Europeans in the nineteenth century, missionaries continued to supervise the churches.

From Madagascar we must pass to other islands in the vicinity of Africa. So small were they and their populations that in the broad scope of our story we can give to them only the briefest mention. Yet that much we must do if our narrative is to be geographically complete. Moreover, the vitality of the impulses which wrought for Christianity its astonishing expansion in the nineteenth century is all the more vividly apparent when we recall that even in these small dots of land the faith was carried partly by European settlers and partly by missionaries who came primarily for that purpose.

Not far from Madagascar is the island of Mauritius. French in the eighteenth century, when active Roman Catholic missions firmly established Christianity, it passed into British control during the Napoleonic Wars and remained under the British flag. To its population of French and Negroes were added a sprinkling of British stocks and, after the emancipation of the Negro slaves in the 1830's, an extensive importation of Indian coolies to provide labour for the sugar plantations which were the chief source of the island's wealth. Of the total of more than 375,000 in 1921, one of the densest on the earth's surface,

---

[69] *Madagascar en 1913* (Paris, Société des Missions Évangéliques, no date, pp. 103), pp. 1-6; *Madagascar for Christ. Impressions of Nine Missionary Visitors to Madagascar July to October, 1913* (London, L.M.S. and F.F.M.A.; Paris, P.M.S., 1914, pp. 68), pp. 52ff.; Griffith, *Madagascar*, p. 49.

[70] Sibree, *Fifty Years in Madagascar*, p. 173.

[71] Sibree, *op. cit.*, p. 174.

about three-fourths were of Indian ancestry. There were a few thousand Chinese. Religiously the majority of the Indians were Hindus and the minority Moslems.

At the time when their possession of Mauritius was confirmed by treaty, the British undertook to give government support to the Roman Catholic clergy. These, however, proved too few adequately to care for the nominally Christian Negro population. To make good this lack, the Vicar Apostolic, a Benedictine, called in (1842), shortly after emancipation, the Fathers of the Holy Ghost, that order dedicated primarily to Negroes. Famous among them was Jacques Désiré Laval, priest and physician, who is said to have converted 67,000 Negroes and who so won the reverence of the islanders that his grave became a place of pilgrimage.[72] Jesuits also arrived, and sisters. About 10,000 Indians were won and the Roman Catholic population reached about 110,000.[73] In 1854 the Church of England consecrated a bishop for Mauritius.[74] Both the Society for the Propagation of the Gospel in Foreign Parts[75] and the Church Missionary Society sent missionaries, and hundreds of converts were made, notably among the Indian coolies.[76] Protestants, however, constituted only a minority of the Christians of the island.

The much smaller island of Rodriguez, east of Mauritius, had a predominantly Roman Catholic population.

Réunion (earlier Bourbon), larger than Mauritius but with a considerably smaller population, except for a short period during the Napoleonic Wars remained in French hands. Its population was prevailingly of French extraction, but with an intermixture of Malagasy and Negro blood. Lazarists had served it in the eighteenth century, but in 1820, because of the vicissitudes of the French Revolution and the Napoleonic Wars, only four priests were left and they were aged. Soon after 1835 two French priests arrived, one of them a colleague of Libermann, the founder of that Congregation of the Holy Heart of Mary which united with the Congregation of the Holy Ghost primarily for missions to Negroes. By 1848, when emancipation came, most of the Negroes of Réunion were professedly Roman Catholic. An influx of Indian labourers introduced a non-Christian element. In 1850 a diocese was established on the island. The priests were trained at Paris in the Seminary of the Fathers of the

[72] Schwager, *Die katholische Heidenmission der Gegenwart*, pp. 152, 153; Marie, *Histoire des Instituts Religieux et Missionaires*, p. 243.

[73] Schwager, *op. cit.*, pp. 152, 153.

[74] Vincent W. Ryan, *Mauritius and Madagascar: Journals of an Eight Years' Residence in the Diocese of Mauritius, and of a Visit to Madagascar* (London, Seeley, Jackson, and Halliday, 1864, pp. ix, 340), p. 8.

[75] Pascoe, *Two Hundred Years of the S.P.G.*, p. 371.

[76] Stock, *The History of the Church Missionary Society*, Vol. II, pp. 470-472.

Holy Ghost and the Holy Heart of Mary. Sisters of St. Joseph and Daughters of Mary were also on the island.[77] The island had only a few Protestants.[78]

The Comoro Islands, lying between Madagascar and the coast of Africa, of volcanic and coral origin and inhabited by a mixture of Malagasy, Negro, and Arab stocks, came progressively under French control in the half century beginning in 1841. The Fathers of the Holy Ghost found here another of their fields.[79]

The Seychelles, an archipelago lying north of Madagascar, was French in the eighteenth century, but became a British possession in consequence of the Napoleonic Wars. Its population was a mixture of French creoles from Mauritius and Réunion, Negroes, Chinese, Indians, and British. In the eighteenth century, the Negro slaves had conformed to the Roman Catholic faith of their French masters. The disorders attendant upon the French Revolution wrought decline in morals and religion. In the first half of the nineteenth century emancipation brought here as elsewhere serious problems for both whites and blacks. It is said that no priest had been there since the French Revolution. In 1852 the islands were made a prefecture apostolic and in 1880 a vicariate apostolic. Massaia, who arrived in 1852, was compelled to leave on suspicion of arousing an anti-British movement. In 1863 the islands were entrusted to the Capuchins of Savoy. The Capuchins entered energetically on their task and began systematically to cover the islands. Marist Brothers and Sisters of St. Joseph of Cluny came to their aid. The large majority of the population were Roman Catholics.[80] Through the Society for the Propagation of the Gospel in Foreign Parts[81] and the Church Missionary Society,[82] the Church of England won a following, but on only one of the islands were they in the majority.[83]

The lonely and bleak group of volcanic peaks in the South Atlantic, a British possession bearing the name of Tristan da Cunha, had only a few score inhabitants, nineteenth-century immigrants from several sources, chiefly Europe and America, and their descendants. Even to this remote spot with its mere handful of people came missionaries. Beginning in the 1850's clergymen of the Church of England, mostly aided by the Society for the Propagation of

[77] Schwager, op. cit., pp. 151, 152; The Catholic Encyclopedia, Vol. XIII, p. 344.

[78] P. Beaton, Six Months in Reunion: A Clergyman's Holiday, and How He Passed It (London, Hurst and Blackett, 2 vols., 1860), passim.

[79] Schwager, op. cit., p. 158.

[80] Schwager, op. cit., pp. 158-160; The Catholic Encyclopedia, Vol. XII, p. 312; Capucins Missionaires. Missions Françaises, p. 31.

[81] Pascoe, op. cit., pp. 368-370.

[82] Stock, op. cit., Vol. II, pp. 470, 472, Vol. III, p. 549.

[83] Pascoe, op. cit., p. 373a.

the Gospel in Foreign Parts, arrived in a somewhat irregular succession, and ministered medically, intellectually, and spiritually to the population.[84]

St. Helena, also of volcanic origin, beginning in the seventeenth century became continuously a part of the British Empire. Its few hundred inhabitants were of several stocks. The Church of England was the most active of the Christian communions. In 1847 the Society for the Propagation of the Gospel in Foreign Parts began to help with the support of clergy, but before then there had been a colonial chaplain. In 1859 a bishop was consecrated. Conversions were made among the liberated slaves. The island was divided into parishes. In 1865 nine-tenths of the population were counted as members of the Church of England.[85] In the 1840's a Dissenting missionary of Baptist convictions attracted a following.[86]

Another volcanic island, Ascension, north-west of St. Helena, like the latter, British, but with a smaller population, was included in the Anglican diocese of St. Helena. To it the Society for the Propagation of the Gospel in Foreign Parts sent at least one missionary.[87]

The Spanish island of Fernando Po lies so close to the mainland and racially is so predominantly Negro that we must defer an account of it to the next chapter.

São Tomé and the much smaller Principe, both of volcanic origin and in the Gulf of Guinea and both of them possessions of Portugal since the days of that country's commercial might, had a mixed population in which Negro blood predominated. Christianity was introduced by the Portuguese in the sixteenth century. Indeed, in 1584 a diocese was created for São Tomé. In the nineteenth century the Christianity of the islands suffered severely. Economic depression was followed by unrest. The forcible dissolution of the religious orders in Portugal in 1834 deprived the islands of much of their accustomed oversight. The see fell vacant in 1847. Yet early in the twentieth century about half the population were still counted as Roman Catholics.[88]

The Cape Verde Islands, with a population which was mainly Negro and mulatto, had been Portuguese since the fifteenth century and had been a

[84] Douglas M. Gane, *Handbook of Tristan da Cunha* (no place or date of publication, pp. 40), *passim*; K. M. Barrow, *Three Years in Tristan da Cunha* (London, Skeffington & Son, 1910, pp. xii, 280), *passim*; Rose Annie Rogers, *The Lonely Island* (London, George Allen & Unwin, 1926, pp. 223), *passim*.

[85] Pascoe, *op. cit.*, pp. 319-321b; Lewis and Edwards, *Historical Records of the Church of the Province of South Africa*, pp. 385-388.

[86] Edwin F. Hatfield, *St. Helena and the Cape of Good Hope: or, Incidents in the Missionary Life of the Rev. James M'Gregor Bertram, of St. Helena* (New York, Edward H. Fletcher, 1852, pp. 220), pp. 115ff.

[87] Pascoe, *op. cit.*, p. 897.

[88] Schwager, *op. cit.*, p. 110; *The Catholic Encyclopedia*, Vol. XIII, p. 381.

diocese since the first half of the sixteenth century. In the nineteenth and twentieth centuries its inhabitants were reckoned as Roman Catholics, although their faith was said to be mixed with many non-Christian superstitions.[89]

In the islands off the African coast as in Africa itself and largely throughout the world, the religious complexion was in part dependent upon political affiliations. French or Portuguese ownership meant the presence of Roman Catholic Christianity. British connexions favoured Protestantism. Where the European overlord had first been French and then British, under nineteenth-century British tolerance Roman Catholicism persisted. Yet never was this religious conformity automatic. Always Christianity owed its persistence and often its very existence to faithful souls who out of self-forgetful devotion strove to win non-Christians, to give spiritual care to the Christians, to provide education, and, often, to promote the physical welfare of their charges. Connexion with one or another of the colonial empires of European powers facilitated the entrance of Christianity and largely determined the kind of Christianity which spread, but here as elsewhere it was through individuals who had been captured by the inherent power of Christianity that the faith was propagated and the Christian communities nourished.

[89] *The Catholic Encyclopedia,* Vol. XIII, p. 467.

Chapter XI

AFRICA SOUTH OF THE SAHARA. THE WHITE CHURCHES IN SOUTH AFRICA: MISSIONS TO THE NON-WHITES IN SOUTH AFRICA: GERMAN SOUTH-WEST AFRICA: BECHUANALAND: RHODESIA: NYASALAND: ANGOLA: PORTUGUESE EAST AFRICA: GERMAN EAST AFRICA: BRITISH EAST AFRICA: UGANDA: THE BELGIAN CONGO: FRENCH EQUATORIAL AFRICA: RIO MUNI: FERNANDO PO: CAMEROON: NIGERIA: DAHOMY: TOGO: THE GOLD COAST: THE IVORY COAST: LIBERIA: SIERRA LEONE: FRENCH GUINEA: PORTUGUESE GUINEA: GAMBIA: SENEGAL: UPPER SENEGAL: NIGER: SUMMARY

IT IS fitting that this volume should be concluded (except for a brief summary) with a chapter on Africa south of the Sahara. In the earlier chapters we have ranged over a wide expanse of territory and over many tribes and nations. The common tie which has given unity to the diversity has been the impact of white peoples upon peoples of primitive cultures. Whether in Canada, Greenland, the West Indies, Latin America, the Islands of the Pacific, the Malay Archipelago, or Madagascar, we have found Europeans or those of European descent impinging upon folk in the primitive stages of civilization. Nearly everywhere those of European stock formed settlements. Always they became politically and culturally dominant. In several areas they founded new nations. Christianity entered as the hereditary faith of the Europeans. With the abounding vitality which characterized it in the nineteenth century, it perpetuated itself through churches, some of them very vigorous, among those of white stock. It also was propagated among the primitive peoples, usually with amazing rapidity. In Africa south of the Sahara was the largest congeries of primitive folk on the planet. The nineteenth century witnessed the penetration of this vast region by white explorers and merchants, and the partition of almost all the territory among European powers. It saw the rise of a new nation in South Africa, ruled by a white minority several hundred thousand strong. In the course of that century Christianity ceased to be confined to the coastal margins where it had been planted in the preceding three hundred

319

years and was carried into the interior. Here Christianity faced on the largest scale the problems thrust upon it by the white exploitation of primitive folk.

This chapter is restricted to Africa south of the Sahara. That is because, in a rough way, this part of Africa is a unity. The Sahara forms a barrier which divides the continent into two parts. The northern shores and the Red Sea littoral belong culturally to the basin of the Mediterranean and Western Asia. Africa south of the Sahara is fairly distinct. Racially it was and is a mixture. Cultural and racial infusions entered it from the North and East. However, its peoples were mostly blacks. Some were pygmies. Many were Negroes. Some were Hottentots and Bushmen. Large numbers were Bantu, a term implying linguistic rather than racial relationship. Such states as arose were ephemeral. Tribal organization prevailed. There was much of agriculture and cattle-raising. Religion was mainly animism. Here and there Islam was making gains, often through contacts with Moslem traders. Its chief strength was on the east coast, in the Sudan, and on the southern borders of the Sahara. Usually writing was unknown. It is with this vast primitive Africa that we have here to do.

Christianity, as we have seen,[1] reached the Africa south of the Sahara late in the fifteenth century. In the following three centuries both Roman Catholic and Protestant Christianity were introduced, the former by the Portuguese and the latter through the Dutch and the English and, to a less extent, through French Huguenot exiles and the Moravians. The Christianity was mostly Roman Catholic and was to be found only on the fringes of the continent. With the decay of Portuguese power in the seventeenth and eighteenth centuries it had dwindled. In some areas it had disappeared. In other areas it persisted, but unenergetically.

Before the nineteenth century, the chief contact of European peoples with Africa south of the Sahara was through the slave traffic. Here was the most extensive selfish exploitation of one set of races by another which history has seen. Hundreds of thousands of blacks were forcibly carried to servitude in the Americas and thousands to the islands adjacent to Africa. The slaves were recruited chiefly by inter-tribal wars, in themselves destructive of life and order. The slave caravans to the coast and the trans-Atlantic passage were a succession of horrors. Much of the plantation life in the New World was accompanied by degradation and cruelty. That this colossal evil was the work of peoples whose nominal faith was Christianity was an indictment of that religion which cannot be brushed aside. If in any way Christianity was responsible for the energy and courage which led to the discovery and settlement

[1] Vol. III, chap. 7.

of the Americas by Europeans, it was to some degree, even though slightly, a cause of Negro slavery, for it was the need of cheap labour on the white man's plantations which gave rise to the institution. While Christianity did something to ameliorate the lot of the slaves and in time the majority of the transplanted blacks adopted it, the faith long failed to abolish either slavery or the slave trade. Black Africa's early contacts with professedly Christian peoples were far from happy.

In the nineteenth century revolutionary changes occurred. As we have seen,[2] largely because of impulses issuing from Christianity, the slave trade was brought to an end and slavery itself was wiped out, in the British Empire in the 1830's and in the United States in the 1860's. It disappeared in the possessions of the other European powers and in Latin America, although not always so clearly because of the Christian conscience as in Anglo-Saxon lands. In the world-wide expansion of European peoples which marked the nineteenth century, white men made themselves masters of Africa south of the Sahara and divided it among themselves. In this series of annexations the British, the French, the Portuguese, the Germans, and the Belgians were the chief beneficiaries. The Spaniards and the Italians picked up small fragments.

Missionaries entered in increasing numbers, sometimes ahead of white governments, sometimes following them. In general, although by no means entirely, their distribution reflected the political patterns imposed by Europeans. Roman Catholicism was strongest in Portuguese, French, German, and Belgian territories. Protestantism was most prominent in British and German possessions. Protestant missionaries were chiefly from the major colonial power, Great Britain. In lesser numbers they came from Germany, partly to German colonial possessions, and from France, the United States, and Scandinavia. Roman Catholic missionaries were mainly from France, which was next to Great Britain in the proportion of African territory acquired. Protestantism was off to a somewhat earlier start than was the revival of Roman Catholic activity. By 1914 the two great wings of the Christian movement were not far from the same numerical strength in the totals of converts from among non-Christians.

As we describe the spread of Christianity in this nineteenth-century Africa, we will move from the South to the North and then to the West. We will begin at the Cape of Good Hope.

At the Cape of Good Hope, on the southern tip of Africa, there had arisen,

[2] Vol. IV, pp. 158, 159, 345-351.

before 1800, a colony of Protestant whites. It was predominantly Dutch, but with a sprinkling of French Huguenots. In 1795, when in the course of the Napoleonic Wars the British seized the Cape, the population numbered 21,000 whites, all of whom were professedly Christian and the large majority of whom were connected with the Dutch Reformed Church. They were served by seven congregations and ten ministers.[3] The salaries of the latter were paid by the Dutch East India Company.[4] The churches and the clergy were under the Classis of Amsterdam.[5] There was also a population of slaves, and several hundreds of these had been baptized.[6] In the eighteenth century a few converts were made by the Moravian, George Schmidt, among the Hottentots.[7]

Between 1795, when the British first established their rule in South Africa, and 1914, there developed a state, the Union of South Africa, somewhat akin to Canada, Australia, and New Zealand in that it had a substantial proportion of British blood and was a self-governing dominion within the British Empire.

In spite of its resemblance to the other major dominions of the British Empire, South Africa presented striking differences which gave it distinct characteristics and which profoundly affected its religious history and complexion. In South Africa those of European stock were in the minority. Blacks of various tribes, coloured, and small enclaves of Asiatics, mainly from India, together constituted more than two-thirds of the whole. In Canada, Australia, and even New Zealand by 1914 the aboriginal peoples were only a small minority. In consequence, Christianity was confronted by extensive bodies of non-Christians and by a race problem which, while changing in its expressions, was persistently grave. Those of European descent were divided. The original Dutch stock with its admixture of French Huguenots multiplied and remained distinct in language and faith. Although not reinforced by immigration, it flourished through the large families made possible by the frontier agricultural economy. It had features similar to those of the French in Canada and Newfoundland. Like these French, it continued apart in tongue and religion. Its inherited Dutch speech became Afrikaans. As in Canada and Newfoundland the Roman Catholic Church was both a symbol and a bond of the French elements, so in South Africa the Dutch Reformed churches were in part a channel and a tie for the common life of the Afrikanders. They were the repository of Dutch traditions. They were the guardian of the Dutch language

[3] McCarter, *The Dutch Reformed Church in South Africa*, p. 13.
[4] Du Plessis, *The Life of Andrew Murray of South Africa*, p. 78.
[5] McCarter, *op. cit.*, pp. 20, 21.
[6] Du Plessis, *op. cit.*, p. 78.
[7] Du Plessis, *A History of Christian Missions in South Africa*, pp. 50ff.

against the encroaching English and were an expression of the national strivings of the Boers.[8] In Canada the Roman Catholic Church, a bulwark of French nationalism, tended to be conservative. For somewhat similar reasons the Dutch Reformed churches of South Africa were tenacious of tradition. The Afrikanders had a stormier history than did the French of Canada and Newfoundland. To be free from British rule some of them in the 1830's went on what came to be termed the Great Trek which gave rise to the semi-independent Transvaal and Orange Free State. Repeated friction with the British culminated in the Boer or South African War (1899-1902), on a scale never seen among the French in Canada. Roman Catholicism was proportionately much less strong than in Canada, Newfoundland, or Australia. No French enclave supported it as in Canada and Newfoundland and no large Irish immigration existed for its basis as in Australia. Relatively it was weaker even than in New Zealand.

If in some aspects which affected its religious life South Africa differed from the other dominions of the British Empire, in the Christianity of the British elements of its population it was singularly like them. The Church of England was prominent. Presbyterianism, as the faith of most of the Scotch settlers, was present. The Methodists were strong. Baptists and Congregationalists were small minorities, but the Baptists were more numerous than the Congregationalists.[9]

We must first address ourselves to the story of Christianity among the white population of South Africa and to the manner in which those of European descent were held to their hereditary faith. We shall then be in a better position to recount the spread of Christianity among the non-European majority.

Of the white communions, the first to claim our attention must be that of the original settlers, the Dutch Reformed Church.

In a manner reminiscent of the treatment of the Roman Catholic Church in Canada when that territory passed into British hands, the articles of capitulation which in 1795 transferred the Cape to Great Britain provided for the maintenance of the existing religious privileges of the population. The British Government continued the salaries of the clergy.[10] In the brief revival of Dutch rule (1803-1806) a Church Order was adopted which provided for a general church assembly or synod every two years, but which stipulated the

[8] Du Plessis, The Life of Andrew Murray of South Africa, p. 7.
[9] In 1911, of the European stock, 54.37 per cent. were listed as Dutch Reformed, 20.03 per cent. as Anglicans, 4.59 per cent. as Presbyterians, 6.43 per cent. as Methodists, 1.18 per cent. as Baptists, 1.05 per cent. as Congregationalists, 1.85 per cent. as Lutherans, 4.22 per cent. as Roman Catholics, and .15 per cent. as Greek Orthodox.—Union of South Africa. Official Year Book No. 9, 1926-1927, p. 289.
[10] McCarter, op. cit., p. 34.

presence of two commissioners of the state and gave them the power to suspend at any point the gathering's actions until the will of the Governor could be learned. This procedure was retained when, in 1806, the British regime was renewed. The restraint proved annoying. In 1843, following an incident in which a Governor withheld his approval of the synod's decisions, a "Church Ordinance" was obtained which granted all but complete autonomy to the Dutch Reformed Church in forming and implementing its decisions.[11] In 1843, moreover, the principle of voluntarism was introduced. Congregations established after 1850 received no state aid.[12]

To the Dutch Reformed Church came leadership from Holland and especially from Scotland[13] which brought contact with the potent fresh currents of religious life in nineteenth-century Protestantism. In the fore part of the nineteenth century the Dutch Reformed Church in South Africa suffered from a dearth of clergy. George Thom, who came to South Africa under the London Missionary Society, became minister of one of the Dutch congregations. In 1821, when he went to Great Britain on furlough, he was commissioned by the Governor of the colony to seek clergy and teachers. He obtained several, chiefly from the Church of Scotland, for that body, being of the Reformed family of Protestantism, was akin to the Dutch Reformed Church. Among those who came was Andrew Murray. Murray was moved by a sense of mission, identified himself with his adopted people, prayed for revivals, and was the progenitor of a numerous and notable line of clergy.[14] Andrew Murray's sons John and Andrew were sent to Scotland to be educated. There they lived in the home of an uncle, a clergyman who became a leader in the Free Church, and were brought in touch with the revival movement led by William C. Burns, later a missionary to China. They decided to enter the ministry. For theological training they went to Holland, to the University of Utrecht. Here they became members of an inner circle which had sprung from the rising tide of religious life in that country.[15] Not far from the same time there arrived in Holland some other South African students who held views similar to those of the Murrays.[16] John Murray eventually became one of the first professors in the theological seminary which was opened in Stellenbosch (1859) and was therefore in a position to exert a marked influence upon his church.[17] In the

[11] Du Plessis, *The Life of Andrew Murray of South Africa*, pp. 79, 80, 209; McCarter, *op. cit.*, pp. 36-40.

[12] Du Plessis, *op. cit.*, p. 264; McCarter, *op. cit.*, p. 43.

[13] Du Plessis, *op. cit.*, pp. 210-212.

[14] Du Plessis, *op. cit.*, pp. 1-33, 80, 81; Douglas, *Andrew Murray and His Message*, p. 15.

[15] Du Plessis, *op. cit.*, pp. 31-70.

[16] Du Plessis, *op. cit.*, p. 70.

[17] Douglas, *op. cit.*, pp. 17-19; Du Plessis, *op. cit.*, pp. 173, 174, 184.

course of a long life, his brother Andrew (1828-1917) became the most widely known of the ministers of the South African church. Warmly evangelistic, placing great emphasis upon the devotional life, prizing the *Theologia Germanica* and other writings of Christian mystics, Andrew Murray the younger had a striking effect upon the Boer church.[18] In 1889, for example, with his active assistance the Cape General Mission (becoming in 1894, through amalgamation with the South-east Africa Evangelistic Mission, the South Africa General Mission) came into being with the object of furthering, chiefly among the whites, "absolute surrender" to the will of God.[19] Through him and others like him, the Dutch Reformed Church, in addition to being conservative theologically, stressed a warm inner life.

To the Dutch Reformed Church the Boers who founded the new settlements in the Transvaal, the Orange Free State, and Natal presented much the same problem as that which confronted the churches on the frontier in the United States and Canada. In contrast, however, with the frontiersmen of the United States, the large majority of those who went on the Great Trek had had religious instruction and were members of the Church. Most of the families possessed a Bible and hymn book. In many of the encampments Sunday was observed and religious services were held.[20] However, there was a great dearth of clergy. To meet the need some of the Cape ministers went to the frontier. In 1849 the younger Andrew Murray, then only twenty-one years of age, became the first pastor of the congregation at Bloemfontein. He also itinerated widely among the Boer farmers scattered on their lonely ranches, pushing his journeys into what became the Transvaal.[21] Some clergy arrived directly from Holland.[22] In 1860, at the instance of Andrew Murray, Jr., a group of ministers sent a representative who was to go to Europe, and, if necessary, to America, to recruit reinforcements. He found most of the clergy in Holland too liberal theologically to meet his requirements, but he obtained two there, several from the Free Church of Scotland, and at least one Swiss.[23] In Natal until ministers of their own faith arrived the Boers were served religiously by an American missionary and by representatives of the Berlin Missionary Society.[24] Eventually in all three areas, the Orange Free State, the Transvaal, and Natal, the Dutch churches became well organized and provided with clergy.

[18] Du Plessis, *op. cit.*, pp. 260, 394, 436, 480, 526-535.
[19] Du Plessis, *op. cit.*, pp. 381-387.
[20] Du Plessis, *op. cit.*, pp. 415-418.
[21] Du Plessis, *op. cit.*, pp. 85-102, 107, 117.
[22] Du Plessis, *op. cit.*, p. 124.
[23] Du Plessis, *op. cit.*, p. 188.
[24] McCarter, *op. cit.*, pp. 95-97.

To South Africa there came, at the request of Afrikanders, teachers from the United States. One of these, George Ferguson, headed a missionary training institution founded by the younger Andrew Murray.[25] Others were women, largely from Mt. Holyoke Seminary,[26] for whose founder and ideals Andrew Murray had conceived a high admiration.[27]

In the 1890's the Dutch Reformed Church began to feel itself confronted with the problem of the "poor whites," those of European blood who, because of competition with slave labour, were without regular means of subsistence. In 1894 the Synod discussed means of improving their condition and of providing them with suitable employment.[28]

Partly in consequence of these various efforts, the Dutch Reformed Church remained the largest of the religious bodies among the South African whites. In the course of the nineteenth century it developed a strong organization and, thanks in no small degree to ministers who early came from Holland and Scotland, in time it supplied and trained its own staff.

Next to the Dutch Reformed Church in numerical strength among the white population of South Africa was the Anglican communion.

In the early years of the British occupation Anglican chaplains served the garrison.[29] We hear that one of them aroused the ire of the Dutch Reformed Church by baptizing infants and adults who were not of the garrison.[30] In 1820, preceded by smaller contingents in 1817 and 1818, a substantial immigration arrived from the British Isles.[31] The Society for the Propagation of the Gospel in Foreign Parts felt called upon to make provision for the spiritual care of the settlers. In 1820 it began according financial assistance. The Society for Promoting Christian Knowledge also helped.[32] The government provided support.[33] In 1825 there were six Anglican clergy at the Cape.[34] Church buildings were erected. Occasional visits were paid by bishops of Calcutta, who were given jurisdiction in the area.[35]

The vigorous life of the Anglican communion in South Africa began with

[25] Du Plessis, *op. cit.*, p. 293.

[26] See Vol. IV, p. 420.

[27] Du Plessis, *op. cit.*, pp. 275-286, 398.

[28] Du Plessis, *op. cit.*, p. 405.

[29] Clarke, *Constitutional Church Government*, pp. 320, 321; Lewis and Edwards, *Historical Records of the Church of the Province of South Africa*, pp. 4-11.

[30] Lewis and Edwards, *op. cit.*, p. 7.

[31] *The Cambridge History of the British Empire*, Vol. VIII, pp. 234, 235.

[32] Allen and McClure, *Two Hundred Years: The History of the Society for Promoting Christian Knowledge, 1698-1898*, pp. 347-355.

[33] Lewis and Edwards, *op. cit.*, pp. 13ff.; Pascoe, *Two Hundred Years of the S.P.G.*, pp. 269ff.

[34] Anderson-Morshead, *A Pioneer and Founder . . . Robert Gray*, p. 24.

[35] Lewis and Edwards, *op. cit.*, pp. 18-21.

the appointment of the first resident bishop, Robert Gray, in 1847.[36] The creation of the See of Cape Town was a result of the Oxford Movement, and Gray was in sympathy with the attitudes of that religious awakening. He was both able and devoted. As soon as he landed he sent out an appeal for clergymen, for there were 5,000 troops in Kaffraria without a chaplain and 800 settlers in Natal without a priest. Almost at once he began training candidates for Holy Orders and made plans for missions to Moslems and pagans. Within two years the number of clergy in the diocese increased from fourteen to forty-two and more than twenty churches were being built.[37] By 1850 fifty clergy were at work.[38] Gray travelled indefatigably over the vast distances of his diocese, even to lonely St. Helena. In 1853 his huge see was divided by the creation of the dioceses of Grahamstown and Natal. Gray thereupon became Metropolitan of the (ecclesiastical) Province of South Africa.[39] In 1857, in an effort to give to the Anglican communion in his jurisdiction a conscious corporate life, he convened a synod. This was something of an innovation and precipitated a controversy which was taken to the civil courts.[40] When he died, in 1872, it was clear that Gray had been one of the outstanding bishops in the Anglican communion.

Gray was succeeded by another man of marked ability, William West Jones, who was Metropolitan from 1874 to 1908 and eventually had the title of Archbishop of Capetown. Under him the Anglican communion in South Africa enjoyed continued growth. It also made further strides, through distressing legal struggles, to an ecclesiastical independence which retained full spiritual fellowship with the mother Church of England.[41]

The young diocese of Natal early came into unhappy prominence through a controversy which was famous in its day but which could not but weaken the nascent Church of England in that colony. The first bishop, John William Colenso, was energetic. He was also unconventional. He adopted and openly advocated positions which were at such variance with those of his communion that they scandalized many. He was indulgent towards the baptism of polygamists among native converts. He taught a view of the Holy Communion which was anathema to men of High Church views. Accepting the methods

---

[36] Day, *Robert Gray, First Bishop of Cape Town, passim;* Anderson-Morshead, *op. cit., passim.*

[37] Day, *op. cit.,* p. 12.

[38] *Church in the Colonies. No. 27, Diocese of Cape Town. Part II. A Journal of the Bishop's Visitation Tour Through the Cape Colony in 1850* (London, Society for Promoting Christian Knowledge, 1851), p. 204.

[39] Lewis and Edwards, *op. cit.,* pp. 37-63, 66.

[40] Day, *op. cit.,* pp. 14-16; Clarke, *op. cit.,* p. 322.

[41] Wood, *A Father in God. The Episcopate of William West Jones, passim.*

of Biblical criticism which were then beginning to arouse fears among the orthodox, he challenged the generally accepted convictions concerning the authorship and authenticity of some of the books of the Old Testament. Bishop Gray brought him to trial before the church courts. He was condemned, deposed, and excommunicated. He took his case to the civil courts, appealing it eventually to the highest tribunal in the Empire, the Judicial Committee of the Privy Council. There he won, but in doing so precipitated the issue of the control of the state over the Church of England in the colonies. In 1869, while Colenso was still living and in spite of the fact that the civil courts gave him control of the church buildings in his diocese, a successor, Macrorie, the choice of Gray, was consecrated by the Anglican communion in South Africa. Colenso still had a following, and the division continued even after his death (1883).[42]

Other dioceses were formed.[43] Some of these were chiefly for missions among the blacks, but spiritual care was also given to white settlers.

Since, in general, it was the Society for the Propagation of the Gospel in Foreign Parts and the Society for Promoting Christian Knowledge which were the most active of the missionary organizations of the Church of England in promoting the Anglican cause in South Africa, and since Gray owed much to the Oxford Movement, the Church of England in that area was prevailingly Anglo-Catholic in tone. It is not surprising, therefore, to find represented the religious communities which were among the fruits of the Anglo-Catholic awakening in England. In the 1860's Gray led the way by encouraging the formation, by volunteers from England, of St. George's Sisters, for the care of the sick, education, and the winning of pagans and Moslems.[44] In the 1880's there was founded in the Diocese of Grahamstown by Cecile Isherwood the Community of the Resurrection of Our Lord.[45] In the 1870's there arrived in Bloemfontein a member of the Sisterhood of St. Thomas the Martyr, Oxford,

[42] Baynes, *South Africa*, pp. 54-85, 171-204 (a neutral account); Lewis and Edwards, *op. cit.*, pp. 159-172, 310-328; Pascoe, *op. cit.*, pp. 328-335 (these two are critical of Colenso); George W. Cox, *The Life of John William Colenso, D.D., Bishop of Natal* (London, W. Ridgway, 2 vols., 1888, favourable to Colenso), *passim;* A. W. L. Rivett, *Ten Years' Church Work in Natal* (London, Jarrold & Sons, 1890, pp. viii, 333, by a clergyman opposed to Colenso), pp. 192ff.; Florence Gregg, *The Story of Bishop Colenso, the Friend of the Zulus* (London, The Sunday School Association, 1892, pp. 144), *passim*, friendly to Colenso.

[43] Baynes, *op. cit.*, pp. 96ff.; Lewis and Edwards, *op. cit.*, pp. 394ff. On the Diocese of Pretoria see J. A. I. Agar-Hamilton. *A Transvaal Jubilee, passim.*

[44] Lewis and Edwards, *op. cit.*, pp. 106ff.

[45] *Mother Cecile in South Africa, 1883-1906, Foundress of the Community of the Resurrection of Our Lord, Compiled by a Sister of the Community* (London, Society for Promoting Christian Knowledge, 1930, pp. ix, 305), *passim.*

who became the nucleus of the Community of St. Michael and All Angels.[46] In the 1860's, at the request of the first Bishop of the Orange Free State, seven men from the Society of St. Augustine migrated from England and began a unit of their brotherhood.[47] In the 1880's came the Cowley Fathers, of the Society of St. John the Evangelist.[48] In 1903 priests of the Community of the Resurrection (Mirfield) arrived in the Transvaal.[49] We hear, too, of the Society of St. John the Divine, of the Sisters of the Church, and of the Community of St. Mary the Virgin.[50] These and other communities which arose out of the Anglo-Catholic revival aided in conserving the faith among the whites and in spreading it among the non-whites.

A unique Anglican enterprise, assisted financially from Great Britain and South Africa, was the South African Church Railway Mission, conducted for the widely scattered employees of the railways who, by the nature of their occupation, were deprived of normal parish life. Begun in 1892 in a humble way, it gradually achieved a wide extension.[51]

Another undertaking was a "Mission of Help," made up of thirty-six clergymen sent from Great Britain in 1904. Its members made tours through the Anglican congregations of South Africa to reinforce and quicken the religious life of the region.[52]

Presbyterianism, if one does not include in that term the closely related Dutch Reformed churches, was much weaker in South Africa among the whites than in Canada, Australia, or New Zealand. What is said to have been the first congregation of that communion was organized in Cape Town in 1813. However, it was composed largely of troops from a particular regiment and when, in 1814, that unit was transferred, the congregation languished and later became Congregationalist. In 1827 or 1828 a Presbyterian church, St Andrews, was founded in Cape Town. Other congregations were eventually begun as branches of St. Andrews and in 1893 the parent body and its offspring instituted a presbytery. Eventually other presbyteries were formed. In 1892 a Federal Council was constituted and met annually until 1897, when it was

---

[46] Lewis and Edwards, *op. cit.,* pp. 416ff.

[47] Lewis and Edwards, *op. cit.,* pp. 401ff.

[48] Lewis and Edwards, *op. cit.,* pp. 99, 100.

[49] Lewis and Edwards, *op. cit.,* p. 605.

[50] Lewis and Edwards, *op. cit.,* pp. 338, 562.

[51] Dorothy F. Ellison, *God's Highwaymen. The Story of the South African Church Railway Mission* (London, Society for Promoting Christian Knowledge, 1931, pp. 157), *passim.*

[52] Arthur W. Robinson, *The Mission of Help to the Church in South Africa* (London, Longmans, Green, and Co., 1906, pp. ix, 152).

succeeded by a General Assembly. At the outset financial assistance was given from Scotland to some of the congregations.[53]

Methodism was somewhat stronger in South Africa among those of European stock than was Presbyterianism. It had its inception in 1806 with Sargeant Kendrick, a class leader and local preacher, in one of the British regiments sent to the Cape. Kendrick began holding services among his comrades, had converts, and asked the Wesleyan Missionary Committee in England for a minister. One was sent, sailing with the wide-ranging Thomas Coke. He landed in 1814. As required by law, he applied to the Governor for permission to hold services. He was refused, and went on to Ceylon.[54] The next Wesleyan minister appointed to South Africa arrived in 1816. He, too, was denied the right to conduct services. When he persisted, the colonel of the regiment ordered his chapel burned. Another was built, but, discouraged, the minister went as a missionary to the Hottentots.[55] Among the British immigration of 1820 were Methodists. Indeed, a group took with them a minister, William Shaw, who saw in the invitation the opportunity to fulfil a long cherished desire to become a missionary.[56] Shaw and a number of lay preachers travelled widely among the British whites. A Methodist colony settled at Salem.[57] Grahamstown, the oldest and for many years the largest town in the eastern districts of the Cape Colony, early had a strong Methodist contingent.[58] By 1844 eighteen Wesleyan churches had been built.[59] In the 1840's Methodism entered Natal through a minister who accompanied the troops in 1842.[60] It was reinforced by immigration from the British Isles. Ministers, too, were sent from England.[61] In 1872 two towns in the Orange Free State had Wesleyan congregations.[62] In 1871 a minister was appointed for the diamond miners who were pouring into Kimberley.[63] Until the 1880's, Methodism grew slowly in the Transvaal, but from 1881 to 1885 it enjoyed a rapid increase. With the influx of the British to the gold fields of the Rand Methodism flourished.[64] In 1866 the ubiquitous American Methodist, William Taylor, arrived in South

[53] Balfour, *Presbyterianism in the Colonies*, pp. 282-291; *Union of South Africa. Official Year Book No. 9, 1926-1927*, pp. 294, 295.
[54] Whiteside, *History of the Wesleyan Methodist Church of South Africa*, p. 35.
[55] Whiteside, *op. cit.*, pp. 36-47.
[56] *Memoir of William Shaw*, pp. 10ff.; Shaw, *The Story of My Mission in South-eastern Africa*, pp. 4, 5.
[57] Shaw, *op. cit.*, pp. 86ff.; Whiteside, *op. cit.*, pp. 93-108.
[58] Whiteside, *op. cit.*, p. 109.
[59] Whiteside, *op. cit.*, p. 112.
[60] Whiteside, *op. cit.*, p. 358.
[61] Whiteside, *op. cit.*, pp. 361-365.
[62] Whiteside, *op. cit.*, pp. 346, 355.
[63] Whiteside, *op. cit.*, pp. 157-166.
[64] Whiteside, *op. cit.*, pp. 419-438.

Africa. His preaching stimulated the white churches, but had especially marked effects among the blacks.[65]

Until after the close of the nineteenth century South African Methodism was aided financially by British Methodism through the Wesleyan Methodist Missionary Society. During most of that century it was also controlled from Great Britain. Beginning in 1873 triennial meetings were held of representatives of all five of the Methodist districts. In 1883, with the approval of the British Conference, the first meeting of the South African Conference convened. This had under its jurisdiction all the churches and missions south of the Vaal River. The district north of the Vaal remained under the British Conference. A gradually diminishing financial grant, terminating in 1902, continued to be given from the mother body. In 1927 the South African Conference became fully independent and autonomous.[66] Methodism was being firmly planted in South Africa.

In spite of its extensive missions among the non-whites of South Africa (to which we are to come in a moment) Congregationalism was numerically weak among those of European stock. About the middle of the nineteenth century, the London Missionary Society, which had been conducting the missions in South Africa, began steps to make these self-supporting.[67] In 1859 the Evangelical Voluntary Union was formed and in 1877 the Congregational Union of South Africa was constituted. The European churches were in the minority in South African Congregationalism.[68] Financial aid continued to come from Great Britain through the Colonial Missionary Society.[69]

Baptist history in South Africa began with the 1820 immigration from the British Isles. Among the settlers were Baptists and in time these organized a church in Grahamstown. By 1877 there were five more churches. In that year the Baptist Union of South Africa was formed. To British membership there were in time added Germans and Afrikanders.[70]

Lutherans were present in South Africa before the British occupation. In the eighteenth century many of the garrison were Germans of that faith. In the 1770's permission was given to build a church. In the nineteenth century the

[65] William Taylor, *Christian Adventures in South Africa* (London, Jackson, Walford, and Hodder, 1868, pp. xiv, xv, 557), *passim;* Taylor, *Story of My Life,* pp. 337-500; Whiteside, *op. cit.,* pp. 263-278.

[66] Whiteside, *op. cit.,* pp. 406-417; *Union of South Africa. Official Year Book No. 9, 1926-1927,* pp. 292, 293.

[67] Lovett, *The History of the London Missionary Society,* Vol. I, pp. 572 ff.

[68] *Union of South Africa. Official Year Book No. 9, 1926-1927,* pp. 296; *The Christian Handbook of South Africa,* pp. 27, 28.

[69] *The Colonial Missionary Society, Seventy-Eighth Annual Report, 1914,* pp. 15, 16.

[70] E. Baker in *The Chronicle,* Vol. I, pp. 122-124.

Lutherans increased through immigration. Churches arose in the Transvaal and Natal. The Hermannsburg Mission sent colonists to co-operate with the missionaries in winning the blacks. Although this method was abandoned in 1869, the German communities continued.[71]

The Seventh Day Adventists organized their South Africa Union Conference in 1902.[72]

In 1912 the Christian Scientists counted five societies and churches. Apparently they were primarily among those of British stock, for their leaders had English, not Dutch names.[73]

The Mormons entered in 1903, carrying on their enterprise, as was their wont, through young men, volunteer missionaries from the United States. They confined their efforts to the whites.[74]

The Salvation Army began work in 1887 among the white population.[75]

We hear, too, of the Plymouth Brethren, primarily among the whites.[76]

The Greek Orthodox Church entered South Africa in 1907, but had only a handful of members.[77]

In 1911 Roman Catholics of European blood numbered about 54,000, or 4.22 per cent. of the white population.[78] The first Roman Catholic priests who were permitted to officiate at the Cape were three who landed in 1805 during the brief restoration of Dutch rule. They were expelled in 1806 when the British resumed their occupation. In 1818 the Cape of Good Hope was included in a new vicariate apostolic which embraced Mauritius. In 1820 permission was obtained from the government to organize the Roman Catholics and the bishop left a priest in Cape Town. In 1837 the Cape was given its own vicariate apostolic, and in 1847 this was divided. By 1892 additional vicariates apostolic had been created for Natal, the Orange Free State, and the Transvaal.[79] Eventually clergy were trained from among the native-born whites. In 1850 a school was opened in Grahamstown. In it the first two South African born bishops were educated.[80]

[71] McCarter, *The Dutch Reformed Church in South Africa*, pp. 115-117; *The Christian Handbook of South Africa*, pp. 38-40; Haccius, *Erlebnisse und Eindrücke Meiner Zweiten Reise durch das Hermannsburger Missionsgebiet in Südafrika (1912-1913)*, pp. 5-8.
[72] *The Christian Handbook of South Africa*, p. 36.
[73] *The Christian Science Journal*, Vol. XXX, p. iii.
[74] *The Christian Handbook of South Africa*, p. 26.
[75] *The Christian Handbook of South Africa*, p. 46.
[76] *The Union of South Africa. Official Year Book No. 9, 1926-1927*, p. 289.
[77] *Ibid.*
[78] *Ibid.*
[79] *The Catholic Directory of British South Africa*, 1910, p. 1; *Cambridge History of the British Empire*, Vol. VIII, p. 848; *Missiones Catholicae . . . MDCCCXCII*, p. 346-355.
[80] *The Catholic Directory of South Africa, 1931*, p. 25.

The effects of Christianity upon the white population of South Africa were about what our observations in other parts of the world would lead us to expect. In the course of the nineteenth century the churches grew with the population. Increasingly they produced their own leadership and provided for their own financial support. Before 1914 the majority of the congregations were in churches which were independent of control from outside South Africa. As we are to see a few paragraphs below, some of the churches engaged in active efforts to win to their faith the coloured and black peoples of Africa. These efforts multiplied as the century advanced. Much was done through the churches to further education and to make it available for all.[81] We hear of a Methodist leaving by bequest a large sum to found an orphanage under the Conference.[82] In the 1880's some of the Dutch Reformed clergy began to advocate total abstinence—but at first this aroused bitter opposition from wine-producing farmers.[83] As was to be anticipated from an institution which was a bulwark of Boer communal life, the Dutch Reformed Church was one of the means of promoting the use of Afrikaans.[84]

South Africa left its distinctive mark upon the Christianity of the area. As we saw a few moments ago, the Dutch Reformed churches were more conservative than many of their sister Reformed churches in Holland and the United States. This seems to have been in part because they were the institutions of a population which was seeking to preserve its own life against assimilation to that of the dominant British Empire. It was in accordance with this characteristic that in the South African War (1899-1902) the clergy of the Dutch Reformed Church were ardent supporters of the Boer cause and that Boer nationalism, fanned by the conflict, led to an added devotion to that church.[85] It is not surprising to read that some of the Afrikanders maintained that England was a horn of the beast mentioned in the Apocalypse (Rev. 17:12)[86] or that some of the Boers who had trekked to the North-east expected soon to move on to Jerusalem as a chosen people.[87] In the 1850's there developed in the Transvaal the *Nederduits Hervormde Kerk* which the Volksraad made the established church of that state.[88] One of the reasons for separating

[81] Whiteside, *History of the Wesleyan Methodist Church of South Africa*, pp. 117, 118; Du Plessis, *The Life of Andrew Murray of South Africa*, pp. 34, 288.
[82] Whiteside, *op. cit.*, p. 84.
[83] Du Plessis, *op. cit.*, pp. 345-349.
[84] Du Plessis, *op. cit.*, pp. 407-409.
[85] Du Plessis, *op. cit.*, pp. 424-428.
[86] Du Plessis, *op. cit.*, p. 123.
[87] Du Plessis, *op. cit.*, p. 103.
[88] Du Plessis, *op. cit.*, pp. 139-145; McCarter, *The Dutch Reformed Church in South Africa*, p. 94; *Union of South Africa. Official Year Book No. 9, 1926-1927*, p. 291.

from the Dutch Reformed Church was that in the Cape the latter enjoyed financial assistance from the local colonial government, which was British.[89] The original leaders of the *Nederduits Hervormde Kerk* came from Holland to minister to the settlers and were accused of rationalism by their fellow clergy in the Cape.[90] Many of the members of the *Nederduits Hervormde Kerk* left it to join the ultra-conservative Reformed Church of South Africa (*Gereformeerde Kerk*). This sprang in part from dissatisfaction with the revival spirit, deemed Methodistic, which was coming into the Cape, and in part through the labours of a clergyman commissioned by the similar ultra-conservative body in Holland.[91] Clinging to the psalms in public worship, the Reformed Church of South Africa eschewed the use of the hymns which were espoused by the majority body of the Cape.[92] With it were affiliated at least some of the Doppers, a strictly Calvinistic group.[93] On the other hand, the majority body, the Dutch Reformed Church (*Nederduits Gereformeerde Kerk*), while responsive to the religious awakenings of Europe, Great Britain, and the United States,[94] after fierce internal struggles dissociated itself from the theological liberalism which was seeping in from Europe. Thus D. P. Faure, descended from the Huguenots who had migrated to the Cape in pre-British times, and who while studying theology in Holland and after an agonizing struggle at readjustment became committed to the liberal views which he found there and in the writings of the American Unitarian, Theodore Parker, was barred from the Dutch Reformed Church and organized in Cape Town the Free Protestant Church.[95] Between 1867 and 1870 the growing strength of liberalism in the Dutch Reformed Church was curbed by the refusal of ordination to candidates affected by it, by the influx of young men trained at Stellenbosch under John Murray and Nicolaas Hofmeyr, and by other actions.[96]

The Dutch Reformed Church, in spite of the two major secessions, was

---

[89] *Church in the Colonies. No. 27. Diocese of Capetown. Part II. A Journal of the Bishop's Visitation Tour through the Cape Colony in 1850* (London, Society for Promoting Christian Knowledge, 1851), p. 25.

[90] McCarter, *op. cit.*, p. 94.

[91] *Union of South Africa. Official Year Book No. 9, 1926-1927*, pp. 290, 291; Du Plessis, *op. cit.*, pp. 175-179.

[92] McCarter, *op. cit.*, p. 94.

[93] Du Plessis, *op. cit.*, p. 89.

[94] The Moody and Sankey movement had repercussions in South Africa and Andrew Murray, Jr., held evangelistic meetings.—Du Plessis, *op. cit.*, p. 322. See also, Growing out of the Moody and Mildmay movements, a fairly wide-spread activity recorded in M. S. Osborn-Howe, *By Fire and Cloud, or Life Experiences in India and South Africa* (London, Hodder and Stoughton, 1895, pp. viii, 262) pp. 61ff.

[95] D. P. Faure, *My Life and Times* (Cape Town, J. C. Juta & Co., 1907, pp. 232, iii), *passim;* Du Plessis, *op. cit.*, p. 231.

[96] Du Plessis, *op. cit.*, pp. 208-236, 249.

strong in the Cape Colony, the Orange Free State, the Transvaal, and Natal. It had a synod in each. The achievement of the Union of South Africa in the political structure of the area stimulated a movement to bring about a union of the four synods. Although all four agreed, the terms of an enabling bill passed by Parliament in 1911 were not immediately met. Yet in time there came into being a federation of the synods through a Council of Churches (*Raad van die Kerke*) whose powers were chiefly advisory.[97]

The effect of the environment was not confined to the Dutch churches. It was also seen in the Anglican communion. The majority of the Anglicans were in the Church of the Province of South Africa, a body in full communion with the Church of England but organizationally independent of it and of the royal supremacy. However, a minority were in the Church of England in South Africa, an association which maintained its allegiance to Canterbury and remained bound by decisions of the Privy Council in matters of faith and doctrine.[98] Each of such communions as the Baptists, Methodists, and Congregationalists developed a regional organization to conform to the political structure of the country.

Christianity among the South African whites, especially among the Dutch, bore clearly the stamp of its environment.

From the spread of Christianity in South Africa through the immigration of Europeans and the foundation and growth of churches for whites, we turn to what must be the major part of our account of Africa south of the Sahara, the propagation of the faith among non-Europeans.

The kinds of Christianity which were carried to non-Europeans were Protestantism and Roman Catholicism. During most of the nineteenth century Protestantism, as in so much of the non-European world, was the more aggressive. In 1914 Protestants outnumbered Roman Catholics among the blacks almost two to one.[99] By that year, however, Roman Catholics had begun to increase their forces and their missionary staff was slightly larger than that of the Protestants.[100] Roman Catholic missionaries were almost entirely from the Continent of Europe. Protestant missionaries were from the United States, the British Isles, the Continent of Europe, and the white churches of South Africa. Those from the United States were only about a fifth of the total. British were

[97] Du Plessis, *op. cit.*, pp. 366-369.
[98] *The Christian Handbook of South Africa*, pp. 23, 24.
[99] Beach and St. John, *World Statistics of Christian Missions*, pp. 59, 103.
[100] *Ibid.*

slightly more numerous than Continentals. Those from the Continent were chiefly from Germany, but Scandinavia, France, and Switzerland were also represented.[101] The Continentals were overwhelmingly Lutheran. Among the British, Anglicans, Presbyterians, and Methodists predominated, but the Congregationalists were prominent and there were sprinklings of other groups. Among the Americans, most of the standard denominations were present. Of the South African bodies, the Dutch Reformed churches had the largest number of missionaries. It was, then, a multiform Christianity which was introduced. It showed variety both in its ecclesiastical and in its national traditions.[102]

The reasons for the spread of Christianity among the non-Europeans were several. They were to be found in part in the prestige of the white man. Many Africans gave consideration to Christianity because it was associated with the conquering race and culture. Then, too, some colonial governments accorded direct or indirect assistance to missions, mainly through subsidies to schools. Always there were the zeal and the devotion of missionaries which constrained them to undertake the hardships and to brave the dangers entailed. Back of the missionaries was the financial support of constituencies in Europe, Great Britain, and America. Both the missionaries and the financial support must be attributed to the vigour in nineteenth-century Christianity.

In the geographic pursuit of our story, we begin, as our programme demands, with South Africa. By this we mean what in 1914 was the Union of South Africa and some enclosed or adjacent lands. It embraced the four provinces, Cape Colony, Transvaal, Orange Free State, and Natal. In South Africa we also include Basutoland and Swaziland, although these were not in the Union, and part of Bechuanaland.

The non-European peoples of South Africa were principally in three racial groups. First on the scene were the Bushmen, wandering hunters utilizing caverns for shelters and having no permanent homes. They were short and dark. Presumably they, like most races, were of mixed origin and may have perpetuated the blood of still earlier inhabitants. They were akin to somewhat similar peoples of pygmy stature found in scattered pockets in much of Central Africa, Southern Asia, and the East Indies. Because of their primitive culture they were unable to persist before the competition of more advanced peoples

---

[101] Beach and St. John, op. cit., pp. 69-71.
[102] For an interesting description of the characteristics and methods of the various Protestant groups, see Richter, Geschichte der evangelischen Mission in Afrika, pp. 772-774.

and survived only in less accessible and undesirable regions. They suffered severely at the hands of the white settlers of South Africa and in 1914 seemed on the way to extinction. Next were the Hottentots, mainly of Bushman stock, but slightly more advanced in culture, subsisting partly on flocks and herds, using iron and copper, and building huts. The Hottentots did not disappear as did the Bushmen. However, in the Cape Colony they were thrown more and more into intimate contact with Europeans, their tribal organization disintegrated, and they were eager to learn the white man's ways. This meant that they were fairly easily won to the Christian faith.[103] Third were the Bantus. They were recent arrivals in South Africa, migrants from the North-east, who began pouring into what was eventually the Union of South Africa late in the sixteenth century, or after the first contacts of Europeans with that region. Ultimately they constituted the bulk of the population. While still near the primitive stage of culture, they had progressed beyond the Hottentots. They were much more skilled in the use of metals. They were better potters and built more substantial huts. Although dependent on cattle, they had also commenced agriculture. Divided into many branches and tribes, in the following pages they will be met under several names. Collectively they were often denominated Kaffirs, from a designation meaning heathen which was applied to them by the Arab traders who preceded the Europeans.[104] In religion the Bantus paid great reverence to their ancestors, for they conceived of these as still living and as intimately connected with the details of every-day life. They believed in the existence of other spirits, usually local and associated with natural objects. They also acknowledged the reality of an overruling creative power or being, of whom, however, their conceptions were ill-defined. In their practice there was much of magic and witchcraft.[105]

Between these black races and the whites bitter rivalry existed, especially over land. The whites, and particularly the Boers, who, being prevailingly farmers, lived by the soil, found the black an encumbrance or an unendurable nuisance. The blacks were progressively dispossessed. They contested the white advance. Here and there they delayed it. Eventually, however, they were usually constrained to yield.

By the end of the nineteenth century most of the blacks were on reserva-

---

[103] Gevers, *Die Kulturarbeit der deutschen evangelischen Missionen in Südafrika*, pp. 12ff.

[104] I. Schapera, editor, *The Bantu-Speaking Tribes of South Africa. An Ethnological Survey* (London, George Routledge & Sons, 1937, pp. xv, 453), *passim;* Du Plessis, *A History of Christian Missions in South Africa*, pp. 5, 6.

[105] W. C. Willoughby, *The Soul of the Bantu* (Garden City, Doubleday, Doran and Co., 1928, pp. xxv, 476), *passim;* W. C. Willoughby, *Nature-Worship and Taboo* (Hartford Seminary Press, 1932, pp. x, 293), *passim.*

tions, were scattered in small groups as labourers on the farms of the whites, or were unskilled workers and servants in the cities. Only among those on reservations did the tribal life and old customs have a chance to survive. Elsewhere the blacks were uprooted from their old culture.

South Africa contained several non-European immigrant minorities. In the Cape Colony there was what was known as the coloured population. It was a composite of many strains and had its origin in the days of Dutch rule. Into it entered slaves brought from Madagascar and from the west and east coasts of Africa, slaves from the East, principally Malays, convicts, chiefly Malays, from Dutch possessions in the East, Hottentots, deracinated by contact with Europeans, and a certain amount of white blood, much in the minority, from miscegenation, largely between Dutch males and Hottentot women. The predominantly Asiatic elements of the coloured folk were Moslems by faith.[106] Beginning in 1860 indentured labourers were introduced from India with government assistance to the sugar plantations of Natal. In time, anti-Indian feeling arose among the whites and in 1911 the Government of India forbade further recruiting.[107] In 1913, however, the Indian population was 115,457,[108] most of it African-born. Commencing in 1904, Chinese were imported, eventually to the total of about 50,000, to work in the mines of the Witwatersrand.[109] Here were non-Christian groups who constituted a challenge to Christians, not only because they were non-Christians to be won, but also because of the discrimination against them and their exploitation by the whites.

To South Africa we are to give a larger proportion of our space than the population or the size of the area would warrant. This is because by 1914 about two-fifths of the black and coloured Christians and more than half of the total number of Christians, black and white, in the Africa south of the Sahara were in that region.

The rapid progress of Christianity was due partly to a concentration of missionary activity on South Africa, partly to white settlement, and partly to the fact that the disintegration of tribal life and the old customs had proceeded further than elsewhere. With this distintegration went the tendency to conform to the dominant European culture, including Christianity.

The Christianity propagated in South Africa was overwhelmingly Protestant. Roman Catholics expended most of their effort in other parts of Africa.

Before the nineteenth century, when South Africa was still in the hands of the Dutch, a few attempts had been made to win non-Europeans to the

[106] Hofmeyr, *South Africa*, pp. 30, 41, 42.
[107] Hofmeyr, *op. cit.*, pp. 173ff.
[108] Hosking, *The South African Year-Book, 1914*, p. 670.
[109] Hofmeyr, *op. cit.*, p. 179.

Christian faith. In the seventeenth century, in the first twenty-five years after the establishment of the Dutch colony, active efforts were put forth to propagate Christianity among the slaves held by the Dutch and among the children of adjacent Hottentots. Many of the children of the slaves were baptized.[110] In the latter part of the seventeenth and the first part of the eighteenth century, however, the Dutch exerted themselves very little to win converts. The missionary fervour of the settlers declined.[111] From 1737 until 1744 a Moravian, George Schmidt, laboured among the Hottentots, but felt constrained to leave because of the insistence of the Dutch authorities that his converts be baptized by the Cape clergy rather than by himself.[112] In 1786 there came to the pastorate of a Cape Town congregation Van Lier, whose warm faith led him to seek the religious instruction of the slaves and Hottentots. His early death (1793) cut short his activities, but some of the Dutch were aroused by him to a sense of responsibility for these groups. Moreover, a Cape-born youth, Michiel Christiaan Vos, who after years of training and pastoral experience in Holland returned home (1794) to take charge of a congregation, made the subject of his first sermon in his new charge the obligation to "preach the Gospel to every creature," and persistently urged upon his parishioners the duty of instructing their slaves in the Christian faith. By the close of the Napoleonic Wars, when treaty authorization was finally given by the British occupation, not a little was being done by the Cape Dutch to win the non-Christians in the vicinity of their settlements.[113] We hear of at least one school, run by devout women, for teaching slaves and free blacks to read.[114] The tide of religious life which was so evidently rising in Europe and the United States was also having its effect in the Dutch churches of South Africa and was stimulating interest in the religious welfare of non-Christians.

It was not, however, from the Dutch churches that the major efforts for the conversion of the non-Europeans were to issue. They were, rather chiefly from enterprises founded by missionaries from the British Isles, Europe, and the United States.

A number of factors militated against the initiation of such projects by Afrikanders. During the fore part of the nineteenth century the Dutch churches suffered from a dearth of clergy. Until the 1840's they were under a supervision

---

[110] Du Plessis, *A History of Christian Missions in South Africa*, pp. 19-35; Van der Merve, *The Development of Missionary Attitudes in the Dutch Reformed Church in South Africa*, pp. 7ff.

[111] Van der Merve, *op. cit.*, pp. 30ff.

[112] Du Plessis, *op. cit.*, pp. 36-59.

[113] Du Plessis, *op. cit.*, 61-69; Van der Merve, *op. cit.*, pp. 73ff.

[114] Ingram Cobbin, *Memoir of Mrs. Christiana Louisa Thom* (London, J. Nisbet, 1822, pp. viii, 100), p. 14.

by the state which proved an incubus.[115] When the great migrations to the North occurred, the provision of religious privileges for the settlers absorbed much of the churches' energy. Moreover, by the very nature of the economic and social structure of their life the Boers were separated from the blacks by chronic enmities. They were frontiersmen, on the border of conflict between races. The situation was similar to that in the Americas, Australia, and New Zealand in the initial stages of white settlement. Most of the Boers were farmers and ranchers. They made their living from the land. In occupying the land they came into competition with the aborigines. The Bushmen long proved annoying, for they stole the settlers' cattle. Repeatedly mass efforts were made to exterminate these human pests,[116] much as in some lands the settlers joined in killing the rabbits which threatened their crops. Many blacks were reduced to servitude on the Boers' farms. Under these circumstances, the Dutch churches played a relatively minor rôle in reaching the non-Christians.

In spite of these untoward circumstances, numerous efforts were made by the Dutch for the non-Christians about them. Eventually, too, missions were inaugurated by the Dutch churches in distant parts of Africa. Some of the Dutch Reformed joined in the inter-denominational South African Missionary Society, initiated in 1799 by Vanderkemp, of whom we are to hear more in a moment, and by Vos. This organization planned to train a native clergy and attempted to win the Moslems. However, several of the more strict of the Dutch Reformed opposed it because it did not teach exclusively the Reformed faith and co-operated with the London Missionary Society. Later, however, it became more nearly Dutch Reformed.[117] At its first synod, in 1824, the Dutch Reformed Church appointed a committee on missions. In 1826 a missionary to non-Christians was ordained.[118]

In the second half of the nineteenth century the Dutch Reformed churches became much more energetic in propagating their faith. Partly through the efforts of the younger Andrew Murray and his contemporaries, religious zeal was rising. Local church consistories undertook missions.[119] Individual farmers and their sons taught their slaves and adjacent free blacks.[120] In the Cape Colony, the Orange Free State, the Transvaal, and Natal, the various synods fostered missions.[121] Although because of a paucity of missionaries from among

[115] Du Plessis, op. cit., pp. 252, 253.
[116] Van der Merve, op. cit., p. 76; Du Plessis, op. cit., pp. 264-269.
[117] Van der Merve, op. cit., pp. 141-145.
[118] Du Plessis, op. cit., p. 254.
[119] Du Plessis, op. cit., p. 291.
[120] Uplifting the Zulus, p. 48; Du Plessis, op. cit., p. 29; Van der Merve, op. cit., p. 169.
[121] Du Plessis, op. cit., pp. 290-293.

the Afrikanders catechists had at first to be obtained from Holland,[122] in 1869 the Dutch Reformed Church had ten mission stations within the Cape Colony and two beyond it.[123] In 1877 a training school for missionaries was organized.[124] We hear of farmers in the northern marches of the Cape Colony who provided the salary of a missionary to natives who were preying on their herds.[125] There were missions in the Transvaal[126] and just outside of the Transvaal, to the west, in Bechuanaland.[127]

In contrast with the British missionaries, who in dealing with the blacks tended to make liberty and equality their watchwords, the Afrikanders regarded the natives as children to be treated paternalistically.[128] Often a congregation of blacks was attached to a white congregation, supervised by the latter's pastor, and served by native helpers.[129] However, separate native congregations arose, and eventually formed autonomous synods distinct from those of the whites.[130]

Missions were also undertaken by the Boers outside of what in time became the Union of South Africa. They were still in Africa, for the Afrikander Christians felt themselves peculiarly responsible to the non-Christians of that continent, but they were on soil almost as foreign as though it had been in another hemisphere. By 1914 the Dutch churches of South Africa were supporting enterprises in Rhodesia, Nyasaland, and Nigeria.[131]

Before the end of the eighteenth century the Moravians resumed the mission which had been begun by Schmidt. In 1792, not quite half a century after Schmidt's unhappy departure, a party arrived to reopen the mission. To their amazement and joy, the new-comers found an aged woman whom Schmidt had baptized. Where Schmidt had laboured alone they founded a station to which was given the healing name Genadendal. There they and their successors served the Hottentots. Other centres were opened. In 1818 (although due to war it was interrupted and did not become continuous until ten years later) an enterprise was commenced farther east in the Cape Colony, among the Kaffirs. In the West and especially to the East and the North-east as far

[122] Du Plessis, *op. cit.*, p. 291.
[123] McCarter, *The Dutch Reformed Church in South Africa*, p. 42.
[124] Du Plessis, *op. cit.*, p. 292.
[125] Du Plessis, *op. cit.*, p. 293.
[126] Du Plessis, *op. cit.*, pp. 285-287.
[127] Andrew Murray, *"Made Exceeding Glad"* (London, James Nisbet & Co., 1897, pp. 63. The Life and Letters of William Neethling), *passim.*
[128] Du Plessis, *The Life of Andrew Murray of South Africa*, p. 417.
[129] Richter, *Geschichte der evangelischen Mission in Afrika*, p. 400.
[130] Du Plessis, *A History of Christian Missions in South Afrika*, pp. 292, 293; Strong and Warnshuis, *Directory of Foreign Missions*, p. 155.
[131] Van der Merve, *op. cit.*, pp. 192-194; Du Plessis, *op. cit.*, pp. 287-290.

as the borders of the Orange River State and Natal, stations were multiplied.[132] A characteristic method was to acquire a grant of land from the government. Here the blacks came, drawn by various motives. Here they were taught agriculture and simple industries and schools were opened. A community arose with the church as its nucleus. In at least one station members of reciprocally hostile tribes were induced to settle down and dwell together in peace.[133] At Genadendal a normal school was developed.[134] There was a striking similarity to the paternalistic missions of the Spaniards of an earlier day on the frontier in Latin America. The Moravians also undertook the care of a leper asylum.[135]

A leader to whom the entire South African enterprise was deeply indebted was Bishop Hans Peter Hallbeck (1784-1840). A Swede by birth and rearing, in his student days Hallbeck came in touch with the Moravians, was won to them, and offered himself to their overseas service. In 1817 he went to South Africa. He became the leader of the mission. Energetic, an organizer and administrator, under him forward strides were taken in opening new stations and in developing the educational programme at Genadendal.[136]

Nor did the enterprise lag after death withdrew his strong hand. It continued to flourish.[137] In spite of major and minor wars which from time to time brought anxiety, the growth in numbers was fairly constant. In 1911, 12,422 baptized, of whom 3,685 were full members, were counted.[138]

Before the end of the eighteenth century another enterprise, that of the recently organized London Missionary Society, was inaugurated in South Africa. It was to have much more extended effects than were the sturdy but

[132] Th. Bechler, *Hundert Jahre Kaffernmission der Brüdergemeine. Gabe zum 20 Mai 1928* (Herrnhut, Missionsbuchhandlung, 1928, pp. 31), *passim*; E. Van Calker, *Menschenwege und Gotteswege. Aus der hundertjahrigen Kaffernmissionsarbeit der Brüdergemeine* (Herrnhut, Missionsbuchhandlung, 1928, pp. 93), *passim*; C. I. Latrobe, *A Journal of a Visit to South Africa, with some Account of the Missionary Settlements of the United Brethren, near the Cape of Good Hope* (London, L. B. Seeley, 1821, pp. xi, 580), *passim*; P. Moths, *Ein Held auf dem Missionsfeld. Heinrich Meyer, der Pioneer der neueren Kaffernmission der Brüdergemeine* (Herrnhut, Missionsbuchhandlung, 1920, pp. 56); Du Plessis, *A History of Christian Missions in South Africa*, pp. 81-90, 242-245; Schulze, *200 Jahre Brüdermission*, Vol. I, pp. 182-196, Vol. II, pp. 362-460; Hutton, *A History of Moravian Missions*, pp. 266-299.

[133] Cory, *The Rise of South Africa*, Vol. VI, p. 346; Evan Calker, *Die Grantstationen in Süd-Afrika* (Herrnhut, Missionsbuchhandlung, 1909, pp. 24), *passim*.

[134] Gevers, *Die Kulturarbeit der deutschen evangelischen Missionen in Südafrika*, pp. 22ff.

[135] Du Plessis, *op. cit.*, pp. 243, 244.

[136] Carl Anshelm, *Biskop Hans Peter Hallbeck, den Förste Svenska Missionären i Afrika* (Lund, C. W. K. Gleerups Förlag, 2 vols., 1927), *passim*.

[137] For pictures of the mission at two different intervals, given by official visitors from Herrnhut, see E. Buchner, *Acht Monate in Südafrika* (Gütersloh, C. Bertelsmann, 1894, pp. 187), and H. Kluge, *Hin und her in Südafrika* (Herrnhut, Missionsbuchhandlung, 1912, pp. 268).

[138] Schulze, *op. cit.*, Vol. II, p. 407.

intensive efforts of the *Unitas Fratrum*. Indeed, through the most famous of its recruits, David Livingstone, it was to do much to shape the map and the future of all Africa south of the Sudan and east of the Gulf of Guinea.

It is not surprising that the London Missionary Society early turned its attention to South Africa. The first British occupation of the Cape and the formation of the society were in the same year, 1795. From the outset the directors of the society had the Cape of Good Hope in view as a possible field.[139] Opportunely for their purpose, John Theodore Vanderkemp, whose strange spiritual pilgrimage we noted in the last volume,[140] heard of the society and offered himself for the South African project. Coming from Holland and with his warm religious experience, in spite of the fact that he was nearing his half-century he seemed admirably fitted to pioneer the new mission. With three companions, Vanderkemp reached the Cape in 1799. He cherished a strong desire to inaugurate a mission among the Kaffirs. He succeeded in effecting a temporary entrance to one of their tribes, but because of the in-flamed state of the relations between Kaffirs and colonists, felt constrained to withdraw. He therefore turned to the Hottentots, who were suffering from the demoralization attendant upon the impact of the whites. He founded a centre, Bethelsdorp, on Algoa Bay, about 400 miles east of Cape Town. He made it a refuge for blacks. In theory he required them to labour, but his critics complained that idlers and ne'er-do-wells battened on him. Possibly influenced by the then prevalent views of Rousseau which idealized the "noble savage," Vanderkemp lived in many ways like a native and bought from slavery and took to wife a girl of seventeen whose mother was a black from Madagascar. The incompatibility of this union is said to have saddened his later years and to have shortened his life.[141]

Vanderkemp died in 1811. Before that date numbers of additional mission-aries had been sent under the auspices of the London Missionary Society. Partly through Vanderkemp's influence some married Hottentot women. Here and there, as in the pioneer days of the London Missionary Society in the South Seas, an appointee proved unworthy of his calling and lived in immorality.[142] However, the majority of the recruits were men of unselfish zeal. Through them stations were opened, partly among the Bushmen, but

[139] Lovett, *The History of the London Missionary Society,* Vol. I, p. 481.

[140] Vol. IV, p. 89.

[141] A. D. Martin, *Doctor Vanderkemp* (Westminster, The Livingstone Press, no date, pp. 195), *passim;* D. C. van der Kemp, *Levensgeschiedenis van den Med. Doctor Johannes Theodorus van der Kemp* (Amsterdam, J. H. & G. van Heteren, 1864, pp. 147), *passim;* Du Plessis, *A History of Christian Missions in South Africa,* pp. 120-136; Lovett, *op. cit.,* Vol. I, pp. 481-517.

[142] Lovett, *op. cit.,* Vol. I, pp. 534-536.

mainly among the Hottentots, both north and south of the middle and lower reaches of the Orange River, in Great and Little Namaqualand, and in Griqualand among the Namaquas, the Griquas (part white or Bastaard groups), and the Bechuana.[143]

In 1820 John Philip, who had come to South Africa the previous year, was appointed superintendent of the London Missionary Society's enterprise in South Africa. For thirty years, or until 1850, he was to hold the post. Forty-four years of age when he arrived, Philip came from the pastorate of an important congregation in Aberdeen and was therefore a man of maturity and experience. Keen of mind, of strong will, and of seemingly inexhaustible physical energy, Philip brought to the superintendency vigour and initiative. He did more. He had been nourished in a Great Britain in which the anti-slavery agitation was on its triumphant course. Emancipation in the colonies, including South Africa, was enacted in 1833, while he was in mid-career. Coming from such a background, Philip was an outspoken and indefatigable champion of the blacks. When he had been at his post a few years, he had published in London a work, *Researches in South Africa,* in which he portrayed in no uncertain terms what he believed to be the injustices and oppression suffered by the natives at the hands of the whites. He came out flatly with the assertion that by nature the blacks were the equals of the whites and that given the same opportunities, as demonstrated in the schools maintained by the missions, would show the same development.[144] His advocacy in Great Britain and the Cape was an important factor in the "humanitarian" policy of treaties with the native chiefs to end the wars which were troubling the frontier and of setting up on the borders native states under the control of the chiefs. His hope was that from these enclaves all whites would be excluded except missionaries and those approved by the missionaries. The natives would thus be saved from the lawless white traders and adventurers who have so often been the vanguard of the white advance against non-Europeans. In the Cape he did much to obtain the emancipation of the Hottentots and fought the sale of liquor to the natives. For these views and their bold and reiterated expression, Philip was heartily hated by many in the Cape Colony, especially the Boers. Feelings ran high over the racial issue and he was not one to seek to allay them by tact or soft speech. His was a stormy career, not unlike that of Las Casas.[145]

[143] Lovett, *op. cit.,* Vol. I, pp. 518-532; Du Plessis, *op. cit.,* pp. 108-119. For a picture of the London Missionary Society's South African enterprise in 1812-1814, see Robert Philip, *The Life, Times, and Missionary Enterprises of the Rev. John Campbell* (London, John Snow, 1841, pp. xiv, 590), pp. 392-510.

[144] John Philip, *Researches in South Africa, Illustrating the Civil, Moral, and Religious Condition of the Native Tribes* (London, James Duncan, 2 vols., 1828).

[145] Lovett, *op. cit.,* Vol. I, pp. 539-571; Du Plessis, *op. cit.,* pp. 137-153; Robert Philip, *The Elijah of South Africa; or the Character and Spirit of the late Rev. John Philip, D.D., Unveiled and Vindicated* (London, John Snow, 1851, pp. 72), *passim.*

One of the most famous of the emissaries sent by the London Missionary Society to Africa was Robert Moffat. Born in Scotland in 1795, of humble parents, his formal education was necessarily brief. While a gardener in England he applied to the London Missionary Society and was accepted. At the age of twenty-one he was sent to South Africa. Of great mental and physical powers, simple-hearted, sanguine, unselfish, fearless, forceful, and attractive, Moffat made an ideal pioneer. For a time he served in Great Namaqualand. There he lived in the camp of a Hottentot, Africaner, who, from being a feared marauder, had been won by his Christian conversion into a life of peace. Most of Moffat's missionary service was on an oasis north of the Orange River, near the southern edge of the Kalahari Desert, where a huge spring of sweet water gushed out and fed the Kuruman River. Here Moffat's labours were for the Bechuana, a loose congeries of Bantu tribes. He reduced the language to writing, translated the Bible into it, and prepared and printed other literature. With his gardener's training, he taught his converts to work, gave them improved tools, and made Kuruman blossom. He undertook numerous journeys, among them one to begin a mission among the Matabele, south of the Zambesi, but it was to Kuruman that he returned. The population in his neighbourhood was sparse. At no one time did he have more than 200 converts about him. Yet when, in 1870, an old man, he returned to Great Britain for the long evening of his life (he died in 1883), he was regarded as one of the greatest of missionaries.[146]

More distinguished than Moffat, and, indeed, one of the greatest and most influential missionaries in the history of mankind, was David Livingstone.[147]

[146] Out of the fairly large literature on or by Moffat, the following are the most important for his biography: John S. Moffat, *The Lives of Robert and Mary Moffat* (London, T. Fisher Unwin, 1886, pp. xxii, 468); Robert Moffat, *Missionary Labours and Scenes in Southern Africa* (London, John Snow, 1842, pp. xv, 624); and Edwin W. Smith, *Robert Moffat, One of God's Gardeners* (London, Student Christian Movement, 1925, pp. 251).
A biography of a son of Moffat who served for a time as a missionary and later as a government official in South Africa, Southern Rhodesia, and Bechuanaland Protectorate is Robert V. Moffat, *John Smith Moffat, C.M.G., Missionary. A Memoir* (New York, E. P. Dutton and Co., 1921, pp. xix, 388).
[147] Of the huge literature on Livingstone, the best biographies are W. Garden Blaikie, *The Personal Life of David Livingstone* (Chicago, Fleming H. Revell Co., no date, preface 1880, pp. 508), and R. J. Campbell, *Livingstone* (London, Ernest Benn, pp. 360). The latter is later and more critical. See also H. H. Johnston, *David Livingstone* (London, Charles H. Kelly, no date, pp. 372). Livingstone's own account in *Missionary Travels and Researches in South Africa* (London, John Murray, 1857, pp. ix, 687) is an invaluable source for the early part of his career. Briefer are *Dr. Livingstone's Cambridge Lectures*, edited by William Monk (Cambridge, Deighton, Bell and Co., 1858, pp. vii, xxx, cxiii, 181). Other first hand sources are *Some Letters from Livingstone 1840-1872*, edited by David Chamberlin (Oxford University Press, 1940, pp. xxvii, 280), and David and Charles Livingstone, *Narrative of an Expedition to the Zambesi and Its Tributaries and the Discovery of the Lakes Shirwa and Nyassa, 1858-1864* (London, John Murray, 1865,

Livingstone, like Moffat, was a Scot. His father was of Highland and his mother of Lowland stock. They were poor, but independent, hard-working, and deeply religious. Livingstone was born in 1813 in Blantyre, in a tenement attached to a large cotton mill. At the tender age of ten he went to work in the factory, with hours from six in the morning until eight at night. The lad proved avid for learning. With part of his first wages he bought a Latin primer. He attended a night school and propped a book on the spinning jenny which engrossed his days. He read such works of science and travel as he could lay his hands on. Reared first in the established church and then in an Independent chapel, as a youth he entered upon a warm religious experience and resolved to become a medical missionary to China. To this end he studied medicine and theology. The London Missionary Society appealed to him because of its undenominational character. Friction between Great Britain and China prevented him from going to the land of his first desire. He was, instead, appointed to South Africa. In 1840 he sailed for Cape Town and the continent of his reluctant second choice. He was partly reconciled by the challenge which came from Moffat during a meeting in England, when the older man expressed the hope that he would not settle in one of the existing mission centres, but would go north where vast reaches were as yet untouched by the faith and where on any clear morning there could be seen the smoke of a thousand villages in which the name of Christ had not been heard. The appeal touched a responsive chord. Arrived at the Cape, Livingstone was disappointed by the concentration of missionaries among relatively small populations. He believed that once churches were founded, native leadership should be trained, self-support achieved, and the missionary pass on to repeat the process in virgin territory. With the frankness which was one of his enduring characteristics, Livingstone spoke his mind. Already the principles which were to determine all his future course were shaping themselves.

Livingstone first went to Moffat's station at Kuruman, then near the northerly fringe of his society's African enterprise. However, he could not think of that as a permanent residence. The lure of travel and of discovery which had shown itself in his boyhood reading grew with the years. The urge which sent some

pp. xiv, 608). Important for the latter part of Livingstone's career is *The Last Journals of David Livingstone in Central Africa from Eighteen Hundred and Sixty-Five to His Death* (New York, Harper & Brothers, 1875, pp. 541). Important, too, is Henry M. Stanley, *How I Found Livingstone* (New York, Charles Scribner's Sons, 1913, pp. xliii, 736. The original edition was 1874). A book of reminiscences is A. Z. Fraser, *Livingstone and Newstead* (London, John Murray, 1913, pp. xii, 263). An early biography, based largely on Livingstone's writings, is J. E. Chambliss, *The Life and Labors of David Livingstone* (Philadelphia, Hubbard Bros., 1875, pp. 805). It is upon these books that the following account is based.

of his race to climbing unscaled mountains, penetrating trackless wildernesses, and inaugurating empires was in his blood. Only in him it was transmuted by his Christian faith into a passion to open the way for the Christian Gospel into regions where it had never been preached and to pave the way for the righting of wrongs and the healing of festering social sores. He wished to raise the tone of all African life. This he would do by introducing commerce and whatever was wholesome in European civilization. If this confidence in Western culture seemed naïve to a later generation which, after 1914, saw the havoc wrought by the unmet colossal ills born of the nineteenth-century Occident, Livingstone at least shared it with many other able minds and noble spirits of his and the following generation. Various characteristics fitted Livingstone for his mission. Apparently he did not know fear. In spite of periods of gloom he was generally hopeful and had a quiet humour which lightened the tension under which he often lived. He had an indomitable will power which propelled a body often racked by fever and spent with dysentery. He was skilful in dealing with the aborigines. He was a keen and accurate observer and kept voluminous day by day records of what he saw. He always had at heart the interest of the Africans. He told the Christian story to those whom he touched on his wide travels. His Christian faith sustained him through his hardships, kept him humble, and towards the end softened some of the native asperities of his character.

Early in 1845 Livingstone married Moffat's daughter Mary, but his obligations to his wife and to the children which came in due course did not deter him from what appeared to him a prior duty, that of the explorer.

Moved in part by a desire to escape the restraints placed by the Boers on his attempts to found mission stations in areas touched by them, Livingstone crossed the Kalahari Desert and in 1849 reached Lake Ngami, being its white discoverer, and penetrated to the better watered country beyond it. Twice he took his family on the perilous journey to the North. Once this was at the cost of the life of his youngest child. The other time all were brought to the verge of death. He now (1852) sent his wife and children to Great Britain while he pursued his dangerous path without them.

Livingstone resolved that he would open the way to the interior or perish. His resolution was strengthened by contact with the devastation wrought by the raids and wars which were the means of recruiting the slave market. In an effort to find a route which would avoid the wastes of the Kalahari Desert and the barriers imposed by the Boers, he pushed up the Zambesi and across to the west coast. The trip was made in spite of perils from the natives and recurring illness. Having attained his goal, Livingstone might easily have accepted the opportunity given at São Paulo de Loanda to return to England in a British ship. Instead, because of his word given to his bearers to see them safely home, he turned back into the wilderness. Crossing the continent, he gave the name of Victoria Falls to the great cataract on the Zambesi, and reached the east coast at the delta of that river. Thence he sailed for England and was greeted with high acclaim. It was his challenge at a public lecture at Cambridge, "Do you carry on the work which I have begun. I leave it with you," which called forth the Universities' Mission to Central Africa of which we are shortly to hear more.

Livingstone now severed his connexion with the London Missionary Society, not because he had changed his purpose, but because he believed that he could better fulfil it under the British Government. In 1858 he was back on the Zambesi, hoping to find that stream a navigable water-way to the interior. Frustrated in this design by cataracts, he pushed north and discovered Lake Nyasa. Disaster after disaster overtook him, culminating (1862) in the death of Mrs. Livingstone. In 1864 he returned to Great Britain for his second and last visit, telling of the atrocities of the slave trade as he had observed them, particularly in Portuguese territory, and seeking to rouse public opinion to end them. In 1866 he once more headed for Africa, bent on exploring the watershed of the continent and finding the sources of the Nile. He discovered Lake Bangweulu, but not the springs of the Nile. He further brought to the attention of the world the devastation wrought by the slave trade. When at a low extremity of destitution and health and long lost to the sight of the Western world, he was reached by Henry M. Stanley, who had been sent for that purpose by James Gordon Bennett, Jr., of *The New York Herald*. His faith and life made a deep impression upon Stanley. Livingstone might now have returned to Europe, but with characteristic perseverance he pursued his quest for the headwaters of the Nile and died, without having accomplished it, alone, in the interior, in 1873. His faithful native servants buried his heart in the Africa that he had loved. The rest of his body they carried to the coast and delivered into British hands. His journeys ended in Westminster Abbey.

Livingstone's life and travels, and through him the Christian faith which was his inspiration and his sustaining strength, had profound effects. It was an age of African exploration. Had Livingstone not penetrated to the regions which he first revealed to the European world some others of the white race would shortly have done so. The exactitude and the wealth of his observations on the land he traversed, its peoples, and its flora and fauna, were amazing, but eventually someone else would have gathered that information. It was Livingstone's peculiar contribution to pursue his travels with an unselfish devotion to the well-being of the Africans which set a high moral standard for the inevitable impact of the whites. That impact, he maintained, must have as a dominant motive the welfare of the natives. He was unusually successful in dealing with the blacks and his reputation for integrity and fair-dealing spread even into districts which he never saw. It was he who, although quite unintentionally, led Stanley to Africa. He was, therefore, responsible for the latter's explorations. In no small degree it was his influence which did much to determine Stanley's benevolent attitude towards the natives and to make of Stanley's travels an opening wedge for Christian missions. Moreover, many of the missions which we are to find in Central Africa owed their inception to Livingstone's appeal or to his example. More than any other one man, Livingstone was the path-breaker for Christianity in Africa south of the Sahara.

The London Missionary Society strove to rise to the opportunity opened by its greatest emissary. Deeming its task there completed, gradually, although more slowly than Livingstone advocated in his first ardour, it withdrew from the Cape Colony. In the 1850's it initiated steps in that direction. In the 1870's and the early part of the 1880's it ceased its financial aid to the churches. It encouraged the natives who had settled on the lands allotted them by the government to purchase their holdings and become proprietors. Most of the churches successfully made the transition to independence. Fewer of the cultivators of the soil did so. Many of them failed to complete their payments and resumed the status of tenants.[148] As among the Negro Christians in the West Indies, the illegitimacy rate was high.[149] Yet in general the black and coloured Christian communities in the Cape Colony were graduating from the tutelage of the white man. In the twentieth century only one station with missionaries supported from Great Britain remained. This possessed an institution for the training of coloured boys and girls, most of whom became teachers in primary schools.[150] The London Missionary Society maintained a centre near Ngami, the lake which was Livingstone's first striking discovery.[151] Partly, although not entirely because of the impetus given by Livingstone, an enterprise was inaugurated among the Matabele, a Bantu tribe, in what was later Southern Rhodesia.[152] There was, too, an abortive adventure, arising out of an invitation to Livingstone to send missionaries, among the Mokololo, on the Zambesi

[148] Lovett, *The History of the London Missionary Society*, Vol. I, pp. 572ff.
[149] *The One Hundred and Seventh Report of the London Missionary Society* (1902), p. 239.
[150] *The One Hundred and Fourteenth Report of the London Missionary Society* (1909), p. 210.
[151] Lovett, *op. cit.*, Vol. I, p. 638; Hepburn, *Twenty Years in Khama's Country*, pp. 35-96, 181-209, 259ff.
[152] Lovett, *op. cit.*, Vol. I, pp. 618-631.

north of Lake Ngami.[153] It was the stimulus given by Livingstone's life and vision, moreover, which led his society, after his death, to begin a mission in Central Africa, near Lake Tanganyika, in the general region of the great pioneer's later explorations.[154]

We must also mention an undertaking of the London Missionary Society among the Bamangwato, to the west of the Transvaal. Here a chief, Khame or Khama, became famous for his efforts to govern his people according to Christian principles. Khame sought to abolish the purchase of slaves, fought drink, advocated marriage by the free choice of the young people instead of the customary bride price, and promoted prosperity. He was the most prominent chief of his generation in Bechuanaland, and lived for nearly a century, dying in 1923 at the age of ninety-five.[155]

It was a missionary of the London Missionary Society, John Mackenzie, who, moved in part by the well-grounded fear of Boer aggression and exploitation of the blacks,[156] had a share in bringing Bechuanaland under British rule.[157]

The Methodists were the next of the British bodies to undertake to win the South African blacks. Eventually they attained a far larger numerical strength than did the older society. In 1816 Barnabas Shaw reached Cape Town. That same year he made his way to the Namaquas, Hottentots south of the Orange River, and there established himself for ten years. Reinforcements came. Efforts were made to expand beyond the Orange River. For a time these were frustrated through the murder by Bushmen of the pioneer, but in 1834 a mission was opened north of the river.[158]

As was to be expected in view of their record in the West Indies and else-

---

[153] Maud Isabella Slater, *Isabella Price, Pioneer* (London, The Livingstone Press, 1931, pp. 184), pp. 57ff.; Lovett, *op. cit.*, Vol. I, pp. 618-623.

[154] Lovett, *op. cit.*, Vol. I, pp. 649ff.

[155] Lovett, *op. cit.*, Vol. I, pp. 634-644; Hepburn, *op. cit.*, pp. 1-34, 124-180, 304ff.; W. Douglas Mackenzie, *John Mackenzie* (London, Hodder and Stoughton, 1902, pp. xii, 564), pp. 96-178; John Mackenzie, *Ten Years North of the Orange River* (Edinburgh, Edmondston and Douglas, 1871, pp. xix, 523), pp. 355ff.; John Mackenzie, *Day-Dawn in Dark Places: a Story of Wanderings and Work in Bechwanaland* (London, Cassell & Co., preface, 1883, pp. viii, 278), pp. 152ff.; Julian Mockford, *Khama: King of the Bamangwato* (London, Jonathan Cape, 1931, pp. 322), *passim*.

[156] On an instance of this, see Cochrane, *Memoirs and Remains of the Reverend Walter Inglis*, pp. 68ff.

[157] John Mackenzie, *Austral Africa. Losing It or Ruling It* (London, Low, Marston, Searle & Rivington, 2 vols., 1887), *passim*.

[158] Barnabas Shaw, *Memorials of South Africa* (London, J. Mason, 1840, pp. 371), pp. 76ff.; Findlay and Holdsworth, *The History of the Wesleyan Methodist Missionary Society*, Vol. IV, pp. 242ff.; Du Plessis, *A History of Christian Missions in South Africa*, pp. 167-173.

where, the Methodists early exerted themselves to serve religiously the coloured population, free and slave, in Cape Town and its vicinity.[159]

It was not to the north and in and around Cape Town that Methodism had its chief extension among the blacks, but to the east and north-east.[160] William Shaw, the Methodist minister who in 1820 came with a group of colonists to Algoa Bay, early began preaching to the Hottentots who were part of the British garrison at Grahamstown.[161] Eventually, under the supervision of white ministers, Methodist classes were established and congregations gathered among various groups of natives in the vicinity of white settlements.[162] Indeed, some Methodist circuits included both white and native congregations.[163] Within his first year in Africa, Shaw wrote to his society expressing his hope that a chain of stations would be created from Algoa Bay to Natal and Delagoa Bay.[164] In 1823 he himself began a mission among the Kaffirs.[165] In the course of the years, although not until after his death, Shaw's dream was largely realized. In some ways it was more than fulfilled, for stations were opened far north of Delagoa Bay, in Rhodesia. By 1831 Methodists had six stations among the Bantu, stretching 200 miles from Wesleyville, east of Grahamstown, almost to the Natal border.[166] Centres were later begun among the Pondos.[167] In the 1820's a mission was inaugurated in Bechuanaland, among the Barolongs.[168] A member of the mission, John W. Appleyard, compiled a Kaffir grammar and was chiefly responsible for a translation of the Bible into a Kaffir tongue.[169] Before Shaw retired to England (1856) the Methodist enterprise for the blacks had been extended to Natal.[170] The year 1851 saw a native church gathered in Bloemfontein.[171] When, after the discov-

[159] Holden, A Brief History of Methodism and Methodist Missions in South Africa, pp. 249, 250, 255.

[160] For the life of one whose activity covered much of the North and North-east of South Africa, see Thornley Smith, The Earnest Missionary: a Memoir of the Rev. Horatio Pearse (London, Hamilton, Adams & Co., 1864, pp. vii, 277), passim.

[161] Shaw, The Story of My Mission in South-Eastern Africa, pp. 276-280.

[162] Shaw, op. cit., pp. 286-313.

[163] Reminiscences of the Early Life and Missionary Labours of the Rev. John Edwards, Fifty Years a Wesleyan Missionary in South Africa (London, T. Woolmer, 2d ed., 1886, pp. xii, 242), pp. 164ff.

[164] Shaw, op. cit., p. 315; Findlay and Holdsworth, op. cit., Vol. IV, p. 252.

[165] Shaw, op. cit., pp. 337ff. For a missionary who co-operated with Shaw and served the Kaffirs, see Shrewsbury, Memorials of the Rev. William J. Shrewsbury, pp. 207-432.

[166] Shaw, op. cit., pp. 468-516; Findlay and Holdsworth, op. cit., Vol. IV, p. 259.

[167] Findlay and Holdsworth, op. cit., Vol. IV, pp. 308, 309.

[168] Shaw, op. cit., pp. 557-562; Holden, op. cit., pp. 364ff.; Findlay and Holdsworth, op. cit., Vol. IV, pp. 260ff.

[169] Thornley Smith, Memoir of the Rev. John Whittle Appleyard (London, Wesleyan Missionary Society, 1881, pp. vi, 139), pp. 46-83.

[170] Shaw, op. cit., pp. 562ff.; Holden, op. cit., pp. 406ff.

[171] Findlay and Holdsworth, op. cit., Vol. IV, pp. 310, 311.

ery of diamonds at Kimberley, in 1870, native labourers, herded into compounds, were used to work the mines, the Methodists preached to them.[172] In the 1880's Methodist efforts for the natives spread to the Transvaal and Swaziland, on the Transvaal-Natal border.[173] In 1891 the Methodists inaugurated operations in Rhodesia.[174]

Methodists, too, sought to reach the coloured population in and near Cape Town.[175] In 1862 a missionary was brought from India to the Hindus of Natal.[176]

Methodism early began schools and the training of native ministers and teachers.[177] One of its products, from Cape Colony, was the Bantu, John Tengo Jabavu (1859-1921). Teacher, preacher, editor, champion of the rights of the blacks, and promoter of education for members of his race, Jabavu was one of the outstanding blacks of his day.[178] Financial support came in part from the state. The natives themselves made contributions.[179]

In 1886, three years after their South African Conference was formed, the Methodists organized the South African Missionary Society.[180] Eventually this had connected with it more missionaries and communicants than any other society labouring in South Africa.[181]

Although Scotch Presbyterians were active in the predominantly Congregational London Missionary Society, organizations chiefly or entirely Presbyterian did not have as large a share in bringing Christianity to the blacks of South Africa as did the Methodists or even as the numerical strength of white Presbyterian churches in that region would have led one to expect. Moreover, most of the missionaries were from Scotland and not from the white churches of South Africa. Yet through educational institutions which they founded Scotch Presbyterians made a major contribution. Moreover, they had extensive missions and Christian communities in the north-eastern part of the Cape Colony and in Natal.

[172] Findlay and Holdsworth, op. cit., Vol. IV, pp. 312, 313.

[173] Findlay and Holdsworth, op. cit., Vol. IV, pp. 327ff.; Amos Burnet, A Mission to the Transvaal (London, Robert Culley, pp. 127), passim.

[174] Findlay and Holdsworth, op. cit., Vol. IV, pp. 379ff. For the life of one of the missionaries in Rhodesia see C. F. Andrews, John White of Mashonaland (London, Hodder and Stoughton, 1935, pp. 316).

[175] Whiteside, History of the Wesleyan Methodist Church of South Africa, pp. 72-76.

[176] Findlay and Holdsworth, op. cit., Vol. IV, p. 305.

[177] William Eveleigh, editor, The Story of a Century (Capetown, Methodist Publishing House and Book Depot, 1923, pp. 67), pp. 22ff.

[178] D. D. T. Jabavu, The Life of John Tengo Jabavu (Lovedale Institution Press, 1922, pp. 154).

[179] Richter, Geschichte der evangelischen Mission in Afrika, pp. 346, 347.

[180] Strong and Warnshuis, Directory of Foreign Missions, p. 156.

[181] Beach and Fahs, World Missionary Atlas, pp. 89, 111.

Something of the formal record of the Scotch Presbyterians among the blacks of South Africa is quickly told. In 1818, in response to a plea from a chief for missionaries, a clergyman (who later went into the service of the London Missionary Society) came from Scotland to the Kaffirs.[182] Three years later two men arrived sent by the Glasgow Missionary Society.[183] Others followed. In spite of frontier wars, several centres were opened. In 1837, because of the division of the parent society between the Church of Scotland and the Relief Church, a separation occurred in the missionary body in South Africa, but relations between the two groups remained friendly.[184] The Relief Church later joined in the United Presbyterian Church.[185] In 1844, after the Disruption in Scotland, the Glasgow Missionary Society transferred its South African staff to the Foreign Mission Committee of the Free Church of Scotland.[186] When, in 1900, the United Presbyterians and the Free Church merged to form the United Free Church, the South African enterprise, except for a small minority, followed the union.[187] Stations extended in a discontinuous line from a centre north of Algoa Bay, through the north-eastern portion of the Cape Colony, across much of Natal,[188] to the northern part of the Transvaal, among the Vendas.[189]

Outstanding among the Presbyterian educational institutions was the one at Lovedale.[190] It was founded in 1841 in connexion with an existing mission station as a small school for natives and sons of missionaries. While primarily for the former, until in 1896, when a ruling of the colonial government made this imposible, it included among its pupils youths of European stock. In its programme it was deeply indebted to a visit of Alexander Duff, whom we are to meet again in the next volume as a distinguished missionary educator in India. In its curriculum it ranged from primary grades to preparation in theology and for teaching. It made much of training in handicrafts and

[182] Lennox, *The Story of Our Missions. South Africa*, p. 20.

[183] Lennox, *op. cit.*, p. 21.

[184] Lennox, *op. cit.*, pp. 26, 27.

[185] On the life of one of the missionaries who first went out under the United Presbyterian Church, see W. P. Livingstone, *Christina Forsyth of Fingoland* (London, Hodder and Stoughton, no date, pp. xiii, 236), *passim*.

[186] Lennox, *op. cit.*, p. 27.

[187] Lennox, *op. cit.*, p. 43.

[188] Lennox, *op. cit.*, map and pp. 19-59.

[189] D. A. McDonald, *With Christ in Africa* (London, Marshall, Morgan & Scott, no date, pp. 158. An autobiography), pp. 73ff.

[190] *Lovedale South Africa. Illustrated by Fifty Views from Photographs, with Introduction by James Stewart* (Edinburgh, Andrew Elliot, 1894, pp. viii, 110), *passim;* Robert Young, *African Wastes Reclaimed, Illustrated in the Story of the Lovedale Mission* (London, J. M. Dent & Co., 1902, pp. xi, 268), *passim;* Shepherd, *Lovedale, South Africa. The Story of a Century, 1841-1941, passim;* Stewart, *Dawn on the Dark Continent*, pp. 180-196; Macdonald, *Light in Africa*, pp. 12-24.

agriculture. It conducted medical work. It emphasized the Church. It had a press which became an important publishing agency. Although long deriving most of its support from the Free Church of Scotland, and, later, the United Free Church, it eventually drew its pupils not only from many tribes but also from the missions of several denominations.

In 1916, partly through the initiative of those connected with Lovedale and at Fort Hare, adjoining Lovedale, on land donated by the United Free Church of Scotland, there was inaugurated a college to give higher education to natives from all South Africa. Fort Hare was a joint enterprise of the leading churches and missionary societies and of the governments and protectorates of South Africa. Thus the chief institution for advanced education for the natives of all South Africa was Christian in character and largely an outgrowth of Lovedale.[191]

The second principal of Lovedale, and the outstanding figure in creating and developing the educational policy which became characteristic of the institution, was James Stewart (1831-1905).[192] He went to Africa in 1861 and for a time was a companion of Livingstone on the Zambesi. With one white companion he explored the Shiré highlands where later missions of the Scottish churches were to rise. Returning to Scotland, the better to fit himself for a missionary career Stewart added a medical course to the one in divinity which he had already taken. In 1867, accompanied by his bride, he arrived at Lovedale. In 1874 and 1875, taking advantage of the devotion roused in the Scottish churches by the death of Livingstone, he inaugurated the Livingstonia mission of the United Free Church. He was, however, identified chiefly with Lovedale. In 1870 he became its principal, and served in that capacity until his death, in 1905. Lovedale was his lengthened shadow. In 1871 and 1872 he founded the East Africa mission of the Church of Scotland, between Mombasa and Lake Victoria. He was a conciliator between conflicting sides in the chronically inflamed racial situation in South Africa and a champion of the rights of the natives against the injustices inflicted by the whites.

A child of Lovedale and of Stewart was the Blythswood Institution. Intended to perform for the Fingo peoples east of the Kei what Lovedale was doing west of that river, it arose out of the invitation of the Fingoes and a local magistrate. In its founding the Fingoes contributed a substantial sum and the Free Church of Scotland matched their contribution.[193]

[191] Shepherd, *op. cit.*, pp. 275-293.

[192] Wells, *The Life of James Stewart, passim;* Shepherd, *op. cit.*, pp. 152ff.; Stewart, *Dawn on the Dark Continent,* pp. 180-239.

[193] Stewart, *Dawn on the Dark Continent,* pp. 196-207; Wells, *op. cit.*, pp. 112-122; Macdonald, *op. cit.*, pp. 44ff.

An outstanding product of the Presbyterian missions was Tiyo Soga.[194] The son of a Kaffir chief, he was educated at Lovedale and then in Scotland. He was ordained in Scotland (1856) in the United Presbyterian Church and married a Scot. Back in Africa, as the first of the Kaffirs to receive so advanced a Western education he was a marked man. His health proved unequal to the strain of the vigorous religious work among his own people to which he subjected it, and he died in his early forties.

Most of the Presbyterian missionary enterprise in South Africa was financed and staffed from Scotland. When, in 1897, the white Presbyterian churches convened a general assembly and constituted the Presbyterian Church of South Africa, formal provision was made for spreading the faith among the blacks.[195] Yet in 1914 only one missionary family was on the staff.[196] The burden was still left for the churches of the mother country.

The Anglicans were somewhat tardy in undertaking efforts to win the blacks and the coloured of South Africa. The chaplains assisted by the Society for the Propagation of the Gospel in Foreign Parts long seem to have cared little for any beside the white population.[197] In the 1830's, before his heroic ventures in South America, Allen F. Gardiner spent a time in Natal[198] and interested the Church Missionary Society in the project. However, the enterprise of that organization proved brief and troubled.[199]

With the coming of the first bishop, the vigorous and able Robert Gray, the neglect was remedied. Gray actively pushed missions to non-Europeans, both in the western part of the Cape Colony, in and around Cape Town, and in the eastern part, among the Kaffirs. In this he was assisted, as in his labours for the whites, by the Society for the Propagation of the Gospel in Foreign Parts.[200]

As in the attempts to reach the whites, so in those to win the blacks, the extension of the Anglican communion was intimately dependent upon the

[194] John A. Chalmers, *Tiyo Soga* (By a friend and including much of Soga's journals and correspondence. Edinburgh, Andrew Elliot, 1877, pp. viii, 488). On Soga's widow and grave, see C. H. Malan, *Rides in the Mission Field of South Africa* (London, Morgan and Scott, 1872, pp. 154), pp. 71ff.

[195] Strong and Warnshuis, *Directory of Foreign Missions*, p. 154.

[196] Beach and St. John, *World Statistics of Christian Missions*, p. 70.

[197] Pascoe, *Two Hundred Years of the S.P.G.*, pp. 269-273.

[198] Allen F. Gardiner, *Narrative of a Journey to the Zoolu Country in South Africa* (London, William Crofts, 1836, pp. 412), *passim*.

[199] Stock, *The History of the Church Missionary Society*, Vol. I, pp. 354, 355; *The Diary of the Rev. Francis Owen, Missionary with Dingaan in 1837-38*, edited by Geo. E. Cory (Capetown, The Van Riebeeck Society, 1926, pp. 189), *passim*. Owen was prominent in the Church Missionary Society's brief undertaking.

[200] Pascoe, *Two Hundred Years of the S.P.G.*, pp. 276, 306; Victor, *The Salient of South Africa*, pp. 59-65.

episcopate. Most of the bishops directed and supervised enterprises for all races within their respective dioceses.[201] We hear, too, of an archdeacon making a visitation which included whites and blacks.[202]

In reaching the non-Europeans the Anglicans employed a number of methods. One was the creation of Christian settlements on blocks of land obtained for this purpose. Another was seeking non-Christians in their existing habitats and encouraging the Christians to remain, as a leaven, in their hereditary surroundings. Still another was periodical visits to the blacks who were employed on the scattered farms of the whites.[203] Then, too, efforts were made to reach those who were in the towns and cities, including Cape Town, the diamond workings at Kimberley, and the gold mines centring in Johannesburg.[204] We hear, moreover, of Christianity spreading from native to native, even though in garbled form.[205] Unlike the Dutch Reformed, but like the Methodists, the Anglicans did not draw a sharp colour line in their churches. Although some congregations were purely white and some exclusively black or coloured, many had both black and white members and both races were represented in the synods.[206] In view of the predominantly Anglo-Catholic character of South African Anglicanism, it is not surprising that various orders of men and women were prominent.[207] As in the case of most of the other communions, much use was made of schools for the laity and for the training of teachers, catechists, and clergy.

By 1914 the Anglicans had missions for the blacks in all four provinces of the Union of South Africa.[208] We must not give the space to a description of all of them, but must content ourselves with singling out a few somewhat at random.

We cannot well omit from such a selection the diocese of Kaffraria, primarily for the Kaffirs in the north-eastern part of the Cape Colony. At the

---

[201] This is made especially evident by such a survey as Baynes, *Handbooks of English Church Extension, South Africa*. On the general structure of the missionary organization, see J. L. Fuller, *South African Native Missions* (Leeds, Richard Jackson, 1907, pp. 61), pp. 44-56.

[202] *The Kafir, the Hottentot, and the Frontier Farmer: Passages of Missionary Life from the Journals of the Venerable Archdeacon Merriman* (London, George Bell, 1853, pp. 200), *passim*.

[203] Browne, *Here and There with the S.P.G. in South Africa*, pp. 57-67.

[204] Browne, *op. cit.*, p. 74.

[205] Agar-Hamilton, *Transvaal Jubilee*, p. 119.

[206] Victor, *op. cit.*, pp. 66-69; Du Plessis, *A History of Christian Missions in South Africa*, p. 359.

[207] Victor, *op. cit.*, p. 88.

[208] For a vivid description of some of the work in the Cape Colony, including Kaffraria, see Robert Furley Callaway, *Letters from Two Fronts* (Brighton, The Southern Publishing Co., 1917, pp. 98), pp. 1-81.

outset its missionary personnel was provided by the Episcopal Church of Scotland. Its first bishop was Henry Callaway. Although reared in the Church of England, Callaway had for some years been a member of the Society of Friends. While a Quaker he had taken a medical course and had practised in England. In his late thirties he returned to the Church of England, offered himself to Bishop Colenso of Natal for the pioneer enterprise in that colony, was ordained, and went to Africa. There he gave years of valiant devotion to the Bantu. In 1873, when he was fifty-six years of age, he was consecrated Bishop of Kaffraria, and served until 1886. During his episcopate the staff was largely augmented and the foundations were laid for future expansion.[209] Callaway's successor, Bransby Lewis Key, brought to the post long experience in the mission, was an indefatigable traveller through the diocese, and stressed the training of a native clergy.[210] In this diocese sprang up the Community of St. Cuthbert, which in 1904 joined the Society of St. John the Evangelist (the Cowley Fathers[211]).

In the diocese of Grahamstown, bordering that of Kaffraria on the west,[212] there came into being in the 1880's the Community of the Resurrection of Our Lord, of women. Eventually it served natives as well as whites, especially in education.[213]

In the Transvaal not much was done by the Anglicans for the natives until the 1880's. In the course of the following three decades fairly extensive efforts were made, in part for those in the towns, in part for those in the country, and in part for the thousands of labourers in the gold mines which centred in Johannesburg.[214] In 1902, at the invitation of Bishop Carter of Pretoria, the Community of the Resurrection, Mirfield, sent an initial contingent. Within

[209] Marian S. Benham, *Henry Callaway, M.D., D.D., First Bishop of Kaffraria. His Life-History and Work* (London, Macmillan and Co., 1896, pp. xix, 368), *passim*.

[210] Godfrey Callaway, *A Shepherd of the Veld. Bransby Lewis Key, Bishop of St. John's, Kaffraria* (London, Wells Gardner, Darton & Co., 1912, pp. xxii, 214), *passim*.

[211] Godfrey Callaway, *Pioneers in Pondoland* (The Lovedale Press, no date, pp. ix, 199), *passim;* Godfrey Callaway, *The Fellowship of the Veld* (London, Society for Promoting Christian Knowledge, 1926, pp. viii, 114), *passim;* Lewis and Edwards, *Historical Records of the Church of the Province of South Africa*, pp. 560ff.; Godfrey Callaway, *Sketches of Kafir Life* (Oxford, A. R. Mowbray & Co., 1905, pp. xv, 154), *passim;* Godfrey Callaway, *Building for God in Africa* (London, Society for Promoting Christian Knowledge, 1936, p. 207); *passim;* Pascoe, *Two Hundred Years of the S.P.G.,* pp. 316b, 316c.

[212] On the first Bishop of Grahamstown and his work for the natives, see T. T. Carter, *A Memoir of John Armstrong, D.D., Late Lord Bishop of Grahamstown* (Oxford, John Henry and James Parker, 1857, pp. xvi, 436), pp. 268ff.

[213] *Mother Cecile in South Africa, 1883-1906. . . . Compiled by a Sister of the Community* (London, Society for Promoting Christian Knowledge, 1930, pp. ix, 308), *passim*.

[214] Agar-Hamilton, *op. cit.,* pp. 119-125, 132, 133; Edwin Farmer, *The Transvaal as Mission Field* (London, Wells Gardner, Darton & Co., no date, pp. vi, 140. By a missionary to the Transvaal), pp. 77ff.

three years it was covering forty-three mine compounds. Eventually its activities were extended to the country districts. It depended much on native catechists.[215]

In the uplands on the western slopes of the Drakensberg Mountains, on the borders of what was for part of the nineteenth century the Orange Free State, was Basutoland. Here, at the request of the great chief of the Basutos, Moshesh, but not until after the death of that prince, two Anglican centres were established in the 1870's. In spite of wars, the enterprise grew.[216]

Efforts for the Zulus began in the 1850's. In 1870 a bishop was consecrated for Zululand. The attempt was made to reach the entire non-Christian community by encouraging the converts to remain with their own people. Famous was a huge stone church erected at Rorke's Drift, a place made memorable in a war between the Zulus and the British.[217] It was from Zululand that the Anglicans penetrated to Swaziland, to the north.[218]

Anglicans did not confine to the blacks their efforts to reach non-Christians. They also ministered to the coloured population and sought to win the Moslem Malays in and near Cape Town.[219] They conducted numerous schools and had converts among the Indians of Natal.[220]

A development peculiar to the Anglican Communion in South Africa was the Order of Ethiopia. In 1892 some blacks broke away from the Wesleyans and called themselves Ethiopians. Two years later they were joined by James Mata Dwane, a Bantu of high rank. For a time they maintained close con-

---

[215] Agar-Hamilton, *op. cit.*, p. 125; Latimer Fuller, *The Romance of a South African Mission* (Westminster, The Society for the Propagation of the Gospel in Foreign Parts, 1917, pp. 101), *passim*.

[216] Baynes, *op. cit.*, pp. 116, 117; Bishop Montgomery, *Francis Balfour of Basutoland, Evangelist and Bishop* (Westminster, The Society for the Propagation of the Gospel in Foreign Parts, 1925, pp. 104), *passim*; John Widdicombe, *In the Lesuto. A Sketch of African Mission Life* (London, Society for Promoting Christian Knowledge, 1895, pp. iv, 349), *passim*; Maria S. B. Burton, *Happy Days and Happy Work in Basutoland* (London, Society for Promoting Christian Knowledge, 1902, pp. 64), *passim*; Pascoe, *op. cit.*, pp. 324-327d.

[217] A. W. Lee, *Charles Johnson of Zululand* (Westminster, The Society for the Propagation of the Gospel in Foreign Parts, 1930, pp. viii, 347), *passim*; Anne Mackenzie, editor, *Mission Life among the Zulu-Kafirs. A Memoir of Henrietta, wife of the Rev. R. Robertson* (London, Bemrose & Sons, 1875, pp. viii, 244), *passim*; G. H. Mason, *Zululand. A Mission Tour of South Africa* (London, James Nisbet & Co., 1862, pp. viii, 232), *passim*; E. & H. W., *Soldiers of the Cross in Zululand* (London, Bemrose & Sons, 1906, pp. xv, 192), *passim*; Moore, *The Land of Good Hope*, pp. 281-284; Pascoe, *op. cit.*, pp. 335-342.

[218] E. & H. W., *op. cit.*, p. 63; C. C. Watts, *Dawn in Swaziland* (Westminster, The Society for the Propagation of the Gospel in Foreign Parts, 1922, pp. viii, 127), pp. 86ff.

[219] A. W. Blaxall, *Between Two Mill Stones* (*The Coloured People of South Africa*) (Westminster, The Society for the Propagation of the Gospel in Foreign Parts, 1932, pp. 23), *passim*; Browne, *Here and There with the S.P.G. in South Africa*, pp. 82-84.

[220] Browne, *op. cit.*, pp. 112, 113; Moore, *op. cit.*, pp. 257-259.

nexions with the African Methodist Episcopal Church, an American Negro body. However, Dwane came in contact with an Anglican who cast doubt upon the validity of his ordination. Accordingly in 1900 he and his followers sought admission and were received into the Anglican fellowship. They were known as the Order of Ethiopia, Dwane was confirmed as their head under the title of provincial, and they maintained a separate corporate existence.[221]

The bodies with which we have thus far concerned ourselves—the London Missionary Society, the Methodists, the Presbyterians, and the Anglicans— were the major British agencies in the extensive efforts to win the non-Christians of South Africa. Some other British bodies were at work, among them the Salvation Army,[222] the Plymouth Brethren,[223] at one station the Primitive Methodists,[224] and "faith" missionaries who were not supported by any denomination,[225] but they were very much in the minority. Among the undenominational "faith" enterprises was the South African Compounds and Interior Mission. It was begun in 1896 by A. W. Baker, a Natal lawyer, and obtained substantial assistance from Australia. Its programme was much influenced by the China Inland Mission.[226] We hear, too, of the South Africa General Mission, interdenominational, supported from Great Britain and the United States, but with Andrew Murray as president for twenty-eight years. It embodied the warm type of evangelism represented by Murray and the Keswick centre in England. It was founded in 1889 and eventually had stations in Natal, Swaziland, the Cape Province, and outside the Union of South Africa in Portuguese East and West Africa, Nyasaland, and Northern Rhodesia.[227] The white Baptists of South Africa, chiefly of British birth or descent, formed, in 1892, the South African Baptist Missionary Society and conducted enterprises in the north-eastern part of the Cape Province, Natal, and the Transvaal. Some aid came in personnel from Australia. There were also independent native Baptist churches.[228] In 1903 the Reformed Baptist churches of Canada began a small mission.[229]

[221] Wood, *A Father in God*, pp. 322ff.; Nunns, *The Land of Storms and Hope* (Wynberg, The Rustica Press, 1921, pp. 125), pp. 94-99.

[222] *Christianity and the Natives of South Africa*, pp. 239-242; *Uplifting the Zulus*, pp. 40-42.

[223] Beach and St. John, *World Statistics of Christian Missions*, p. 70.

[224] *Sixty-fifth Annual Report of the Primitive Methodist Missionary Society*, pp. xlviii, xlix.

[225] For one of these, who for a time was with the Salvation Army, see Wm. F. P. Burton, *When God Makes a Missionary* (*Being the Life Story of Edgar Mahon*), (London, Victory Press, 1936, pp. ix, 124). See also *Uplifting the Zulus*, pp. 38, 39.

[226] Du Plessis, *A History of Christian Missions in South Africa*, pp. 398, 399.

[227] *Christianity and the Natives of South Africa*, pp. 242-245.

[228] *Christianity and the Natives of South Africa*, pp. 308-312.

[229] *Christianity and the Natives of South Africa*, pp. 313, 314.

To South Africa came missionaries from the United States. Although American whalers and traders were frequenting South Africa, Americans had no political interest in the land. It was perhaps for that reason that American missions were less prominent than were those of the Afrikanders or the British. Yet they were fairly numerous.

Outstanding among the enterprises from the United States was that of the American Board of Commissioners for Foreign Missions. As early as 1825 the American Board, as the long name of this society is conveniently abbreviated, began active steps towards undertaking a mission to Africa.[230] In the 1830's it landed missionaries on both the west coast and in the South.[231] The latter region seems to have been entered through a suggestion of John Philip, superintendent of the London Missionary Society's undertakings at the Cape.[232] The objective of the American Board's South African mission was the Zulus. The plan called for two parties, one to go overland from Cape Town and the other to land somewhere north of Port Natal on the east coast. Both parties arrived in 1835.[233] The one which went overland eventually joined that in Natal. Natal was so troubled by unrest that in 1843 the home authorities decided to discontinue the seemingly futile venture.[234] However, the extension of British rule to Natal (1843-1845) brought improvement. Gradually stations were inaugurated among the Zulus north and south of Durban, schools were opened, medical work was begun, the Bible was translated into Zulu, churches were gathered, and a native ministry was trained.[235] Use was made of the method of receiving grants of land from the state and settling Africans on them. Eventually these holdings became a source of friction with the native cultivators on the one hand and the government on the other. The natives wished individual ownership and the government long demurred.[236] A secession of pastors and Christians induced by the desire to be freed from foreign super-

---

[230] *Report of the American Board of Commissioners for Foreign Missions,* 1825, p. 23.
[231] Strong, *The Story of the American Board,* pp. 125-132.
[232] *Report of the American Board of Commissioners for Foreign Missions,* 1834, p. 40.
[233] For journals of one of the original group, see Sarah E. Champion, *Rev. George Champion, Pioneer Missionary to the Zulus. Sketch of His Life and Extracts from His Journal, 1834-8* (New Haven, privately printed, 1896, pp. 51).
[234] Strong, *op. cit.,* pp. 132-136; Grout, *Zulu-land,* pp. 201-212, 227-237; Du Plessis, *A History of Christian Missions in South Africa,* pp. 219-229. On some of the first missionaries, see Mary W. Tyler Gray, *Stories of the Early American Missionaries in South Africa* (No place or date of publication, pp. 71), *passim.*
[235] Grout, *op. cit.,* pp. 213-226; Gertrude R. Hance, *The Zulu Yesterday and To-day. Twenty-nine Years in South Africa* (Chicago, Fleming H. Revell Co., 1916, pp. 274), *passim;* Strong, *op. cit.,* pp. 136-139, 281-289, 426-435; Taylor, *The American Board Mission in South Africa,* pp. 9-12; *The Autobiography of the Rev. Lewis Grout* (Brattleboro, Clapp & Jones, no date, pp. ix, xi, 74), *passim.*
[236] Taylor, *op. cit.,* pp. 50-54.

vision troubled the churches.[237] Yet the Christian communities increased in numbers.[238] Moreover, it was partly through the initiative or assistance of Zulu Christians that important expansion was achieved. Zulu young men who went to Johannesburg to work in the mines organized themselves into a congregation and it was this which led to the sending of American missionaries to that city for what eventually became an outstanding piece of social and religious service.[239] It was partly with the help of Zulu Christians as missionaries that the American Board embarked, in the 1890's, on a new enterprise in the later Southern Rhodesia.[240] In the first decade of the twentieth century Zulu preachers from Natal went to Delagoa Bay, in Portuguese East Africa, to serve Christian centres which had arisen from the labours of natives who had been converted in Pretoria.[241] The efforts of the American Board were bearing increasing fruitage.

We must not pause long on the other American organizations represented in South Africa. Ethiopianism, which sought to establish black churches independent of the support or control of the white man and which in its extreme form dreamed of driving the white man off African soil, found, as we have hinted, a sympathetic hearing from the African Methodist Episcopal Church. Dwane, its first leader, went to the United States and returned with the title of General Superintendent in South Africa for that body. The visit in 1898 of H. M. Turner, a bishop of the African Methodist Episcopal Church, gave marked impetus to the movement. In 1900 the general conference of the American body made the Ethiopian Church one of its districts and appointed a resident bishop.[242] By 1914 the African Methodist Episcopal Church counted in the four provinces of South Africa 98 ordained and 475 unordained ministers and a membership of about 18,000.[243] In the 1890's American Negro Baptists sent their first missionaries to South Africa and later could point to

[237] Taylor, op. cit., pp. 28, 29.
[238] Josiah Tyler, Forty Years among the Zulus (Boston, Congregational Sunday-School and Publishing Society, 1891, pp. 300), pp. 163-180.
[239] Taylor, op. cit., pp. 16, 17.
[240] Strong, op. cit., pp. 341-345; South African Deputation Papers (For the American Zulu Mission, Natal, and the East Central African Mission, Rhodesia, 1904, pp. 131), pp. 103ff.; Report of the Deputation sent by the American Board to its Missions in South Eastern Africa in 1903 (Boston, Congregational House, 1904, pp. 60), pp. 37ff.; George A. Wilder, The White African (Bloomfield, N. J., The Morse Press, 1933, pp. 192), pp. 56ff.
[241] Strong, op. cit., pp. 431, 432.
[242] Lea, The Native Separatist Church Movement in South Africa, pp. 29, 34; Berry, A Century of Missions of the African Methodist Episcopal Church, pp. 158ff.
[243] The Twenty-fifth Annual Report of the Parent Home and Foreign Missionary Department of the African Methodist Episcopal Church, 1912-1916, p. 26.

churches in Cape Town and Pondoland.[244] In the 1880's the Free Methodists sent missionaries to Natal. Eventually they had a missionary force almost as numerous as that of the American Board. Younger, by 1914 they had not gathered so large a body of converts.[245] The Seventh Day Adventists entered in 1892 and in 1914 could count a few adherents among the natives.[246] The Brethren in Christ were at work both in the Union of South Africa and in Rhodesia.[247] In 1910 the Nazarenes entered Swaziland.[248] In Swaziland, too, was an enterprise of the Scandinavian Alliance Mission of North America, dating from the 1890's. Later that body also became active in Natal and the Transvaal.[249] If the African Methodist Episcopal Church be excluded, in 1914 the American Board's missions had about twice as many communicants as the combined totals of all the other American societies.[250]

In South Africa missions were begun from France, Switzerland, Germany, and Scandinavia. Like those from the United States, they did not arise out of political connexions, for these were non-existent, but were purely from the desire to propagate the Christian faith. In 1914 they had even more missionaries and a larger body of native Christians affiliated with them than did those issuing from Great Britain.

Of the Continental European organizations represented in South Africa, one of the three with the largest staffs was the Paris Evangelical Missionary Society. It had its stronghold among the Basuto, in Basutoland. Indeed, in time the form of Christianity introduced by these Frenchmen became a kind of national church of the Basuto. From Basutoland and by Basuto under the direction of French missionaries, Christianity was carried to the upper reaches of the Zambesi.

It was in 1829 that the first men sent by the Paris Evangelical Missionary Society arrived in South Africa. That organization, formed in 1822 and having several candidates trained and ready, was looking for a field. Philip, the large-visioned superintendent of the London Missionary Society's enterprise

[244] *Thirty-second Annual Report of the Foreign Mission Board of the National Baptist Convention, 1912*, pp. 10ff., 24.

[245] *Proceedings of the General Missionary Board of the Free Methodist Church and of the Woman's Foreign Missionary Society, October, 1914, passim;* Barritt, *The Story of Fifty Years*, pp. 43ff.

[246] *Statistical Report of the Seventh-Day Adventist Conferences and Missions for . . . 1912*, p. 8; Anderson, *On the Trail of Livingstone*, pp. 17ff.

[247] *Handbook of Missions Home and Foreign of the Brethren in Christ, 1919, passim.*

[248] Lula Schmelzenbach, *The Missionary Prospector. A Life Story of Harmon Schmelzenbach, Missionary to South Africa* (Kansas City, Nazarene Publishing House, 1937, pp. 204), pp. 43ff.

[249] T. Olsen in *Christianity and the Natives of South Africa*, p. 271.

[250] Beach and St. John, *World Statistics of Christian Missions*, p. 70.

in South Africa, was in England seeking more missionaries, learned of the quest of the Paris society, and suggested South Africa. The decision followed.[251]

At the request of the descendants of the Huguenot refugees, one of the original contingent devoted himself to the Hottentot slaves of these colonials of French ancestry.[252] The two others went to Bechuanaland, where they had the friendly aid of Moffat. They established a station near Kuruman.[253] Neither of these enterprises attained large dimensions.

It was through Philip that the opportunity came which led to the most striking achievement of the French mission, that in Basutoland. Moshesh, head of the Basuto, while still a petty chief and near the outset of the career which made him one of the greatest leaders which his race has produced, expressed the wish for missionaries. This was probably not from religious reasons, but because of the quite secular advantages which he felt would accrue. The information reached Philip. He told of the opening to the second contingent sent by the Paris society. They saw in it the hand of Providence and responded.[254] Their mission among the Basuto dated from 1833. A combination of fortunate circumstances led to an unusually successful development. In the course of a long life (born ante 1800, died 1870), Moshesh welded the scattered Basuto tribes into something approaching a nation which in 1914 numbered not far from half a million. Frequent hostilities with the Boers brought difficulties both for him and the mission, but, under British suzerainty, Basutoland was preserved as a kind of native state, or reserve, from which most whites were excluded. Physically Basutoland lent itself to that status. Its heart was lofty plateaux and fertile mountain valleys partly encircled by the great Drakenberg Range. Its climate was bracing and its people were sturdy mountaineers.[255] Moshesh himself did not become a Christian, unless it was in his last months,[256] but he was friendly to missionaries. The mission staff included some able and devoted men who, thanks to longevity, gave to the enterprise continuity, experience, and stability. Among these were two of the original pioneers, Thomas Arbousset (1810-1877)[257] and Eugène Casalis (1812-1891).[258]

[251] Jousse, *La Mission Française Évangélique au Sud de l'Afrique,* Vol. I, pp. 17-19.
[252] Casalis, *The Basutos,* pp. 1, 2; Jousse, *op. cit.,* Vol. I, pp. 37, 38.
[253] Jousse, *op. cit.,* Vol. I, pp. 59-98.
[254] Casalis, *op. cit.,* pp. 8-10; Jousse, *op. cit.,* Vol. I, pp. 99ff.; Ellenberger, *Un Siècle de Mission au Lessouto,* pp. 11ff.
[255] Godfrey Lagden, *The Basutos* (London, Hutchinson & Co., 2 vols., 1909. By a former resident commissioner of Basutoland), *passim.*
[256] Ellenberger, *op. cit.,* p. 193.
[257] Georges Galliene, *Thomas Arbousset* (Paris, Société des Missions Évangéliques, no date, pp. 344), *passim;* Thomas Arbousset, *Voyage d'Exploration aux Montagnes Bleues* (Paris, Société des Missions Évangéliques, no date, p. 253); T. Arbousset, *Narrative of an Exploratory Tour to the North-east of the Colony of the Cape of Good Hope,*

There were also Adolphe Mabille (1836-1894),[259] who married a daughter of Casalis[260] and was the real leader of the mission after 1860, and François Coillard (1834-1904),[261] who not only spent many years in Basutoland but also was the creator of the child of the Basuto church, the mission in Northern Rhodesia. The mission extended its field to East Griqualand, on the east side of the Drakenbergs, for Basuto were likewise found there.[262] Mabille was largely responsible for enlarging the territory of the mission, inaugurating a native pastorate, and starting a normal school, a printing establishment, and a book depot. It was he who early dreamed of the mission on the Zambesi and had much to do with the coming of the Swiss mission of which we are to speak in a moment. Again and again the progress of Christianity was retarded and even set back by the wars which troubled the land, but long before 1914 these had abated and substantial growth was recorded. The Roman Catholics, the Anglicans, and the Ethiopian movement each had a following.[263] Yet the church founded by the Paris Evangelical Missionary Society was essentially that of the Basuto people. In 1914 it counted 22,233 communicants.[264] By their counsel, their schools, and the Christian faith of which they were the channel, the French missionaries had a large share in enabling the Basuto to accommodate themselves to the white man's world.

An offshoot of the mission to Basutoland was one to Barotseland, on the upper courses of the Zambesi. Although geographically this should fall later in the chapter, because of its close connexion with the mission to Basutoland we can more properly speak of it here. Its great leader was François Coil-

---

translated by J. C. Brown (London, John C. Bishop, 1852, pp. 453. In part a translation of the preceding work).

[258] Eugène Casalis, *Mes Souvenirs* (Paris, Société des Missions Évangéliques, new edition, 1922, pp. 355). There is an English translation, by J. Brierley, *My Life in Basutoland* (London, The Religious Tract Society, 1889, pp. 293), *passim;* H. Dieterlen, *Eugène Casalis* (Paris, Société des Missions Évangéliques, 1930, pp. 261), *passim.*

[259] Edwin W. Smith, *The Mabilles of Basutoland* (London, Hodder and Stoughton, 1939, pp. 382); H. Dieterlen, *Adolphe Mabille* (Paris, Société des Missions Évangéliques, new edition, no date, pp. xvi, 318), *passim.*

[260] J. E. Siordet, *Adèle Mabille, née Casalis* (Paris, Société des Missions Évangéliques, 1933, pp. 286), *passim.*

[261] Edouard Favre, *Les Vingt-cinq Ans de Coillard au Lessouto* (Paris, Société des Missions Évangéliques, 1931, pp. 363), *passim.* For other books on Coillard see note 265.

[262] Eugene Hotz, *Paul Ramseyer, Missionnaire, 1870-1929* (Paris, Société des Missions Évangéliques, 1930, pp. 279), pp. 51ff.

[263] Ellenberger, *op. cit.,* pp. 354-357.

[264] Ellenberger, *op. cit.,* p. 350. Also on the Basuto mission see *Livre d'Or de la Mission du Lessouto* (Paris, Maison des Missions Évangéliques, 1912, pp. xxviii, 689); V. Ellenberger, *Sur Les Hauts-Plateaux du Lessouto* (Paris, Société des Missions Évangéliques, 1930, pp. 234); C. H. Malan, *South African Missions* (London, James Nisbet & Co., 1876, pp. xii, 298), pp. 103ff.

lard.[265] In 1872 Mabille urged upon the Christian Basuto the importance of carrying the Christian message to other parts of Africa. A preliminary effort by four Basuto north of the Limpopo River miscarried because of the opposition of the Boers. It became necessary to have a European as the head of the enterprise. That man was found in Coillard. Born in 1834, of peasant stock, tempered by a youth of poverty and hardship to the work of a pioneer, and kindled by the revivals which arose from the labours of Robert Haldane among the French,[266] Coillard came to Africa in 1857 under the Paris Evangelical Missionary Society. For nearly twenty years he served an important apprenticeship among the Basuto. He seemed the logical man to captain the new mission. He and his Basuto colleagues first went to the Banyai, a tribe north of the Limpopo, but failed to win the consent of Lobengula, the paramount chief of the Matabele, the dominant people in the region, and were constrained to leave. They then made their way to the Barotse, a folk who had acquired the language of the Basuto from contact with conquering migrants of that stock. Coillard first reached the Barotse in 1877. It was not until 1887, when he was in his early fifties, that he succeeded in raising the necessary funds and began a continuing effort in the region. In the meantime Arnot, a Scotch missionary explorer, one of the Plymouth brethren, whom we are to know later as a founder of important missions in Central Africa, had spent about two years with Lewanika, the chief of the Barotse, and had made an impression on him.[267] Lewanika welcomed Coillard, probably moved by the material benefits which he hoped would follow, but did not himself become a Christian. Before his death, in 1904, Coillard had the satisfaction of seeing Chris-

[265] The standard life of Coillard is Édouard Favre, *François Coillard* (Paris, Société des Missions Évangéliques, 3 vols., 1908-1913). Shorter accounts by Édouard Favre are *La Vie d'un Missionnaire Français, François Coillard, 1834-1904* (Paris, Société des Missions Évangéliques, 1922, pp. 320), *Un Futur Missionnaire, François Coillard, 1834-1857* (Paris, Société des Missions Évangéliques, 1934, pp. 138), and *Un Combattant. Episodes de la Vie de François Coillard* (Paris, Société des Missions Évangéliques, 1936, pp. 186). A well written life in English is Edward Shillito, *François Coillard* (London, Student Christian Movement, 1923, pp. 235). An early biography, based in part upon the journals and letters of Coillard and his wife, is C. W. Mackintosh, *Coillard of the Zambesi. The Lives of François and Christina Coillard . . .* (1858-1904) (New York, The American Tract Society, 1907, pp. xix, 484). Another account is Alfred Bertrand, *En Afrique avec le Missionnaire Coillard* (Geneva, Ch. Eggimann et Cie, 2d ed., no date, pp. 203). See also C. Rey, *Une Femme Missionnaire. Souvenirs de la Vie et de la Mort de Madame Coillard* (Paris, Maison des Missions Évangéliques, 2d ed., 1892, pp. 125). By Coillard himself is *Sur la Haut-Zambese. Voyages et Travaux de Mission* (Paris, Berger-Levrault et Cie, 1899, pp. xxix, 694), translated into English by C. W. Mackintosh as *On the Threshold of Central Africa* (New York, American Tract Society, 1903, pp. xxxiv, 663).
[266] Vol. IV, pp. 131, 133.
[267] Baker, *The Life and Explorations of F. S. Arnot*, pp. 66-103; Arnot, *Missionary Travels in Central Africa*, pp. 13-24.

tianity make marked progress among the Barotse. The faith had, moreover, saved the Barotse from some of the worst of the evils accompanying the invading white culture and, partly through training in handicrafts[268] and partly through moral and religious means, had assisted them towards a wholesome adjustment to the new order.[269]

Closely associated in its inception with the mission of the Paris society was a Swiss enterprise in South Africa.[270] In 1869 two young men offered themselves as missionaries to the Synod of the Free Church of Canton Vaud. They were accepted and, because of the intimate relations between the French and Swiss Reformed churches, were sent to Basutoland and collaborated with the French. Thence, in the mid-1870's, they went to the northern part of the Transvaal and inaugurated a new undertaking.[271] Unexpected difficulties with the Transvaal Government brought embarrassment. However, these were removed and prosperity followed. In the 1880's the Free Churches of Neuchâtel and Geneva joined with those of Vaud in constituting a new society, the *Mission des Églises Libres de la Suisse Romande*, so that the South African field became that of the Free Churches of all French Switzerland. In the 1880's and 1890's centres were opened in Portuguese East Africa, near Delagoa Bay. They adjoined the Transvaal territory of the mission and with the latter constituted a fairly continuous field. Excellent schools were conducted, the New Testament was translated, and converts were made. Since some of their Christians went as labourers to Johannesburg and Pretoria, Swiss missionaries followed them and established residences in these cities.[272]

John Philip, who had so much to do with the inception of the South

[268] For the life of a Scotchman who assisted the mission, see J. MacConnachie, *W. T. Waddall* (Edinburgh, Oliphant, Anderson & Ferrier, no date, pp. 156), translated by L. Sautter (Paris, Maison des Missions Évangéliques, 1912, pp. 172).

[269] On another member of the mission see Jacques Liènard, *Lettres et Fragments* (Cahors, A. Couesland, 1902, pp. 304) and Jacques L. Liènard, *Notre Voyage au Zambéze* (Cahors, Imprimerie A. Couesland, pp. xxiii, 226). See also on the Barotse mission J. Bouchet, *Comment l'Évangile Agit au Zambèse* (Paris, Société des Missions Évangéliques, 1922, pp. 122) and Adolphe Jalla, *Pionniers parmi les Ma-Rotse* (Florence, Imprimerie Claudienne, 1903, pp. 359).

[270] Henri R. Junod *et alii*, *Fünfzig Jahre Schweizer Mission in Südafrika* (Zürich, Wandererverlag, 1928, pp. 52), *passim;* Jean Rambert, *Arthur Grandjean, Secrétaire Général de la Mission Suisse dans l'Afrique du Sud* (Lausanne, Mission Suisse dans l'Afrique du Sud, no date, pp. 62), *passim.* Grandjean, *La Mission Romande, passim;* Valentin Nuesch, *Die Geschichte der schweizer Mission in Südafrika* (Zürich, Wandererverlag, 1933, pp. 259), *passim;* Du Plessis, *A History of Christian Missions in South Africa*, pp. 330-335.

[271] For a first hand account by pioneers in the Transvaal, see *Lettres Missionnaires de M. & Mme Paul Berthoud de la Mission Romande, 1873-1879* (Lausanne, Georges Bridel & Cie, 1900, pp. 525), *passim.*

[272] An excellent history of the mission, by its general secretary, is Grandjean, *La Mission Romande, passim.*

African enterprises of the American Board and the Paris Evangelical Missionary Society, was also influential in the inauguration of the activities in South Africa of the Rhenish Missionary Society.[273] In the two chapters before the last we met this society in a notable group of enterprises in the Netherlands Indies and in New Guinea. Earlier than any of these undertakings was one in South Africa. The combination of a favourable climate, a Protestant governing power, the prevalence of Dutch, a language related to that of the lower Rhine, and the knowledge that Philip was soon to return to the Cape with a missionary party, induced the Rhenish committee to send out with him (1829) their own first foreign contingent. North of Cape Town lands were obtained in two centres and Hottentots were induced to settle on them. The kind of orderly, industrious communities were gradually developed which we have noted in the Moravian stations. There was, too, a centre at Stellenbosch in co-operation with the Dutch. Within a few years operations were extended still farther north of Cape Town, on both sides of the Orange River, among the Hottentots and Bantu in Little and Great Namaqualand, and, still northward, among the Herero, a Bantu folk. The coming of German rule (1884) to the west coast north of the Orange River brought costly wars between the natives and the new overlords. However, the mission made progress.

A few years after the Rhenish society, the first contingents of the Berlin Missionary Society arrived (1834).[274] Eventually the Berlin organization built up a far larger staff in South Africa than did the other. Long before 1834 missionaries had been coming to South Africa who had been trained in Jänicke's school in Berlin,[275] but they had served under other bodies, largely the London Missionary Society.[276] By 1850, or within less than two decades, emissaries of the Berlin society were to be found in stations in the Cape Colony, in what eventually was a part of the Cape Colony, Kaffraria, in what became the Orange Free State, and in Natal.[277]

---

[273] Bonn, *Ein Jahrhundert Rheinische Mission*, pp. 32-42; Du Plessis, *A History of Christian Missions in South Africa*, pp. 200-210, 336-342; Wangemann, *Die evangelische Missionsarbeit in Südafrika*, Vol. I, pp. 184-186, 233-239.

[274] Du Plessis, *op. cit.*, p. 212; Krakenstein, *Kurze Geschichte der Berliner Mission in Südafrika*, p. 9.

[275] On Jänicke's school see Vol. IV, p. 92.

[276] Du Plessis, *op. cit.*, p. 211; Wangemann, *op. cit.*, Vol. I, pp. 239ff.; Johann Leonhardt Ebner, *Reise nach Süd-Afrika und Darstellung meiner während acht Jahren daselbst als Missionair unter den Hottentotten gamachten Erfahrungen* (Berlin, L. Oehmigke, 1829, pp. xvi, 318), *passim.*

[277] Du Plessis, *op. cit.*, pp. 211-218; E. Pfitzner and Wangemann, *Wilhelm Posselt, der Kaffern-Missionar* (Berlin, Buchhandlung der Berliner evangelischen Missionsgesellschaft, 1891, pp. 209), *passim;* Käthe Kühne, *Tagebuchblätter bescrieben während der Jahre 1891 bis 1895 in Südafrika* (Berlin, Buchhandlung der Berliner evangelischen Missionsgesellschaft, 2d ed., 1897, pp. 110), *passim.*

In the 1860's the society extended its activities to the Transvaal. Here it became the leading missionary agency among the blacks and achieved its greatest triumphs. Suspicious of British missionaries, the Boers welcomed the Germans, from whom no unpleasant political complications were to be anticipated.[278] The initial attempt, among the Swazi, was frustrated by the hostility of the paramount chief.[279] However, an opportunity was found among the Basuto, for the Transvaal was long the home of that people and remnants remained after the majority had taken refuge in what became Basutoland. The Berlin pioneer in the Transvaal, Alexander Merensky, inaugurated a centre at Botshabelo, east of Pretoria, which, after initial discouragements, under his able leadership became the most prominent station of his society.[280] In the 1870's a station was founded in the northern part of the Transvaal, among the Bavenda. A new language had to be mastered and wars between the Bavenda and the Boers made missionary efforts difficult. Eventually, after Boer rule was established, the enterprise prospered.[281] From the Transvaal the Berlin society moved northward into Mashonaland, in Southern Rhodesia, but in 1907 this enterprise was turned over to the Dutch Reformed Church.[282] Concentrating chiefly on the Transvaal, the Berlin Missionary Society was responsible for one of the largest bodies of Christians among the South African blacks. Progress, although at times so slow as to be almost discouraging, was made towards giving the native congregations a share in the direction of the collective body, in the training of a native ministry, and in self-support.[283]

Later in origin than the Berlin Missionary Society and still later in entering South Africa was the Hermannsburg Mission. However, by 1914, while having a smaller body of missionaries than the older organization, it counted more native Christians.[284]

The Hermannsburg Mission had its inception in Hanover, through a revival which broke out in the revolutionary year of 1848 under the preaching of a Lutheran pastor, Ludwig Harms. The parish to which Harms ministered was largely peasant. Harms dreamed of sending out bands of farmers and missionaries who would form communities which would hold all things in common

---

[278] Du Plessis, *op. cit.*, pp. 342, 343; Krakenstein, *op. cit.*, pp. 159ff.; Wangemann, *op. cit.*, Vol. IV, pp. 109ff.

[279] Merensky, *Erinnerungen aus dem Missionsleben in Transvaal, 1859-1882*, pp. 6-17.

[280] Merensky, *op. cit., passim;* Hermann Petrich, *Alexander Merensky* (Berlin, Buchhandlung der Berliner evangelischen Missionsgesellschaft, no date, pp. 216), *passim;* Schlunk, *Grosse Missionsführer der Kirchengeschichte*, pp. 127-139.

[281] W. Gründler, *Geschichte der Bawenda Mission in Nord-Transvaal* (Berlin, Buchhandlung der Berliner evangelischen Missionsgesellschaft, no date, pp. 102), *passim.*

[282] Du Plessis, *op. cit.*, pp. 349, 350.

[283] *Christianity and the Natives of South Africa*, pp. 282-284.

[284] Beach and St. John, *World Statistics of Christian Missions*, p. 70.

and by their example and preaching would win the non-Christians about them. In him the democratic idealism of 1848 found religious and missionary expression.[285]

In the 1850's two attempts, both unsuccessful, were made to effect a foothold among the Gallas, on the East Coast of Africa, immediately south of Abyssinia.[286]

Before the second of these efforts had come to naught, a settlement, Hermannsburg, was made in Natal. Eventually a number of centres were opened in Natal and in Zululand, an area later incorporated into Natal. Within less than two decades the communistic phase of the enterprise broke down. The Zulu wars brought difficulties. The presence of other societies prevented the development of a consistent programme over an extensive area. Moreover, due to a schism in the constituency in Germany which gave rise to the Free Church of Hanover, some of the missionaries in Natal separated from their colleagues and formed the nucleus of the Free Hanoverian Mission in South Africa. Yet converts were made by both branches, congregations were built up, and schools were conducted.[287]

The Hermannsburg Mission had its most extensive development in the Transvaal. It was at the invitation of its president that the Hermannsburgers entered the Boer republic. An attempt just west of the Transvaal did not have a continuing life and the field was left to the London Missionary Society, although that convert, Khame, was baptized who later contributed so notably to the growth of Christianity among his own people.[288] In the Transvaal proper the outcome was more fortunate. Here, in the South-west, was a fairly large area in which no other society was at work. Here, too, at Bethany, about twenty miles west of Pretoria, was a black who as a labourer in the Cape Colony had been won by the Wesleyans and on his return home had brought many of his people to his faith. The chief of the tribe, as a result, wished a resident white missionary. It was, accordingly, at Bethany, under these favouring circumstances, that the Hermannsburg Mission developed its chief Transvaal centre. Other stations were opened, schools were conducted, and congre-

---

[285] Du Plessis, op. cit., pp. 373, 374.

[286] Speckmann, Die Hermannsburger Mission in Afrika, pp. 12-54.

[287] Du Plessis, op. cit., pp. 374, 375, 378, 379; Speckmann, op. cit., pp. 178-551; Heinrich Wiese, Auf schwerem Posten im Zululand. Lebenserfahrungen des Missionars F. Volker, nach Aufzeichnungen seiner Gattin (Hermannsburg, Missionshandlung, 1928, pp. 63), passim; David Wolff, Unter den Sulu. Mancherlei Mitteilungen aus dem praktischen Missionsdienst (Hermannsburg, Missionshandlung, 1914, pp. vii, 142), passim; Gevers, Die Kulturarbeit der deutschen evangelischen Missionen in Südafrika, pp. 27-40.

[288] Du Plessis, op. cit., pp. 375, 376.

gations were gathered. In this fairly compact area there were counted, on the eve of 1914, not far from 60,000 Christians.[289]

The Free Church of Hanover was also represented in the Transvaal.[290]

Although here and there a Scandinavian had served in South Africa under a non-Scandinavian society, the first representative of a Scandinavian organization to reach Africa was Hans Paludan Smith Schreuder.[291] In 1843 Schreuder and a companion were sent as the first agents of the recently organized Norwegian Missionary Society, a fruit of the rising revival spirit associated with the labours of Hans Nilson Hauge. It seems to have been a knowledge of Robert Moffat which attracted them to South Africa. Failing to obtain the permission of the paramount chief to begin a mission among the Zulus, Schreuder went to China, hoping there to find an open door through the recent treaties between that empire and Western powers. Disappointed again—for he was told that his fair hair and blue eyes would handicap his effort to enter the land quietly in Chinese dress—he returned to Natal. Through his skill in healing the leading Zulu chief, Schreuder obtained access to territory hitherto closed to him, but conversions were late in beginning. Not until 1858 was the first baptism celebrated. Wars and persecutions made progress slow. Yet, in the 1880's, as these subsided, growth ensued.[292] In 1866 Schreuder was consecrated bishop. However, in 1873, unhappy over his relations with it, he withdrew from the Norwegian Missionary Society. Thereafter he was supported by a committee from the Church of Norway. Only a small minority of the Zululand enterprise went with him. Schreuder died in 1882, but the Church of Norway Mission, as the new movement which he had founded was called, continued. Nils Astrup, who was sent out in 1883 to succeed him, was eventually (1902) consecrated bishop.[293] Schreuder had inaugurated two continuing Christian movements among the Zulus.

The inception of the Church of Sweden Mission was also connected with Schreuder. This organization came into being in Sweden in 1874. Its first

---

[289] Du Plessis, *op. cit.*, pp. 376-378; Haccius, *Erlebnisse und Eindrücke meiner zweiten Reise durch das Hermannsburger Missionsgebiet in Südafrika (1912-1913)*, pp. 9-48, 101-151.

[290] *Christianity and the Natives of South Africa*, p. 288.

[291] A. Olsen, *Missionsbiskop Hans Paludan Smith Schreuder hans Liv og Virke* (Copenhagen, O. Lohse, 1917, pp. 6ff.); Burgess, *Unkulunkulu in Zululand*, pp. 104-166.

[292] O. Stavem, *The Norwegian Missionary Society: a Short Review of Its Work among the Zulus* (Stavanger, The Norwegian Missionary Society, 1918, pp. 76. By a former superintendent of the mission), *passim;* Halfdan E. Sommerfelt, *Den Norske Zulumission. Et Tilbageblik paa de forste 20 Aar af det Norske Missionsselskabs Virksomhed* (Christiania, 1865, pp. xv, 359), *passim.*

[293] Du Plessis, *A History of Christian Missions in South Africa*, p. 384; Burgess, *op. cit.*, pp. 168ff.; H. J. S. Astrup, *Mørke-bliv lys. Fra den første norske hedningemisjon Litt om den Schreuderske misjon* (Oslo, Thronsen & Co., 1934, pp. 77), *passim.*

representative in South Africa arrived in 1876 or 1877 and at the outset was associated with Schreuder. Like the latter, its original objective was Zululand. Because of the obstacles which at that time made the propagation of Christianity in that area difficult, a farm was purchased in Natal near the Zulu border. A few years later a centre was opened in Dundee, in the north-western part of Natal, where coal mines brought together a large number of natives. Eventually access was had to Zululand. In 1902 a missionary was stationed at Johannesburg, where labourers from many parts of Africa presented a challenge and where natives who had been in touch with Lutheran enterprises in their home tribes in Zululand and Natal constituted a peculiar obligation. In 1903 a beginning was made in Southern Rhodesia. As was usual in most of the other missions, emphasis was placed upon schools and upon the development of a church led by its own clergy.[294]

Other Scandinavian societies can be mentioned only briefly. The Swedish Holiness Union, dating from 1887, in the early years of its existence sent its first missionary to South Africa (1891). It developed a field in Natal and Zululand.[295] A family from the Swedish Holiness Union began an enterprise in Southern Rhodesia and called it the Swedish Free Church Mission.[296] The South African pioneer of the Swedish Alliance Mission reached Durban in 1901 and proceeded to the Transvaal. There a centre was chosen from which out-stations were opened over a considerable area.[297] In 1880 a revival swept Norway. Frederick Franson,[298] in the course of the travels in which he sought to bring to others his vision of the world-wide spread of the Christian faith, helped to direct some of the devotion born of the awakening into efforts outside Scandinavia. As an outgrowth of the revival, the Norwegian Mission Union was formed (1884). At first it confined its labours to Norway, but in 1889 it sent some young people to Natal. There and in Zululand it found its field.[299] The Scandinavian Independent Baptist Mission entered Natal in 1892. Assisted by Swedish Baptists in the United States, it extended its operations to Zululand, the Transvaal, and Portuguese East Africa.[300] Finnish friends of missions long contributed to a Swedish society. However, they eventually de-

[294] *Christianity and the Natives of South Africa*, pp. 253-257; J. E. Norenius, *Bland Zuluer och Karanger. Femtio Ars Missionshistoria på Svenska Kyrkans Fält i Sydafrika* (Stockholm, Svenska Kyrkans Diakonistyrelses Bokförlag, 1924, pp. 183), *passim;* Thora Hellgren, *Efter 40 Ar. En Blick på Svenska Kyrkans Missionsarbete i Zuluernas Land* (Stockholm, Svenska Kyrkans Diakonistyrelses Bokförlag, 1919, pp. 111), *passim.*
[295] *Christianity and the Natives of South Africa*, pp. 257-259.
[296] *Christianity and the Natives of South Africa*, p. 259.
[297] *Christianity and the Natives of South Africa*, pp. 260-263.
[298] Vol. IV, p. 276.
[299] *Christianity and the Natives of South Africa*, pp. 264-267.
[300] *Christianity and the Natives of South Africa*, pp. 269, 270.

cided to undertake a field of their own. At the suggestion of a Rhenish missionary they turned their attention to the Ovambo, in the northern part of what a few years later became German South-West Africa. Their first party arrived in 1869, but did not enter Ovamboland until 1870.[301]

Roman Catholicism, numerically weak in South Africa, in 1912 could count in all that area, including not only the Union of South Africa, but also Basutoland, Rhodesia, and German South-West Africa, less than 90,000, both whites and blacks.[302] While not in all ecclesiastical divisions were separate statistics kept for the two races,[303] blacks may have constituted two-thirds of the whole. If that is true, they were considerably less than one-tenth of the Protestant natives.[304]

Several Roman Catholic bodies ministered to the blacks. In the vicinity of Cape Town the Sisters of the Holy Cross and the Salesians of Don Bosco cared for some of the coloured population.[305] North of Cape Town, among the scattered Hottentots in the discouraging Little Namaqualand, the Lyons Seminary was given a field in 1873. The following decade this was transferred to the Oblates of Troyes.[306] North of the Orange River, in what in 1884 became German South-West Africa, in the 1890's the Oblates of Mary Immaculate were entrusted with an equally difficult assignment.[307] To the eastern part of the Cape Colony came the Jesuits, in the 1870's. To them were added, in the same decade, Dominican Sisters from Augsburg. In spite of the pre-emption of the area by the Protestants, and although much of their energy was devoted to the whites, the Jesuits made some progress among the Kaffirs.[308] In 1850 the vicariate of Natal (which, incidentally, at first was much larger than that province) was committed to the Oblates. Their first contingent arrived in 1852. Although they directed much of their energy towards the whites, by 1904 they had ten centres for the blacks in Natal, Zululand, and Kaffraria.[309] In Durban, too, was a school for Indians.[310]

The most famous of the Roman Catholic missions in South Africa was Mariannhill, in Natal. Here, in 1882, on a site commanding a view of Durban and the sea, Trappists (Reformed Cistercians) from Germany bought a large tract of land. On this they induced the blacks to settle. They cared for them

[301] *Christianity and the Natives of South Africa*, pp. 273, 274.
[302] Streit, *Atlas Hierarchicus*, p. 102.
[303] *Christianity and the Natives of South Africa*, p. 307.
[304] Beach and St. John, *World Statistics of Christian Missions*, p. 70.
[305] Martindale, *African Angelus*, pp. 47-49.
[306] Schwager, *Die katholische Heidenmission der Gegenwart*, pp. 134, 135.
[307] Schwager, *op. cit.*, pp. 132-134.
[308] Schwager, *op. cit.*, pp. 137, 138; Martindale, *op. cit.*, pp. 66ff.
[309] Schwager, *op. cit.*, pp. 138, 139.
[310] Martindale, *op. cit.*, p. 101.

physically, conducted schools for them, and, after winning their confidence, introduced them to the Roman Catholic faith. In 1885 there came to the assistance of the Trappists Sisters of the Precious Blood. In 1905 about 7,000 Roman Catholics had been gathered. Around Mariannhill as a centre was developed a beehive of industrial, normal, and other schools, a printing establishment, and a hospital.[311]

To Basutoland in 1862 went Oblates of Mary Immaculate. A station was established near the residence of Moshesh. Although the French Protestants had preceded them, and in spite of the disturbing wars of the earlier years of their mission, the Oblates could point to a substantial growth in the 1880's and 1890's, and by 1913 could count about 15,000 Roman Catholics.[312]

In the Orange River Free State and the Bechuanaland Protectorate there were, in 1914, few native Roman Catholics.[313] So, too, in the Transvaal, by 1914 only a small number of black Roman Catholics had been gathered, even in the congested mining city of Johannesburg.[314]

Before we move on to other parts of the continent, this long section on the progress of Christianity among the non-Europeans of South Africa demands a summary. As usual, that can best be given under our accustomed categories.

The Christianity which spread among non-Europeans in South Africa was more varied than that to be found in any other part of Africa, or even than among the Negroes of the United States. Dutch, English, Scotch, American, French, Swiss, German, and Scandinavian Protestantism were active. Anglicanism, the Reformed faith in its Dutch, Scotch Presbyterian, and French forms, Methodism of at least three kinds, Congregationalism, Lutheranism of several traditions, the Baptists, numerous strains of the nineteenth century revival movements which had partly or entirely broken from existing ecclesiastical patterns, the Salvation Army, and the Seventh Day Adventists were all present. To these were added Roman Catholicism and churches of local origin.

The reasons for the spread of Christianity were multiform. They were found largely in the penetration of South Africa by the white man. Here whites, although in the minority, were more numerous than elsewhere in Africa. Politically and economically they were dominant. They were professedly Christian, and, accordingly, that faith came to the blacks with the prestige

[311] Schwager, op. cit., pp. 139-141; Martindale, op. cit., pp. 107-126; P. D. von Blomberg, Allerlei aus Süd-Afrika (Gütersloh, C. Bertelsmann, 1899, pp. vi, 184), pp. 157-176.

[312] Schwager, op. cit., pp. 142, 143; Johannes Rommerskirchen, Missionsbilder aus dem Basutoland (Hünfeld, Verlag der Oblaten, 1927, pp. 111).

[313] Schwager, op. cit., pp. 143, 144.

[314] Schwager, op. cit., pp. 144, 145.

which attaches to the culture of ruling peoples. White conquest and settlement were inevitably followed by the disintegration of the inherited structure of non-European life. Indian and Malay immigrants were somewhat affected, although, as enclaves on the defensive, they did not quickly or entirely conform to white culture. The tribal life of the blacks tended to break up. In some areas, notably in the vicinity of the oldest white settlements, those in and around Cape Town, and in the great mining centres of Kimberley and Johannesburg, its disappearance was almost if not entirely complete. Thousands of individuals, deracinated, were cast adrift, and were, especially if encouraged by Christians, inclined to conform to the white man's religion along with the rest of his culture. In areas more remote from the main concentrations of white peoples, and notably on the reserves, lands which were kept for the blacks, tribal structure persisted. Yet even here it underwent changes and progressively offered less resistance to the faith associated with the surrounding white culture. Often a chief took the lead in asking that a missionary reside among his people. Presumably he felt that this kind of white man, friendly and free from the motive of selfish exploitation of which other whites were suspect, would be able to give the tribe the education and advice which would enable it to make a successful adjustment to the new world brought by the European irruption. Added to these reasons were the numbers and the zeal of the missionaries. Being under the religiously neutral and at times friendly British rule, in the fore part of the nineteenth century South Africa was one of the relatively few places where non-Christian Europeans were accessible to Protestant enterprise. The rapidly rising tide of missionary devotion, therefore, found here a congenial and open, although difficult field. Once having been attracted, Protestant effort continued, even after additional portions of the world became accessible. Probably, too, climate was a factor. Certainly it was more favourable to white missionary residence than in most of the other sections of Africa.

The processes by which Christianity spread were likewise numerous. Often the white master, especially the Boer farmer, instructed his native servants in his faith. Many a pastor of a white congregation felt a responsibility for the non-whites of the neighbourhood and sought to reach them. On more than one occasion Christianity had its first contacts through black converts who carried to their own people the religion which they had received elsewhere from white men. The white missionary and the blacks whom he trained and directed were the most common agents. Roman Catholics and Protestants of many different denominations acquired tracts of land, on them built mission stations, induced the natives to settle around them, and there, under careful tutelage, developed new communities in which, cut off from the old tribal ways, Christian *mores* could be inculcated. These were akin to the missions among American Indians and Australian aborigines with which we have already become familiar. Other missionaries made their home with a tribe and endeavoured to lead its members to accept the faith while in their accustomed environment and gradually to transform the tribe without destroying it. Still others went to the blacks whom they found, uprooted, in the white man's cities. Everywhere the school was an instrument for propagating Christianity and both prepared the black for the new day thrust on him by the white man and trained its pupils in the faith. Languages were reduced to writing, the Bible was translated into them, and other literature prepared as a means of spreading the faith and of rearing the Christians in it.

The effects of Christianity upon the non-European stock of South Africa are not either easily determined or appraised. We cannot be sure as to how many of the blacks were professed Christians. One set of figures based upon the census of 1911 declares that in the Union of South Africa out of 4,697,152 persons of non-European stock 1,438,075 were Protestants and 37,242 were Roman Catholics.[315] To these must be added, according to the census figures of that same year, 69,080 Christians in Basutoland (out of a Bantu population of 401,807), of whom 44,695 were connected with the French Protestant mission, 7,801 with the Anglican communion, and 13,107 with the Roman Catholics.[316] Ecclesiastical returns gave for Basutoland 48,060 for the French mission, 5,226 Anglicans, and 11,621 Roman Catholics.[317] In Swaziland, out of 98,735 Bantus, 2,925 were Christians.[318] The proportion of Christians varied with the province. By the census of 1911, of the Bantu population, in the Cape Province 31.08 per cent., in Natal 14.79 per cent., in the Transvaal 23.15 per cent., and in the Orange Free State 48.5 per cent. were Christians.[319] Of the Bantu Christians in the Union of South Africa, by that same census, nearly 40 per cent. were Wesleyans, slightly over 15 per cent. were Anglicans, about 11 per cent. Lutherans, about 7 per cent. Congregationalists, and about 6 per cent. Dutch Reformed.[320] By the census of 1904, in the Cape Colony, of the non-whites 43 per cent. were Christians, and in the western part of the province, where tribal organization had most nearly disappeared and assimilation to white culture was most advanced, 253,379 were connected with the churches,

[315] Richter, *Geschichte der evangelischen Mission in Afrika*, p. 532.
[316] A. G. S. Gibson in *The East and the West*, Vol. XI, p. 389.
[317] *Ibid.*
[318] *Ibid.*
[319] *Ibid.*
[320] *Ibid.*

24,548 were counted as pagans and 18,595 as Moslems.[321] The greater part of this growth was in the fifty years preceding 1914. A set of figures for the mid-1870's gives about 70,000 baptized native Christians in all South Africa.[322] This coincides with what was happening in much of the rest of the world. The nineteenth-century spread of Christianity gained momentum as it went on. As a result of the missions of the nineteenth century, South Africa contained a larger number of Christians of African stock than were to be found in any one country outside the United States.

As to what Christianity meant to those who professed it and to South African non-European society in general, some results are fairly obvious. To Christian missionaries was due the reduction of several of the languages to writing. Missionaries, too, produced much of such literature as appeared, notably translations of the Bible, grammars, and dictionaries. Most of the schools which gave a European type of education and so prepared their pupils to live in the new world of the white man were founded and conducted by Christians.[323] The missionaries stoutly opposed polygamy.[324] Many stood against the sale and use of alcoholic beverages. They insisted upon a high standard of sex relations. The movement against slavery was heavily indebted to them. The belief of many of the missionaries, especially British and Americans, in the capacity of the native for development, and the zeal to give him education and civil rights stemmed in part from Romanticism, but it also had its roots in the Christian faith.[325] By stressing what he believed to be Christian standards the missionary hastened the disintegration of tribal life and native institutions. Sometimes he encouraged the Christians to don European clothes.[326] Yet the old *mores* would have disappeared had the missionary never come and had Christianity never been taught. Sooner or later contact with the aggressive white man would have brought it about. The contribution of Christianity was positive as well as negative. It destroyed much of the old, but it built a new community. Here and there a Christian chief, of whom Khame was an outstanding example,

---

[321] Richter, *op. cit.*, p. 533.

[322] J. E. Carlyle, *South Africa and Its Mission Field* (London, James Nisbet & Co., 1878, pp. viii, 325), p. 310.

[323] In the Union of South Africa in 1927 and 1928, 96.4 per cent. of the schools for the natives were under the missions.—Gevers, *Die Kulturarbeit der deutschen evangelischen Missionen in Südafrica*, p. 78.

[324] There were degrees of strictness with which monogamy was required of those who at conversion had more than one wife. Colenso, for instance, opposed the enforced separation of wives from their husbands.—Cox, *The Life of John William Colenso*, Vol. I, pp. 64, 122. The Rhenish missionaries in what became German South-west Africa differed among themselves.—Driessler, *Die Rheinische Mission in Südwest Afrika*, pp. 119-122.

[325] As an example of this see H. Calderwood, *Caffres and Caffre Missions* (London, James Nisbet and Co., 1858, pp. xii, 234), pp. 103ff.

[326] Driessler, *op. cit.*, p. 115.

was able to lead his people collectively into the new day without the sacrifice of tribal identity. As always, moreover, the characteristic fruits of Christianity were seen in the lives of individuals who were transformed, partly by the training given in church and school, and partly by the inner compulsion of the faith.

What effect did Christianity have upon the non-missionary contacts of whites with blacks in South Africa? Any comprehensive answer to this question is impossible, for it presupposes what is in turn impracticable, an accurate appraisal of the place of Christianity in Western European culture. That there was some effect is clear. For instance, the idealism of Cecil Rhodes, who was potent in extending the British Empire in South Africa, seems to some degree to have had its roots in his rearing in the home of a Christian clergyman. In his mature life much of his childhood's religion dropped away. Yet along with his belief that the Anglo-Saxons, as the superior race, should govern, there was also the conviction that their rule should be for the welfare of the subject peoples. The predominance of the Anglo-Saxons Rhodes believed to be God's purpose as a means to justice, liberty, and peace, and he set himself to further the accomplishment of what he was convinced was God's will.[327] Earlier than Rhodes, Sir George Grey, who was also a builder of empire and was as well a champion of native peoples and a sincere and dauntless advocate of full opportunity for them, drew his inspiration in part from the Romanticism of which Rousseau was a distinguished spokesman and in part from a warm Evangelical faith. The latter not only helped to give him his vision but also sustained him in arduous labours.[328]

An incident in the South African scene which was to have repercussions elsewhere was the struggle of the Indians for what they believed to be their rights. In this a leader was found in a young lawyer, Gandhi. Here that amazing figure worked out the main outlines of the programme of passive resistance which he was later to apply on a much larger scale in India. During some of the acute phases of the struggle he found haven and unflinching support in the home of a Christian clergyman.[329] How far, if at all, he was influenced by this friendship, a friendship of which he was deeply appreciative, it would be impossible to say.

The environment had its effect upon the Christianity of the blacks. To a large extent the colour bar which existed outside the churches found its way

---

[327] Basil Williams, *Cecil Rhodes* (London, Constable and Co., 1921, pp. xi, 353), pp. 49-52.

[328] Henderson, *Sir George Grey*, pp. 2-4, 19, 20, 275-278.

[329] C. F. Andrews, editor, *Mahatma Gandhi at Work. His Own Story Continued* (New York, The Macmillan Co., 1931, pp. 406), pp. 231-237.

into the churches. In some congregations both natives and whites were admitted to membership and to the same communion table. Many other congregations were formed on racial lines.[330] In the 1880's and especially in the 1890's a trend began which was to result in a number of native churches independent of white control. A few pages back we noted the fashion in which this led to the Order of Ethiopia in the Anglican communion and to the coming of the African Methodist Episcopal Church. Before 1914 several other independent native groups arose.[331] After 1914 their number greatly increased. They were akin to similar movements elsewhere in Africa, in the islands of the Pacific, the Netherlands East Indies, and the Philippines, and among the Indians of the Americas. Yet in South Africa in 1914 the majority of the native Christians were still in churches in which the influence of the missionary continued to be strong and which reproduced in large measure the creeds, organizations, and forms of worship transplanted from the lands from which the missionaries came.

The multiplicity of the forms in which Christianity was brought to South Africa could not but arouse in some the effort towards co-operation. By 1914 a beginning had been made. In 1857 a branch of the Evangelical Alliance, then in the heyday of its youth in Europe, was formed in South Africa. In 1872, at the suggestion of Andrew Murray, an interdenominational conference of churches and missionary societies was held.[332] Beginning in 1904, three triennial General Missionary Conferences were convened. In education denominational lines here and there were overpassed.[333] In general, however, but little progress had been made towards a united approach by the Christian forces.

As we proceed northward in our geographic survey we come to what, from 1884 to the War of 1914-1918, was German South-west Africa. It was an extensive area, more than half again as large as the Germany which annexed it. It occupied the region along the west coast and the adjacent highlands between the Cape Colony and Angola. In many ways it was a forbidding land. It possessed no natural harbours of consequence and much of it was desert or

---

[330] Gerdener, *Studies in the Evangelisation of South Africa*, p. 91.

[331] Gerdener, *op. cit.*, pp. 46-53; Lea, *The Native Separatist Church Movement in South Africa, passim;* Du Plessis, *A History of Christian Missions in South Africa*, pp. 453-459; Richter, *Geschichte der evangelischen Mission in Afrika*, pp. 375-380; Taylor, *The American Board Mission in South Africa*, pp. 28, 29.

[332] G. B. A. Gerdener, *Two Centuries of Grace* (Stellenbosch, The Students' Christian Association of S. A., 1937, pp. 52), pp. 39-44.

[333] Gerdener, *Studies in the Evangelisation of South Africa*, pp. 145ff.; Du Plessis, *op. cit.*, p. 405.

semi-desert. Its population was made up of Bushmen, Hottentots (chiefly the Nama or Namaqua), the Herero (a Bantu folk, late arrivals), and some slight intermixture of Boer and other white stocks. At the dawn of the twentieth century the population was supposed to total about 200,000. Because of wars, however, by the end of the first decade it is said to have declined to about 50,000 or 100,000.[334]

Through much of its nineteenth and twentieth century history the region was so closely connected with what, in the preceding pages, we have termed South Africa, that we have already almost unavoidably covered the introduction and growth of Christianity among its peoples. Here, therefore, we must content ourselves with the briefest of recapitulations.

In the first quarter of the nineteenth century both the London Missionary Society and the British Wesleyans penetrated the land. The major and continuing Protestant effort was by the Rhenish Missionary Society. In 1842 representatives of this body crossed the Orange River into Great Namaqualand. Two years later they approached the Herero, in the northern part of the region. Hugo Hahn, the pioneer among the Herero, brought in a colony of German artisans, who he hoped would introduce handicrafts. He endeavoured to establish a trading company which would undergird the economic life of the Herero. He also founded an institute for the training of native teachers and evangelists. Some of the Bastaards, as they were known, a mixture of white and native blood, were led from Little Namaqualand to a station just north of the Orange River and there formed a settlement. In the 1870's Protestant Christianity registered substantial progress. Several hundreds of converts were made. The missionaries sought to induce the blacks to lead a settled, agricultural existence, but the frequent droughts made the traditional life of the herdsman more attractive. In the 1880's wars handicapped the missions. By 1903, however, 5,000 members of congregations were counted among the Namaqua and 5,100 Christians among the Herero. In 1904 the natives rose against the whites. In the resulting hostilities the tribal organization was broken past repair and the population reduced by about half. The missions suffered severely. They were accused by some of the Germans of causing the uprising, and, as whites, were distrusted by many of the natives. Yet they continued and gradually adjusted their methods to the new conditions.[335]

[334] Schmidlin, *Die katholischen Missionen in den deutschen Schutzgebieten*, p. 91; *The Encyclopædia Britannica*, 11th ed., Vol. XI, p. 800.

[335] Driessler, *Die Rheinische Mission in Südwest Afrika, passim;* Richter, *Geschichte der evangelischen Mission in Afrika*, pp. 497-514; Carl Paul, *Die Mission in unsern Kolonien. Drittes Heft, Deutsch-Südwestafrika* (Dresden, C. Ludwig Ungelenk, 1905, pp. 166), *passim;* H. Irle, *Unsere Schwarzen Landsleute in Deutsch-Südwestafrika* (Gütersloh, C. Bertelsmann, 1911, pp. 175), pp. 120ff.; Hedwig Irle, *Wie ich die Herero lieben lernte* (Gütersloh, C. Bertelsmann, 1909, pp. 170), *passim.*

In the 1870's the Finnish Missionary Society, which was seeking an opening, at Hahn's suggestion entered the country. It found its field among the Ovambo, just south of Angola, but did not achieve much numerical success until after 1914.[336]

Early in the twentieth century the Anglicans of South Africa explored the possibility of a mission but postponed further action.[337]

Roman Catholics were later than Protestants in entering German South-west Africa. In 1879 the Holy Ghost Fathers attempted to establish a mission in the northern portion, but two years later, because of the Protestant pre-emption of the territory, they were constrained to withdraw. In 1892 the area was given by Rome to the Oblates of Mary Immaculate. The southern part was presumably in the Prefecture Apostolic of Namaqualand, entrusted in 1873 to the Lyons Missionaries (the Society of African Missions) and nine years later transferred to the Oblates of Troyes. However, because of the policy of the German Government which sought to prevent competition between the various confessions by allowing only one branch of the Church among a particular tribe, Roman Catholics, being last on the field, were long kept from the Herero. The Oblates at first had to content themselves with a few Roman Catholic settlers and with Bechuana who had come in from the British possessions on the east. Not until after the disruption of the old tribal structure by the war of 1904-1907 could they make much headway. In Great Namaqualand in the 1880's the Oblates obtained a grant of land and began collecting on it poverty-stricken Hottentots. After the war of 1904-1907 several new centres were opened and on them were gathered some remnants of the Hottentots.[338] On the eve of 1914 the number of Roman Catholics in German South-west Africa was not far from 5,000. Of these about 2,000 were natives.[339]

Immediately to the east and about two-thirds the size of German South-west Africa was, in 1914, the Bechuanaland Protectorate. Much of it was embraced in the Kalahari Desert and it was but sparsely settled. While not included in the entity known as the Union of South Africa, from the first half of the nineteenth century it was subject to influences issuing from the British posses-

---

[336] Hermann Tönjes, *Ovamboland, Land, Leute, Mission* (Berlin, Martin Warneck, 1911, pp. viii, 316), pp. 248ff.

[337] Alan G. S. Gibson, *Between Capetown and Loanda. A Record of Two Journeys in South West Africa* (London, Wells Gardner, Darton & Co., 1905, pp. xvi, 203), *passim*.

[338] Schmidlin, *op. cit.*, pp. 91-107; Schwager, *Die katholische Heidenmission der Gegenwart*, pp. 131-136; Josef Gotthardt, *Auf zum Okawango* (Hünfeld, Verlag der Oblaten, 1927, pp. 87), *passim*.

[339] Streit, *Atlas Hierarchicus*, p. 102.

sions on the south and from the Boer colonies on the east. In the second half of the century Great Britain brought the area under its control. Indeed, in 1895 the southern portion, under the title of British Bechuanaland, was made a part of the Cape Colony.

Because the penetration of Bechuanaland by Christianity was intimately connected with the spread of the faith in what we have called South Africa, we have covered the story, so far as our space allows, in earlier pages of this chapter. It was in what became British Bechuanaland that Kuruman was situated, memorable for Moffat and the early African years of Livingstone. In what was eventually the Bechuanaland Protectorate was the home of Khame or Khama, the noted Christian chief. The Christianity represented was almost entirely Protestant, for the Jesuits whose territory embraced most of its northern portion confined their efforts mainly to Rhodesia, and the Oblates of Mary Immaculate, to whom was entrusted the southern section, reached only its eastern fringes.[340] The chief Protestant foreign agency was the London Missionary Society.[341] The Dutch Reformed and the Hermannsburg missions were on the eastern fringes, and the Paris Evangelical Missionary Society was in British Bechuanaland. The Wesleyans had also been active.[342]

North of the Limpopo River, which separated it from the northernmost unit of the Union of South Africa, stretched what after 1895 was officially denominated Rhodesia. An inland region, it was made up largely of elevated plateaux and was cut off from the sea by Portuguese possessions to its west and east. From the standpoint of natural boundaries, it was an artificial entity, the creation of European empire-building of the last quarter of the nineteenth century. It was a northward extension of British South Africa, carved out between the Portuguese territories on either coast and the German and Belgian possessions in Central Africa. That it became British was due chiefly to him whose name it bore, Cecil Rhodes, whose ambition it was to see a solid block of British territory extending from the Cape of Good Hope to Egypt. It was he who led in the organization of the British South Africa Company (1889), under which, until after 1914, the area was administered. Rhodesia was about a third larger than German South-west Africa. It was much more populous than the latter, having a total of not far from 2,000,000. The overwhelming majority of these were Bantu.

[340] Streit, op. cit., Map No. 22.
[341] Elliott, South Africa, pp. 6off.
[342] Samuel Broadbent, A Narrative of the First Introduction of Christianity among the Barolong Tribe of Bechuanas, South Africa (London, Wesleyan Mission House, 1865, pp. 204), passim.

Rhodesia fell naturally into two main divisions, eventually reflected in its governmental structure. The separating line was the Zambesi. The portion south of that river became known as Southern Rhodesia and that on the north as Northern Rhodesia. The former was about half the size of the latter. Nearer to the white settlements in South Africa and having important gold deposits, it attracted more of European blood. Its native population was about two-thirds that of its northern neighbour.

In Southern Rhodesia during much of the nineteenth century the ruling power was that of the Matabele, a Bantu people akin to the Zulus. In the 1830's, in flight from the Boers, they migrated north of the Limpopo and, being sturdy warriors, dominated the earlier inhabitants until, in the 1890's, their power was broken by the British. More numerous than the Matabele were a group of tribes termed the Mashona. From them the north-eastern part of the region took its name.

Christianity first penetrated to what was later Southern Rhodesia in the sixteenth century.[343] It was Roman Catholicism, conveyed under the auspices of the then expanding Portugal. It was also present in the seventeenth century.[344] Although more than one chief was baptized, by the dawn of the nineteenth century most traces of the faith had disappeared.

The reintroduction of Christianity was by Protestantism. It was through that bold pioneer, Robert Moffat, of the London Missionary Society, that this was achieved. In 1829 and again in 1835, while they were still in the Transvaal,[345] Moffat visited the Matabele. In 1854 he went to what was later Southern Rhodesia to the kraal of the head chief of that people.[346] In 1857 he again visited this chief,[347] and in 1859 he led a party which included his own son, John Smith Moffat, and which established a residence among the Matabele north of the Limpopo.[348] For more than thirty years the mission met very slight tangible success. With the coming of British rule a striking change occurred. An eager demand for white teachers arose, presumably from the desire to achieve accomnodation to the white man's regime. In the first decade of the twentieth century there was a rapid rise in schools and church members.[349]

---

[343] Essen in Descamps, *Histoire Générale Comparée des Missions*, p. 315; Kilger, *Die erste Mission unter den Bantustämmen Ostafrikas*, pp. 108ff.

[344] Goyau in Descamps, *op. cit.*, pp. 484, 485.

[345] Moffat, *The Lives of Robert and Mary Moffat*, pp. 161, 162, 186-198.

[346] Moffat, *op. cit.*, pp. 304ff.

[347] Elliott, *South Africa*, p. 108.

[348] Moffat, *John Smith Moffat*, pp. 78-115; Lovett, *The History of the London Missionary Society*, Vol. I, pp. 624, 625.

[349] Elliott, *op. cit.*, pp. 94-101. On the story of the London Missionary Society in Southern Rhodesia, see an account by one who spent several years in the enterprise, W. A. Elliott, *Gold from the Quartz* (London, The London Missionary Society, 1910, pp. 223), pp. 39ff.

For many years the London Missionary Society was the only Christian agency with resident representatives in what became Southern Rhodesia. In the 1870's two efforts, both of them foiled, were made from Basutoland, one of them led by Coillard.[350] In the 1880's the American Board of Commissioners for Foreign Missions attempted to enter the territory of a chief which was on the border of Portuguese East Africa and Southern Rhodesia, but did not succeed.[351]

The next to gain a continuing foothold were the Roman Catholics. In 1879 the Society of Jesus was assigned a vast area on the Zambesi which included much of the later Rhodesia. That same year Jesuits obtained permission from Lobengula, the head chief of the Matabele, to establish a mission in his territory.[352] Here, for about a decade, they laboured, but in 1889 withdrew from what appeared a hopelessly stony field.[353]

In 1890 the Union Jack was hoisted over Mashonaland, a part of Southern Rhodesia. With the extension of British authority, several branches of the Church inaugurated missions in the region. The British South Africa Company welcomed them and gave them large grants of land.[354] One of the Roman Catholic priests who had left in 1889 returned as chaplain of the pioneer column which set up British rule. The Jesuits thus resumed the enterprise from which they had temporarily retreated.[355] In 1902 the Roman Catholic forces were augmented by Trappists from Mariannhill.[356]

It was in 1891 that the Church of England actively entered Southern Rhodesia. For a time it forebore going to the Matabele, partly because it did not wish to seem to compete with the London Missionary Society. However, with the influx of white settlers it came in to care for those of its communion and later extended its efforts among the natives.[357] In 1888, G. W. H. Knight-Bruce, the Bishop of Bloemfontein, aided by representatives of the London Missionary Society, had made an approach to the country. In 1891 a diocese was created for Mashonaland and the adjacent regions. Knight-Bruce became the first incumbent. He travelled extensively and obtained large grants of land, hoping to keep them as reserves for the natives in which the latter might continue to pursue a livelihood after their own fashion if they were crowded out of their

[350] Du Plessis, A History of Christian Missions in South Africa, pp. 323-325.
[351] Annual Reports of the American Board of Commissioners for Foreign Missions, 1880, pp. 16-19; 1881, pp. 15-25; 1882, pp. 16-19.
[352] Verwimp, Thirty Years in the African Wilds, pp. 45-51.
[353] Verwimp, op. cit., p. 182; Schwager, Die katholische Heidenmission der Gegenwart, pp. 146, 147.
[354] Richter, Geschichte der evangelischen Mission in Afrika, p. 485.
[355] Verwimp, op. cit., p. 182.
[356] Schwager, op. cit., p. 148.
[357] Pascoe, Two Hundred Years of the S.P.G., pp. 362ff.

possessions elsewhere. Originally intending to confine himself to Mashonaland and to leave the Matabele to the London Missionary Society, he later felt it wise to extend his activities to the entire region.[358] Eventually the Church of England drew a larger number of natives into its membership than did any other of the Christian bodies.[359] A. S. Cripps, poet and missionary, who for a time served under the Society for the Propagation of the Gospel in Foreign Parts, lived almost as did the blacks, fought to save for them their lands, championed them in the courts, and strove for better relations between the races.[360]

The year 1891 also saw the entrance of the Wesleyan Methodist Missionary Society, hastened by the promise of a subsidy from the British South Africa Company. Extensive grants of land were made by the same generous patron. In the course of time several strong centres were established, each with a surrounding circle of out-stations. Occasionally Methodism spread without the presence of a white missionary. Like the Anglicans, it served both white and black. Some clergymen had both races in their parishes. One of the leading missionaries was a peacemaker in the wars of the 1890's between the British and the Matabele. In the course of time the Wesleyans stood next to the Church of England in the number of black communicants.[361]

For years members of the Dutch Reformed Church who maintained a mission in the northern part of the Transvaal looked longingly across the Limpopo. The extension of British authority over the region gave them their opportunity, and in 1891 a station named hopefully *Morgenster* (Morning Star) was opened near the ancient and mysterious ruins of Zimbabwe. Additional missionaries were sent, more centres were begun, and in 1907 three stations founded by the Berlin Missionary Society as an extension of its enterprise in the Transvaal were added.[362] Eventually this child of the Dutch Reformed Church of South Africa maintained a larger staff, both white and native, than any other mission in Southern Rhodesia. Its membership, however, was less than that of at least three other bodies.[363]

---

[358] G. W. H. Knight-Bruce, *Journals of the Mashonaland Mission 1888 to 1892* (Westminster, Society for the Propagation of the Gospel in Foreign Parts, 1892, pp. viii, 99), *passim;* G. W. H. Knight-Bruce, *Memories of Mashonaland* (London, Edward Arnold, 1895, pp. 242), *passim.*

[359] Smith, *The Way of the White Fields,* appendix IV.

[360] Arthur Shearly Cripps, *The Sabi Reserve. A Southern Rhodesia Native Problem* (Oxford, Basil Blackwell, 1920, pp. 56), *passim;* A. S. Cripps, *Lyra Evangelistica. Missionary Verses of Mashonaland* (Oxford, B. H. Blackwell, 1911, pp. viii, 128), *passim;* Andrews, *John White of Mashonaland,* pp. 71, 72.

[361] Findlay and Holdsworth, *The History of the Wesleyan Methodist Missionary Society,* Vol. IV, pp. 378-413; Andrews, *John White of Mashonaland, passim.*

[362] *Die Koningsbode,* Vol. LIV, pp. 227ff.; *Jubileum van die Ned. Ger. Kerk Sending in Mashonaland, 1941* (Gt. Zimbabwe, Sending Drukpers Morgenster, 1941, pp. 40), *passim.*

[363] Smith, *op. cit.,* appendix IV.

In 1893 the American Board of Commissioners for Foreign Missions inaugurated a station at Mt. Selinda, on a high upland not far from the Portuguese border. Here Cecil Rhodes obtained for it a large grant of land and here education, including industrial features, was developed.[364]

In 1895 the Seventh Day Adventists, of American origin, acquired a tract of land. They made much of agricultural and industrial training.[365]

In 1897 still another American organization, the Methodist Episcopal Church, entered Southern Rhodesia. Under the direction of the widely travelled William Taylor, beginnings had been made in the Congo Free State, Angola, and Portuguese East Africa. In 1896 Taylor retired from the active episcopate and was succeeded in the African assignment by Joseph Crane Hartzell. Hartzell's imagination was fired by the imperial plans of Rhodes. He believed that his denomination should accompany the extension of Anglo-Saxon power. In 1897 he journeyed inland from Portuguese East Africa and selected as a field the beautiful Umtali Valley, north of Mt. Selinda. Here white settlers had recently penetrated and here extensive lands were assigned the mission by the British South Africa Company. By 1914 other centres had been added, schools had been developed, including training in agriculture, and medical service had been begun.[366]

In 1897 one more American body, the Brethren of Christ, intent upon inaugurating a foreign mission, sent a party to Africa. They, too, were attracted by the northward expanding frontier of British power. In 1898 they obtained land in the Matopo Hills, in the Matabele country. There they developed a centre from which they spread into the surrounding region.[367]

In 1897 the South Africa General Mission reached into Rhodesia, hoping thence to penetrate Portuguese East Africa.[368]

Other bodies which by 1914 had entered Rhodesia were the Presbyterian Church of South Africa, the Church of Sweden[369] and the Salvation Army.[370]

It was to be expected that the area later embraced in Northern Rhodesia, more remote from the white settlements in South Africa and on the east coast,

---

[364] *Sketch of the East Central African Mission. Gazaland* (Boston, American Board of Commissioners for Foreign Missions, 1903, pp. 36), *passim;* Strong, *The Story of the American Board,* pp. 343-345, 435, 436; Jones, *Education in East Africa,* p. 247.

[365] Anderson, *On the Trail of Livingstone,* pp. 62ff.

[366] Henry I. James, *Missions in Rhodesia under the Methodist Episcopal Church 1898-1934* (Old Umtali, The Rhodesia Mission Press, 1935, pp. 138), *passim;* Springer, *The Heart of Central Africa,* pp. 19-53; Hunnicut and Reid, *The Story of Agricultural Missions,* pp. 16, 123-129.

[367] Davidson, *South and South Central Africa,* pp. 19-234.

[368] Smith, *op. cit.,* pp. 68, 69.

[369] Smith, *op. cit.,* pp. 69, 70.

[370] Du Plessis, *A History of Christian Missions in South Africa,* p. 401.

would be somewhat later in being penetrated by Christianity than was Southern Rhodesia.

The first continuous mission in the area was that of the Paris Evangelical Missionary Society, led by Coillard, in Barotseland, in the western part of the region, and begun in the 1880's. This we described a few pages back.

The next to enter was that pioneer of so much of British Protestant enterprise, the London Missionary Society. Here was the last major African mission to be begun by that organization. It dated from the 1870's and was directed towards the central region which had been first revealed to the white man by David Livingstone. Indeed, it owed its inception to the impressive funeral of the explorer in Westminster Abbey and the desire worthily to commemorate him. The initial expedition left Zanzibar in 1877. The following year, after a heart-breaking journey, Ujiji, on the shores of Lake Tanganyika, made memorable by the sufferings of Livingstone's later days, was reached. Several stations were founded. In the 1880's, with great labour, a steamer was dragged overland in sections, was put together, and was launched on the lake. Another followed. The undertaking proved costly in missionary life and health. Yet, with fine courage, the society persevered. In 1887 a station was opened on the high ground between Lakes Tanganyika and Nyasa on the extreme northern border of what later became Northern Rhodesia. The centres on and near Lake Tanganyika were discontinued and from this healthier neighbourhood advances were made, with the creation of schools and churches. Industrial training and medical care were also undertaken.[371]

The Roman Catholics were not far behind the pioneers of Protestant Christianity. In the 1880's the Jesuits made an effort, fleeting as it proved, to found a mission among the Barotse, on the upper reaches of the Zambesi.[372] The first continuing Roman Catholic enterprise was by the White Fathers, or, to give them their longer and official name, the *Société des Missionnaires de Notre Dame d'Afrique*. The White Fathers counted as their founder Charles Martial Allemand Lavigerie, of whom we are to hear more in the next volume as the outstanding leader of the renewed Roman Catholic Church in North Africa. They were intended not only for the conversion of the Moslems, but also, through the wide-ranging vision of Lavigerie, for the pagan blacks. The society's mother house was opened, near Algiers, in 1871.[373] Before the decade was out, in 1879, the White Fathers had established a centre near Lake

[371] *The One Hundred and Nineteenth Annual Report of the London Missionary Society*, 1914, pp. 269-280; Lovett, *The History of the London Missionary Society*, Vol. I, pp. 649-670; Johnson, *Light and Morning in Dark Africa*, pp. 22-44, 97-108, 209-222.
[372] Schwager, *Die katholische Heidenmission der Gegenwart*, p. 146.
[373] Attwater, *The White Fathers in Africa*, p. 16.

Tanganyika.[374] As they multiplied their efforts in Central Africa they stretched southward, and in 1891 they were in the northern part of Northern Rhodesia. By 1914 they had spread quite widely in the section in and around Lake Bangweulu.[375] In 1913 the area was made a separate mission.[376] In the meantime, in 1905, the Jesuits had begun a station in the south-western region.[377]

In the 1890's the Primitive Methodists arrived, a British denomination. For two decades they had been in the Cape Colony and the Orange Free State, but wished a field which was not so congested with missions as were these areas. Partly at the suggestion of Coillard they came to the then nearly virgin territory north of the Zambesi and there, in the south-west of the later Northern Rhodesia, eventually opened several stations. A grammar was produced and translations of hymns and of the New Testament were begun.[378]

Into Northern Rhodesia spread from their main centres in Nyasaland the mission of the United Free Church of Scotland.[379] Of that undertaking we are to hear more in a moment.

In the closing years of the nineteenth century the Dutch Reformed Church of the Orange Free State, wishing to join in the enterprise which had been developed in Nyasaland by the Dutch Reformed Church of South Africa, chose an area immediately to the west of Nyasaland. There in the course of the years it built up one of the largest missions in Northern Rhodesia, especially strong in its village schools.[380]

In our description of the French mission among the Barotse we had occasion to notice the pioneer travels of F. S. Arnot, of the Plymouth Brethren. Beginning in 1881 and ending with his death, in 1914, Arnot made nine journeys into Africa. Out of them came an extensive enterprise of the Christian Missions in Many Lands, as the Brethren denominated their foreign activities, which spanned a region in the southern portion of the Belgian Congo and a northern section of Rhodesia.[381] Moreover, it was Arnot who first directed to Africa the attention of Daniel Crawford. Crawford came out with Arnot in

[374] Attwater, op. cit., p. 21.

[375] Smith, The Way of the White Fields, pp. 80, 81.

[376] Bouniol, The White Fathers and Their Missions, pp. 278ff.

[377] Schwager, op. cit., p. 147.

[378] Smith, op. cit., pp. 81-83 (Smith was once a member of this mission); William Chapman, A Pathfinder in South Central Africa. A Story of Missionary Work and Adventure (London, W. A. Hammond, 1910, pp. xv, 385), passim.

[379] Smith, op. cit., pp. 84, 85.

[380] Smith, op. cit., p. 87; Hofmeyr, Het Land Langs het Meer, p. 159.

[381] Baker, The Life and Explorations of F. S. Arnot, passim; Arnot, Missionary Travels in Central Africa, passim; F. S. Arnot, Garengantze; or, Seven Years' Pioneer Mission Work in Central Africa (Chicago, Fleming H. Revell, no date, pp. viii, 276), passim; A Central African Jubilee or Fifty Years with the Gospel in "the Beloved Strip" (London, Pickering and Inglis, 1931, pp. 192), passim; Smith, op. cit., pp. 88, 89.

1889. He later made a remarkable record as an explorer and missionary in Central Africa.[382]

In 1903 the Seventh Day Adventists inaugurated a station on a five thousand acre farm purchased from the government not far from where the Jesuits were soon to open a centre, on the Batoka plateau between the Zambesi and Kafue rivers.[383]

In 1905 Baptists expanded to Northern Rhodesia an enterprise, originally called the Nyasa Industrial Mission, which in the early 1890's had been begun in Nyasaland. Support for the latter had first been derived from Australia, but later came from England. In 1914 the Rhodesian field was assumed by the Baptists of South Africa. The territory occupied was among a tribe hitherto untouched by Christianity. The language was reduced to writing, medical care was given, and in the mission schools training in manual labour was provided.[384]

In 1906 two ladies from the Brethren in Christ, the American body already at work in Southern Rhodesia, came to the Batoka plateau and began an enterprise which later was expanded.[385]

In 1910 the Anglican communion entered Northern Rhodesia through the Universities' Mission to Central Africa. It had been earlier represented by the South African Church Railway Mission, but the services of that organization had been confined chiefly to railroad employés.

The Universities' Mission to Central Africa had come into being in 1858 in response to Livingstone's memorable appeal at the Senate House in Cambridge in 1857 reinforced by the energy of Robert Gray, the first Bishop of Cape Town. At first it had included only Cambridge and Oxford. Later it drew support also from the Universities of Dublin and Durham.[386] The initial party was led by Charles Frederick Mackenzie, who had been archdeacon in Natal under Bishop Colenso and who after reaching Africa as head of the new mission was consecrated bishop by the episcopate of South Africa. The purpose

[382] G. E. Tilsley, *Dan Crawford. Missionary and Pioneer in Central Africa* (London, Oliphants, pp. xix, 609), *passim;* Daniel Crawford, *Thinking Black. 22 Years without a Break in the Long Grass of Central Africa* (London, Morgan and Scott, 1912, pp. xvi, 485, 18), *passim.*

[383] Anderson, *On the Trail of Livingstone,* pp. 164ff.

[384] Masters, *In Wild Rhodesia,* pp. 191ff.; Du Plessis, *The Evangelisation of Pagan Africa,* pp. 310, 311; Smith, *op. cit.,* p. 90.

[385] Davidson, *South and South Central Africa,* pp. 237ff.; Smith, *op. cit.,* p. 91.

[386] Wilson, *The History of the Universities' Mission to Central Africa,* pp. 1-4. On the initial years of the mission by one of its early staff, see Henry Rowley, *The Story of the Universities' Mission to Central Africa, from its Commencement, under Bishop Mackenzie, to its Withdrawal from the Zambesi* (London, Saunders, Otley and Co., 1866, pp. xii, 493), *passim.*

was to bring the Christian faith to the tribes in the vicinity of Lake Nyasa and the Shiré River. Livingstone helped guide the party into the interior. Headquarters were established between the Shiré and Lake Shirwa, slightly south of Lake Nyasa. Misfortune dogged the undertaking. Somewhat unwittingly the missionaries became involved in native wars. Mackenzie died of fever (January 31, 1862). Death thinned the remaining ranks.[387]

When the news of these disasters reached him, Gray hurried to England. Partly through him a new bishop, William George Tozer, was chosen. A new site, also near the Shiré, was selected but proved unhealthy. Headquarters were thereupon removed to Zanzibar. From this coign of vantage it was planned to penetrate the interior.[388] Tozer resigned in 1873 and his friend, the extraordinarily able Edward Steere, succeeded him. A cathedral was erected on the site of a former slave market in Zanzibar, a striking symbol of the triumph of Christianity. Stations were established on the mainland and eventually, as we shall see in a few moments, reached up into the highlands around Lake Nyasa which had been the mission's original objective.[389]

Northern Rhodesia, adjacent as it was to Nyasaland, seemed a logical field into which to expand the efforts of the Universities' Mission. In pursuance of the policy of having from the outset episcopal direction for a new enterprise, John Edward Hine, who had successively been bishop in Nyasaland and Zanzibar, was chosen to head the undertaking. By the year 1914 promising beginnings had been made.[390]

Aided by F. S. Arnot, in 1910 the South Africa General Mission determined on a site in Northern Rhodesia. By the year 1914 it had only barely begun operations.[391]

It is not surprising that the Wesleyans reached northward from their fields in Southern Rhodesia. In 1908 a Methodist clergyman from South Africa crossed the Zambesi with the purpose of beginning a mission without financial

[387] Harvey Goodwin, *Memoir of Bishop Mackenzie* (Cambridge, Deighton, Bell and Co., 2d ed., 1865, pp. xii, 388, 7), *passim;* Frances Awdrey, *An Elder Sister. A Short Sketch of Ann Mackenzie, and Her Brother the Missionary Bishop* (London, Bemrose and Sons, 1878, pp. v, 261), *passim;* R. Coupland, *Kirk on the Zambesi* (Oxford, The Clarendon Press, 1928, pp. vi, 286), pp. 185ff; Wilson, op. cit., pp. 5-18.

[388] *Letters of Bishop Tozer and his Sister together with some other records of the Universities' Mission from 1863-1873.* Edited by Gertrude Ward (London, Office of the Universities' Mission to Central Africa, 1902, pp. xv, 304), *passim;* Anderson-Morshead, *The History of the Universities' Mission to Central Africa,* pp. 43ff.; Wilson, op. cit., pp. 19-34.

[389] R. M. Heanley, *A Memoir of Edward Steere, D.D., LL.D., Third Missionary Bishop in Central Africa* (London, George Bell and Sons, 1888, pp. xii, 446), *passim;* Wilson, op. cit., pp. 35ff.

[390] Hine, *Days Gone By,* pp. 251-282; Wilson, op. cit., pp. 143-148.

[391] Smith, *The Way of the White Fields,* p. 95.

support from home or from England. In a few months he was dead. In 1912, following an invitation from a chief who had become a Christian while a labourer in the mines in Southern Rhodesia, the Wesleyan Methodist Missionary Society pushed north and under these friendly auspices established a centre.[392]

The record of Rhodesia gives striking evidence of the energy and rapidity with which Christian agencies penetrated Africa in the third of a century preceding 1914. Until the last quarter of the nineteenth century only the London Missionary Society had established a continuing enterprise in that area. Beginning in the 1870's society after society, chiefly Protestant, but also Roman Catholic, entered, reduced languages to writing, began the preparation of a Christian literature, pioneered in modern European medicine, multiplied schools, and gave rise to churches. By the year 1914 Christianity was making rapid headway. A little later, in the 1920's, Southern Rhodesia had about 59,000 Protestants and about 28,000 Roman Catholics,[393] and the 1921 census reported in Northern Rhodesia 65,531 Protestants and 76,084 Roman Catholics.[394]

To the east of Northern Rhodesia there was, in 1914, a much smaller political subdivision, since 1891 formally under British protection, Nyasaland. It lay west and south of Lake Nyasa, about 520 miles in length and varying from 50 to 100 miles in width. Its most important physical features were Lake Nyasa, mountains and plateaux west of Lake Nyasa, the valley of the Shiré, and, to the south of Lake Nyasa and east of the Shiré, the fertile Shiré Highlands. In 1915 the population was estimated to be 1,137,000, a rapid increase during the British administration. A number of tribes were represented. Bantu stock predominated, although traces existed of earlier Hottentot-Bushmen types.[395] The relatively high altitude of much of the region made for greater health than in some other portions of equatorial Africa. Religiously the overwhelming majority were animists, but Islam had begun to make its way in from the east coast.[396] Indeed, some British colonial officials favoured Islam on the

[392] Findlay and Holdsworth, *The History of the Wesleyan Methodist Missionary Society*, Vol. IV, pp. 408-410.
[393] Smith, *op. cit.*, p. 145.
[394] Smith, *op. cit.*, p. 161.
[395] Johnston, *British Central Africa*, pp. 52-55.
[396] *Nyasaland* (London, H.M. Stationery Office, 1920, pp. 90), pp. 1-19. The increase in population came partly because, with the establishment of a settled government, natives flocked in from adjoining territories.—Norman, *Nyasaland without Prejudice*, p. 108.

assumption that it was better than paganism and more suited to the natives than Christianity.[397] When the first Christian missionaries penetrated the land the tribal system and its authority had suffered partial disintegration through extensive slave raids. The new faith, therefore, met with less resistance than it would otherwise have encountered.[398]

Christianity came somewhat earlier to Nyasaland than to Northern Rhodesia. As in the case of Rhodesia, the penetration by Protestant Christianity was in the nature of an extension of the South African efforts. The explorations of Livingstone, originally begun from South Africa, gave the incentive for the introduction of Protestantism. Several of the leading bodies at work were also present in South Africa. In proportion to the population Protestantism made somewhat more rapid progress than in either of the Rhodesias.[399]

The Universities' Mission to Central Africa was first on the scene. However, as we saw a few paragraphs above, its initial efforts were followed by retreat. That retreat was only temporary. From the headquarters on the island of Zanzibar beginnings were made on the adjacent mainland.[400] The original objective of the mission was not forgotten. Aided by one of Livingstone's old servants, Bishop Steere sought to reach Lake Nyasa by way of the Ruvuma River (1875). Part way in, not far from the north bank of that stream, in 1876 a centre was founded at Masasi with a nucleus of Christian freed slaves.[401] From Masasi as a base, in 1881 William Percival Johnson, with a companion, arrived at Lake Nyasa. Left alone by his colleague's death, Johnson continued. The son of a lawyer who died when the child was three years old, Johnson had been reared by his mother, at Oxford had a record about the average in scholarship and athletics, and was headed for the Indian civil service. But while at Oxford he heard the call of the Universities' Mission. He spent more than half a century as a missionary, preached, started schools, translated the entire Bible and the Book of Common Prayer into one of the tongues of Nyasaland and part of the Bible into another, and did some translating into three other

[397] Barnes, *Johnson of Nyasaland*, p. 126; Chirgwin, *An African Pilgrimage*, p. 110.
[398] Norman, *op. cit.*, p. 178.
[399] In the 1920's Nyasaland is estimated to have had 110,000 Protestants.—Roome, *A Great Emancipation*, p. 67. For a picture of non-Anglican Protestantism in 1910 given by a visitor to the country, see Charles Inwood, *An African Pentecost. The Record of a Missionary Tour in Central Africa* (London, Marshall Brothers, pp. 79), pp. 17-62. In 1912 it and Northern Rhodesia had about 6,000 Roman Catholics.—Streit, *Atlas Hierarchicus*, p. 102. In 1927 the White Fathers were said to have in Nyasa 19,513 neophytes.— Bouniol, *The White Fathers and their Missions*, p. 273.
[400] Heanley, *A Memoir of Edward Steere*, p. 137; Anderson-Morshead, *The History of the Universities' Mission to Central Africa*, pp. 54ff.
[401] Heanley, *op. cit.*, pp. 138-152, 189-196; Anderson-Morshead, *op. cit.*, pp. 111ff.

tongues. He accomplished these feats in spite of the loss of one eye when he was about thirty years of age and with imperfect vision in the other.[402]

In time various centres were opened in Nyasaland, chiefly along the east shore of the lake. The main station was on Likoma, an island about equidistant from both ends of Lake Nyasa.[403] For a number of years the Nyasa mission was supervised from Zanzibar and Smythies, as bishop, four times made the difficult journey.[404] In 1892 a bishop was consecrated for Nyasaland, Wilfrid Bird Hornby, who had been one of the founders of the Oxford Mission to Calcutta. In about two years ill health compelled him to resign.[405] He was succeeded in the episcopate by a veteran, Chauncy Maples, a close friend of Johnson since university days and a pioneer at Masasi and Likoma. On his way in, after his consecration, Maples was drowned in Lake Nyasa through the foundering of a mission boat.[406] He was followed as bishop by Hine, who had served his missionary apprenticeship on Likoma.[407] Significantly the cathedral at Likoma was erected on ground which had been used for the burning of witches.[408] Here as in Zanzibar the bishop's seat testified to the triumph of the faith over dark evils.

The mission had the customary accompaniments of schools,[409] medical care,[410] the training of teachers,[411] and, in time, the ordination of native clergy.[412] Like the Anglican communion in South Africa, with which in its beginnings it was closely connected, the Universities' Mission represented the Catholic wing of the Church of England. This fact helped to determine its programme,

---

[402] Heanley, op. cit., pp. 323-332; Bertram Herbert Barnes, Johnson of Nyasaland (Westminster, Universities' Mission to Central Africa, 1933, pp. 258), pp. 37ff.; Johnson, My African Reminiscences, pp. 78ff.; Anderson-Morshead, op. cit., pp. 127ff.

[403] Johnson, op. cit., pp. 115-149; Wilson, The History of the Universities' Mission to Central Africa, pp. 59-73.

[404] Ward, The Life of Charles Alan Smythies, p. 148.

[405] Wilson, op. cit., pp. 91, 92, 98.

[406] Chauncy Maples. . . . A Sketch of His Life with Selections from His Letters by His Sister (London, Longmans, Green and Co., 1897, pp. viii, 403), passim.

[407] Hine, Days Gone By, pp. 72ff., 145ff.

[408] Hine, op. cit., p. 81.

[409] Mills, What We Do in Nyasaland, pp. 28ff., 179ff., 209ff.

[410] Mills, op. cit., pp. 108ff.

[411] Arthur Douglas, Missionary on Lake Nyasa, the Story of His Life, compiled by B. W. Randolph (Westminster, Universities' Mission to Central Africa, 1912, pp. viii, 312), pp. 254, 255.

[412] See the autobiography of one such priest who had been reared in Islam, was sold as a slave, freed by a British gunboat, turned over to the mission for instruction, went to Nyasaland as a teacher, and later was ordained—in Augustine Ambali, Thirty Years in Nyasaland (Westminster, Universities' Mission to Central Africa, no date, pp. 64), passim. See the life of another in D. Y. Mills, An African Priest and Missionary, being a Sketch of the Life of Leonard Mattiya Kamungu (Westminster Universities' Mission to Central Africa, 1914, pp. 87), passim.

but did not prevent it from bearing in many of its features a likeness to other enterprises which did not hold to that tradition.[413]

As the Universities' Mission had owed its inception in part to Livingstone and in part to Bishop Gray of Cape Town, so what was eventually the Livingstonia Mission of the United Free Church of Scotland in Nyasaland sprang in part from the great explorer and in part from James Stewart, whom we have come to associate with Lovedale, in South Africa. To obtain funds for the enterprise, Stewart sold his family plate and most of his patrimony. He made a trip up the Zambesi and the Shiré to meet Livingstone and in 1874, a month after the funeral in Westminster Abbey, proposed to his church that a mission, to be named Livingstonia, be sent to Nyasa. A Glasgow committee made itself responsible for raising funds for the first five years, and in 1875 the initial party set out.[414] Lake Nyasa was explored and a centre selected near the southern end.[415] Before many years the entire west side of the lake was claimed as a field and a strong station was developed at Bandawé, near the middle, almost directly across from Likoma, where the Universities' Mission eventually built its cathedral. In 1894 the headquarters were placed at Livingstonia, on an elevation about 3,000 feet above the lake and near its northern end.[416]

He who became the outstanding leader of the mission, Robert Laws, was one of the pioneer party. Born in humble circumstances, of a father who had dedicated him from birth for the life of a missionary, from a child Laws cherished the ambition to follow that calling. Through a hard struggle with poverty he acquired a university education and training in theology and medicine. He was determined to go to Central Africa and over obstacles obtained appointment to be one of the inaugurators of the enterprise. It was Laws who was chiefly responsible for founding and developing at Livingstonia a central educational institution, not unlike the one at Lovedale, in South Africa, with training in many branches, including industries and handicrafts, and with a hospital.[417]

---

[413] For the life of a young priest, cut off by illness after eighteen months of service in Africa, see *The Life and Letters of Arthur Fraser Sim* (Westminster, Universities' Mission to Central Africa, 1897, pp. xiv, 278), *passim*.

[414] Laws, *Reminiscences of Livingstonia*, pp. 5, 6; Fraser, *Livingstonia*, pp. 3, 4; Stewart, *Daybreak in the Dark Continent*, pp. 223ff.

[415] Accounts of the expedition and the early years by members of the party are E. D. Young, *Nyassa; a Journal of Adventures whilst Exploring Lake Nyassa, Central Africa, and Establishing the Settlement of Livingstonia* (London, John Murray, 1877, pp. xii, 239), *passim*; Laws, *op. cit.*, pp. 1-23.

[416] Laws, *op. cit.*, pp. 53-111, 146-178; Fraser, *op. cit.*, p. 14; Roome, *A Great Emancipation*, p. 39; Jack, *Daybreak in Livingstonia*, pp. 134ff.

[417] Laws, *op. cit.*, *passim*; W. P. Livingstone, *Laws of Livingstonia* (London, Hodder and Stoughton, 1921, pp. xi, 385. Based upon the extensive papers of Laws), *passim*;

The opening decades of the mission of the Free Church were very arduous. Slave-traders and native wars brought difficulties. Some of the chiefs welcomed the foreigners, for they saw in their presence an opportunity for trade and wealth, but others were jealous of those who were so favoured. Converts were slow in coming. After fifteen years all Nyasaland held only sixty native communicants.[418]

The extension of British rule over the country, in the form of a protectorate, in 1891, brought a change.[419] The coming of order, British prestige, and the faithful work of missionaries combined to produce movements, some of them *en masse*, towards the new faith. Schools and churches were multiplied.[420] In 1914 there were 49 European missionaries, 9,517 communicants, 900 schools, 1,618 teachers, and 57,000 scholars.[421] Ten languages were reduced to writing and a large amount of material was printed in them. Native Christians carried their faith to adjoining regions and tribes.[422]

Prominent among those who served in the years of the mission's growing prosperity and who yet shared in pioneering in some of its outposts was Donald Fraser. A son of the manse, he was caught up in the youth of the Student Christian Movement and became active in promoting an interest in missions. He arrived in Africa in 1896.[423]

Almost simultaneously with the Livingstonia mission, in which the Free Church of Scotland predominated, the Church of Scotland began an enterprise in what was later Nyasaland. It, too, had been stirred by the death of Livingstone. With the party which went out in 1875 to found the Livingstonia undertaking there travelled a representative of the Church of Scotland. After surveying the country, he deemed the most favourable centre the Shiré High-

---

James Johnston, *Robert Laws of Livingstonia* (Glasgow, Pickering and Inglis, no date, new ed., pp. 206. For young people), *passim;* Jack, *op. cit.,* pp. 337ff.; Jones, *Education in East Africa,* pp. 62, 205-208.

[418] Fraser, *op. cit.,* pp. 18-25.

[419] Johnston, *British Central Africa,* pp. 80-151, by one who was a leader in the enforcement of British authority.

[420] For an account by a missionary which begins in the difficult days and continues into more successful ones, see W. A. Elmslie, *Among the Wild Ngoni, being Some Chapters in the History of the Livingstonia Mission in British Central Africa* (Chicago, Fleming H. Revell Co., 1899, pp. 319), *passim.* See also Donald Fraser, *Winning a Primitive People* (New York, E. P. Dutton & Co., 1914, pp. 320), *passim.* On a convert, later a teacher and evangelist, trained from a boy in the mission, see Donald Fraser, *Autobiography of an African. Retold in Biographical Form & in the Wild African Setting of the Life of Daniel Mtusu* (London, Seeley, Service & Co., 1925, pp. 210), *passim.*

[421] Livingstone, *Laws of Livingstonia,* p. 349.

[422] Fraser, *Livingstonia,* pp. 32-34.

[423] Agnes R. Fraser, *Donald Fraser of Livingstonia* (London, Hodder and Stoughton, 1934, pp. ix, 325), *passim;* Donald Fraser, *African Idylls. Portraits and Impressions of a Central African Mission Station* (London, Seeley, Service & Co., 1923, pp. 229), *passim.*

lands.[424] In 1876 the first contingent arrived. It was composed of a medical officer and five artisans. These were intended to teach the natives the useful crafts of civilization while leading them into the Christian faith. On the Shiré Highlands a location was blocked out and given the name of Blantyre, after the birthplace of Livingstone.[425]

The opening years of the mission were not happy. The artisans, inexperienced, ran afoul of tribal feuds and were accused of undue severity towards the natives and of arrogating to themselves civil authority.[426] The General Assembly of the Church of Scotland sent a committee of investigation. In consequence of the report of the committee a new beginning was made. In 1881 a well-trained clergyman, David Clement Scott, was appointed to lead the mission. He achieved reorganization. Blantyre was retained and industrial education continued prominent in the programme, but the initial abuses had passed.[427]

In 1883 there arrived at Blantyre Alexander Hetherwick. A man of outstanding ability, in 1898 he succeeded to the headship of the mission.[428] In the course of time other stations were opened and the field was extended into Portuguese East Africa.[429] The original purpose of combining religious, medical, educational, and industrial activities was maintained. At Blantyre an institution similar to the ones at Livingstonia and Lovedale was developed. It became the centre of a system of schools. It trained not only teachers but also artisans, clerks, and overseers of plantations.[430] In the first decade of the twentieth century the beginnings of a native ministry were made.[431]

By the mid-1920's the Nyasaland enterprises of the Free Church of Scotland and the Church of Scotland were not far from the same numerical strength in missionaries and church members. The former had more native workers and more pupils in its schools.[432]

[424] Hetherwick, *The Romance of Blantyre*, pp. 14-19.

[425] Hetherwick, *op. cit.*, pp. 20-22.

[426] Johnston, *op. cit.*, p. 68; Hetherwick, *op. cit.*, pp. 23-32.

[427] Hetherwick, *op. cit.*, pp. 33ff.

[428] W. P. Livingstone, *A Prince of Missionaries. The Rev. Alexander Hetherwick C.B.E., D.D., M.A., of Blantyre, Central Africa* (London, James Clarke & Co., 1931, pp. 206), *passim*. See also Alexander Hetherwick, *The Gospel and the African* (Edinburgh, T. & T. Clark, 1932, pp. xi, 176), *passim*.

[429] W. Henry Rankine, *A Hero of the Dark Continent. Memoir of Rev. W^m. Affleck Scott* (Edinburgh, William Blackwood and Sons, 1896, pp. x, 313) is the biography of one of the missionaries of this period.

[430] Jones, *Education in East Africa*, pp. 202-204.

[431] Hetherwick, *The Romance of Blantyre*, pp. 167-176. A biography of one who engaged in theological teaching is *Robert Hellier Napier in Nyasaland. Being His Letters to His Home Circle.* Edited by Alexander Hetherwick (Edinburgh, William Blackwood and Sons, 1925, pp. iv, 158), *passim*.

[432] Roome, *A Great Emancipation*, final statistical table.

An interesting undertaking designed to operate in connexion with the Scottish missions was the Livingstonia Central African Trading Company, organized in the mother country for the purpose of relieving the missions of the burden of transportation into the interior and of developing the commerce and resources of Central Africa in a fashion which would benefit the natives. In time it became the African Lakes Corporation and had much to do with the extension of British authority in the region.[433]

We must add that the three British missionary societies and their friends brought much pressure on their government to induce it to take possession of Nyasaland, for they feared the threatened Portuguese control.[434] To what degree they were responsible for the final action seems uncertain.

The Dutch Reformed Church of South Africa entered Nyasaland. In 1886, partly at the instance of Andrew Murray and of the brother-in-law of James Stewart, some of the ministers of that communion organized a missionary union. The first missionary sent was from the Murray clan. He arrived in Nyasaland in 1888 and collaborated with the Livingstonia Mission.[435] Eventually the South African enterprise had more missionaries than either of the Scottish societies. The more southerly stations of the Livingstonia Mission were transferred to them.[436] Much use was made of native evangelists. Schools, a press, and medical service were maintained in addition to the building of congregations and the instruction of neophytes in the faith.[437] Schools were made ancillary to religious activities and much stress was placed on agriculture and simple village industries.[438] By 1909 about 2,000 Christians had been gathered.[439] Relieved of the care of the southern part of its field, the Livingstonia Mission was able to push farther north.[440]

The Nyasa Industrial Mission, which we found in Northern Rhodesia, was inaugurated in the Shiré Highlands in the early 1890's by Australian Baptists. Its purpose was to give instruction in industries and the cultivation of the soil with the hope of arousing an interest in the Christian message. In 1898 a second station was opened. In 1905 a mass movement towards Christianity began which spread largely by native initiative.[441]

[433] Livingstone, Laws of Livingstonia, pp. 144, 145; Stewart, Dawn on the Dark Continent, pp. 216-223; Hetherwick, op. cit., p. 42; Jack, Daybreak in Livingstonia, pp. 215ff.
[434] Jack, op. cit., pp. 296, 297, 300, 301; Livingstone, op. cit., pp. 49-56.
[435] Hofmeyr, Het Land Langs het Meer, pp. 118-121; Livingstone, op. cit., pp. 247, 248; Jack, op. cit., p. 176; Laws, Reminiscences of Livingstonia, p. 203.
[436] Livingstone, op. cit., pp. 265, 266.
[437] Hofmeyr, op. cit., pp. 131ff.
[438] Jones, Education in East Africa, p. 211.
[439] Hofmeyr, op. cit., p. 159.
[440] Fraser, Livingstonia, p. 31.
[441] Masters, In Wild Rhodesia, pp. 191-194.

Early in the 1890's, the Zambesi Industrial Mission, an undenominational body, acquired a large tract of land near Blantyre. It later opened additional centres. By means of its large plantations of coffee and cotton, around which its activities revolved, it sought to be self-supporting.[442]

We hear, too, of a similar enterprise, the Baptist Industrial Mission, with assistance from Scotland.[443]

In 1898 the South Africa General Mission commenced activities in the southern part of Nyasaland, but for years made little headway.[444]

The Seventh Day Adventists purchased a plantation not far from Blantyre (1902), but the beginnings were made difficult by the illness or death of the pioneers. For a time the estate was under the direction of American Negroes.[445]

In a region pre-empted by as strong Protestant missions as was Nyasaland, Roman Catholics found entrance difficult. In 1889, before the final determination had been made as to whether title to the country should go to Great Britain or to Portugal, with authorization from Lisbon, Lavigerie consecrated several White Fathers for the region. Meeting with varied obstacles, this initial contingent withdrew. It was not until 1901 that the White Fathers returned. Then they opened a station not far from one of the Dutch Reformed. They planned to establish a chain of centres across Nyasaland and Rhodesia. In 1907 the first baptisms were administered. By 1911 five posts were in operation. In 1913 Nyasa was made a separate vicariate apostolic.[446] In 1910 the De Montfort Fathers arrived, coming in from the South. By 1914 a separate vicariate had arisen out of their efforts at the southern end of the lake.[447] Since they had obtained so late a start, the Roman Catholics did not display a large growth until after 1914.

At the dawn of the nineteenth century the Portuguese held, as remnants of the colonial empire acquired in the fifteenth, sixteenth, and seventeenth centuries, footholds on approximately opposite sides of Africa, on the west coast south of the Congo and on the east coast north of Natal. When, in the last quarter of the nineteenth century, the European scramble for African territories became acute, they attempted to join their possessions by the acquisition of a broad belt of land across the continent. In this ambition they were

---

[442] Roome, op. cit., pp. 43, 44; Du Plessis, The Evangelisation of Pagan Africa, pp. 309, 310.
[443] Roome, op. cit., pp. 45, 46.
[444] Roome, op. cit., p. 44; Du Plessis, op. cit., pp. 311, 312.
[445] Du Plessis, op. cit., p. 311.
[446] Jack, op. cit., p. 304; Bouniol, The White Fathers and Their Missions, pp. 260ff.
[447] Bouniol, op. cit., pp. 263-266.

frustrated by the British. However, they extended their borders and through a series of agreements with other Western powers obtained recognition of claims which gave them extensive areas. Their holdings on the west coast south of the Congo were collectively known as Angola and those on the east coast as Portuguese East Africa or Mozambique.

The two colonies were of unequal size and population. Portuguese East Africa was smaller than Angola, with an area of 293,500 square miles as against the 480,000 square miles of the latter. It had, in 1909, slightly over 3,000,000 inhabitants, while Angola's total in 1906 was a little over 4,000,000. Both were predominantly Bantu, but in Angola there was a strong mixture of Negro blood and in its south were Bushmen.[448] In the latter part of the nineteenth century both faced a quickening of European penetration with the consequent disintegration of traditional native life.

In Angola, beginning in the 1880's, Portugal made more effective its nominal control of the hinterland and broke the power of some of the chiefs. Portuguese traders penetrated the region with rum and fire-arms. The slave trade was accentuated to obtain labour for the developing plantations of sugar and cacao.[449]

The area embraced in Angola had been the scene of some of the most spectacularly successful of the Roman Catholic missions of the fifteenth, sixteenth, and seventeenth centuries.[450] By the eighteenth century, however, decay had set in. Yet Christianity did not completely die out. There were whites and mixed bloods who professed to be Roman Catholics and some of the blacks held to a nominal connexion with the faith. Towards the close of the nineteenth century one estimate placed the number at 250,000.[451] In the nineteenth century a local seminary prepared secular clergy.[452] Capuchins had been in the area, but in the 1830's the last of their number left and in 1865 they surrendered the mission.[453] Thereupon the area was assigned to the Holy Ghost Fathers. Since these were French, the Portuguese authorities distrusted them and difficulty was encountered in gaining a foothold. However, in 1873 a station was opened at Landana, in the small Portuguese enclave north of the mouth of the Congo. There institutions of various kinds and great plantations

[448] *The Encyclopædia Britannica*, 11th ed., Vol. II, pp. 38, 39, Vol. XXII, pp. 163, 165.
[449] Richter, *Geschichte der evangelischen Mission in Afrika*, p. 219.
[450] Vol. III, pp. 242-244.
[451] Louvet, *Les Missions Catholiques au XIX Siècle*, p. 390. In 1880 the Bishop of Loanda declared the number of Roman Catholics to be 1,000,000, but this was judged excessive.
[452] Schwager, *Die katholische Heidenmission der Gegenwart*, p. 118.
[453] Schmidlin-Braun, *Catholic Mission History*, p. 648; *Missiones Catholicae . . . MDCCCXCII*, p. 344.

were developed. Schools and a theological seminary were begun.[454] South of the Congo spiritual care was given to the nominally Christian blacks and centres were opened for work among non-Christians.[455] In 1879 the Holy Ghost Fathers were given charge in the southern part of Angola. The first few years were discouraging and were marked by deaths in the missionary staff. By the year 1914, partly with the aid of state subventions, stations and schools were multiplied and progress was achieved among a robber tribe. At Huilla, in the South, schools, orphanages, hospitals, a seminary for priests, and a novitiate for lay brothers were built up.[456] By 1913 the Holy Ghost Fathers were counting in all Angola 29,200 native Roman Catholics in their care.[457]

Protestant missionaries entered Angola somewhat later than the Holy Ghost Fathers. They became more numerous than the latter, but they did not gather so large a body of Christians.[458] The first to arrive were the English Baptists, in 1878. They established their headquarters at San Salvador, made famous by early Roman Catholic enterprise. Further stations were eventually opened, all in the northern part of Angola.[459] In 1880 came the American Board of Commissioners for Foreign Missions. It chose as its centre Bihé, inland from Benguella and at an elevation of about 5,000 feet. The first party included an American Negro who had been educated at Hampton Institute. In 1884 an unfriendly chief drove the missionaries out, but, supported by the Portuguese governor, they were soon back. Progress was slow. It was eight years before the first church was organized and at the end of twenty-five years the entire mission could count only 283 baptized Christians. Not until after 1914 was rapid growth experienced.[460] To the aid of the American Board, in 1886, came the Canadian Congregationalists.[461] In 1889 Plymouth Brethren landed, led by the intrepid F. S. Arnot. In that year he headed a party which went inland to the vicinity of Bihé, not far from the place where the American Board was to establish its headquarters. From there into Northern Rhodesia a chain of sta-

[454] Schwager, op. cit., p. 117.

[455] Schwager, op. cit., p. 118.

[456] Schwager, op. cit., pp. 126-128.

[457] Streit, Atlas Hierarchicus, p. 101.

[458] In 1931 Protestants had 239 foreign missionaries and 21,461 full members as against 137 Roman Catholic foreign missionaries and 295,216 Roman Catholic Christians.—Tucker, Angola, pp. 141, 143.

[459] Tucker, op. cit., pp. 38-42; R. H. Carson Graham, Under Seven Congo Kings (London, The Carey Press, no date, pp. xii, 293), passim.

[460] Strong, The Story of the American Board, pp. 336-340; Tucker, op. cit., p. 42; Tucker, in The International Review of Missions, Vol. XIX, pp. 256-265.

[461] H. W. Barker, The Story of Chisamba. A Sketch of the African Mission of the Canadian Congregational Churches (Toronto, Canada Congregational Foreign Missionary Society, 1904, pp. 132), pp. 44ff.; L. M. Silcox, The Story of Chisamba Re-told (Toronto, Canada Congregational Foreign Missionary Society, 1916, pp. 212), pp. 58ff.

tions was created. The Christian message was preached, slaves were rescued, and medical work undertaken. Reinforcements came until the mission had a larger foreign staff than any other Protestant group in Angola.[462] In 1884 William Taylor, whom we have previously met in Latin America, Australia, and South Africa, was elected by the Methodist Episcopal Church bishop for Africa. Influenced by the report of a German exploring expedition, he decided on Angola as a field for a new mission. In 1885 he arrived at Loanda with a party of recruits. His plan, as in South America, was to make the enterprise self-supporting. Stations were opened, languages were reduced to writing, and schools, industrial training, and widespread preaching were undertaken.[463] In 1897 there came to the northern part of the colony the Angola Evangelical Mission, an undenominational organization supported from Great Britain.[464] Heli Chatelain, who went out in 1885 with Taylor as a linguist, later, in 1897, established the independent Mission Philafricaine, financed by friends in Switzerland. Following Taylor's plan, it was designed to be self-supporting. It was manned largely by artisans. The death toll was heavy and the enterprise was small.[465] In 1910 came the Christian and Missionary Alliance.[466] In 1914 the South Africa General Mission entered by way of the Northern Rhodesian frontier.[467] By the year 1914, then, Protestantism had been introduced to several parts of Angola. No systematic plan was adopted for a complete permeation of the country, but much of the land was being touched.

In Portuguese East Africa the sixteenth and seventeenth centuries had seen aggressive Roman Catholic missions by Jesuits, Dominicans, Augustinians, and seculars,[468] but the eighteenth century had been marked by decline. The expulsion of the Jesuits (1759) was a severe blow. The suppression of the religious orders in the second quarter of the nineteenth century was a further

[462] Arnot, *Missionary Travels in Central Africa*, pp. 105ff., 127ff.; Baker, *The Life and Explorations of Frederick Stanley Arnot*, pp. 238ff., 274ff., 285ff.; Tucker, *op. cit.*, pp. 54-61; Arnot, *Bihé and Garenganze*, pp. 5-48.

[463] Taylor, *Story of My Life*, pp. 695-713; *Annual Report of the Board of Foreign Missions of the Methodist Episcopal Church for the Year 1914*, pp. 229-236. For a short biographical sketch of one of the missionaries, see *In Jesus' Name. Memoirs of the victorious life and triumphant death of Susan Talbott Wengatz*, compiled by Sadie Louise Miller (no place or date of publication, pp. 85).

[464] Tucker, *op. cit.*, p. 404.

[465] Heli Chatelain, *Folk-Tales of Angola* (Boston, Houghton Mifflin and Co., 1894, pp. xii, 315), pp. v-vii; Tucker, *op. cit.*, pp. 69, 70.

[466] Tucker, *op. cit.*, p. 67.

[467] Tucker, *op. cit.*, p. 70.

[468] Thauren, *Die Missionen der Gesellschaft des Göttlichen Wortes in den Heidenländern. Die Mission in Mozambique*, etc., pp. 9, 10. Laurenz Kilger, *Die erste Mission unter den Bantustämmen Ostafrikas* (Münster, Verlag der Aschendorffschen Buchhandlung, 1917, pp. vii, 208), *passim*; Schebesta, *Zum ersten Missionsanfang am Sambesi*, in *Zeitschrift für Missionswissenschaft*, Vol. XIV, pp. 88-99.

disaster. The few seculars, mostly from the Portuguese Indian centre, Goa, could scarcely halt the disintegration.[469]

It was not until 1881 that Jesuits, by re-entering, were able to bring renewed life to the languishing Roman Catholic cause. Within a few years they had opened a number of stations.[470] However, climate and disease took a severe toll[471] and led to a reduction in the number of centres.[472] Portuguese seculars were provided by the Seminary of Sernache, but they confined their attention almost entirely to the small white population. In 1898 came the first of the Portuguese Franciscans. Side by side with them laboured the Franciscan Missionaries of Mary.[473] Christian literature was prepared in the vernaculars, including a translation of the Bible and a catechism. A meteorological observatory was inaugurated and studies were made of the flora and fauna.[474] In 1910, with the founding of the Portuguese republic and the adoption of an anti-clerical policy, the Jesuits were ordered out of the colony. The Society of the Divine Word replaced them and by 1914 had sent in several priests and lay brothers. Sisters also came. In 1912 the Sisters of the Holy Ghost succeeded the Josephines of Cluny.[475] Because of the late renewal of their missions and the political vicissitudes which embarrassed them, by the year 1914 the Roman Catholics could count less than 5,000 Christians among the natives.[476]

Protestants were earlier in attempting to reach the non-Christians of Portuguese East Africa than were the revived Roman Catholic missions. In the 1820's the British Methodists placed a missionary at Delagoa Bay, but the unhealthfulness of that region led to the early abandonment of the enterprise. Not until the 1880's was it resumed. Then it was by a native of Lourenço Marques who had become a Christian while in South Africa, had joined the Wesleyans, and was moved by a burning desire to carry his new faith to his own country. In 1896 he was deported on the charge of complicity with a native revolt. When released he went to South Africa. British missionaries were put in charge of the enterprise which he had begun.[477] In 1879 the American Board of Commissioners for Foreign Missions decided to send a

[469] Schwager, *Die katholische Heidenmission der Gegenwart*, p. 148.
[470] Thauren, *op. cit.*, p. 10.
[471] *Catalogus Patrum ac Fratrum qui in Missione Zambesiae in territorio Lusitanae ditionis vita functi sunt ab anno 1881 ad annum 1913* (Brussels, Typ. E. Daem, 1913, pp. 7), *passim*.
[472] Thauren, *op. cit.*, pp. 10, 11.
[473] Thauren, *op. cit.*, p. 11.
[474] *Ibid.*
[475] Thauren, *op. cit.*, pp. 12-15.
[476] Thauren, *op. cit.*, pp. 12, 15; Streit, *Atlas Hierarchicus*, p. 102.
[477] Findlay and Holdsworth, *The History of the Wesleyan Methodist Missionary Society*, Vol. IV, pp. 241, 251, 252, 261-263, 348, 357; Moreira, *Portuguese East Africa*, pp. 23-25.

contingent to the east side of the continent. The initial attempt miscarried, and it was not until 1883 that a foothold was obtained at Inhambane. That port proved insalubrious and the mission was moved inland, to Rhodesia.[478] However, from the Rhodesia stations, situated as they were not far from the boundary, missionaries and natives carried the Christian message into Portuguese territory,[479] and in 1914 plans were formulated for placing resident missionaries at Beira, on the coast.[480] In 1885, through contact with American Board missionaries from Inhambane, Free Methodists from the United States established a centre across the bay from that town. Activities were extended into the surrounding countryside. Some of the native helpers had become Christians while labourers in the mines at Johannesburg.[481] When the American Board retired from Inhambane, representatives of the Methodist Episcopal Church succeeded it (1890), partly with the assistance of a missionary of the former organization who felt that he could not abandon his flock.[482] By the year 1914 central schools and a mission farm had been developed and seventy out-stations had been opened.[483] In the 1870's members of what later joined with others in forming the Swiss Romande mission established themselves among blacks who had been driven by war from Portuguese East Africa to the Transvaal. Transvaal converts carried the Christian message to their relatives north of Lourenço Marques. European missionaries followed. In time other stations were opened.[484] In 1893 a bishop of the Anglican communion was consecrated for a new diocese which embraced the southern part of Portuguese East Africa. This was done by the bishops of South Africa. Financial assistance came from England. Headquarters were established at Inhambane and other centres were occupied. At first confined to the care of white residents, in 1895 the Anglican mission began efforts to reach the blacks. Early, too, care was given to the religious needs of the English population at Beira, the coastal port for the railway which ran inland to Rhodesia.[485] In spite of its

[478] Strong, *The Story of the American Board*, pp. 341-343; W. C. Wilcox, *The Man from an African Jungle* (New York, The Macmillan Co., 1925, pp. 248), *passim*.

[479] *Annual Report of the American Board of Commissioners for Foreign Missions*, 1913, p. 48.

[480] *Annual Report of the American Board of Commissioners for Foreign Missions*, 1914, pp. 38-41.

[481] Moreira, *op. cit.*, pp. 20, 21; John Wesley Haley, *Life in Mozambique and South Africa* (Chicago, The Methodist Publishing House, 1926, pp. 174), *passim*; Burritt, *The Story of Fifty Years*, pp. 23-40.

[482] Moreira, *op. cit.*, p. 21.

[483] *Annual Report of the Board of Foreign Missions of the Methodist Episcopal Church for the Year 1914*, pp. 223-228.

[484] Grandjean, *La Mission Romande*, pp. 114-198; Henri-Philippe Junod, *Henri—A—Junod, Missionnaire et Savant, 1863-1934* (Lausanne, Mission Suisse dans l'Afrique du Sud, 1934, pp. 89), *passim*; Moreira, *op. cit.*, pp. 22,23.

[485] Pascoe, *Two Hundred Years of the S.P.G.*, pp. 246ff.

connexion with a predominantly Roman Catholic country, Portuguese East Africa, like Angola, became a field for several Protestant agencies.

North of Portuguese East Africa lay what from the 1880's until the World War of 1914-1918 was German East Africa. With an area of about 364,000 square miles, it was larger than the former but not so large as Angola. In it were highlands and mountain ranges which included the loftiest peaks in Africa, those of Kilimanjaro. Three of the great lakes of Africa, Victoria Nyanza, Tanganyika, and Nyasa, formed part of its borders. Its population, estimated as being about 8,000,000, was larger than that of both Portuguese possessions combined. Like the latter, its peoples were predominantly Bantu. It contained a small Arab minority. On the coast were the Swahili, mainly a mixture of Bantu and Arab blood, and Moslem by faith. There were traces of pre-Bantu pygmy and Bushman stocks. The religion of the Bantu majority was animism in one of its many varieties. During their heyday, in the sixteenth century, the Portuguese wrested possession of the coast from the Arabs, but in their decline, in the eighteenth century, lost it again to that people. For a time in the fourth quarter of the nineteenth century British influence, dominant in Zanzibar, was strong, but by agreements between Great Britain and Germany made in the 1880's and in 1890 the latter recognized the former's claim, acquired through exploration and a number of concessions, to what became British East Africa, the later Kenya, and the former acquiesced in the latter's title to the region which we are considering in these paragraphs. Great Britain also, it may be added, established a protectorate over Zanzibar, consisting of the islands of Zanzibar and Pemba.[486]

The first contact of the area with Christianity had, presumably, been through the Portuguese. By the dawn of the nineteenth century, however, all traces of the faith seem to have disappeared.

In the nineteenth century the initial attempt to propagate Christianity in the region was by Johann Ludwig Krapf. Born in 1810, in Württemberg, of God-fearing farmer folk, Krapf early determined to be a missionary. He received his training at Basel, entered the service of the Church Missionary Society, and thus was one of those many Germans who helped to recruit the staffs of that organization and of the London Missionary Society.[487] He hoped to penetrate Africa by way of Abyssinia. Frustrated in that effort, in the 1840's he moved southward, visited and preached at Zanzibar, and lived for a time

---

[486] *The Encyclopædia Britannica,* Vol. XI, pp. 771-774.
[487] Claus, *Dr. Ludwig Krapf,* pp. 1ff.

at Mombasa, in what was later British East Africa. He learned the Swahili tongue and translated the New Testament into it. Reinforcements were sent him, also Germans. He dreamed of a chain of mission stations across Africa. He and some of his colleagues, notably J. Rebmann, undertook tours of exploration. These revealed snow-capped Kilimanjaro to an incredulous European world. They also were pursued along the coast of what was later German East Africa. However, the central station which Krapf established was not in this area, but in what was eventually British East Africa.[488] In the 1860's the mission was at a low ebb.[489] In the 1870's the death of Livingstone and the concern for the slave trade revived the interest. From then on a great extension of the operations of the Church Missionary Society occurred.[490] This was chiefly in the later British East Africa and in Uganda, but out of a half-way post to the latter a field was developed west of Zanzibar near the centre of German East Africa.[491]

The main Anglican activity in German East Africa was not by the Evangelicals through the Church Missionary Society but by the Anglo-Catholics through the Universities' Mission to Central Africa. Indeed, in the course of time the Universities' Mission had the largest foreign staff and the most numerous body of Christians of any of the non-Roman Catholic agencies in the colony. In 1864, as we saw a few paragraphs above, headquarters were established on Zanzibar. Although the original objective, Nyasaland, was not surrendered, fields in what became German East Africa were also developed. These were north of the Ruvuma River, in and near Masasi, *en route* to Lake Nyasa, and near the coast north-west of Zanzibar. Moreover, the Nyasa enterprise extended into German territory on the north-east side of the lake.

We must also remind ourselves that the Universities' Mission was the largest and almost the only non-Roman Catholic Christian organization represented in the British protectorate which included the islands of Zanzibar and Pemba.[492]

---

[488] Claus, *op. cit.*, pp. 64-129, 149-163; Krapf, *Travels*, pp. 126-410; Stock, *The History of the Church Missionary Society*, Vol. II, pp. 125-139.

[489] Stock, *op. cit.*, Vol. II, pp. 430-434.

[490] Stock, *op. cit.*, Vol. III, pp. 73ff.

[491] Stock, *op. cit.*, Vol. IV, pp. 77-80; J. H. Briggs, *In the East Africa War Zone* (London, Church Missionary Society, 1918, pp. 88), *passim*; G. A. Chambers, *Tanganyika's New Day* (London, Church Missionary Society, 1931, pp. vi, 68), *passim*.

[492] Wilson, *The History of the Universities' Mission to Central Africa*, pp. 24-133; Hine, *Days Gone By*, pp. 109-124, 179-194; Gertrude Ward, *Letters from East Africa*, (2d ed., 1901, pp. 240), *passim*; Dora S. Yarnton Mills, compiler, *Where We Live and What We Do* (London, Universities' Mission to Central Africa, 1909, pp. xii, 340), *passim*; Buchanan, *The Shiré Highlands*, pp. 233-257, Ward, *The Life of Charles Alan Smythies*, *passim*; William Carmichael Porter, *Missionary* (Westminster, Universities' Mission to Central Africa, no date, pp. 72), *passim*; Gertrude Ward, *Father Woodward of U.M.C.A.* (Westminster, Universities' Mission to Central Africa, 1927, pp. 64), *passim*;

The other non-Roman Catholic enterprise in the protectorate was that of the English Friends. It centred about a plantation on Pemba, an industrial mission.[493] One more British society was represented in German East Africa. The London Missionary Society, as we saw in our account of Northern Rhodesia, inaugurated, at heavy cost in life, an enterprise in the vicinity of Lake Tanganyika. Eventually its centres in German territory were either abandoned or were turned over to the Moravians.[494]

The Africa Inland Mission was begun in 1895 by Peter C. Scott, who had served for a time in the Congo and then revived Krapf's dream of a chain of stations from the east coast across the continent. A beginning was made in British East Africa, but a succession of misfortunes brought the undertaking to a low ebb. However, reinforcements came, the Church Missionary Society transferred to it part of its field in German territory, and a supporting committee in London was added to the one in America.[495]

The British societies, save for the partially British African Inland Mission, inaugurated their activities in the area before German rule was extended over it.

During the course of the German ownership, the only Protestant organizations which entered the country, with the exception noted above, were German. The assumption of authority by Germany was followed in church circles in the Fatherland by a sense of responsibility for the blacks thus brought within their sphere of influence. A Continental missionary conference held in Bremen in 1885 made plans to cover all the various possessions which were being acquired by Germany in Africa.[496]

In 1886 there was formed, with headquarters in Berlin, the Evangelical Missionary Society for German East Africa. To distinguish it from earlier missionary societies whose centre was in that city it was known as Berlin III. Since Bodelschwingh, a pastor, became its leading figure, eventually its home office was moved to his institutions in Bethel bei Bielefeld, and it came to be known by one or another of these names.[497] Its first undertaking was in 1887, at Dar-es-Salaam, the capital of the colony. There it planned to care both for

---

H. Maynard Smith, *Frank Bishop of Zanzibar. Life of Frank Weston, D.D. 1871-1924* (London, Society for Promoting Christian Knowledge, 1926, pp. xi, 326), *passim*; Egbert C. Hudson, *A Central African Parish* (Cambridge, W. Heffer & Sons, 1914, pp. 96), *passim*.

[493] Henry Stanley Newman, *Banani: The Transition from Slavery to Freedom in Zanzibar and Pemba* (London, Headley Brothers, 1898, pp. vii, 216), pp. 159ff.

[494] Lovett, *The History of the London Missionary Society*, Vol. I, pp. 649ff.; Edward Coode Hore, *Tanganyika. Eleven Years in Central Africa* (London, Edward Stanford, 1892, pp. xii, 306), *passim*; Johnson, *Night and Morning in Dark Africa*, pp. 22-44, 97-108, 209-222.

[495] Du Plessis, *The Evangelisation of Pagan Africa*, pp. 329, 330.

[496] Merensky, *Deutsche Arbeit am Njassa, Deutsch-Ostafrika*, p. 23.

[497] Richter, *Geschichte der evangelischen Mission in Afrika*, pp. 581, 582.

Germans and natives. It also extended its operations in the neighbourhood of that port. Before long it had found an additional field near the northern coast of the colony, first in Tanga and then in the uplands of Usambara.[498] In 1907 it went into Ruanda, thickly populated highlands west of Victoria Nyanza and immediately east of Lake Kivu.[499] In 1903 it turned over its work in Dar-es-Salaam and vicinity to that older Berlin Missionary Society which we have already met in South Africa.[500]

In the meantime, in 1891, this Berlin Missionary Society, through an initial expedition led by A. Merensky, a veteran of South Africa, entered the back part of the German domains, near the northern end of Lake Nyasa.[501] There it developed stations among several tribes, with literature, schools, and medical care. By 1914 it had in all German East Africa 22 stations, 57 missionaries, and 2,308 communicants.[502]

Also in the region north of Lake Nyasa laboured the Moravians. They were encouraged by a substantial legacy to undertake this new enterprise and from the outset planned collaboration and the division of the field north of Lake Nyasa with the Berlin society. The pioneer party went to Africa in the same year, 1891, as did that of the sister organization. Stations were opened, Christians were gathered around them into villages, translation was done, schools were developed, and leper settlements were founded. In 1898 the Moravians took over from the London Missionary Society an enterprise south of Victoria Nyanza, for it was isolated from other fields of the British organization and the latter was eager to transfer it to a like-minded German body.[503] By 1914

[498] Paul Döring, *Morgendämmerung in Deutsch-Ostafrika. Ein Rundgang durch die ostafrikanische Mission (Berlin III)* (Berlin, Martin Warneck, 1900, pp. vii, 191), *passim*; Siegfried Delius, *Gute Saat auf hartem Boden. Bilder aus Missionsarbeit in Tanga* (Bethel b. Bielefeld, Verlag der Evangelischen Missions-Gesellschaft für Deutsch-Ostafrika, 2d ed., 1911, pp. 92), *passim*.

[499] E. Johansen, *Ruanda. Kleine Anfänge-Grosse Aufgaben der Evangelischen Mission im Zwischenseengebiet Deutsch-Ostafrikas* (Verlagshandlung der Anstalt Bethel bei Bielefeld, 1912, pp. 210), *passim*.

[500] Ludwig Weichert, *Zehn Jahre Berliner Missionsarbeit in Daressalam* (Berlin, Buchhandlung der Berliner evang. Missionsgesellschaft, 1913, pp. 44), *passim*.

[501] Merensky, *op. cit.*, pp. 28ff. On a later stage of the Nyasa mission, see P. Gröschel, *Zehn Jahre christlichen Kulturarbeit in Deutsch-Ostafrika. Dargestellt in Briefen aus den Jahren 1898-1908* (Berlin, Buchhandlung der Berliner evang. Missionsgesellschaft, 1911, pp. 228), *passim*.

[502] K. Axenfeld, *Küste und Inland. Ein Ueberblick über die Entwicklung und die Aufgaben der Berliner-Mission in Deutsch-Ostafrika* (Berlin, Buchhandlung der Berliner evangel. Missionsgesellschaft, 1912, pp. 48), *passim*; K. Axenfeld, *Wegweiser durch die Berliner Mission in Deutsch-Ostafrika* (Berlin, Buchhandlung der Berliner evangel. Missionsgesellschaft, 1909, pp. 24), *passim*; Du Plessis, *The Evangelisation of Pagan Africa*, pp. 324, 325.

[503] J. Taylor Hamilton, *Twenty Years of Pioneer Missions in Nyasaland. A History of Moravian Missions in German East Africa* (Bethlehem, Pa., Bethlehem Printing Co., 1912, pp. 192), *passim*.

the Moravians had 15 stations, 28 missionaries, and 1,780 baptized Christians.[504] This wide-ranging fellowship had established itself in central Africa.

In 1893 the Leipzig Missionary Society (*Evangelisch-lutherische Missionsgesellschaft zu Leipzig*) assumed responsibility for what had been begun by the Church Missionary Society in the highlands near the foot of Kilimanjaro. The latter organization withdrew because of friction with the German colonial authorities. Building on this foundation the Leipzig representatives rapidly developed an extensive enterprise, with schools, a teacher training institution, medical care, and handicrafts. In 1911 it had 34 missionaries in 11 stations and counted 2,210 Christians and 8,119 children in school.[505] This was in spite of the violent death at the hands of the natives of two of the pioneers.[506]

By the year 1914 the German branch of the Seventh Day Adventists was at work east of Victoria Nyanza.[507] In 1911 the Breklum Mission and the Neukirchen Orphanage and Missionary Institution entered the region south of Ruanda along Lake Tanganyika and within a short time had opened a number of stations.[508]

The spread of Roman Catholic Christianity to East Africa was by way of Réunion. In 1859 Bishop Maupoint of that island also held the title of Apostolic Delegate for East Africa and because of that office sent his vicar with two seculars, a physician, and three Sisters of Mary to Zanzibar. There they were welcomed by the Moslem sultan and opened a hospital and school.[509] In 1863 the enterprise was entrusted to the Holy Ghost Fathers. Since Zanzibar was then a slave mart, the missionaries gave themselves to the care of the unfortunates and to the purchase of slave children for the purpose of rearing them as Christians. One of the two first Holy Ghost Fathers in Zanzibar, Stefan Bauer, lived to celebrate half a century in East Africa. It was he who extended the mission to the mainland and founded a station in Bagamojo, opposite Zanzibar. From there additional centres were opened as far north as the British border and Kilimanjaro. Schools were multiplied and a press issued Christian literature. By 1914 two vicariates apostolic had come into being which together counted 25 stations, 43 priests, 29 brothers, 50 sisters, and nearly 20,000 Christians.[510]

---

[504] Du Plessis, *op. cit.*, p. 323.

[505] H. Adolphi and Johannes Schanz, *Am Fusse der Bergriefen Ostafrikas. Geschichte der Leipziger Mission am Kilimandjaro und in den Nachbargebirgen* (Leipzig, Verlag der evang.-luth. Mission, 1912, pp. xii, 212), *passim*.

[506] C. v. Schwartz, *Karl Segebrock und Ewald Ovir. Zwei früh vollendete Missionare der Evangelisch-lutherischen Mission zu Leipzig* (Leipzig, 1897, pp. 97), *passim*.

[507] Richter, *Tanganyika and Its Future*, p. 25.

[508] Richter, *op. cit.*, p. 34.

[509] Schwager, *Die katholische Heidenmission der Gegenwart*, p. 166.

[510] Schwager, *op. cit.*, pp. 166-168; Schmidlin, *Die katholischen Missionen in den deutschen Schutzgebieten*, pp. 124-136.

In the southern part of German East Africa a vicariate apostolic bearing the name of Dar-es-Salaam was developed. It was the work of Benedictines. The pioneers, nine brothers and four sisters under a prefect apostolic, arrived in 1888. In time a cathedral was erected in Dar-es-Salaam and a number of stations were opened. In 1905 a rebellion brought death to the vicar apostolic and temporary ruin to several of the stations, but the reverse was followed by fresh expansion. True to the tradition which made them effective creators of civilization in the European Middle Ages, the Benedictines stressed agriculture, with plantations of rice, cacao, coffee, bananas, and cotton, and cattle raising. They also had schools, a leper asylum, hospitals, and Christian villages. In 1911 they counted 23 priests, 35 brothers, 49 sisters, 199 catechists, 174 schools with more than 12,000 pupils, and over 9,000 Christians.[511]

The entire eastern part of German East Africa was the field of the White Fathers. Together with contiguous territories in Uganda, the Belgian Congo, Northern Rhodesia, and Nyasaland it formed a solid block of territory served by these spiritual children of Lavigerie. In contrast with North Africa, where because of the dominance of Islam and the certain hostility which would be aroused by open attempts to win converts Lavigerie did not permit the direct teaching of the Christian faith, in Central Africa active religious instruction was encouraged.[512] Here as for Protestants it was the journeys of Livingstone which aroused interest and opened the way. It was in 1878 that the first contingent left Marseilles. Early in the following year the White Fathers sighted Lake Tanganyika.[513] Difficulty was encountered, largely at the hands of the Arabs and because of the White Fathers' opposition to the slave trade by which the Arabs thrived. However, before many years several stations were established. In the course of time catechists were trained, schools were multiplied, care of the sick and of children was undertaken, and on the mission farms various crops were raised. In 1913 four vicariates apostolic existed in the German domains and 33,685 Christians were counted.[514] It was at first deemed unsafe for women to go to Central Africa. As the scene became more peaceful,

[511] Schmidlin, op. cit., pp. 113-124.
[512] Bouniol, The White Fathers and Their Missions, pp. 93-99.
[513] Florentin Loriot, Explorations et Missions dans l'Afrique Equatoriale (Paris, Gaume et Cie, 1890, pp. 375), pp. 272ff.
[514] Bouniol, op. cit., pp. 215-254; Schmidlin, op. cit., pp. 136ff.; l'Assaut des Pays Nègres. Journal des Missionnaires d'Alger dans l'Afrique Équatoriale (Paris, l'Oeuvre des Écoles d'Orient, 1884, pp. 342), passim; A. Le Roy, Au Kilima-Ndjaro. Histoire de la Fondation d'une Mission Catholique en Afrique Orientale (Paris, l'Oeuvre d'Auteuil, 1914, pp. 379), passim; Près des Grands Lacs, par les Missionnaires de S. Ém. le Cardinal Lavigerie (Lyon, Bureau des Missions Catholiques, 1886, pp. 195), passim; G. Leblond, Le Père Auguste Achte des Missionnaires d'Afrique (Pères Blancs), Missionnaire au Nyanza Septentrional (Algiers, Maison Carrée, 1912, pp. xiv, 444), passim.

in 1894 a company of White Sisters set out and was soon followed by others.[515] Both men and women joined in making the mission a success. Steps were taken to train a native priesthood, but it was not until after 1914 that the first black was ordained to that office.[516]

The year 1914 found Christianity spreading in German East Africa at an accelerated pace. At the middle of the nineteenth century it had scarcely been introduced. Most of the organizations and the foreign staff engaged in its propagation entered in the last third of a century before 1914. Here, as in so much of the rest of the continent south of the Sahara, the penetration of the interior by European culture and by the Christian faith was mostly after three-quarters of the nineteenth century had passed and was only well begun when the World War of 1914-1918 broke out. In German East Africa, in contrast with most of the British possessions thus far surveyed, Roman Catholic Christianity was making greater progress than were the Protestant forms of the faith.

Immediately to the north and east of German East Africa was what in 1914 was known as British East Africa, the later Kenya. In area it was about two-thirds and in population less than half the size of its southern neighbour. The fact that most of it was an elevated plateau seemed to make it, in spite of the fact that it lay across the equator, a possible region for extensive settlement by Europeans. However, while immigration had only well begun in 1914, it never attained the dimensions which some of the optimistic had anticipated. The native population was heterogeneous. It included Swahili, Bantus, Hamitic folk, and primitive pygmies. Arabs had been present from early times. Some Indians had come in. Europeans were largely owners of farms and plantations. It was not until the last quarter of the nineteenth century that British influence became strong. In the 1880's the British East Africa Company did much to extend British control. However, a variety of difficulties led to the transfer of the possession to the crown (1895) and it became a British protectorate.[517]

Except for possible contacts in the pre-nineteenth century days when the

---

[515] *Mère Marie Claver, Assistante Générale des Sœurs Missionnaires de N.-D. d'Afrique . . . Notes et Souvenirs recueillis par son frère le Colonel de l'Éprevier* (Paris, Gabriel Beauchesne, 2d ed., 1927, pp. viii, 376), pp. 291ff. On the work of the sisters see Pia Kühn and Ignatia Engel, *Auf Gottes Saatfeld. Erlebnisse und Beobachtungen aus der Ruandamission* (Trier, Paulinus-Druckerei, 1928, pp. 143), *passim.*

[516] For the biography of one of the earliest of these clergymen who entered the seminary in 1904 and was ordained priest in 1917, see J. Paas, *Padri Donatus Leberaho. Werden und Werken eines Negerpriesters* (Trier, Paulinus-Druckerei, 1927, pp. 179), *passim.*

[517] Norman Leys, *Kenya* (London, The Hogarth Press, 1925, pp. 409), *passim; The Encyclopædia Britannica,* 11th ed., Vol. IV, pp. 601-606.

Portuguese, at the height of their power, had footholds on the coast and still earlier but more shadowy times when Nestorians and Jacobites may have come as merchants, the first efforts to introduce Christianity seem to have been by Krapf and Rebmann, in the 1840's. These pioneers established themselves at Mombasa, and, very shortly, in a station a few miles inland from that port.[518] Their journeys into the interior did much to open the region to Europeans. Ill-health compelled Krapf's return to Europe in 1853. He made two other trips to Africa, in 1861 and 1867, but his days of long sojourn there were over and it was in Europe that he died, in 1881.[519] Rebmann remained in East Africa, reduced three languages to writing, and prepared a dictionary in each. Not until 1874, blind and infirm, did he retire to Europe.[520]

Meanwhile African slaves who had been rescued by British ships, taken to India, and there won by missionaries to the Christian faith, were sent to Mombasa to become the nucleus of a Christian community.[521] Following the abolition, through British pressure, of slavery in Zanzibar (1873), at the suggestion of Sir Bartle Frere, who had been the British agent in bringing about that step, the Church Missionary Society founded, near Mombasa, Frere Town, a colony for freed slaves.[522] With the extension of British power, in the 1880's, the Church Missionary Society sent reinforcements who carried the Christian message to additional villages in the vicinity of the older stations and still farther inland.[523]

In 1862, largely through the instrumentality of Krapf, the United Methodist Free Churches began a mission near Mombasa. Later they extended their labours to the Tana River, farther north.[524]

Through Krapf, moreover, a German mission was induced to enter the region, but in 1914 it turned over its enterprises, never large, to the Africa Inland Mission.[525]

In 1891 what was called the East African Scottish Industrial Mission was inaugurated. This was done on the initiative of directors, themselves Scotch,

---

[518] Krapf, *Travels,* pp. 126ff.; Claus, *Dr. Ludwig Krapf,* pp. 64ff.

[519] Claus, *op. cit.,* pp. 190-243.

[520] Philp, *A New Day in Kenya,* p. 13; Stock, *The History of the Church Missionary Society,* Vol. III, pp. 77, 84.

[521] Stock, *op. cit.,* Vol. III, pp. 431, 432.

[522] Stock, *op. cit.,* Vol. IV, pp. 83-92.

[523] Stock, *op. cit.,* Vol. IV, pp. 428-433, 731, 732; Vol. V, pp. 75-77; *East Africa* (London, Church Missionary Society, 1929, pp. 66), pp. 27-36; E. May Crawford, *By the Equator's Snow Peak. A Record of Medical Missionary Work and Travel in East Africa* (London, Church Missionary Society, 1913, pp. 176), *passim.*

[524] Richter, *Geschichte der evangelischen Mission in Afrika,* p. 612; Philp, *op. cit.,* p. 64; Joseph Kirsop, *Life of Robert Moss Ormerod, Missionary to East Africa* (London, Andrew Crombie, 1901, pp. 144), *passim.*

[525] Richter, *op. cit.,* pp. 612, 613.

of the British East Africa Company, for they felt a philanthropic responsibility for the region. They obtained the experienced leadership of James Stewart, distinguished for his development of Lovedale and as a pioneer in Nyasaland. Stewart could not remain permanently, but he selected a site about 200 miles inland. The first superintendent was David Charters, who had served his missionary apprenticeship with the English Baptists on the Congo.[526] After some years of heart-breaking effort, the enterprise was moved farther into the interior, among the Kikuyu, a Bantu folk. In the first decade of the twentieth century the undertaking was transferred to the Church of Scotland. Leadership came from the seasoned staff of Blantyre, and some of the features of the Nyasaland mission were reproduced.[527]

In 1902 American Friends sent an initial contingent which bought a tract of land far inland, east of Victoria Nyanza, and there began agricultural, industrial, and educational work. The agricultural phase of the enterprise was especially successful.[528]

The Africa Inland Mission, which we met in German East Africa, had stations in British East Africa.[529] Into the Kikuyu country came, in 1902, the Gospel Missionary Society, an offshoot of the Africa Inland Mission.[530] Early in the twentieth century Seventh Day Adventists entered, pressing towards the interior.[531] On the Tana River was a small enterprise, begun in 1887, of the Neukirchen Mission, of German Congregationalists.[532] We hear, too, of an independent mission by Mr. and Mrs. Stuart Watt, who first came to Africa under the Church Missionary Society, who later were pioneers in the Kikuyu uplands, and who, when constrained by ill-health to leave, turned over their station to the Africa Inland Mission.[533]

To bring these various Protestant agencies together for co-operation and for the prevention of overlapping of territories, conferences were held in 1908, 1909, and 1913. The 1909 gathering endorsed a project for the creation of a

[526] Victoria T. Coats, *David Charters, Engineer, Doctor and Missionary 1864-1894* (London, A. & C. Black, 1925, pp. viii, 184), *passim.*

[527] *Kikuyu: 1898-1923. Semi-Jubilee Book of the Church of Scotland Mission, Kenya Colony* (Edinburgh, William Blackwood and Sons, 1923, pp. 96), *passim;* Horace R. A. Philp, *God and the African in Kenya* (London, Marshall, Morgan & Scott, no date, pp. 189), *passim.*

[528] Philp, *A New Day in Kenya,* pp. 20, 21.

[529] Richter, *op. cit.,* pp. 613, 614; Willis R. Hotchkiss, *Then and Now in Kenya Colony. Forty Adventurous Years in East Africa* (New York, Fleming H. Revell Co., 1937, pp. 160), *passim.*

[530] Philp, *op. cit.,* p. 61.

[531] Philp, *op. cit.,* p. 52; Richter, *op. cit.,* p. 614.

[532] Philp, *op. cit.,* p. 64; Richter, *op. cit.,* p. 615.

[533] Mrs. Stuart Watt, *In the Heart of Savagedom. Reminiscences of Life and Adventure during a Quarter of a Century of Pioneering Missionary Labours in the Wilds of East Equatorial Africa* (London, Pickering & Inglis, 3d ed., no date, pp. 422), *passim.*

united African church, but this ambitious undertaking did not win the consent of the supporting constituencies. In 1913 a programme for federation was discussed but not adopted.[534]

Provision was made by Protestants for the religious needs of the white settlers, with churches, schools, and a Young Men's Christian Association.[535]

Roman Catholics were also active in British East Africa, although, except for the pre-nineteenth century Portuguese, somewhat more tardily than the Protestants. Eventually, however, they became about as strong as the latter, both in size of staff and in numbers of converts.[536] The Holy Ghost Fathers, to whom Zanzibar had been assigned by the Holy See in 1863, developed, as we saw a few paragraphs above, an extensive enterprise on the neighbouring mainland, mostly in what became German territory. In 1891 they acquired a foothold at Mombasa. In the closing years of the century they also established a head station at Nairobi, the capital of the protectorate, where, on the railway and in the uplands, a European town was arising.[537] In the highlands of Kenya, where Protestant missionaries had preceded them in considerable numbers, representatives of the institution newly founded at Turin, the Fathers *della Consolata*, arrived in 1902. In 1906 the region was created a prefecture apostolic and, a few years later, a vicariate apostolic.[538]

The largest of the Roman Catholic enterprises in British East Africa was that of an English organization, St. Joseph's Society of Mill Hill.[539] Its field was in the far western part of the protectorate, where the vicariate apostolic of the Upper Nile was carved out for it. The first contingent arrived in 1895, led by a bishop. Already there were some Roman Catholics in the region, largely migrants from the prosperous missions of the White Fathers in Uganda. Here, as in Uganda, a mass movement towards Christianity quickly set in. Although a catechumenate of from three to four years was required, with careful religious instruction, in 1905, at the end of the first decade of the mission, 18,747 baptized Christians were counted, and 13,707 catechumens.[540]

It is natural now to move on to Uganda, immediately to the west of British East Africa and north of German East Africa. Here in the last third of a century before 1914 an amazing growth of the Christian Church was witnessed.

[534] Philp, *op. cit.*, pp. 34-37.
[535] Philp, *op. cit.*, pp. 25, 26.
[536] Philp, *op. cit.*, pp. 155, 169.
[537] Schwager, *Die katholische Heidenmission der Gegenwart*, p. 170.
[538] Schwager, *op. cit.*, p. 171.
[539] Vol. IV, p. 55.
[540] Schwager, *op. cit.*, pp. 192, 193.

This was through Anglican and Roman Catholic missions which entered almost simultaneously.

Uganda, in 1914 a British protectorate, had as its nucleus the kingdom of Buganda, from which the name commonly used by Europeans was derived. The Baganda were the ruling people.[541] They were Bantu, but with an intermixture of Hamitic blood. Their reigning dynasty probably had been in power from early in the fifteenth century. Although in the third quarter of the nineteenth century still animists, the Baganda had made advances towards civilization. In spite of the fact that the equator crossed it, their territory, because of its altitude, possessed a climate which was not adverse to culture. It was among the Baganda that the chief gains of Christianity were registered. One is reminded by this of Madagascar, where the dominant Hòva were the people among whom Christianity first made headway. In their rapid acceptance of Christianity, the Baganda, like the Hòva, appear to have been moved by the desire to learn from what appealed to them as the powerful civilization of the white man and so to acquire the religion which seemed to them an integral part of that culture. In addition to the Baganda, British Uganda included numbers of other peoples—pygmies, Bantus of various tribes, Nile Negroes, and some tribes of Hamitic stock.

The first contact of the Baganda with Christianity came in consequence of the dreams and labours of Livingstone. Henry M. Stanley, whose successful search for the great explorer we noted a few pages back, although he hated Africa and the discomforts and perils of travel in what was to him the Dark Continent, felt called by the death which so stirred the Anglo-Saxon world to carry on the uncompleted work of him who had made so profound an impression upon him.[542] In 1874, therefore, he once more entered Africa, on a notable expedition which brought him to Uganda. There he saw much of Mtesa, the king of the Baganda, and found him eager to learn the secret of the white man's civilization. To Mtesa, half pagan and half Moslem, Stanley taught some of the principles of the Christian faith. In this he was aided by Colonel Linant de Bellefonds, a French Protestant who had been sent south from the Sudan by General Charles G. Gordon.[543] Stanley also translated part of the Bible for Mtesa.[544] Mtesa believed the white man to be better than the Arab, partly because of his mechanical inventions and partly because, unlike the Arab, he did not enslave men.[545] He professed himself to be a Christian, sought

[541] On the Baganda see John Roscoe, *Twenty-Five Years in East Africa* (Cambridge University Press, 1921, pp. xvi, 288), pp. 75-100, 134-194.

[542] Hird, *H. M. Stanley, passim;* Stanley, *Through the Dark Continent*, Vol. I, pp. 1-3.

[543] Stanley, *op. cit.*, Vol. I, pp. 192-210; Hird, *op. cit.*, pp. 140-143.

[544] Stanley, *op. cit.*, Vol. I, pp. 321-324.

[545] Stanley, *op. cit.*, Vol. I, pp. 321, 324.

to prove his faith by sparing, at Stanley's instance, an enemy whom he had in his power, and erected a church building.[546] Stanley wrote to Great Britain and the United States of these events and called for Christian missionaries to follow up what he had thus auspiciously begun.[547]

In England the response to the appeal was immediate. Money and offers of personal service poured into the Church Missionary Society.[548] In the spring of 1876, less than six months after the publication of Stanley's letter, a large party sailed for Zanzibar. It was not until the summer of 1877 that those who survived the difficult journey into the interior reached Mtesa. The king received them cordially. He still professed himself a Christian.[549] Reinforcements came, some of them by way of the Nile.[550]

The enterprise which opened so hopefully suffered many unhappy vicissitudes.[551] To be sure, some converts were soon won and beginnings were made in creating a Christian literature. However, the arrival, in 1879, of White Fathers, of which we are to say more in a moment, brought division and rivalry in the Christian forces. Arab traders offered opposition. Mtesa became timorous, fearing that the missionaries were the forerunners of European aggression. Disease took a heavy toll.[552] Although Mtesa more than once asked for baptism, he was troubled by the conflicts between the various religions which sought him and never made the decisive step. On his death, in 1884, he was succeeded by his son, Mwanga, a lad of eighteen, who had studied Christianity with both Protestants and Roman Catholics. Moved by the Arabs to panic at the prospect of having his territories annexed by Europeans, Mwanga instituted a persecution in which numbers of native Christians were killed.[553] In 1885 the first Anglican Bishop of Eastern Equatorial Africa, Hannington, was murdered on his way inland from Mombasa, presumably on the order of Mwanga. Hannington, who had joined the mission in his thirties and whom ill-health had forced to return to England after a first attempt in Africa, had

---

[546] Stanley, op. cit., Vol. I, pp. 325, 335-337, 417.

[547] Stanley, op. cit., Vol. I, pp. 209, 210.

[548] Stock, The History of the Church Missionary Society, Vol. III, pp. 95-98. One of the appeals aroused by Stanley was Edward Hutchinson, The Victoria Nyanza, a Field for Missionary Enterprise (London, John Murray, 1876, pp. 137), passim.

[549] Stock, op cit., Vol. III, pp. 98-102.

[550] Stock, op. cit., Vol. III, p. 105.

[551] For one sketch of the period of hardship see Sarah Geraldina Stock, The Story of Uganda and the Victoria Nyanza Mission (London, The Religious Tract Society, 1892, pp. 223), passim. For another of this period see Julius Richter, Uganda. Ein Blatt aus der Geschichte der evangelischen Mission und der Kolonialpolitik in Centralafrika (Gütessloh, C. Bertelsmann, 1893, pp. 268), passim.

[552] Stock, op. cit., Vol. III, pp. 105, 106.

[553] Stock, op. cit., Vol. III, pp. 410-412.

been consecrated bishop, and had sought to reach Uganda by a new route.[554] For a time in 1886 and 1887 one of the original party, Alexander M. Mackay, was the only European left in the Anglican mission in Uganda. Late in 1888 the Moslem party succeeded in gaining control and in expelling both Protestant and Roman Catholic missionaries. The leading Christian chiefs were either put to death or driven from the country. In 1890 Mackay succumbed to fever. Mackay, a successful engineer, had been sent to help inaugurate the Uganda enterprise. His faithfulness had contributed much to the persistence of the mission. Now he was gone.[555] In 1886 a new Anglican bishop, H. P. Parker, was consecrated, but within seventeen months he, too, was dead.[556]

In the struggle for Africa which was then in progress Uganda was caught in the maelstrom of titanic forces and was thrown into internal confusion. French, English, Germans, and Arabs contended for the mastery. For a time the pagan party induced Mwanga to act against both Moslems and Christians. The Moslem Arab party expelled Mwanga. Protestant and Roman Catholic native Christians united in putting him back on the throne (1889).[557] Protestant missionaries sought to further English influence, while the Roman Catholic missionaries saw their hope in French or German control.[558] Civil war broke out between the Protestant, pro-British faction and the Roman Catholic, pro-French party. Mwanga favoured now one and now the other.[559] The Anglo-German treaty of 1890 assigned Uganda to the British, but in 1891 the latter seemed on the point of withdrawal. Public opinion in Great Britain, in part the creation of the missionary forces, and the raising of a special fund by popular subscription, also partly at missionary initiative, led to the retention of British claims and in 1894 Uganda was declared a British protectorate.[560] Even that act did not at once end internal disorder. In a fresh outbreak in 1897 George Pilkington, the mission's chief linguist, was killed.[561] Before the close of the century, however, Mwanga was deported. In 1902 a railway was com-

[554] E. C. Dawson, *James Hannington . . . A History of his Life and Work, 1847-1885* (New York, Anson D. F. Randolph & Co., pp. xi, 472), *passim; The Last Journals of Bishop Hannington, being Narratives of a Journey through Palestine in 1884 and a Journey through Masai-Land and U-Soga in 1885.* edited by E. C. Dawson (London, Seeley & Co., 1888, pp. xii, 239), *passim.*

[555] *A. M. Mackay, Pioneer Missionary of the Church Missionary Society to Uganda. By his Sister* (London, Hodder and Stoughton, 1890, pp. viii, 488), *passim.*

[556] Tucker, *Eighteen Years in Uganda and East Africa,* Vol. I, pp. 23-25.

[557] Tucker, *op. cit.,* Vol. I, pp. 26-28.

[558] Tucker, *op. cit.,* Vol. I, pp. 28, 29.

[559] Tucker, *op. cit.,* Vol. I, pp. 171-180, 243-252.

[560] Stock, *op. cit.,* Vol. III, pp. 441-448.

[561] Harford-Battersby, *Pilkington of Uganda,* pp. 335, 336. For an account of a fellow missionary of Pilkington whose term of service spanned the period of Pilkington's death, see *"In Full and Glad Surrender." The Story of the Life and Work of Martin J. Hall . . . by his Sister* (London, Hodder and Stoughton, 1905, pp. xvi, 386), pp. 179ff.

pleted from the coast to Victoria Nyanza. Order was established under effective British rule.

In spite of these many hardships, Protestantism, with the representatives of the Church Missionary Society as its directing agents, made rapid gains. The Anglicans were fortunate in the choice of their third bishop, Alfred R. Tucker. Tucker was consecrated in 1890 and during the more than two decades of his episcopate, a tenure terminated in 1911 by ill-health, he gave notable leadership. Born in 1849, the son of artist parents, Tucker had himself become a painter of some distinction when, at the age of twenty-nine, he decided to enter Oxford to prepare for holy orders. He became deeply interested in Uganda and after eight years of parish work in England was chosen for the vacant bishopric. Of rugged physique, unflinching courage, bold initiative, sound judgment, organizing ability, and single-hearted devotion, Tucker made an ideal head of the enterprise.[562] With the establishment of British rule and the internal peace which ensued, a mass movement to Christianity set in. When Tucker arrived in Uganda his flock of baptized Christians numbered only about 200. In 1908 it was 62,867.[563] Reinforcements came to the missionary staff. The Bible was translated into the vernacular, largely by Pilkington.[564] An educational system was developed which included the industrial training inaugurated by Mackay.[565] There were schools for girls as well as boys. A beginning was made in secondary education which, it was hoped, would grow into a university course.[566] Medical work became part of the programme of the mission.[567] A native staff was trained, composed of teachers, evangelists, and clergy.[568] Hundreds of places of worship, including a huge cathedral, were built.[569] The Baganda churches were largely self-supporting, erecting their own structures and paying the stipends of the native staff. A diocesan organization, heading up in a synod, was gradually developed, with the native Christians having a large share in it.[570] The Baganda, active and intelligent, proved eager missionaries. More than once their enterprise led to the introduction of the faith to neighbouring tribes. Europeans joined in the extension

---

[562] Arthur P. Shepherd, *Tucker of Uganda, Artist and Apostle, 1849-1914* (London, Student Christian Movement, 1929, pp. 206), *passim*.

[563] Tucker, *op. cit.*, Vol. II, p. 359.

[564] Harford-Battersby, *op. cit.*, pp. 264-271.

[565] Tucker, *op. cit.*, Vol. II, pp. 146-158.

[566] Tucker, *op. cit.*, Vol. II, pp. 327-331; C. W. Hattersley, *The Baganda at Home* (London, The Religious Tract Society, 1908, pp. xvi, 227. By the secretary of the C.M.S. Board of Education in Uganda), pp. 154-199.

[567] Tucker, *op. cit.*, Vol. II, p. 157.

[568] Tucker, *op. cit.*, Vol. II, p. 361.

[569] Tucker, *op. cit.*, Vol. II, p. 362.

[570] Weatherhead, *Uganda*, pp. 57, 58.

of the Christian message to other peoples. Group conversions to Christianity were witnessed.[571] In the region where Hannington had been killed one of them took place. Hannington's son baptized a son and daughter of his father's murderer.[572] Within less than a generation Protestant Christianity, through the agency of the Church Missionary Society, had made amazing headway. In 1914 the number of baptized Christians was 98,477.[573]

In Uganda, as in so many others of the lands of primitive peoples which we have surveyed in this volume, an indigenous movement arose which combined some features of Christianity with others from the native environment. Not far from the year 1914 a sect came into being, led by a chief, which professed to be based upon the Bible. It eschewed medicine and doctors, depended upon faith for healing, admitted polygamists to baptism on the ground that monogamy was not taught in the Scriptures, and did not insist upon a prolonged catechumenate before administering the rite. For a time it attracted throngs, but within a few months appeared to be waning.[574]

Roman Catholics were not far behind Protestants in entering Uganda. As one of his first official acts, Pope Leo XIII, in February, 1878, authorized the mission of the White Fathers to Central Africa.[575] In spite of a personal appeal to Lavigerie by a secretary of the Church Missionary Society not to send to Uganda what would, in the nature of the case, prove a competing Christian enterprise,[576] the pioneer party of White Fathers went on its way. Early in 1879, about a year and a half after the coming of the first agents of the Church Missionary Society, the contingent of White Fathers assigned to Uganda reached the court of Mtesa.[577]

The Roman Catholic undertaking suffered from many of the adversities that troubled the first decade and a half or more of the Protestant mission. Disease and hardship took their toll.[578] Civil strife, partly aroused and greatly

[571] Weatherhead, *op. cit.*, pp. 45-50; Tucker, *op. cit.*, Vol. II, pp. 159-197, 209-251; A. R. Tucker, *Toro. Visits to Ruwenzori "Mountains of the Moon"* (London, Church Missionary Society, 1899, pp. 51), *passim;* R. D. Pierpoint, *In Uganda for Christ: The Life Story of the Rev. John Samuel Callis, B.A., of the Church Missionary Society* (London, Hodder and Stoughton, 1898, pp. viii, 196), pp. 131ff.; Albert B. Lloyd, *Uganda to Khartoum* (New York, E. P. Dutton & Co., 1906, pp. xii, 312), pp. 30-80, 111-116; Martin J. Hall, *Through My Spectacles in Uganda* (London, Church Missionary Society, 1898, pp. 104), pp. 71-75, 81, 82.
[572] Richter, *Geschichte der evangelischen Mission in Afrika*, p. 641.
[573] *Proceedings of the Church Missionary Society . . . 1914-15*, p. xvi. On the situation in Uganda in 1913 see J. J. Willis, Bishop of Uganda, *The Church in Uganda* (London, Longmans, Green and Co., 1914, pp. 24), *passim.*
[574] *Proceedings of the Church Missionary Society . . . 1914-15*, pp. 65, 66.
[575] Hallfell, *Uganda*, p. 22; Philippe, *Au Cœur de l'Afrique. Ouganda*, p. 32.
[576] Stock, *The History of the Church Missionary Society*, Vol. III, p. 105.
[577] Hallfell, *op. cit.*, p. 29.
[578] Hallfell, *op. cit.*, pp. 26-28; Philippe, *op. cit.*, p. 35.

accentuated by religious differences between pagans, Moslems, Protestants, and Roman Catholics, made the initial years difficult. Some of the early converts paid for their faith with their lives.[579] Yet with fine heroism the missionaries persisted. One of the original party, Simeon Lourdel, had access to both Mtesa and Mwanga, treated them medically, shared the exile which at one stage was forced on the foreign staff, and died, in 1890, of fever, before the British protectorate brought security.[580]

Yet the Roman Catholic mission, like the Protestant, prospered. In Livinhac, leader of the initial party and the first bishop, it had an able head. In 1890 Livinhac became the superior general of the entire society of the White Fathers, but he did not forget Uganda. When, in 1894, the international struggle for Uganda was terminated by the formal act which made the land a British protectorate, Livinhac was emphatic in denying that either he or his colleagues had ever acted as representatives of France or that they had spoken of their faith as the religion of France.[581] Further to remove the suspicion of a French taint from the Roman Catholic mission, in 1894 the north-eastern part of Uganda was made a separate vicariate apostolic and was entrusted to an English society, the Mill Hill Fathers.[582] To aid them, in 1902 there came Franciscan nuns from Mill Hill.[583] For the Roman Catholics as well as for the Protestants the mass movement towards Christianity brought thousands into the Church. Not far from the year 1912 the White Fathers counted 113,811 Christians in their vicariate and the Mill Hill Fathers 22,393 in theirs.[584] Favour shown by Mwanga at one stage of his erratic career gave an early impetus to the growth,[585] but most of the increase occurred after 1895.[586] The White Fathers did not admit the converts to baptism indiscriminately. True to the injunctions of their founder, they required a four years' catechumenate.[587] Much emphasis was placed upon training native assistants. Scores of catechists were prepared; sisters were recruited from among the blacks, some for a congrega-

---

[579] Henri Streicher, *Les Bienheureux Martyrs de l'Ouganda* (Algiers, Maison-Carrée, 1925, pp. vii, 37), *passim*. Several of the martyrs were beatified in 1920.

[580] Nicq, *Le Père Siméon Lourdel de la Société des Pères Blancs et les premières années de la Mission de l'Ouganda* (Algiers, Maison-Carrée, 1922, pp. viii, 546), *passim;* F. A. Forbes, *Planting the Faith in Darkest Africa. The Life Story of Father Simeon Lourdel* (London, Sands & Co., 1926, pp. x, 126), *passim*.

[581] Bouniol, *The White Fathers and Their Missions*, pp. 199, 200.

[582] Bouniol, *op. cit.*, p. 200.

[583] F. M. Dreves, *The African Chronicles of Brother Giles* (London, Sands & Co., 1929, pp. 293), *passim*.

[584] Streit, *Atlas Hierarchicus*, p. 102. Philippe, *op. cit.*, p. 132, gives the number of Christians for 1914, presumably in the White Fathers' vicariate, as 102,456.

[585] Schwager, *Die katholische Heidenmission der Gegenwart*, p. 187.

[586] Philippe, *op. cit.*, p. 133.

[587] Schwager, *op. cit.*, p. 87.

tion whose first novitiate was under the White Sisters, and some for a congregation of cloistered nuns; and beginnings were made of the long preparation for the priesthood.[588] Children reared as Christians were admitted to their first communion between the ages of seven and ten.[589] From the outset the mission had been placed under the special protection of the Virgin Mary, and the Christians, accordingly, showed marked devotion to her.[590] Much stress was laid on the creation of families which would conform to Christian standards.[591] Increasing attention was paid to education, although in 1914 less than one-third as many pupils were enrolled in Roman Catholic schools as in those of the Protestants.[592] Attempts, too, were made to render the mission self-supporting, partly through plantations.[593] In numerical terms in 1914 the Uganda mission of the White Fathers was the strongest of any of the vicariates apostolic in Africa south of the Sahara.

The valley of the largest of the rivers of Africa, the Congo, was opened to Europeans chiefly as a result of the inspiration given by Livingstone. As early as the 1480's the Portuguese had discovered the mouth of the river. In the first six decades of the nineteenth century various explorers had pushed part way up the stream. But it was Livingstone who, under the impression that he was at the headwaters of the Nile, traced portions of the courses of some of the rivers of the upper part of the Congo system. And it was Henry M. Stanley who, pursuing his purpose to carry further the mission of Livingstone, did most to reveal to the white men the Congo basin.

Politically by the year 1914 the valley of the Congo had been divided among European powers into three unequal holdings. Small sections of the lower portions of the valley were in the possession of Portugal. These we have already noted in our survey of the Angola. On the north side a considerable area was in the hands of the French. The most substantial slice was Belgian.

In the Belgian Congo we come to the largest population of any of the political divisions of Africa with the possible exception of Nigeria and Egypt. The majority of the peoples were of Bantu stock, divided into many tribes. There were traces of some other races, among them pygmies.

[588] Philippe, *op. cit.*, pp. 151-161.
[589] Bouniol, *op. cit.*, p. 204.
[590] Hallfell, *op. cit.*, pp. 200-202.
[591] Hallfell, *op. cit.*, pp. 202-209.
[592] Protestants had 73,291 pupils (*Proceedings of the Church Missionary Society . . . 1914-15*, p. xxv), as compared with 21,745 in Roman Catholic schools (Streit, *op. cit.*, p. 102).
[593] Hallfell, *op. cit.*, pp. 136-138, 213ff.

The political evolution which led to the creation of the Belgian Congo was chiefly due to Leopold II, the King of the Belgians. In 1876 Leopold began actively to interest himself in the Congo. By a series of agreements with various European powers, including the actions of an international conference in Berlin in 1884, recognition was given to a political entity known as the Congo Free State which was under the personal rule of the King. The avowed purpose of the arrangement was the development of the region for the benefit of the natives. By international agreement complete freedom was given for all religious, charitable, and scientific enterprises irrespective of nationality or form of worship. The area thus became especially inviting to Protestant and Roman Catholic missions. In the course of time abuses developed in connexion with the economic exploitation of the land under Leopold, with marked cruelty to the natives. Partly in consequence of the criticism aroused in various countries and partly for a combination of other reasons, in 1908 Belgium assumed sovereignty and the Congo Free State became the Belgian Congo.[594]

Religiously, at the outset of the nineteenth century the valley of the Congo was overwhelmingly animist. In the course of the century, Islam made advances, notably in the eastern portions, through Arabs from Zanzibar.[595] European exploration and the establishment of European rule paved the way for Christianity. The growing missionary zeal which characterized both Roman Catholics and Protestants in the closing decades of the nineteenth century saw in the vast area thus opened an opportunity and a challenge. By 1914 numbers of organizations had inaugurated enterprises for the winning of the peoples of the Congo to the Christian faith.

Since Belgian influence was dominant, and since Belgium was overwhelmingly Roman Catholic, that form of the faith was strongly represented. In the 1870's and the 1880's, before the Congo Free State came into being, the Holy Ghost Fathers, to whom portions of the Portuguese domains on the west coast had been allotted in the 1860's, opened stations at several points in the lower part of the valley.[596] In the fore part of the twentieth century they were also given a field in the southern portion of Congo Belge.[597] The large-visioned Lavigerie saw in the Congo an opening for his White Fathers. The assignment (1878) to the White Fathers by the Pope of territory in Central Africa included part of the basin of the Congo. Leopold II was not happy over this programme, for it had French leadership and he feared that it might entail

[594] The Encyclopædia Britannica, 11th ed., Vol. IV, pp. 917-922; Stonelake, Congo Past and Present, pp. 18-22.
[595] Belgian Congo, pp. 45-49.
[596] Schwager, Die katholische Mission der Gegenwart, p. 119; Belgian Congo, p. 41.
[597] Streit, Atlas Hierarchicus, p. 101.

political complications. To resolve the friction, in 1886 Rome created the Vicariate Apostolic of the Upper Congo, in the Free State on the west side of Lake Tanganyika. It was entrusted to the White Fathers. To satisfy Leopold, Lavigerie constituted a Belgian branch of his society and gave to it the care of the vicariate.[598]

To obtain Belgian missionaries, Leopold had already (1876) appealed to the recently founded[599] Congregation of the Immaculate Heart of Mary, whose headquarters were at Scheutveld. For the time being the Scheutveld Fathers had their energies absorbed in Mongolia, their first field. However, in 1888 they felt strong enough to assume responsibility for the Vicariate Apostolic of the Belgian Congo which was created in that year.[600] In 1901 a section in the southern part of the Congo Free State was made a separate mission of the Scheutvelders. It was given the name of a major tributary of the Congo, the Kassai. Within a few years it was constituted a vicariate apostolic.[601] Although in the course of the next few years parts of their field were transferred to other organizations, in 1912 the Scheutveld Fathers had a larger foreign staff than all the other Roman Catholic missions in Congo Belge combined.[602] They employed a method which they were using in Mongolia and developed Christian colonies. To these they brought children and freed salves. Moreover, they won many converts in the centres of white civilization, such as Leopoldville. There the blacks in the service of the state as soldiers and labourers, removed from their accustomed surroundings and wishing to conform to the ways of the dominant Europeans, were susceptible to Christian instruction.[603]

Leopold early asked the Belgian Jesuits for help, but their resources were strained by their mission in populous Bengal and not for some years could they heed the royal call. Early in the 1890's, however, their first contingent came. For the Jesuits the prefecture apostolic of Kwango was created in the region immediately east of Leopoldville. Side by side with the Jesuits were the Sisters of Our Lady, charged with the education of girls. In the course of the years a number of centres were opened.[604]

[598] Lechartrain in *Revue d'Histoire des Missions,* Vol. VIII, p. 186.

[599] Vol. IV, p. 54.

[600] Lechartrain in *Revue d'Histoire des Missions,* Vol. VIII, pp. 185-187.

[601] Schwager, *op. cit.,* p. 123.

[602] Streit, *Atlas Hierarchicus,* p. 101.

[603] Schwager, *op. cit.,* p. 120.

[604] E. Laveille, *L'Évangile au Centre de l'Afrique. Le P. Van Hencxthoven, S.J., Fondateur de la Mission du Kwango (Congo Belge) (1852-1906)* (Louvain, Museum Lessianum, 1926, pp. 401), pp. 88ff.; E. Laveille, *Étudiant et Missionnaire. Xavier van den Peereboom de la Compagnie de Jésus* (Liége, H. Dessain, 1928, pp. vi, 182), *passim;* E. Verwimp, *Thirty Years in the African Wilds* (Bro. Francis de Sadeleer, S.J.), adapted from the Flemish (London, Alexander Ouseley, 1938, pp. 198), pp. 118ff.

In 1898 there arrived the first group of the Priests of the Sacred Heart of Jesus. Theirs was a new organization and this was their first foreign missionary enterprise. To them was entrusted a region in the north-eastern portion of the Congo Free State which later became the Vicariate Apostolic of Stanley Falls.[605]

The list of the additional Roman Catholic agencies which entered the Belgian Congo before 1914 is indicative of the attention the vast possession attracted and of the devotion expended. In 1894 came the Trappists, in 1896 the Premonstratensians, in 1899 the Redemptorists, in 1905 the Mill Hill Fathers, in 1910 Benedictines and Capuchins, in 1911 Dominicans and Salesians, in 1909 the Brothers of Christian Schools, in 1910 the Brothers of Charity of Gand, in 1911 the Marist Brothers, in 1891 the Sisters of Charity of Gand, in 1895 the Sisters of Our Lady of Namur, in 1895 the White Sisters, in 1896 the Franciscan Missionaries of Mary, in 1899 the Sisters of the Sacred Heart of Mary of Berlaer, and in 1911 the Daughters of the Cross of Liége. In 1914 more different Roman Catholic bodies were at work than in any political entity in Africa south of the Sahara. Most of the personnel was Belgian. Increasingly the religious energy of the small but populous, wealthy, and loyally Roman Catholic Belgium was being directed to this, the country's sole colonial possession.[606] For the various congregations of priests territories were carved out which in time became prefectures apostolic and then vicariates apostolic. By the year 1914 the Roman Catholic enterprise was only beginning to get into its stride. Yet in 1912 the number of Roman Catholic converts was already in excess of 100,000.[607] After the World War of 1914-1918 the growth was to be spectacular.

Protestants were as prompt to take advantage of the opening of the Congo as were the Roman Catholics. Although the terms of the international agreements setting up the Congo Free State included the promise of religious liberty, the fact that in Belgium they were a very small minority placed Protestants at a disadvantage. In contrast with the Roman Catholics, practically all the Protestant missionaries were non-Belgians. Roman Catholics could plead, therefore, that they rather than their "separated brethren" should have the support of the ruling power. Particularly after the area passed from the personal control of the King to the state of Belgium, they claimed special privileges on the ground that they were the national religion.[608] Sometimes, notably after 1914, under

---

[605] V. Jeanroy, *Vingt-cinq Ans de Mission au Congo* (Brussels, Action Catholique, 1923, pp. 208), *passim;* G. Kanters, *le T.R.P. Léon Dehon, Fondateur de la Congrégation des Prêtres du Coeur de Jésus* (Brussels, A. Dewit, 1930, pp. 94), p. 45.

[606] Alfred Corman, *Annuaire des Missions Catholiques au Congo Belge . . . 1924* (Brussels, Albert Dewit, 1924, pp. 228), pp. 7, 8.

[607] Streit, *op. cit.*, p. 101.

[608] Hemmens, *George Grenfell*, pp. 224-227.

pro-Roman Catholic administrations, they were favoured as against the Protestants. Yet eventually more Protestant than Roman Catholic organizations were in Congo Belge.

Almost simultaneous in beginning enterprises in the Congo were the Livingstone Inland Mission and the (English) Baptist Missionary Society. The Livingstone Inland Mission was largely the creation of H. Grattan Guinness and his wife. The Guinnesses had been intimately associated with that Hudson Taylor who in the 1860's had created the China Inland Mission, which had as its objective the Chinese untouched by the Christian message. The Livingstone Inland Mission wished to perform something of the same function for those Africans whom Henry M. Stanley's travels were revealing to Europeans. It came into being late in 1877 and, like the China Inland Mission, was undenominational and did not guarantee fixed salaries. The first representative of the Livingstone Inland Mission reached the mouth of the Congo in February, 1878. Reinforcements rapidly followed. Centres were opened on the lower course of the river and, a few years later, aided by a mission steamer, on the upper reaches of the great stream.[609] In 1884 the Livingstone Inland Mission transferred its Congo enterprise to the American Baptist Missionary Union (later the American Baptist Foreign Mission Society). That body was seeking a field in Africa and for various reasons the Livingstone Inland Mission deemed it wise to turn over its work to it. The change was facilitated by the fact that most of the existing missionaries were Baptists.[610] The American Baptists vigorously built upon the foundations which had been laid.[611] In 1888, however, the Guinnesses resumed operations in the Congo. They were eager to see new stations opened beyond the limits to which the American Baptists felt that their own efforts should be confined. A combination of circumstances directed their attention to the Balolos, south of the great northern bend of the Congo. The Congo Balolo mission was, accordingly, begun as a branch of the Regions Beyond Missionary Union. The first party sailed in 1889.[612] To the assistance of the Swedes who had been under the Livingstone Inland Mission there came the *Svenska Missionsförbundet*, or Swedish Missionary Union. Its field was on the lower reaches of the Congo. The first con-

---

[609] Guinness, *The New World of Central Africa*, pp. 175ff.; Madame R. Saillens, *Au Pays des Ténèbres. Histoire de la Première Mission Chrétienne au Congo* (Paris, Librairie Fischbacher, 1889, pp. 116), *passim*.

[610] Guinness, *op. cit.*, pp. 391ff.; *American Baptist Missionary Union: Seventy-first Annual Report . . . 1885*, pp. 122-124.

[611] For the status in 1914 see *One Hundredth Annual Report. American Baptist Foreign Mission Society . . . 1914*, pp. 145-150.

[612] Guinness, *op. cit.*, pp. 461ff.; Mrs. H. Grattan Guinness, *Congo Recollections* (London, Hodder and Stoughton, 1890, pp. 115), *passim*.

tingent, which arrived in 1881, contained Nils Westlind, who became a distinguished linguist and translated the New Testament into the tongue of the area.[613] The death rate was heavy, but the Swedes persisted.[614]

British Baptists owed the impulse which sent them to the Congo in part to the devoted and eccentric Robert Arthington (1823-1900). Arthington might well have been mentioned earlier in these pages, for his beneficence made itself felt in more than one portion of the world which we have already covered as well as in some which we are still to traverse. Born of Quaker stock and in a wealthy family, he devoted his inherited fortune chiefly to foreign missions. He reduced his personal expenses to the absolute minimum, living the life of a recluse and an ascetic. By saving and by wise investment he increased what had come to him. He gave largely to projects designed to carry the Christian message to areas and peoples where, at least in its Protestant form, it had never been heard. He did this because he was convinced that when the Gospel had been preached to all nations, Christ would return and set up his righteous rule.[615] In pursuance of this conviction, in 1877 Arthington offered the Baptist Missionary Society £1,000 to send an expedition to the Congo which, he hoped, would be followed by a steamer on that river.[616] Two pioneers (1878) of the undertaking were George Grenfell (1849-1906)[617] and Thomas J. Comber (1852-1887),[618] who were missionaries of the society in Cameroon, and who had been wishing to go to the Congo when the instructions from the London committee reached them. Comber's career was cut short in 1887 by fever. Grenfell's was longer and was distinguished for extensive exploration in the area, for assisting in the delimitation of the boundary between the Congo Free State and the Portuguese possessions, for founding new stations, and for protests against the exploitation of the blacks. Another of the pioneers was W. Hol-

[613] J. E. Lundahl, *Nils Westlind* (*Stockholm, Svenska Missionsförbundets Förlag*, 1915, pp. 165), *passim*.

[614] J. A. Swedberg, *Bland Kongonegrer och Kanaker. C. F. Johnson, den Första Svenska* (Stockholm, B.-M:s Bokförlags A.-B., no date, p. 115); E. Berlin, *Tagesanbruch Svenska Missionären: Kongo* (Stockholm, B.-M:s Bokförlags A.-B., no date, p. 115); E. Berlin, *Tagesanbruch am Kongo. Die fünfundzwanzigjährige Missionsarbeit des "Swedischen Missionsbundes" in Niederkongo* (Berlin, Buchhandlung der Berliner evang. Missionsgesellschaft, 1912, pp. 83), *passim*.

[615] A. M. Chirgwin, *Arthington's Million. The Romance of the Arthington Trust* (London, The Livingstone Press, no date, pp. 160), pp. 1-37.

[616] Fullerton, *The Christ of the Congo River*, pp. 22, 23.

[617] Hemmens, *George Grenfell*, *passim*; Johnston, *George Grenfell and the Congo*, *passim*; George Hawker, *The Life of George Grenfell, Congo Missionary and Explorer* (New York, Fleming H. Revell Co., 1909, pp. xxv, 587), *passim*.

[618] Ernest H. Hayes, *Comber, the Congo Pioneer* (London, The Livingstone Press, 1927, pp. 128), *passim*; John Brown Myers, *Thomas J. Comber, Missionary Pioneer to the Congo* (New York, Fleming H. Revell, no date, pp. 160), *passim*.

man Bentley (1855-1906).[619] He went out in 1877, reduced one of the languages to writing, prepared a dictionary and grammar for it, and translated the New Testament into it. Other reinforcements came. Their withdrawal from Cameroon after the German occupation of that region (1884) led the British Baptists to concentrate more of their efforts on the Congo. The toll of disease was heavy. Half of those sent in the first decade died within ten years and nearly a fourth returned home.[620] Converts were slow in coming. Yet steamers were brought out and operated, stations were opened both in the lower valley (in the vicinity of the old Roman Catholic centre, San Salvador, in Portuguese territory) and on the upper river, more missionaries came to fill the ranks depleted by the African fevers, the health rate improved, and gradually schools were opened, Christian literature prepared, medical care developed, and churches organized.[621]

Other societies followed fairly rapidly. Under the leadership of F. S. Arnot, the enterprise of the Plymouth Brethren, which we have had occasion to notice in both Northern Rhodesia and Angola, also extended into the south-eastern part of the Congo.[622] Daniel Crawford, whom we met in Northern Rhodesia, spent part of his African career in the portion of the Congo which lay adjacent to that British possession. Arnot was also the means of bringing to the Congo the brilliant physician, Walter Fisher.[623] In 1885 A. B. Simpson, out of whose labours in the United States came what was eventually the Christian and Mis-

[619] W. Holman Bentley, *Pioneering on the Congo* (Chicago, Fleming H. Revell Co., 2 vols., 1900), *passim;* H. M. Bentley, *W. Holman Bentley* (London, The Religious Tract Society, 1907, pp. xx, 446), *passim.*

[620] C. C. Chesterman in *The International Review of Missions,* Vol. XXVI, p. 378.

[621] Robert Glennie, *The Congo and Its People* (London, The Carey Press, no date, pp. 89), *passim;* H. Sutton Smith, *"Yakuso."* *The Very Heart of Africa. Being some account of the Protestant Mission at Stanley Falls, Upper Congo* (London, Marshall Brothers, no date, pp. xviii, 288), *passim;* Thomas Lewis, *These Seventy Years. An Autobiography* (London, The Carey Press, no date, pp. xii, 300), *passim;* William Brock, *A Young Congo Missionary: Memorials of Sidney Roberts Webb, M.D.* (London, H. R. Allenson, 1897, pp. vii, 120), *passim;* H. L. Hemmens, *Congo Journey* (London, The Carey Press, 1938, pp. 160), *passim;* Fullerton, *op. cit., passim;* John Brown Myers, *The Congo for Christ. The Story of the Congo Mission* (Chicago, Fleming H. Revell Co., 1895, pp. 163), *passim;* Joseph Tritton, *Baptist Missionary Society. Rise and Progress of the Work on the Congo River* (London, The Baptist Missionary Society, 1884, pp. 63), *passim;* George Hawker, *An Englishwoman's Twenty-Five Years in Tropical Africa: being the Biography of Gwen Elen Lewis, Missionary to the Cameroons and the Congo* (London, Hodder and Stoughton, 1911, pp. xiv, 352), pp. 82ff.; John Bell, *A Miracle of Modern Missions. The Story of Matula, a Congo Convert* (Chicago, Fleming H. Revell Co., no date, pp. 139), *passim.*

[622] Arthur G. Ingleby, *Pioneer Days in Darkest Africa* (London, Pickering & Inglis, pp. 176), *passim;* Fred S. Arnot, *Garenganze; or Seven Years Pioneer Mission Work in Central Africa* (Chicago, Fleming H. Revell, 1889, pp. viii, 276), pp. 133ff.; Arnot, *Bihé and Garenganze,* pp. 49ff.

[623] Stonelake, *Congo, Past and Present,* p. 43.

sionary Alliance, sent his first band to the Congo. Illness brought to the venture a tragic interruption, but in 1888 another party came and succeeded in establishing a station which was the beginning of a continuous undertaking.[624] In 1890 the (Southern) Presbyterian Church in the United States sent its two pioneers, a Negro and a white man, to found what in time became one of the largest Protestant missions in the Congo. To avoid overlapping with other Protestant societies, they chose a field in the upper portion of the valley of the Kassai. The white member of the initial pair of missionaries, S. N. Lapsley, died shortly after making secure government permission to occupy the area. The news of his death stimulated others to offer their services. Among those who came were both Negroes and whites. A constituency was rapidly built up among freed slaves. The manumission of some of these was purchased by the mission. Schools were developed, among them ones for training in agriculture and industry. Western medicine was introduced.[625] One of the leading languages was reduced to writing and a dictionary, a grammar, and Christian literature were prepared in it, notably by W. M. Morrison.[626] The Presbyterians assisted other missions which entered their areas—the Wescott (Plymouth) Brethren, the Congo Inland Mission (Mennonites), and the Southern Methodists.[627] In 1914 the Southern Methodists took as their responsibility the Atetela tribe.[628] In 1897 the Disciples of Christ sent their first representatives to the Congo. A field was sought, but the Belgian officials were not encouraging. However, the American Baptists turned over to the Disciples (1899) one of their stations, and from this centre the enterprise spread.[629] Pursuing its

[624] Mrs. Alexander Macaw, *Congo, the First Alliance Mission Field* (Harrisburg, Christian Publications, pp. 168), pp. 43ff.

[625] Robert Dabney Bedinger, *Triumphs of the Gospel in the Belgian Congo* (Richmond, Presbyterian Committee of Publication, no date, pp. 218), *passim;* William H. Sheppard, *Presbyterian Pioneers in Congo* (Richmond, Presbyterian Committee of Publication, no date, pp. 157), *passim;* Samuel P. Verner, *Pioneering in Central Africa* (Richmond, Presbyterian Committee of Publication, 1903, pp. ix, 500), *passim.*

[626] T. C. Vinson, *William McCutchan Morrison. Twenty Years in Central Africa* (Richmond, Presbyterian Committee of Publication, 1921, pp. 201), *passim.*

[627] Stonelake, *op. cit.*, pp. 46, 47. On the Mennonites see Alma E. Doering, *Leopard Spots or God's Masterpiece. Which?* (Cleveland, "Malembe" Publisher, 1916, pp. 197), *passim.*

[628] Thomas Ellis Reeve, *In Wembo-Nyama's Land. A story of the thrilling experiences in establishing the Methodist Mission among the Atetela* (Nashville, Publishing House of the M. E. Church South, 1921, pp. 208), *passim.*

[629] Mrs. Eva N. Dye, *Bolenge. A Story of Gospel Triumphs on the Congo* (Cincinnati, Foreign Christian Missionary Society, 1910, pp. 233), *passim;* Andrew F. Hensey, *A Master Builder on the Congo. A Memorial to the Service and Devotion of Robert Ray Eldred and Lillian Byers Eldred* (Chicago, Fleming H. Revell Co., 1916, pp. 192), *passim;* Andrew F. Hensey, *Opals from Africa* (Cincinnati, E. W. Allen, 1910, pp. 64), *passim;* Andrew F. Hensey, *My Children of the Forest* (New York, George H. Doran Co., 1924, pp. 221), *passim;* Stephen J. Corey, *Among Central African Tribes* (Cincinnati, Foreign Christian Missionary Society, 4th ed., 1912, pp. 157), *passim.*

plan to open a chain of stations across the continent, in 1912 and 1913 the African Inland Mission, which we have found in German East Africa and British East Africa, expanded its efforts to the western shores of Lake Albert, near the north-easterly corner of Congo Belge.[630] A convert of the Moody movement, Charles T. Studd, after serving under the China Inland Mission and in India, in 1912 founded the Heart of Africa Mission in an attempt to plant a chain of stations from the north-eastern part of the Belgian Congo to Lake Chad. In 1913 the initial party, led by Studd and including his future son-in-law, went to the Congo.[631] In 1913 the (Northern) Methodist Episcopal Church undertook to reach the labourers in a mining camp in the southern portion of the Belgian Congo. The pioneers were John M. Springer and his wife, who had already served in Rhodesia.[632] In connexion with the American Baptist Missionary Union, the Lott Carey Baptist Foreign Missionary Convention, an American Negro organization, sent representatives to the Congo.[633] In 1914 the Assemblies of God entered through the Congo Evangelistic Mission.[634] Belgian Protestants, being few, were late in beginning a mission. In 1910 they organized a society for the Congo and in 1911 sent a man to find a field, but in 1914 residence had not been established.[635]

One last word must be added to this summary of the spread of Christianity in the Congo. Missionaries, both Roman Catholic[636] and Protestant,[637] but especially the latter, contributed to bringing to the attention of the world the cruel exploitation of the natives under the administration of the Congo Free State. Aroused public opinion forced reform.

French Congo, in 1910 officially renamed French Equatorial Africa, in 1914 was comprised of three administrative units—Gabun, on the coast north of the

---

[630] Stonelake, op. cit., pp. 47, 48.

[631] Thomas B. Walters, Charles T. Studd, Cricketer and Missionary Pioneer (London, The Epworth Press, 1930, pp. 126), passim; Norman P. Grubb, C. T. Studd, Cricketer and Pioneer (London, The Religious Tract Society, 1933, pp. 256), pp. 126ff.

[632] John McKendree Springer, Pioneering in the Congo (The Methodist Book Concern, 1916, pp. xx, 311), passim; John M. Springer, The Heart of Central Africa (Cincinnati, Jennings and Graham, 1909, pp. 223), passim.

[633] C. C. Boone, Congo as I Saw It (New York, J. J. Little and Ives Co., 1927, pp. viii, 96), passim.

[634] E. Hodgson, Fishing for Congo Fisher Folk (London, Assemblies of God, no date, pp. 181), passim; Stonelake, op. cit., p. 51.

[635] Richter, Geschichte der evangelischen Mission in Afrika, pp. 211, 212.

[636] Stonelake, op. cit., p. 21; Witte, Monseigneur Augouard, p. 70.

[637] Conditions in the Congo State. Grounds for Action by the United States Government (Washington, Judd & Detweiler, 1904, pp. 39), p. 7; H. R. Fox Bourne, Civilisation in Congoland: a Story of International Wrong-doing (London, P. S. King & Son, 1903, pp. xvi, 311), pp. 198, 199, 205-226.

Congo River, Middle Congo, on the west bank of that river, and Ubangi-Shari-Chad, north of Middle Congo. The physical geography was varied. The unity was due to the French occupation. The population was far from uniform and was made up of many tribes and peoples, chiefly Negroes, Arabs, Hausa, and Fula, the latter two probably being mixtures of Negro with other strains. Estimates of the total number in the area in the first few years of the twentieth century ranged from 3,652,000 and 9,000,000 to 15,000,000. In the second quarter of the nineteenth century the French obtained a foothold on the coast, but it was not until after 1850 that explorers, some of them French, revealed the interior to Europeans. It was only in the 1880's and 1890's that French political control was extended over the region.[638]

Because of the French prominence in Roman Catholic missions in the nineteenth century, it was to be expected that in this colony of France that branch of the Church would be stronger than Protestantism. In 1844 missionaries sent through Libermann, the converted Jew who was outstanding in the founding of the Holy Ghost Fathers,[639] reached Gabun.[640] In 1849 they were followed by Sisters of the Immaculate Conception of Castres.[641] In 1849 Jean Remy Bessieux (1803-1876), the first priest who came through Libermann, was consecrated bishop over a vicariate which embraced Senegambia and the two Guineas. He made his residence at Gabun and is said to have been instrumental in holding the territory for France when, as a result of the Franco-Prussian War of 1870, there was thought of ceding it to Great Britain.[642] On the coast south of Gabun, still in French territory, the vicariate apostolic of Loango was created in 1886. It likewise was in charge of the Holy Ghost Fathers. As was usual in their missions, the Holy Ghost Fathers made much of educating the blacks in handicrafts and agriculture on extensive plantations. There were numbers of experiment stations for the introduction and testing of tropical plants.[643] The vicariate apostolic of Ubangi, which embraced a large area on the north bank of the Congo, was created in 1890. It, too, was entrusted to the Holy Ghost Fathers. Even before the vicariate was created, financial assistance came from the French Government.[644] The vicariate had as its first

[638] *The Encyclopædia Britannica*, 11th ed., Vol. XI, pp. 99-102; *French Equatorial Africa* (London, H. M. Stationery Office, 1920, pp. 71), *passim*.

[639] Vol. IV, pp. 54, 111, 112.

[640] Marie-Germaine, *Le Christ au Gabon*, p. 33.

[641] Marie-Germaine, *op. cit.*, p. 44; Maurice Briault, *Un Sœur Missionnaire: La Sœur St. Charles . . . Missionnaire au Gabon . . . 1859 à 1911* (Paris, P. Téqui, 1914, pp. 228), *passim*.

[642] Marie-Germaine, *op. cit.*, pp. 38-43.

[643] Schwager, *Die katholische Heidenmission der Gegenwart*, p. 115.

[644] Goyau, *Monseigneur Augouard*, p. 66.

bishop Prosper Philippe Augouard.[645] Explorer, able administrator, versatile, and energetic, Augouard was very prominent in the founding and development of the mission and eventually was given the title of archbishop. In 1909 there was created in the northern part of the French Congo, also for the Holy Ghost Fathers, the prefecture apostolic of Ubangi-Shari.[646] On the eve of 1914 there were in all of French Equatorial Africa not far from 30,000 Roman Catholics, of whom the majority were in the Vicariate Apostolic of Gabun.[647] Beginnings were made of a native staff. A black sister began her novitiate in 1886 and in 1911 a community of native sisters was inaugurated.[648] In 1856 a seminary was founded at Libreville and in 1899 there was an ordination to the priesthood.[649]

Protestant missions, while eventually weaker, were slightly earlier in what became French Equatorial Africa than were Roman Catholic missions. Stimulated in part by the project of the American Colonization Society, in 1833 and 1834 the American Board of Commissioners for Foreign Missions started an enterprise at Cape Palmas, on the eastern border of Liberia. In 1842 and 1843 this mission was moved to the lower reaches of the Gabun River.[650] In spite of the heroism of those who manned it, its course was very discouraging.[651] In 1870 the New School Presbyterians reunited with the Old School and withdrew from the American Board.[652] In the ensuing division of fields between Congregationalists and Presbyterians the Gabun mission became the property of the latter.[653] In the meantime, in 1850, the Old School (American) Presbyterians had gained a foothold on the small island of Corisco (recently annexed by Spain) not far from the mouth of the Gabun River, hoping that from this

[645] Schwager, op. cit., p. 116; Jehan de Witte, Un Explorateur et un Apôtre du Congo Français, Monseigneur Augouard (Paris, Émile-Paul Frères, 1924, pp. x, 372), passim; Augouard, 44 Années au Congo. Suite de "28 Années" et "36 Années au Congo" et fin des Lettres de Mgr. Augouard 1905-1914-1921, Vol. IV (Evreux, M. Poussin, 1934, pp. 512), passim; Goyau, op. cit., passim; G. G. Beslier, L'Apôtre du Congo, Mgr. Augouard (Paris, Éditions de la Vraie France, 1926, pp. 263), passim.

For the life of one of the missionaries of the vicariate who served under Augouard, see Le Père Édouard Épinette, Missionnaire au Congo (Paris, Procure des Missionnaires du Saint-Esprit, 1913, pp. xii, 394), passim.

[646] Streit, Atlas Hierarchicus, p. 101.

[647] Ibid.

[648] Marie-Germaine, op. cit., pp. 137-140.

[649] Marie-Germaine, op. cit., pp. 143-154.

[650] Strong, The Story of the American Board, pp. 124-131; Report of the American Board of Commissioners for Foreign Missions, 1843, p. 83.

[651] On the life of the pioneer of the Gabun mission see Hampden C. DuBose, Memoirs of Rev. John Leighton Wilson, D.D., Missionary to Africa, and Secretary of Foreign Missions (Richmond, Presbyterian Committee of Publication, 1895, pp. 336), passim.

[652] Vol. IV, p. 88.

[653] Strong, op. cit., pp. 280, 281; Annual Report of the American Board of Commissioners for Foreign Missions, 1870, p. 7.

vantage the continent might be penetrated.[654] In 1871 the Gabun and Corisco missions were merged.[655] Because of the insistence of the colonial authorities as part of their general educational policy that no language except French be used in the schools, in the 1890's the American Presbyterians turned over some of their work in French territory to the Société des Missions Évangéliques of Paris.[656] In 1913 the rest was transferred to the French society.[657] The French Protestants developed the enterprise thus acquired.[658] In 1913 they had in five stations 1,908 Christians and 1,976 catechumens.[659]

To this French Protestant mission there came, in 1913, one of the most famous of the many who assisted in the spread of Christianity in Africa, Albert Schweitzer.[660] The son of a pastor, as a boy Schweitzer had heard from his father tales of Casalis, one of the pioneers of their church to South Africa. Born in 1875, Schweitzer had already achieved distinction as a scholar in philosophy, as the author of a fresh and daring study known in its English translation as *The Quest of the Historical Jesus*, as an organist, and as an authority on Bach, when in 1905 he entered upon a medical course to prepare himself for service in Africa. The step meant eventually surrendering his pastorate, his teaching post in the University of Strasbourg, and the headship of a theological faculty. He embarked on what seemed to his friends his mad venture because of what he believed to be the compulsion of the words of Jesus and because of a published appeal for personnel for the French Equatorial African mission of his church. During part of his medical course he continued his teaching and preaching. He raised the funds needed for his support in

---

[654] Brown, *One Hundred Years*, p. 213. For an intimate picture of that mission in 1864 see Wilson, *George Paull*, pp. 113ff.

[655] Brown, *op. cit.*, p. 216. For the mission from 1874 to 1893 see Robert Hamill Nassau, *My Ogowe, Being a Narrative of Daily Incidents During Sixteen Years in Equatorial West Africa* (New York, The Neale Publishing Co., 1914, pp. 708), *passim.* See also Parsons, *A Life for Africa*, pp. 30-159. For some of the continuing enterprise, see John Frederick Hinkhouse, editor, "*The Beloved.*" *An Iowa Boy in the Jungles of Africa, Charles Warner McCleary, His Life, Letters and Work* (Fairfield, Iowa, 1909, pp. 294), *passim.*

[656] Brown, *op. cit.*, p. 217.

[657] *The Seventy-Sixth Annual Report of the Board of Foreign Missions of the Presbyterian Church in the United States of America*, 1913, pp. 57, 58.

[658] Société des Missions Évangéliques de Paris, *Nos Champs de Mission*, pp. 67ff. On one of the missionaries, see *In Memoriam. Madame Edouard Lantz, Née Valentine Ehrhardt, 1873-1906* (Paris, Maison des Missions Évangéliques, 1907, p. 116), *passim.*

[659] F. Grébert, *Au Gabon* (Paris, Société des Missions Évangéliques de Paris, 1922, pp. 216), p. 180.

[660] Albert Schweitzer, *Aus Meinem Leben und Denken* (Leipzig, Felix Meiner, 1932, pp. 211), pp. 1-125 (there is an English translation, *Out of My Life and Thought. An Autobiography*, by C. T. Campion. New York, Henry Holt & Co., 1933, pp. 288); Albert Schweitzer, *On the Edge of the Primeval Forest*, translated by C. T. Campion (London, A. & C. Black, 1922, pp. 180), *passim;* Magnus C. Ratter, *Albert Schweitzer* (London, Allenson & Co., no date, pp. 260), pp. 1-56.

Africa. In spite of the timorous reluctance of some of the directors of the society, who feared his radical scholarship, he was given appointment to Lambaréné.

The *Svenska Missionsförbundet*, which we have met in the Belgian Congo, extended its operations into adjacent portions of French Equatorial Africa.[661]

On the coast north of French Equatorial Africa there was, by the year 1914, a small Spanish protectorate called Rio Muni or Muni River Settlements. It had become Spanish territory in the nineteenth century and especially during the partition of Africa in the 1880's. Its population was said to be between 100,000 and 150,000.[662]

In 1865 an American Presbyterian missionary, George Paull, using the island of Corisco as his base, opened a station on the mainland in the later Spanish territory. Within three months he was dead,[663] but others made permanent the enterprise which he had begun. Eventually several churches were organized and hundreds of converts were gathered.[664]

In 1889 the Holy Ghost Fathers obtained a foothold at the main port, Bata. The hinterland became the charge of the Congregation of the Immaculate Heart of Mary. Financial support was accorded by the Spanish Government to Roman Catholic missionaries. The missionaries were also in part supported by their prosperous plantations.[665] By the year 1913 there were about 1,500 native Roman Catholics in the protectorate.[666]

Only a short distance off the coast north of Rio Muni was Fernando Po, a mountainous island of volcanic origin. Before 1778 it had belonged to Portugal. In that year it came into the hands of Spain and was used in connexion with the slave trade. For a time in the second quarter of the nineteenth century it was administered by Great Britain as a centre for the suppression of the slave trade. Not far from the middle of the century Spain again took over control. During the British occupation numbers of freedmen came to the island from the West Indies, Sierra Leone, and elsewhere, and a kind of English became the prevailing tongue on the coast. In the interior was a primitive Bantu people.[667]

[661] Georges Bruel, *l'Afrique Équatoriale Française* (Paris, Émile Larose, 1918, pp. ix, 558), p. 484.
[662] *Spanish Guinea*, p. 6; *The Encyclopædia Britannica*, 11th ed., Vol. XIX, p. 9.
[663] Wilson, *George Paull*, pp. 224ff.
[664] Brown, *One Hundred Years*, pp. 213-215.
[665] Schwager, *Die katholische Heidenmission der Gegenwart*, p. 112.
[666] Streit, *Atlas Hierarchicus*, p. 101.
[667] *Spanish Guinea*, pp. 4-14; Johnston, *George Grenfell and the Congo*, Vol. I, pp. 18-23.

Protestant missionaries entered during the British period. In 1841 came representatives of the (English) Baptist Missionary Society.[668] Their programme called for a staff of whites and of natives of the West Indies and for the utilization of Fernando Po as a base from which stations could be established on the mainland.[669] In 1858, after nearly two decades on the island, the Baptist missionaries were expelled by the Spanish authorities.[670] However, Protestant communities continued and in 1870 the Spanish government allowed Primitive Methodists to come in. The Methodists were placed under embarrassing restrictions, but they not only served the existing Protestants but also reached out to the aborigines in the interior.[671]

Roman Catholics seem to have been somewhat later than Protestants in caring for Fernando Po. In 1855 the island was entrusted to seculars from the archdiocese of Toledo. In 1857 it was transferred to the Jesuits and made a prefecture apostolic. In 1870 the Society of Jesus withdrew because of the heavy toll which disease had made in their ranks and because of difficulties with the government brought by the revolution of 1868 in Spain. In 1883 there was only one priest on the island. In that year the prefecture apostolic was revived and assigned to the Congregation of the Immaculate Heart of Mary. In spite of a terrifying death rate, this congregation persisted. Schools were opened, industrial training was given, and converts were gathered. To the assistance of the men came Sisters of the Immaculate Conception. The gains were chiefly among the mixed population rather than among the primitive peoples in the interior. The missionaries were Spanish and enjoyed the support of the government.[672]

North of Rio Muni there was, in 1914, the German possession, Cameroon. Its area was fairly extensive—about 292,000 square miles. The larger part of the centre and south was a plateau rising from 1,000 to 10,000 feet. The configuration of the colony varied from a low, swampy, coastal plain to the volcanic Cameroon Mountains over 13,000 feet in height. Of the river systems, one drained south, another into the Niger, and still another into Lake Chad. The population, estimated in 1915 to be over 2,600,000, was of several stocks—

[668] *The Annual Report of the Committee of the Baptist Missionary Society*, 1841, p. 33.
[669] *The Annual Report of the Committee of the Baptist Missionary Society*, 1842, pp. 29-31, 1843, pp. 35-37.
[670] *The Annual Report of the Committee of the Baptist Missionary Society*, 1859, pp. 6-8; Johnston, *op. cit.*, Vol. I, pp. 18-24.
[671] Johnston, *op. cit.*, Vol. I, p. 24.
[672] Schwager, *op. cit.*, p. 111; *The Catholic Encyclopedia*, Vol. XVI, p. 83; *Revista de la Exposición Misional Española*, Nov., 1928, pp. 69-74.

Bantu, Negro, pygmy, and Hamitic—and of numerous tribes. In the South, animism prevailed. In the North, a veneer of Islam overlaid more primitive beliefs and practices. In the fifteenth century Portuguese explored the coast. In the middle of the nineteenth century, partly because of the Baptist missions of which we are to say more in a moment, the British regarded Cameroon as in their empire. However, they did not actively pursue their advantage, and in 1884 the German flag was raised. With characteristic thoroughness the Germans explored the country, organized an administration, and sought to develop the economic resources.[673]

The first attempt to plant Christianity in the region later embraced in Cameroon seems to have been by the English Baptists. In pursuance of the purpose of using Fernando Po as a base for penetrating the continent, beginning with 1845 their missionaries on that island began visits to the neighbouring shore, over which the lofty Cameroon Mountains towered with impressive abruptness. There, on a promontory, in 1848 they established a station. When, in 1858, constrained by the Spanish authorities, the Baptist missionaries left Fernando Po, they augmented their efforts on the mainland. Led by their great pioneer, Alfred Saker (1814-1880), who, except for infrequent visits to Great Britain, was in Africa from 1844 to 1876, they reduced languages to writing, prepared literature, including a translation of the Bible, erected buildings, conducted schools, and gathered converts.[674] To Cameroon there came, in 1875, George Grenfell, soon to become the outstanding trail-blazer of his society on the Congo. In Cameroon he showed his mettle as an explorer.[675] In 1887, when the region passed under the German flag, the new rulers, unhappy because of the vigorous efforts of the English missionaries to prevent the annexation, their influence with the natives, and the latter's discontent with the transfer of authority, made the situation so difficult that the Baptist Missionary Society turned over its enterprise to the Basel Mission.[676]

Almost as soon as the transfer was made a mass movement set in towards Christianity, possibly because the blacks associated the faith with the new order being established by the Germans. As the government built roads to the

[673] *Cameroon* (London, H. M. Stationery Office, 1920, pp. 83), *passim.*

[674] Edward Bean Underhill, *Alfred Saker, Missionary to Africa: a Biography* (London, The Baptist Missionary Society, 1884, pp. xiii, 168), *passim;* E. M. Saker, *Alfred Saker, the Pioneer of the Cameroons* (London, The Religious Tract Society, 1908, pp. 224), *passim;* Johnston, *op. cit.,* Vol. I, pp. 27-62. On a black missionary from Jamaica, see Robert Glennie, *Joseph Jackson Fuller, An African Christian Missionary* (London, The Carey Press, no date, pp. 64), *passim.*

[675] Johnston, *op. cit.,* Vol. I, pp. 43-62.

[676] Johnston, *op. cit.,* Vol. I, pp. 61, 62; *The Annual Report of the Committee of the Baptist Missionary Society,* 1886, pp. 54-57; Harry R. Rudin, *Germans in the Cameroons, 1884-1914* (Yale University Press, 1938, pp. 456), pp. 24, 51, 52, 55, 56, 69-73.

interior, the Basel Mission extended its work inland. Several tribes asked for catechists and schools, not so much because they desired Christianity, as because they wished instruction in the new culture to which they knew they must adjust themselves. In 1914 the Basel society counted 16 head stations, 67 missionaries, 9 missionary sisters, 384 schools with 21,622 pupils, and 15,112 baptized Christians.[677]

The American Presbyterians, already in Rio Muni and French Equatorial Africa, and, since 1879, in what later was German territory, saw in the German occupation of Cameroon an opportunity. In the 1880's they began expanding in the southern coast region of Cameroon. In the 1890's they extended their operations eastward and inland. In contrast with the Basel Mission, the Presbyterians centred their efforts around a few strongly manned stations from which extensive preaching could be carried on in the surrounding country. By 1914 they had about 5,000 baptized Christians.[678]

In 1891 German Baptists undertook a mission in Cameroon.[679] Early in 1914, on the eve of the changes wrought by the World War of 1914-1918, came the first Gossner missionary.[680]

Roman Catholics were later in entering Cameroon than were Protestants. By 1914, however, they counted not far from as many converts. After the German occupation a French society sought in vain for permission to enter and Jesuits and Trappists declined to undertake the pioneering task. In 1890 German Pallotti Fathers from Limburg accepted the responsibility for the prefecture apostolic which was created in that year. In spite of a heavy mortality, they rapidly built up a foreign staff—in 1912 31 priests, 33 lay brothers, and 30 sisters in 14 head stations. In 1912 they counted 20,277 Christians in their communities. In the early years of the mission they acquired slave children and settled them in villages where they gave them Christian instruction.

[677] P. Steiner, *Kamerun als Kolonie und Missionsfeld* (Basel, Verlag der Basler Buchhandlung, 1909, pp. 134), pp. 65ff.; Emanuel Kellerhals, *Ich will sie mehren und nicht mindern. Fünfzig Jahre Basler Mission in Kamerun* (Stuttgart, Evang. Missionsverlag, 1936, pp. 99), *passim;* Richter, *Geschichte der evangelischen Mission in Afrika*, pp. 173-180.

[678] Richter, *op. cit.*, pp. 181-184; Parsons, *A Life for Africa*, pp. 167ff.; Brown, *One Hundred Years*, pp. 217, 218; *The Testing of a Mission. A Ten-Year Policy 1904-1913 in the West Africa Mission* (New York, Board of Foreign Missions of the Presbyterian Church in the U.S.A., 1913, pp. 19), *passim;* Robert H. Milligan, *The Jungle Folk of Africa* (Chicago, The Fleming H. Revell Co., 1908, pp. 380), pp. 19-169; Jean Kenyon Mackenzie, *Black Sheep. Adventures in West Africa* (Boston, Houghton Mifflin Co., 1916, pp. viii, 314), *passim.*

[679] Richter, *op. cit.*, p. 180; E. Scheve, *Die Mission der deutschen Baptisten in Kamerun (West-Afrika) (von 1884 bis 1901)* (Missions-Gesellschaft der deutschen Baptisten, no date, pp. 125), *passim.*

[680] Richter, *op. cit.*, p. 184.

Later they established schools in many non-Christian villages as a means of winning and instructing the on-coming generation. For a time paucity of funds and weaknesses of the native teachers forced retrenchment, but by 1914 these losses had been more than made good. The Pallotti Fathers undertook careful studies of the customs of the tribes to which they went and sought so far as was consistent with their faith to adapt themselves to them.[681]

In 1914 in the three decades which had elapsed since the German occupation, Christianity, both Protestant and Roman Catholic, had made phenomenal headway.

West of Cameroon, in 1914, was a British possession, Nigeria. In area it was somewhat larger than Cameroon, about 336,000 square miles. In population it was much more important, having probably between 15,000,000 and 20,000,000 inhabitants. Its peoples were of many tribes and languages. The overwhelming majority were of Negro blood, but in large numbers this blood mingled with other strains. Prominent were the Hausa and the Fulani, both widespread in the North. There were also minorities of Bantus and pygmies. In the South Negroes were much more predominant than in the North. Before the British occupation several strong native states had arisen, some of them, as was so usual in Africa, being ephemeral. There were, too, at least a score of cities each with 20,000 people or more. Religiously, the South was overwhelmingly pagan. In the North, penetrated as it was by trade routes from the southern shores of the Mediterranean and the Nile Valley, Islam had been present for centuries and had won at least the nominal allegiance of a large proportion of the population, especially the ruling classes.[682]

The spread of Christianity was determined in large part by the physical geography. The North looked towards the Sahara and North Africa. The South faced the Gulf of Guinea. In the North, therefore, Moslem influence predominated. It was in the South, more remote from the Moslem world, that animism persisted. From the South, moreover, with its frontage on the ocean, came the currents of European life and, with them, Christianity. It was here that Christianity, finding access easier and the opposition of Islam less marked, had its chief growth.

From the close of the eighteenth century the British were more potent on the coast than any other European people. It was a Scot, Mungo Park (1771-

[681] Schwager, *Die katholische Heidenmission der Gegenwart,* pp. 107-110; Schmidlin, *Die katholischen Missionen in den deutschen Schutzgebieten,* pp. 75-89.
[682] *Nigeria,* pp. 1-13, 20.

1806?), who was the most famous of the white explorers of the Niger River.[683] During the first half of the nineteenth century the British were active, but it was in the second half and particularly in the fourth quarter of the nineteenth century that they rapidly extended their authority. It was early in the 1840's that an enterprise combining commercial and philanthropic objectives for the introduction of European civilization to the Niger and associated with the name of Thomas Fowell Buxton, prominent in the emancipation of the slaves within the British Empire, and with its centre at Lokoja on the Niger, had its brief and disastrous course.[684] In 1851 the British occupied Lagos. The United African Company, formed in 1879, energetically pushed British interests in the Niger Valley. In 1885 the British proclaimed a protectorate over the coast from Lagos to Cameroon. In 1906 this was united administratively with Lagos. In 1900, as an outgrowth of the United African Company and its successor, the National African Company, Northern Nigeria was made a British protectorate. On January 1, 1914, this was amalgamated with Lagos and Southern Nigeria.[685]

In the 1840's Christianity was introduced to the later Nigeria by the Anglicans through the Church Missionary Society, the Wesleyans, and the Presbyterians.

The Church Missionary Society was slightly earlier than the others. Prominent among its organizers were Evangelicals who were also committed to the anti-slavery movement and who shared in the founding of Sierra Leone, a centre for freedmen. Its original title, Society for Missions to Africa and the East,[686] indicated the place which Africa held in the minds of the founders. As we are to see a few pages below, one of its earliest projects was in Sierra Leone. It is not surprising, therefore, that two of its emissaries accompanied, in 1841, the ill-starred Niger expedition sponsored by Buxton.[687] One of these was the remarkable African, later Anglican bishop in the Niger, Samuel Adjai Crowther. As a lad Crowther was rescued by a British boat from a slave ship, was taken to Sierra Leone, and was educated there and in England.[688]

A continuing enterprise by the Church Missionary Society arose in what was known as the Yoruba country, in the later Lagos, in connexion with freedmen from Sierra Leone. Between 1839 and 1842 several hundred former

[683] Stephen Gwynn, *Mungo Park and the Quest of the Niger* (New York, G. P. Putnam's Sons, 1935, pp. 269), *passim;* Walker, *The Romance of the Black River*, pp. 9-13.

[684] Stock, *The History of the Church Missionary Society*, Vol. I, pp. 451-455.

[685] *Nigeria*, pp. 14-19.

[686] Charles Hole, *The Early History of the Church Missionary Society for Africa and the East* (London, Church Missionary Society, 1896, pp. xxxviii, 677), pp. 40-42.

[687] *Journals of the Rev. James Frederick Schön and Mr. Samuel Crowther, who, with the Sanction of Her Majesty's Government, Accompanied the Expedition up the Niger, in 1841, in Behalf of the Church Missionary Society* (London, Hatchard and Son, 1842, pp. xxii, 393), *passim;* Walker, *The Romance of the Black River*, pp. 14-30.

[688] Page, *The Black Bishop*, pp. 1-67.

slaves returned from Sierra Leone to their own people, whom they found in and near the city of Abeokuta, some distance inland from the ports of Lagos and Badagry. Since in Sierra Leone they had been in touch with emissaries of the Church Missionary Society, that body sought to follow them and to find through them an open door into a new area.[689] In 1842 and 1843 Henry Townsend, a representative of the society, made his way to Abeokuta.[690] Late in 1844 a party which included Townsend, C. A. Gollmer and his wife,[691] and Crowther left Sierra Leone to inaugurate a mission in Abeokuta. Crowther met his mother and sisters after more than two decades of separation and his mother was among the first to be baptized.[692] Crowther gave notable service in preparing a grammar and dictionary in the Yoruba tongue and in translating part of the Bible into that language.[693] The British occupation of Lagos (1851) was followed by the founding there of an Anglican mission.[694] In 1853 David Hinderer and his wife established a station at Ibadan, inland from Abeokuta.[695] In 1853 and 1854 Crowther accompanied an expedition up the Niger.[696] In 1857 the Church Missionary Society placed a steamer, the *Dayspring*, on that river. Crowther went on it with several other African Christians.[697] In the attempt to found a native church manned by African clergy, in 1864 Crowther was consecrated in Canterbury Cathedral as Bishop of the Niger Territories.[698] He served in that post until his death, in 1891. A man of rugged constitution who seemed all but immune to the diseases of Africa, an incessant worker, intellectually alert and eager, and optimistic, Crowther was singularly adapted to his pioneer task. Under him Christianity spread rapidly and he ordained a number of Africans. However, while his own moral character was above reproach, and cannibalism, human sacrifices, and the murder

[689] [Sarah] Tucker, *Abbeokuta; or Sunrise within the Tropics: an Outline of the Progress of the Yoruba Mission* (London, James Nisbet and Co., 1853, pp. vi, 278), pp. 39ff.

[690] George Townsend, *Memoir of the Rev. Henry Townsend* (London, Marshall Brothers, 1887, pp. xv, 186), pp. 24ff.

[691] *Charles Andrew Gollmer . . . by His Eldest Son* (London, Hodder and Stoughton, 1889, pp. xv, 220), p. 14.

[692] Page, *op. cit.*, pp. 95-97. For the scene in one village see M. A. S. Barber, *Oshielle: or, Village Life in the Yoruba Country; from the Journals and Letters of a Catechist there; Describing the Rise of a Christian Church in an African Village* (London, James Nisbet and Co., 1857, pp. xxiv, 222), *passim*.

[693] Walker, *op. cit.*, p. 110.

[694] Walker, *op. cit.*, pp. 75, 76.

[695] *Seventeen Years in the Yoruba Country. Memorials of Anna Hinderer* (London, Seeley, Jackson, and Halliday, 1872, pp. xii, 342), pp. 51ff.

[696] Walker, *op. cit.*, pp. 85-93.

[697] Samuel Crowther and John Christopher Taylor, *The Gospel on the Banks of the Niger. Journals and Notices of the Native Missionaries accompanying the Niger Expedition of 1857-1858* (London, Church Missionary House, 1859, pp. x, 451), *passim*.

[698] Page, *op. cit.*, pp. 183ff.

of new-born twins were fought, in his declining years, largely through weaknesses of the native clergy and catechists, laxity of moral standards crept into the growing church.[699] It seemed wise to choose a white bishop as his successor. The diocese of Western Equatorial Africa was created and to it was consecrated (1893) Joseph Sidney Hill, who had had experience in New Zealand and in Great Britain. Soon after landing at Lagos, Hill and his wife were dead (January, 1894).[700] Herbert Tugwell was appointed in his place.[701] Gradually order and discipline were restored.[702] Growth in membership continued.[703]

When, in 1900, Northern Nigeria was made a British protectorate, the Church Missionary Society extended its operations into the vast area. Already, in the 1890's, the society had been reaching out into the Upper Niger and the independent Hausa Association had sent in a party to study the Hausa language.[704] In 1900 the Church Missionary Society assigned a contingent to the North. In spite of hardships and difficulties, footholds were gradually established.[705] In 1904 there was formed the Cambridge University Mission Party, which later became affiliated with the Church Missionary Society and which in 1907 began operations in the Central Sudan.[706]

In 1914 the Church Missionary Society counted 51,750 baptized in Nigeria. Of these approximately four-fifths were in its oldest fields, in the Yoruba country. Only 499 were in the northern provinces.[707]

The Wesleyans entered the later Nigeria almost simultaneously with the Anglicans. Among the Yorubas who, as freedmen, returned to their own people in Abeokuta in the 1830's and 1840's were those who while in Sierra Leone had been in contact with Wesleyans. From Abeokuta they sent an

---

[699] Page, op. cit., pp. 194ff; Walker, op. cit., pp. 130-155.

[700] Rose E. Faulkner, *Joseph Sidney Hill, First Bishop in Western Equatorial Africa* (London, H. R. Allenson, 1895, pp. 223), *passim*.

[701] Walker, op. cit., p. 167.

[702] Walker, op. cit., pp. 169-172; *Letters of Henry Hughes Dobinson, Late Archdeacon of the Niger in the Diocese of Western Equatorial Africa* (London, Seeley and Co., 1899, pp. vi, 230), *passim*.

[703] For the life of one who gave herself largely to the education of girls, see G. T. Basden, *Edith Warner of the Niger* (London, Seeley, Service & Co., 1927, pp. 91), *passim*.

[704] Charles Henry Robinson, *Hausaland, or, Fifteen Hundred Miles through the Central Sudan* (London, Sampson Low, Marston and Co., 1896, pp. xv, 304), *passim;* Florence Robinson, *Charles H. Robinson* (Westminster, The Society for the Propagation of the Gospel in Foreign Parts, 1928, pp. xii, 143), pp. 45-99.

[705] W. R. S. Miller, *Reflections of a Pioneer* (London, Church Missionary Society, 1936, pp. 227), *passim*.

[706] Walker, op. cit., p. 229.

[707] *Proceedings of the Church Missionary Society for Africa and the East . . . 1914-15,* pp. xx, xxi.

appeal to Sierra Leone for missionaries.[708] In response there came, in 1842, a remarkable man, Thomas Birch Freeman (1809-1890). Freeman was born in England, the son of a Negro father and a white mother. As a boy he took his stand with the Methodists. By occupation he was a gardener. He acquired a fair education and had the dignity and poise of a gentleman. In 1837 he offered himself for service in Africa to take the place of missionaries who had perished in the adverse physical surroundings. In contrast with the heavy toll which death exacted of the early staffs, Freeman lived to a great age. As we shall see a few pages below, he was a pioneer on the Gold Coast. From there he came to the Yoruba country and was the advance agent for Methodism in Abeokuta and Badagry.[709] Until 1878 Lagos and the Yoruba country were administered in connexion with the older mission on the Gold Coast. Under John Milum, the chairman of the new district which was created for Lagos and who served until 1881, a rapid growth was witnessed and the Niger was reached, although only temporarily.[710] The Wesleyans did not expand as widely in Nigeria as did the Anglicans, and were confined chiefly to the Lagos region. In 1913 they counted a Christian community of 7,221.[711]

East of the Niger, on the Old Calabar River, the United Presbyterian Church of Scotland began a mission in 1846. This arose out of the initiative of a presbytery in Jamaica. Hope Masterton Waddell, a clergyman of the United Secession Church, had been sent in 1829 to Jamaica as a missionary. Early in the 1840's the presbytery of which he was a member began dreaming of a mission to Africa. Waddell was appointed by it to arouse interest in Scotland. In 1846 the first party, which included Waddell, landed near the mouth of the Old Calabar River.[712] The initial contingent had in it a Jamaican mulatto.[713] In addition to Scotch missionaries, some of whom had previously seen service in Jamaica,[714] several of Negro blood later came as reinforcements from that West Indian isle.[715] The mission early began to combat the

[708] Findlay and Holdsworth, *The History of the Wesleyan Methodist Missionary Society,* Vol. IV, p. 158.

[709] Walker, *Thomas Birch Freeman,* pp. 11-28, 114-159; Milum, *Thomas Birch Freeman,* pp. 9-30, 93-105.

[710] Findlay and Holdsworth, *op. cit.,* Vol. IV, pp. 202-207.

[711] *The One Hundredth Report of the Wesleyan Methodist Missionary Society (1914),* p. 257. See also on the history of the mission, C. R. Johnson, *Bryan Roe* (London, Charles H. Kelly, 1896, pp. 272), *passim.*

[712] Waddell, *Twenty-nine Years in the West Indies and Central Africa,* pp. 15, 206-266.

[713] Luke, *Pioneering in Mary Slessor's Country,* pp. 24, 25.

[714] Luke, *op. cit.,* p. 18; Alex. Robb, *The Gospel to the Africans. A Narrative of the Life and Labours of the Rev. William Jameson in Jamaica and Old Calabar* (Edinburgh, Andrew Elliot, 2d ed., no date, pp. x, 299), *passim;* William Marwick, *William and Louisa Anderson. A Record of Their Life and Work in Jamaica and Old Calabar* (Edinburgh, Andrew Elliot, 1897, pp. viii, 664), *passim.*

[715] Luke, *op. cit.,* pp. 33, 34.

destruction of new-born twins, the killing of the aged, and other native customs abhorrent to Christian ethics.[716] It was befriended by the local chief, who, while never becoming a Christian, supported the missionaries in many of their efforts and was a regular attendant at their services.[717] For many years the labours of the missionaries were confined to the Efik people. These folk held a monopoly of the trade with the interior and were unwilling to have the white men go inland.[718] It was only in the 1880's, when the establishment of the British protectorate broke Efik control, that much expansion to the hinterland was possible.[719] In the meantime the Efik tongue was reduced to writing, a dictionary prepared, and the Bible translated into it.[720] The beginnings of a native ministry were made.[721] In the 1880's stations were opened farther inland.[722] One of the most remarkable members of the mission was Mary Slessor (1848-1915).[723] Born in Aberdeen, as a girl and young woman a factory labourer in Dundee, she came to the Calabar mission in 1876. There she put in much of her nearly forty years in pioneering. Courageous and vigorous, she fought the chronic social evils of the region, saving twins, opposing the poison ordeal, and sheltering runaway slaves. The Presbyterian mission had a fairly steady growth. In 1914 it counted 3,412 communicants and a Christian community of 10,792.[724]

In 1849, not many years after their separation from the Northern Baptists, the Southern Baptists of the United States sent two missionaries to Africa with the Yoruba country as their destination. One of them died in Liberia. The other, Thomas J. Bowen, reached Abeokuta in 1850. He had hoped to go farther inland, but for a time was prevented and employed the interval to study the Yoruba language. Reinforcements came, among them some of Negro blood. Several centres were opened, but, as was all too usual in the initial days of missions in so much of equatorial Africa, disease again and again depleted the ranks. Moreover, the unhappy coincidence of the Civil War in the United States and a devastating war in Yorubaland almost extinguished the mission in the 1860's and the early 1870's. However, in 1875 the renewal of the staff

[716] Waddell, op. cit., pp. 444-449, 483, 484, 511; Luke, op. cit., p. 43.

[717] Goldie, Calabar and Its Mission, pp. 210, 202.

[718] Goldie, op. cit., p. 270; Richter, Geschichte der evangelischen Mission in Afrika, p. 155.

[719] Richter, op. cit., p. 157.

[720] Goldie, op. cit., p. 304; Luke, op. cit., p. 20.

[721] Dickie, Story of the Mission in Old Calabar, p. 77.

[722] Dickie, op. cit., pp. 83, 84.

[723] W. P. Livingstone, Mary Slessor of Calabar (London, Hodder and Stoughton, 1916, pp. xi, 347), passim; Cuthbert McEvoy, Mary Slessor (London, The Carey Press, no date, pp. 62), passim.

[724] United Free Church of Scotland. Report on Foreign Missions for 1914 (Edinburgh, T. and A. Constable, 1915, pp. 130), p. 107.

began. Lost centres were eventually regained and new ones opened. One of the strongest churches was at the port of Lagos. In the 1880's a movement arose which sought independence of the white man and which was found in more than one denomination. Several Baptist congregations withdrew from association with the white missionary. In 1914, 31 Baptist churches, of which 14 were independent, were enumerated, with 2,880 members.[725]

Between the Old Calabar River and the Niger was a small stream, the Qua Iboe, which emptied into the Gulf of Guinea and so afforded a highway to part of the interior. In 1886, while on a trading excursion to Calabar, natives of the Qua Iboe region were brought in contact with the Christians in that vicinity. A white merchant, moreover, who had settled among them gathered them together on Sundays for Christian instruction. This led to an appeal for a resident missionary. The request came into the hands of H. Grattan Guinness, whom we met a few pages above as one of the initiators of Protestant missions in the Congo Free State. Guinness spoke of it to his students and one of them, Samuel A. Bill, who was seeking an opening as a missionary abroad, responded. In 1887 Bill reached the Qua Iboe. In 1888 he was joined by another missionary. By the year 1890 he had gathered a small church. A little financial assistance came from Guinness, but in 1891, while on a visit to his native North Ireland, Bill aroused interest in his enterprise and an inter-denominational council of friends was formed to support the mission with funds and personnel. New centres were progressively opened, chiefly in the valley of the Qua Iboe. Native pastors were trained and eventually the churches were required to support all of the non-white staff.[726]

In 1893 the Primitive Methodists, their field on the neighbouring island of Fernando Po becoming restricted, opened a new one on the mainland, near Calabar. With the settlement of political boundaries, they found themselves in German Cameroon. Accordingly they moved across the line into British territory. There in time they developed a fairly extensive mission.[727]

In 1911 four representatives of the leading Protestant societies in Southern Nigeria, the Church Missionary Society, the United Free Church of Scotland, the Qua Iboe Mission, and the Primitive Methodists, met and planned con-

[725] Louis M. Duval, *Baptist Missions in Nigeria* (Richmond, Educational Department, Foreign Mission Board, Southern Baptist Convention, 1928, pp. 212), pp. 39-159; S. G. Pinnock, *The Romance of Missions in Nigeria* (Richmond, Educational Department, Foreign Mission Board, Southern Baptist Convention, 1917, pp. 176), *passim;* Elkin Lightfoot Lockett, *Basil Lee Lockett. A Beloved Physician* (Richmond, Foreign Mission Board, Southern Baptist Convention, 1936, pp. xii, 206), pp. 37-113.
[726] M'Keown, *Twenty-Five Years in Qua Iboe*, pp. 52ff.
[727] Maxwell, *Nigeria*, pp. 97, 98.

certed action for a comprehensive approach to the region, the training of native evangelists, and the discipline of church members.[728]

Difficult Northern Nigeria proved a challenge to daring spirits. After 1890, in addition to the Church Missionary Society, three new bodies entered the region. In 1893 the Sudan Interior Mission, with headquarters in Canada, sent its first contingent. It found one tribe which had been prepared by a Christian native for the missionaries' message and, after 1900, made rapid advance.[729] The Sudan United Mission entered Nigeria in 1904. It had been founded in 1904 by Karl Kumm, a son-in-law of H. Grattan Guinness, and was international in its support and personnel. It drew many of its staff from the Dutch churches of South Africa and the United States.[730] In 1905 a Mennonite who had come to Africa under the Sudan Interior Mission began an enterprise for his own denomination, an American body.[731]

To Nigeria also came the Seventh Day Adventists. On the eve of 1914 their widely flung missions were extended to this field.[732]

As was to be anticipated where the British were the dominant European influence, Roman Catholics were much less numerous in Nigeria than Protestants. It is possible that a few vague memories survived into the nineteenth century of the Roman Catholic Christianity propagated along the Guinea coast by the Portuguese and Spaniards in the days of their might.[733] However, the renewal did not come until after the introduction of Protestant Christianity. In the 1860's there arrived at Lagos former slaves from Brazil who were professedly Roman Catholic. A freedman, Antonio, laboured to hold them true to their faith until European missionaries should come. He also baptized a number of pagans.[734]

The larger part of Nigeria became the field of the Society of African Missions. This organization was a child of the French missionary impulse of the nineteenth century. It was founded in 1856 by Marion Brésillac, a scion of the old nobility. As its name indicates, it had Africa as its objective. Its headquarters were a seminary in Lyons. Brésillac became Vicar Apostolic of Sierra Leone, but within a few weeks after landing at his post (1859) he and all but one of those who came with him were dead. After this depressing beginning, Sierra Leone was abandoned, but in 1860 the Vicariate Apostolic of Benin and

---

[728] M'Keown, *op. cit.*, p. 101.

[729] Maxwell, *op. cit.*, pp. 98-100.

[730] Maxwell, *op. cit.*, pp. 100, 101 ; Richter, *op. cit.*, p. 153.

[731] Maxwell, *op. cit.*, p. 101.

[732] Maxwell, *op. cit.*, p. 102.

[733] Teilhard de Chardin, *La Guinée Supérieure et ses Missions*, pp. 174-176.

[734] Teilhard de Chardin, *op. cit.*, p. 192.

Dahomey was created and given to the society.[735] In this charge was part of the later Nigeria. In 1868 missionaries arrived at Lagos.[736] Although there was a heavy mortality among the pioneers, the enterprise flourished. The British gave it (1877) a peninsula on which a plantation and headquarters of the mission were developed.[737] New centres were opened. In 1913 the society had charge of one vicariate and two prefectures apostolic in Nigeria with a total Roman Catholic population of about 10,000.[738]

Before 1900 the Holy Ghost Fathers from Gabun established themselves on the east side of the lower reaches of the Niger. After 1900 they made fairly rapid progress. They had the satisfaction of seeing one of their catechists chosen as a chief and remain true to his faith.[739] In 1913 there were said to be 4,789 Roman Catholics in their part of Nigeria.[740]

Dahomey, on the coast of the Gulf of Guinea immediately to the west of Nigeria, was French in 1914. In the first three-quarters of the nineteenth century traders of various nationalities possessed forts along its littoral. A strong native state ruled much of the area and with its army of Amazon-like women proved formidable. Not until the mid-1880's did the region become indisputably French. The population, totalling somewhat less than 1,000,000, belonged to several reciprocally unrelated tribes.[741]

In the second half of the seventeenth century, Spanish Capuchins inaugurated in the region a mission whose life proved very brief.[742] In the nineteenth century very few traces of its effects could be discovered.[743] The European forts contained professing Christians, but their faith seems not to have spread to the blacks.

However, it was in Dahomey that the Society of African Missions had the strongest and most prosperous of its West African missions. In 1913 it counted 11,440 Roman Catholics served by 34 European priests, 1 European lay brother,

[735] Teilhard de Chardin, op. cit., pp. 176-181; J. Mouren, Een Pionier van het Moderne Missieapostolaat de inlandsche Geestelijkheid, Mgr. Melchior de Marion-Bresillac (Missiehuis der Afrikaansche Missiën Cadier en Keer [Limburg], 1927, pp. 96), passim.
[736] Teilhard de Chardin, op. cit., p. 191.
[737] Teilhard de Chardin, op. cit., p. 194.
[738] Streit, Atlas Hierarchicus, p. 101.
[739] Schwager, Die katholische Heidenmission der Gegenwart, pp. 104-106.
[740] Streit, op. cit., p. 101.
[741] Dahomey (London, H. M. Stationery Office, 1920, pp. 41), pp. 5-11.
[742] Henri Labouret and Paul Rivet, Le Royaume d'Arda et son Évangelisation au XVIIe Siècle (Paris, Institut d'Ethnologie, 1929, pp. 62), passim.
[743] Teilhard de Chardin, op. cit., pp. 174-176.

and 22 Sisters of Our Lady of the Apostles for African Missions.[744] In 1861 its first missionaries gained a foothold in one of the ports. However, opposition was great and mortality heavy. The earliest converts were from among Portuguese half-breeds. From 1871 to 1884 the witch-doctors were strong enough to compel the abandonment of the centre. Not until the 1890's did the mission achieve substantial gains.[745]

The nineteenth century renewal of Christian missionary effort was begun earlier by Protestants than by Roman Catholics. The Wesleyan mulatto Freeman, whom we met a few paragraphs above in the Yoruba country, visited the region in 1843 and 1854.[746] Yet it was not until 1880 that the Wesleyans were able to begin a continuing enterprise and in 1912 they had less than 750 members.[747] They were the only Protestant mission in the colony.

In the year 1914 Togo, or Togoland, adjoining Dahomey on the west, had been a German possession for about three decades. Portuguese, German, British, and French merchants had frequented the coast, but in the scramble for Africa in the 1880's the Germans obtained exclusive title. The population was said to be about 1,000,000 and was made up of a number of tribes.[748] Paganism prevailed, but there was a sprinkling of Islam.

In Togo, as in Dahomey, in the nineteenth century Protestant missions were first on the scene. Here, too, the pioneer was Freeman. He visited part of the coast in 1843.[749] He did not establish a continuing enterprise. In the 1870's the Wesleyans reappeared.[750] After the German occupation they made considerable progress.[751]

More prominent than the British were the German Protestants. In 1847 the North German Missionary Society, which had been organized in 1836, sent a group of missionaries to West Africa. An attempt to gain a foothold in Gabun was foiled by the French authorities. Encouraged by the friendly Wesleyans, the Germans made their next effort in what became Togoland. The initial years were discouraging. Disease and climate made alarming inroads on

[744] Streit, op. cit., p. 101; Guilcher, Un Ami des Noirs, Augustin Planque, pp. 155ff.; Deux Soeurs Noires (Paris, Librairie Bloud et Gay, 1931, pp. 239), passim.
[745] Schwager, op. cit., pp. 100-102; Teilhard de Chardin, op. cit., pp. 182-191.
[746] Findlay and Holdsworth, The History of the Wesleyan Methodist Missionary Society, Vol. IV, pp. 159, 162; Walker, Thomas Birch Freeman, pp. 160-179.
[747] Findlay and Holdsworth, op. cit., Vol. IV, p. 205.
[748] Togoland (London, H. M. Stationery Office, 1920, pp. 55), pp. 1-18.
[749] Findlay and Holdsworth, op. cit., Vol. IV, p. 160.
[750] Findlay and Holdsworth, op. cit., Vol. IV, p. 205.
[751] Findlay and Holdsworth, op. cit., Vol. IV, pp. 216-218.

the staff. Wars brought disturbed conditions. Not until 1853 was a continuing centre established. Eventually, however, persistence and faith had their reward. The German occupation made for a more favourable environment. In 1914 7,140 baptized were counted, chiefly in the Ewe language belt. The Basel Mission, expanding from the adjacent Gold Coast, had also achieved gains when the World War of 1914-1918 brought an altered political *milieu.*[752]

In the fore part of the nineteenth century a few nominal Roman Catholics with Portuguese names were to be found. From time to time they were visited by Portuguese priests.[753] For some years after 1860 the Society of African Missions had Togo in its assignment. Its priests cared for the few Roman Catholics in the country. In the 1880's it maintained a station in the region, but opposition by non-Christians compelled withdrawal.[754] In 1892 Rome entrusted Togo to the Society of the Divine Word, which was predominantly German in its personnel. In the little over two decades before the World War of 1914-1918 intervened, the society opened a number of stations. In 1914 it had 19,740 Roman Catholics in its care, 198 schools with 7,911 pupils, and a staff of 47 priests, 15 lay brothers, and 30 sisters.[755]

In Togo, as in so much of the rest of Africa, Christianity was making rapid gains in the closing years of the era.

In 1914 the Gold Coast was a British possession. It stretched about 340 miles along the shore of the Gulf of Guinea west of Togo and reached inland approximately 300 miles. Somewhat larger than either Togo or Dahomey, in 1914 it had a population estimated at 1,500,000. It was divided into many tribes of Negro and Negroid blood. Chief in the western coastal regions were the Fanti. Related to the Fanti were the Ashanti, who in the eighteenth century built a powerful state with its capital at Kumasi. Coming in the latter part of the fifteenth century, the Portuguese seem to have been the first Europeans to establish themselves on the coast. Attracted by the gold which gave the region the name by which the white man knew it, English, Dutch, French, Danes, Swedes, and Brandenburgers followed. The Dutch were especially powerful.

[752] Gustav Müller, *Geschichte der Ewe-Mission* (Bremen, Verlag der Norddeutschen Missions-Gesellschaft, 1904, pp. 288), *passim;* Martin Schlunk, *Die Norddeutsche Mission in Togo* (Bremen, Verlag der Norddeutschen Missions-Gesellschaft, 2 vols., 1910), *passim;* Carl Paul, *Die Mission in unsern Kolonien. Erstes Heft: Togo und Kamerun* (Leipzig, Fr. Richter, 1898, pp. iv, 214), pp. 50-109.

[753] Schmidlin, *Die katholischen Missionen in den deutschen Schutzgebieten,* p. 61.

[754] *Ibid.*

[755] Joh. Thauren, *Die Mission in der ehemaligen deutschen Kolonie Togo* (Missionsdruckerei Steyl, 1931, pp. 44), *passim;* Matthias Dier, *Unter den Schwarzen* (Missionsdruckerei Steyl, 2d ed., 1901, pp. 397), pp. 129ff.

The British, however, gradually extended their interests and in the seventeenth century built a number of forts. Early in the nineteenth century they began exercising territorial rights. Gradually they increased their authority. In the 1870's they obtained the Dutch forts and defeated the Ashanti. In 1899 they annexed the Ashanti state and then reached northward.[756]

Through the numerous contacts with Europeans, Christianity arrived on the Gold Coast long before the nineteenth century. The Portuguese introduced it, but not in such fashion that it persisted. In the eighteenth century the heroic and wide-ranging Moravians had a mission there, but their enterprise also lapsed.[757] The Anglicans entered through the Society for the Propagation of the Gospel in Foreign Parts. In 1752 Thomas Thompson came, under appointment from that organization. He made his headquarters at Cape Coast Castle. One of the Negroes whom he sent to England for education was ordained and, returning to the Gold Coast, continued there as a missionary until death, in 1816. Two white successors were appointed, but in 1824 the society's connexion with the Gold Coast lapsed for several decades.[758] In the 1740's the Dutch conducted a mission through a native clergyman who had been ordained in Amsterdam.[759]

The renewal of active Protestant effort was in 1828, through the Basel Mission. The Basel enterprise was begun in connexion with the Danish interests on the Gold Coast. After twelve years the undertaking seemed a failure. Apparently all that it had to show for itself was the graves of eight missionaries. The one survivor, Andreas Riis, was in Germany pleading the desperate cause. The attempt was next made to continue through Negroes from the West Indies who would come as colonists. This, too, proved disappointing. However, Riis returned to Africa, additional whites reinforced the staff, and some of the new-comers proved more than equal to the climate and had long terms of service. The Bible was translated into at least two of the tongues. The mission developed plantations of coffee and tobacco, brought in new fruits, and trained artisans. It maintained a trading company partly to eliminate, if possible, the firms which were introducing liquor and gunpowder. New stations were opened. Physicians fought disease. A system of schools was gradually created and a native staff was nurtured for the Church. Cocoa was introduced. Its cultivation spread widely and led to a rapid increase in wealth which was not

[756] *Gold Coast* (London, H. M. Stationery Office, 1920, pp. 66), *passim.*
[757] Müller, *200 Jahre Brüdermission*, Vol. 1, pp. 164-170.
[758] Pascoe, *Classified Digest of the Records of the Society for the Propagation of the Gospel in Foreign Parts*, pp. 254-258.
[759] Richter, *Geschichte der evangelischen Mission in Afrika*, p. 96.

an unmixed blessing. In 1913, 24,374 Christians were connected with the Basel Mission.[760]

To the Basel Mission were added, beginning in 1834, the Wesleyans. They came as the outgrowth of grants of Bibles to school-boys in the British Cape Coast Castle by the British and Foreign Bible Society which had created a desire to know more of the Christian faith. As was all too often the experience in the pioneer days of missions in equatorial Africa, the initial Wesleyan appointees were quickly stricken. It was Thomas Birch Freeman who first had a long period of service and who laid the foundations for a continuing enterprise. By his courtesy, friendliness, and respect for the chiefs, Freeman won the confidence of the Africans. Utilizing his gardener's training, he created a model farm and introduced coffee, cinnamon, ginger, mangoes, and olives. Between 1834 and 1844 there was a striking numerical advance. Natives, especially Fanti, had a prominent part in spreading the faith. From this popularity something of a reaction occurred. However, a recovery was made and growth was resumed.[761] In 1912 the Wesleyans claimed 16,300 Christians.[762] They, too, had schools and began a native pastorate. They created a Christian literature. In contrast with the Basel Mission, which was strong in the eastern part of the colony, the Wesleyans had their largest growth in the central and western sections.[763]

In 1898 what remained a small undertaking, the Baptist Church and Mission, was inaugurated by a Negro clergyman.[764] In 1898 the African Methodist

[760] Richter, op. cit., pp. 96-107; Schlatter, Geschichte der Basler Mission, Vol. III, pp. 19-195; P. Steiner, Im Heim des afrikanischen Bauern. Skizzen aus der Basler Mission im Buschland (Basel, Missionsbuchhandlung, 1903, pp. 113), passim; Dark and Stormy Days at Kumassi, 1900; or Missionary Experience in Ashanti, According to the Diary of Rev. Fritz Ramseyer (London, S. W. Partridge & Co., 1901, pp. 240), passim; Missionar J. G. Christaller, Erinnerungen aus seinem Leben (Stuttgart, Evang. Missionsverlag, 1929, pp. 64), passim; Ramseyer and Kühne, Four Years in Ashantee (New York, Robert Carter and Brothers, 1875, pp. xv, 320); Henri Perregaux, Edmond Perregaux, Missionnaire, d'après sa Correspondence 1868-1905 (Neuchâtel, Delachaux & Niestlé, 1906, pp. 282), passim; C. Stromberg, Minnen och Bilder från Guldkusten (Lund, Berlingska Boktryckeri, 1890, pp. 252), passim; R. Fisch in K. W. Braun, Modern Medical Missions (Burlington, Lutheran Literary Board, 1932, pp. 176), pp. 19-29.

[761] Findlay and Holdsworth, The History of the Wesleyan Methodist Missionary Society, Vol. IV, pp. 151ff.; Walker, Thomas Birch Freeman, pp. 35ff.; Milum, Thomas Birch Freeman, pp. 31ff.; Arthur E. Southon, Gold Coast Methodism (London, The Cargate Press, 1934, pp. 158), passim; Thomas West, The Life and Journals of the Rev. Daniel West (London, Hamilton, Adams, and Co., 1857, pp. viii, 287), pp. 123ff.; Dennes Kemp, Nine Years at the Gold Coast (London, Macmillan and Co., 1898, pp. xv, 279), passim; Thomas B. Freeman, Journal of Two Visits to the Kingdom of Ashanti (London, John Mason, 1843, pp. viii, 196), passim.

[762] Cooksey and McLeish, Religion and Civilization in West Africa, p. 138.

[763] Cooksey and McLeish, op. cit., p. 145.

[764] The Baptist Church and Mission and the Christian Army of the Gold Coast. Year-Book and Report (London, George Tucker, 1913, pp. 127), passim.

Episcopal Zion Church, of American Negro origin, entered.[765] About four years later the Society for the Propagation of the Gospel in Foreign Parts once more began operations in the region.[766] In 1914 it had 3,890 baptized Christians in the colony.[767] Not far from the year 1914 the Seventh Day Adventists came.[768]

Although in 1841 a priest, presumably a secular, seems to have given some care to the nominal Roman Catholics along the coast, continuous efforts to revive Roman Catholic Christianity were not made until the 1880's. In 1879 the region was entrusted to the Society of African Missions, and in 1881 a centre was opened. A church building dating from Portuguese times was re-occupied.[769] In 1913 there were said to be 10,797 Roman Catholics in the colony.[770]

The Ivory Coast, immediately to the west of the Gold Coast, although with a population not far from the size of that of the latter, need detain us but a moment, for by the year 1914 Christianity had made much less progress in it than in its neighbours to the east and west. The Ivory Coast was a French possession. French control dated from the 1780's, but during much of the nineteenth century it had not been pressed and at one period seemed about to be transferred to Great Britain. In the 1880's, however, it was revived and strengthened.[771]

The active propagation of Christianity appears not to have begun on an extensive scale, if at all, until the 1890's. In 1895 the region was assigned by Rome to the Society of African Missions (the Lyons Seminary). In its first three years in the colony the society lost ten of its staff by death, but in 1901, so undauntedly did it persist, it had six stations. As French authority was extended inland, the missionaries pressed into the interior. In spite of the anticlerical policy of the government, schools were developed. A printing establishment was opened. A steamer, named, appropriately, from the Roman Catholic apostle to Negro slaves, *Peter Claver,* plied between the stations on the coast.[772] In 1913 there were said to be about 2,400 native Christians.[773]

[765] Cameron-Chesterfield Alleyne, *Gold Coast at a Glance* (New York, The Hunt Publishing Co., 1931, pp. 143), pp. 100-119; Cooksey and McLeish, *op. cit.,* p. 141.
[766] *Report of the year 1904 of the Society for the Propagation of the Gospel in Foreign Parts,* p. 176.
[767] *Report of the year 1914 of the Society for the Propagation of the Gospel in Foreign Parts,* p. 224.
[768] Cooksey and McLeish, *op. cit.,* p. 143.
[769] Schwager, *Die katholische Heidenmission der Gegenwart,* pp. 95, 96.
[770] Streit, *Atlas Hierarchicus,* p. 101.
[771] *Ivory Coast* (London, H. M. Stationery Office, 1920, pp. 39), pp. 1-9.
[772] Schwager, *op. cit.,* pp. 94, 95.
[773] Streit, *op. cit.,* p. 101.

Protestantism was late in appearing in this French domain. However, in 1913 there began an amazing mass movement under indigenous leadership which after 1914 was to bring tens of thousands into the Christian faith here and on the Gold Coast. It was one of several somewhat similar phenomena in Africa after 1914 led by men who were sometimes denominated prophets and who owed at least part of their impulse to contact with Christianity. The Ivory Coast prophet was William Wadé Harris. Harris was from the adjoining Liberia, from the vicinity of Cape Palmas, not far from the western border of the Ivory Coast. There he had come to the Christian faith through a spiritual succession which owed much to the Protestant Episcopal mission. About the year 1913 he began preaching on the Ivory Coast. This he did quite on his own initiative and without any backing by a white man's organization. He believed himself called of God. He went clad in a white robe and wearing and carrying a cross. He demanded the destruction of fetishes and all other symbols of paganism, and taught a belief in one God, the observance of Sunday, and the prohibition of adultery. He baptized his converts. He wanted no money, but encouraged his followers to build churches and to hope and pray for missionaries who would teach them more fully the way of God.[774] Since the Harris movement had its chief fruition after 1914, we must wait until our last volume to tell of its spread and its outcome. We shall then find it a very striking phenomenon.

Liberia, west of the Ivory Coast, was deeply indebted to Christianity. As a political entity it was the child of the American Colonization Society which, as we saw in the last volume,[775] was sprung largely from the Christian impulse. In the course of the nineteenth century, chiefly between 1820 and 1860, several thousand Negroes from the United States were planted in a number of colonies along the coast. The hope had been to solve the problem of slavery and the related tension between the races by removing the Negro to the continent of his ancestors. Some, moreover, dreamed of using the footholds thus acquired to bring the Christian message to Africa.

From the beginning, some of the more earnest Christians of the United States were deeply interested in the project. Samuel J. Mills, outstanding in the inauguration of foreign missions from that country, died while on an expedition to seek sites for colonization. Ashmun, prominent in the early stages of

[774] W. J. Platt, *An African Prophet* (London, Student Christian Movement Press, 1934, pp. 157), pp. 40-65; William J. Platt, *From Fetish to Faith* (London, Edinburgh House Press, 1935, pp. 159), pp. 78-88.

[775] Vol. IV, pp. 344, 345.

the settlement, had been a home missionary and had once planned to be a foreign missionary.[776]

When Liberia was being founded, Protestantism was much more influential in the United States than Roman Catholicism. Most of the Negro colonists, so far as they had ecclesiastical affiliations, were Protestants. Protestant missions, therefore, were much more active than Roman Catholic missions. Some of them were from the white and some from the Negro churches. They were chiefly to the Negroes from the United States, their descendants, and the relatively small proportion of the population which conformed to the imported culture. However, they were also in part to the aborigines who constituted the large majority of the population.

The Negroes, Lott Carey and Colin Teague, who went to Liberia in 1821, began the Baptist enterprise.[777] In 1846, not long after its formation, the Foreign Mission Board of the Southern Baptist Convention appointed missionaries to Liberia. A decade later the American Baptist Missionary Union, now the organ of the Northern Baptists, transferred to the southern board the undertaking which it had developed before the separation. With the Civil War in the United States, support from American white Baptists lapsed. The churches which had been founded continued, but in the 1870's the decision was made to concentrate on the Yoruba country and to close the Liberia mission.[778] However, the Lott Carey Baptist Foreign Mission Society[779] and the Foreign Mission Board of the National Baptist Convention,[780] both supported by Negroes in the United States, maintained connexions in Liberia. The churches in Liberia calling themselves Baptist were said to outnumber those of any other denomination.[781]

In 1827, in response to a general appeal by Ashmun for missionaries, the Basel Mission designated representatives to Liberia. In 1832, however, the project was discontinued.[782]

[776] Ralph Randolph Gurley, *Life of Jehudi Ashmun, Late Colonial Agent in Liberia* (Washington, James C. Dunn, 1835, pp. 396, 160), *passim*.

[777] Miles Mark Fisher, in *The Journal of Negro History*, Vol. VII, pp. 380-418.

[778] Mary Emily Wright, *The Missionary Work of the Southern Baptist Convention* (Philadelphia, American Baptist Publication Society, 1902, pp. xix, 412), pp. 143-152; T. J. Bowen, *Central Africa. Adventures and Missionary Labors in Several Countries in the Interior of Africa, from 1849 to 1856* (New York, Sheldon, Blakeman and Co., 1857, pp. 359), pp. 27-82; R. B. Medbery, *Memoir of William G. Crocker* (Boston, Gould, Kendall & Lincoln, 1848, pp. 300), *passim*.

[779] *Annual Report of the Corresponding Secretary of the Lott Carey Baptist Foreign Mission Society, 1922-1923*.

[780] *The Fifty-first Annual Report of the Foreign Mission Board of the National Baptist Convention, 1931*, p. 6.

[781] *Ibid.*

[782] Schlatter, *Geschichte der Basler Mission*, Vol. III, pp. 9-16.

In 1833 there arrived in Liberia Melville B. Cox, the first foreign missionary sent to any land by the Methodist Episcopal Church. The following year the Liberian Annual Conference was organized. From time to time reinforcements were despatched. Negroes were appointed bishops. For a period in the second half of the century the mission was at a low ebb, but William Taylor, while Bishop for Africa, revived it, and his successor, Hartzell, strengthened it. Within the Methodist purview were not only the immigrant Negroes but also the aborigines.[783] Negroes from the United States as well as whites were on the staff.[784] Two of the large American Negro Methodist bodies, the African Methodist Episcopal Church[785] and the African Methodist Episcopal Zion Church, notably the former, found fields in Liberia.[786]

It was to Liberia, too, that the first agent of an American Presbyterian society to reach a foreign land came in 1833. He was an appointee of the Western Foreign Missionary Society.[787] The enterprise did not prosper. In the 1890's assistance ceased to be given from the United States to the twelve Presbyterian churches then in existence.[788]

In 1833 there arrived, as well, representatives of the American Board of Commissioners for Foreign Missions. There followed the establishment of stations in the vicinity of Cape Palmas. However, within a decade the undertaking was discontinued.[789]

Two of the stations founded by the American Board were turned over to the Protestant Episcopalians, also from the United States. In the 1820's there had been two attempts by the Episcopalians to send missionaries to Liberia, but both of these had miscarried. In 1835 the Episcopalians appointed a Negro who was acting as lay reader in a church of their faith in Monrovia. White

[783] *Annual Report of the Board of Foreign Missions of the Methodist Episcopal Church for the year 1914*, pp. 214-219; *Brown's Abridged Journal, Containing a Brief Account of the Life, Trials and Travels of Geo. S. Brown, Six Years a Missionary in Liberia* (Troy, Prescott & Wilson, 1849, pp. 392), *passim;* Agnes McAllister, *A Lone Woman in Africa* (New York, Hunt & Eaton, pp. 295), *passim;* J. C. Hartzell, *American Methodism in Africa*, in *The Missionary Review of the World*, Vol. XXXII, pp. 565ff.

[784] For an account by one of the Negroes, see Alexander Priestley Camphor, *Missionary Story Sketches. Folk-Lore from Africa* (Cincinnati, Jennings and Graham, 1909, pp. 346), *passim.*

[785] *The Twenty-Fifth Quadrennial Report of the Parent Home and Foreign Missionary Department of the African Methodist Episcopal Church, 1912-1916*, pp. 22-26; *A Century of Missions of the African Methodist Episcopal Church*, p. 151.

[786] *Quadrennial Report, Board of Foreign Missions of the African Methodist Zion Church in America*, 1924, pp. 6-10.

[787] For this society see Vol. IV, p. 88.

[788] E. P. Swift, *A Memoir of the Rev. Joseph W. Barr* (Pittsburgh, R. Patterson, 1833, p. 291), *passim;* Brown, *One Hundred Years*, pp. 205-209.

[789] Strong, *The Story of the American Board*, pp. 124-128.

missionaries followed. Several stations were opened. In 1851 one of the staff, John Payne, was consecrated bishop. He served until 1871. Under his long and able direction the mission prospered. Then followed lean years under a succession of episcopates made brief by disease and death. In 1884, however, a Negro clergyman, Samuel D. Ferguson, was consecrated bishop. During his extended tenure, for he served until 1916, the mission increased in schools and in the development of a native ministry.[790]

The first missionaries to Liberia of the Lutheran Church (General Synod) of the United States arrived in 1860. There followed a slow but solid growth.[791]

Roman Catholics were early in Liberia, but did not attract large numbers. A few were among the initial settlers at Cape Palmas, and the Plenary Council of Baltimore of 1833 wished the Jesuits to take charge. When that plan proved abortive, the Archbishop of Philadelphia sent his Vicar General, Edward Barron, to West Africa on a tour of investigation. Following his visit to Africa, Barron went to Europe. There he interested Libermann, who had an important part in the development of the Holy Ghost Fathers. Barron was appointed Vicar Apostolic of the two Guineas, but did not serve long. Attempts to enter Liberia proved fruitless until 1884, when Holy Ghost Fathers arrived from Sierra Leone. The deadly climate was too much for the staff. In 1903 came Marists, but by 1905 fever had brought their effort to an end. In 1906 the discouraging field was entrusted to the Society of African Missions. By 1914 it had gathered only a handful of followers.[792]

In 1914, in spite of nearly a century of effort, Christianity in Liberia was only a minority movement. The descendants of the immigrants from the United States were professedly Christian, but they were mainly on the coast. The natives who were influenced by them to adopt the imported culture were inclined to be open-minded to the associated religion. Beginnings had been

[790] Mrs. E. F. Hening, *History of the African Mission of the Protestant Episcopal Church in the United States* (New York, Stanford and Swords, 1850, pp. 300), *passim;* Charles Clifton Penick, *Our Mission Work in Africa* (no date or place of publication, pp. 16), *passim; Handbooks of the Missions of the Episcopal Church, No. IV Liberia* (New York, The National Council of the Protestant Episcopal Church, 1924, pp. 122), *passim;* S. H. Tyng, *Memoir of Rev. Erasmus J. P. Messinger* (Philadelphia, American Sunday School Union, 1856, pp. 240), *passim;* George Townshend Fox, *A Memoir of the Rev. C. Colden Hoffman, Missionary to Cape Palmas, West Africa* (London, Seeley, Jackson and Halliday, 1868, pp. xxiii, 365), *passim;* Anna M. Scott, *Day Dawn in Africa; or, Progress of the Prot. Epis. Mission at Cape Palmas, West Africa* (New York, Protestant Episcopal Society for the Promotion of Evangelical Knowledge, 1858, pp. 314), *passim.*

[791] Gertrude Simpson Leonard, *Our Africa Story. An Account of the Work of the Woman's Home and Foreign Mission Society at Muhlenberg Mission, Liberia, Africa, Lutheran Church (General Synod)* (Baltimore, General Literature Committee, no date, pp. 40), *passim.*

[792] Schwager, *Die katholische Heidenmission der Gegenwart*, pp. 85, 92-94.

made among some of the pagan tribes. However, the vast majority of the inhabitants, including practically all those in the *hinterland*, were untouched.

Sierra Leone, north-west of Liberia, as a colony was the prototype of the latter. The Portuguese had frequented it in the days of their might, but had left few if any traces of their Roman Catholic Christianity. In the closing decades of the eighteenth century a settlement was formed near the spacious harbour as a refuge for slaves freed in England and for freedmen from Nova Scotia who were refugees from the Thirteen Colonies during the American War of Independence. English philanthropists, Evangelicals active in the anti-slavery movement and the formation of the Church Missionary Society, were prominent in the founding of Sierra Leone.[793] When, under the impetus given by the reforming Evangelicals, the British took the leadership in suppressing the slave trade, British cruisers brought to Freetown many of those whom they liberated. The population was, accordingly, a mixture of many tribes. Uprooted from its hereditary habitats, it was easily assimilated to the white man's ways, acquired English, and was responsive to missionaries, affiliated, as these were, with the dominant culture. The colony proper remained small in area and in population. The latter never reached 100,000. However, the British extended their authority, notably towards the close of the nineteenth century, in the form of a protectorate over the *hinterland*, peopled by many tribes, mostly pagan, and numbering not far from one and a third millions.[794]

Begun by Evangelicals and not far from the time of the organization of the Church Missionary Society for Africa and the East, it was almost inevitable that the colony of Sierra Leone should early be a mission field of that society and that Anglican Christianity of the Evangelical type should become the dominant faith. It was to Sierra Leone that the first appointees of the Church Missionary Society went (1806).[795] They were Germans, graduates of Jänicke's school in Berlin. In 1797 the London Missionary Society and the Glasgow and Edinburgh Missionary Societies had joined in sending a contingent to West Africa which landed at Sierra Leone, but it had only a brief and unfortunate life.[796] The Church Missionary Society, like the others, did not intend to make the freedmen in Sierra Leone its field, but planned to push inland to uncivi-

---

[793] Hole, *The Early History of the Church Missionary Society*, pp. 16-18.

[794] *Sierra Leone* (London, H. M. Stationery Office, 1920, pp. 58), *passim*; F. A. J. Utting, *The Story of Sierra Leone* (London, Longmans, Green and Co., 1931, pp. viii, 178), *passim*; E. G. Ingham, *Sierra Leone after a Hundred Years* (London, Seeley and Co., 1894, pp. xi, 368), *passim*.

[795] Stock, *The History of the Church Missionary Society*, Vol. I, pp. 81-86.

[796] Lovett, *The History of the London Missionary Society*, Vol. I, pp. 479, 480.

lized tribes. It was on the Rio Pongo, among the Susu, that the initial stations were opened.[797] The Rio Pongo enterprise proved disappointing and was eventually abandoned.

Not long after the year 1815 the settlements of freedmen in Sierra Leone became a field of the Church Missionary Society. The government divided them into parishes and subsidized ministers and schoolmasters.[798] Famous among the early missionaries was the German, William Augustine Bernard Johnson, who came to the colony in 1816 and died in 1823. Under him a remarkable mass movement to Christianity was witnessed.[799] The society hoped to make the church in Sierra Leone self-supporting and served by its own clergymen. Partly to this end it maintained schools, among them Fourah Bay College. It also pressed for the founding of a bishopric. The first Bishop of Sierra Leone, Owen Emeric Vidal, was consecrated in 1852, but died in 1854. His successor, John William Weeks, had less than two years in the post before death supervened.[800] The third bishop, the greatly loved John Bowen, had also not served two years when an African fever claimed him.[801] However, some of the later bishops had much longer tenures of office.[802] Gradually native clergymen were trained and ordained. What was termed the Sierra Leone Pastorate Church came into being under its own ministers. The society eventually discontinued white clergy and financial assistance except in the schools. In 1875 the government withdrew its subsidies.[803] The society pushed on into the interior[804] but found its chief field in the Yoruba country and the Niger Valley. The native church organized a missionary society for the purpose of reaching some of the tribes on the mainland.[805] The overwhelming majority

[797] Stock, op. cit., Vol. I, p. 157.

[798] Stock, op. cit., Vol. I, pp. 156-163; Henry Seddall, The Missionary History of Sierra Leone (London, Hatchards, 1874, pp. ix, 246), pp. 77-106.

[799] Stephen H. Tyng, A Memoir of the Rev. W. A. B. Johnson (New York, Robert Carter & Brothers, 1853, pp. 385), passim; [Maria Louisa Charlesworth], Africa's Mountain Valley; or the Church in Regent's Town, West Africa (London, Seeley, Jackson, and Halliday, 1856, pp. vi, 272), passim.
On the early history of the mission, see also Samuel Abraham Walker, The Church of England in Sierra Leone (London, Seeley, Burnside, and Seeley, 1846, pp. xlviii, 589), passim.

[800] Stock, op. cit., Vol. II, pp. 100, 121, 122.

[801] Memorials of John Bowen, LL.D., Late Bishop of Sierra Leone. Compiled from His Letters and Journals by His Sister (London, James Nisbet & Co., 1862, pp. x, 633), passim.

[802] E. G. Walmsley, John Walmsley, Ninth Bishop of Sierra Leone: A Memoir for His Friends (London, Society for Promoting Christian Knowledge, 1923, pp. 159), passim; E. L. Langston, Bishop Taylor Smith (London, Marshall, Morgan & Scott, 1939, pp. 288), pp. 48-102; Maurice Whitlow, J. Taylor Smith (London, The Lutterworth Press, 1938, pp. 191), pp. 42-85.

[803] Stock, op. cit., Vol. II, pp. 101, 102, 447, 448.

[804] Stock, op. cit., Vol. II, p. 103.

[805] Stock, op. cit., Vol. III, p. 102.

of the Anglicans were among the English-speaking descendants of the freed-men.

It is not surprising that Sierra Leone attracted the British Wesleyans. The colony was launched in the days of Methodism's youth. John Wesley and Thomas Coke were both interested in it. In 1795 Coke sent to Sierra Leone mechanics and local preachers, hoping that they would become missionaries to the neighbouring tribes. In this he was disappointed. Not until 1811 was a missionary contingent sent of which a good account could be given. Progress was retarded by heavy mortality among the reinforcements, by the gulf which separated the Negro immigrants from the native tribes, and by the continuing influx of newly freed slaves, poverty-stricken and bewildered. Yet growth was registered. Schools were founded. A ministry was trained from among the local members. The congregations became self-supporting. Less and less per-sonnel from the British Isles was needed. Eventually, too, efforts were made to reach the native tribes of the protectorate. Methodism was gaining.[806]

Other forms of Methodism were also represented in Sierra Leone. We hear of the United Methodist Church, of the African Methodist Episcopal Church,[807] and of the Wesleyan Methodist Church, an American organization which in 1889 formed a connexion with an existing congregation in Sierra Leone and before many years reached out to the non-Christian tribes.[808] The Countess of Huntingdon's Connexion was also present.[809]

In the 1840's the American Missionary Association began an enterprise in the Mendi country, in what eventually was the southern part of the protec-torate of Sierra Leone.[810] This had arisen through the return to that area of some Negroes who had been captured by a Spanish slaver, when near Cuba had gained their liberty by taking possession of the ship, had made their way to the United States, and had had their liberty confirmed through a famous appeal to the courts. The friends of the freedmen enabled them to go back to their homes and with them sent missionaries. The American Missionary

---

[806] Findlay and Holdsworth, *The History of the Wesleyan Methodist Missionary Society*, Vol. IV, pp. 73-117; Fox, *A Brief History of the Wesleyan Missions on the Western Coast of Africa*, *passim*.

[807] Cooksey and McLeish, *Religion and Civilization in West Africa*, p. 113; *A Century of Missions of the African Methodist Episcopal Church*, pp. 136ff.

[808] George H. Clarke and Mary Lane Clarke, *American Wesleyan Methodist Missions of Sierra Leone, W. Africa* (Syracuse, Wesleyan Methodist Publishing Association, no date, p. 257), pp. 39ff.

[809] Cooksey and McLeish, *op. cit.*, p. 113.

[810] Beard, *A Crusade of Brotherhood*, pp. 23-48; *Thompson in Africa; or, an Account of the Missionary Labors, Sufferings, Travels, and Observations, of George Thompson, in Western Africa, at the Mendi Mission* (New York, 1854, pp. 356), *passim;* George Thompson, *The Palm Land; or West Africa, Illustrated* (Cincinnati, Moore, Wilstach, Keys & Co., 1858, pp. 456), *passim*.

Association continued the undertaking. Gradually several stations were opened and a number of churches came into being. In 1882 the enterprise was transferred to the United Brethren in Christ. In 1855 that body had inaugurated a mission on Sherbro Island, south of Freetown, not far from the Mendi country.[811] It was, therefore, the logical successor to the American Missionary Association when the latter withdrew. Beginning in the 1880's rapid growth was registered.[812]

In Sierra Leone were also the Society of Friends,[813] the Seventh Day Adventists,[814] and the Christian and Missionary Alliance.[815] The Christian and Missionary Alliance established stations inland with the purpose of penetrating into the upper part of the Niger Valley. This hope was eventually to be fulfilled, but not until after 1914.[816]

Roman Catholic missions were not strong in the overwhelmingly Protestant colony of Sierra Leone. In 1820 a portion of Freetown was a Roman Catholic quarter known as the Portuguese city. In 1844 Barron visited the colony, but the death of his missionaries and his own return to America prevented the founding of a continuing enterprise. The creation of the Vicariate Apostolic of Sierra Leone in 1858 and its assignment to the Society of Africa were made abortive by the early death of the missionary staff. In 1864 the Holy Ghost Fathers took charge of the abandoned mission. Growth was slow and Freetown was long the only centre, but in the 1890's a foothold was acquired on Sherbro Island and in the course of time stations were opened on the mainland.[817] In 1913, 3,250 Roman Catholics were reported.[818]

By 1914 the bulk of the descendants of the Negro immigrants to Sierra Leone were Christians, most of them Protestants, and the faith was making

[811] A. W. Drury, *History of the Church of the United Brethren in Christ* (Dayton, United Brethren Publishing House, rev. ed., 1931, pp. 832), pp. 438, 591, 592; D. K. Flickinger and Wm. McKee, *Missions of the United Brethren in Christ. History of the Origin, Development and Condition of Missions among the Sherbro and Mendi Tribes in Western Africa* (Dayton, United Brethren Publishing House, 1885, pp. 120), *passim;* D. K. Flickinger, *Ethiopia; or, Thirty Years of Missionary Life in Western Africa* (Dayton, United Brethren Publishing House, 1885, pp. 329), *passim.*

[812] J. S. Mills, *Mission Work in Sierra Leone, West Africa* (Dayton, United Brethren Publishing House, 1898, pp. 253), pp. 73ff.; S. S. Hough, *Report of a Visit to Sierra Leone, West Africa* (Dayton, The Foreign Mission Society, United Brethren in Christ, c. 1913, pp. 24), *passim.*

[813] Cooksey and McLeish, *op. cit.,* p. 114.

[814] Cooksey and McLeish, *op. cit.,* p. 115.

[815] *The Seventeenth Annual Report of the Christian and Missionary Alliance . . . 1914,* pp. 20, 32.

[816] R. S. Roseberry, *The Niger Vision* (Harrisburg, Christian Publications, 1934, pp. 254), pp. 35ff.

[817] Schwager, *Die katholische Heidenmission der Gegenwart,* pp. 90-92.

[818] Streit, *Atlas Hierarchicus,* p. 101.

headway among the native tribes on the mainland. Moreover, as we saw a few pages above, some who had found a temporary refuge in Sierra Leone, when returning to their ancestral homes in the Yoruba country had afforded a door of entrance into Nigeria.

What in 1914 was known as French Guinea was north and west of Sierra Leone. The population, not far from 2,000,000 in numbers, was predominantly Moslem by religion, although traces survived of a pre-Islamic paganism. French control was not extended definitively over the region until the second half of the nineteenth century. Indeed, it was not consummated until the 1880's, the period of the partition of Africa.

Aside from some earlier contacts through the Portuguese, Christianity seems first to have entered the country through the Anglicans. As we saw a few paragraphs above, it was here, on the Rio Pongo among the Susu, that the Church Missionary Society had its first agents in Africa. In the second decade of the nineteenth century, after only a few years of effort, the undertaking was given up, largely because of the hostility of the local chiefs.[819] However, in the 1850's Anglicans again appeared, this time from the West Indies. They came from Barbados, some of them trained in Codrington College under the saintly Rawle.[820] The first leader of the mission was H. J. Leacock, a native of Barbados, but of white stock. He and a Negro colleague reached West Africa in 1855.[821] Leacock found a field on the Rio Pongo, but less than a year after his arrival succumbed to one of the African diseases. Reinforcements, chiefly Negroes, arrived, and in 1874 the West Indian bishops made the mission the special foreign responsibility of their church. The enterprise, however, did not enjoy a large growth and the French occupation led it to remove much of its effort to British territory in the adjoining Sierra Leone.[822]

Roman Catholic efforts in French Guinea, like the Protestant ones, began on the Rio Pongo among the Susu. In 1878 the Holy Ghost Fathers, through the opening given by the education in their school in Dakar of sons of one of the families of chiefs, established a station near the mouth of that stream.

[819] Stock, *The History of the Church Missionary Society*, Vol. I, pp. 157-161.

[820] Pascoe, *Two Hundred Years of the S.P.G.*, pp. 260, 261.

[821] Henry Caswell, *The Martyr of the Pongas: being a Memoir of the Rev. Hamble James Leacock* (London, Rivingstons, 1857, pp. xvi, 294), *passim*.

[822] Pascoe, *op. cit.*, pp. 263-267b; A. H. Barrow, *Fifty Years in Western Africa: Being a Record of the Work of the West Indian Church on the Banks of the Rio Pongo* (London, Society for Promoting Christian Knowledge, 1900, pp. 157), *passim;* Mather and Blagg, *Bishop Rawle, a Memoir*, pp. 147ff.

Subsequently additional centres were opened and industrial and plantation schools were begun.[823] By 1913, 5,670 Roman Catholics were reported.[824]

Portuguese Guinea, to the north of French Guinea, was a remnant of holdings acquired in consequence of fifteenth-century explorations under Prince Henry the Navigator. In the second half of the nineteenth century boundaries were defined. The population, estimated to be between 100,000 and 800,000, was made up of a number of tribes, partly Moslem and partly animists.

Ecclesiastically the region belonged to a diocese whose seat was on the Cape Verde Islands. It was divided into a number of parishes whose priests were subsidized by the state. The disestablishment of the church in 1912 was followed by the withdrawal of at least some of the clergy.[825] There seems to have been no Protestant mission.

Gambia was in 1914 a narrow British enclave made up of a colony and a protectorate in the valley of the Gambia River and flanked on both sides by French Senegal. British influence dated from early in the seventeenth century and the colony, with varying boundaries, had been British continuously since 1816. The population, apparently numbering not far from 150,000, was of several tribes, Negroid and Negro, predominantly pagan but with a potent infiltration of Islam.[826]

The first attempts to propagate Christianity in Gambia seem to have been by the Wesleyans. Two Wesleyan missionaries arrived in 1821, while the chief British settlement, Bathurst, was still young. From time to time reinforcements came, but sickness and death depleted the staff and prevented much continuity of service. By 1914 the Christian community numbered only a few hundred.[827]

The Church of England was represented by chaplains. In Bathurst, to which Anglican activity was chiefly confined, the native Christians gave support to a succession of clergymen, but there was no marked growth.[828]

[823] Schwager, op. cit., pp. 89, 90; R. Lerouge, Un fils du Vénérable Libermann: Le Père Arsène Mell (Paris, Editions Spes, 1927, pp. 205), passim.

[824] Streit, op. cit., p. 101.

[825] The Catholic Encyclopedia, Vol. XIII, p. 467.

[826] Gambia (London, H. M. Stationery Office, 1920, pp. 36), pp. 7-13.

[827] Findlay and Holdsworth, The History of the Wesleyan Methodist Missionary Society, Vol. IV, pp. 121-146; John Morgan, Reminiscences of the Founding of a Christian Mission on the Gambia (London, Wesleyan Mission House, 1864, pp. 124), passim; William Fox, A Brief History of the Wesleyan Missions on the Western Coast of Africa (London, Aylott and Jones, 1851, pp. xx, 624), pp. 259ff.

[828] John Laughton, Gambia (London, S.P.G., 1938, pp. 38), pp. 22-25.

Gambia was included in territory assigned by the Holy See to the Holy Ghost Fathers, but Roman Catholic Christianity made only slight headway.[829]

North of Gambia and for a short distance south of it was an extensive French territory, in 1914 part of French West Africa and known as Senegal. French influence along the coast dated from the seventeenth century, but it was in the nineteenth century that the chief French expansion occurred. The population included many of Negro blood. Islam was strong.[830]

Roman Catholic Christianity entered through the French before 1800 and was further developed in the nineteenth century. In the eighteenth century spiritual care was given to the whites in the French posts. In 1765 a prefecture was erected for the two trading centres, St. Louis and Gorée, but apparently without systematic attempts to reach the Negroes. In 1819 the foundress of the Sisters of St. Joseph of Cluny sent nuns to St. Louis and in 1822 accompanied them personally to Gorée. In 1833 came Holy Ghost Fathers. In spite of a heavy death rate among the missionaries, advance was registered. In 1863 the Vicariate Apostolic of Senegambia was created. New centres were opened. A seminary was founded from which by 1902 ten native priests had gone out. A congregation of native sisters was developed. Schools were maintained.[831] In 1913 there were nearly 17,000 native Christians.[832]

Protestant Christianity entered Senegal in 1862. This was through the Société des Missions Évangéliques of Paris. The staff was never large and only a few converts were gathered.[833] We hear, too, of travels through the country of a representative of the National Bible Society of Scotland.[834]

East of Senegal stretched a vast region which was part of the huge empire acquired by France in the nineteenth century between the Mediterranean and the Gulf of Guinea. Politically it was made up of Upper Senegal and Niger. It included part of the Niger Valley and reached to Lake Chad. It bordered the Sahara on the south and embraced part of that desert. The population was

---

[829] Schwager, op. cit., pp. 87, 88.

[830] Senegal (London, H. M. Stationery Office, 1920, pp. 49), pp. 1-12.

[831] Schwager, op. cit., pp. 86-89.

[832] Streit, op. cit., p. 101.

[833] Société des Missions Évangéliques de Paris, Nos Champs de Mission, pp. 23-28; Benjamin Escande, Missionnaire au Sénégal et à Madagascar. Souvenirs Intimes Extraits de Son Journal et de Sa Correspondance (Geneva, J. H. Jeheber, no date, pp. 288), passim.

[834] Campbell, Wanderings in Widest Africa, passim.

a mixture of races, with much of Negro blood. Islam was very strong, conveyed along the trade routes from the northern shores of Africa.

Here and there individual Christians seem to have come in from Mediterranean lands,[835] but the active propagation of the faith appears to have been
undertaken first by the spiritual sons of Lavigerie. In 1868 the region was
assigned by Rome to Lavigerie as Apostolic Delegate. He first brought in the
Jesuits, but in 1872 these were replaced by the White Fathers. The great
pioneer was Hacquard. He had already had experience in the Sahara when, in
the 1890's, he was sent into the region. In 1898 he was consecrated bishop to
be Vicar Apostolic of the Sahara and the Sudan. Stations were opened, among
them one at Timbuktu. In one centre a nucleus was obtained through freed
slaves who were entrusted to the mission. Progress in numbers was slow,
partly because of the difficulties presented by Islam, but in 1913 about 1,300
were said to be Christians.[836]

This completes our geographic survey of the spread of Christianity in the
nineteenth century in Africa south of the Sahara. We must now essay a summary of a chapter which has been so long and so full of necessary details as
at times to be confusing.

The Christianity which spread to Africa in the nineteenth century was
Roman Catholic and Protestant. The Roman Catholic Christianity was chiefly
from France and secondarily from Germany and Belgium, with some slight
assistance from Italy, Portugal, and Spain. The Protestant Christianity was
predominantly from the British Isles, but substantial missions came from
France, Switzerland, Germany, Scandinavia, the United States, and the white
churches of South Africa. Of the Protestant communions the ones having the
widest extension were the Anglicans, the Methodists, various branches of the
Reformed and Presbyterian churches, and the Lutherans. Through the London
Missionary Society British Congregationalism had an important part, especially in the early stages of the Protestant advance.

The reasons for the spread of Christianity were manifold. The penetration
of Africa and the partition of the continent by the whites were major factors.
Many of the chiefs, more or less vaguely seeing the necessity of their peoples
adapting themselves to the new order brought by the white man, wished
missionaries, not because of the latters' religion but because of material ad-

---

[835] Campbell, *op. cit.*, p. 54.
[836] Eug. Marin, *Mgr. Hacquard des Pères Blancs (1860-1901)* (Paris, Maison de la
Bonne Press, 1919, pp. 109), *passim;* Bouniol, *The White Fathers and Their Missions,*
pp. 148-153; Schwager, *op. cit.*, pp. 106, 107; Streit, *op. cit.*, p. 101.

vantages accruing from the presence of these white emissaries and of a desire for guidance in making the inescapable adjustments. The awakenings in the churches in Europe, Britain, and the United States which were among the outstanding features of the nineteenth century and which, as the century wore on, issued in a vast increase in missionary effort, impelled hundreds to give their lives to carrying the Christian Gospel to Africa. In some missionaries the lure of adventure was undoubtedly an incentive. However, the cost in health and lives was appalling, especially in the pioneer days, and only devotion and faith sprung from profound religious conviction are sufficient to account for the continued offering of men and women for the task.

The processes through which the expansion was accomplished were also varied. Always there was the communication of the tenets of the Christian faith through teaching, preaching, and the printed page. The length of time covered by the period of pre-baptismal instruction differed from group to group. The White Fathers and some of the Protestants had a prolonged catechumenate. Others had a briefer requirement. Nearly always the language was given a written form if none had previously existed. Schools were conducted. Hospitals and dispensaries were maintained. Mass movements towards the Church, sometimes led by the chiefs, were frequent. Now and again financial assistance came from the colonial governments. This was notably the case in Roman Catholic missions in Belgian and Portuguese territories, but in numbers of instances the British also gave subsidies in the form of land or of grants to schools. With some striking exceptions, Protestantism was the prevailing form of Christianity in British possessions and Roman Catholicism in French, Belgian, Portuguese, and Spanish territories. Yet Roman Catholicism was permitted in British lands and was introduced into them all, and in only a few of the areas controlled by predominantly Roman Catholic countries was Protestantism so discriminated against as to make its propagation impossible.

The effects of Christianity were numerous. Clearly one of them was the growth of the Christian communities. This growth was rapidly accelerated as the century went on and was preliminary to an even greater increase after 1914. The reduction of languages to writing, the translation of the Bible[837] and the preparation of other literature, with the coming of the printed page and the development of schools built upon the printed page and the white man's ways, were fairly constant results. The overwhelming majority of the schools for blacks were begun and maintained by missionaries.[838] The white man's

[837] Richter, *Geschichte der evangelischen Mission in Afrika*, pp. 706-711, says that in 1920 the entire Bible had been translated into 22, the New Testament into 36, and parts of the Bible into 92 African languages.

[838] Jones, *Education in East Africa*, pp. 46, 47.

medicine was introduced. Often plantations were developed and new culti-vated trees and plants were brought in.[839]

All this meant that Christianity hastened the disintegration of the native African cultures. In a number of other ways Christianity contributed to that process. Most missionaries prohibited polygamy. Many taught that the existing marriage customs, with their "bride-price," were wrong.[840] Missionaries were especially vigorous against what they deemed sex offenses[841] and for this reason usually opposed the traditional rites by which the young, especially the boys, were initiated into adulthood.[842] In doing so, they dealt a blow to one of the most influential forms of African education. Missionaries aided in introducing a money economy.[843] They fought murder and the ritual killing which some-times attended the burial of prominent people.[844] They opposed witchcraft.[845] They undermined the belief in the activity of the spirits of the ancestors and of the tribal gods which was part of the cement of the old life.[846] Missionaries were among the most prominent of the white explorers and nearly always were among the pioneers of the white man's culture. Sometimes they de-signedly hastened the annexation of a particular region by a European power.

Yet it must be remembered that had never a missionary come to Africa the penetration of the continent by the white man would have taken place in the nineteenth century, and the dissolution of the inherited cultures would have occurred and probably at not far from the same pace which was actually witnessed. The commercial and political expansion of European peoples would have brought this about.

While the missionary assisted in the disintegration, he led in the constructive adaptation of the African to the new culture. Most of the instruments which he employed which contributed to the disappearance of the old also had posi-tive value in helping to build a better life. The missionary fought the exploita-tion of the African by the white man. He opposed the introduction of liquor. Especially did he contend against slavery and the slave traffic. It was the Chris-tian conscience which was primarily responsible for abolishing the trans-

---

[839] Livingstone, *A Prince of Missionaries*, p. 99; Berg, *Die katholische Heidenmission als Kulturträger*, Vol. I, pp. 302, 318.

[840] On the varying attitudes of missions towards marriage, see J. K. Macgregor in *The International Review of Missions*, Vol. XXIV, pp. 379-391; Berg, *op. cit.*, Vol. I, p. 239; Schapera, *Western Civilization and the Natives of South Africa*, pp. 70, 71.

[841] Livingstone, *op. cit.*, p. 46.

[842] Ward, *Father Woodward*, p. 20.

[843] Fraser, *Donald Fraser*, pp. 127, 128.

[844] Hemmens, *George Grenfell*, p. 138; Hetherwick, *The Gospel and the African*, p. 53; Berg, *op. cit.*, Vol. I, p. 231.

[845] Hetherwick, *op. cit.*, p. 81.

[846] Schapera, *op. cit.*, pp. 67-69.

oceanic slave trade and Negro slavery in the Americas. It also set itself against the slave trade and slavery in Africa, in the main successfully. For decades the campaign was waged almost exclusively by Protestants. Much later in the nineteenth century, after it was largely won, the Roman Catholics joined in it. Lavigerie was an outstanding leader in the struggle.[847] Some missionaries, foreseeing the demoralization which would ensue, opposed the recruiting of labour, even though free, for the great mining centres.[848]

While these rather obvious effects of Christianity are being noted, others, no less real but more difficult to determine, might easily escape us. They are qualities of life which at the outset of Christianity Paul declared to be the characteristic fruits of the faith—love, joy, peace, longsuffering, kindness, goodness, faithfulness, meekness, self-control. That as a result of the coming of Christianity these emerged in the lives of thousands of Africans, or, where they already existed, were strengthened, is clear. That they were of major importance must also be obvious. However, they defy accurate measurement. We can know only of their presence.

As between the two great wings of Christianity which were most active in spreading the faith, Protestantism and Roman Catholicism, some differences in effect were seen. In general, the Roman Catholic black was more docile, more dependent on the white man, and more submissive to him. The Protestant black was inclined to be more independent, to think for himself, and to be more self-reliant. The Roman Catholic regarded the Protestant attitude as breeding rampant individualism, vagaries, and rebellions. The Protestant adjudged the Roman Catholic methods to be producing automata, to be cramping the rightful development of human life, and to be making for a continuation of servitude, even though in a mild and benevolent form.

By the year 1914 the African environment was producing some change in the transplanted Christianity. This was true among the white Dutch churches of South Africa. Probably in part because these bodies were a bulwark of the Boers against the encroaching British, they were conservative. It was certain that the blacks, with their radically different background,[849] would make alterations in the faith which the white man had transmitted to them. However, in 1914 Christianity was, in general, so largely a recent importation that the black had not as yet made many obvious changes in it. These were to appear more rapidly after 1914 and especially, as might have been expected

[847] Richard F. Clarke, editor, *Cardinal Lavigerie and the African Slave Trade* (London, Longmans, Green and Co., 1889, pp. viii, 379), *passim*. See also on Roman Catholic opposition to slavery, Berg, *op. cit.*, Vol. I, pp. 247, 248, 289.

[848] Livingstone, *op. cit.*, pp. 105-108.

[849] Hetherwick, *The Gospel and the African*, pp. 2-5.

from what was said in the preceding paragraph, in Protestant ranks. To be sure, in South Africa a number of independent movements were beginning to emerge.[850] Moreover, the African mind placed its own interpretation upon what the missionary taught and the latter sometimes discerned a lack of comprehension of what he was trying to say.[851] The African, too, was inclined to carry over his old conceptions of the, to him, novel ecclesiastical polity.[852] Here and there a missionary was seeking to adapt European practices to African ways.[853] Yet, in the main, the effects of the environment were to become much more marked after 1914. We must wait until our last volume to record them.

In the year 1914 Christianity, like the white man's culture with which it was so closely associated, was making rapid strides in Africa. In most sections it was still a recent arrival, but it was growing rapidly and already was having marked effects. It was bringing a new life and was modifying in important and, in general, thoroughly wholesome and beneficent ways the impact of the European upon the African.

[850] *Union of South Africa. Report of Native Churches Commission, passim;* Shepherd, *Lovedale,* pp. 245, 246; Lee, *Charles Johnson of Zululand,* p. 184; Moreira, *Portuguese West Africa,* pp. 31-33.
[851] Fraser, *Donald Fraser,* p. 53.
[852] Laws, *Reminiscences of Livingstonia,* p. 137.
[853] Fraser, *op. cit.,* p. 89; Laws, *op. cit.,* p. 143; Lewis, *These Seventy Years,* p. 122.

Chapter XII

BY WAY OF BRIEF SUMMARY AND ANTICIPATION

TO ONE who has had the patience to read them from beginning to end or even to skim through them, the preceding chapters may well seem a jumbled mass of detail. Even if, as a preliminary to the others, he has perused the introductory chapter and so has acquired a kind of *vade-mecum* through the maze, the reader may end with a sense of bewildered weariness. So many and varied have been the areas covered that at times it seems hard to detect the common features through which they were inter-related. So numerous were the individuals and the enterprises by which Christianity was spread that even the incomplete summary contained in this volume has had to be condensed in such rigorous fashion that it gives the appearance of a *staccato* catalogue of names and events.

However, a unity exists, even though not always apparent. As we said at the outset, in this volume and in the portions of its predecessor which dealt with the United States of America we have had to do with the impact of European peoples and of the accompanying Christianity upon folk of primitive cultures. Except in portions of Latin America and of the East Indies, before the advent of the white man those with whom these chapters have been concerned were in various stages of what is usually described as primitive life. That does not mean that these cultures were unaltered survivals of what mankind had known in its childhood. They might be very old. Yet they were probably nearer to the ways of primeval mankind than the advanced civilizations of North Africa and Asia. Unlike the latter, they were unable to present a prolonged resistance to what was brought by the white man but rapidly disintegrated before it. In areas fitted by climate for extensive white populations, notably the United States, Canada, portions of Latin America, Australia, New Zealand, and South Africa, the white man through immigration and rapid reproduction brought into being new communities of European blood and culture. The primitive folk survived only as minorities. In regions which the white man found less salubrious, the non-whites remained in the majority. Under the initial force of the impact their numbers usually declined and their cultures went to pieces. As a rule, after the first shock of the contact passed, their numbers tended to recover and even to mount. However, the old cultures had gone, presumably forever, and, instead, the white man's civilization was copied, albeit imperfectly.

The impingement of Europeans upon primitive peoples had begun long before the nineteenth century. As we saw in our third volume, it had proceeded very far in the sixteenth, seventeenth, and eighteenth centuries, particularly in the Americas and the Philippines. However, in the nineteenth century it was renewed and accelerated and extended over a much wider area.

Christianity was in part the cause of this expansion of European peoples. Precisely how far it was the cause is not clear. Obviously the Christian missionary was at times a pioneer of the white man's penetration. Sometimes, most spectacularly in Livingstone in Africa, he was the initial explorer who blazed the trails. Occasionally, as in Uganda, he urged annexation·by a European government and was at least partially responsible for the political complexion of the white man's rule. However, the missionary was never the sole impulse in the coming of the white man. The economic and political forces at work among European peoples would have brought it had never a missionary embarked upon his task. At most the missionary only slightly hastened the white man's advance and that merely in particular areas.

What is less clear is the part of Christianity in giving rise to the implements and the inner urge through which European peoples became the masters of the nineteenth-century world. That to some degree the Christian faith which they professed made European peoples the authors of modern science and the creators of the machines which revolutionized the life of mankind seems fairly certain. That it also was a factor in sending many Europeans upon their voyages of adventure and settlement is apparent. What we do not know is whether but for Christianity science, the machine, and the white man's geographic progress would not have been.

However, it is indisputable that Christianity was an important element in the new nations of European blood which arose from the expansion of European peoples and that it modified profoundly the impact of Europeans upon non-Europeans.

In the preceding volume we saw the important and growing place which Christianity had in the life and culture of the United States. The course of Christianity in the United States was in large degree paralleled by the rôle of the faith in the new nations which arose in the nineteenth century under the British flag in Canada, Australia, New Zealand, and South Africa. Here, as in the United States, Christianity was successfully transplanted. With decreasing aid in funds and personnel from the churches of the mother country, and except in the early years with no financial assistance from the state, a healthy ecclesiastical structure came into being. Support and leadership were chiefly from the colonists and their descendants. The overwhelming majority of the population professed some kind of affiliation with one or another of the churches. As in the United States, although not to the same degree as there, Christianity was varied and complex. The effect upon the moral standards of the population, impossible to measure accurately, was clearly great. Family life was moulded. The trend towards democracy, with its emphasis upon the rights and responsibilities of the individual, was strengthened. Education was fostered, especially in its beginnings and in its more advanced forms. Millions had their eyes lifted, even if only for brief moments and imperfectly, to a horizon of life which was infinitely broader than food, clothing, and physical comforts.

In Latin America the course was somewhat different. Here in the new nations which came into being in the nineteenth century under a leadership which was predominantly white, the Roman Catholic Christianity introduced in the preceding period was sadly weakened by the upheavals which ushered in the century. Largely because of the fashion in which it had been transplanted, that Christianity was dependent on a continuing stream of fresh blood from Europe. For a time the revolutions which brought political independence interrupted that stream. They also disturbed the existing intimate ties between Church and state. The attempts of the new governments to achieve the kind of control over the Church which the colonial regime had exercised gave rise to recurring conflicts which were accentuated by an anti-clericalism reinforced by contacts with similar movements in Europe. By the latter part of the nineteenth century recovery was well under way. Roman Catholic missionaries were once more entering from Europe. The violence of the controversies between Church and state had abated. Protestant Christianity had entered, mainly from Great Britain, the United States, and Germany. It was spreading rapidly, particularly in Mexico and Brazil, partly by immigration but mainly through missionaries from the United States. In Latin America Christianity came to the year 1914 on a mounting tide.

Among the primitive folk whom we have met in this volume Christianity was having a growth which was becoming more marked as the century drew towards its close. In several regions, such as Canada, Greenland, the West Indies, and many of the islands of the Pacific, by the year 1914 the overwhelming majority professed to be Christian. In others, mainly parts of the interior of South America, some of the larger islands of the Pacific, Madagascar, and Africa, only a minority had assumed the Christian name. Yet in most of these islands and regions the numbers of Christians were increasing.

The growth of Christianity among primitive peoples was in part because of the desire to ease the strain brought by the coming of the white man by conforming to the ways of the invader. It was also due to the zeal of missionaries. The outpouring of missionary life was amazing. Thousands of missionaries, Roman Catholic and Protestant, went from the white man's churches to the dusky races. In spite of the hardships involved and the heavy toll taken by disease and climate, particularly among the pioneers, the missionary forces mounted. They were not evenly apportioned. For example, although the populations of the two areas were not far from the same size, in 1914 the missionary staff in Africa was more than twice that in Latin America. However, the missionary army touched every land and the large majority of the tribes in the vast extent of territory surveyed in this volume. It gave vivid witness to the enormous vitality not only of the white races but also of the Christian faith in the nineteenth century.

The effect of Christianity upon the primitive folk was, in the main, in the direction of making the conflict in cultures issue in good for the coloured races rather than evil. Usually the introduction of Christianity contributed to the disintegration of the old culture. At times harm followed. In general, however, missionaries fought the exploitation of non-Europeans by non-missionary whites. In this they were supported by the consciences of many of their fellow-countrymen, made sensitive and active by the Christian faith. This, it will be recalled, had also been true in the preceding period and had given birth to humanitarian measures, notably in the Spanish Laws of the Indies. The nineteenth century witnessed the abolition of the African slave trade and slavery, attempts to curb the sale to primitive folk of intoxicating liquors and fire-arms, and movements to help primitive peoples adapt themselves to the new world by creating for them schools after the white man's pattern, teaching them appropriate handicrafts, introducing plants and better methods of agriculture, and applying the new medical skill of the latter part of the nineteenth century to the healing and prevention of disease. Moreover, as the nineteenth century progressed, the attitude crystallized in the phrase "the white man's burden" became increasingly characteristic of empire-builders and colonial administrations. The white man's rule, so this maintained, should be for the benefit of the governed. Much of this varied activity for the well-being of races subject to the white man was directly and clearly traceable to Christianity. Much of it arose from a widespread humanitarianism which was not so demonstrably from Christianity but which seems to have been indebted to it. We must remember, however, that neither Christianity nor nineteenth-century humanitarianism completely prevented the selfish and at times colossal exploita-

tion of non-European by European peoples or fully annulled the suffering
which accompanied the cultural dislocation brought by the impinging white
civilization. Christianity partly allayed the agony and eventually abolished or
reduced some of the more palpable evils. It did not succeed in making the
coming of the white man an unmixed blessing.

So rapid and so recent was the spread of Christianity in most of the areas
covered in this volume that the environment had not fully made itself felt
before the year 1914. However, it had begun to have its effect. The variety and
the predominantly British complexion of the Christianity of Canada, Australia,
and New Zealand arose from the source of the white populations of these
dominions. The prominence in South Africa of the Dutch Reformed Church
was due to the origin of the first white settlers. The trend towards co-operation between the Protestant bodies in Canada was partly the outgrowth of the
frontier, principally that in the West. The predominantly French character of
the Roman Catholic Church in Canada and the leadership of the Irish in
Australian Roman Catholicism were so obviously from the nature of the immigration that to call attention to them seems almost a banality. The conservatism
of the Roman Catholic Church in Canada and of the Dutch Reformed Church
in South Africa was in part to be attributed to the fact that each of these
bodies was a symbol and tie of a group which had once been conquered and
felt itself on the defensive against the dominant British.

As Christianity gained headway among primitive peoples it began to reflect
its new *milieu*. It did this in ways which defy accurate recording. Converts
brought with them preconceptions from their traditional heritage and in the
light of these interpreted their new faith. Yet as a rule they were unconscious
or only semi-conscious of what they were doing. Here and there movements
broke out, partly under the impulse of the new faith and embodying elements
or attitudes from the old. They were to be found in South America, in several
of the islands of the Pacific, including New Zealand and the Philippines, and
in South Africa. Some were attempts to achieve ecclesiastical independence of
the white man. Others were of a messianic character. By the latter, peoples
who deemed themselves oppressed by the white man or by adverse economic
conditions responded to a leader who preached sudden miraculous deliverance.
These movements were to increase after 1914, especially in Africa and the East
Indies.

Never before in a period of equal length had Christianity or any other
religion penetrated for the first time as large an area as it had in the nineteenth century in the regions covered by this volume. In many of the countries,
regions, and islands which we have here surveyed Christianity had been previ-

ously present. In still more, however, it was now freshly introduced. Its course was the more rapid not only because of the religious awakenings in Europe and America which gave to it impulse and renewed vigour but also because it was borne by an extensive migration of professedly Christian peoples and accompanied the impact of a powerful advanced civilization upon primitive cultures which offered brief but inadequate resistance.

In the following volume we are to turn to another phase of our story. We are still to be dealing with the nineteenth century. We are, however, to have to do with the northern and north-eastern shores of Africa and with Asia. Here we shall be in areas in which Christianity had previously been represented. In some of them it had been present continuously for many centuries. In others it had once been present but had dwindled or disappeared. Moreover, here Christianity confronted the rival before which it had suffered its greatest territorial losses, Islam, and from which it had regained far less ground than it had surrendered. It also was faced with ancient civilizations. To be sure, it met as well some peoples of primitive culture. Among several of the latter it registered notable gains. The advanced cultures were more resistant. Although by 1914 they were beginning to crumble under the impact of the Occident, at times spectacularly, their disintegration was not yet nearly so marked as that of the primitive cultures with which the present volume has been so largely concerned. Opposed by the grudgingly yielding front presented by these cultures, Christianity made slower progress than among primitive folk. In 1914 it could point only to small minorities which had arisen from its nineteenth-century missionary activity. However, although its missionary staffs in Asia were larger than those engaged in efforts for non-Europeans recorded in this volume, in proportion to the populations approached they were smaller. Moreover, by the year 1914 Christianity's numerical gains in much of Asia were being greatly accelerated and the effects upon Asiatic cultures were rapidly mounting. In Asia as in the Americas, the Pacific, and Africa the period from 1815 to 1914 was the great century.

BIBLIOGRAPHY

IN THE present volume the same procedure has been followed in compiling the bibliography as in the preceding two. Items have been listed alphabetically by author, or when no author is given, by title. Only those books have been included to which more than one reference has been made in the footnotes. To those mentioned only once the appropriate data of place of publication, date, and number of pages have been given with the citation. This method has considerably shortened the bibliography, for to have included the books used only once would have about doubled the length of the list. A list of titles on any subject covered in the volume may be quickly obtained by turning to the footnotes of the section in which the topic is treated. If a book is used only once in the volume, the pertinent information is with its citation. If it is utilized more than once, the full information can be had from the bibliography.

Annual Reports of the Aborigines' Protection Society (London, 1838ff.).

Agar-Hamilton, J. A. I., *A Transvaal Jubilee. Being A History of the Church of the Province of South Africa in the Transvaal* (London, Society for Promoting Christian Knowledge, 1929, pp. ix, 165). By a teacher of history in the Transvaal. A sympathetic account.

Allen, W. O. B., and McClure, Edmund, *Two Hundred Years: The History of The Society for Promoting Christian Knowledge, 1698-1898* (London, Society for Promoting Christian Knowledge, 1898, pp. vi, 551). The standard history, based upon records, letter-books, reports, and minutes.

Alzona, Encarnacion, *A History of Education in the Philippines 1565-1930* (Manila, University of the Philippines Press, 1932, pp. xi, 390). Fairly scholarly: based upon a variety of printed sources.

Amelunxen, C. P., *De Geschiedenis van Curaçao* (no place or date of publication. Preface 1929, pp. 227).

Annual Reports of the American Bible Society (New York, 1838ff.).

Anderson, James S. M., *The History of the Church of England in the Colonies and Foreign Dependencies of the British Empire* (London, Rivingtons, 2d ed., 3 vols., 1856).

Anderson, Rufus, *The Hawaiian Islands: their Progress and Condition under Missionary Labors* (Boston, Gould and Lincoln, 1865, pp. 450). By a secretary of the American Board of Commissioners for Foreign Missions.

Anderson, Rufus, *History of the Sandwich Islands Mission* (Boston, Congregational Publishing Co., 1870, pp. xxiv, 408).

Anderson, W. H., *On the Trail of Livingstone* (Mountain View, Cal., Pacific Press

Publishing Association, 1919, pp. 351). Largely an autobiographical narrative of the experiences of early Seventh Day Adventist missionaries.

Anderson-Morshead, A. E. M., *A Pioneer and Founder. Reminiscences of Some who Knew Robert Gray, D.D., First Bishop of Cape Town and Metropolitan of South Africa. With Preface by the Right Rev. Allan B. Webb, D.D., Dean of Salisbury* (London, Skeffington & Son, 1905, pp. xxiii, 268). By a woman who knew him.

Anderson-Morshead, A. E. M., *The History of the Universities' Mission to Central Africa 1859-1909* (London, Universities' Mission to Central Africa, revised ed., 1909, pp. xxix, 448).

Andrews, C. F., *John White of Mashonaland* (New York, Harper and Brothers, 1935, pp. viii, 205).

Annales de l'Association de la Propagation de la Foi (Lyon, 1837ff.).

Anuario Católico Argentino 1933. Publicacion de la Junta Nacional de la Accion Catolica Argentina (Buenos Aires, 1933, pp. 737).

Arms, Goodsil F., *History of the William Taylor Self-Supporting Missions in South America* (New York, The Methodist Book Concern, 1921, pp. 263). Based upon manuscript and printed sources by one long a member of the missions.

Armstrong, E. S., *The History of the Melanesian Mission* (New York, E. P. Dutton & Co., 1900, pp. xxviii, 372). Based upon personal knowledge and printed and manuscript sources.

Arnot, Fred. S., *Bihé and Garenganze; or, Four Years' Further Work and Travel in Central Africa* (London, J. E. Hawkins & Co., 1893, pp. viii, 150).

Arnot, F. S., *Missionary Travels in Central Africa* (London, Alfred Holness, 1914, pp. xix, 159).

Asia (New York, 1901ff.). A monthly magazine for a popular constituency.

Attwater, Donald, *The Catholic Eastern Churches* (Milwaukee, Wis., The Bruce Publishing Co., 1935, pp. xx, 308). By a Roman Catholic. Contains excellent bibliographies.

Attwater, Donald, *The White Fathers in Africa* (London, Burns, Oates & Washbourne, 1937, pp. xii, 116). A semi-popular account.

Australasian Catholic Directory for 1907. Containing the Ordo Divini Officii, the Fullest Ecclesiastical Information and an Alphabetical List of the Clergy of Australasia (Sydney, F. Cunninghame & Co., pp. lii, 241).

Australasian Catholic Directory for 1910 . . . (Sydney, William Brook & Co., pp. liv, 244).

Australasian Catholic Directory for 1921 . . . (Sydney, William Brook & Co., pp. lxxxviii, 304).

Australasian Catholic Directory for 1929 (Sydney, St. Mary's Cathedral, pp. lxxi, 412).

The Australian Encyclopædia (Sydney, Angus & Robertson, 2 vols., 1925, 1926).

The Autobiography of a Wesleyan Methodist Missionary (Formerly a Roman Catholic) (Montreal, E. Pickup, 1856, pp. 407).

Ayarragaray, Lucas, *La Iglesia en América y la Dominación Española. Estudio de la Época Colonial* (Buenos Aires, J. Lajouane & Cia, 1920, pp. 321). In addition to narrative, the book contains a number of documents.

Backhouse, James, *A Narrative of a Visit to the Australian Colonies* (London, Hamilton, Adams and Co., 1843, pp. xviii, 560, cxliv).

Baker, Archibald G., *Christian Missions and a New World Culture* (Chicago, Willett, Clark & Co., 1934, pp. xiii, 322). An interpretation of modern missions by a liberal expert.

Baker, Ernest, *The Life and Explorations of Frederick Stanley Arnot* (London, Seeley, Service & Co., 1921, pp. 334). Made up largely of Arnot's own journals, letters, and other writings.

Balangero, Gio. Battista, *Australia e Ceylan. Studi e Ricordi di tredici anni di Missione* (Turin, G. B. Paravia e Comp., 1897, pp. xiv, 386). A kind of missionary autobiography.

Balfour, R. Gordon, *Presbyterianism in the Colonies with Special Reference to the Principles and Influence of the Free Church of Scotland* (Edinburgh, Macniven & Wallace, 1899, pp. xi, 341). The author was convenor of the Free Church Colonial Committee from 1874 to 1881. Based upon various printed sources and secondary accounts. Very few exact references to sources.

The Baptist Missionary Society Annual Reports (Earlier numbers called *Periodical Accounts*) (London, 1793ff.).

Baring-Gould, S., and Bampfylde, C. A., *A History of Sarawak under the Two White Rajahs 1839-1908* (London, Henry Sotheran & Co., 1909, pp. xxiii, 464).

Barnes, Bertram Herbert, *Johnson of Nyasaland. A Study of the Life and Work of William Percival Johnson, D.D., Archdeacon of Nyasa, Missionary Pioneer 1876-1928* (Westminster, Universities' Mission to Central Africa, 1933, pp. 258). By a colleague.

Barrows, David P., *History of the Philippines* (London, George G. Harrap & Co., revised ed., 1924, pp. v, 406).

Baynes, A. Hamilton, *Handbooks of English Church Expansion. South Africa* (London, A. R. Mowbray & Co., 1908, pp. xv, 219). By a former Bishop of Natal.

Beach, Harlan P., and St. John, Burton, editors, *World Statistics of Christian Missions* (New York, The Committee of Reference and Counsel of the Foreign Missions Conference of North America, 1916, pp. 148). Authoritative.

Beard, Augustus Field, *A Crusade of Brotherhood. A History of the American Missionary Association* (Boston, The Pilgrim Press, 1909, pp. xii, 334). The author was a secretary of the American Missionary Association.

Beets, Henry, *Toiling and Trusting. Fifty Years of Mission Work of the Christian Reformed Church among Indians and Chinese with chapters on Nigeria and South America* (Grand Rapids, Grand Rapids Printing Co., 1940, pp. 325). By a director of missions.

Belgian Congo (London, H. M. Stationery Office, 1920, pp. 135).

Bennett, Wendell C., and Zingg, Robert M., *The Tarahumara. An Indian Tribe of Northern Mexico* (The University of Chicago Press, 1935, pp. xix, 412). An objective study of contemporary culture based upon residence and careful investigation.

Berg, Ludwig, *Die katholischen Heidenmission als Kulturträger* (Second edition, Aachen, Aachener Missionsdruckerei, 3 vols., 1927). Carefully supported by references to authorities, which as a rule are standard German experts and missionary periodicals. Warmly pro-Roman Catholic and critical of Protestants.

Berry, L. L., *A Century of Missions of the African Methodist Episcopal Church 1840-1940* (New York, Gutenberg Printing Co., 1942, pp. 333). An official history.

Bickford, James, *An Autobiography of Christian Labour in the West Indies, Demerara, Victoria, New South Wales, and South Australia, 1838-1888* (London, Charles H. Kelly, 1890, pp. viii, 446).

Bickford, James, *Christian Work in Australasia: with Notes on the Settlement and Progress of the Colonies* (London, Wesleyan Conference Office, 1878, pp. vii, 344). By a Methodist missionary to Australia. Written for a popular audience.

Bill, I. E., *Fifty Years with the Baptist Ministers and Churches of the Maritime Provinces* (Saint John, N. B., Barnes & Co., 1880, pp. 778). By one who had a part in much of what he narrates. Contains many documents and summaries of documents.

Bingham, Hiram, *A Residence of Twenty-one Years in the Sandwich Islands; or the Civil, Religious, and Political History of those Islands* (Hartford, Hezekiah Huntington, 2d ed., 1848, pp. 616). By a missionary to the islands.

Birkeli, Emil, *Fra tamarinderes land* (Stavanger, Det Norske missionsselskaps forlag, 1913, pp. viii, 236). A mission study textbook.

Birt, Henry Norbert, *Benedictine Pioneers in Australia* (London, Herbert & Daniel, 2 vols., 1911).

Blackman, William Fremont, *The Making of Hawaii. A Study in Social Evolution* (New York, The Macmillan Co., 1899, pp. xii, 266).

Blair, Emma Helen, and Robertson, James Alexander, *The Philippine Islands 1493-1803. Explorations of Early Navigators, Descriptions of the Islands and their Peoples, the History and Records of the Catholic Missions, as Related in Contemporaneous Books and Manuscripts, Showing the Political, Economic, Commercial and Religious Conditions of those Islands from their Earliest Relations with European Nations to the beginning of the Nineteenth Century* (Cleveland, The Arthur H. Clark Co., 55 vols., 1903-1907). A standard collection.

Blanc, J., *L'Héritage d'un Évêque d'Océanie* (Toulon, Imprimerie Sainte-Jeanne d'Arc, 1921, pp. 310). By a Vicar Apostolic of Central Oceania.

Blanc, Joseph, *Histoire Religieuse de l'Archipel Fidjien* (Toulon, Imprimerie Sainte-Jeanne d'Arc, 2 vols., 1926).

Bliss, Mrs. Theodora, *Micronesia. Fifty Years in the Island World* (Boston, American Board of Commissioners for Foreign Missions, 1906, pp. viii, 167). By a missionary to Micronesia.

Boissevain, H. D. J., editor, *De Zending in Oost en West Verleden en Heden* (Gravenhage, Algemeene Boekhandel voor Inwendige en Uitwendige Zending, 1934, pp. 210).

Bompas, William Carpenter, *Diocese of Mackenzie River* (London, Society for Promoting Christian Knowledge, 1888, pp. 108). By a bishop of the diocese.

Bonn, Alfred, *Ein Jahrhundert Rheinische Mission* (Barmen, Missionshaus, 1928, pp. 320). Popularly written official account.

Bouniol, J., editor, *The White Fathers and Their Missions* (London, Sands and Co., 1929, pp. 334). A popular account, not especially scholarly.

Bracq, Jean Charlemagne, *The Evolution of French Canada* (New York, The Macmillan Co., 1924, pp. viii, 467). Sympathetic and careful.

Braga, Erasmo, and Grubb, Kenneth G., *The Republic of Brazil. A Survey of the Religious Situation* (London, World Dominion Press, 1932, pp. 184). Braga was executive secretary of the Committee on Cooperation in Brazil. Grubb spent a good deal of time there to collect information.

Brasseur de Bourbourg, *Histoire du Canada de son Église et de ses Missions* (Paris, Sagnier et Bray, 2 vols., 1852). By a Vicar-General of Boston, formerly Professor of Ecclesiastical History at the Seminary of Quebec.

British Guiana (London, H. M. Stationery Office, 1920, pp. 97).

Broughton, William Grant, *Sermons on The Church of England: Its Constitution, Mission and Trials: edited with a prefatory memoir by Benjamin Harrison* (London, Bell and Daldy, 1857, pp. xliv, 360).

Brown, Arthur Judson, *One Hundred Years. A History of the Foreign Missionary Work of the Presbyterian Church in the U. S. A., With Some Account of Countries, Peoples and the Policies and Problems of Modern Missions* (New York, Fleming H. Revell Co., 1937, pp. 1140). An official history by a secretary emeritus of the board.

Brown, Arthur Judson, *The New Era in the Philippines* (New York, Fleming H. Revell Co., 1903, pp. 314).

George Brown, D.D., Pioneer-Missionary and Explorer. An Autobiography. A Narrative of Forty-Eight Years' Residence and Travel in Samoa, New Britain, New Ireland, New Guinea, and the Solomon Islands (London, Hodder and Stoughton, 1908, pp. xii, 536).

[Browne, A. R. Langford], *Here and There with the S. P. G. in South Africa* (Westminster, Society for the Propagation of the Faith, 1917, pp. 115). A popular summary.

Browning, Webster E., *The River Plate Republics. A Survey of the Religious, Economic and Social Conditions in Argentina, Paraguay and Uruguay* (London, World Dominion Press, 1928, pp. 139). By the executive secretary of the Committee on Cooperation, Buenos Aires.

Browning, Webster E., Ritchie, John, and Grubb, Kenneth G., *The West Coast Republics of South America, Chile, Peru and Bolivia* (London, World Dominion Press, 1930, pp. vi, 183). An excellent survey, especially of Protestant missions. Browning was long a missionary in Chile. Ritchie long lived in Peru. Grubb writes of Bolivia.

Brummitt, Robert, *A Winter Holiday in Fiji* (London, Charles H. Kelly, 1914, pp. 173).

Buchanan, John, *The Shiré Highlands (East Central Africa) as a Colony and Mission* (Edinburgh, William Blackwood and Sons, 1885, pp. vi, 260).

Buller, James, *Forty Years in New Zealand: Including a Personal Narrative, an Account of Maoridom, and of the Christianization and Colonization of the Country* (London, Hodder and Stoughton, 1878, pp. viii, 503).

Burgess, Andrew, *Unkulunkulu in Zululand* (Minneapolis, The Board of Foreign Missions, 1934, pp. 263).

Burgess, Andrew, *Zanahary in South Madagascar* (Minneapolis, The Board of Foreign Missions, 1932, pp. xii, 250). By a Lutheran missionary to Madagascar.

Burritt, Carrie T., *The Story of Fifty Years* (Winona Lake, Ind., Light and Life Press, pp. 213). The mission of the Free Methodist Church.

Burton, J. W., *The Call of the Pacific* (London, Charles H. Kelly, 1912, pp. xiv, 286). A study textbook for the churches.

Burton, John Wear, *The Fiji of To-Day* (London, Charles H. Kelly, 1910, p. 304). By a Methodist missionary.

Burton, J. W., and Deane, Wallace, *A Hundred Years in Fiji* (London, The Epworth Press, pp. 144).

Burton, William Westbrooke, *The State of Religion and Education in New South Wales* (London, J. Cross and Simpkin and Marshall, 1840, pp. vii, 321, cxxxvi). By a justice of the supreme court of New South Wales. Has a strong Anglican bias.

[Busk, H. W.], *A Sketch of the Origin and the Recent History of the New England Company by the Senior Member of the Company* (London, Spottiswoode & Co., 1884, pp. 89).

Callcott, Wilfrid Hardy, *Liberalism in Mexico, 1857-1929* (Stanford University Press, 1931, pp. xiii, 410). A careful piece of work.

Camargo, G. Baez, and Grubb, Kenneth G., *Religion in the Republic of Mexico* (London, World Dominion Press, 1935, pp. 166). Pro-Protestant.

The Cambridge History of the British Empire. Vol. VIII. South Africa, Rhodesia, and the Protectorates (Cambridge University Press, 1936, pp. xxv, 1005).

Cameron, James, *Centenary History of the Presbyterian Church in New South Wales* (Sydney, Angus and Robertson, 1905, pp. xxii, 449). An official history based on documents.

Campbell, A. J., *Fifty Years of Presbyterianism in Victoria* (Melbourne, M. L. Hutchinson, 1889, pp. 240). Written at the request of the General Assembly's Jubilee Committee.

Campbell, Dugald, *Wanderings in Widest Africa* (London, The Religious Tract Society, 1930). The autobiographical account of a journey into the Sahara of an agent of the National Bible Society of Scotland.

Le Canada Ecclésiastique. Annuaire du Clergé. Fondé par feu L.-J.-A.-Derome. Pour l'Année 1932. Quarante-Sixième Année (Montreal, Librairie Beauchemin, 1932, pp. 963).

The Canada Year Book 1912. Published by Authority of the Hon. George E. Foster, M.P., Minister of Trade and Commerce (Ottawa, C. H. Parmelee, 1913, pp. xvi, 470).

Canton, William, *A History of the British and Foreign Bible Society* (London, John Murray, 5 vols., 1904-1910).

Capuchins Missionnaires. Missions Françaises. Notes Historiques et Statistiques (Paris, Société et Librairie Coopératives St. François, 1926, pp. iv, 86). No author given. A popular summary.

Carey, S. Pearce, *William Carey, D.D., Fellow of Linnaean Society* (New York,

George H. Doran Co., preface 1923, pp. xvi, 428). By a great-grandson. A standard biography.

Carrington, Hugh, *Life of Captain Cook* (London, Sidgwick & Jackson, 1939, pp. ix, 324). Based upon careful research, much of it in manuscript sources.

Carruthers, J. E., *Lights in the Southern Sky. Pen Portraits of Early Preachers and Worthies of Australian Methodism with some Sketches from Life of Humbler Workers* (London, The Epworth Press, 1924, pp. 160). Made up partly of personal reminiscences.

Carruthers, J. E., *Memories of an Australian Ministry 1868 to 1921* (London, The Epworth Press, 1922, pp. 339). By a prominent Methodist minister, president of the General Conference of the Methodist Church of Australasia, 1917-1920.

Cartas Edificantes de los Misioneros de la Compañia de la Jesus en Filipinas 1898-1902 (Barcelona, Imprenta de Henrich y Compañia en Comandita, 1903, pp. 379).

Casalis, E., *The Basutos; or, Twenty-Three Years in South Africa* (London, James Nisbet & Co., 1861, pp. xix, 355).

The Catholic Directory of South Africa for the Year 1931. Eighteenth Issue (Cape Town, Salesian Press, pp. xvi, 256).

The Catholic Encyclopedia (New York, 16 vols., 1907-1913). Written for informative and apologetic purposes.

Census of the Philippine Islands Taken under the Direction of the Philippine Legislature in the year 1918 (Manila, Bureau of Printing, 4 vols., 1920-1921).

The Centennial Book. One Hundred Years of Christian Civilization in Hawaii 1820-1920. A Symposium published by the Central Committee of the Hawaiian Mission Centennial (Honolulu, 1920, pp. 90). By several authors. It includes American Board, Episcopalian, Methodist, and Roman Catholic enterprises.

The Central American Bulletin (Paris, Texas, 1895ff.). Organ of The Central American Mission.

The Christian Century (Chicago, 1894ff.).

The Christian Science Journal (Boston, 1883ff.).

The Christian World. Magazine of the American and Foreign Christian Union (New York, 1850-1884).

Christianity and the Natives of South Africa. A Year-Book of South African Missions. Compiled and edited by J. Dexter Taylor. Published under the auspices of the General Missionary Conference of South Africa (The Lovedale Institution Press, no date, pp. xii, 499).

The Chronicle. A Baptist Historical Quarterly (Scottdale, Penn., The American Baptist Historical Society, 1938ff.).

The Church in Canada. A Journal of Visitation to the Western Portion of his Diocese by the Lord Bishop of Toronto in the Autumn of 1842 (London, S. P. G., 1844, pp. iv, 60).

Proceedings of the Church Missionary Society for Africa and the East (London, 1801ff.).

Clark, John, Dendy, W., and Philippo, J. M., *The Voice of Jubilee. A Narrative of the Baptist Mission, Jamaica, from its Commencement: with Biographical Notices of its Fathers and Founders* (London, John Snow, 1865, pp. xx, 359).

Clarke, Henry Lowther, *Constitutional Church Government in the Dominions Beyond the Seas and in Other Parts of the Anglican Communion* (London, S. P. C. K., 1924, pp. xvi, 543). Containing a large number of documents; by a former Archbishop of Melbourne.

Clarke, John, *Memorials of Baptist Missionaries in Jamaica, Including a Sketch of the Labours of Early Religious Instructors in Jamaica* (London, Yates & Alexander, 1869, pp. xi, 234). Based upon fairly extensive research.

Claus, W., Dr. *Ludwig Krapf, weil Missionar in Ostafrika* (Basel, C. F. Spittler, no date, pp. 243).

Coan, Titus, *Life in Hawaii. An Autobiographic Sketch of Mission Life and Labors (1835-1881)* (New York, Anson D. F. Randolph & Co., 1882, pp. viii, 340).

Cochrane, William, *Memoirs and Remains of the Reverend Walter Inglis, African Missionary and Canadian Pastor* (Toronto, C. Blackett Robinson, 1887, pp. 325). By a friend; based largely on first-hand information.

Annual Reports of the Colonial Missionary Society (London, 1837ff.).

Colwell, James, editor, *A Century in the Pacific: Scientific, Sociological, Historical, Missionary, General* (London, Charles H. Kelly, 1914, pp. xi, 781). By various authors. Deals chiefly with the history of Methodism.

Colwell, James, *The Illustrated History of Methodism. Australia: 1812 to 1855. New South Wales and Polynesia: 1856 to 1902* (Sydney, William Brook & Co., 1904, pp. 669). Compiled from official records and other sources. Contains a good many quotations from sources.

Commons, John R., *Races and Immigrants in America* (New York, The Macmillan Co., new ed., 1920, pp. xxix, 242). By a distinguished scholar.

Comrie, W. J., *The Presbytery of Auckland. Early Days and Progress* (Dunedin, A. H. and A. W. Reed, 1939, pp. 261).

Condliffe, J. B., *A Short History of New Zealand* (Christ Church, I. M. Isitt, 1925, pp. xvi, 239). A textbook for elementary and secondary schools, by a competent scholar.

The Annual Reports of the Congregational Home Missionary Society for New South Wales (Sydney, 1851ff.).

Cooksey, J. J., and McLeish, Alexander, *Religion and Civilization in West Africa. A Missionary Survey of French, British, Spanish, and Portuguese West Africa, with Liberia* (London, World Dominion Press, 1931, pp. 277).

Coolsma, S., *De Zendingseeuw voor Nederlandsch Oost-Indië* (Utrecht, C. H. E. Breijer, 1901, pp. xii, 892).

Cooper, Clayton Sedgwick, *The Brazilians and Their Country* (New York, Frederick A. Stokes Co., 1917, pp. xvi, 403).

Cornish, George H., *Cyclopædia of Methodism in Canada: Containing Historical, Educational, and Statistical Information, Dating from the Beginning of the Work in the Several Provinces of the Dominion of Canada, and Extending to the Annual Conferences of 1880* (Toronto, Methodist Book and Publishing House, 1881, pp. 850).

Cory, Geo. E., *The Rise of South Africa. A History of the Origin of South African Colonisation and of its Development towards the East from the Earliest Times to 1857* (London, Longmans, Green and Co., Vol. 5, 1930, pp. xiv, 520). Lacking in references to authorities, but apparently fairly scholarly.

Cousins, George, *Isles Afar Off: An Illustrated Handbook to the Missions of the London Missionary Society in Polynesia* (London, London Missionary Society, 1914, pp. 104).

Cowper, William Macquarie, *The Autobiography and Reminiscences of William Macquarie Cowper, Dean of Sydney* (Sydney, Angus & Robertson, 1902, pp. 258).

Cox, George W., *The Life of John William Colenso, D.D., Bishop of Natal* (London, W. Ridgway, 2 vols., 1888). Largely a defense of Colenso.

Creighton, Louise, *G. A. Selwyn, D.D., Bishop of New Zealand and Lichfield* (London, Longmans, Green and Co., 1923, pp. xi, 180).

Crétineau-Joly, J., *Histoire, Religieuse, Politique et Littéraire de la Compagnie de Jésus. Composée sur les Documents Inédits et Authentiques* (Third edition, Paris, Jacques Lecoffre et Cie, 6 vols., 1859). Well written; not always critical; some documents given, at least in part; laudatory of the Jesuits.

Crowe, Frederick, *The Gospel in Central America; Containing a Sketch of the Country, Physical and Geographical—Historical and Political—Moral and Religious: A History of the Baptist Mission in British Honduras and of the Introduction of the Bible into the Spanish American Republic of Guatemala* (London, Charles Gilpin, 1850, pp. xii, 588).

Currey, L. E., *Borneo* (Westminster, The Society for the Propagation of the Gospel in Foreign Parts, 1933, pp. 96).

Davidson, H. Frances, *South and Central Africa. A Record of Fifteen Years' Missionary Labors among Primitive Peoples* (Elgin, Brethren Publishing House, 1915, pp. 481). By a pioneer member of the mission.

Dawson, C. A., *Group Settlement. Ethnic Communities in Western Canada* (Vol. VII of *Canadian Frontiers of Settlement*) (Toronto, The Macmillan Co. of Canada, 1936, pp. xx, 395). Deals with Doukhobors, Mennonites, Mormons, German Catholics, and French Canadians.

Day, E. Hermitage, *Robert Gray, First Bishop of Cape Town* (London, Society for Promoting Christian Knowledge, 1930, pp. 32). A popular, brief account.

Delmas, Siméon, *Essai d'Histoire de la Mission des Iles Marquèses (Océanie) jusqu'en 1881* (Paris, Annales des Sacrés Coeurs, 1929, pp. 358). By one of the Picpus Fathers, a missionary on the Marquesas. Ardently pro-missionary and not very scholarly, but contains some documents.

Denis, Pierre, *Brazil.* Translated, with a historical chapter, by Bernard Miall and a supplementary chapter by Dawson A. Vindin (London, T. Fisher Unwin, 1911, pp. 388).

Department of Commerce, Bureau of the Census, *Religious Bodies 1916* (Washington, Government Printing Office, 2 vols., 1919).

Descamps, Baron, *Histoire Générale Comparée des Missions* (Paris, Librairie Plon, 1932, pp. viii, 760). Seven other writers have contributed. A standard survey, by Roman Catholic scholars, of Roman Catholic mission history from the beginning, together with chapters on the spread of Protestantism and of some other religions.

Dibble, Sheldon, *History of the Sandwich Islands* (Lahainaluna, Press of the Mission Seminary, 1843, pp. viii, 464). By an early missionary teacher.

Dickie, William, *Missions of the United Presbyterian Church. Story of the Mission in Old Calabar* (Edinburgh, United Presbyterian Church, 1894, pp. 99).

Dickson, John, *History of the Presbyterian Church of New Zealand* (Dunedin, J. Wilkie & Co., 1899, pp. xviii, 532). Based upon reminiscences of individuals, church records, and other sources. Not so much an organized account of the church as a whole, as the story town by town and district by district.

Dictionary of American Biography (New York, Charles Scribner's Sons, 21 vols., 1928-1937). The standard work.

Dijkstra, H., *Het Evangelie in Onze Oost. De Protestantsche Zending in het tegenwoordige Nederlandsch Indië van de eerste Vestiging tot op Onzen Tijd* (Leiden, D. Donner, 2d ed., 2 parts, 1900).

Dodds, James, *Records of the Scottish Settlers in the River Plate and Their Churches* (Buenos Aires, Grant & Sylvester, 1897, pp. xiv, 460). By one who had some share in the enterprise.

Los Dominicos en el Extremo Oriente. Provincia del Santísimo Rosario de Filipinas. Relaciones publicadas con motivo del Séptimo Centenario de la confirmación de la Sagrada Orden de Predicadores (no date or place of publication, pp. 391). Done by a commission. No names of authors given.

Donne, T. E., *The Maori, Past and Present* (London, Seeley Service & Co., 1927, pp. 287). Much of the material derived from the personal observation of the author.

Dorland, Arthur Garratt, *A History of the Society of Friends (Quakers) in Canada* (Toronto, The Macmillan Company of Canada, 1927, pp. xiii, 343).

Douglas, W. M., *Andrew Murray and His Message. One of God's Choice Saints. Compiled from Materials Supplied by Miss Murray from various Letters and Recollections and by Miss Mary Murray from her large Manuscript* (London, Oliphants, [no date], pp. 334). By a friend. The personal side of Murray's life. Intended to supplement Du Plessis' account.

Drach, George, editor, *Our Church Abroad. The Foreign Missions of the Lutheran Church in America* (Philadelphia, The United Lutheran Publication House, 1926, pp. 277). An official description of the missions of the various Lutheran bodies of the United States.

Driessler, Heinrich, *Die Rheinische Mission in Südwestafrika* (Gütersloh, C. Bertelsmann, 1932, pp. viii, 318). Volume 2 of the *Geschichte der Rheinischen Mission*. By the *Missionsinspektor* in Barmen.

Drury, A. W., *History of the Church of the United Brethren in Christ* (Dayton, United Brethren Publishing House, revised edition, 1931, pp. 832). By one long connected with the church. Based upon personal knowledge and extensive research.

Dubois, *Les Missions Maristes d'Océanie* (Paris, no publisher, 1926, pp. 32).

[Dubois, Henri], *La Mission de Madagascar Betsiléo. PP. Jesuites Français* (Lille, Procure des Missions, 1925, pp. 94).

Duncan, Peter, *A Narrative of the Wesleyan Mission to Jamaica; with Occasional*

Remarks on the State of Society in that Colony (London, Partridge and Oakey, 1849, pp. xii, 396). By a missionary to Jamaica.

Du Plessis, J., *The Evangelisation of Pagan Africa. A History of Christian Missions to the Pagan Tribes of Central Africa* (Cape Town and Johannesburg, J. C. Juta & Co., 1930, pp. xii, 408). By a competent scholar, but with few references to sources.

Du Plessis, J., *A History of Christian Missions in South Africa* (London, Longmans, Green and Co., 1911, pp. xx, 494). Well done, but with few references to sources.

Du Plessis, J., *The Life of Andrew Murray of South Africa* (London, Marshall Brothers, 1919, pp. xvi, 553). Not only the standard biography, but also virtually a history of the Dutch Reformed Church in South Africa in the nineteenth and the early part of the twentieth century.

Dwight, Henry Otis, *The Centennial History of the American Bible Society* (New York, The Macmillan Co., 2 vols., 1916). By a secretary of the society.

E. and H. W., *Soldiers of the Cross in Zululand* (London, Bemrose & Sons, 1906, pp. xv, 192).

The East and the West. A Quarterly Review for the Study of Missionary Problems (Westminster, The Society for the Propagation of the Gospel in Foreign Parts, 1903-1927).

Eaton, Arthur Wentworth, *The Church of England in Nova Scotia and the Tory Clergy of the Revolution* (London, James Nisbet & Co., 2d ed., 1892, pp. viii, 320).

Eckhardt, Carl Conrad, *The Papacy and World-Affairs as Reflected in the Secularization of Politics* (University of Chicago Press, 1937, pp. xiv, 310).

Elder, John Rawson, editor, *The Letters and Journals of Samuel Marsden, 1765-1838, Senior Chaplain in the Colony of New South Wales and Superintendent of the Mission of the Church Missionary Society in New Zealand* (Dunedin, Coulls Somerville Wilkie, 1932, pp. 580). Edited in a thoroughly scholarly fashion.

Elder, John Rawson, *The History of the Presbyterian Church in New Zealand, 1840-1940* (Christ church, Presbyterian Bookroom, no date, c. 1940, pp. xv, 464). Based upon extensive research, but without footnote references to the sources.

Ellenberger, V., *Un Siècle de Mission au Lessouto (1833-1933)* (Paris, Société des Missions Évangéliques, no date, pp. 444). There is an English translation by E. M. Ellenberger (Morija, Sesuto Book Depot, 1938, pp. 380). Undocumented; by a missionary.

Elliott, Arthur Elwood, *Paraguay. Its Cultural Heritage, Social Conditions and Educational Problems* (New York, Bureau of Publications, Teachers College, Columbia University, 1931, pp. xiv, 210). A scholarly study. From the standpoint of missionary education.

Elliott, W. A., *South Africa* (London, London Missionary Society, 1913, pp. 115).

Ellis, J. B., *The Diocese of Jamaica. A Short Account of Its History, Growth, and Organisation* (London, Society for Promoting Christian Knowledge, 1913, pp. 237). By one who was for a time a member of the staff.

Ellis, John Eimeo, *Life of William Ellis, Missionary to the South Seas and to Madagascar* (London, John Murray, 1873, pp. xxiv, 310). By a son.

Ellis, William, *History of Madagascar* (London, Fisher, Son & Co., 2 vols., c. 1839). Embodying some first hand material.

Ellis, William, *Madagascar Revisited, Describing the Events of a New Reign and the Revolution which Followed* (London, John Murray, 1867, pp. xviii, 502).

Ellis, William, *The Martyr Church: A Narrative of the Introduction, Progress, and Triumph of Christianity in Madagascar* (London, John Snow and Co., 1870, pp. x, 404). By one with first hand knowledge of events.

Ellis, William, *Polynesian Researches during a Residence of Nearly Eight Years in the Society and Sandwich Islands* (London, Fisher, Son & Jackson, 2d ed., 4 vols., 1831). By a missionary.

The Encyclopædia Britannica (New York, The Encyclopædia Britannica, 11th ed., 25 vols., 1910, 1911).

The Encyclopædia Britannica (London, The Encyclopædia Britannica, 14th ed., 24 vols., 1929).

Engelhardt, Zephyrin, *The Missions and Missionaries of California* (San Francisco, The James H. Barry Co., 4 vols., 1908-1915).

Espey, P. Cletus, *Festschrift zum Silberjubiläum der Wiedererrichtung der Provinz von der Unbefleckten Empfängnis im Süden Brasiliens 1901-1926* (Werl i. Westf. Franziskus-Druckerei, 1929, pp. 175).

Every, E. F., *The Anglican Church in South America* (London, Society for Promoting Christian Knowledge, 1915, pp. 155). By a bishop in that area.

Every, E. F., *South America Memories of Thirty Years* (London, Society for Promoting Christian Knowledge, 1933, pp. vi, 210). By an Anglican bishop.

Every, E. F., *Twenty-Five Years in South America* (London, Society for Promoting Christian Knowledge, 1929, pp. vii, 212).

Farrar, Thomas, *Notes on the History of the Church in Guiana* (Berbice, Wm. Macdonald, 1892, pp. xi, 226). By an Anglican clergyman in British Guiana.

Fensham, Florence A., and Tuthill, Beulah Logan, *The Old and the New in Micronesia* (Chicago, Woman's Board of Missions of the Interior, 1907, pp. 91).

Fergusson, E. Morris, *Historic Chapters in Christian Education in America. A Brief History of the American Sunday School Movement and the Rise of the Modern Church School* (New York, Fleming H. Revell Co., 1935, pp. 192). Based partly on archives and personal recollections.

Fides News Service (Rome, c. 1926ff.). A mimeographed set of news release notes on current happenings in Roman Catholic missions, compiled in close co-operation with the Association for the Propagation of the Faith.

Fijen, H. J. H., and Hamelijnck, S. C. A., *Missie-Schetsen uit Tropisch Nederland* (Hertogenbosch, L. C. G. Malmberg, 1928, pp. 196).

Findlay, G. G., and Holdsworth, W. W., *The History of the Wesleyan Methodist Missionary Society* (London, The Epworth Press, 5 vols., 1921-1924). An official history, based largely upon the manuscript records of the society.

Fitch, E. R., editor, *The Baptists of Canada. A History of their Progress and Achievements* (Toronto, The Standard Publishing Co., 1911, pp. 304).

Forbes, W. Cameron, *The Philippine Islands* (Boston, Houghton Mifflin Co., 2 vols., 1928).

Fox, William, *A Brief History of the Wesleyan Missions on the Western Coast of Africa* (London, Aylott and Jones, 1851, pp. xx, 624).

Franken-VanDriel, Pietertje Magdalena, *Regeering en Zending in Nederlandsch-Indië* (Amsterdam, A. H. Kruyt, 1923, pp. 128). A doctoral dissertation.

Fraser, Agnes R., *Donald Fraser of Livingstonia* (London, Hodder and Stoughton, 1934, pp. ix, 325). A charmingly written biography by the widow.

Fraser, Donald, *Livingstonia* (Edinburgh, Foreign Mission Committee of the United Free Church of Scotland, 1915, pp. 88).

Fullerton, W. Y., *The Christ of the Congo River* (London, The Carey Press, no date, pp. 216).

Galarreta, *Vida del Martir Ilmo. Fr. Jerónimo Hermosilla, Obispo del Orden de Predicadores Vicario Apostolico del Tonquin, Beatificado por S. S. el Papa Pio X, en 20 Mayo, 1906* (Barcelona, Tip. Ariza, 1906, pp. 336).

Gamio, Manuel, *Mexican Immigration to the United States* (University of Chicago Press, 1930, pp. xviii, 262). Summarizing a scholarly investigation.

Gammon, Samuel R., *The Evangelical Invasion of Brazil: or a Half Century of Evangelical Missions in the Land of the Southern Cross* (Richmond, Presbyterian Committee of Publication, 1910, pp. 179). The author was for twenty years a missionary in Brazil.

Gates, E. H., *In Coral Isles* (Washington, Review and Herald Publishing Association, 1923, pp. 256). An account of Seventh Day Adventist missions in the Pacific Islands.

Geary, Gerald J., *The Secularization of the California Missions (1810-1846)* (Washington, The Catholic University of America, 1934, pp. x, 204). A doctoral dissertation.

Gerdener, G. B. A., *Studies in the Evangelisation of South Africa* (London, Longmans, Green and Co., 1911, pp. xvii, 212).

Gevers, Gottfried, *Die Kulturarbeit der deutschen evangelischen Missionen in Südafrika. Das Eingeborenenschulwesen der deutschen evangelischen Missionen in der Südafrikanischen Union* (Göttingen, Universitätsverlag von Robert Noske in Borna-Leipzig, 1929, pp. ix, 79). A doctoral dissertation based upon a little less than fifty books, periodicals, and reports.

Ghéon, Henri, *The Secret of Saint John Bosco*. Translated by F. J. Sheed (New York, Sheed & Ward, 1936, pp. 203). An admiring biography for popular reading.

Giles, R. A., *The Constitutional History of the Australian Church* (London, Skeffington & Son, 1929, pp. 320). Scholarly.

Gill, William, *Gems from the Coral Islands; or, Incidents of Contrast between Savage and Christian Life of the South Sea Islands* (London, Ward and Co., 2 vols., 1856). By a missionary of the London Missionary Society.

Gill, W. Wyatt, *Jottings from the Pacific* (London, The Religious Tract Society, 1885, pp. 248). Chiefly a travelogue by a missionary.

Gillies, William, *The Presbyterian Church Trust: The Documents Relating to the Title and Administration of the Trust Property of the Presbyterian Church of*

Otago and Southland; with Historical Narrative (Dunedin, Reith & Wilkie, 1876, pp. 108).

Goldie, Hugh, *Calabar and Its Mission* (Edinburgh, Oliphant Anderson & Ferrier, 1890, pp. 328). By a pioneer of the mission, and so in large part from first hand knowledge.

Gomes, Edwin H., *Seventeen Years among the Sea Dyaks of Borneo* (London, Seeley & Co., 1911, pp. 343).

Goodman, George, *The Church in Victoria during the Episcopate of the Right Reverend Charles Perry, First Bishop of Melbourne, Prelate of the Order of St. Michael and St. George* (London, Seeley & Co., 1892, pp. xxiv, 476). By a clergyman who had worked under Bishop Perry. Quotes extensively from documents, such as Mrs. Perry's letters.

Gordon, Charles W., *The Life of James Robertson, Missionary Superintendent in Western Canada* (Toronto, The Westminster Co., 2d ed., 1908, pp. 412).

Gould, S., *Inasmuch. Sketches of the Beginnings of the Church of England in Canada in Relation to the Indian and Eskimo Races* (Toronto, no publisher given, 1917, pp. xiv, 285).

Goyau, Georges, *Monseigneur Augouard* (Paris, Librairie Plon, 1926, pp. vii, 213).

Grace, Thomas Samuel, *A Pioneer Missionary among the Maoris 1850-1879. Being the Letters and Journals of Thomas Samuel Grace.* Edited by S. J. Brittan, G. F., C. W., and A. V. Grace (Palmerston North, G. H. Bennett & Co., no date, pp. xv, 314).

Grandjean, A., *La Mission Romande. Ses Racines dans le Sol Suisse Romand. Son Épanouissement dans la Race Thonga* (Lausanne, Georges Bridel & Cie, 1917, pp. viii, 328). By the General Secretary of the mission.

Green, Eda, *Borneo. The Land of River and Palm* (Westminster, Society for the Propagation of the Gospel in Foreign Parts, new ed., 1912, pp. xvi, 172).

Greenland (London, H. M. Stationery Office, 1920, pp. 37).

Gregg, William, *Short History of the Presbyterian Church in the Dominion of Canada from the Earliest to the Present Time* (Toronto, printed for the author by C. Blackett Robinson, 1892, pp. viii, 248). By the professor of church history in Knox College.

Griffith, Robert, *Madagascar. A Century of Adventure* (London, London Missionary Society, 1919, pp. 79).

Grose, Howard B., *Advance in the Antilles. The New Era in Cuba and Porto Rico* (New York, Young People's Missionary Movement of the United States and Canada, 1910, pp. xii, 256).

Grout, Lewis, *Zulu-land; or Life among the Zulu-Kafirs of Natal and Zulu-land, South Africa* (Philadelphia, Presbyterian Publication Committee, 1864, pp. 351).

Grubb, Kenneth G., *Religion in Central America* (London, World Dominion Press, 1937, pp. 147). By an expert on missionary surveys.

Guilcher, René F., *Un Ami des Noirs, Augustin Planque. Premier Supérieur Général Société des Missions Africaines de Lyon* (Lyons, Imprimerie des Missions Africaines, 1928, pp. 297).

Guinness, Mrs. H. Grattan, *The New World of Central Africa. With a History of the First Christian Mission on the Congo* (New York, Fleming H. Revell,

1890, pp. xx, 537). By one who helped promote a pioneer Protestant mission to the Congo.

Gulick, Orramel Hinckley, *The Pilgrims of Hawaii. Their Own Story of Their Pilgrimage from New England and Life Work in the Sandwich Islands, now known as Hawaii* (New York, Fleming H. Revell Co., 1918, pp. 351). Made up largely of excerpts from letters of missionaries.

Gulick, Sidney L., *Mixing the Races in Hawaii. A Study of the Coming Neo-Hawaiian American Race* (Honolulu, The Hawaiian Board Book Rooms, 1937, pp. xiii, 220). Well done.

Gunn, William, *The Gospel in Futuna* (London, Hodder & Stoughton, 1914, pp. xvii, 308).

Haccius, Georg, *Erlebnisse und Eindrücke meiner zweiten Reise durch das Hermannsburger Missionsgebiet in Südafrika (1912-1913)* (Hermannsburg, Missionshandlung, 1913, pp. 152).

Hagspiel, Bruno, *Along the Mission Trail* (Techny, Mission Press, S.V.D., 5 vols., 1925-1927). A travelogue by a priest of the Society of the Divine Word.

Hallfell, Matthias, *Uganda. Eine Edelfrucht am Missionsbaum der katholischen Kirche zu Ehren der seligen Ugandamärtyrer* (Freiburg im Breisgau, Herder & Co., 1921, pp. viii, 230). Fairly carefully done, by a White Father, but without footnote references to the sources.

Hamilton, Robert, *A Jubilee History of the Presbyterian Church of Victoria, or the Rise and Progress of Presbyterianism from the Foundation of the Colony to 1888* (Melbourne, M. L. Hutchinson, 1888, pp. xx, 495, xxx). By one of the oldest surviving pioneer Presbyterian ministers of Victoria, who depended partly on his memory and largely on the original church records.

Handbooks of the Missions of the Episcopal Church. No. VI. South America: Brazil, Colombia, Panama, Canal Zone (New York, The National Council of the Protestant Episcopal Church, Department of Missions, 1927, pp. 125).

Handbooks of the Missions of the Episcopal Church. No. VII. Mexico (New York, The National Council of the Protestant Episcopal Church, Department of Missions, 1927, pp. 111).

Hands, W. J., *Polynesia* (Westminster, The Society for the Propagation of the Gospel in Foreign Parts, 1929, pp. 54).

Harford-Battersby, Charles F., *Pilkington of Uganda* (London, Marshall Brothers, pp. xvi, 346, v).

Harper, Henry W., *Letters from New Zealand, 1857-1911. Being some Account of Life and Work in the Province of Canterbury, South Island* (London, Hugh Rees, 1914, pp. 357).

Harrop, A. J., *The Amazing Career of Edward Gibbon Wakefield* (London, George Allen & Unwin, 1928, pp. 253). Based largely upon Wakefield's unpublished papers and published writings.

Harrop, A. J., *England and New Zealand from Tasman to the Taranaki War* (London, Methuen & Co., 1926, pp. xxiv, 326). Carefully done.

Harvey, F. G., *Notes on Australian Church History* (Ms). Based upon extensive research.

Annual Reports of the Hawaiian Evangelical Association (Honolulu, 1823ff.).

Hawkins, Ernest, *Historical Notices of the Missions of the Church of England in the North American Colonies, Previous to the Independence of the United States, Chiefly from the Ms. Documents of the Society for the Propagation of the Gospel in Foreign Parts* (London, B. Fellowes, 1845, pp. xix, 447).

Hay, Alexander, *Jubilee Memorial of the Presbyterian Church of Queensland, 1849-1899* (Brisbane, Alex. Muir & Co., 1900, pp. viii, 220). Written at the request of the General Assembly of the Presbyterian Church of Queensland.

Hayes, Ernest H., *David Jones: Dauntless Pioneer. An Epic Story of Heroic Endeavour in Madagascar* (London, The Livingstone Press, 1923, pp. 127). A popular biography, but carefully done and checked with the sources and by men who knew well the history of the period.

Heanley, R. M., *A Memoir of Edward Steere, D.D., LL.D., Third Missionary Bishop in Central Africa* (London, George Bell and Sons, 1888, pp. xii, 446).

Heeney, Wm. Bertol, editor, *Leaders of the Canadian Church* (Toronto, The Mission Book Co., 1918, pp. 319). By various authors.

Hemmens, H. L., *George Grenfell, Pioneer in Congo* (London, Student Christian Movement, 1927, pp. 248). By an assistant home secretary of the Baptist Missionary Society, written with warm enthusiasm for Grenfell.

Henderson, G. C., *Fiji and the Fijians 1835-1856* (Sydney, Angus and Robertson, 1931, pp. xi, 333). Written to elucidate the journal of the Rev. Thomas Williams, Wesleyan Methodist missionary in Fiji, 1840-1853, and based upon collections of original documents in Australia, Fiji, and England. Favourable to missions.

Henderson, Geo. C., *Sir George Grey, Pioneer of Empire in Southern Lands* (London, J. M. Dent & Co., 1907, pp. xxiv, 315). Without footnote reference to authorities, but based upon original documents.

Henderson, G. C., editor, *The Journal of Thomas Williams, Missionary in Fiji, 1840-1853* (Sydney, Angus and Robertson, 1931, pp. li, 606). Scholarly; by an emeritus professor of history in Adelaide University.

Henderson, George E., *Goodness and Mercy. A Tale of a Hundred Years* (Kingston, The Gleaner Co., 1931, pp. ix, 169). By a pastor of one of the Jamaican churches.

Hepburn, J. D., *Twenty Years in Khama's Country and Pioneering among the Batauana of Lake Ngami* (London, Hodder and Stoughton, 1895, pp. xiii, 393). Compiled by C. H. Lyall from Hepburn's letters.

Herskovits, Melville J., *Life in a Haitian Valley* (New York, Alfred A. Knopf, 1937, pp. xvi, 350, xix).

Hetherwick, Alexander, *The Gospel and the African* (Edinburgh, T. and T. Clark, 1932, pp. xi, 176). The author was formerly head of the Blantyre Mission, Nyasaland.

Hetherwick, Alexander, *The Romance of Blantyre. How Livingstone's Dream Came True* (London, James Clarke & Co., no date, pp. 260).

Hine, J. E., *Days Gone By. Being Some Account of Past Years Chiefly in Central Africa* (London, John Murray, 1924, pp. xii, 313). Autobiographical.

Hinton, John Howard, *Memoir of William Knibb, Missionary in Jamaica* (London, Houlston and Stoneman, 1847, pp. viii, 562).

Hird, Frank, *H. M. Stanley. The Authorized Life* (London, Stanley Paul & Co., 1935, pp. 320). Based on Stanley's diaries, letters, papers, and note-books. Admiring but not uncritical.

Hirst, W. A., *Argentina* (New York, Charles Scribner's Sons, 1910, pp. xxviii, 302).

Hislop, John, *History of the Knox Church, Dunedin* (Dunedin, J. Wilkie & Co., 1892, pp. xviii, 160, 21). By one of the elders of the church.

Hocken, Thomas Morland, *Contributions to the Early History of New Zealand [Settlement of Otago]* (London, Sampson Low, Marston and Co., 1898, pp. xiii, 342). Based largely upon journals and memories of early settlers.

Hofmeyr, Ds. A. L., *Het Land Langs Het Meer* (Stellenbosch, De Christen Studenten Vereniging van Zuid Afrika, 1910, pp. 161).

Hofmeyr, Jan H., *South Africa* (London, Ernest Benn, 1931, pp. vi, 331). By an outstanding South African.

Hogbin, H. Ian, *Experiments in Civilization. The Effects of European Culture on a Native Community of the Solomon Islands* (London, George Routledge & Sons, 1939, pp. xvii, 268). By a trained anthropologist.

Holden, W. Clifford, *A Brief History of Methodism, and of Methodist Missions in South Africa* (London, Wesleyan Conference Office, 1877, pp. viii, 519). Based upon printed sources, and, for Natal, the author's own experiences.

Hole, Charles, *The Early History of the Church Missionary Society for Africa and the East to the end of A.D. 1814* (London, Church Missionary Society, 1896, pp. xxxviii, 677). Very full. Based upon extensive and careful research.

Horne, M., *Til Seier Gjennem Nederlag. Mission paa Sydostkysten af Madagascar* (Stavanger, Det Norske Missionsselskap Forlag, 1912, pp. 200).

How, F. D., *Bishop John Selwyn. A Memoir* (London, Isbister and Co., 1899, pp. x, 268).

Howley, M. F., *Ecclesiastical History of Newfoundland* (Boston, Doyle & Whittle, 1888, pp. 426). Roman Catholic, by the Prefect Apostolic of St. George's, Newfoundland.

Hughes, Katherine, *Father Lacombe, The Black-Robe Voyageur* (New York, Moffat, Yard and Co., 1911, pp. xxi, 467). Sympathetic, popularly written, based upon manuscript material.

Hunnicutt, Benjamin H., and Reid, William Watkins, *The Story of Agricultural Missions* (New York, Missionary Education Movement of the United States and Canada, 1931, pp. ix, 180). A study book for adults. Hunnicutt was an agricultural missionary in Brazil and Reid was active in the International Association of Agricultural Missions.

Huonder, Anton, *Der einheimische Klerus in den Heidenländern* (Freiburg im Breisgau, Herdersche Verlagshandlung, 1909, pp. x, 312). Based upon fairly wide reading.

Hutton, J. E., *A History of Moravian Missions* (London, Moravian Publication Office, 1923, pp. 550).

Inglis, John, *Bible Illustrations from the New Hebrides. With Notices of the Progress of the Mission* (London, Thomas Nelson and Sons, 1890, pp. 356).

Inglis, John, *In the New Hebrides. Reminiscences of Missionary Life and Work,*

Especially on the Island of Aneityum from 1850 till 1877 (London, T. Nelson and Sons, 1887, pp. xvi, 352).

The International Review of Missions (London, 1912ff.). The standard Protestant journal on foreign missions.

International Survey of the Young Men's and Young Women's Christian Associations. An Independent Study of the Foreign Work of the Christian Associations of the United States and Canada (New York, The International Survey Committee, 1932, pp. vi, 425). A survey made by technical experts and largely written by F. Ernest Johnson.

Jack, James W., *Daybreak in Livingstonia. The Story of the Livingstonia Mission, British Central Africa* (Edinburgh, Oliphant, Anderson & Ferrier, 1901, pp. 371).

Jacobs, Henry, *New Zealand. Containing the Dioceses of Auckland, Christchurch, Nelson, Waiapu, Wellington, and Melanesia* (London, Society for Promoting Christian Knowledge, 1887, pp. xvi, 480). By the Dean of Christchurch, New Zealand. Has chiefly to do with the history of the development of the ecclesiastical organization of the Church of England in New Zealand.

Jacomb, Edward, *The Future of the Kanaka* (Westminster, P. S. King & Son, 1919, pp. 222).

Jarves, James Jackson, *History of the Hawaiian Islands* (Honolulu, Charles Edwin Hitchcock, 3d ed., 1847, pp. 240).

Johnson, Harry, *Night and Morning in Dark Africa* (London, London Missionary Society, no date, pp. 222). Popular account for young people of the London Missionary Society's enterprise near Lakes Nyasa and Tanganyika, by a member of the mission.

Johnson, Johs., *Det første Hundredaar av Madagaskars Kirkehistorie. En Studiebok* (Stavanger, 1914, pp. 238).

Johnson, William Percival, *My African Reminiscences 1875-1895* (Westminster, Universities' Mission to Central Africa, 1924, pp. 235). By the archdeacon of Nyasa.

Johnston, Harry, *George Grenfell and the Congo* (London, Hutchinson & Co., 2 vols., 1908). Based on the diaries and researches of Grenfell.

Johnston, Harry H., *British Central Africa. An Attempt to Give Some Account of a Portion of the Territories under British Influence North of the Zambesi* (London, Methuen & Co., 1898, pp. xix, 544).

Johnstone, S. M., *A History of the Church Missionary Society in Australia and Tasmania* (Sydney, The Church Missionary Society, 1925, pp. 415, vii).

Johnstone, S. M., *Samuel Marsden, A Pioneer of Civilization in the South Seas* (Sydney, Angus & Robertson, 1932, pp. xiii, 256).

Jones, Thomas Jesse, *Education in East Africa. A Study of East, Central and South Africa by the Second African Education Commission under the Auspices of the Phelps-Stokes Fund, in Coöperation with the International Education Board* (New York, Phelps-Stokes Fund, London, Edinburgh House Press, no date, pp. xxxiii, 416). The commission was in Africa in 1924.

The Journal of Negro History (Lancaster, Pa., The Association for the Study of Negro Life and History, 1916ff.).

Jousse, Théophile, *La Mission Française Évangélique au Sud de l'Afrique, son Origine et son Développement jusqu'a nos jours* (Paris, Librairie Fischbacher, 2 vols., 1889). By a former missionary.

Kahn, Morton C., *Djuka. The Bush Negroes of Dutch Guiana* (New York, The Viking Press, 1931, pp. xxiv, 233).

Kanters, G., *Le T.R.P. Léon Dehon, fondateur de la Congrégation des Prêtres du Coeur de Jésus Esquisse Biographique* (Brussels, A. Dewit, Paris, G. Beauchesne, 1930, pp. 94).

Keeling, Anne E., *What He Did for Convicts and Cannibals. Some Account of the Life and Work of the Rev. Samuel Leigh, the first Wesleyan Missionary to New South Wales and New Zealand* (London, Charles H. Kelly, 1896, pp. xvii, 216).

Keesing, Felix M., *The Changing Maori* (New Plymouth, N. Z., Thomas Avery and Sons, 1928, pp. xvi, 198). *Memoirs of the Board of Maori Ethnological Research*, Vol. IV. Written in popular style and without many footnotes. It has, however, a bibliography and apparently is based on sound scholarship. Sympathetic with the Maori.

Keesing, Felix M., *Modern Samoa. Its Government and Changing Life* (London, George Allen & Unwin, 1934, pp. 506). Carefully and objectively done.

Keesing, Felix M., and Keesing, Marie, *Taming Philippine Headhunters. A Study of Government and of Cultural Change in Northern Luzon* (London, George Allen and Unwin, 1934, p. 288). The result of six months' intensive study in the Philippines.

Keirstead, Charles Wesley, *The Church History of the Canadian North-west* (Ms. doctoral dissertation at Yale).

Kiek, Edward Sidney, *An Apostle in Australia. The Life and Reminiscences of Joseph Coles Kirby, Christian Pioneer and Social Reformer* (London, Independent Press, 1927, pp. 316). Based largely upon Kirby's own memoranda.

Kilger, Laurenz, *Die erste Mission unter den Bantustämmen Ostafrikas* (Münster, Verlag der Aschendorffschen Buchhandlung, 1917, pp. vii, 212). Well documented.

King, Joseph, *W. G. Lawes of Savage Island and New Guinea* (London, The Religious Tract Society, 1909, pp. xxvi, 388). By a close friend, from manuscript and printed sources and with the assistance of Lawes's family.

Die Koningsbode (Stellenbosch, 1888ff.).

Krakenstein, Ed., *Kurze Geschichte der Berliner Mission in Südafrika* (Berlin, Missionshaus, 3d ed., 1887, pp. 319).

Krapf, J. Lewis, *Travels, Researches, and Missionary Labours during an Eighteen-Years' Residence in Eastern Africa* (London, Trübner and Co., 1860, pp. li, 566).

Kruijf, E. F., *Geschiedenis van het Nederlandsche Zendelinggenootschap en zijne Zendingsposten* (Groningen, J. B. Wolters, 1894, pp. xv, 695).

A Lady Member of the Melanesian Mission, *The Isles that Wait* (London, Society for Promoting Christian Knowledge, 1912, pp. 128).

Lang, John Dunmore, *An Historical and Statistical Account of New South Wales from the Founding of the Colony in 1788 to the Present Day* (London, Sampson Low, 4th ed., 2 vols., 1875).

Langridge, A. K., *The Conquest of Cannibal Tanna. A Brief Record of Christian Persistency in the New Hebrides Islands* (London, Hodder and Stoughton, 1934, pp. 200). By the secretary of the John G. Paton Mission.

Langridge, A. K., and Paton, Frank H. L., *John G. Paton. Later Years and Farewell* (London, Hodder and Stoughton, 1910, pp. xv, 286).

Langtry, J., *History of the Church in Eastern Canada and Newfoundland* (London, Society for Promoting Christian Knowledge, 1892, pp. 256). By a Toronto clergyman.

Laubach, Frank Charles, *The People of the Philippines. Their Spiritual Progress and Preparation for Spiritual Leadership in the Far East* (New York, George H. Doran Co., 1925, pp. 515).

La Vaissière, de, *Histoire de Madagascar Ses Habitants et Ses Missionnaires* (Paris, Librairie Victor Lecoffre, 2 vols., 1884). By a Jesuit.

Lawry, Walter, *Friendly and Feejee Islands: A Missionary Visit to Various Stations in the South Seas in the Year MDCCCXLVII* (London, John Mason, 1850, pp. 303).

Lawry, Walter, *A Second Missionary Visit to the Friendly and Feejee Islands, in the Year MDCCCL* (London, John Mason, 1851, pp. viii, 217).

Laws, Robert, *Reminiscences of Livingstonia* (Edinburgh, Oliver and Boyd, 1934, pp. xvi, 272).

Lea, Allen, *The Native Separatist Church Movement in South Africa* (Capetown, Juta & Co., no date, pp. 84). By the General Missionary Secretary of the Wesleyan Methodist Church of South Africa.

Leenhardt, Maurice, *La Grande Terre Mission de Nouvelle-Calédonie* (Paris, Société des Missions Évangéliques, new ed., 1922, pp. 168).

Lemmens, Leonhard, *Geschichte der Franziskanermissionen* (Münster i.W., Aschendorffschen Verlagsbuchhandlung, 1929, pp. 376). Carefully done, by a Franciscan.

Lennox, John, *The Story of Our Missions. South Africa* (Edinburgh, Offices of the United Free Church of Scotland, 1911, pp. 87).

Lesourd, Paul, editor, *L'Année Missionnaire 1931* (Paris, Desclée de Brouwer et Cie, pp. 667).

Lewis, Cecil, and Edwards, G. E., *Historical Records of the Church of the Province of South Africa* (London, Society for Promoting Christian Knowledge, 1934, pp. xviii, 821). A history of the Anglican communion in South Africa, based upon careful research and incorporating excerpts from many documents.

Lewis, Thomas, *These Seventy Years. An Autobiography by Thomas Lewis, Missionary in Cameroons and Congo, 1883-1923* (London, The Carey Press, 1930, pp. xii, 300).

Lindsey, Charles, *Rome in Canada. The Ultramontane Struggle for Supremacy over the Civil Authority* (Toronto, Lovell Brothers, 1877, pp. 398). Anti-Roman Catholic and especially against ultramontanism in Canada.

Livingstone, W. P., *Laws of Livingstonia* (London, Hodder and Stoughton, 1921, pp. xi, 385).

Reports of the London Missionary Society (London, 1796ff.).

Louvet, Louis-Eugène, *Les Missions Catholiques au XIXme Siècle* (Lyon, Œuvre de la Propagation de la Foi, 1895, pp. xvi, 543, 46). Popular account. Must be used with discrimination.

Lovett, James, *James Chalmers: His Autobiography and Letters* (New York, Fleming H. Revell Co., no date, pp. 511).

Lovett, Richard, *The History of the London Missionary Society 1795-1895* (London, Henry Frowde, 2 vols., 1899).

Lübeck, Konrad, *Die russischen Missionen* (Aachen, Xaverius-Verlagsbuchhandlung, 1922, pp. 68). Careful and objective, by a Roman Catholic scholar.

Luke, James, *Pioneering in Mary Slessor's Country* (London, The Epworth Press, 1929, pp. 271). Largely personal reminiscences.

The Lutheran World Almanac and Annual Encyclopedia for 1921 (New York, The Lutheran Bureau, 1920, pp. 966).

MacBeth, R. G., *Our Task in Canada* (Toronto, The Westminster Co., 1912, pp. 146). Prepared for the Home Mission Board of the Presbyterian Church in Canada.

McCarter, John, *The Dutch Reformed Church in South Africa with Notices of other Denominations* (Edinburgh, W. and C. Inglis, 1869, pp. vi, 147). The author was for several years a pastor among the Dutch.

Macdonald, Frederick C., *Bishop Stirling of the Falklands* (London, 1929). A sympathetic biography.

Macdonald, James, *Light in Africa* (London, Hodder and Stoughton, 1890, pp. viii, 263). Largely from the author's own experience in the Scottish mission in South Africa.

MacDougall, Donald, *The Conversion of the Maoris* (Philadelphia, Presbyterian Board of Publication and Sabbath-School Work, 1899, pp. viii, 216).

McFarlane, S., *Among the Cannibals of New Guinea: Being the Story of the New Guinea Mission of the London Missionary Society* (London, London Missionary Society, 1888, pp. 192).

Mackay, John A., *The Other Spanish Christ. A Study in the Spiritual History of Spain and South America* (London, Student Movement Press, 1932, pp. xv, 288). By a scholarly Protestant missionary executive, long a missionary in Peru.

Mackenzie, Jean Kenyon, *Black Sheep. Adventures in West Africa* (Boston, Houghton Mifflin Co., 1916, pp. vii, 313).

McKeown, Robert L., *Twenty-five Years in Qua Iboe. The Story of a Missionary Effort in Nigeria* (London, Morgan & Scott, 1912, pp. vii, 170).

M'Kerrow, John, *History of the Foreign Missions of the Secession and United Presbyterian Church* (Edinburgh, Andrew Elliott, 1867, pp. ix, 518). Drawn largely from the *Missionary Record of the United Presbyterian Church*.

Mackinnon, Ian F., *Settlements and Churches in Nova Scotia, 1749-1776* (Montreal, The Walker Press, 1930, pp. ix, 111). Well done.

McMahon, E. O., *Christian Missions in Madagascar* (Westminster, The Society for the Propagation of the Gospel in Foreign Parts, 1914, pp. viii, 179). By an Anglican archdeacon in Imèrina.

McNeill, George, *United Free Church of Scotland. The Story of our Missions. The West Indies* (Edinburgh, Foreign Mission Committee, 1911, pp. 93).

McNeill, John Thomas, *The Presbyterian Church in Canada, 1875-1925* (Toronto, General Board, Presbyterian Church in Canada, 1925, pp. xi, 276). By a Professor of Church History in Knox College.

Mann, Cecil W., *Education in Fiji* (Melbourne University Press, 1935, pp. 138). From a special visit for the Methodist Missionary Society of Australia by a lecturer at the Teachers College, Sydney.

Chauncy Maples, D.D., F.R.G.S., Pioneer Missionary in East Central Africa for Nineteen Years and Bishop of Likoma, Lake Nyasa, A.D. 1895. A Sketch of his Life with Selections from his Letters by his Sister (London, Longmans, Green and Co., 1897, pp. viii, 403).

Marie-Germaine, *Le Christ au Gabon* (Louvain, Museum Lessianum, 1931, pp. xx, 168). Written by one of Soeurs Bleues de Castres.

Marsden, J. B., editor, *Memoirs of the Life and Labours of the Rev. Samuel Marsden of Paramatta, Senior Chaplain of New South Wales, and of His Early Connexion with the Missions to New Zealand and Tahiti* (London, The Religious Tract Society [no date, c. 1858], pp. viii, 326). The editor was not related to Samuel Marsden. Based upon the correspondence and journals of S. Marsden, and a Ms. life by Sadleir of Paramatta.

Marsden, Joshua, *The Narrative of a Mission to Nova Scotia, New Brunswick, and the Somers Islands; with a Tour to Lake Ontario. To which is added, The Mission, an Original Poem, with Copious Notes, also, a Brief Account of Missionary Societies* (Plymouth, Dock, J. Johns, 1816, pp. xiv, 289). By a Methodist missionary.

Marsh, John W., *Narrative of the Origin and Progress of the South American Mission; or "First Fruits" Enlarged* (London, South American Missionary Society, 1883, pp. 160).

Martin, K. L. P., *Missionaries and Annexation in the Pacific* (Oxford University Press, 1924, pp. 101). Somewhat critical of missionaries, but attempting to be objective.

Martin, Lady, *Our Maoris* (London, Society for Promoting Christian Knowledge, 1884, pp. iv, 220). Partly from personal experience and observation.

Martindale, C. C., *African Angelus. Episodes and Impressions* (London, Sheed & Ward, 1932, pp. xvi, 436).

Masters, Henry and Walter E., *In Wild Rhodesia. A Story of Missionary Enterprise and Adventure in the Land where Livingstone Lived, Laboured, and Died* (London, Francis Griffiths, 1920, pp. 246).

Maston, A. B., editor, *Jubilee Pictorial History of Churches of Christ in Australasia* (Melbourne, Austral Publishing Co., 1903, pp. 423).

Mather, George, and Blagg, Charles John, *Bishop Rawle. A Memoir* (London, Kegan Paul, Trench, Trübner & Co., 1890, pp. xii, 421).

Mathews, Basil, *John R. Mott, World Citizen* (New York, Harper & Brothers, 1934, pp. xiii, 469). A warmly appreciative biography by a personal friend, based upon careful research and upon data provided by Dr. Mott.

Mathieson, William Law, *The Sugar Colonies and Governor Eyre 1849-1866* (London, Longmans, Green and Co., 1936, pp. xiv, 243). Well documented.

Matthews, C. H. S., *A Parson in the Australian Bush* (London, Edward Arnold, 1908, pp. xiv, 311).

Maxwell, J. Lowry, *Nigeria. The Land, the People and Christian Progress* (London, World Dominion Press, no date, pp. 164). By a member of the Sudan United Mission in Northern Nigeria.

Mecham, J. Lloyd, *Church and State in Latin America* (Chapel Hill, University of North Carolina Press, 1934, pp. viii, 550). Objective. Based largely upon printed sources.

Meigs, Peveril, 3d, *The Dominican Mission Frontier of Lower California* (Berkeley, University of California Press, 1935, pp. vi, 192). Excellent.

Merensky, A., *Deutsche Arbeit am Njassä, Deutsch-Ostafrika* (Berlin, Buchhandlung der Berliner evangelischen Missionsgesellschaft, 1894, pp. vi, 368). By a director, a pioneer of the Berlin Missionary Society in German East Africa.

Merensky, A., *Erinnerungen aus den Missionsleben in Transvaal* (Berlin, Buchhandlung der Berliner evangelischen Missionsgesellschaft, 2d ed., 1900, pp. 414).

Annual Report of the Board of Foreign Missions of the Methodist Episcopal Church (Earlier ones under the title, *Annual Report of the Missionary Society of the Methodist Episcopal Church*) (New York, 1820ff.).

Michelsen, Oscar, *Misi* (London, Marshall, Morgan and Scott [no date, c. 1934], pp. xvi, 238). An autobiography of a missionary to the New Hebrides.

Mills, Dora S. Yarnton, compiler, *What We Do in Nyasaland* (London, Universities' Mission to Central Africa, 1911, pp. x, 266).

Milum, John, *Thomas Birch Freeman, Missionary Pioneer to Ashanti, Dahomey, and Egba* (Chicago, Fleming H. Revell Co., no date, pp. 160). By a pioneer missionary who knew Freeman.

The Missionary Herald (Boston, 1821ff.). An official organ of the American Board of Commissioners for Foreign Missions.

Missiones Catholicae cura S. Congregationis de Propaganda Fide Descriptae in Annum MDCCCXCII (Rome, S. C. de Propaganda Fide, 1892, pp. xxxvi, 682).

Missiones Catholicae cura S. Congregationis de Propaganda Fide Descriptae Statistica. Data Statistica Referunter ad diem 30 Juni 1926 (Rome, Typis Polyglottis Vaticanis, 1930, pp. xii, 534). Official and full figures and summary descriptions.

Missions (New York, 1910ff.). An organ of Northern Baptists.

Moffat, John S., *The Lives of Robert and Mary Moffat* (London, T. Fisher Unwin, new edition, 1886, pp. xxii, 468). By their son.

Moffat, Robert U., *John Smith Moffat C.M.G. Missionary. A Memoir* (New York, E. P. Dutton and Co., 1921, pp. xix, 388). By a son.

Mondain, Gustave, *Un Siècle de Mission Protestante à Madagascar* (Paris, Société des Missions Évangéliques, 1920, pp. xii, 372).

Montgomery, Henry Hutchinson, *The Light of Melanesia: a Record of Fifty Years' Mission Work in the South Seas, Written after a Personal Visitation* (London, Society for Promoting Christian Knowledge, 1896, pp. xii, 254).

Moore, Herbert, *The Land of Good Hope* (Westminster, Society for the Propagation of the Gospel in Foreign Parts, 1912, pp. viii, 372). A study book.

Moreira, Eduardo, *Portuguese East Africa. A Study of its Religious Needs* (London, World Dominion Press, 1936, pp. 104).

[Morice, A. G.], *Fifty Years in Western Canada. Being the Abridged Memoirs of Rev. A. G. Morice, O.M.I., by D.L.S.* (Toronto, The Ryerson Press, 1930, pp. x, 267).

Morice, A. G., *History of the Catholic Church in Western Canada from Lake Superior to the Pacific (1659-1895)* (Toronto, The Musson Book Co., 2 vols., 1910). Sympathetic, based upon manuscript archives and printed sources.

Moulton, J. Egan, with co-operation of W. Fiddian Moulton, *Moulton of Tonga* (London, The Epworth Press, 1921, pp. 169). By members of the family.

Mountain, Armine W., *A Memoir of George Jehoshaphat Mountain, D.D., D.C.L., Late Bishop of Quebec, Compiled (at the Desire of the Synod of that Diocese) by his Son* (Montreal, John Lovell, 1866, pp. 477).

Müller, Karl, *200 Jahre Brüdermission. 1 Band. Das erste Missionsjahrhundert* (Herrnhut, Missionsbuchhandlung, 1931, pp. viii, 380).

Mullins, J. D., *Our Beginnings: being a Short Sketch of the History of the Colonial and Continental Church Society* (no date or place, c. 1923, pp. 35). By a secretary of the society.

Murray, A. W., *The Bible in the Pacific* (London, John Nisbet & Co., 1888, pp. vi, 296). By one who spent forty years as a missionary in the Pacific.

Murray, A. W., *Forty Years' Mission Work in Polynesia and New Guinea from 1835 to 1875* (London, John Nisbet & Co., 1876, pp. xvi, 509). An autobiographical record of a representative of the London Missionary Society.

Murray, A. W., *The Martyrs of Polynesia. Memorials of Missionaries, Native Evangelists, and Native Converts, Who have Died by the Hand of Violence, from 1799 to 1871* (London, Elliott Stock, 1885, pp. xiv, 223).

Murray, A. W., *Missions in Western Polynesia: Being Historical Sketches of these Missions, from Their Commencement in 1839 to the Present Time* (London, John Snow, 1863, pp. xi, 489).

Nederlandschen Studenten Zendings-Bond, *Hedendaagsche Zending in Onze Oost* (The Hague, Boekhandel van den Zendings-Studie-Raad, 1909, pp. 267).

Needham, J. S., *White and Black in Australia* (London, Society for Promoting Christian Knowledge, 1935, pp. 174). By the head of the Australian Board of Missions who for a time was a missionary among the blacks. The first two chapters are by other authors.

Nigeria (London, H. M. Stationery Office, 1920, pp. 82).

Nijland, E., *Schetsen uit Insulinde* (Utrecht, C. H. E. Breijer, 1893, pp. vii, 411).

Nolte, Ferdinand, *Missions-Annalen der Missionare von der Hl. Familie. Brasilianisches Missionsfeld* (Betzdorf, Missionshaus Heilige Familie, Vol. I, 1931, pp. xxiv, 251).

Norman, L. S., *Nyasaland without Prejudice. A Balanced, Critical Review of the Country and its Peoples* (London, East Africa, 1934, pp. viii, 186). A popular account, friendly to missions.

Northcott, Cecil, *John Williams Sails On* (London, Hodder and Stoughton, 1939, pp. 255).

Notizie Statistiche. Delle Missioni di Tutto il Mondo Dipendenti dalla S. C. de Propaganda Fide (Rome, Coi Tipi della S. C. de Propaganda Fide, 1844).

O'Brien, Eris M., *The Dawn of Catholicism in Australia* (Sydney, Angus & Robertson, 2 vols., 1928). The years covered are 1816-1821. The narrative, written by an ardent Catholic, is based on extensive research in the appropriate documents. It treats chiefly of the priest, Jeremiah O'Flynn.

Oliver, Edmund H., *The Winning of the Frontier* (Toronto, The United Church Publishing Co., 1930).

O'Rorke, Benjamin C., *Our Opportunity in the West Indies* (Westminster, Society for the Propagation of the Gospel in Foreign Parts, 1913, pp. 136).

Osias, Camilo, and Lorenzana, Avelina, *Evangelical Christianity in the Philippines* (Dayton, The United Brethren Publishing House, 1931, pp. xx, 240). By Protestants; pro-Filipino; made up chiefly of excerpts from a few well-known books.

Page, Jesse, *The Black Bishop, Samuel Adjai Crowther* (New York, Fleming H. Revell Co., no date, pp. xv, 440).

Pannier, Jacques, and Mondain, Gustave, *L'Expansion Française Outre-Mer et Les Protestants Français* (Paris, Société des Missions Évangéliques, 1931, pp. 179). Contains excellent bibliographical notes.

Paradela, B., *Resumen Histórico de la Congregación de la Misión en España, desde 1704 a 1868* (Madrid, G. Hernández y Galo Sáez, 1923, pp. xv, 477). By a Lazarist, and a volume in the *Biblioteca San Vincente de Paul*.

Parker, Joseph I., editor, *Directory of World Missions* (New York, International Missionary Council, 1938, pp. xi, 255).

Parker, Joseph I., editor, *Interpretative Statistical Survey of the World Mission of the Christian Church* (New York, International Missionary Council, 1928, pp. 323).

Pascoe, C. F., *Two Hundred Years of the S. P. G. An Historical Account of the Society for the Propagation of the Gospel in Foreign Parts, 1701-1900* (London, Published at the Society's Office, 1901, pp. xli, 1429). Very detailed; by an assistant secretary of the Society.

Pascoe, C. F., *Classified Digest of the Records of the Society for the Propagation of the Gospel in Foreign Parts, 1701-1892* (London, at the Society's Office, 1893, pp. xvi, 980).

Paton, Frank H. L., *The Kingdom in the Pacific* (London, London Missionary Society, 1913, pp. viii, 166).

Paton, Frank H. L., *Patteson of Melanesia. A Brief Life of John Coleridge Patteson, Missionary Bishop* (London, Society for Promoting Christian Knowledge, [1930], pp. ix, 209). Based chiefly upon the biography by Miss Yonge.

Patterson, George, *Missionary Life among the Cannibals: Being the Life of the Rev. John Geddie, D.D., First Missionary to the New Hebrides; with the History of the Nova Scotia Presbyterian Mission on that Group* (Toronto, James Campbell & Son, etc., 1882, pp. xiv, 512).

Payne, Ernest A., *Freedom in Jamaica. Some Chapters in the Story of the Baptist Foreign Missionary Society* (London, The Carey Press, 1933, pp. 112).

Peers, E. Allison, *Spain, the Church and the Orders* (London, Eyre and Spottiswoode, 1939, pp. xi, 219). By an Anglican. Sympathetic. Derived from long residence and some reading.

Pérez, Rafael, *La Compañía de Jesus en Colombia y Centro-América despues de su Restauración. Parte Primera desde el llamamiento de los PP. de la Compañía de Jesus á la Nueva Granada en 1842, hasta su expulsión y dispersión en 1850* (Valladolid, Luis n. de Gavivia, 1896, pp. xx, 453). By a Jesuit.

Philippe, Anthony, *Au Coeur de l'Afrique. Ouganda. Un Demi-Siècle d'Apostolat au Centre Africain, 1878-1928* (Paris, Dillen & Cie, 1929, pp. 191). By one of the White Fathers. A popular account.

The Philippine Liberal (Manila, 1933). An organ of the Philippine Independent Church.

Philippo, James M., *Jamaica: Its Past and Present State* (London, John Snow, 1843, pp. xvi, 487). By one long a Baptist missionary in Jamaica.

Philp, Horace R. A., *A New Day in Kenya* (London, World Dominion Press, 1936, pp. vi, 188). By a missionary of the Church of Scotland with long experience in Kenya.

Pierson, Delavan L., *The Pacific Islanders. From Savages to Saints. Chapters from the Life Stories of Famous Missionaries and Native Converts* (New York, Funk & Wagnalls, 1906, pp. ix, 354). Popularly written.

Pinfold, James T., *Fifty Years in Maoriland* (London, The Epworth Press, 1930, pp. 200). Chatty, not very well organized, made up in part of reminiscences but chiefly of notes concerning the history of New Zealand.

Piolet, J. B., *Les Missions Catholiques Françaises au XIXe Siécle* (Paris, Librairie Armand Colin, 5 vols., no date, last vol. to 1902). By various authors.

Pitts, Herbert, *The Australian Aboriginal and the Christian Church* (London, Society for Promoting Christian Knowledge, 1914, pp. 133).

Playter, George F., *The History of Methodism in Canada* (Toronto, Anson Green, 1862, pp. viii, 414).

Pompallier, Jean Baptiste François, *Early History of The Catholic Church in Oceania* (Auckland, H. Brett, 1888, pp. 83). By a Vicar Apostolic of Western Oceania. The narrative was compiled from the author's diary, part of his report to the Holy See.

Price, Ernest, *Bananaland. Pages from the Chronicles of an English Minister in Jamaica* (London, The Carey Press, 1930, pp. x, 186). By a Principal of Calabar College and Headmaster of Calabar High School, in Kingston, Jamaica.

Pride, Andrew, and Cowell, A. J., *South America. A Handbook of the Work of the South American Missionary Society* (London, South American Missionary Society, 2d ed., no date, pp. 67).

Protestant Missions in South America (New York, Student Volunteer Movement for Foreign Missions, 1900, pp. vii, 239). By several authors.

Purchas, H. T., *A History of the English Church in New Zealand* (Christchurch, Simpson & Williams, 1914, pp. xviii, 252). Based upon careful research.

Ramsden, Eric, *Marsden and the Missions. Prelude to Waitangi* (Sydney, Angus & Robertson, 1936, pp. xix, 295). Based largely upon the original sources.

Rankin, Melinda, *Twenty Years among the Mexicans. A Narrative of Missionary Labor* (Cincinnati, Chase & Hall, 1875, pp. 199). An important source for early Protestant missions in Mexico.

Rasmussen, Knud, *The People of the Polar North. A Record Compiled from the Danish Originals and Edited by G. Herring* (London, Kegan Paul, Trench, Trübner & Co., 1908, pp. xix, 358). From first hand observations.

Raucaz, L. M., *In the Savage South Solomons. The Story of a Mission* (The Society for the Propagation of the Faith, 1928, pp. 270). By a Vicar Apostolic of the South Solomon Islands.

Rauws, Joh., *Overzicht van het Zendingswerk in Ned. Oost- en West-Indië overdruk uit "Mededeelingen" tijdschrift voor Zendingswetenschap* (Oegstgeest Zendingsbureau, 1930-1931, pp. 73).

Rauws, Joh., Kraemer, H., Van Hasselt, F. J. F., and Slotemaker de Bruine, N. A. C., *The Netherlands Indies* (London, World Dominion Press, 1935, pp. 186). By Dutch experts on missions.

Restarick, Henry Bond, *Hawaii 1778-1920 from the Viewpoint of a Bishop* (Honolulu, Paradise of the Pacific, 1924, pp. 413). Carefully done.

Revista de la Exposición Misional Española, Barcelona, 1929 (Barcelona, 1928-1930). A periodical published in connexion with the missionary exposition which formed part of a general exposition at Barcelona.

Revue d'Histoire des Missions (Paris, 1924ff.).

Richter, Julius, *Die evangelische Mission in Fern- und Südost-Asien, Australien, Amerika* (Gütersloh, C. Bertelsmann, 1932, pp. xii, 488). Readable. Few references to sources, but occasional bibliographies.

Richter, Julius, *Die evangelische Mission in Niederländisch-Indien* (Gütersloh, C. Bertelsmann, 1931, pp. 167). The only general history, except in Dutch, of missions in the Netherlands East Indies. Somewhat lacking in footnote references to the sources.

Richter, Julius, *Geschichte der evangelischen Mission in Afrika* (Gütersloh, C. Bertelsmann, 1922, pp. 813). The standard account of the history of Protestant missions in Africa. The book suffers somewhat from a paucity of footnote references to authorities for statements made. The author has decided convictions which occasionally make themselves manifest. His German nationality and sympathies are at times obvious.

Richter, Julius, *Tanganyika and Its Future* (London, World Dominion Press, 1934, pp. 112).

Rink, Henry, *Danish Greenland. Its People and Its Products.* Edited by Robert Brown (London, Henry S. King & Co., 1877, pp. xvii, 468). Somewhat critical of the missionaries.

Rippy, J. Fred, and Nelson, Jean Thomas, *Crusaders of the Jungle* (Chapel Hill, University of North Carolina Press, 1936, pp. x, 401). The story of missions in tropical South America during the colonial period. Semi-popular in style, scholarly.

Rivers, W. H. R., editor, *Essays on the Depopulation of Melanesia* (Cambridge University Press, 1922, pp. xviii, 116).

Rivers, W. H. R., *The History of Melanesian Society* (Cambridge University Press, 2 vols., 1914).

Roberts, Stephen H., *Population Problems of the Pacific* (London, George Routledge & Sons, 1927, pp. xx, 411). Scholarly, friendly to missions.

Robertson, James, *History of the Mission of the Secession Church to Nova Scotia and Prince Edward Island from its Commencement in 1765* (Edinburgh, John Johnstone, 1847, pp. 285). By the pastor of the Portsburgh Church, Edinburgh. Based chiefly upon minutes, letters, and other first hand information. Some of the documents are quoted *in extenso*. A valuable source.

Robson, George, *Missions of the United Presbyterian Church. The Story of Our Jamaica Mission with a Sketch of Our Trinidad Mission* (Edinburgh, United Presbyterian Church, 1894, pp. 135).

Rodgers, James B., *Forty Years in the Philippines. A History of the Philippine Mission of the Presbyterian Church in the United States of America* (New York, The Board of Foreign Missions of the Presbyterian Church in the United States of America, 1940, pp. viii, 205). By a pioneer of the mission.

Rodway, James, *Guiana: British, Dutch, and French* (London, T. Fisher Unwin, 1912, pp. 318).

Rogers, Edgar, *Canada's Greatest Need* (Westminster, Society for the Propagation of the Gospel in Foreign Parts, 1913, pp. xi, 365). A mission study text.

Roome, Wm. J. W., *A Great Emancipation. A Missionary Survey of Nyasaland, Central Africa* (London, World Dominion Press, 1926, pp. 64). By an agent of the British and Foreign Bible Society who had travelled much in Africa.

Ross, C. Stuart, *Churches and Church Workers in Fiji* (Greelong, H. Thacker, 1909, pp. 108). Outgrowth of a visit in 1876, as an agent of the Presbyterian church in New Zealand.

Ross, C. Stuart, *Colonization and Church Work in Victoria* (Melbourne, Melville, Mullen & Slade, 1891, pp. 368). Chiefly Presbyterian, by a clergyman.

Ross, C. Stuart, *The Story of the Otago Church and Settlement* (Dunedin, Wise, Caffin & Co., 1887, pp. x, 449). Based upon the literature accessible in Otago; by a clergyman.

Røstvig, L., *Sakalaverne og deres Land* (Stavanger, Det Norske Missionsselskabs Forlag, 1886, pp. 114).

Rutter, Owen, *British North Borneo. An Account of its History, Resources and Native Tribes* (London, Constable & Co., 1922, pp. xvi, 404).

Ryan, Archie Lowell, *Religious Education in the Philippines* (Manila, The Methodist Publishing House, 1930, pp. xiv, 205).

Ryan, Edwin, *The Church in the South American Republics* (New York, The Bruce Publishing Co., 1932, pp. viii, 119). By a Roman Catholic priest; popular in style, but scholarly.

[Ryerson, Egerton] *"The Story of My Life." By the Late Rev. Egerton Ryerson, D.D., LL.D. (Being Reminiscences of Sixty Years' Public Service in Canada).* Edited by J. George Hodgins (Toronto, William Briggs, 1883, pp. 613).

Salinis, de, *Marins et Missionnaires. Conquête de la Nouvelle-Calédonie 1843-1853*

(Paris, Pierre Tequi, 2d ed., 1927, pp. 296). Based partly on manuscript sources; by a Jesuit.

Sanderson, J. E., *The First Century of Methodism in Canada* (Toronto, Wm. Briggs, 2 vols., 1908). Exact references to sources not always given, but containing much first hand material. Largely in the form of annals.

Schapera, I., editor, *Western Civilization and the Natives of South Africa. Studies in Culture Contact* (London, George Routledge and Sons, 1934, pp. xiv, 312). By various authors.

Schlatter, Wilhelm, *Geschichte der Basler Mission 1815-1915* (Basel, Basler Missionsbuchhandlung, 3 vols., 1916). Based especially upon unpublished sources.

Schlunk, Martin, *Grosse Missionsführer der Kirchengeschichte* (Leipzig, Quelle & Meyer, 1931, pp. 152). Popularly written sketches.

Schmidlin, Joseph, *Katholische Missionsgeschichte* (Steyl, Missionsdruckerei, 1924, pp. xi, 598). A standard work by a distinguished Roman Catholic specialist on missions, with extensive bibliographical notes.

There is an English translation by Matthias Braun (Mission Press, Techny, Ill., 1933, pp. xiv, 862) which makes additions to the bibliographies, especially of more recent works and works in English, and here and there adds to the text and footnotes. In some portions, therefore, it is fuller and better than the German original.

Schmidlin, J., *Die katholischen Missionen in den deutschen Schutzgebieten* (Münster in Westfalen, Aschendorffsche Verlagsbuchhandlung, 1913, pp. xiv, 304).

Schoenrich, Otto, *Santo Domingo. A Country with a Future* (New York, The Macmillan Co., 1918, pp. xiv, 418).

Scholefield, Guy H., *Captain William Hobson, First Governor of New Zealand* (Oxford University Press, 1934, pp. 227). By a Dominion Archivist and Parliamentary Librarian of New Zealand.

Schrieke, B., editor, *The Effect of Western Influence on Native Civilisations in the Malay Archipelago* (Batavia, G. Kolff & Co., 1929, pp. vii, 247). Scholarly.

Schulze, Adolf, *200 Jahre Brüdermission. II Band, Das zweite Missionsjahrhundert* (Herrnhut, Verlag der Missionsbuchhandlung, 1932, pp. xii, 715). Well documented.

Schwager, Friedrich, *Die katholische Heidenmission der Gegenwart im Zusammenhang mit ihrer grossen Vergangenheit* (Steyl, Missionsdruckerei, 1907, pp. 446). A standard work.

Memoir of William Shaw, Late Superintendent of the Wesleyan Missions in South-Eastern Africa. Edited by His Oldest Surviving Friend (London, Wesleyan Conference Office, 1874, pp. vi, 463).

Shaw, William, *The Story of My Mission in South-Eastern Africa* (London, Hamilton, Adams, and Co., 1860, pp. ix, 576). By the real founder of South African Methodism.

Shepherd, Robert H. W., *Lovedale South Africa. The Story of a Century 1841-1941* (Lovedale, The Lovedale Press, 1941, pp. xiv, 531). A thorough, careful work, friendly to Lovedale.

Shortt, Adam, and Doughty, Arthur G., editors, *Canada and Its Provinces* (Toronto, Glasgow, Brook and Co., 23 vols., 1914-1917).

Shrewsbury, John V. B., *Memorials of the Rev. William J. Shrewsbury* (London, Hamilton, Adams & Co., 2d ed., 1869, pp. viii, 528). By a son.

Shrimpton, A. W., and Mulgan, Alan E., *Maori & Pakeha. A History of New Zealand* (Auckland, Whitcombe & Tombs, 1921, pp. 399).

Sibree, James, *Fifty Years in Madagascar. Personal Experiences of Mission Life and Work* (London, George Allen & Unwin, 1924, pp. 359). By a distinguished missionary of the London Missionary Society.

Sibree, James, *The Madagascar Mission* (London, London Missionary Society, 1907, pp. 103). By a veteran missionary.

Silcox, Claris Edwin, *Church Union in Canada, Its Causes and Consequences* (New York, Institute of Social and Religious Research, 1933, pp. xvii, 493). Carefully done.

Silva Cotapos, Carlos, *Historia Eclesiástica de Chile* (Santiago de Chile, Imprenta de San José, 1925, pp. viii, 387). By a bishop.

Sissons, C. B., *Egerton Ryerson. His Life and Letters* (Toronto, Clarke, Irwin & Company, Vol. I, 1937, pp. x, 601).

Smith, C. Henry, *The Mennonites of America* (Scottdale, Pa., Mennonite Publishing House, 1909, pp. 484). Based upon extensive research, by a well-trained scholar.

Smith, Edwin W., *The Way of the White Fields in Rhodesia. A Survey of Christian Enterprise in Northern and Southern Rhodesia* (London, World Dominion Press, 1928, pp. 172). By a competent scholar who had been a missionary in that area.

Smith, James Porter, *An Open Door in Brazil. Being a brief survey of the Mission Work carried on in Brazil since 1869 by the Presbyterian Church in the United States* (Richmond, Presbyterian Committee on Publication, 1925, pp. 235).

Société des Missions Évangéliques . . . établie à Paris (Annual Reports, Paris, 1835ff.).

Société des Missions Évangéliques, *Nos Champs de Mission* (Paris, Société des Missions Évangéliques, 2d ed., 1908, pp. xxiv, 144).

The Society of Friends in Australasia. List of Members Constituting the General Meeting for Australia. With a List of the Members of the Society in New Zealand, 1st December, 1906. Also (separately) editions of the above, 1st February, 1908, and 1st December, 1908.

South American Missionary Society, Annual Reports (London).

Spanish Guinea (London, H. M. Stationery Office, 1920, pp. 60).

Speckmann, F., *Die Hermannsburger Mission in Afrika* (Hermannsburg, Missionsdruckerei, 1876, pp. x, 560).

Spiecker, J., *Die Rheinische Mission auf Sumatra, Nias und den andern westlich von Sumatra gelegenen Inseln* (Barmen, Verlag des Missionshauses, 1913, pp. 288).

Spring, Gardiner, *Memoirs of the Rev. Samuel J. Mills, Late Missionary to the South Western Section of the United States and Agent of the American Colonization Society Deputed to Explore the Coast of Africa* (New York, New York Evangelical Missionary Society, 1820, pp. 247). By a friend; in part made up of letters and journals of Mills.

Springer, John M., *The Heart of Central Africa* (Cincinnati, Jennings and Graham, 1909, pp. 223).

[Staley, T. N.], *Five Years Church Work in the Kingdom of Hawaii* (London, Rivington's, 1868, pp. 126). Based upon documents.

Stanley, Henry M., *Through the Dark Continent* (New York, Harper & Brothers, 2 vols., 1878).

The Statistical Year-book of Canada for 1890. Sixth Year of Issue. Published by the Department of Agriculture. Compiled by Sydney C. D. Roper (Ottawa, printed by Brown Chamberlain, 1891, pp. 628).

Stead, Francis Herbert, *The Story of Social Christianity* (London, James Clarke and Co., 2 vols., [no date]). Laudatory of the social changes wrought in the world by Christianity.

Stewart, D. Macrae, *The Presbyterian Church of Victoria. Growth in Fifty Years, 1859-1909. Issued by Authority of the General Assembly* (Melbourne, D. W. Paterson & Co., pp. vi, 129).

Stewart, James, *Dawn in the Dark Continent, or Africa and Its Missions* (Chicago, Fleming H. Revell Co., 1903, pp. 400). By the distinguished head of the Lovedale Institution in South Africa.

Stewart, Walter Sinclair, *Later Baptist Missionaries and Pioneers,* Vol. II (Philadelphia, 1929). Popular account.

Stock, Eugene, *The History of the Church Missionary Society: Its Environment, Its Men, and Its Work* (London, Church Missionary Society, 4 vols., 1899-1916). The standard history, by a secretary of the Society.

Stocker, Harry Emilius, *A Home Mission History of the Moravian Church in the United States and Canada (Northern Province)* ([No place], The Special Publication Committee of the Moravian Church, 1924, pp. 256).

Stonelake, Alfred R., *Congo Past and Present* (London, World Dominion Press, 1937, pp. 202). By an experienced missionary to the Congo.

Stowell, Jay S., *Between the Americas* (New York, Council of Women for Home Missions, 1930, pp. vi, 180). A Missionary Education Movement Text-book.

Strachan, Alexander, *The Life of the Rev. Samuel Leigh, Missionary to the Settlers and Savages of Australia and New Zealand; with a History of the Origin and Progress of the Missions in those Colonies* (London, The Wesleyan Mission House, 1870, pp. vi, 418).

Streit, Carolus, *Atlas Hierarchicus* (Typographia Bonifaciana, Paderborn, 1913, pp. 128, 37, 35).

Strong, Esther Boorman, and Warnshuis, A. L., editors, *Directory of Foreign Missions, Missionary Boards, Societies, Colleges, Coöperative Councils, and Other Agencies of the Protestant Churches of the World* (New York, International Missionary Council, 1933, pp. xii, 278).

Strong, William Ellsworth, *The Story of the American Board: An Account of the First Hundred Years of the American Board of Commissioners for Foreign Missions* (Boston, The Pilgrim Press, 1910, pp. xv, 523). A semi-official history.

Stuntz, Homer C., *The Philippines and the Far East* (Cincinnati, Jennings and Pye, 1904, pp. 514).

Survey of Service. Organizations Represented in International Convention of Dis-

ciples of Christ (St. Louis, Christian Board of Publication, 1928, pp. 723). Various authors have contributed, writing from first hand knowledge, describing the work of the denomination.

Sutherland, Alexander, *The Methodist Church and Missions in Canada and Newfoundland* (Toronto, The Department of Missionary Literature of the Methodist Church, Canada, 1906, pp. 316).

The Twenty-Second Report of the Tasmanian Colonial Missionary and Christian Instruction Society in Connection with the Tasmanian Congregational Union (Hobart Town, Burnet, 1858, pp. 16).

Thirty-third Report of the Tasmanian Missionary Society, 1859 (Hobart Town, Burnet, 1860, pp. 7).

Taylor, James Dexter, *The American Board Mission in South Africa. A Sketch of Seventy-five Years* (Durban, John Singleton & Sons, 1911, pp. 97).

Taylor, Richard, *The Past and Present of New Zealand; with its Prospects for the Future* (London, William Macintosh, 1868, pp. viii, 331). By an Anglican missionary.

Taylor, William, *Our South American Cousins* (New York, Phillips & Hunt, 1882, pp. 366). A first hand account of a missionary journey.

Taylor, William, *Story of My Life,* edited by John Clark Ridpath (New York, Hunt & Eaton, 1895, pp. 750).

Teilhard de Chardin, *La Guinée Superieure et Ses Missions* (Keer-lez-Maastricht, Collège Apostolique des Missions Africaines, 1888, pp. 235).

Thauren, Johannes, *Die Missionen der Gesellschaft des Göttl. Wortes in den Heidenländern. Die Mission in Mozambique, de Negermission in der Vereinigten Staaten und die Indianermissionen Paraguays und Brasiliens* (Steyl, Missionsdruckerei, 1931, pp. 40).

Theile, F. Otto, *One Hundred Years of the Lutheran Church in Queensland* (South Brisbane, United Evangelical Lutheran Church in Australia, 1938, pp. 290).

Thompson, R. Wardlaw, *My Trip in the "John Williams"* (London, London Missionary Society, 1900, pp. xii, 208).

Thomson, Basil, *The Fijians. A Study of the Decay of Custom* (London, William Heinemann, 1908, pp. xx, 396). By one who was a British official in the islands.

Tucker, Alfred R., *Eighteen Years in Uganda & East Africa* (London, Edward Arnold, 2 vols., 1908). Autobiographical, by a distinguished Anglican bishop of that region.

Tucker, Hugh C., *The Bible in Brazil. Colporter Experiences* (New York, Fleming H. Revell Co., 1902, pp. 293).

Tucker, H. W., *Memoir of the Life and Episcopate of George Augustus Selwyn, D.D., Bishop of New Zealand, 1841-1869; Bishop of Litchfield, 1867-1878* (London, William Wells Gardner, 2 vols., 1879). Based upon original sources.

Tucker, John T., *Angola. The Land of the Blacksmith Prince* (London, World Dominion Press, 1933, pp. viii, 180). By an experienced missionary in Angola.

Tucker, Leonard, *"Glorious Liberty." The Story of a Hundred Years Work of the Jamaica Baptist Mission* (London, The Baptist Missionary Society, 1914, pp. vii, 168).

Tucker, L. Norman, *From Sea to Sea the Dominion* (Toronto, Prayer and Study Union of the M.S.C.C., 2d ed., 1911, pp. 181).

Turner, George, *Nineteen Years in Polynesia: Missionary Life, Travels, and Researches in the Islands of the Pacific* (London, John Snow, 1861, pp. xii, 548).

Turner, J. G., *The Pioneer Missionary: Life of the Rev. Nathaniel Turner, Missionary in New Zealand, Tonga, and Australia* (London, The Wesleyan Conference Office, 1872, pp. viii, 335). By a son.

Ullathorne, W., *The Catholic Mission in Australasia* (London, Keating and Brown, 1838, 3d ed., pp. 58). By the vicar general of a Vicar Apostolic of New Holland and Van Dieman's Land.

Ullathorne, W., *A Reply to Judge Burton of the Supreme Court of New South Wales on "The State of Religion" in the Colony* (Sydney, W. A. Duncan, 1840, pp. xi, 98).

Union of South Africa, *Report of Native Churches Commission* (Cape Town, Cape Times, 1925, pp. 38). The members of the Commission were Alex. W. Roberts, Chairman, L. A. S. Lemmer, C. T. Loram, and P. v. d. Merwe.

Union of South Africa, Union Office of Census and Statistics, *Official Year Book of the Union and of Basutoland, Bechuanaland Protectorate, and Swaziland, No. 9, 1926-1927* (Pretoria, The Government Printing and Stationery Office, 1928, pp. xix, 1157).

Uplifting the Zulus. Seventy-Five Years' Mission Work in Natal and Zululand (Durban, John Singleton & Sons, pp. 52). Prepared on the initiative of the Natal Missionary Conference, an interdenominational body.

Vandenbosch, Amry, *The Dutch East Indies: Its Government, Problems, and Politics* (Grand Rapids, Mich., Wm. B. Eerdmans Publishing Co., 1933, pp. 385). Scholarly; based upon wide reading and upon travel in The Netherlands and the East Indies.

Van der Merve, Willem Jacobus, *The Development of Missionary Attitudes in the Dutch Reformed Church in South Africa* (Cape Town, Ivasionale Pers BPK, 1936, pp. x, 279). A doctoral dissertation.

Van der Velden, J. H., *De Roomsch-Katholieke Missie in Nederlandsch Oost-Indië, 1808-1908. Eene historische schets* (Nijmegen, L. C. G. Malmberg, 1908, pp. 397).

The First Report of the Van Dieman's Land Home Missionary and Christian Instruction Society (Hobart Town, William Gore Elliston, 1837, pp. 16). Also the 4th report of the Independents (Congregationalists).

Verguet, Léopold, *Histoire de la Première Mission Catholique au Vicariat de Mélanésie* (Carcassone, P. Labau, 1854, pp. 319).

Vernon, C. W., *The Old Church in the New Dominion. The Story of the Anglican Church in Canada* (London, Society for Promoting Christian Knowledge, 1929, pp. viii, 215). Semi-popular.

Verwimp, E., *Thirty Years in the African Wilds (Bro. Francis de Sadeleer, S. J.).* Adapted from the Flemish by W. Peters and M. Hannan (London, Alexander Ouseley, 1938, pp. 198). There is also a German translation.

Victor, Osmund, *The Salient of South Africa* (Westminster, Society for the Propagation of the Gospel in Foreign Parts, 1931, pp. vii, 190). A popular survey of the work of the Anglicans in South Africa by a member of the Community of the Resurrection.

Waddell, Hope Masterton, *Twenty-Nine Years in the West Indies and Central Africa: a Review of Missionary Work and Adventure, 1829-1858* (London, T. Nelson and Sons, 1863, pp. 681). In part autobiographical.

Walker, F. Deaville, *The Call of the West Indies: The Romance of Methodist Work and Opportunity in the West Indies and Adjacent Regions* (London, The Cargate Press, [no date], pp. 190).

Walker, F. Deaville, *The Romance of the Black River. The Story of the C. M. S. Nigeria Mission* (London, Church Missionary Society, 1930, pp. xvi, 267). A popular account, without footnote references to authorities, but based upon several earlier books and on articles in the C. M. S. magazine.

Walker, F. Deaville, *Thomas Birch Freeman* (London, Student Christian Movement, 1929, pp. 221). Based upon careful research in manuscript sources.

Walker, James Backhouse, *Early Tasmania* (Tasmania, John Vail, 1902, pp. viii, 289). Based upon the sources. Carefully done.

Walter, George, *Australien. Land, Leute, Mission* (Limburg, Druck und Verlag der Kongregation der Pallottiner, 1928, pp. 261).

Wangemann, *Geographisch-geschichtliche Übersichtskarte über die Evangelische Missionsarbeit in Süd-Afrika* (Berlin, Missionshaus, 1881).

Ward, Gertrude, *Father Woodward of U. M. C. A.* (Westminster, Universities' Mission to Central Africa, 1927, pp. 64). Made up largely of Woodward's letters.

Ward, G., *The Life of Charles Alan Smythies, Bishop of the Universities' Mission to Central Africa.* Edited by Edward Francis Russell (London, Universities' Mission to Central Africa, 1899, pp. xvii, 271).

Warneck, Gustav, *Abriss einer Geschichte der protestantischen Missionen von der Reformation bis auf die Gegenwart, mit einem Anhang über die katholischen Missionen* (Berlin, Martin Warneck, 10th ed., 1913, pp. x, 624).

Warneck, Joh., *50 Jahre Batakmission in Sumatra* (Berlin, Martin Warneck, 1912, pp. 301).

Watsford, John, *Glorious Gospel Triumphs as Seen in My Life and Work in Fiji and Australasia* (London, Charles H. Kelly, 1900, pp. xiii, 328).

Watson, Charles H., *Cannibals and Head-Hunters. Victories of the Gospel in the South Seas* (Washington, Review and Herald Publishing Association, 1926, pp. 287). A description of Seventh Day Adventist Missions.

Watters, Mary, *A History of the Church in Venezuela, 1810-1930* (Chapel Hill, The University of North Carolina Press, 1933, pp. ix, 260). Carefully done; based upon the sources.

Weatherhead, H. T. C., *Uganda: a Chosen Vessel. A Missionary Study Text-book on Uganda* (London, Church Missionary House, 1913, pp. 62).

Webster, A. N., *Madagascar* (Westminster, The Society for the Propagation of the Gospel in Foreign Parts, 1932, pp. 71). By an archdeacon of Imèrina.

Welles, Sumner, *Naboth's Vineyard. The Dominican Republic, 1844-1924* (New York, Payson & Clarke, 2 vols., 1928). By an American Commissioner to the Dominican Republic.

Wells, James, *The Life of James Stewart* (London, Hodder and Stoughton, 1909, pp. xi, 419).

West, Thomas, *Ten Years in South-Central Polynesia: Being Reminiscences of a Personal Mission to the Friendly Islands and Their Dependencies* (London, James Nisbet & Co., 1865, pp. xv, 500).

White, Charles L., *A Century of Faith: . . . Centenary Volume Published for the American Baptist Home Mission Society* (Philadelphia, The Judson Press, 1932, pp. 320).

White, Gilbert, *Round About the Torres Straits. A Record of Australian Church Missions* (London, Society for Promoting Christian Knowledge, 1917, pp. vii, 95).

White, Ralph J., *Six Years in Hammock Land* (Philadelphia, The United Lutheran Publication House, 1922, pp. 123). Lutheran missions in British Guiana.

Whiteside, J., *History of the Wesleyan Methodist Church of South Africa* (London, Elliott Stock, 1906, pp. viii, 479). By a Methodist minister. Excellent; sympathetic.

Whitington, F. T., *William Grant Broughton, Bishop of Australia, with Some Account of the Earliest Australian Clergy* (Sydney, Angus & Robertson, 1936, pp. xiv, 300).

Whitington, T., *Augustus Short, First Bishop of Adelaide. The Story of a Thirty-Four Years' Episcopate* (London, Wells Gardner, Darton & Co., 1888, pp. xxi, 301). By a clergyman ordained by Bishop Short. Based largely upon Short's papers.

Wilks, Mark, *Tahiti: Containing a Review of the Origin, Character, and Progress of French Roman Catholic Efforts for the Destruction of English Protestant Missions in the South Seas.* From the French (London, John Snow, 1844, pp. 134).

Williams, John, *A Narrative of Missionary Enterprises in the South Sea Islands* (New York, D. Appleton & Co., 1837, pp. xxii, 525).

Williams, Joseph J., *Voodoos and Obeahs. Phases of West India Witchcraft* (New York, Dial Press, 1933, pp. xvii, 257). By a Jesuit; based upon extensive research, including first hand observations.

Williams, Thomas, and Calvert, James, *Fiji and the Fijians* (London, Alexander Heylin, 2 vols., 1860). By eminent Methodist missionaries to Fiji.

Williams, William, *Christianity among the New Zealanders* (London, Seeley, Jackson, and Halliday, 1868, pp. vi, 384). By an Anglican bishop, one of the most distinguished of the pioneer missionaries to the Maoris.

Wilson, George Herbert, *The History of the Universities' Mission to Central Africa* (Westminster, Universities' Mission to Central Africa, 1936, pp. xvi, 278).

Wilson, Roland, *Official Year Book of the Commonwealth of Australia, No. 32, 1939* (Canberra, L. F. Johnston, 1940, pp. xxxii, 990).

Wilson, Samuel, *George Paull, of Benita, West Africa. A Memoir* (Philadelphia, Presbyterian Board of Publication, 1872, pp. 288). Made up almost entirely of the letters of Paull.

Winton, George B., *Mexico To-day, Social, Political and Religious Conditions*

(New York, Missionary Education Movement of the United States and Canada, 1916, pp. x, 227).

Witte, Jehan de, *Monseigneur Augouard* (Paris, Émile-Paul Frères, 1924, pp. x, 372).

Wood, John, *Memoir of Henry Wilkes, D.D., LL.D., His Life and Times* (Montreal, F. E. Grafton & Sons, 1887, pp. iv, 280). By an intimate friend and based largely on autobiographical notes by Wilkes.

Wood, Michael H. M., *A Father in God. The Episcopate of William West Jones, D.D.* (London, Macmillan and Co., 1913, pp. xxviii, 500). Based upon careful research in the sources. Sympathetic.

Woodsworth, James S., *Strangers Within Our Gates or Coming Canadians* (Toronto, Methodist Mission Rooms, 1909, pp. 335).

Wynne, G. Robert, *The Church in Greater Britain* (Westminster, Society for the Propagation of the Gospel in Foreign Parts, 3d ed., revised, 1911, pp. viii, 204). Semi-popular.

Yonge, Charlotte Mary, *Life of John Coleridge Patteson, Missionary Bishop of the Melanesian Islands* (London, Macmillan and Co., 2 vols., 1888). Based largely upon Patteson's letters; by a cousin.

Young, Robert, *From Cape Horn to Panama. A Narrative of Missionary Enterprise among the Neglected Races of South America, by the South American Missionary Society* (London, 2d ed., South American Missionary Society, 1905, pp. xii, 212).

Yzendoorn, Reginald, *History of the Catholic Missions in the Hawaiian Islands* (Honolulu, Honolulu Star-Bulletin, 1927, pp. xiv, 254). By a missionary in the islands; based upon research in the archives.

Zeitschrift für Missionswissenschaft (Münster, i. W., 1911ff.).

INDEX

Abel, Charles W., 242
Abeokuta, 437, 438
Aborigines' Friends' Association, 164
Aborigines' Inland Mission, 165
Aborigines of Australia, 161-165, 169, 170
Aborigines' Protection Society, 181
Acadia, 14
Acadia College, 28n
Adat, 287
Adelaide, 152-154, 168
Adriani, 290, 291
Africa, 319-470
Africa Inland Mission, 405, 410, 411, 427
African Lakes Corporation, 396
African Methodist Episcopal Church, in Canada, 36; in Jamaica, 57, 61; in Africa, 359, 361, 451, 455
African Methodist Episcopal Zion Church, 65, 451
Africaner, 345
Afrikaans, 322, 333
Afrikanders, 322, 326
Aglipay, Gregorio, y Labayan, 267
Aguinaldo, 267
Aitutaki, 209
Alberdi, 110
Albert, Lake, 427
Algoa Bay, 343, 351
All Saints College, Bathurst, 171n
Alline, Henry, 25, 28
Amazon Valley, 96
Ambali, Augustine, 392n
Amboina, 279
Ambrose, Ethel, 154n
Ambrym, 232
American and Foreign Christian Union, 114, 116, 117, 119, 122, 125
American Baptist Home Mission Society, 116
American Baptist Missionary Union, 423, 427, 450
American Bible Society, in Latin America, 113, 114, 115, 116, 117, 118, 120, 121, 124

American Board of Commissioners for Foreign Missions, in Mexico, 114; in the Marquesas, 207; in Hawaii, 247-252; in Micronesia, 256-258; in the Philippines, 271; in Africa, 360, 361, 385, 399, 401, 429, 451
American Home Missionary Society, 20
American Missionary Association, 19, 56, 455
American Seamen's Friend Society, 106, 113, 119
American Tract Society, 114
Amsterdam, Classis of, 322
Anderson, William and Louisa, 439n
Aneityum, 228, 230, 234
Angmagssalik, 47
Angola, 397-400
Aniwa, 229
Antanànarìvo, 302, 305, 307, 308
Anthing, F. L., 283
Anti-Burghers, 25
Antonio, 442
Appleyard, John W., 351
Araucanians, 104
Arbousset, Thomas, 363
Argentina, 83, 96, 110, 111, 113, 119, 120
Armentia, Nicholas, 95
Armstrong, John, 357n
Armstrong, Richard, 251
Arnot, F. S., 365, 387, 389, 399, 425
Arthington, Robert, 424
Ascension, 317
Ashanti, 445, 446
Ashmun, Jehudi, 449
Assemblies of God, 427
Associate Synod of the Secession Church, 18, 25, 26
Association of Christian Workmen, 283
Astrolabe Bay, 245
Astrup, Nils, 370
Atetela, 426
Auckland, 188, 191, 193
Augouard, Prosper Philippe, 429
Augustinians, 79, 94

Austin, William Pierce, 63
Austral Islands, 208
Australasian Board of Missions, 160, 230, 242
Australasian Wesleyan Methodist Connexion, 143, 174
Australia, 130-176
Australian Church Missionary Society, 135
Australian Methodist Missionary Society, 217

Badagry, 437, 438
Bagamojo, 407
Baganda, 413, 416
Bahamas, 60
Bahia, 97
Bailey, Jacob, 16n
Baker, A. W., 359
Baker, Moses, 53
Baker, Shirley, 212
Baker, Thomas, 222
Balfour, Francis, 358n
Balolos, 423
Bamangwato, 350
Bandawé, 393
Bangweuiu, Lake, 348, 387
Banjermasin, 280
Banks Islands, 231
Bantus, 337, 381, 390, 398, 403, 419, 433
Banyai, 365
Baptist Canadian Missionary Society, 20
Baptist Industrial Mission, 397
Baptist Missionary Society, 54, 423, 424, 432, 433
Baptist Union of Western Australia, 156
Baptists, in Canada, 6, 20, 23, 24, 27, 28, 32, 34; in Jamaica, 53, 54; in Latin America, 116, 118, 122, 123, 124; in Australia, 143, 148, 151, 154, 156, 158; in New Zealand, 192; in the Philippines, 270; in Africa, 331, 388, 396, 399, 423, 424, 432-434, 440, 441, 450
Bara, 308
Barbados, 60, 61
Barclay, P., 190
Barker, Frederic, 138
Barolongs, 351
Barotse, 365, 366
Barotseland, 364, 365, 386
Barr, Joseph W., 451n
Barron, Edward, 452
Basel Mission, 107, 136, 149, 158, 278, 434, 446, 450

Bastaards, 379
Basuto, 368
Basutoland, 358, 363, 364, 373
Bata, 431
Bataillon, 214, 217, 219, 225
Bataks, 280, 287-289, 300
Batavia, 277, 280, 283
Batavia River, 164
Bathurst, 458
Batoka plateau, 388
Batu, 289
Bauer, Stefan, 407
Bauro, 237
Bavenda, 368
Bay of Islands, 179-181
Beaton, P., 316n
Bechuanaland, 341, 350
Bechuanaland Protectorate, 380, 381
Beira, 402
Belgians, in Canada, 10
Belize, 61, 62
Bellefonds, Linant de, 413
Benedictines, in Latin America, 73, 97; in Australia, 169; in Africa, 408, 422
Bennett, James Gordon, Jr., 348
Bentley, W. Holland, 425
Berlin III, 405
Berlin Missionary Society, 367, 368, 406
Bermuda, 60
Berthoud, Paul, 366n
Bertram, James M'Gregor, 317n
Bessieux, Jean Remy, 428
Bethany, 369
Bethel bei Bielefeld, 405
Bethelsdorp, 343
Bethlehem Church, Berlin, 158
Bètsilèo, 306, 308, 312
Bianquis, 311n
Bible, translation of, 204, 209, 213, 221, 228, 250, 270, 287, 304, 351, 391, 401, 404, 416, 425, 433, 437, 440, 461
Bible Christians, 27n
Bickersteth, J. Burgon, 32n
Bihé, 399
Bill, Samuel A., 441
Bingham, Hiram, 258
Bismarck Archipelago, 239
Black, John, 32
Black, William, 27
Blackbirding, 235, 237
Blanco, Gúzman, 79

Blancos, 85
Blantyre, 346, 395
Bligh, William, 207
Bloemfontein, 325, 328, 351
Blythswood Institution, 354
Bodelschwingh, 405
Boer, de, 293
Boer War, 323, 333
Boers, in South America, 108; in Africa, 322-335, 337, 340
Boga, Lake, 164
Bogotá, 110
Bolivar, Simon, 71, 78
Bolivia, 81, 82, 94, 95, 118
Bolivian Indian Mission, 104
Bompas, William Carpenter, 37
Bonaire, 49
Borneo, 280, 296-298
Bosco, John, 96
Botshabelo, 368
Bounty, 207
Bourbon, Isle of, 305, 315
Bowen, John, 454
Bowen, Thomas J., 440
Boyle, Robert, 52
Brazil, 85, 86, 96, 97, 106, 107, 120-123
Breklum Mission, 407
Brent, Charles H., 271
Brésillac, Marion, 442
Brethren in Christ, 385
Brett, William Henry, 64
Bride price, 462
Bridgman, Wellington, 33n
Brisbane, 156, 157, 169, 174
British and Foreign Bible Society, in Jamaica, 57, 61; in British Guiana, 65; in Latin America, 109, 110; in Australia, 136, 142; in the Philippines, 269, 270
British and Foreign Society, 171
British Columbia, 4, 19, 31, 32, 34
British East Africa, 409-412
British East Africa Company, 409, 411
British Honduras, 61, 62
British North America, 3-45
British North Borneo Company, 296
British South Africa Company, 381, 383, 385
Brooke, Charles, 297
Brooke, James, 296
Brotherhood of St. Andrew, 53
Brothers of Charity of Gand, 422
Brothers of Christian Schools, 306, 422

Broughton, William Grant, 138, 145, 150
Brown, George, 238, 239, 242
Brown, George S., 451n
Brownsville, 114
Brunei, 296
Buchanan, Francis de Sales, 243n
Buenos Aires, 105, 106, 110, 111, 113, 120
Buganda, 413
Bulgarians, 15
Bumby, John Hewgill, 180n
Burdett-Counts, Miss, 32, 135
Burghers, 25
Burgos, 74
Burns, Thomas, 189
Burns, William C., 324
Burton, Maria S. B., 358n
Bury, Herbert, 62n
Bush Brotherhoods, 174
Bush Negroes, 66, 67
Bushmen, 336, 340, 344
Butler, John Wesley, 114
Buxton, Thomas Fowell, 50, 436
Buzacott, A., 209n

Cagliero, Giovanni, 96
Calabar, 439, 440
Callao, 106, 117, 118
Callaway, Godfrey, 357n
Callaway, Henry, 357
Callaway, Robert Furley, 356n
Callis, John Samuel, 417n
Calvert, James, 222
Cambridge University Mission Party, 438
Camden College, 143
Cameroon, 432-435
Campbell, John, 344n
Canada, 3-45
Canada Congregational Missionary Society, 23
Canada Education and Home Missionary Society, 23
Canadian Baptists in Bolivia, 112, 118
Canadian Congregationalists, in Africa, 399
Canal Zone, 108, 116
Canterbury, New Zealand, 187, 190
Canterbury Association, 187, 196
Cape Coast Castle, 446, 447
Cape Colony, 338, 341, 344, 349
Cape Town, 332, 334, 339, 351, 372
Cape Verde Islands, 317, 458
Cape York, 47

Capuchins, 73, 91, 93, 94, 95, 100, 257, 316, 422, 443
Carey, Jabez, 279
Carey, Lott, 450
Carey, William, 202
Carghill, William, 189
Cargill, David, 221
Carolines, 257, 258
Carpentaria, 159
Carrera, 77
Carvosso, Benjamin, 151
Casalis, Eugène, 363, 386
Case, William, 22n
Castro, 95
Cayenne, 86
Celebes, 279, 290
Central America, 77, 78, 91, 115, 116
Central American Mission, 116
Chaco, 92, 103, 104
Chamorros, 257
Champion, George, 360n
Chanel, Pierre Louis Marie, 214
Charters, David, 411
Chatelain, Heli, 400
Chatham Islands, 184
Chevron, 213
Chiapas, 115
Chile, 82, 83, 95, 119
Chillán, 92, 95
China Inland Mission, 238
Chinese, 62, 63, 66, 161, 297
Chiriguanos, 92
Chisamba, 399n
Christaller, J. G., 447n
Christchurch, 187, 192, 193
Christian and Missionary Alliance, 119, 120, 125, 271, 400, 425, 456
Christian Missions in Many Lands, 111, 119
Christian Reformed Church, 284, 293
Christian Science, 149, 332
Chubut, 106
Church Manse and Building Fund, 33
Church Missionary Society, in Canada, 17, 37; in Jamaica, 52; in British Guiana, 63; in Australia, 160, 163; in New Zealand, 179-182, 184; in Madagascar, 307; in Mauritius, 315; in Seychelles, 316; in Africa, 405, 407, 410, 414-417, 436-438, 453-455, 457
Church of England, in Canada, 5, 17, 20, 21, 25, 26, 31, 32, 36, 37, 42, 43; in the West Indies, 50-61; in British Honduras, 62; in British Guiana, 63, 64; in South America, 105, 106; in Australia, 135, 137-139, 145, 146, 149, 150, 152, 155, 157, 159, 160, 163, 172-174; in New Zealand, 178-184, 186, 187; in the Pacific Islands, 213, 225, 230, 231, 243, 253, 254; in Africa, 326-329, 335, 355-359, 383, 384, 388, 389, 391-393, 404, 405, 407, 410, 414-417, 436-438, 453-455, 457
Church of England Society for Newfoundland and the Colonies, 17
Church of God, 57, 61
Church of Norway Mission, 370
Church of Scotland, in Canada, 19, 21, 26, 43; in Australia, 140, 141, 155; in New Zealand, 188, 190; in Africa, 394
Claver, Marie, 409n
Clergy reserves, 21, 42, 43
Clow, James, 146, 147
Codner, Samuel, 17
Codrington, Christopher, 60
Codrington College, 457
Coillard, François, 364, 365, 383, 387
Coke, Thomas, 54, 60, 142, 330
Colegio de Ultramar, 74
Colenso, John William, 327, 328
Collegio Pio-Latino-Americano Pontificio, 73
Colombia, 79, 80, 94, 117
Colonial and Continental Church Society, 17, 135
Colonial Bishoprics Fund, 135
Colonial Church and School Society, 17
Colonial Church Union, 52, 53
Colonial Committee of the Church of Scotland, 136, 146
Colonial Missionary Society, 33, 136, 143, 148, 151, 154, 158, 161, 331
Colorados, 85
Colorum, 268
Coloured, 338, 352
Comber, Thomas J., 424
Commission for the Affairs of the Protestant Churches in the Netherlands East and West Indies, 277
Committee of Assistance for the Christian School for Daughters of the Javanese Nobility, 285
Committee on Co-operation in Latin America, 125

Community of St. Mary the Virgin, 329
Community of St. Michael and All Angels, 329
Community of the Resurrection (Mirfield), 329
Community of the Resurrection of Our Lord, 328, 357
Comoro Islands, 305, 316
Comte, Auguste, 70
Condah, Lake, 163
Congo Balolo Mission, 423
Congo, Belgian, 419-427
Congo Evangelistic Mission, 427
Congo Free State, 420
Congregation of the Immaculate Heart of Mary, 273, 421, 431, 432
Congregational Church Extension Society of Western Canada, 34
Congregational Union in London, 19
Congregational Union of Upper Canada, 23
Congregationalism, in Canada, 6, 19, 23, 24, 32, 33, 44; in Jamaica, 56; in Australia, 136, 143, 148, 151, 154, 161, 174; in New Zealand, 192; in South Africa, 331
Conselheiro, Antonio, 128n
Convicts, in Australia, 132, 137, 144, 149, 166, 167
Cook Islands, 208-210
Cook, James, 130, 131, 177, 198, 202, 247
Coolen, 292, 293
Coope, Anna, 105
Corisco, 429
Corn Island, 108
Costa Rica, 78, 108
Countess of Huntingdon's Connexion, 455
Couppé, 239
Cowie, William Garden, 188n
Cowley Fathers, 329
Cowper, William Macquarie, 169n
Cox, Melville B., 451
Crawford, Daniel, 387, 425
Crees, 38
Creoles, 68, 71
Cripps, A. S., 384
Crocker, William G., 450n
Crosby, Thomas, 38n
Crowe, 110
Crowther, Samuel Adjai, 436, 437
Cuarteron, 297
Cuba, 89, 124
Culture system, 280

Curaçao, 49
Curling, Joseph James, 29n

Dahomy, 443, 444
Dalmond, 305
Damien, Joseph, 256
Danish Lutherans, in Greenland, 46-48
Danks, Benjamin, 239
Dar-es-Salaam, 405, 406, 408
Darwin, Charles, 104
Daughters of Mary, 316
Daughters of the Cross of Liége, 422
Davao, 271
Dayaks, 280, 297
Dayspring, 229, 437
Dehon, Léon, 422n
Delagoa Bay, 351, 361, 366
Demerara, 62-64
De Montfort Fathers, 397
Depok, 285
Depok Central Committee, 285
Derwent, 149
Deutscher Verein für Pastoration in Brazil, 107
Diáz, 76, 77
Diocesan Church Society, in Upper Canada, 21
Disciples of Christ, in Jamaica, 56; in Argentina, 120; in Australia, 144, 149, 151, 154, 156, 158; in the Philippines, 271; in Africa, 426n
Disney, H. P., 30n
Disruption, in Scotland, 22, 26, 141
Dixon, 167
Dobinson, Henry Hughes, 438n
Dogura, 243
Dolamore, 192
Dole, Sanford B., 253
Dominica, 59
Dominican Republic, 88
Dominican Sisters, 372
Dominicans, in Trinidad, 58; in Latin America, 73, 79, 91, 94, 97; in the Philippines, 267, 273; in Africa, 422
Doppers, 334
Douarre, 234
Douglas, Arthur, 392n
Doukhobors, 15, 35
Drees, Charles W., 114n
Drysdale River, 169
Duff, 202, 203, 211

Duff, Alexander, 353
Duncan, James, 184n
Dundee, 371
Dunedin, 189, 192, 193
Durban, 372
Dutch East Indies, 276-295
Dutch Guiana, 65-67
Dutch Reformed Church, 322-335, 339-341, 384, 387, 396
Dutch Reformed Missionary Union, 284
Dutton, Joseph, 256
Dwane, James Mata, 358, 359

East African Scottish Industrial Mission, 410
East India Company, Dutch, 276-278
East Indies, 275-300
East London Mission Institute, 111
Easter Island, 206
Eastern Orthodox, in Canada, 15; in Latin America, 101; in Australia, 170; in South Africa, 332
Ebon, 258
Ecuador, 80, 81, 94, 117
Education, in Canada, 41, 42; in Australia, 171; in Africa, 375, 376, 416, 425
Edwards, John, 351n
Efate, 229
Efik, 440
Egreja Episcopal Brasileira, 123
Ehrhardt, Valentine, 430n
Eimeo, 203
Eldred, Robert Ray and Lillian Byers, 426n
Ellice Islands, 218
Elliott, W. A., 382n
Ellis, Mrs. Mercy, 203n
Ellis, William, 203n, 304, 305, 307
Elroy, Louis, 217
El Salvador, 77
Emancipation of Negroes, in West Indies, 50, 51; in Africa, 344, 463
Embde, 292, 293
Enggano, 289
Épalle, 235
Epi, 229, 230
Épinette, Édouard, 428n
Ermelo, 283, 293
Erromanga, 227, 228
Erskine, George, 142
Eskimos, 14, 15, 30, 36, 37, 46-48
Espiritu Santo, 232

Esser, J. P., 293
Ethical policy, 281
Ethiopia, Order of, 358, 359
Ethiopianism, 361
Eustatius, 49
Evangelical Alliance, 378
Evangelical Missionary Society for German East Africa, 405
Evangelical Union of South America, 111
Evangelical Union of the Philippine Islands, 272
Evangelicalism, in Australia, 137, 138
Evans, James, 38
Every, E. F., 106n

Falklands, Bishop of the, 105
Fanti, 445, 447
Farquhar, Governor, 303
Faure, D. P., 334
Federation de Circulos Católicos de Obreros, 126
Feild, Edward, 29, 30
Ferdinand VII, 72, 73
Ferguson, George, 326
Ferguson, Samuel D., 452
Fernando Po, 431
Fiji Islands, 219-226
Fingoes, 354
Finnish Missionary Society, 380
Finns, 35
Fisher, Walter, 425
Fletcher, William, 219
Flierl, Johann, 244
Flores, 295
Floridas, 237
Fly River, 241
Forbes, James, 146
Foreign Evangelical Society, 119
Forrest River, 164
Forsyth, Christina, 353
Fort Hare, 354
Fotuna, 214, 234
France, in Madagascar, 310-314
Francia, 84
Franciscan Missionaries of Mary, 401, 422
Franciscans, in Latin America, 73, 74, 91, 92, 94, 96, 97, 100; in New Zealand, 193; in Africa, 401
Franson, Frederick, 371
Fraser, C., 190
Fraser, Donald, 394

Free Baptists, 28
Free Church of Scotland, in Canada, 18, 26; in Australia, 141, 147, 155; in New Zealand, 188-190; in Africa, 353, 393, 394
Free Church, on the Tonga Islands, 212, 213
Free Hanoverian Mission, 369, 370
Free Methodists, 362, 387, 402
Free Presbyterian Synod of Australia Felix, 146
Freeman, Thomas Birch, 439, 444, 447
Freemasonry, 86
Freetown, 456
Fremantle, 155
French, in Canada, 4, 8-14; in Tahiti, 205; in the Marquesas, 208; on Wallis Island, 214
French Equatorial Africa, 427-431
French Guiana, 86
French Guinea, 457
Frere, Sir Bartle, 410
Frere Town, 410
Friar lands, 272
Friendly Islands, 202, 210-213, 215, 216, 221
Friends. See Quakers
Friends Foreign Mission Association, 307
Frontier, in Canada, 6, 7, 12-14, 31-34
Fulani, 435
Fuller, Joseph Jackson, 433n
Futuna, 227

Gabun, 427, 429
Gachupines, 71
Galicians, 35
Gallas, 369
Gallicanism, in Canada, 11
Gambia, 458
Gambier Islands, 205, 206
Gandhi, 377
Gardiner, Allen Francis, 102, 103, 355
Geddie, John, 227, 228
Genadendal, 341
General Associate Synod, 26
General Missionary Conferences, South Africa, 378
George, David, 28
George, King. See Tufaahau
Gereformeerde Kerk, 334
German East Africa, 403-409
German Protestants in Brazil, 106, 107

German South-west Africa, 378-380
Germans, in Canada, 10, 13, 34
Gibson, William, 151
Gifford, A., 30n
Gilbert Islands, 258, 259
Gill, William, 209n
Gippsland, 146
Glasgow Colonial Society, 18, 26
Glasgow Missionary Society, 353
Glass, Frederick C., 111n
Godley, John Robert, 186
Gold Coast, 445
Gollmer, C. A., 437
Gordon, George Nichol, 228
Gordon, James Douglas, 228
Gospel Missionary Society, 411
Gossner, 283, 290, 434
Gossner, Johannes E., 158
Goulburn, 139
Grahamstown, 327, 328, 330, 332, 351, 357
Gran Chaco, 92, 103, 104
Grandjean, Arthur, 366
Gray, Robert, 327, 328, 355, 388, 389
Great Awakening, 25
Great Britain, in the Pacific Islands, 220, 224
Great Colombia, 78-80
Great Namaqualand, 379
Great Trek, 323, 325
Greek Independent Church, 36
Greek Orthodox, in Canada, 15; in Latin America, 101; in Australia, 170; in South Africa, 332
Greenland, 46-48
Greenland Board of Trade, 47
Gregory XVI, 73
Gregory, William Edward, 312n
Grela, Ignacio, 71
Grenada, 59
Grenfell, George, 424, 433
Grenfell, Wilfred, 30, 31
Grey, Sir George, 182, 195n, 377
Gribble, John Brown, 163
Gribble, J. R., 163
Griquas, 344
Grout, Lewis, 360n
Grubb, W. Barbrooke, 103
Guadalcanar, 237
Guam, 257
Guardia de Honor, 269
Guatemala, 77, 116

Guiana, British, 62, 63; Dutch, 65, 66;
     French, 86, 87
Guinness, H. Grattan, 423, 441, 442

Haabai, 210-212
Hacquard, 460
Hagenauer, August, 164
Hahn, Hugo, 379
Haiti, 87, 88, 124
Hale, Archdeacon, 163
Haley, John Wesley, 402n
Hall, Martin J., 415n
Hallbeck, Hans Peter, 342
Halmahera, 290
Hannington, James, 414, 415, 417
Harper, Henry John Chitly, 187
Harris, James, 228
Harris, William Wadé, 449
Hartzell, Joseph Crane, 385, 451
Hau Hau, 183
Hauge, Hans Nilson, 308, 370
Hausa, 435
Hausa Association, 438
Hawaii, 207, 246-256
Hawaiian Evangelical Association, 208, 251
Haweis, T., 202
Heart of Africa Mission, 427
Help for Brazil Mission, 111
Hemmen, 283
Henricksen, 104
Herero, 367, 379
Hermannsburg, 144, 149, 158, 368, 369
Herrero, Andreas, 94, 95
Hervey Islands, 208-210
Hetherington, Irving, 147
Hetherwick, Alexander, 395
Hickey, James, 114
Hidalgo, 71
Highlanders, in Canada, 10, 11, 26, 32
Hill, John C., 116
Hill, Joseph Sidney, 438
Hiltrup, 258
Hinderer, Anna, 437
Hinderer, David, 437
Hine, John Edward, 389, 392
Hines, J., 37n
Hinteröcker, Johann Nep., 166n
Hispaniola, 87, 88, 124
Hobart, 149-152, 168
Hobson, William, 181, 182
Hoevell, W. R., Baron van, 280

Hoffman, C. Colden, 452n
Hofmeyr, Nicolaas, 334
Hokianga, 180
Holiness Church of California, 117
Holy Family, Missionaries of the, 73
Holy Ghost Fathers, 87, 97; in Madagascar,
     312; in Mauritius, 315; on the Comoro
     Islands, 316; in Africa, 380, 398, 399, 407,
     412, 420, 428, 429, 431, 443, 456, 457, 459
Holy Ghost, Missionaries of the, 73
Home Mission and Church Extension Fund
     of Queensland, 136
Honduras, 77
Honolulu, 250, 253
Hoover, James M., 297
Hopkins, Henry, 148, 151
Horden, John, 37
Hornby, Wilfrid Bird, 392
Hottentots, 337, 338, 339, 341, 344, 367, 380,
     390
Houlder, J. A., 309n
Hòva, 302-314
Howard, C. B., 152
Hudson Bay, 37
Hudson Bay Company, 4, 12, 32
Huilla, 399
Hungarians, 35
Hunt, John, 221
Hutchins, William, 150

Ibadan, 437
Icelanders, in Canada, 35
Iglesia Filipina Independiente, 268
Igorots, 271
Imèrina, 302, 303, 306
Immigration, into Latin America, 98-101
Independent Catholic Church of the Philip-
     pines, 268
Indians, in Canada, 13-15, 36-39; in Latin
     America, Roman Catholic mission to,
     89-97; Protestant missions to, 102-105
Indians (East), immigrants in West Indies,
     56, 59; in British Guiana, 62, 64; in Dutch
     Guiana, 66; in the Fijis, 224; on Mauri-
     tius, 315; in South Africa, 338, 352, 358,
     372, 376
Inglis, Charles, 26
Inglis, John, 228
Inhambane, 402
Inquisition, 71

International Grenfell Association, 31
Ipswich, 158
Irish, in Canada, 10, 11; in Australia, 166
Irish Presbyterian Church, 18
Irwin, Frederick Chidley, 135
Isherwood, Cecile, 328
Islam, 290, 292, 320, 390, 414-418, 433, 470
Issoudun, Congregation of the Holy Heart of Jesus of, 239, 245
Italians, in Canada, 10
Ivory Coast, 448, 449

Jabavu, John Tengo, 352
Jacobite Uniates, 100
Jänicke's school, 278
Jamaica, 50-57
Jamaica Baptist Missionary Society, 54
Jamaica Home and Foreign Missionary Society, 52
Jameson, William, 439n
Japanese, in Brazil, 100, 108
Jarrett, W., 143
Java, 291-293
Java Committee, 283, 293
Javanese, in Dutch Guiana, 65
Jefferson, Selby, 30n
Jeffreys, J., 303n
Jellesma, J. E., 293
Jesuits, in Canada, 8, 14; in Jamaica, 51; in Latin America, 73, 94, 97; in the Dutch East Indies, 295; in Madagascar, 306; in Africa, 383, 387, 400, 401, 421
Jivaros, 94
Johannesburg, 356, 357, 361, 371, 373
Johnson, C. F., 424n
Johnson, Charles, 358
Johnson, Richard, 137
Johnson, William and Lucy S., 310n
Johnson, William Augustine Bernard, 454
Johnson, William Percival, 391
Jones, David, 303
Jones, John, 29
Jones, William West, 327
Joseph, Sisters of St., 100
Josephites, 93
Juárez, 74
Judd, Gerrit Parmele, 250
Jugendbund für Entschiedenes Christentum, 258
Junod, Henri A., 402n

Kaffirs, 337, 341, 343, 353, 355-357
Kaffraria, 356, 357
Kaiser Wilhelm's Land, 245
Kalahari Desert, 347, 380
Kalahaua, 254
Kalley, Robert Reid, 111
Kam, Joseph Carel, 278, 279
Kamehameha I, 247
Kamehameha IV, 253
Kamunga, Leonard Mattiya, 392n
Kanakas, 156, 157, 161, 238
Kapiolani, 249
Kassai, 426
Kei Islands, 295
Kendrick, 330
Kennedy, William, 156n
Kennion, George Wyndon, 153
Kenya, 409-412
Key, Bransby Lewis, 357
Khame, 350, 369, 376, 381
Kidder, Daniel Parish, 121n
Kikuyu, 411
Kilauea, 249
Kilimanjaro, 403, 404
Kimberley, 352, 356
King, Copland, 243n
King, Johannes, 67n
King Movement, 183
Kinsolving, L. L., 123
Kirton, W., 190
Kleinschmidt, Samuel, 47
Knibb, William, 53
Knight-Bruce, G. W. H., 383
Knox Church, Winnipeg, 33
Koperamana, Lake, 164
Krapf, Johann Ludwig, 403, 404, 410
Kruyt, A. C., 290, 291
Kuching, 296, 298
Kumm, Karl, 442
Kuruman, 345, 346, 363, 381
Kusaie, 257, 258
Kuyper, Abraham, 281
Kwato, 242

Labour movement, in Australia, 172
Labrador, 4, 14, 30, 31
Labuan, 296, 297
Lacombe, Albert, 13
Lagos, 436, 439
Lakemba, 221, 225
Lallave, 270

Lambaréné, 431

Lancastrian Educational Society, 109

Landana, 398

Lang, John Dunmore, 139-141, 146, 150, 157, 158

Languages, reduction of to writing, 390, 394, 410, 425, 426, 433, 440

Lapsley, S. N., 426

La Salette, Missionaries of, 312

Latin America, 68-129; independence of, and the Church, 71-88

LaTrobe, Charles Joseph, 145

Launceston, 151

Laval, Jacques Désiré, 315

Lavigerie, Charles Martial, 386, 397, 420, 460

Lawes, W. G., 210, 241

Lawry, Walter, 142, 211

Laws, Robert, 393

Lazarists, 73, 267, 312

Leacock, H. J., 457

Leberaho, Donatus, 409n

Leigh, Samuel, 142, 151, 160, 180, 211

Leipzig Missionary Society, 407

Le Jolle, Mrs., 283, 292

Leo XIII, 417

Leopold II, 420, 421

Leopoldville, 421

Lewis, Gwen Elen, 425n

Lewis, Thomas, 425n

Liberia, 449-452

Libermann, 315, 428, 452

Libreville, 429

Liebenzell Mission, 257

Liele, George, 53

Liénard, Jacques, 366n

Lifu, 240, 241

Likoma, 392

Liliuokalani, 254

Limbrock, Eberhard, 245

Limpopo River, 365, 381, 382

Lisle, George, 53

Little Sisters of Mary, 234

Little Sisters of the Poor, 234

Little Sunda Islands, 295

Livingstone, David, 345-349, 386, 391, 393, 413, 419

Livingstone Inland Mission, 423

Livingstonia Central African Trading Company, 396

Livingstonia Mission of the United Free Church of Scotland, 393, 394

Livinhac, 418

Loanda, 348, 400

Loango, 428

Lobengula, 365, 383

Lockett, Basil Lee, 441n

Lofthouse, J., 36n

Lokoja, 436

London Missionary Society, in Canada, 19; in Jamaica, 56; in Trinidad, 59; in British Guiana, 64, 65; in Tahiti, 202-205; in Cook Islands, 208, 209; in Niue, 210; in Tongatabu, 211; in Samoa, 215; in the New Hebrides, 227-229; in the Loyalty Islands, 233; in New Guinea, 240-242; in the East Indies, 279; in Madagascar, 303-311; in South Africa, 342-350, 381; in the rest of Africa, 405, 406

López, Carlos Antonio, 84

López, Francisco Solano, 84

Lott Carey Baptist Foreign Missionary Convention, 427

Lourdel, Simeon, 418

Lourenço Marques, 402

Lovedale, 353, 354

Low Archipelago, 206

Lower California, 77, 93

Lower Canada, 3, 4, 20-24

Loyalists, 20, 28, 60

Loyalty Islands, 233, 234

Lund, Eric, 270

Lundie, George Archibald, 215n

Lutheran Free Church, 308

Lutherans, in Canada, 5, 32, 34, 35; in British Guiana, 65; in Dutch Guiana, 66; in Brazil, 107; in Australia, 154, 158, 165; in South Africa, 331; in Liberia, 452

Lyman, Henry, 280, 287

Lyon, James, 18

Lyons Seminary. See Society of African Missions

Lyth, Richard Burdsall, 221

Lyttelton, 190

Mabille, Adolphe, 364, 365

Macao, Bishop of, 295

MacArthur, Archibald, 150

McCleary, Charles Warner, 430n

McCulloch, Thomas, 26

McDonald, Alexander, 34
McDonald, D. A., 353n
Macdonnell, Alexander, 10n
McDougall, Francis Thomas, 296
McDowall, Robert, 18
Macfarlane, 188
McFarlane, 240, 241
MacGregor, James, 26
Machray, Robert, 32
McKaeg, John, 143
Mackay, Alexander M., 415
McKean, Thomas S., 205n
Mackenzie, Ann, 389n
Mackenzie, Charles Frederick, 388
Mackenzie College, 123
Mackenzie, John, 350
Maclaren, Albert Alexander, 243
McNabb, D., 169
Macquarie, 137, 142
Macrorie, 328
Madagascar, 301-314
Madura, 293
Mahon, Edgar, 359n
Mala, 237, 238
Malagasy, 301-314
Malays, 338, 358
Mallicollo, 232
Mamaia, 205
Manila, 267, 270
Manitoba, 14, 33-35, 41
Manitoba College, 33
Manua, 215
Maori Mission Board, 184
Maoris, 177-185, 194, 195
Maples, Chauncy, 392
Maré, 233
Marianas, 257
Mariannhill, 372, 383
Marist Brothers, 316, 422
Marists, 180, 181, 193, 213, 214, 225, 232, 234-236
Maritime Provinces, 24-28
Marmoiton, Blaise, 234
Maronites, in Brazil, 100
Marquesas, 202, 203, 207
Marriage, 313
Marrons, 66, 67
Marsden, Samuel, 137, 142, 143, 163, 178, 179
Marshall Islands, 258

Masasi, 391, 404
Mashonaland, 383
Mason, Etta, 231n
Massaia, 316
Matabele, 345, 349, 365, 382-384
Matopo Hills, 385
Matthews, Thomas T., 309n
Matto Grosso, 97
Matula, 425n
Maupoint, 407
Mauritius, 302-304, 314, 315
Maximilian, 74
Medhurst, 279, 280
Medical missions, 309, 416, 425
Melanesian Mission, 231, 235
Melanesians, 225-233, 239
Melbourne, 144-148
Mell, Arsène, 458
Menabe, 307n
Mendi, 455
Mennonite Missionary Union, 282, 293
Mennonites, 34, 35, 442
Mentawei, 289
Mercedarians, 73, 91
Merensky, Alexander, 368, 406
Mereweather, John Davies, 175n
Merino, 88
Merriman, 356n
Messinger, Erasmus J. P., 452n
Methodism, in Canada, 5, 19, 22, 23, 27, 28, 31, 33, 38, 44; in Jamaica, 54, 55; in Trinidad, 58, 59; in others of the West Indies, 60; in Demerara, 64, 65; in Latin America, 113, 114, 116, 118, 119, 121, 122, 124; in Australia, 136, 141-143, 147, 148, 151, 153, 155-157, 159, 160, 164, 173; in New Zealand, 180, 191, 192; in Tonga Islands, 211-213; in Samoa, 216; on Rotuma, 219; in Fiji, 221-224; in the Solomon Islands, 238; in the Bismarck Archipelago, 239; in New Guinea, 242, 243; in Hawaii, 254, 255; in the Philippines, 270; in the East Indies, 286; in Africa, 330, 350-352, 384, 385, 387, 389, 390, 400, 401, 402, 410, 426, 432, 438, 439, 442, 444, 447, 451, 455, 458
Methodist Evangelical Church of the Philippines, 272
Methodist Immigrants' Home, 147
Methodist New Connexion, 19

Mexico, and the Roman Catholic Church, 71, 72, 76, 77, 91, 93; and Protestantism, 113-115
Meyer, Heinrich, 342n
Michelsen, Oscar, 230
Micmacs, 14
Micronesia, 256-259
Milan, Foreign Missionary Society of, 236
Millennial Dawn, 57
Miller, Frederick, 151
Miller, W. R. S., 438
Mill Hill, 193, 273, 297, 412, 418, 422
Mills, Samuel J., 113, 248, 449
Milne, Peter, 229
Miltrup, 240
Milum, John, 439
Minahassa, 279, 285, 287, 294
Miquelon, 3
Mission of Help, 329
Mission Philafricaine, 400
Mission to the Free Coloured Population of Canada, 18
Missions Consulate, 285
Missouri Synod, 107, 144, 158
Mitchell River, 164
Moffat, John Smith, 345n, 382
Moffat, Mary, 347, 348
Moffat, Robert, 345, 346, 363, 370, 381, 382
Mohawks, 20
Mokololo, 349
Molokai, 256
Moluccas, 278, 295
Mombasa, 404, 410, 412
Monterey, 114
Montgomery, Henry, 150
Montreal, 8
Moody, Dwight L., 30
Moosenee, 37
Moran, Patrick Francis, 168, 172
Moravians, in Canada, 20; in Labrador, 30, 36; in Greenland, 46-48; in the Danish West Indies, 49, 50; in Jamaica, 55; in Dutch Guiana, 66, 67; in Central America, 104, 105; in Australia, 164; in Africa, 322, 339, 341, 342, 406
Morelos, 71
Moreno, García, 80, 81, 94
Moreton Bay, 157, 158
Morgenster, 384
Mormons, in Canada, 35; in New Zealand, 184; in Tahiti, 206; on Easter Island,

206; in Samoa, 216; in Hawaii, 254; in South Africa, 332
Morning Star, 258
Morris, J. W., 123
Morris, William Case, 111
Morrison, W. M., 426
Morton, J., 59
Moshesh, 358, 363
Mosquera, Tomás, 79, 80
Mosquito Coast, 104
Mott, John R., 136
Moulton, J. E., 212, 213
Mozambique, 400-403
Mtesa, 413, 414, 417, 418
Mt. Holyoke Seminary, 326
Mtusu, Daniel, 394n
Muhlenberg, Henry Melchior, 34
Mullens, Joseph, 306n
Muni River Settlements, 431, 432
Munson, Samuel, 280, 287
Murphy, Francis, 168
Murray, A. W., 241
Murray, Andrew, 324
Murray, Andrew, Jr., 324-326, 340, 359, 378, 396
Murray, John, 324
Murray Island, 241
Murray River, 153
Mwanga, 414, 415, 418
Myalism, 57

Nairobi, 412
Namaquas, 344, 350, 379, 380
Napier, 190
Napier, Robert Hellier, 395n
Nassau, Robert Hamill, 430n
Natal, 325, 327, 328, 330, 355, 360, 361, 369, 370
National African Company, 436
Navigators Islands, 214-217
Nazarene, Church of the, 118, 362
Nederduits Gereformeerde Kerk, 334
Nederduits Hervormde Kerk, 333, 334
Needham, Hester, 288
Neethling, William, 341n
Negroes, in Canada, 5, 28; in West Indies, British Honduras, and the Guianas, 50-66; in Latin America, 97
Nelson, 186, 187, 190
Nesbit, R., 121
Netherlands Bible Society, 284, 287

Netherlands Indies Missionary Alliance, 285
Netherlands Indies Missionary Conference, 285
Netherlands Missionary Society, 278, 279, 282, 283, 290, 291, 293
Netherlands Missionary Union, 283
Neubronner van der Tuuk, 287
Neuendettelsau, 144, 149, 244
Neukirchen Mission, 293, 411
New Brunswick, 4, 24-28
New Brunswick, N. J., Presbytery of, 18
New Caledonia, 233, 234
New England Company, 17, 37
New Georgia, 238
New Granada, 79
New Guinea, 240-246, 290, 295
New Hebrides, 226-233
New Norcia, 169
New Plymouth, 192
New Pomerania, 239
New South Wales, 131, 136-144, 167, 168
New York Conference, 19
New Zealand, 177-197
New Zealand Church Society, 186
New Zealand Company, 186, 187, 196
Newcastle, 138
Newfoundland, 4, 5, 9, 10, 11, 17, 28, 29
Newfoundland and British North America Society for Educating the Poor, 17
Newman, J. E., 122
Ngami, Lake, 347, 349
Nguna, 229
Nias, 289, 295, 299
Nieuwindt, M. J., 49
Niger River, 436-442, 459, 460
Nigeria, 435, 443
Nile, 348
Nisbet, James, 38
Niuatobatabu, 214
Niue, 210
Nixon, Francis Russell, 150
Nommensen, Ludwig Ingwer, 289
Norfolk Island, 167, 231, 236
North German Missionary Society, 184, 444, 445
North Pacific Institute, 252
Northern Australia, 159
North-west Fur Company, 12
North-west Territories, 31
Norwegian Missionary Society, 308, 311, 370

Nossi Bé, 305
Nova Scotia, 4, 18, 24-28
Nukapu, 231
Nyasa, Lake, 348, 390-397
Nyasa Industrial Mission, 388, 396
Nyasaland, 390-397

Obeah, 49, 57, 59, 62, 88
Oblates of Mary Immaculate, 12-14, 372, 373, 380
Oblates of Troyes, 372, 380
Obookiah, Henry, 248
Ocapa, 92, 94
O'Donel, James Louis, 10
O'Flynn, Jeremiah Francis, 167
Ogilvie, John, 20
Ogle, J. Furniss, 103
Okumura, Takie, 252n
Ono-i-lau, 221
Ontario, 3, 18, 20-24, 35, 42
Orange Free State, 323, 325, 330
Ormerod, Robert Moss, 410n
Orton, James, 142, 147, 148
Oruba, 49
Otago, 189-191
Otaheite, 202
Oudenbosch, 295
Ovambo, 372, 380
Ovir, Ewald, 407n
Owen, Francis, 355n
Oxford Movement, 327, 328

Paama, 229, 230
Pacific Islands, 198-263
Pai Marire, 183
Pallotines, 73, 97, 100, 170, 434
Pallotti, Vincent Mary, 100
Palmas, Cape, 451
Panama, 78, 108
Papacy, and Latin America, 71-88
Papua, 240-246
Paraguay, 84, 96, 120
Parent, Amand, 11n
Paris Evangelical Missionary Society, 205, 233, 311, 362-366, 383, 386, 429, 430, 459
Paris, Peace of, 3
Park, Mungo, 435
Parker, H. P., 415
Parker, Theodore, 334
Parramatta, 164, 179

Passionists, 169
Patagonia, 96, 102, 106
Patagonian Missionary Society, 102
Paton, John G., 229
Paton, Maggie Whitecross, 229n
Patronato de Indias, 72-88
Patteson, John Coleridge, 231, 235
Paull, George, 431
Paumotu, 206
Payne, John, 452
Pearse, Horatio, 351n
Pearse, John, 309n
Peck, E. J., 37n
Pedro II, 86
Peeredoom, Xavier van der, 421n
Pele, 249
Pemba, 404
Penrhyn Islands, 209, 210
Pentecostal Holiness, 57
Penzotti, Francisco G., 117, 118
Perregaux, Edmond, 447n
Perry, Charles, 145
Perth, 156
Peru, 81, 82, 94, 117
Peter Claver, 448
Pétion, 124
Philadelphia, Associate Synod of, 18
Philip, John, 344, 362, 363, 366
Philippine Islands, 264-274
Philips, Mrs., 292
Phillippo, James Mursell, 54n
Phillips, J. Garland, 103n
Picpus Fathers, 205, 206, 208, 209, 256
Pilkington, George, 415
Pines, Isle of, 233, 234
Pitcairn Island, 207
Pius IX, 73
Planque, Augustin, 444n
Plessis, 9
Plymouth Brethren, 112, 119, 359, 365, 387, 399, 400, 425
Polding, John Bede, 167, 168, 180
Poles, in Canada, 10, 13
Polygamy, 376, 462
Polynesians, 200-263
Pomare, 203
Pomare II, 203, 204
Pomare IV, 205
Pompallier, Jean Baptiste François, 181, 193, 213, 214, 219, 225

Ponape, 257
Pond, Theodore S., 116
Population, decline of, in the Pacific Islands, 200
Pormalim, 288
Port Chalmers, 192
Port Darwin, 169
Port Jackson, 132
Port Moresby, 241
Port Nicholson, 191
Port of Spain, 58, 59
Port Phillip, 145, 146, 148
Porter, William Carmichael, 404n
Portland, Australia, 145
Portuguese, in Hawaii, 256
Portuguese East Africa, 400-403
Portuguese Guinea, 458
Portuguese West Africa, 397-400
Positivism, 70, 86
Posselt, Wilhelm, 367n
Posso, 290
Potosi, 95
Premonstratensians, 422
Presbyterian Church Society of Australia Felix, 160
Presbyterians, in Canada, 5, 18, 21, 22, 25-27, 32, 33, 38, 44; in Jamaica, 56; in Latin America, 114, 116, 117, 122; in Australia, 135, 136, 139-141, 146, 147, 150, 153, 155, 157, 160, 164, 173; in New Zealand, 188-191; in the New Hebrides, 227-229; in the Philippines, 270; in Africa, 329, 352-355, 393-395, 426, 429-431, 434, 439, 440
Presbyterians, Canadian, in Trinidad, 59
Price, Isabella, 350n
Primitive Methodists, 19, 147
Prince Edward Island, 4, 24-28
Principe, 317
Protestant Church in the Netherlands Indies, 286, 287
Protestant Episcopal Church, in Latin America, 115, 123; in Hawaii, 253, 254; in the Philippines, 271; in Liberia, 451, 452
Protestantism, in Canada, 15-45; in Latin America, 101-125; in Australia, 133-165; in the Pacific Islands, 200-263; in the Philippines, 269-272; in the Dutch East Indies, 276-293
Provencher, 12, 13
Puerto Rico, 123, 124

Qua Iboe, 441
Quakers, in Canada, 24, 28; in Mexico, 115; in Central America, 116; in Australia, 144, 149, 151; in New Zealand, 192; in Madagascar, 307, 311; in Africa, 411, 456
Quateron, 297
Quebec, 4, 8, 9, 11, 20-24
Quebec Act, 8
Queensland, 156-158
Queensland Kanaka Mission, 237, 238
Quito, 94

Raad van die Kerke, 335
Radàma I, 302, 303
Radàma II, 305, 306
Raiatea, 204
Ramseyer, Fritz, 447n
Ramseyer, Paul, 364n
Rànavàlona, 303-305
Rànavàlona II, 306
Rankin, Melinda, 114
Ransom, J. J., 122
Rarotonga, 209
Ràsohèrina, 306
Rawle, Richard, 58, 60
Rebmann, J., 404, 410
Recollets, 77
Red River Settlement, 12, 17, 32, 33
Redemptorists, 13, 73, 193, 422
Reed, W. E., 117
Reformed, in Canada, 34
Reformed Church of God, 57
Regina, 13
Regions Beyond Missionary Union, 111, 423
Regular Baptists, 28
Religious liberty, in Canada, 8
Rennie, George, 189
Reno, Leon M., and Alice W., 122n
Restarick, Henry Bond, 254
Réunion, 305, 315
Reyes, Don Isabelo de los, y Florentino, 268, 270
Rhenish Missionary Society, in New Guinea, 245; in the East Indies, 280, 286-289; in Africa, 367, 379
Rhodes, Cecil, 377, 385
Rhodesia, 381-390
Richards, William, 251
Ride, John, 147
Ridley, W., 164
Riedel, Johann Friedrich, 279

Riemenschneider, I. Fr., 184n
Riis, Andreas, 446
Rio de Janeiro, 121, 123
Rio Muni, 431, 432
Rio Pongo, 454, 457
Rivadavia, Bernadino, 83
Rives, Jean, 255
Rivett, A. W. L., 328
Rizal, 264
Robertson, Henrietta, 358n
Robertson, James, 33
Robinson, Charles H., 438
Rockhampton, 157
Rodriguez, 315
Roe, Bryan, 439n
Roman Catholicism, in Canada, 4, 5, 7-15, 42; in the West Indies, 49-61; in British Honduras, 61, 62; in British Guiana, 63; in Latin America, 69-101; in Australia, 165-170; in New Zealand, 180, 181, 192, 193; in Tahiti, 205; in Paumotu, 206; on Easter Island, 206; in the Marquesas, 208; in the Tonga Islands, 213; on Wallis Island, 214; in Samoa, 217; on Rotuma, 219; in the Fijis, 225, 226; in the New Hebrides, 232; in New Caledonia, 234; in the Solomon Islands, 235, 236; in New Guinea, 245, 246; in the Bismarck Archipelago, 239, 240; in Hawaii, 255, 256; in Micronesia, 257, 258; in the Philippines, 272, 273; in the Dutch East Indies, 294, 295; in Madagascar, 305-313; in South Africa, 332, 372, 373; in German Southwest Africa, 380; in Rhodesia, 383, 386, 387; in Nyasaland, 397; in Angola, 398, 399; in Mozambique, 400, 401; in German East Africa, 407, 408; in British East Africa, 412; in the Belgian Congo, 420-422; in French Equatorial Africa, 418, 419; in Cameroon, 434; in Nigeria, 442, 443
Romanticism, 377
Rondon, 97
Rorke's Drift, 353
Rosario, 110
Rosas, Juan Manuel de, 83
Ross, John Miller, 141
Rotuma, 218, 219
Rousseau, 377
Rowlands, Thomas, 309n

Royal National Mission to Deep Sea Fishermen, 31
Ruanda, 406
Rumanians, 15
Rupert's Land, 4, 32
Rurutu, 208
Russian Orthodox in Latin America, 101
Ruthenians, 13, 35, 36, 100
Ruvuma River, 391, 404
Ryan, Bishop, 307
Ryerson, Egerton, 23n, 41

Saba, 49
Sacred Heart of Jesus, Priests of, 422
Sadeleer, Francis de, 421n
Sadrach, 292
Sainte Marie, 305
Sakalava, 307n, 308
Saker, Alfred, 433
Salatiga Mission, 283, 292
Salem, 330
Salesians of Don Bosco, in Latin America, 73, 79, 94, 96, 97; in Africa, 372, 422
Salvado, 169
Salvation Army, in Canada, 28, 41; in Latin America, 118; in Australia, 144, 148, 154; in New Zealand, 194; in Hawaii, 255; in the East Indies, 286; in Africa, 332, 385
Samoa, 214-217
San Bartolomé, college of, 79
San Blas Indians, 105
San Pedro Mission, 104
San Salvador, 399, 425
Sangi and Talaud Committee, 284
Sangi Islands, 290
Santa Cruz Islands, 231, 235
Santo Tomás, University of, 267, 273
São Paulo de Loanda, 348, 400
São Tomé, 317
Sapalada, 269
Sarawak, 296
Sargeant, George, 55
Saskatchewan, 35, 38
Saunders, John, 143
Savaii, 215
Scandinavian Alliance Mission, 117, 362
Scheutvelders, 273, 421, 431, 432
Schmelzenbach, Harmon, 362n
Schmidt, George, 322, 339, 341
Schön, James Frederick, 436n
Schools, in Pacific Islands, 205

Schreuder, Hans Paludan Smith, 370
Schwartz, Johann Gottlieb, 279
Schweitzer, Albert, 430
Scofield, C. I., 116
Scots Church, Melbourne, 146, 147
Scott, David Clement, 395
Scott, Peter C., 405
Scott, Thomas Hobbes, 138
Scott, William Affleck, 395n
Secularization of missions in Latin America, 90, 91
Segebrock, 407n
Selinda, Mt., 385
Selkirk, Earl of, 12
Selwyn, George Augustus, 182, 183, 186, 187, 196, 230, 231, 237
Selwyn, John, 231, 235, 236
Seminary of Saints Peter and Paul, 93
Senegal, 459
Senegambia, 459
Separatist churches in South Africa, 378
Seraphimites, 13
Sernache, Seminary of, 401
Seventh Day Adventists, in Jamaica, 57; in British Guiana, 65; in Latin America, 116-120, 123, 125; in Australia, 144, 149, 151, 156; in New Zealand, 192; in Islands of the Pacific, 206, 207, 216, 225, 237, 243, 255; in the Philippines, 271; in the East Indies, 286; in Africa, 332, 362, 385, 388, 397, 407, 456
Seychelles, 316
Shaftesbury, Lord, 18
Shaw, Barnabas, 350
Shaw, William, 330, 351
Sherbro Island, 456
Shiré, 389, 390
Shiré Highlands, 394, 395
Short, Augustus, 153, 163
Shrewsbury, William J., 351n
Sibree, James, 306n
Sierra Leone, 453-457
Sierra Leone Pastorate Church, 454
Sierro, Candidus, 97n
Silcox, J. B., 34
Silliman Institute, 270
Sim, Arthur Fraser, 393n
Simpson, A. B., 425
Sisterhood of St. Thomas the Martyr, 328
Sisters of Charity of Gand, 422
Sisters of Our Lady, 421

Sisters of Our Lady of Mercy, 193
Sisters of Our Lady of Namur, 422
Sisters of Our Lady of the Mission, 193
Sisters of St. Joseph, 306, 316
Sisters of St. Joseph of Cluny, 226, 234, 459
Sisters of St. Joseph of Nazareth, 193
Sisters of the Church, 329
Sisters of the Holy Ghost, 401
Sisters of the Immaculate Conception, 432
Sisters of the Immaculate Conception of Castres, 428
Sisters of the Sacred Heart, 193
Sisters of the Sacred Heart of Mary of Berlaer, 422
Slater, 167
Slave trade, 303, 313
Slavery, 320, 321, 344, 348, 368, 408, 463
Slessor, Mary, 440
Smith, George Herbert, 307n
Smith, John, 65
Smith, J. Taylor, 454n
Smythies, Charles Alan, 392
Société des Missions Étrangères of Paris, 294
Société des Missions Évangéliques, 205, 233, 311, 362-366
Society for Home and Foreign Missions, 283, 290
Society for Promoting Christian Knowledge, in Canada, 16; in the West Indies, 52-61; in Australia, 135; in South Africa, 326, 328
Society for the Conversion and Religious Instruction and Education of the Negro Slaves in the British West Indies, 52
Society for the Propagation of the Gospel in Foreign Parts, in Canada, 16, 17, 20, 25, 26, 32, 34, 37; in Newfoundland, 29; in the West Indies, 52-61; in British Guiana, 63, 64; on the Mosquito Coast, 105; in Australia, 135, 146, 149, 152, 155, 157; in New Zealand, 186; in Madagascar, 307; in Mauritius, 315; in Seychelles, 316; in St. Helena, 317; in South Africa, 326, 355; in Rhodesia, 384; on the Gold Coast, 446, 448
Society Islands, 202-205
Society of African Missions (Lyons Seminary), 372, 380, 442-445, 448, 452, 456
Society of St. John the Divine, 329

Society of the Divine Word, in Latin America, 73, 96, 97; in New Guinea, 245; in the Philippines, 273; in the Dutch East Indies, 295; in Africa, 401, 445
Soemba, 293
Soga, Tiyo, 355
Solages, Henri de, 305
Solomon Islands, 235-238
Soren, Francisco Fulgencio, 122n
South Africa General Mission, 325, 359, 385, 389, 397, 400
South Africa, missions to blacks in, 338-378
South Africa, whites in, 321-335
South African Baptist Missionary Society, 359
South African Church Railway Mission, 329, 388
South African Compounds and Interior Mission, 359
South African Conference, 331
South American Evangelical Mission, 111
South American Missionary Society, 102-105, 110, 340
South Australia, 152-154
South Sea Evangelical Mission, 237, 238
Southern Baptist Convention, 122
Spanish-American War, 264, 265
Springer, John M., 427
Spurgeon, C. H., 154
St. Augustine's College, Canterbury, 138, 139
St. Croix, 49
St. George's Sisters, 328
St. Helena, 317, 327
St. John, 49
St. John's College, 187
St. Johns, Newfoundland, 10
St. Kitts, 59
St. Martin, 49
St. Pierre, 3
St. Thomas, 49
Staley, T. N., 253
Stanley Falls, 422
Stanley, Henry M., 348, 413, 419
Steere, Edward, 389, 391
Stellenbosch, 324, 334, 367
Stewart, Charles James, 17
Stewart, James, 354, 393, 396, 411
Stirling, Waite Hockin, 103, 106
Stow, T. Q., 154
Stuart, John, 20

Studd, Charles T., 30, 427
Studd, J. E., 30
Stundists, 108
Sudan Interior Mission, 442
Suisse Romande mission, 366, 402
Sumatra, 287-289, 295
Sumba, 293
Sun Yat-sen, 254
Sunday School Union, 271
Sura, 236
Surabaia, 292
Sustentation Fund Scheme, 141
Susu, 454, 457
Swahili, 403, 404
Swaziland, 352, 362
Sweden, Church of, in Africa, 370, 371
Swedish Free Church Mission, 371
Swedish Holiness Mission, 371
Swedish Missionary Union, 423, 431
Swiss Baptists, 108
Swiss mission, 366, 402
Sydney, 132, 139, 141, 168, 174
Synge, Edward, 139
Synod of Australia, 140, 141
Synod of Eastern Australia, 141
Synod of New South Wales, 140
Synod of the Presbyterian Church of New Brunswick, 27
Syrian Orthodox in Latin America, 101
Syrians, in Jamaica, 52

Taché, Alexander Antonin, 13
Taft, William Howard, 272
Tahiti, 202-206
Talaud Islands, 290
Tamate, 241
Tamils, 62
Tana River, 410, 411
Tanga, 406
Tanganyika, Lake, 386
Tanna, 227
Tarahumara, 93
Tarata, 95
Tarija, 92, 95
Tasmania, 149-152
Taufaahau, 211-213, 216, 222
Taylor, John Christopher, 437n
Taylor, William, 118, 119, 121, 136, 330, 385, 400, 451
Taylor, William George, 143
Te Whiti, 184

Teague, 450
Thakombau, 222
Thoburn, 270
Thom, Mrs. Christiana Louis, 339n
Thom, George, 324
Thomas, John, 211
Thompson, George, 455n
Thompson, Thomas, 446
Thomson, James, 81, 109, 117
Thomson, John Francis, 110
Thomson, W. Burns, 309n
Thursday Island, 245
Thurston, Asa, 248n
Thurston, Lucy Goodale, 248n
Tierra del Fuego, 102, 103
Timbuktu, 460
Timor, 295
Timor Archipelago, 293
Tobou College, 212
Togoland, 444, 445
Tokelau, 218
Tonga Islands, 202, 210-213, 215, 216, 221
Tongatabu, 202, 203, 210-213
Tongoa, 229
Toradjas, 290, 291
Toronto, 21
Toronto, University of, 42
Torres Islands, 231, 232
Townend, Joseph, 147
Townsend, Henry, 437
Tozer, William George, 389
Tractarianism, in Australia, 138, 153
Transit and Building Fund Society, 118
Transvaal, 323, 325, 330, 333, 341, 352, 368, 369
Trappists, 170, 372, 383, 422
Trinidad, 58, 61
Tristan da Cunha, 316
Trumbull, David, 119
Tsizehena, John, 311n
Tubuai, 208
Tucker, Alfred R., 416
Tucker, Hugh C., 121n
Tugwell, Herbert, 438
Tungud movement, 269
Turin, Fathers *della Consolata*, 412
Turner, H. M., 361
Turner, Nathaniel, 180n
Turner, Peter, 216
Tutuila, 215

Tyers, Lake, 163
Tyrrell, William, 138

Ubangi, 428
Ucayali, 92
Uganda, 412-419
Ujiji, 386
Ulawa, 237
Ullathorne, 167, 168
Umtali Valley, 385
Union for Christian Dutch Education for
the Native Population in the Netherlands
Indies, 285
Union Theological Seminary, Manila, 272
Unitarians, 35
United Aborigines' Mission, 165
United African Company, 436
United Brethren, 123, 271, 456
United Church of Canada, 45
United Foreign Missionary Society, 113
United Methodist Free Church, 147
United Norwegian Lutheran Church, 308
United Presbyterians, in Canada, 22
United States, Christianity in, contrasted with
Canada, 4-7; influence of, upon Canadian
Christianity, 17-22, 27, 28, 42; influence
in Australia, 136; in the Philippines, 265-
275
Universities' Mission to Central Africa, 348,
388, 389, 391-393, 404
Upolu, 215
Upper Canada, 3, 4, 20-24
Upper Canada Baptist Missionary Society,
24
Upper Canada Clergy Society, 17
Upper Senegal, 459
Uruguay, 84, 85, 120
Usambara, 406
Utrecht Missionary Union, 284, 290
Uvea Island, 214

Valparaiso, 119
Van Diemen's Land Colonial Missionary
and Christian Instruction Society, 151, 161
Van Henexthoven, P., 421n
Van Lier, 339
Vancouver, George, 247
Vancouver Island, 19
Vanderkemp, John Theodore, 340, 343
Vaud, Canton, 366
Vavau, 210-212

Vendas, 353
Venezuela, 78, 79, 91, 93, 116
Verjus, 245
Victoria, Australia, 144-149
Victoria, British Columbia, 33, 34
Victoria Falls, 348
Victoria Nyanza, 406
Vidal, Julien, 226
Vidal, Owen Emeric, 454
Villota, Gerard, 74
Viti Levu, 221
Volker, F., 369n
Vollenhoven, Mrs. van, 283, 292
Voluntarism, 139, 324
Voodoo, 49, 88
Vos, Michiel Christiaan, 339, 340

Waddall, W. T., 366n
Waddell, Hope Masterton, 439
Waiapu, 187
Waitangi, Treaty of, 181, 182
Wakefield, Edward George, 185, 186
Waldensees, in South America, 106
Walker, William, 164
Wallis Island, 214
Walmsley, John, 454n
Walter, George, 170
Warne, F. W., 297
Warneck, Gustav, 289
Warneck, Johann, 289
Warner, Edith, 438n
Waterfield, William, 148
Watkins, J. B., 212
Watt, Agnes C. P., 229n
Watt, Stuart, 411
Webb, Sidney Roberts, 425n
Weeks, John William, 454
Welchman, 237n
Wellington, 186, 187, 190, 192, 193
Welsh, in Patagonia, 106
Wengatz, Susan Talbott, 400n
Wescott, Bishop, 174
Wescott Brethren, 426
Wesley, John, 29
Wesleyan Methodist Missionary Society, 55,
331, 384, 390
Wesleyans. See Methodism
Wesleyville, 351
West, Daniel, 447n
West, John, 17
West Indies, 48-61

Western Australia, 155, 156, 170
Western Australia Missionary Society, 135, 155
Westerwoudt, Felix, 298n
Westlind, Nils, 424
Whangaroa Bay, 180
Wheeler, Daniel, 204n
Wheeler, D. H., 115
Wheelwright, I. W., 117
White, Gilbert, 159
White Fathers, 386, 397, 408, 409, 417, 418, 420, 421, 460
White, John, 352n, 384n
White Sisters, 409, 422
Wilkes, Henry, 23
William I, 277
Williams, Henry, 179
Williams, John, 204, 208-211, 215, 218, 221, 227
Williams, Richard, 103n
Williams, Thomas, 222
Williams, William, 179
Willis, Alfred, 213, 254
Willis, J. J., 417n
Willson, Robert William, 168
Wilson, Edward F., 37n
Wilson, James, 202
Wilson, John Leighton, 429n
Winnipeg, 12, 33, 34
Witteveen, H. W., 283

Wood, Leonard, 89
Wood, T. B., 118
Woodsworth, James, 38n
Wray, John, 65n

Yarrabah, 163, 164
Yoruba, 436-438, 440
Youd, Thomas, 63n
Young, Arminius, 30n
Young, Florence S. H., 237, 238
Young, George, 33
Young Men's Christian Association, 41, 120, 123, 124, 194
Young Peoples Societies of Christian Endeavour, 41
Young Women's Christian Association, 41, 120, 144
Ysabel Epalle, 235
Yucatán, 77
Yukon, 31
Yule Island, 245

Zacatecas, 91, 114
Zambesi, 347, 348, 362, 364, 365
Zambesi Industrial Mission, 397
Zamora, Nicolas, 272
Zanzibar, 389, 403, 404, 407, 410
Zapopan, 91
Zimbabwe, 384
Zulus, 358, 360, 369, 370

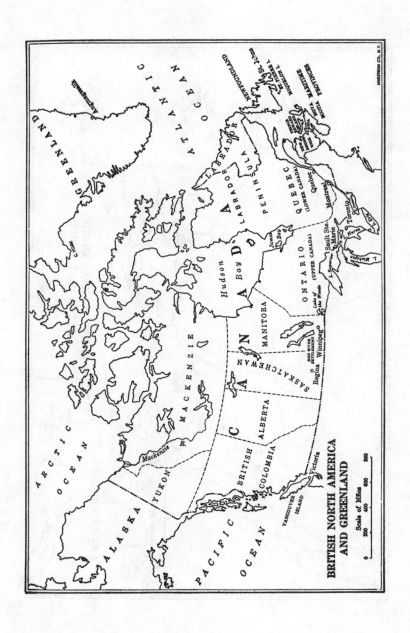

BRITISH NORTH AMERICA
AND GREENLAND

Scale of Miles

0   200   400   600   800

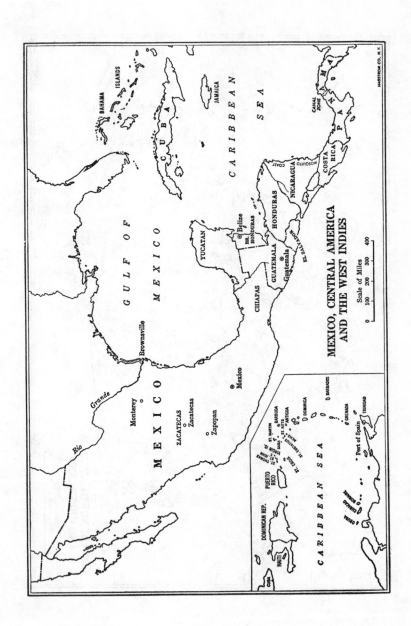

MEXICO, CENTRAL AMERICA
AND THE WEST INDIES

Scale of Miles
0   100   200   300   400

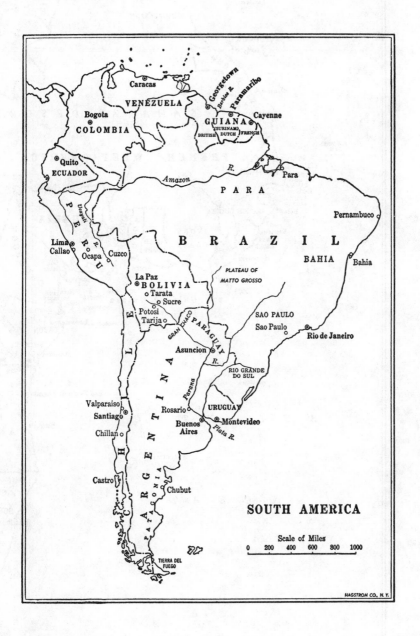

SOUTH AMERICA

Scale of Miles
0   200   400   600   800   1000

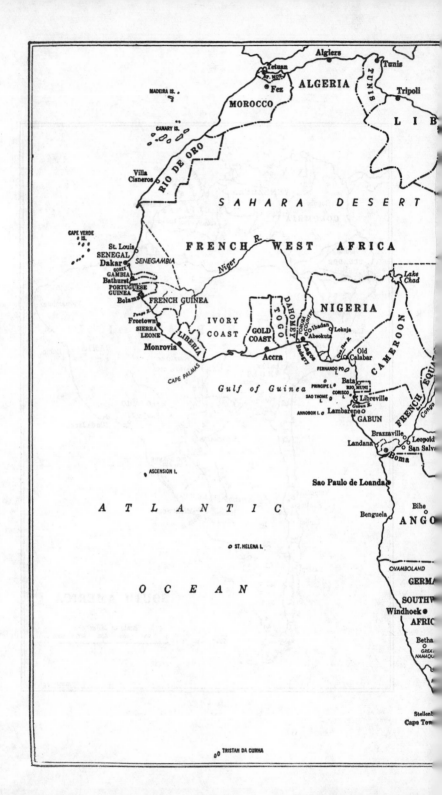

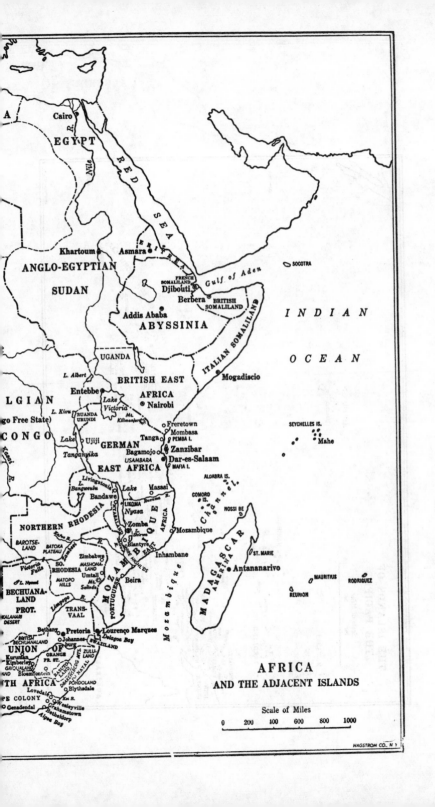

AFRICA
AND THE ADJACENT ISLANDS

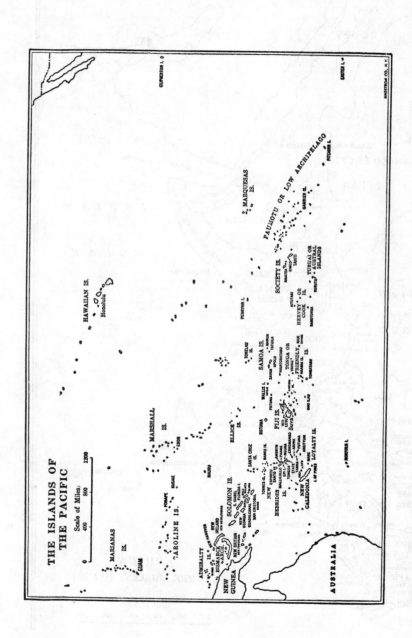

THE ISLANDS OF
THE PACIFIC

Scale of Miles
0   400   800   1200

MARIANAS IS.

GUAM

HAWAIIAN IS.

Honolulu

CAROLINE IS.

PONAPE

KUSAIE

ADMIRALTY

NEW HANOVER

NEW IRELAND

NEW BRITAIN

NEW GUINEA

BISMARCK ARCH.

SOLOMON IS.

MARSHALL IS.

EBON

NAURU

ELLICE IS.

MARQUESAS IS.

PAUMOTU OR LOW ARCHIPELAGO

SOCIETY IS.

TAHITI

TUBUAI OR AUSTRAL ISLANDS

HERVEY OR COOK IS.

RAROTONGA

TOKELAU IS.

SAMOA IS.

WALLIS I.

ROTUMA

FIJI IS.

SUVA

TONGA OR FRIENDLY IS.

SANTA CRUZ IS.

BANKS IS.

NEW HEBRIDES

NEW CALEDONIA

LOYALTY IS.

NORFOLK I.

AUSTRALIA

CLIPPERTON I.

EASTER I.

PITCAIRN I.

GAMBIER IS.

HASSTROM CO., N. Y.

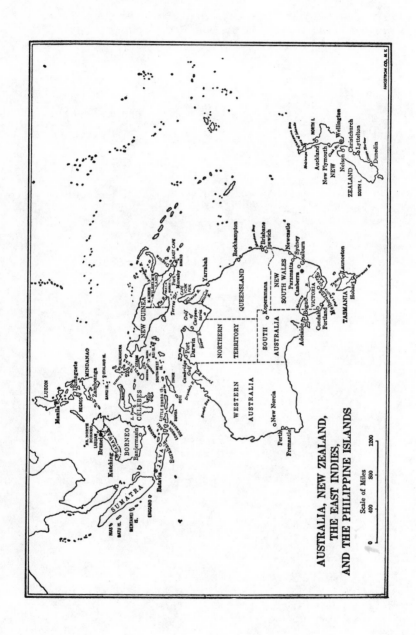

AUSTRALIA, NEW ZEALAND,
THE EAST INDIES,
AND THE PHILIPPINE ISLANDS

Scale of Miles
0   400   800   1200

HAGSTROM CO., N. Y.